Englischer Wortschatz

Biologie

Englischer Wortschatz Biologie

von
Dr. Carola Burgtorf
Melanie Gersdorf
Dr. Peter Menke
Christine Schmeling-Rößler
Ina Ullrich

Ernst Klett Sprachen
Stuttgart

Bildquellennachweis
510 Klett-Archiv (Horst Schneeweiß), Stuttgart; 510 Okapia (D. M. Phillips/PR Science Sc), Frankfurt; 510 Johannes Lieder, Ludwigsburg; 510 Okapia (Biophoto Ass./Science Source), Frankfurt; 510 Okapia (NAS), Frankfurt; 510 Okapia (Lonc. Sc. Films/OSF), Frankfurt; 513 Fotolia LLC (AlienCat), New York; 514 shutterstock (Oguz Aral), New York, NY; 516 shutterstock (Blamb), New York, NY; 521 Klett-Archiv (Rudolf Hungreder), Stuttgart; Nicht in allen Fällen war es uns möglich, den Rechteinhaber der Abbildungen ausfindig zu machen. Berechtigte Ansprüche werden selbstverständlich im Rahmen der üblichen Vereinbarungen abgegolten.

1. Auflage 1 8 7 6 5 | 2023 22 21 20

Alle Drucke dieser Auflage sind unverändert und kçnnen im Unterricht nebeneinander verwendet werden.
Die letzte Zahl bezeichnet das Jahr des Druckes. Das Werk und seine Teile sind urheberrechtlich geschützt. Jede Nutzung in anderen als den gesetzlich zugelassenen Fällen bedarf der vorherigen schriftlichen Einwilligung des Verlags.

© Ernst Klett Sprachen GmbH, Stuttgart 2010. Alle Rechte vorbehalten.
Internetadresse: www.klett-sprachen.de

Autoren: Dr. Carola Burgtorf, Melanie Gersdorf, Dr. Peter Menke, Christine Schmeling-Roeßler, Ina Ullrich

Redaktion: Bettina Höfels
Englisches Fachkorrektorat: Anne Louise McCabe, Cambridge, MA, USA
Layoutkonzeption: Eva Mohklis, Ulrike Wollenberg
Illustrationen: Prof. Jürgen Wirth; Visuelle Kommunikation, Dreieich

Gestaltung und Satz: Dörr + Schiller GmbH, Stuttgart
Umschlaggestaltung: Elmar Feuerbach
Titelbild: Elmar Feuerbach
Druck und Bindung: Salzland Druck, Staßfurt
Printed in Germany
ISBN 978-3-12-580101-1

Inhaltsverzeichnis

Einführung 8
Phonetische Umschrift 10
Abkürzungsverzeichnis 10

I. In the biology classroom 11

1 Basic biology classroom phrases 12
1.1 Tasks and "Operatoren" 12
1.2 Comparisons 13
1.3 Form and function 14
1.4 Terminology 14

2 Biological key words 15
2.1 Areas of study 15
2.2 Life 16
2.3 Organisational levels 16
2.4 Classification 16
2.5 Life forms 17

3 The scientific method 17

4 Experiments and methods 19
4.1 In the lab 19
4.2 The microscope 24
4.3 Lab equipment 27
4.4 In the field 30
4.5 Models 31
4.6 Writing utensils 34
4.7 Writing up 34

5 Graphs and Figures 37
5.1 Illustrations 37
5.2 Statistics and Numbers 38
5.3 Graphs and Charts 41

6 Working with films and computers 45
6.1 Films 45
6.2 Computers 46

II. Basic vocabulary 47

1 Plants 48

2 Animals 49

3 The human body 53

III. Thematic vocabulary 57

1 The human body 58
1.1 Cells, tissue and organs 58
1.2 Covering and movement 61
1.3 Sensory organs 63
1.4 Nervous system 68
1.5 Endocrine system 70
1.6 Sexuality, human reproduction and life cycle ... 71
1.7 Food and diet 75
1.8 Digestion, absorption and use of food 76
1.9 Blood circulatory system 78
1.10 Lymphatic system 80
1.11 Respiratory system 80
1.12 Excretion and the kidneys .. 83
1.13 Immune system 85
1.14 Health and disease 90

2 Plant families 90
2.1 Basic vocabulary: reproduction of plants in general 90
2.2 Reproduction of green algae, bryophyta, and pteridophyta 91
2.3 Common features of gymnosperms and angiosperms 97
2.4 Gymnosperms 98
2.5 Angiosperm plant families: reproduction 101
2.6 Fertilisation and development of embryo 107
2.7 Angiosperm plant families: recognizing angiosperms 109
2.8 Monocots 115
2.9 Dicotyledons 118
2.10 Deciduous tree families 122

3 Metabolism 124
3.1 Physical principles of biological energy transformation 124
3.2 Role of ATP 128
3.3 Enzymes 129
3.4 Regulation of enzyme activities 137
3.5 Industrial and commercial uses of enzymes 139
3.6 Aerobic pathways of glucose metabolism 140
3.7 Anaerobic pathways of glucose metabolism 144
3.8 Photosynthesis 145

4 Cell biology – Cytology 158
4.1 Eukaryotic cells 158
4.2 Prokaryotic cells 161
4.3 Organelles 162
4.4 Chemical content of a cell 164
4.5 Biomembrane 173
4.6 Analysis of cells 176

5 Genetics 179
5.1 Mendelian and Classical Genetics 179
5.2 Cytogenetics 188
5.3 Human genetics 196
5.4 Population genetics 203
5.5 Molecular genetics 204
5.6 Developmental genetics 221
5.7 Immunogenetics 230
5.8 Methods of DNA analysis and more applied genetics 242

6 Biotechnology 255
6.1 Keywords 255
6.2 Gene transfer 258
6.3 Techniques used to generate recombinant DNA 261
6.4 More applications of genetic engineering techniques 269
6.5 Genetic engineering: hopes and fears 278

7 Evolution 280
7.1 Population genetics 280
7.2 Adaptation 281
7.3 Species 283
7.4 Homology, analogy and rudiments 283
7.5 Genealogy 285
7.6 Early Earth 286
7.7 Human evolution 291

8 Ethology 295
8.1 Topics and methods of ethology 295
8.2 Instinct 297
8.3 Learning 298
8.4 Behavioural ethology 303
8.5 Ethology of human behaviour 311

9 Neurobiology 315
9.1 Stimulation and conduction 315
9.2 Connecting neurons 320
9.3 Sensory organs of the nervous system 322
9.4 Nervous system 326

10 Ecology 329
10.1 Abiotic factors affecting all populations 331
10.2 Population ecology 337
10.3 Population dynamics 343
10.4 Feeding relationships 346
10.5 Environmental cycles 347
10.6 Terrestrial ecosystems 353
10.7 Ecosystem forest 353
10.8 Meadow ecosystem 363
10.9 Man-made ecosystems 366
10.10 Examples of aquatic ecosystems 369
10.11 Lake ecosystem 372
10.12 River and stream ecosystem 381
10.13 Wetland ecosystems 391
10.14 Endangered marine ecosystems 394
10.15 Perils threatening our environment 395

11	Reproduction, growth and development	410
11.1	Asexual reproduction	410
11.2	Sexual reproduction	413

Appendix

Englisches Stichwortregister 421
Deutsches Stichwortregister 462
Übersicht über die Infoboxen 504

Illustrations 505

Englischer Wortschatz Biologie

Der vorliegende Wortschatz wurde für den bilingualen Sachfachunterricht konzipiert und ist aus der Unterrichtspraxis heraus entstanden. Entsprechend ist der Wortschatz auf die Themen der aktuellen Lehrpläne für das Fach Biologie ausgerichtet. Dabei wurden die thematischen Ansätze der gängigen Lehrwerke für den deutschsprachigen Biologieunterricht ebenso berücksichtigt, wie auch die Ansätze von Werken, die speziell für den englischsprachigen Unterricht entwickelt wurden.

Darüber hinaus bilden Lehrwerke aus dem angelsächsischen Sprachraum, englischsprachige Fachzeitschriften, Quellen aus dem Internet sowie ein- und zweisprachige Wörterbücher eine wichtige Grundlage für den vorliegenden Wortschatz.

Ziel des Wortschatzes ist es, Lehrenden und Lernenden schnell Zugang zur relevanten Lexik, die für eine reibungslose Kommunikation im Biologieunterricht unabdingbar ist, zu verschaffen. Dabei werden nicht allein Fachtermini der Biologie im thematischen Zusammenhang gelistet. Vielmehr ermöglicht die Kombination aus Fachbegriffen und zahlreichen Redemitteln, Textbausteinen und Beispielsätzen, den korrekten Einsatz des Wortschatzes in schriftlicher und mündlicher Kommunikation.

Der *Englische Wortschatz Biologie* gliedert sich in zwei große Teilbereiche sowie einen umfangreichen Anhang mit Stichwortregistern und illustriertem Wortschatz.

Der erste Teil **In the Biology Classroom** ist der schriftlichen und mündlichen Kommunikation gewidmet. Hier finden sich neben grundlegendem Klassenzimmervokabular Kernbegriffe des Sachfachs und – in Form von Sprachbausteinen und Redemitteln – umfangreicher Wortschatz für alle aktiven Bereiche des Biologieunterrichts. So geht es um die Arbeit im Labor mit Mikroskop und anderen Utensilien, genauso wie um Feldstudien und das Erstellen von Untersuchungsberichten. Der Umgang mit Tabellen, Charts und Grafiken und Maßeinheiten wird ebenso dargestellt wie die Präsentation und Diskussion von Arbeitsergebnissen.

Der zweite Teil **Basic Vocabulary** beinhaltet grundlegenden Wortschatz zu den Bereichen Pflanzen, Tier, Mensch.

Im Zentrum des Buches steht das: **Thematic Vocabulary**. Dieser Teil vermittelt den thematisch geordneten Wortschatz zu den Kernthemen des Biologieunterrichts. Dabei ist jedes Kernthema in Unterthemen gegliedert, in denen der Wortschatz in lernerfreundlichen, übersichtlichen Lerneinheiten präsentiert wird. Die Gliederung in Haupteinträge und davon abgeleitete Untereinträge ermöglicht einen schnellen Überblick über einen Themenbereich sowie eine gründliche Vertiefung. Zahlreiche Fachbegriffe werden mit ihren Synonymen oder weiteren Wortbedeutungen dargestellt. Zusatzinformationen, die einer Vielzahl von Begriffen zugeordnet werden, erleichtern darüber hinaus das Verständnis des komplexen Fachwortschatzes.

Natürlich werden auch im **Thematic Vocabulary** die Fachbegriffe durch Redemittel und Beispielsätze so angereichert, dass die individuelle Sprachproduktion leicht fällt. Schwierig auszusprechende Wörter werden mit der phonetischen Umschrift wiedergegeben.

Um größere Dopplungen im Wortschatz zu umgehen, finden sich bei einzelnen Kapiteln Querverweise auf engverwandte Themenbereiche.

Die Bereiche **In the Biology Classroom**, **Basic Vocabulary** und **Thematic Vocabulary**, enthalten zahlreiche **Infoboxen** zu verschiedenen Themen, die Wortschatz und kontextuelle Informationen fokussiert darstellen. Eine Liste der Infoboxen findet sich im **Anhang**.

Der *Englische Wortschatz Biologie* versteht sich als Lernwortschatz. Seine thematische Aufbereitung ist darauf ausgerichtet, den Wortschatz in leicht zu verarbeitenden Lernportionen zu präsentieren. Dabei können das Pensum und die Vorgehensweise ganz individuell gehandhabt werden. Natürlich empfiehlt es sich hier, wie bei Wortschatzarbeit generell, regelmäßig und in kleinen Einheiten zu lernen. Dazu bietet die vorliegende Zusammenstellung eine ideale Grundlage.

Darüber hinaus ermöglicht der umfangreiche **Anhang** mit **deutschem und englischem Stichwortregister** das schnelle Nachschlagen des hochspezialisierten Fachwortschatzes in beide Sprachrichtungen. Der Verweis auf die entsprechenden Seiten ordnet das Wort jeweils in den spezifischen Kontext ein. Dabei kann ein Begriff mehr als einem Kontext zugeordnet sein. In Kombination mit dem Inhaltsverzeichnis, ist der richtige Zusammenhang schnell gefunden. Schließlich enthält der Anhang einen umfangreichen, vierfarbigen Abbildungsteil, der ausgewähltes Kernvokabular visualisiert und so den Lernerfolg unterstützt.

Wir wünschen viel Erfolg und Spaß
mit dem *Englischen Wortschatz Biologie*!

Das Autorenteam

Phonetische Umschrift

['] folgende Silbe hat die stärkste Betonung: biology [baɪˈɒlədʒi]
[ˌ] folgende Silbe die zweitstärkste Betonung: biotechnology [ˌbaɪətekˈnɒlədʒi]

[ɪ] in
[e] yes
[æ] can
[ʌ] sun
[ɒ] model
[ʊ] good
[ə] water [ˈwɔːtə]
[iː] beetle
[ɑː] chart
[ɔː] organ
[uː] food
[ɜː] bird
[eɪ] male
[aɪ] life
[ɔɪ] oil
[əʊ] bone
[aʊ] now
[p] population
[t] tree
[k] cage
[f] female
[θ] thorn

[s] cell
[ʃ] shape
[h] hormone
[m] muscle
[n] near
[ŋ] lung
[b] blood
[d] down
[g] good
[v] variation
[ð] feather
[z] physical
[ʒ] vision
[l] like
[r] red
[j] yes
[w] wave
[tʃ] channel
[dʒ] gene
[i] react
[u] visual

Abkürzungsverzeichnis

AE	American English – *Amerikanisches Englisch*
adj	adjective – *Adjektiv, Eigenschaftswort*
adv	adverb – *Adverb*
BE	British English – *Britisches Englisch*
n	noun – *Nomen, Substantiv, Hauptwort*
pl	plural – *Plural, Mehrzahl*
sb	somebody – *jemand(es/em/en)*
sg	singular – *Singular, Einzahl*
sth	something – *etwas*
v	verb – *Verb, Zeitwort*
etw.	etwas – something
jmd.	jemand(es/em/en) – somebody
Pl.	Plural, Mehrzahl – plural
Sg.	Singular, Einzahl – singular

I. In the Biology Classroom

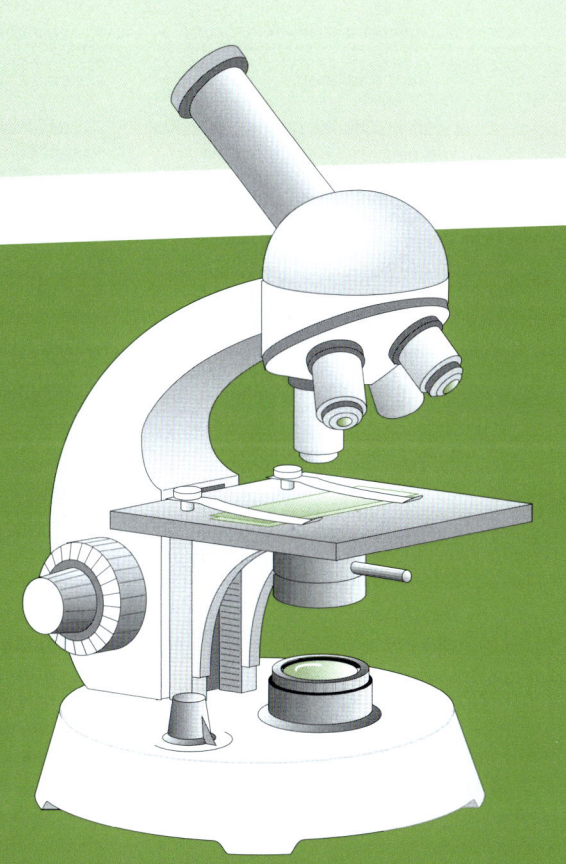

1 Basic biology classroom phrases

1.1 Tasks and "Operatoren"

Your task is to …	Deine / Eure / Ihre Aufgabe ist es,
… collect ideas.	… Ideen zu sammeln.
… think about possible reasons.	… über mögliche Gründe nachzudenken.
… copy the text from the blackboard.	… den Text von der Tafel abzuschreiben.
… state 5 features of endothermic animals.	… 5 Merkmale gleichwarmer Tiere zu nennen.
… analyse the problem.	… das Problem zu analysieren.
… suggest a solution.	… eine Lösung vorzuschlagen.
… infer a solution.	… eine Lösung herzuleiten.
… exemplify the problem of global warming.	… das Problem der Erderwärmung an einem Beispiel zu verdeutlichen.
… give an example of birds of prey.	… ein Beispiel für einen Greifvogel zu nennen.
… list the parts of an animal cell.	… die Bestandteile einer tierischen Zelle aufzulisten.
… label the cell.	… die Zelle zu beschriften.
… define the term molecular genetics.	… den Begriff Molekulargenetik zu definieren.
… give a definition of the term virus.	… eine Definition für den Begriff Virus zu geben.
… present your results.	… eure (Ihre) Ergebnisse dar- / vorzustellen.

describe v	beschreiben
classify v	einordnen / klassifizieren / nach Gruppen ordnen
analyse *BE* / **analyze** *AE* v	analysieren
apply v	anwenden
explain v	erklären
summarise *BE* / **summarize** *AE* v	zusammenfassen

give your view on sth	Stellung zu etw. nehmen
give reasons for sth	etw. begründen

Describe the flight reaction of cockroaches.
Beschreiben Sie den Verlauf der Fluchtreaktion der Schabe.

Classify these hominid skulls in terms of evolution.
Ordnen Sie diese Schädel von Hominiden evolutionsbiologisch ein.

Analyse the phylogenetic tree.
Analysieren Sie den Stammbaum.

Give your view on the following statement.
Nehmen Sie Stellung zur folgenden Aussage.

Apply the Hardy-Weinberg principle to the example.
Wenden Sie auf das Beispiel die Hardy-Weinberg-Regeln an.

Give reasons for this statement using the data given.
Begründen Sie diese Aussage mit Hilfe der vorliegenden Daten.

Explain the low number of species in the habitat.
Erklären Sie die Artenarmut des Habitats.

Summarise the characteristic features of a salt marsh.
Fassen Sie die Merkmale einer Salzmarsch zusammen.

1.2 Comparisons

diagnostic character n	Unterscheidungsmerkmal
characteristic feature n	Erkennungsmerkmal
comparison n	Vergleich
distinguish between v	unterscheiden zwischen
distinct adj	unterschiedlich
confuse v	verwechseln
share (sth) v	(etw.) gemeinsam haben / (etw.) teilen

compare sth with sth	etw. mit etw. vergleichen
tell sth from sth	etw. von etw. unterscheiden

Distinguish between insects and spiders.
Nenne(n Sie) die Unterschiede zwischen Insekten und Spinnen.

There are 4 distinct phases to the cell cycle.
Der Zellzyklus hat 4 unterschiedliche Phasen.

1 Basic biology classroom phrases › 1.3 Form and function

Can you tell apples from pears?
Kannst du Äpfel von Birnen unterscheiden?

Don't confuse legs with antennae.
Verwechsele Beine nicht mit Fühlern.

1.3 Form and function

structure ['strʌktʃə] n	Bau / Struktur
form n	Form / Bau / Struktur
constituent [kən'stɪtjuənt] n	Bestandteil
chief constituent	Hauptbestandteil
order n	Anordnung
function n	Funktion
function (as) v	fungieren (als)

»
be made up of consist of be composed of	bestehen aus
The function of the iris is …	Die Funktion der Iris ist …
Form fits function.	Der Bau passt zur Funktion.

Biological structures are always correlated with functions.
Biologische Strukturen entsprechen immer einer Funktion.

Compare the front limbs of vertebrates in form and function.
Vergleichen Sie die Vorderextremitäten von Wirbeltieren in Bau und Funktion.

1.4 Terminology

term n	Begriff
technical term	Fachbegriff
colloquial term [kə'ləʊkwiəl,tɜːm]	umgangssprachliche Benennung
non-technical term	umgangssprachliche Bezeichnung
non-scientific term	nichtwissenschaftlicher Begriff
name n	Name
scientific name [ˌsaɪən'tɪfɪk,neɪm]	wissenschaftlicher Name
common name	umgangssprachlicher Name
trivial name ['trɪviəl,neɪm]	Trivialname
name v	benennen

2 Biological Key Words

2.1 Areas of study

biology [baɪˈɒlədʒi] n	Biologie
cell biology [ˌselbaɪˈɒlədʒi]	Zellbiologie
marine biology [məˌriːnbaɪˈɒlədʒi]	Meeresbiologie
molecular biology [ˌməˈlekjələbaɪˈɒlədʒi]	Molekularbiologie
microbiology [ˌmaɪkrəʊbaɪˈɒlədʒi]	Mikrobiologie

biologist n	Biologe / Biologin
biological adj	biologisch
bio~ adj	bio~ *(Vorsilbe „Leben")*
biotechnology [ˌbaɪəʊtekˈnɒlədʒi] n	Biotechnologie
biochemistry [ˌbaɪəʊˈkemɪstri] n	Biochemie
bioethics [ˌbaɪəʊˈeθɪks] n	Bioethik
chemistry n	Chemie
physics n	Physik
botany n	Botanik
zoology n	Zoologie
ecology n	Ökologie / Umweltforschung
genetics n	Genetik
molecular genetics	Molekulargenetik
classical genetics	klassische Genetik
Mendelian genetics [menˈdiːliən]	klassische Genetik

» Genetics is a field of much interest for medical research.
Die Genetik ist ein Bereich, der für die medizinische Forschung von großem Interesse ist.

evolution n	Evolution
cytology [saɪˈtɒlədʒi] n	Cytologie
anatomy n	Anatomie
physiology n	Physiologie
ethology [iːˈθɒlədʒi] n	Verhaltensbiologie
behavioural sciences *BE* / behavioral sciences *AE* n pl	Verhaltenswissenschaften / Verhaltensforschung
neurosciences [ˌnjʊərəʊˈsaɪənsɪz] n pl	Neurowissenschaften
anthropology [ˌænθrəˈpɒlədʒi] n	Anthropologie / Menschenwissenschaften
life sciences n pl	Biowissenschaften

2.2 Life

life, *pl* lives n	Leben
metabolism [mə'tæbəlɪzm] n	Stoffwechsel
metabolise *BE* / metabolize *AE* v	Stoffwechsel haben
growth n	Wachstum
grow v	wachsen
movement n	Bewegung
move v	bewegen
reproduction n	Fortpflanzung / Vermehrung
reproduce v	sich fortpflanzen
stimulus ['stɪmjələs], *pl* stimuli ['stɪmjəlaɪ] n	Reiz
reaction (to stimuli) n	Reaktion (auf Reize)
react v	reagieren

2.3 Organisational levels

cell [sel] n	Zelle
tissue ['tɪʃuː] n	Gewebe
organ n	Organ
organism n	Organismus

2.4 Classification

(biological) classification n	Systematik
phylum ['faɪləm], *pl* phyla n	Stamm
class, *pl* classes n	Klasse
order n	Ordnung
family, *pl* families n	Familie
genus ['dʒiːnəs], *pl* genuses; genera ['dʒenərə] n	Gattung
species ['spiːʃiːz], *pl* species n	Art
species name	Artname

Classification – the wolf

phylum: vertebrates	**Stamm**: Wirbeltiere
class: mammals	**Klasse**: Säugetiere
order: carnivors	**Ordnung**: Raubtiere
family: dogs	**Familie**: Hunde
genus: wolves	**Gattung**: Wolfartige
species: wolf	**Art**: Wolf

2.5 Life forms

bacterium [bæk'tɪərɪəm], *pl* bacteria n	Bakterium
fungus ['fʌŋgəs], *pl* fungi ['fʌŋgaɪ] n	Pilz
alga ['ælgə], *pl* algas; algae ['ældʒiː] n	Alge
lichen ['laɪkən] n	Flechte

> Lichens are made up of fungus and alga.
> Flechten bestehen aus Pilz und Algen.

plant n	Pflanze
animal n	Tier
invertebrate [ɪn'vɜːtɪbreɪt] n	Evertebrat / wirbelloses Tier
vertebrate ['vɜːtɪbreɪt] n	Wirbeltier / Vertebrat
arthropod ['ɑːθrəpɒd] n	Gliederfüßer / Arthropode
insect ['ɪnsekt] n	Insekt
arachnid [ə'ræknɪd] n	Spinnentier
myriapod ['mɪrɪəpɒd] n	Tausendfüßer
crustacean [krʌs'teɪʃn] n	Crustacee / Krebstier
fish n	Fisch
reptile ['reptaɪl] n	Reptil / Kriechtier
amphibian [æm'fɪbiən] n	Amphibium / Lurch
bird n	Vogel
mammal ['mæml] n	Säugetier
marsupial [mɑː'suːpɪəl] n	Beuteltier

3 The scientific method

problem n	Problem(stellung)
phenomenon [fɪ'nɒmɪnən], *pl* phenomena; phenomenons n	Phänomen
hypothesis [haɪ'pɒθəsɪs], *pl* hypotheses n	Hypothese »Abb. 1

> | | | | |
> |---|---|---|---|
> | set up ... | | | ... aufstellen |
> | test ... | | | ... überprüfen |
> | verify ... | a hypothesis | eine Hypothese | ... verifizieren |
> | refute ... | | | ... falsifizieren, widerlegen |
> | confirm ... | | | ... bestätigen |
> | reject ... | | | ... verwerfen |

3 The scientific method › 2.5 Life forms

| experiment n | Versuch / Experiment »Abb. 1 |
| experiment v | experimentieren |

design …			entwerfen
set up …	an experiment	einen Versuch…	aufbauen
carry out …			durchführen

result n	Ergebnis
data n pl	Daten
interpretation n	Auswertung / Deutung / Interpretation
interpret (the results) v	(die Ergebnisse) auswerten / deuten / interpretieren
conclude v	schließen / schlussfolgern
conclusion n	Schlussfolgerung

The researchers formulated a problem. Then they set up a hypothesis and gathered data to test it.
Die Forscher formulierten ein Problem. Dann entwickelten sie eine Hypothese und trugen Daten zusammen, um sie zu überprüfen.

We want to find out if …	Wir wollen herausfinden, ob …
Our hypothesis is …	Unsere Hypothese ist …
We suppose that …	Wir glauben, dass …
The experiment shows that …	Der Versuch zeigt, dass …
We conclude that … / Our conclusion is that … / From the experiment can be concluded …	Wir schließen (aus dem Versuch), dass …
Hypothesis 1 is confirmed by our experiment.	Unser Versuch bestätigt Hypothese 1.
Hypothesis 2 is refuted.	Hypothese 2 wurde widerlegt.
Our hypothesis must be rejected.	Unsere Hypothese muss verworfen werden.

4 Experiments and methods

4.1 In the lab

laboratory [ləˈbɒrətri] n	Labor / Fachraum
lab [læb] n	Labor / Fachraum
work bench n	Arbeitstisch / Arbeitsplatte
experiment n	Experiment / Versuch
experimental subject	Versuchsobjekt
experimental plant	Versuchspflanze
experimental animal	Versuchstier

»

carry out an experiment	einen Versuch durchführen
carry out an investigation	eine Untersuchung durchführen

experimenter [ɪkˈsperɪmentə] n	Versuchsleiter(in)
subject / test subject n	Proband(in) / Versuchsperson
participant n	Proband(in) / Teilnehmer(in)
volunteer / study volunteer n	Freiwillige(r)
lab procedure [læbˌprəʊˈsiːdʒə] n	Versuchsanleitung / Vorgehensweise
set up n	Versuchsaufbau
set up of an experiment	Versuchsanordnung

»

The groups presented their lab procedures.
Die Gruppen stellten ihre Versuchsanleitungen vor.

We used different set ups to test the hypotheses.
Wir nutzten verschiedene Versuchsaufbauten, um die Hypothesen zu überprüfen.

precise [prɪˈsaɪs] adj	präzise
feasible [ˈfiːzəbl] adj	machbar / realisierbar / realistisch
reversible [rɪˈvɜːsəbl] adj	reversibel
reproducible adj	reproduzierbar
condition n	Bedingung

Safety

safety precautions [ˈseɪftɪprɪˈkɔːʃnz] n pl	Sicherheitsvorkehrungen
goggles [ɡɒɡlz] / safety goggles n pl	Schutzbrille
protective glasses	Schutzbrille

19

4 Experiments and methods

glove [glʌv] n   Handschuh
lab coat n   Kittel

» You must follow the safety rules.
Man muss die Sicherheitsregeln einhalten.

Remove everything from the work bench.
Entferne(n Sie) alles vom Arbeitstisch.

Solutions, suspensions and liquids

solution n   Lösung
   aqueous solution [ˈeɪkwɪəsfəˌluːʃn]   wässrige Lösung
suspension n   Suspension / Aufschwemmung

» a 10 per cent sugar solution | eine 10-prozentige Zuckerlösung

Pour solution 1 into the test tube. | Schütte(n Sie) Lösung 1 in das Reagenzglas.

emulsify [ɪˈmʌlsɪfaɪ] v   emulgieren
shake v   schütteln
agitate [ˈædʒɪteɪt] v   heftig schütteln / stark rühren
solvent [ˈsɒlvənt] n   Lösungsmittel
solute [ˈsɒljuːt] n   gelöste Substanz
dissolve v   (auf-)lösen
soluble [ˈsɒljəbl] adj   löslich

» Sugar is soluble in water.
Zucker ist löslich in Wasser.
If you dissolve sugar in water, sugar is the solute and water is the solvent.
Wenn man Zucker in Wasser löst, ist Zucker die gelöste Substanz und Wasser das Lösungsmittel.

saturated [ˈsætʃəreɪtɪd] adj   gesättigt
supersaturated [ˌsuːpəˈsætʃəreɪtɪd] adj   übersättigt
saturation point n   Sättigungspunkt
dilute [daɪˈluːt] adj   verdünnt
dilute v   verdünnen

» When you reach the saturation point stop adding salt.
Wenn Sie den Sättigungspunkt erreichen, geben Sie kein weiteres Salz hinzu.
You can dilute a solution by adding more of the solvent.
Man kann eine Lösung verdünnen, indem man mehr vom Lösungsmittel hinzufügt.

saline ['seɪlaɪn] n	Salzlösung
salinity [sə'lɪnəti] n	Salzgehalt
pH [ˌpiː'əitʃ] n	pH-Wert
indicator n	Indikator
litmus paper ['lɪtməsˌpeɪpə] n	Lackmuspapier
acidity [ə'sɪdəti] n	Säuregehalt
acidic [ə'sɪdɪk] adj	sauer
alkaline ['ælklaɪn] n	basisch
neutral ['njuːtrl] adj	neutral

» We tested the pH of solution 1 using litmus paper. It is pH 3, the solution is acidic.
Wir untersuchten den pH-Wert von Lösung 1 mit Lackmuspapier. Der pH-Wert ist 3, die Lösung ist sauer.
Acidity influences enzyme activity.
Der Säuregehalt beeinflusst die Enzymaktivität.

filtration n	Filtration
filtrate n	Filtrat
filter v	filtrieren
evaporate [ɪ'væpəreɪt] v	verdunsten
distillation n	Destillation
distill v	destillieren
decant [dɪ'kænt] v	dekantieren
supernatant [ˌsuːpə'neɪtənt] n	Überstand
centrifuge ['sentrɪfjuːdʒ] n	Zentrifuge
centrifuge / spin v	zentrifugieren
speed of rotation n	Drehgeschwindigkeit *(Zentrifuge)*

» Centrifuge the suspension at high speed.
Zentrifugiere(n Sie) die Suspension bei hoher Geschwindigkeit.
Spin the suspension at high speed, then re-spin the supernatant.
Zentrifugiere(n Sie) die Suspension bei hoher Geschwindigkeit, zentrifugieren Sie dann den Überstand.

4 Experiments and methods › 4.1 In the lab

Heat
boil v   kochen
boiling point n   Siedepunkt
heat v   erhitzen
water bath n   Wasserbad
incubate ['ɪŋkjʊbeɪt] v   inkubieren / bebrüten / heranzüchten

»
heat sth over a flame	etw. über einer Flamme erhitzen
incubate sth for a number of hours / days	etw. für eine bestimmte Anzahl an Stunden / Tagen inkubieren

sterilisation BE / **sterilization** AE   Sterilisation
[ˌsterəlaɪ'zeɪʃn] n
sterilise BE / **sterilize** AE ['sterəlaɪz] v   sterilisieren
sterile ['steraɪl] adj   steril

»
Bring the solution to the boil. (AE: bring sth to a boil)
Bringe(n Sie) die Lösung zum Kochen.
Heat the alcohol in a water bath. / Heat the mixture over the Bunsen burner.
Erhitze(n Sie) den Alkohol im Wasserbad. / Erhitze(n Sie) die Mischung über dem Bunsenbrenner.
Incubate the cultures for 3 days at 37°C (centigrade / degrees Celsius).
Inkubiere(n Sie) die Kulturen 3 Tage lang bei 37°C.

Testing, measuring and examination

test n   Nachweis
test v   untersuchen / nachweisen

»
test sth for sth	etw. auf etw. testen

We tested the potato for starch.
Wir untersuchten die Kartoffel auf Stärke.

Add a few drops of Lugol's solution.
Gib (Geben Sie) ein paar Tropfen Lugol'scher Lösung hinzu.

measure ['meʒə] v   messen
measurable ['meʒrəbl] adj   messbar
measurement error n   Messfehler

quantifiable ['kwɑntɪfaɪəbl] adj	quantifizierbar
examine [ɪɡ'zæmɪn] v	untersuchen
electrophoresis [ɪˌlektrəfə'riːsɪs] n	Elektrophorese
chromatography [ˌkrəʊmə'tɒɡrəfi] n	Chromatografie
chromatogram ['krəʊmətəɡræm] n	Chromatogramm
polymerase chain reaction [ˌpɒlɪmreɪs'tʃeɪnriˌækʃn] n	Polymerase-Kettenreaktion
PCR	PCR

Results and interpretation

decolourise *BE* / decolorize *AE* v	entfärben

» When the chlorophyll leaves the leaf, the leaf decolourises. It loses its original colour.
Wenn das Chlorophyll das Blatt verlässt, wird das Blatt entfärbt. Es verliert seine ursprüngliche Farbe.

We decolourised the leaf.
Wir haben das Blatt entfärbt.

convert into v	umsetzen in
observation n	Beobachtung
observe v	beobachten / feststellen

» We observed a change in colour. | Wir stellten einen Farbumschlag fest.

notice v	bemerken
result n	Ergebnis

» Discuss / Interpret the results. | Diskutiere(n) / Interpretiere(n Sie) die Ergebnisse.
What are your results? | Was ist euer (Ihr) Ergebnis?
What have you found out? | Was habt ihr (haben Sie) herausgefunden?

summarise ['sʌməraɪz] *BE* / summarize *AE* v	zusammenfassen
interpretation n	Interpretation / Deutung / Auswertung
interpret v	interpretieren / deuten
explain v	erklären
evaluate (sth) v	(etw.) auswerten

4 Experiments and methods › 4.2 The microscope

> Explain the results of the experiment by referring to the graph.
> Erkläre(n Sie) die Ergebnisse des Versuchs anhand der Grafik.
>
> Comment on the results of the experiment.
> Erläutern Sie die Ergebnisse des Experiments.
>
> Evaluate the collected data looking at water quality.
> Werte(n Sie) die gewonnenen Daten hinsichtlich der Gewässergüte aus.

4.2 The microscope » Abb. 4–14

microscope [ˈmaɪkrəskəʊp] n	Mikroskop
binocular microscope [baɪˌnɒkjələ ˈmaɪkrəskəʊp] n	Binokular
electron microscope [ɪˌlektrɒn ˈmaɪkrəskəʊp] n	Elektronenmikroskop
use a microscope	mikroskopieren
microscopic [ˌmaɪkrəˈskɒpɪk] adj	mikroskopisch klein
macroscopic [ˌmækrəˈskɒpɪk] adj	makroskopisch
microscopy [maɪˈkrɒskəpɪ] n	Mikroskopie
fluorescence microscopy [flɔːˌresnsmaɪˈkrɒskəpɪ]	Fluoreszenzmikroskopie
bright-field microscopy	Durchlicht-Hellfeldmikroskopie
dark-field microscopy	Durchlicht-Dunkelfeldmikroskopie
phase-contrast microscopy	Phasenkontrastverfahren
polarised-light microscopy	Polarisationsmikroskopie
visible adj	sichtbar
invisible adj	unsichtbar
illuminate v	erleuchten / durchleuchten
direct light / transmitted-light n	Durchlicht
reflected light n	Auflicht
diffracted light [dɪˈfræktɪdˌlaɪt] n	gebeugtes Licht

» Fluorescence microscopy uses blue, green or ultra-violet light to illuminate a sample.
Bei der Fluoreszenzmikroskopie wird das Objekt mit blauem, grünem oder UV-Licht beleuchtet.
In bright-field microscopy the sample is illuminated with visible light.
Bei der Durchlicht-Hellfeldmikroskopie wird das Objekt von sichtbarem Licht durchstrahlt.
The structures of objects appear bright against the dark in dark-field microscopy.
Die Strukturen von Objekten leuchten hell vor dunklem Hintergrund bei Durchlicht-Dunkelfeldmikroskopie.
Phase-contrast microscopy uses the interference between direct and diffracted light.
Das Phasenkontrastverfahren nutzt die Interferenz zwischen direktem und gebeugtem Licht.
In polarised-light microscopy, the sample is illuminated by plane-polarised light.
Im Polarisationsmikroskop wird das Objekt mit linear-polarisiertem Licht beleuchtet.

coarse adjustment knob [kɔːsəˈdʒʌstmənt‿nɒb] n	Grobtrieb
fine adjustment knob n	Feintrieb
eyepiece / ocular (lens) n	Okular
nosepiece / revolving nosepiece n	Revolver / Objektivrevolver
objective n	Objektiv
low power objective	Objektiv mit kleiner Vergrößerung
high power objective	Objektiv mit großer Vergrößerung
lens n	Linse
tube [tjuːb] n	Tubus
microscope stage n	Objekttisch
microscope slide n	Objektträger
illuminating system [ɪˈluːmɪneɪtɪŋ] n	Beleuchtung
diaphragm [ˈdaɪəfræm] n	Blende
specimen [ˈspesəmɪn] n	Objekt
permanent mount [ˌpɜːmənəntˈmaʊnt] n	Dauerpräparat
squash preparation [ˈskwɒʃprəprˌeɪʃn] n	Quetschpräparat

sample [ˈsɑːmpl] n	Untersuchungsobjekt
section [ˈsekʃn] n	Schnitt
cross section	Querschnitt
transverse section [ˈtrænzvɜːzˌsekʃn]	Querschnitt
longitudinal section [ˌlɒndʒɪˈtjuːdɪnlˌsekʃn]	Längsschnitt
section v	Schnitt(e) anfertigen

4 Experiments and methods › 4.2 The microscope

» Cut a cross section. Now section the leaf. Remove any excess water with filter paper.
Fertige(n Sie) einen Querschnitt an. Fertige(n Sie) nun Schnitte vom Blatt an.
Sauge(n Sie) überstehendes Wasser mit etwas Filterpapier ab.

| magnification n | Vergrößerung |
| magnify v | vergrößern |

» smallest, medium, largest magnification | kleinste, mittlere, größte Vergrößerung

Look at the specimen at a magnification of 25 times.
Betrachte(n Sie) das Objekt bei einer 25-fachen Vergrößerung.

Examine the specimen with the next higher magnification.
Untersuche(n Sie) das Objekt mit der nächstgrößeren Vergrößerung.

stain(ing agent) n	Färbemittel
stain v	(an)färben
unstained adj	ungefärbt

» Use methylene blue solution to stain the cheek cells.
Färbt (färben Sie) die Mundschleimhautzellen mit Methylenblau.

Suck the stain solution underneath the cover slip.
Sauge(n Sie) die Färbelösung unter dem Deckgläschen durch.

infusion of hay / hay infusion n	Heuaufguss
microorganism n	Mikroorganismus
paramecium [ˌpærəˈmiːsiəm] n	Pantoffeltierchen / Paramecium
euglena [ˈjuːgliːnə] n	Augentierchen / Euglena
amoeba [əˈmiːbə] n	Amöbe
vorticella [ˌvɔːtəˈselə] n	Glockentierchen / Vorticella
heliozoan [ˌhiːlɪəʊˈzəʊən] n	Sonnentierchen / Heliozoe
radiolarian ˌreɪdiəʊˈlæriən] n	Strahlentierchen / Radiolarie
colpidium [kɒlˈpɪdiəm] n	Heutierchen

label n	Beschriftung
label v	beschriften
sketch n	Skizze
sketch v	skizzieren
drawing n	Zeichnung

> Make a labelled drawing using a sharpened pencil.
> Fertige(n Sie) mit einem gespitzten Bleistift eine beschriftete Zeichnung an.
>
> Draw labelling lines with a ruler.
> Benutze(n Sie) ein Lineal für die Linien zur Beschriftung.
>
> Draw a sketch.
> Mache(n Sie) eine Skizze.

4.3 Lab equipment

lab equipment [ˌlæbɪˈkwɪpmənt] n	Laborgeräte
lab [læb] / laboratory, pl laboratories n	Labor / Fachraum
biology store n	Sammlung

In the lab » Abb. 2–6

dissecting pan [dɪˈsektɪŋˌpæn] n	Sezierwanne
dissecting needle n	Präpariernadel
probe [prəʊb] n	Probe / Sonde
scalpel [ˈskælpl] n	Skalpell
razor (blade) [ˈreɪzə] n	Rasierklinge
tweezers [ˈtwiːzəz] n pl	Pinzette
hand lens n	Stiellupe
magnifying glass [ˈmægnɪfaɪɪŋˌglɑːs] / magnifier n	Vergrößerungsglas / Lupe

microscope [ˈmaɪkrəskəʊp] n	Mikroskop
microscope slide [ˈmaɪkrəskəʊpˌslaɪd] n	Objektträger
coverslip n	Deckgläschen

mortar [ˈmɔːtə] n	Mörser
pestle [ˈpəsl] n	Pistill / Stößel
spatula [ˈspætjələ] n	Spatel
scales / weighing scales n pl	Waage
wash bottle / squeeze bottle n	Spritzflasche

pipette [pɪˈpet] n	Pipette
graduated pipette	Messpipette
micropipette	Mikropipette
pipetteman / pipetteboy n	Peleusball / Pipettierball / Pipettierhilfe

4 Experiments and methods › 4.3 Lab equipment

dropper / Pasteur pipette [pæsˈtɜː] n	Tropfpipette
stirring rod [ˈstɜːrɪŋˌrɒd] / glass stirring rod n	Glasstab
watch glass, *pl* glasses n	Uhrglas
petri dish [ˈpetriˌdɪʃ] n	Petrischale
beaker [ˈbiːkə] n	Becherglas
cylinder glass, *pl* glasses [ˈsɪlɪndəˌɡlɑːs] n	Standzylinder
graduated cylinder [ˈɡrædjueɪtɪdˌsɪlɪndə] / measuring cylinder / graduated glass n	Messzylinder
Erlenmeyer flask [ˈɜːlənmaɪəˌflɑːsk] n	Erlenmeyerkolben
funnel [fʌnl] n	Trichter
separating funnel	Scheidetrichter
test tube n	Reagenzglas
test tube stand / test tube rack	Reagenzglasständer / Reagenzglasgestell
stopper n	Stopfen
crucible tongs [ˈkruːsɪblˌtɒŋz] n pl	Tiegelzange
ring stand n	Stativ
ring clamp / retort ring n	Stativring
tripod [ˈtraɪpɒd] n	Dreifuß
wire gauze [ɡɔːz] n	Drahtnetz
gas supply n	Gaszufuhr
gas valve n	Gashahn
Bunsen burner [ˌbʌnsnˈbɜːnə] n	Bunsenbrenner
gas burner	Gasbrenner
hot plate n	Heizplatte
water bath n	Wasserbad
fume hood [ˈfjuːmˌhʊd] n	Abzug
incubator [ˈɪnkjʊbeɪtə] n	Brutschrank / Inkubator
centrifuge [ˈsentrɪfjuːdʒ] n	Zentrifuge
thermometer [θəˈmɒmɪtə] n	Thermometer
stop watch / stop clock / timer n	Stoppuhr

Everyday tools

scissors n pl	Schere
glue n	Klebstoff
glue stick	Klebestift
tube of glue	Klebstofftube

sticky tape *BE* / adhesive tape *AE* n	Klebeband
Sellotape™ *BE* / Scotch tape™ *AE* n	Tesafilm
rubber band n	Gummiband
paper clip n	Büroklammer
straw n	Trinkhalm
cotton wool n	Watte
cotton (wool) ball / cotton pad n	Watte / Wattebausch / Wattepad
cotton bud *BE* / cotton swab *AE* n	Wattestäbchen

Substances, solutions and tests

substance n	Stoff
solution n	Lösung
solvent ['sɒlvənt] n	Lösungsmittel
alcohol n	Alkohol
ethanol ['eθənɒl] n	Ethanol
water n	Wasser
distilled water	destilliertes Wasser
deionised water [dɪˌaɪənaɪzd'wɔːtə]	entsalztes Wasser
reagent [ˌriːˈeɪdʒənt] n	Reagens
stain(ing agent) n	Färbemittel / Farbstoff
dye [daɪ] n	Farbstoff
Sudan (dye) [suːˈdɑːn (daɪ)] n	Sudan(-farbstoff)
methylene blue solution ['meθliːn] n	Methylenblau
eosin [ˌiːəˈsɪn] n	Eosin
neutral red n	Neutralrot
test substance n	Nachweismittel
indicator n	Indikator
universal indicator	Universalindikator
litmus ['lɪtməs] n	Lackmus
litmus paper	Lackmuspapier
methyl orange ['miːθaɪl] n	Methylorange
Lugol's solution / Lugol's iodine n	Lugolsche Lösung
iodine solution ['aɪədiːn]	Jodlösung
Fehling's test n	Fehlingprobe
Fehling's solution n	Fehlingsche Lösung
biuret test ['beɪjəretˌtest] n	Biuret-Test
biuret reaction n	Biuretreaktion
Ringer's solution n	Ringerlösung

4 Experiments and methods › 4.4 In the field

4.4 In the field

transect n	Transekt
line transect	Linientransekt
belt transect	Flächentransekt
girth [gɜːθ] n	Umfang

» Measure the width, length, depth of the pond.
Miss (Messen Sie) die Breite, Länge und Tiefe des Teichs.

indicator species, *pl* species n	Zeigerart
sample ['sɑːmpl] n	Probe
random sample	Zufallsprobe
kick sample	Kickprobe
soil sample ['sɔɪlˌsɑːmpl]	Bodenprobe
water sample	Wasserprobe
sample size	Probengröße
sampling n	Probenentnahme
sample v	Proben entnehmen
record v	aufzeichnen / festhalten
recording sheet	Ergebnisbogen

»
random sampling	das Nehmen von Zufallsproben
take a sample	eine Probe entnehmen

We will take soil samples. | Wir werden Bodenproben nehmen.

The (river) Fulda was sampled close to its source.
Die Fulda wurde nah der Quelle untersucht.

Five 20 second kick samples were taken.
Es wurden fünf 20-sekündige Kickproben entnommen.

Tools for field studies

field work n	Feldforschung / Untersuchung im Freiland
tool n	Gerät / Arbeitsgerät
net n	Fangnetz
dip net	Kescher
jar [dʒɑː] n	Glas / Aufbewahrungsglas
sample container n	Probengefäß

tweezers ['twiːzəz] n	Pinzette
magnifying glass ['mægnɪfaɪɪŋˌglɑːs] / magnifier n	Lupe / Vergrößerungsglas
hand lens n	Stiellupe
binoculars n pl	Fernglas
soil sampler n	Erdbohrer *(Gerät zum Nehmen von Bodenproben)*
rule / folding rule n	Zollstock
tape measure n	Maßband
quadrate ['kwɒdrət] n	Probequadrat
rubber glove n	Gummihandschuh
waterproofs n pl	Regenkleidung
wellington (boot) [ˌwelɪŋtən'buːt] n	Gummistiefel
first aid kit n	Erste-Hilfe-Tasche

4.5 Models

model n	Modell
scale model	maßstabsgetreues Modell
cell model	Zellmodell
thought model	Gedankenmodell / Denkmodell
fictional model	Modellvorstellung
material model	Anschauungsmodell
functional model	Funktionsmodell
working model	bewegliches Modell
model of a protein molecule [ˌprəʊtiːn'mɒlɪkjuːl]	Modell eines Eiweißmoleküls
evaluation of a model	Modellkritik
model v	modellieren / ein Modell erstellen
modelling n	Modellbildung

» There are material models like Watson and Crick's model of the DNA molecule and fictional models like Bohr's model of the atom.
Es gibt Anschauungsmodelle wie das DNA-Modell von Watson und Crick, sowie Gedankenmodelle wie das Bohr'sche Atommodell.

4 Experiments and methods › 4.5 Models

> A model is …
>
> … an idealised and reduced representation of a complex object, structure, phenomenon.
>
> … a simplification of an abstract phenomenon.
>
> … a copy of a structure.

> Ein Modell ist …
>
> … eine idealisiertes und reduziertes Abbild eines komplexen Objekts, einer Struktur oder eines Phänomens.
>
> … eine Vereinfachung eines abstrakten Phänomens.
>
> … die Nachbildung einer Struktur.

> A model includes (only) the features relevant for answering the question.
> Ein Modell besitzt (nur) die für die Beantwortung der Fragestellung wesentlichen Eigenschaften.
> A model includes features that are absent in the real object.
> Ein Modell besitzt Eigenschaften, die im realen Objekt nicht vorhanden sind.
> Is a stuffed animal a model of this animal?
> Ist ein ausgestopftes Tier ein Modell dieses Tieres?

> A model you can
> … use to explain sth.
> … design.
> … develop (from experiments).
> … improve.
> … describe.
> … compare with sth.
> … plan.
> … construct.
> … build.
> … manipulate.
> … implement.
> … interpret.
> … evaluate.
>
> Ein Modell kann man …
> … anwenden, um etw. zu erklären.
> … entwickeln.
> … (aus Versuchen) entwickeln.
> … verbessern.
> … beschreiben.
> … mit etw. vergleichen.
> … entwerfen, planen.
> … konstruieren, bauen.
> … bauen, basteln.
> … bedienen, betätigen.
> … anwenden, einsetzen.
> … interpretieren.
> … beurteilen.

»

A model is used to	Ein Modell wird benutzt um komplexe Phänomene / Strukturen / Beobachtungen zu …
… understand …	…verstehen.
… illustrate …	…veranschaulichen.
… explain …	…erklären.
… investigate …	…untersuchen.
… simulate …	…simulieren.
… analyse …	…analysieren.
complex phenomena / structures / observations.	

»

With a model you can perform (thought) experiments / simulations.
Mit einem Modell kann man (Gedanken-) Experimente / Simulationen durchführen.

»

A model can be	Ein Modell kann
… good.	…gut …
… weak.	…schwach …
… suitable.	…passend …
… reduced.	…reduziert …
… adequate.	…geeignet … sein.
A model can have …	Ein Modell kann …
… weaknesses.	… Schwächen …
… limitations.	… Grenzen …
… validity.	… Aussagekraft … haben.

»

Evaluate the model's validity.
Beurteile(n Sie) die Aussagekraft des Modells.

Structure x in the model represents y in reality.
Die Struktur x im Modell entspricht y in der Realität.

In our model, the oil represents the fat layer of the seal.
In unserem Modell entspricht das Öl der Fettschicht der Robbe.

4.6 Writing utensils

graph paper n	Millimeterpapier
drawing paper n	Zeichenpapier
jotter ['dʒɒtə] n	Notizheft / Kladde
notebook n	Notizbuch
notepad n	Notizblock
ruler n	Lineal
set square n	Geodreieck
rubber *BE* / eraser *AE* [ɪ'reɪzə] n	Radiergummi
pencil n	Bleistift
mechanical pencil	Druckbleistift
pencil sharpener n	Spitzer

4.7 Writing up

lab report n	Versuchsbeschreibung *(kurzes ausformuliertes Versuchsprotokoll)*
write-up n	Untersuchungsbericht *(Text, der die Untersuchung zusammenfasst)*
write up v	aufschreiben *(die Untersuchung in einem Text zusammenfassen)*
investigation [ɪnˌvestɪ'geɪʃn] n	Untersuchung
aim [eɪm] n	Ziel

»
The aim of the project is to find out why …	Das Ziel des Projekts ist es, herauszufinden, warum …
background of the investigation	Hintergrund der Untersuchung

introduction n	Einleitung
hypothesis [haɪ'pɒθəsɪs], *pl* hypotheses [haɪ'pɒθəsiːz] n	Hypothese
site [saɪt] n	Standort / Fundort
study v	untersuchen
investigate [ɪn'vestɪgeɪt] v	untersuchen / ermitteln

»
the site is located at …	der Fundort befindet sich …
sth was studied to investigate sth	etw. wurde untersucht, um etw. zu ermitteln
investigate the effect of …	den Effekt von etw. untersuchen …

outcome (of an investigation) n	Ergebnis (einer Untersuchung)
research v	untersuchen / erforschen
research n	Forschung

»

carry out research	eine Untersuchung durchführen
Further research could include …	Weitergehende Untersuchungen könnten sein …

State clearly the aim of your investigation.
Schreibe(n Sie) das Ziel deiner (Ihrer) Untersuchung explizit auf.

In your introduction, present the background of your investigation, give information about the objects or the site. State your hypothesis.
Stelle(n Sie) in der Einleitung den Hintergrund der Untersuchung vor und gib (geben Sie) Informationen über die Objekte oder den Standort. Nenne(n Sie) deine (Ihre) Hypothese.

Two sites located at White Bay were studied to investigate the effect of grazer pressure on macroalgal species richness.
Zwei Standorte in der White Bay wurden untersucht, um die Auswirkungen von Fraßdruck auf den Artenreichtum der Makroalgen zu ermitteln.

method ['meθəd] n	Methode / Vorgehensweise
materials *(equipment)* n pl	Materialien
sample ['sɑːmpl] n	Probe
take a sample	einen Probe nehmen
water sample	Wasserprobe
measure ['meʒə] v	messen
collect data v	Daten sammeln
record v	aufzeichnen / festhalten
result n	Ergebnis
discussion n	Diskussion / Interpretation
possible explanation n	mögliche Erklärung

»

sth was measured	etw. wurde gemessen
record results	die Ergebnisse aufzeichnen
present results in a chart or graph	die Ergebnisse in einem Schaubild oder Diagramm präsentieren
results indicate that	die Ergebnisse zeigen an, dass / weisen darauf hin, dass / lassen erkennen, dass
discuss reasons for sth	Gründe für etw. diskutieren / interpretieren
play an important role	eine wichtige Rolle spielen

4 Experiments and methods › 4.7 Writing up

»
Describe your procedure, methods and materials.
Beschreibe(n Sie Ihre) deine Vorgehensweise, die Methoden und Materialien.
In the results paragraph, give a clear picture of the data you have collected. Use tables and graphs.
Gib (geben Sie) ein klares Bild der gesammelten Daten im Abschnitt über die Ergebnisse. Benutze(n Sie) Tabellen und Grafiken.
In the discussion, interpret the results looking at your hypothesis. Discuss reasons for the outcome of the investigation.
Interpretiere(n Sie) die Ergebnisse im Hinblick auf die Hypothese im Abschnitt „Diskussion". Diskutiere(n Sie) Gründe für das Ergebnis der Untersuchung.

The results are presented below.
Die Ergebnisse sind unten dargestellt.
Our findings are shown in table 1 below.
Unsere Ergebnisse sind unten in Tabelle 1 dargestellt.
The highest number of species was recorded in zone 1.
Die größte Artenzahl wurde in Zone 1 gezählt.
There was no significant difference between zones 1 and 2.
Es gab zwischen Zone 1 und 2 keinen signifikanten Unterschied.
Differences between the sites were found.
Wir stellten Unterschiede zwischen den Standorten fest.
The results indicate that salinity plays an important role in species distribution.
Die Ergebnisse weisen darauf hin, dass der Salzgehalt für die Verteilung der Arten eine wichtige Rolle spielt.

reference n — Literaturangabe
acknowledgements [əkˈnɒlɪʤmənts] n pl — Danksagung
asterisk [ˈæstrɪsk] n — Sternchen *(für Fußnote)*
footnote n — Fußnote
bracket [ˈbrækɪt] v — einklammern

»
In the references paragraph, give details of all the books, articles and other sources you have used.
Gib (geben Sie) in den Literaturangaben alle genutzten Bücher, Artikel und sonstige Quellen genau an.
In your acknowledgements you can thank everyone who has helped you.
In der Danksagung kannst du (können Sie) allen danken, die dir (Ihnen) geholfen haben.

Passive voice

In scientific writing the passive voice is often used. Using the passive voice puts the focus on the action rather than the actor. The scientist as a person remains in the background.
The passive voice: **subject** + **form of** *to be* + **past participle**
Example: **Depth of water was recorded**. *Die Wassertiefe wurde festgestellt.*
You can also use the pronoun *we*; first person singular (*I*) should be avoided.
Example: **We examined the distribution of different species of wracks on the shore.**
Wir untersuchten die Verteilung verschiedener Tangarten am Strand.

Participle constructions

Participle constructions also stress the action and leave the scientist out of focus. Participles can replace subordinate clauses.
Participle constructions:
present participle (ing-form)
Example: **Depth of water was recorded using a rule.** *Die Wassertiefe wurde mit Hilfe eines Zollstocks festgestellt.*
past participle
Examples: **The questions asked are** ... *Die Fragen, die gestellt werden, sind* ...
The plants sampled at the lake were different from those at the stream.
Die Pflanzen, die am See gefunden wurden, sind andere als die am Bach.

5 Graphs and Figures

5.1 Illustrations » Abb. 7–14, 18

figure ['fɪɡə] n	Abbildung
poster n	Plakat / Poster
slide n	Dia
slide projector	Diaprojektor
image n	Aufnahme / Darstellung
microscopic image	mikroskopische Aufnahme
electron microscopic image	elektronenmikroskopische Darstellung
EM-image	EM-Darstellung
fluorescence picture [flɔː'resns‚pɪktʃə] n	Fluoreszenzaufnahme
X-ray photograph ['eksreɪˌfəʊtəɡrɑːf] n	Röntgenaufnahme
by eye adj	unvergrößert
by magnifying glass adj	Ansicht mit Lupe
by microscopy adj	Ansicht unter dem Mikroskop
section ['sekʃn] n	Schnitt
cross section	Querschnitt

5 Graphs and Figures › 5.2 Statistics and Numbers

longitudinal section	Längsschnitt
sagittal section ['sædʒɪtlˌsekʃn]	Sagittalschnitt
midsagittal section ['mɪdˌsædʒɪtlˌsekʃn]	Medianschnitt
serial section	Serienschnitt
view n	Ansicht
inferior view	Ansicht von unten
surface view / top view	Ansicht von oben / Aufsicht
side view	Ansicht von der Seite
sectional view	Schnittansicht

» Here you can see a leaf in surface view.
Hier siehst du (sehen Sie) ein Blatt in Aufsicht.

Figure 1 shows the leaf in inferior view.
Abbildung 1 zeigt das Blatt von unten.

vertical adj	vertikal
horizontal adj	horizontal
laterally inverted adj	seitenverkehrt
three-dimensional adj	dreidimensional

»
In the top left corner you can see …	In der linken oberen Ecke sieht man …
In the top right-hand corner there is / are …	In der oberen rechten Ecke ist / sind …
At the bottom of the picture you can see …	Unten auf dem Bild ist … zu sehen.
In the foreground of the picture you can see …	Im Vordergrund kannst du / können Sie … sehen.
In the background … is discernible.	Im Hintergrund ist … erkennbar.

label n	Beschriftung
label v	beschriften

5.2 Statistics and Numbers

data pl	Daten
empirical [ɪmˈpɪrɪkl] adj	empirisch
qualitative [ˈkwɒlɪtətɪv] adj	qualitativ
quantitative [ˈkwɒntɪtətɪv] adj	quantitativ
set of data n	Datensatz

| data point n | Datenpunkt |
| figure n | Zahl / Ziffer |

empirical		empirische	
qualitative	data	qualitative	Daten
quantitative		quantitative	

Calculate the population development using the data given.
Berechnen Sie die Entwicklung der Population anhand der gegebenen Daten.

statistics n — Statistik
stats coll — Statistik
  statistical significance — statistische Signifikanz
  null hypothesis [nɪlhaɪˈpɒθəsɪs] n — Nullhypothese

chi-square test [ˈkaɪskweəˌtest] n — Chi-Quadrat-Test
t-test / Student's t-test n — t-Test
correlation [ˌkɒrəˈleɪʃn] n — Korrelation
  correlation coefficient [kɒrəˈleɪʃnkəʊɪˌfɪʃnt] — Korrelationskoeffizient
constant [ˈkɒnstənt] n — Konstante
parameter [pəˈræmɪtə] n — Parameter
factor n — Faktor

average [ˈævrɪdʒ] n — Durchschnitt
average adj — durchschnittlich
mean n — Durchschnitt
mean adj — durchschnittlich
  arithmetic mean [ˌærɪθˈmetɪkˈmiːn] — arithmetisches Mittel
deviation [ˌdiːviˈeɪʃn] n — Abweichung
  mean deviation — durchschnittliche Abweichung
median n — Median
total n — Summe
percentage [pəˈsentɪdʒ] n — Prozentsatz
per cent BE / percent AE [pəˈsent] n — Prozent
rate n — Rate
probability n — Wahrscheinlichkeit

The probability of x is 15%. | Die Wahrscheinlichkeit von x ist 15%.

quantity, pl quantities n — Größe / physikalische Größe
unit n — Einheit
  metrical units — metrische Einheiten

5 Graphs and Figures › 5.2 Statistics and Numbers

Quantities and their units

Quantity	Größe	Units	Abbreviation
length	Länge	meter	m
volume	Volumen	litre BE, liter AE	l
mass	Masse	gramme	g
		ton	t
time	Zeit	second	s
		minute	min
		hour	h
electric current	Stromstärke	Ampere	A
voltage	Spannung	Volt	V
resistance	Widerstand	Ohm	Ω
temperature	Temperatur	degrees Kelvin	°K
			0°K = -273 °C
		degrees Celsius	°C
			°C = 5/9 (°F-32)
		degrees Fahrenheit	°F
			°F = 9/5 °C + 32
amount of substance	Stoffmenge	Mol / Mole	mol
luminous intensity	Lichtstärke	Candela	cd
pressure	Druck	Pascal	P

Prefixes and their abbreviations

Prefix		Abbreviation	Value
nano-		n	x 10^{-9}
micro- (deutsch: Mikro-)		µ	x 10^{-6}
milli-		m	x 10^{-3}
centi-		c	x 10^{-2}
deci- (deutsch: Dezi-)		d	x 10^{-1}
hecto- (deutsch: Hekto-)		h	x 100
kilo-		k	x 1000
square- (deutsch: Quadrat-) 10^2 = ten to the power of two zehn hoch zwei		2	
cubic- (deutsch: Kubik-) 18^3 = eighteen cubed (eighteen to the power of three) achtzehn hoch drei		3	
27^{19} = twenty-seven to the power of nineteen siebenundzwanzig hoch neunzehn			
billion		10^9	1.000.000.000 (Milliarde)
trillion		10^{12}	1.000.000.000.000 (Billion)

5.3 Graphs and Charts » Abb. 15–17

graph [grɑːf] n	Diagramm / Grafik
line graph	Kurve(-ndiagramm)
pie graph	Kuchendiagramm / Kreisdiagramm
graph paper n	Millimeterpapier

»
describe		eine	beschreiben
interpret	a graph	Kurve	interpretieren
draw			zeichnen

chart [tʃɑːt] n	Diagramm / Kurve
bar chart	Säulendiagramm
flow chart	Flussdiagramm
pie chart	Kuchendiagramm / Kreisdiagramm
line n	Kurve / Linie
table n	Tabelle
diagram ['daɪəgræm] n	Diagramm / Abbildung

»
Name features 1–5 in the diagram.	Benennen Sie Teile 1–5 der Abbildung.
Fill in the table.	Vervollständige(n Sie) die Tabelle.
Put your findings / results in a table.	Trage deine Ergebnisse in eine Tabelle ein.

curve n	Kurve (mathematische)
axis ['æksɪs], pl axes n	Achse
x axis ['eks͵æksɪs]	X-Achse
y axis ['waɪ͵æksɪs]	Y-Achse
horizontal axis	waagerechte Achse
vertical axis	senkrechte Achse
ordinate n	Ordinate / X-Achse
abscissa [æb'sɪsə], pl abscissas; abscissae n	Abszisse / Y-Achse
variable n	Variable
independent variable	unabhängige Variable
dependent variable	abhängige Variable

Drawing graphs

unit n	Einheit
quantity, pl quantities n	Eigenschaft

» Label the axes.
Beschrifte(n Sie) die Achsen.

Don't forget to include the units.
Vergiss (Vergessen Sie) nicht, die Einheiten anzugeben.

We use the unit gramme for mass.
Wir benutzen die Einheit Gramm für die Masse.

gramme / gram *AE* n	Gramm
legend ['leʤənd] n	Legende
plot v	auftragen
data n pl	Daten
set of data	Datensatz
data point	Datenpunkt
extrapolate [ɪk'stræpəleɪt] v	extrapolieren / die Kurve verlängern
interpolate [ɪn'tɜːpəleɪt] v	interpolieren / zwischen Datenpunkten vermitteln

»
time in minutes	Zeit in Minuten
temperature in degrees Celsius	Temperatur in Grad Celsius
Plot your data.	Trage(n Sie) die Daten auf.

(Don't) connect the data points in different colours for each set of data.
Verbinde(n Sie) die Datenpunkte des jeweiligen Datensatzes (nicht) verschiedenfarbig.

Colour the pie chart.
Male(n Sie) das Kreisdiagramm verschiedenfarbig aus.

Talking and writing about graphs

bell curve n	Optimumskurve
optimum, *pl* optima n	Optimum
maximum, *pl* maxima n	Maximum
global maximum	globales Maximum
local maximum	lokales Maximum
highest value n	höchster Wert
high point n	Hochpunkt
minimum, *pl* minima n	Minimum
lowest value n	niedrigster Wert
low point n	Tiefpunkt
turning point n	Wendepunkt

» | | |
|---|---|
| Give a description of the slope. | Beschreibe(n Sie) den Kurvenverlauf. |
| Mention the title of the graph. | Nenne(n Sie) den Titel der Kurve. |
| Temperature was
… recorded every minute.
… plotted against time. | Die Temperatur wurde
… jede Minute aufgezeichnet.
… gegen die Zeit aufgetragen. |
| In / On the chart you can see / find that / how … | In diesem Diagramm kann man sehen / herausfinden, dass / wie … |

» | | |
|---|---|
| The graph shows | Die Kurve zeigt |
| … the correlation between x and y. | … die Korrelation zwischen x und y. |
| … a comparison between x and y. | … einen Vergleich von x und y. |
| … the survival rate versus medication in 100 patients. | … die Überlebensrate gegen die Medikation bei 100 Patienten. |
| … how species diversity has changed over time. | …, wie sich die Artenvielfalt über die Zeit geändert hat. |
| … the average height of teenagers in years 5 to 10. | … die durchschnittliche Größe von Teenagern in den Klassen 5 bis 10. |
| … the average rainfall in different months of the year in Karlsruhe, Germany. | … die durchschnittliche Regenmenge in verschiedenen Monaten im Jahr in Karlsruhe, Deutschland. |

» | | |
|---|---|
| The graph starts | Die Kurve beginnt |
| … at zero degrees Celsius. | … bei 0°C. |
| … high on the y axis. | … hoch auf der y-Achse. |
| … at 0 minutes and continues to 120 minutes. | … bei 0 Minuten und läuft bis 120 Minuten. |
| … at its maximum height. | … in ihrem Maximum. |

The graphs start at the same height.
Die Kurven beginnen auf der gleichen Höhe.

The graph is curved.
Der Kurvenverlauf ist nicht gerade.

5 Graphs and Figures › 5.3 Graphs and Charts

The graph is in a straight line.
Die Kurve verläuft in einer geraden Linie.

The graph stays flat for about 2 seconds.
Die Kurve bleibt für circa 2 Sekunden ohne Steigung.

The graph ends below its starting point.
Die Kurve endet unterhalb des Ausgangspunktes.

This graph has three parts.
Diese Kurve besteht aus drei Teilen.

The graph has got a maximum and a minimum.
Die Kurve hat ein Maximum und ein Minumum.

The graph has a maximum value of 60 °C at 3 min.
Die Kurve hat bei 3 Min. ein Maximum von 60°C.

There are different maxima for each enzyme.
Die Maxima sind bei allen Enzymen unterschiedlich.

symmetrical [sɪˈmetrɪkl] adj   symmetrisch
asymmetrical [ˌeɪsɪˈmetrɪkl] adj   asymmetrisch
skewed [skjuː] adj   verschoben

» The graph is skewed to the right.   Die Kurve ist nach rechts verschoben.

| The curve / The line | increases / decreases / falls | continually. / at a steady rate. / slightly. / sharply. | Die Kurve | steigt / sinkt / fällt | gleichmäßig. / stetig. / leicht. / stark. |

slope n   Steigung
  zero slope   keine Steigung / ohne Steigung
  a slope of 45 degrees   eine 45-gradige Steigung
slope v   ansteigen / fallen

» | The slope of a graph can be … | … small / large. / … positive. / … negative. / … gentle. / … steep. | Die Steigung einer Kurve kann … | … gering / stark sein. / … positiv sein. / … negativ sein. / … gering sein. / … steil sein. |

upward sloping graph / line   steigende Kurve
downward sloping graph / line   fallende Kurve

When the graph is sloping up, the line has a positive slope.
Wenn die Kurve ansteigt, hat sie eine positive Steigung.

A bigger slope means a steeper line.
Eine größere Steigung führt zu einer steileren Kurve.

Take the angle of the slope into account.
Berücksichtige(n Sie) den Grad der Steigung.

At 7 sec the graph starts to slope down in a straight line.
Bei 7 Sekunden beginnt die Kurve in einer geraden Linie abzufallen.

The line is level / flat.
Die Kurve steigt und fällt nicht.

The line is shallow / steep.
Die Kurve verläuft flach / steil.

The line goes up.
Die Kurve steigt.

The line goes down three units.
Die Kurve fällt um drei Einheiten.

distribution n | Verteilung
  normal distribution | Normalverteilung
  Gaussian distribution [ˈgaʊsɪən] | Gauß'sche Normalverteilung
  bell curve | Glockenkurve
  skewed distribution | verschobene Verteilung
  bimodal distribution | bimodale Verteilung

6 Working with films and computers

6.1 Films

slow motion | Zeitlupe
time-lapse photography | Zeitrafferaufnahme

» This sequence was filmed in time-lapse photography.
Diese Sequenz ist eine Zeitrafferaufnahme.

We'll watch a time-lapse film now.
Wir schauen jetzt einen Zeitrafferfilm an.

We'll watch the film without sound.
Wir schauen den Film ohne Ton an.

Write a voice-over comment for the film.
Schreibe(n Sie) einen Off-Kommentar zum Film.

6 Working with films and computers › 6.2 Computers

Describe the scene.
Beschreibe(n Sie) die Szene.

6.2 Computers

»
boot (up) the computer	den Computer hochfahren
start up / turn on the computer	den Computer starten
shut down the computer	den Computer herunterfahren
switch off the screen	den Bildschirm ausschalten
type in a user name and a password	einen Benutzernamen und ein Passwort eingeben
open the internet explorer	den Internet Explorer öffnen
do a web search	eine Internet-Recherche durchführen

»
Open Google or another search engine for your web search.
Öffne(n Sie) Google oder eine andere Suchmaschine für deine (Ihre) Internetrecherche.
Click on the links to open the sites.
Klicke(n Sie) auf die Links um die Seiten zu öffnen.
You can copy-paste pictures into Word.
Du kannst (Sie können) Bilder in Word kopieren.
Observe copyright.
Beachte(n Sie) das Urheberrecht.
Add the reference.
Gib (Geben Sie) die Quelle an.
"Google" is not a proper reference.
"Google" ist keine richtige Quellenangabe.
A good reference would be for example
http://nobelprize.org/nobel_prizes/lists/2007.html (4th October 2008).
Eine gute Quellenangabe wäre z.B. http://nobelprize.org/nobel_prizes/lists/2007.html
(4. Oktober 2008).
Save your work on a disk, on a memory stick or on the hard drive.
Speichere deine (Speichern Sie Ihre) Arbeit auf Diskette, auf einem Memory-Stick oder auf der Festplatte.
You cannot print at school.
Du kannst (Sie können) in der Schule nicht drucken.
Bring your print-outs to school.
Bringe(n Sie) die Ausdrucke in die Schule mit.

II. Basic Vocabulary

1 Plants » III. 2 Plant families; III. 10 Ecology

plant n	Pflanze
bryophyte ['braɪəˌfaɪt] n	Moos
fern [fɜːn] n	Farn
fungus ['fʌŋgəs], *pl* fungi ['fʌŋgaɪ] n	Pilz
lichen ['laɪkən] n	Flechte

broad-leafed tree [ˌbrɔːdˈliːfˌtriː] / deciduous tree [ˌdɪˈsɪdjuəsˌtriː] n	Laubbaum
maple (tree) ['meɪpl] n	Ahorn
beech (tree) [biːtʃ] n	Buche
birch (tree) [bɜːtʃ] n	Birke
ash (tree) [æʃ] n	Esche
poplar ['pɒplə] n	Pappel
willow ['wɪləʊ] n	Weide
alder ['ɔːldə] n	Erle
basswood ['bæswʊd] / lime (tree) [laɪm] n	Linde

conifer ['kɒnɪfə] n	Nadelbaum
spruce [spruːs] n	Fichte
fir (tree) [fɜː] n	Tanne
pine [paɪn] n	Kiefer
larch [lɑːtʃ] n	Lärche
yew (tree) [juː] n	Eibe

raspberry ['rɑːzbri] n	Himbeere
blackberry n	Brombeere
bilberry ['bɪlbri] n	Heidelbeere
strawberry n	Erdbeere
apple n	Apfel
pear ['peə] n	Birne
peach n	Pfirsich
cucumber ['kjuːkʌmbə] n	Salatgurke
tomato, *pl* tomatoes n	Tomate

meadow ['medəʊ] n	Wiese
grass n	Gras
clover ['kləʊvə] n	Klee
daisy n	Gänseblümchen
marguerite [ˌmɑːgrˈiːt] n	Margerite
chamomile / camomile ['kæməmaɪl] n	Kamille
coltsfoot ['kəʊltsfʊt] n	Huflattich
dandelion ['dændɪlaɪən] n	Löwenzahn

meadow saffron [ˈmedəʊˌsæfrən] n	Herbstzeitlose
orchid [ˈɔːkɪd] n	Orchidee

spring flower / early bloomer n	Frühblüher
spring forest geophyte [ˌsprɪŋˈfɒrɪstˈdʒiːəʊfaɪt] n	Waldfrühblüher
snowdrop n	Schneeglöckchen
snowflake n	Märzenbecher
crocus [ˈkrəʊkəs] n	Krokus
corydalis [ˈkərɪdələs] n	Lerchensporn
anemone [əˈneməni] n	Buschwindröschen
pilewort n	Scharbockskraut

lilac [ˈlaɪlək] n	Flieder
violet [ˈvaɪələt] n	Veilchen
rose n	Rose
privet [ˈprɪvɪt] n	Liguster
(stinging) nettle [ˈstɪŋɪŋˌnetl] n	Brennnessel
deadnettle [ˈdednetl] n	Taubnessel

ivy [ˈaɪvi] n	Efeu
gorse [ˈɡɔːs] n	Ginster / Stechginster
heather [ˈheðə] n	Heide
cactus, *pl* cacti [ˈkæktəs] n	Kaktus

grain [ɡreɪn] n	Getreide
wheat [wiːt] n	Weizen
barley [ˈbɑːli] n	Gerste
oat [əʊt] n	Hafer
rye [raɪ] n	Roggen
rice n	Reis
corn / maize [meɪz] n	Mais
sweetcorn	Zuckermais

2 Animals » III. 10 Ecology; Ecosystems

red deer, *pl* red deer n	Hirsch
roe deer, *pl* roe deer n	Reh
reindeer, *pl* reindeer n	Rentier
moose, *pl* moose [muːs] n	Elch
bear [beə] n	Bär
wolf [wʊlf], *pl* wolves [wʊlvz] n	Wolf
lynx [lɪŋks], *pl* lynxes n	Luchs

2 Animals

wildcat n	Wildkatze
pig n	Schwein
domestic pig	Hausschwein
boar ['bɔː] / wild boar	Wildschwein
fox, *pl* foxes n	Fuchs
badger ['bædʒə] n	Dachs
marten ['mɑːtɪn] n	Marder
hare [heə] n	Hase
rabbit n	Kaninchen
hedgehog ['hedʒhɒg] n	Igel
mole n	Maulwurf
beaver ['biːvə] n	Biber
squirrel ['skwɪrl] n	Eichhörnchen
rat n	Ratte
mouse, *pl* mice n	Maus
bat n	Fledermaus

robin ['rɒbɪn] n	Rotkehlchen
nightingale ['naɪtɪŋgeɪl] n	Nachtigall
sparrow ['spærəʊ] n	Spatz, Sperling
blackbird n	Amsel
tit [tɪt] n	Meise
great tit	Kohlmeise
blue tit	Blaumeise
cuckoo ['kʊkuː] n	Kuckuck
finch [fɪnʃ] n	Fink
Darwin's finches	Darwinfinken
Tree-finch (Small, Medium, Large)	Baumfink (Kleiner, Mittlerer, Großer)
Ground-finch (Small, Medium, Large)	Grundfink (Kleiner, Mittlerer, Großer)
Woodpecker Finch	Spechtfink
Vegetarian Finch	Dickschnabel-Darwinfink
Cocos Island Finch	Kokosfink
Warbler Finch	Waldsängerfink

pigeon ['pɪdʒən] n	Taube
pheasant ['feznt] n	Fasan
woodpecker ['wʊdˌpekə] n	Specht
swift [swɪft] n	Mauersegler
swallow ['swɒləʊ] n	Schwalbe
stork [stɔːk] n	Storch

rook [rʊk] n	Saatkrähe
jackdaw ['dʒækdɔː] n	Dohle
magpie ['mægpaɪ] n	Elster

raven ['reɪvn] n	Rabe

bird of prey n	Raubvogel
scavenger ['skævɪnʤə] n	Aasfresser
owl [aʊl] n	Eule
eagle owl	Uhu
falcon ['fɔːlkn] n	Falke
peregrin falcon	Wanderfalke
buzzard ['bʌzəd] n	Bussard
eagle n	Adler
vulture ['vʌltʃə] n	Geier

duck n	Ente
goose, pl geese n	Gans
grey goose	Graugans
puffin ['pʌfɪn] n	Papageitaucher
cormorant ['kɔːmrənt] n	Kormoran
seagull ['siːgʌl] n	Möwe
herring gull	Heringsmöwe
lesser black backed gull	Silbermöwe
greater black backed gull	Mantelmöwe
gannet ['gænɪt] n	Basstölpel

tortoise ['tɔːtəs]	Schildkröte
turtle n	Seeschildkröte
lizard ['lɪzəd] n	Eidechse
blindworm n	Blindschleiche
grass snake n	Ringelnatter

salamander ['sæləmændə] n	Salamander
newt [njuːt] n	Molch
frog n	Frosch
toad [təʊd] n	Kröte

goldfish, pl goldfish n	Goldfisch
carp [kɑːp], pl carps; carp n	Karpfen
trout ['traʊt], pl trouts; trout n	Forelle
salmon ['sæmən], pl salmons; salmon n	Lachs
pike [paɪk], pl pikes; pike n	Hecht
eel [iːl], pl eels; eel n	Aal

dragonfly, pl dragonflies ['drægnflaɪ] n	Libelle
water strider n	Wasserläufer
water flea [fliː] n	Wasserfloh

2 Animals

freshwater shrimp n	Bachflohkrebs
sandhopper ['sænd‚hɒpə] n	Strandfloh
crayfish ['kreɪfɪʃ] n	Flusskrebs
lobster ['lɒbstə] n	Hummer
barnacle ['bɑːnəkl] n	Seepocke
bivalve ['baɪvælv] n	Muschel
oyster ['ɔɪstə] n	Auster
mussel ['mʌsl] n	Miesmuschel
jellyfish, pl jellyfish n	Qualle
sea urchin ['siː‚ɜːtʃɪn] n	Seeigel
earthworm n	Regenwurm
slug [slʌg] n	Nacktschnecke
snail [sneɪl] n	Schnecke (mit Gehäuse)
spider n	Spinne
garden spider	Gartenkreuzspinne
harvestman, pl harvestmen / daddy longlegs AE n	Weberknecht
woodlouse, pl woodlice n	Kellerassel
locust ['ləʊkəst] n	Heuschrecke
grasshopper n	Grashüpfer
stick insect / walking stick n	Stabheuschrecke
mantis ['mæntɪs], pl mantises n	Gottesanbeterin
cricket ['krɪkɪt] n	Grille
mole cricket	Maulwurfsgrille
cockroach, pl cockroaches n	Küchenschabe
earwig ['ɪəwɪg] n	Ohrwurm
bug n	Wanze
butterfly n	Schmetterling
peacock butterfly	Tagpfauenauge
cabbage butterfly	Kohlweißling
peppered moth	Birkenspanner
brimstone butterfly	Zitronenfalter
mayfly n	Eintagsfliege
caddisfly ['kædɪs‚flaɪ] n	Köcherfliege
mosquito, pl mosquitoes n	Stechmücke
horsefly n	Bremse
housefly n	Stubenfliege
ant n	Ameise
hornet ['hɔːnɪt] n	Hornisse

wasp [wɒsp] n	Wespe
bee n	Biene
bumblebee ['bʌmblbiː] n	Hummel
beetle n	Käfer
stag beetle	Hirschkäfer
ladybird	Marienkäfer
dung beetle	Mistkäfer

3 The human body   » III. 1 The human body » Abb. 19–29

anatomy [əˈnætəmi] n	Anatomie
head n	Kopf
torso [ˈtɔːsəʊ] n	Rumpf
thorax [ˈθɔːræks], pl thoraxes; thoraces n	Brustkorb
abdomen [ˈæbdəmən] n	Bauch
limb [lɪm] n	Gliedmaßen (dtsch. ausschließlich Pl.)
skeleton [ˈskelɪtn] n	Skelett
joint n	Gelenk
muscle [ˈmʌsl] n	Muskel
tendon [ˈtendən] n	Sehne
digestion [daɪˈdʒestʃn] n	Verdauung
mouth n	Mund
saliva [səˈlaɪvə] n	Speichel
salivary gland [ˈsælɪvriˌglænd] n	Speicheldrüse
eosophagus [iːˈsɒfəgəs], pl eosophagi [iːˈsɒfəgaɪ] / esophagus AE n	Speiseröhre
stomach [ˈstʌmek] n	Magen
pancreas [ˈpæŋkriəs] n	Bauchspeicheldrüse
gall bladder n	Gallenblase
duodenum [ˌdjuːəˈdiːnəm] n	Zwölffingerdarm
intestine [ɪnˈtestɪn] n	Darm
small intestine	Dünndarm
large intestine	Dickdarm
anus [ˈeɪnəs], pl anes [ˈeɪniːz] n	After
respiration [ˌrespɪˈreɪʃn] n	Atmung
nose n	Nase
mucosa [mjuːˈkoʊsə], pl mucosae [mjuːˈkoʊsiː] n	Schleimhaut
larynx [ˈlærɪŋks], pl larynxes [ˈlærɪŋksɪz] n	Kehlkopf / Larynx
vocal cord [ˌvəʊklˈkɔːd] n	Stimmband

3 The human body

windpipe ['wɪnpaɪp] n	Luftröhre
lung n	Lunge / Lungenflügel
bronchus ['brɒŋkəs], pl bronchi n	Bronchus / Bronchie
alveolus [ˌælvi'əʊləs], pl alveoli [ælvi'əʊlaɪ] n	Alveole
diaphragm ['daɪəfræm] n	Zwerchfell
circulatory system n	Kreislaufsystem
pulse [pʌls] n	Puls
blood n	Blut
heart n	Herz
atrium, pl atria ['eɪtriəm] n	Vorhof
ventricle ['ventrɪkl] n	Herzkammer
heart valve [ˌvælv] n	Herzklappe
blood vessel ['blʌdˌvesl] n	Blutgefäß
artery ['ɑːtri], pl arteries n	Arterie
aorta [eɪ'ɔːtə], pl aortas; aortae [eɪ'ɔːtəz; eɪ'ɔːtiː] n	Aorta
vein [veɪn] n	Vene
venous valve ['viːnəs ˌvælv] n	Venenklappe
capillary [kə'pɪlri], pl capillaries n	Kapillargefäß
coronary blood vessel ['kɒrənri] n	Herzkranzgefäß
excretion [ɪk'skriːʃn] n	Ausscheidung / Exkretion
kidney ['kɪdni] n	Niere
bladder ['blædə] n	Harnblase
ureter [jʊə'riːtə] n	Harnleiter
urethra [jʊə'riːθrə] n	Harnröhre
genital ['dʒenɪtl] n	Geschlechtsorgan
vulva ['vʌlvə], pl vulvae ['vʌlviː] n	Vulva
labium ['leɪbiəm], pl labia ['leɪbiə] n	Schamlippe
vagina [və'dʒaɪnə], pl vaginae; vaginas n	Scheide / Vagina
clitoris ['klɪtrɪs], pl clitores; clitorides ['klɪtrɪːz; 'klɪtrɪdiːs] n	Klitoris
uterus ['juːtrəs], pl uteruses; uteri n	Gebärmutter / Uterus
fallopian tube [fəˌləʊpiən'tjuːb] / oviduct ['əʊvɪdʌkt] n	Eileiter
ovary ['əʊvri], pl ovaries ['əʊvriz] n	Eierstock
breast n	Brust
nipple n	Brustwarze
mammary gland [ˌmæmri'glænd] n	Milchdrüse / Brustdrüse
penis ['piːnɪs], pl penises n	Penis
foreskin ['fɔːskɪn] n	Vorhaut

glans [ˈglænz], *pl* glandes [ˈglændiːs] n	Eichel
corpus cavernosum [ˌkɔːpəskævəˈnəʊsəm], *pl* corpora cavernosa / **erectile tissue** n	Schwellkörper
prostate [ˈprɒsteɪt] n	Prostata
vas deferens [ˌvæsˈdefərenz] n	Samenleiter
scrotum, *pl* scrota; scrotums [ˈskrəʊtəm] n	Hodensack
testicle n	Hoden

3 The human body

III. Thematic Vocabulary

1 The human body

1.1 Cells, tissue and organs » III. 4 Cell biology – Cytology » Abb. 37–40

The microscope and differentiation of human cells

eukaryotic cell [ˌjuːkærɪɒtɪkˈsel] n	eukaryo(n)tische Zelle *(beinhaltet einen echten Zellkern)*
human cell n	menschliche Zelle
totipotent [təʊˈtɪpətənt] adj	totipotent *(Zelle, die sich noch zu allen Zelltypen entwickeln kann)*
differentiation [ˌdɪfrenʃɪˈeɪʃn] n	Differenzierung
determination [dɪˌtɜːmɪˈneɪʃn] n	Determination
multicellular organism [ˌmʌltiˈseljələ] n	Vielzeller
cell type n	Zelltyp
stem cell n	Stammzelle
omnipotent stem cell	omnipotente Stammzelle *(kann den kompletten Organismus herstellen)*
pluripotent stem cell	pluripotente Stammzelle
multipotent stem cell	multipotente Stammzelle *(kann die Zelltypen des umgebenden Gewebes herstellen)*
adult stem cell	adulte Stammzelle

nerve cell n	Nervenzelle
cartilage cell [ˈkɑːtɪlɪdʒˌsel] n	Knorpelzelle
glandular cell [ˈɡlændjʊləˌsel] n	Drüsenzelle
secretory cell [ˈsekrətriˌsel] n	sekretorische Zelle
bone cell n	Knochenzelle
body cell / somatic cell n	Körperzelle / somatische Zelle
embryonic cell [ˌembrɪˈɒnɪkˌsel] n	Embryo-Zelle
undifferentiated cell n	undifferenzierte Zelle
reproductive cell / germline cell [ˈdʒɜːmlaɪnˌsel] n	Fortpflanzungszelle / Keimbahnzelle
oral mucosa cell [ˌɔːrl mjuːˈkəʊsəˌsel] n	Mundschleimhautzelle

parenchyma cell [pərenjkəməˌsel] n	Parenchymzelle
connective tissue cell n	Bindegewebezelle
epithelial cell [ˌepɪθiːlɪəlˈsel] n	Epithelzelle
bone cell n	Osteocyt
blood cell n	Blutzelle
smooth muscle cell n	glatte Muskelzelle

» The cell is as fundamental to human biology as the atom is to chemistry.
Die Zelle ist für die Humanbiologie genauso grundlegend wie das Atom für die Chemie.
Eukaryotic cells have internal membranes that compartmentalise their functions.
Eukaryotische Zellen haben innere Membranen, die ihre Funktionen aufteilen.
Embryonic cells are undifferentiated cells with the ability to divide.
Embryonale Zellen sind undifferenzierte Zellen mit der Fähigkeit zur Teilung.
Human beings are multicellular organisms.
Menschen sind vielzellige Organismen.
Pluripotent stem cells can produce all cell types but not a complete organism.
Pluripotente Stammzellen können alle Zelltypen herstellen, aber nicht den kompletten Organismus.

organelle [ˌɔːɡənˈel], *pl* **organelles** n	Organelle *(Pl. Organellen)*
cytoplasm [ˈsaɪtəʊplæzm] n	Zellplasma / Cytoplasma
layer of cells n	Zellschicht
tight junction n	Verschlusskontakt *(zwischen Zellen)*
desmosome [ˈdəzməˌsəʊm] n	Desmosom
gap junction n	Kommunikationskontakt *(zwischen Zellen)*

» The cell is a living unit greater than the sum of its parts.
Die Zelle ist eine lebende Einheit, die größer ist als die Summe ihrer Teile.
The emergence of cellular functions is based on the cooperation of many organelles.
Das Erscheinen zellulärer Funktionen basiert auf der Zusammenarbeit vieler Organellen.

Tissues

tissue [ˈtɪʃuː] n	Gewebe
bone tissue / osseous tissue [ˈɒsiəsˌtɪʃuː]	Knochengewebe
connective tissue	Bindegewebe
epithelial tissue [ˌepɪˈθɪliəlˌtɪʃuː]	Epithel
cartilage tissue [ˈkɑːtɪlɪdʒˌtɪʃuː] n	Knorpelgewebe
muscle tissue [ˈmʌslˌtɪʃuː] n	Muskelgewebe
nervous tissue n	Nervengewebe
epidermis [ˌepɪˈdɜːmɪs] n	Epidermis
bone marrow [ˈbəʊnˌmærəʊ] n	Knochenmark
blood n	Blut
keratinised *BE* / **keratinized** *AE* [ˌkerətəˈnaɪzəd] adj	verhornt

1 The human body › 1.1 Cells, tissue and organs

parenchyma [pə'reŋkımə] *(functional parts of an organ in the body)* n
Parenchym *(Funktionsgewebe eines Organs)*
junction n
Anschluss
intercellular adj
zwischenzellulär
    intercellular junctions
    zwischenzelluläre Anschlüsse

» Animal and human tissues are connected via intercellular junctions.
Tierische und menschliche Gewebe sind durch zwischenzelluläre Anschlüsse verbunden.

Organs and organ systems

organ n — Organ
organ system n — Organsystem
circulatory system n — Gefäßsystem / Kreislaufsystem
digestive system n — Verdauungssystem
endocrine system ['endəʊkraın,sıstəm] n — endokrines System
excretory system [ık'skriːtri,sıstəm] n — Exkretionssystem
immune and lymphatic system n — Immun- und Lymphgefäßsystem
integumentary system [ın'təgjəməntəri] n — Integumentsystem
muscular system n — Muskelsystem
nervous system n — Nervensystem
reproductive system n — Fortpflanzungssystem
respiratory system n — Atmungssystem
skeletal system n — Skelettsystem
derivative [dı'rıvətıv] n — Abkömmling / Derivat
thermoregulation n — Thermoregulation

» Different tissues are organised into organs. In some organs, different tissues are organised in layers.
Unterschiedliche Gewebe sind als „Organe" organisiert. In manchen Organen sind die verschiedenen Gewebe in Schichten organisiert.
The integumentary system is based on skin and its derivates (such as hair, claws or skin glands).
Das Integumentsystem basiert auf der Haut und ihren Abkömmlingen (wie Haare, Krallen oder Hautdrüsen).

1.2 Covering and movement

Covering » Abb. 23

skin n	Haut
epidermis [ˌepɪˈdɜːmɪs] n	Epidermis
basal layer n	Stratum basale
dermis [ˈdɜːmɪs] n	Dermis
hypodermis n	Hypodermis
subcutis [sʌbˈkjuːtis] n	Unterhaut
subcutaneous tissue	Unterhautgewebe
adipose tissue n	Fettgewebe
connective tissue n	Bindegewebe
superficial fascia [suːpəˌfɪʃlˈfæʃiə] n	Faszie *(an der Körperoberfläche)*
sensory receptor n	Sinnesrezeptor
heat n	Hitze
light n	Licht
pain n	Schmerz
cold n	Kälte
pressure n	Druck
thermoregulation [θɜːməʊˌreɡjəˈleɪʃn] n	Thermoregulation
body defence mechanism n	Körperabwehrmechanismus
hair n	Haar
keratinous adj	hornig

» Compare the epidermis to the dermis.
Vergleiche(n Sie) die Epidermis mit der Dermis.

A mammalian body is continuously covered by skin.
The human skin is composed of two layers, the epidermis (outer layer) and the dermis (the lower layer).
The basal layer separates the dermis from the epidermis. It is also called stratum basale, which is the deepest layer of the epidermis.
Ein Säugetierkörper ist vollständig mit Haut bedeckt.
Die menschliche Haut setzt sich aus zwei Schichten zusammen, der Epidermis (äußere Schicht) und der Dermis (untere Schicht).
Die basale Schicht trennt die Dermis von der Epidermis. Sie wird auch Stratum basale genannt und ist die tiefste Schicht der Epidermis.

bipedalism [baɪˈpiːdəlizm] n	Bipedie / Zweibeinigkeit
human skeleton n	Menschenskelett » Abb. 19
skull n	Schädel
spine n	Rückgrat / Stachel / Hartstrahl
pectoral girdle [ˈpektərəlˌɡɜːdl] n	Schultergürtel

1 The human body › 1.2 Covering and movement

rib cage n	Brustkorb
pelvic girdle [ˌpelvɪkˈgɜːdl] n	Beckengürtel
arm bone n	Armknochen
hand bone n	Handknochen
leg bone n	Beinknochen
foot bone n	Fußknochen
footprint n	Fußabdruck
normal foot	mormale Fußform
flat foot	Plattfuß
tendon [ˈtendən] n	Sehne
tibia [ˈtɪbɪə] n	Schienbein
tendon of tibial muscle	Sehne des Schienbeinmuskels
plantar aponeurosis [ˈplæntəˌapənuˈrəʊsɪs] n	Plantaraponeurose *(Sehnenplatte im Bereich der Fußsohle)*
bone structure n	Knochenstruktur
epiphysis [ɪˈpɪfəsɪs] / pineal gland n	Epiphyse
diaphysis n	Diaphyse / Knochenschaft / Durchwachsung
joint cartilage n	Gelenkknorpel
red bone marrow n	rotes Knochenmark
trabecula n	Knochenbälkchen / Trabekel
periosteum [ˌperɪˈɒsteˌəm] n	Knochenhaut
yellow bone marrow n	gelbes Knochenmark
bone matrix n	Knochenmatrix
detailed bone structure n	detaillierte Knochenstruktur
bone layers n	Knochenschichten
bone tissue n	Knochengewebe
osteoblast n	Knochenbildungszelle
blood vessel n	Blutgefäß
nerve fibre [ˈnɜːvˌfaɪbə] n	Nervenfaser
joint n	Gelenk
ball-and-socket-joint	Kugelgelenk
hinge joint [ˈhɪndʒˌdʒɔɪnt]	Scharniergelenk
saddle joint	Sattelgelenk
skeletal muscle n	Skelettmuskel
fascia [ˈfæʃɪə] n	Faszie
muscle fibre [ˈmʌslˌfaɪbə] n	Muskelfaser

»	bundle of muscle fibres	Bündel an Muskelfasern

neuromuscular synapse [ˌnjʊərəʊˈmʌskjələˈsaɪnæps] n	neuromuskuläre Synapse
nucleus [ˈnjuːklɪəs], pl nuclei n	Zellkern / Nukleus
cell membrane n	Zellmembran
myofibril [ˌmaɪəˈfaɪbrəl] n	Myofibrille / Muskelfibrille
myosin filament n	dickes Filament / Myosin Filament
actin filament n	dünnes Filament / Aktin Filament
antagonist n	Gegenspieler
relaxed adj	entspannt
contract v	kontrahieren / zusammenziehen
contracted adj	kontrahiert / zusammengezogen
impulse n	Impuls
trigger v	auslösen
response v	Reizbeantwortung

» The long tubular bones have an especially high fracture risk.
Die langen, röhrenartigen Knochen haben ein besonders hohes Brechrisiko.
A stimulus device can be used in a nerve-muscle experiment to trigger an impulse in the nerve which is then passed to the muscle.
Ein reizauslösendes Gerät kann im Nerv-Muskel-Experiment verwendet werden, um im Nerv einen Impuls auszulösen, der dann zum Muskel weiter transportiert wird.
The muscle responds in this experiment, as in the human body, by contracting.
Der Muskel reagiert in diesem Experiment, wie im menschlichen Körper, durch Kontraktion.

1.3 Sensory organs

The human senses » Abb. 23–27

stimulus, pl stimuli n	Reiz
adequate stimulus	adäquater Reiz
chemical n	Chemikalie
light n	Licht
sound waves n	Schallwellen
sensory organ n	Sinnesorgan
sense n	Sinn
sense of vision	Sehsinn
sense of hearing	Hörsinn
sense of smell and taste	Geruchs- und Tastsinn
ear n	Ohr
eye n	Auge
nose n	Nase
tongue n	Zunge
skin n	Haut

1 The human body › 1.3 Sensory organs

supporting structure n	unterstützende Struktur
receptor cell n	Rezeptorzelle
nervous system n	Nervensystem
nerve fibre n	Nervenfaser
transduce [træz'djuːs] v	transduzieren / wandeln / umwandeln
process v	bearbeiten
reference value n	Sollwert
input n	Eingabe des Sollwerts
output n	Istwert
controller n	Regler
sensor n	Fühler
error n	Regelgröße *(Differenz zwischen Ist- und Sollwert)*

» A sensory organ is a highly specialised organ consisting of many receptors (receptor cells, sense cells). It is receptive to stimuli.
Ein Sinnesorgan ist ein hochspezialisiertes Organ, das aus vielen Rezeptoren (Rezeptorzellen, Sinneszellen) besteht. Es ist für Reize empfänglich.

The ear and the nature of sound » Abb. 24–26

sound n	Geräusch / Laut / Schall
sound wave	Schallwelle
pitch n	Tonhöhe / Stufe
amplitude ['æmplɪtjuːd] n	Amplitude
wavelength n	Wellenlänge
frequency n	Frequenz

»
form of energy	Energieform
particles of a medium	Teilchen eines Medium

outer ear n	Außenohr
collection n	Sammeln
middle ear n	Mittelohr
transmission n	Übertragung
inner ear n	Innenohr
transduction [træns'dʌkʃn] n	Transduktion
balance n	Gleichgewicht
semicircular canal n	häutiger Bogengang
macula ['mækjʊlə] n	Macula

gravity n	Schwerkraft
ampulla [æm'pʊlə] n	Ampulle / polische Blase
loop n	Schleife
pinna ['pɪnə] n	Ohrmuschel
ear canal n	Gehörkanal
eardrum n	Trommelfell
gland [glænd] n	Drüse
secrete [sɪ'kriːt] n	Sekret
earwax n	Ohrenschmalz
throat [θrəʊt] n	Rachen
Eustachian tube [juː'steɪʃən,tjuːb] n	Eustachische Röhre
transfer v	übertragen
ear bones n	Gehörknöchelchen
hammer n	Hammer
anvil ['ænvɪl] n	Amboss
stirrup ['stɪrəp] n	Steigbügel
oval window n	ovales Fenster
round window n	rundes Fenster
vestibular apparatus [ves'tɪbjələ,æpə'reɪtəs] n	Gleichgewichtsorgan
vestibular system	Gleichgewichtssystem
vestibular nerve	Nervus vestibularis
auditory nerve n	Gehörnerv
amplify v	verstärken / erweitern

》

The pinna serves to focus ...	Die Ohrmuschel dient der Bündelung der ...
The eardrum helps to transfer ...	Das Trommelfell hilft bei der Übermittlung ...
The earwax is good for keeping ...	Der Ohrenschmalz ist geeignet für die Beibehaltung ...
The ear bones are the smallest bones ...	Die Gehörknöchelchen sind die kleinsten Knochen ...

fluid n	Flüssigkeit
cochlea ['kɒkliə] n	Cochlea / Schnecke
snail shell n	Schneckenhaus
convert v	umwandeln / verwandeln
encode v	verschlüsseln / kodieren
organ of Corti n	Corti-Organ / cortisches Organ
electrical impulse n	elektrischer Impuls

1 The human body › 1.3 Sensory organs

cochlear duct [ˈkɒkliəˌdʌkt] n	häutiger Schneckengang
pressure wave n	Druckwelle
hair cell n	Haarzelle
tectorial membrane n	Tektorialmembran
base n	Basis
apex [ˈeɪpeks] n	Apex / Spitze

The human ear: functional areas

The human ear can be separated into three functional areas:	Das menschliche Ohr kann in drei funktionelle Zonen geteilt werden:
outer ear: collection of sound waves	**Außenohr**: Sammlung der Schallwellen
middle ear: transmission of sound waves	**Mittelohr**: Weiterleitung der Schallwellen
inner ear: transduction of vibrational energy into electrical impulses	**Innenohr**: Reizumwandlung der Vibrationsenergie in elektrische Impulse

The eye and the nature of vision » Abb. 27

cornea [ˈkɔːniə] n	Hornhaut
chamber of the eye n	Augenkammer
front chamber of the eye / anterior chamber of the eye	vordere Augenkammer
back chamber of the eye / posterior chamber of the eye / vitreous cavity	hintere Augenkammer
lens n	Linse
light receptor cell n	Lichtrezeptorzelle
retina [ˈretɪnə] n	Netzhaut / Retina
cone [kəʊn] n	Zapfen
rod n	Stäbchen
rhodopsin [rəˈdɒpsɪn] n	Rhodopsin
decomposition n	Zersetzung
chain n	Kette
spatial adj	räumlich
optic / optical adj	optisch
optic chiasma n	Sehnervenkreuzung
optic fibre n	Sehfaser
optic nerve	Sehnerv
focus (on) v	fokussieren (auf)
horizontally adv	horizontal
contract v	kontrahieren / zusammenziehen
tight adj	fest / straff
phenomenon [fɪˈnɒmɪnən], pl phenomena; phenomenons	Erscheinung / Phänomen

optical axis, *pl* axes n	optische Achse
sclera ['sklɪərə] n	Lederhaut
pupil ['pjuːpl] n	Pupille
iris ['aɪərɪs] n	Iris
ciliary muscle ['sɪliərɪˌmʌsl] n	Ziliarmuskel
eye muscle n	Augenmuskel
suspensory ligament n	Aufhängepparat *(der Augenlinse)*
accommodate (to) v	anpassen (an)
vitreous body ['vɪtriəsˌbɒdɪ] n	Glaskörper
gelatinous [dʒə'lætɪnəs] / jelly adj	gallertartig
yellow spot n	gelber Punkt
fovea ['fɒviə] / central pit n	Fovea / Sehgrube
visual acuity [ˌvɪʒuələ'kjuːəti] n	Sehgenauigkeit
blind spot n	Blinder Fleck
pigment layer n	Pigmentschicht
blood vessel n	Blutgefäß
choroid ['kɔːrɔɪd] n	Aderhaut
pupillary reflex ['pjuːpɪləriˌriːfləks] n	Pupillenreflex
perception [pə'sepʃn] n	Wahrnehmung
detect (sth) / perceive (sth) v	(etw.) wahrnehmen
spatial perception [ˌspeɪʃlpə'sepʃn] n	räumliche Wahrnehmung
visual field n	Gesichtsfeld
succession [sək'seʃn] n	Sukzession
visible adj	sichtbar

»

The sclera serves to …	Die Lederhaut dient der …
The iris is responsible for …	Die Iris ist verantwortlich für …
The suspensory ligament and the ciliary muscle work together to …	Die Zonulafasern und der Ziliarmuskel arbeiten gemeinsam, um …

The light receptors in our retina register optical stimuli.
Die Lichtrezeptoren unserer Retina registrieren optische Reize.

The interpretation of what we look at takes place in our brain.
Die Interpretation der Dinge, die wir ansehen, findet in unserem Gehirn statt.

1.4 Nervous system »Abb. 22, 31–32

Structure and function of the human nervous system

neuron ['njʊərɒn] (nerve cell) n   Neuron (Nervenzelle)
interneuron   Interneuron
sensory neuron   Sensoneuron
motor neuron   Motoneuron

> information processing circuits | informationsverabeitende Kreisläufe

axon ['æksɒn] n   Axon
extracellular body fluid n   Extrazellulärflüssigkeit /
                                              extrazelluläre Körperflüssigkeit
central nervous system (CNS) n   zentrales Nervensystem
brain n   Gehirn »Abb. 22
limbic system n   limbisches System
spine n   Rückgrat
spinal cord n   Rückenmark
spinal ganglion ['spaɪnel‚gæŋɡliən] n   Spinalganglion
spinal nerve n   Spinalnerv
white matter n   weiße Substanz
grey matter n   graue Substanz
bipolar nerve cell n   bipolare Nervenzelle
anterior horn n   Vorderhorn
posterior horn n   Hinterhorn
dorsal root ['dɔːsl‚ruːt] n   Dorsalwurzel
ventral root ['ventrl‚ruːt] n   Ventralwurzel
peripheral nervous system (PNS) n   peripheres Nervensystem
autonomic nervous system /   autonomes Nervensystem /
  vegetative nervous system n   vegetatives Nervensystem
parasympathetic adj   parasympathisch
acetylcholine [‚æsɪtaɪl'kəʊliːn]   Acetylcholin
  (transmitter) n
sympathetic adj   sympathisch
adrenalin [ə'drenəlɪn] / epinephrine   Adrenalin
  [‚epɪ'nefrɪn] AE n
noradrenalin [nɔːrə'drenəlɪn] /   Noradrenalin
  norepinephrine [nɔːrəpə'nefrən] AE n

» The brain and spinal cord together are called the *central nervous system* (CNS).
Gehirn und Rückenmark werden zusammen als Zentrales Nervensystem (ZNS) bezeichnet.

The autonomic nervous system is divided into two functional subsystems: the parasympathetic and sympathetic nervous system.
Das autonome Nervensystem ist in zwei funktionelle Untersysteme geteilt: das parsympathische und das sympathische Nervensystem.

Feelings such as fear, anger and happiness are accompanied by typical body reactions that are initiated by the autonomic nervous system.
Gefühle wie Angst, Zorn und Glück werden von typischen körperlichen Reaktionen begleitet, die vom autonomen Nervensystem ausgelöst wurden.

Methods in brain research:

- electroencephalography (EEG)	- Elektro-Encephalografie (EEG)
- excitatory postsynaptic potentials (EPSP)	- exzitatorische postsynaptische Potentiale (EPSP)
- PET (positron emission tomography)	- Positronen-Emissionstomografie (PET)
- tomography (e.g. magnetic resonance imaging)	- Tomografie (u.a. Kernspintomografie)

cerebrum [sə'riːbrəm] / **telencephalon** n	Großhirn » Abb. 22
cerebral cortex [ˌsərəbrl'kɔːteks] n	Großhirnrinde
hippocampus [ˌhɪpəʊ'kæmpəs] n	Hippocampus
cerebral hemisphere n	Großhirnhemisphäre
right and left hemisphere n	rechte und linke Hemisphäre
corpus callosum [ˌkɔːpəskə'ləʊsem] n	Balken / Corpus callosum
diencephalon [daɪen'səfəˌlɒn] / interbrain n	Diencephalon
thalamus [ˌθæləməs] n	Thalamus / Receptaculum
epiphysis ['epɪphəsɪs] / **pineal gland** n	Epiphyse
hypothalamus [ˌhaɪpə'θæləməs] n	Hypothalamus
hypophysis [haɪ'pəfesɪs] n	Hirnanhangdrüse
hormone n	Hormon
follicle-stimulating hormone (FSH)	follikelstimulierendes Hormon (FSH)
mesencephalon [ˌmezən'sæfələn] / midbrain n	Mesencephalon
cerebellum [ˌserɪ'beləm] n	Cerebellum / Kleinhirn
pons n	Brücke
medulla oblongata [med'ʌləˌɒblɒŋgətə] (elongation of the spinal cord) n	verlängertes Mark
brainstem n	Hirnstamm / Stammhirn

1 The human body › 1.5 Endocrine system

> The human cerebrum consists of the cerebral cortex, which in humans has an enormously enlarged surface, because of the presence of furrows (sulcus, pl sulci), and billions of neurons.
> Das menschliche Großhirn besteht aus der Großhirnrinde, die bei Menschen aufgrund von Furchen (Sulcus, Pl. Sulci) und Milliarden von Neuronen eine enorm vergrößerte Oberfläche bildet.
> The thalamus is also called "the door to the cerebral cortex".
> Der Thalamus wird auch „die Tür zur Großhirnrinde genannt".
> Located below the thalamus is the hypothalamus, which is the control centre of the autonomic nervous system and the hormone system.
> Unterhalb des Thalamus befindet sich der Hypothalamus, der das Kontrollzentrum des autonomen Nervensystems und des Hormonsystems bildet.
> The medulla oblongata together with pons and midbrain are called the *brainstem*.
> Das verlängerte Mark wird zusammen mit der Brücke und dem Mittelhirn als *Stammhirn* bezeichnet.

drug n	Medikament
psychopharmaca [ˌsaɪkəʊˈfɑːməkə] n	Psychopharmaka
endorphin [enˈdɔːfɪn] n	Endorphin

1.5 Endocrine system

Endocrine glands

endocrine gland [ˈendəʊkraɪnˌɡlænd] n	endokrine Drüse
pituitary gland [pɪˈtjuːɪtrɪˌɡlænd]	Hypophyse
thyroid gland [ˈθaɪrɔɪdˌɡlænd]	Schilddrüse
parathyroid gland [pærəˈθaɪrɔɪdˌɡlænd]	Nebenschilddrüse
thymus gland [ˈθaɪməsˌɡlænd]	Thymusdrüse
adrenal gland	Nebenniere
reproductive glands *(ovaries, testes)*	Reproduktionsdrüsen *(Eierstöcke, Hoden)*
pancreas [ˈpæŋkrɪəs] n	Bauchspeicheldrüse
pineal body n	Epiphyse
hormone n	Hormon
pathway n	Reaktionskette
hormonal control pathways	hormonelle Reaktionsketten
blood circulatory system n	Blutkreislaufsystem
regulatory system n	Regulationssystem
behaviour *BE* / behavior *AE* n	Verhalten
homoeostasis *BE* [ˌhəʊmiəʊˈsteɪsɪs] / homeostasis *AE* n	Homöostase *(Erhaltung der Stabilität von Vorgängen im Körper, z.B. Wasserhaushalt)*

> Endocrine means "secreting directly into the bloodstream".
> The hormones circulate to target cells as part of a regulatory system.
> Non-pituitary hormones help regulate homeostasis, metabolism, development and behaviour.
> Endokrin bedeutet „direkt in den Blutkreislauf sekretierend".
> Die Hormone zirkulieren als Teil eines Steuerungssystems zu den Zielzellen.
> Nicht von der Hypophyse stammende Hormone helfen dabei, Homöostase, Stoffwechsel und das Verhalten zu steuern.

1.6 Sexuality, human reproduction and life cycle

Female reproductive anatomy

reproductive organ n	Reproduktionsorgan
sex characteristic n	Geschlechtsmerkmal
primary sex characteristics	primäre Geschlechtsmerkmale
secondary sex characteristics	sekundäre Geschlechtsmerkmale
ovary ['əʊvri], *pl* ovaries ['əʊvriz] n	Eierstock
follicle ['fɒlɪkl] n	Follikel / Balgfrucht
ovulation [ˌɒvjə'leɪʃn] n	Ovulation
corpus luteum [ˌkɔːpəs'luːtɪəm] n	Corpus luteum
oviduct ['əʊvɪdʌkt] / fallopian tube [fæk,əʊpiən'tjuːb] n	Eileiter
uterus ['juːtrəs], *pl* uteruses; uteri n	Uterus / Gebärmutter
endometrium [ˌendəʊ'miːtriəm] n	Gebärmutterschleimhaut / Endometrium
cervix ['sɜːvɪks], *pl* cervixes n	Gebärmuttermund / Zervix
vagina [və'dʒaɪnə], *pl* vaginae; vaginas n	Scheide / Vagina
vulva ['vʌlvə], *pl* vulvae ['vʌlviː] n	Vulva
hymen [haɪmen] n	Hymen / Jungfernhäutchen
vestibule ['vestɪbjuːl] n	Vorhof
labia minora n *(sg uncommon)*	kleine Schamlippen *(Sg. ungebräuchlich)*
labia majora n *(sg uncommon)*	große Schamlippen *(Sg. ungebräuchlich)*
clitoris ['klɪtərɪs] n	Klitoris
Bartholin's gland n	Bartholin-Drüse
mammary gland [ˌmæməri'glænd] n	Brustdrüse / Milchdrüse

> Mammary glands are present in both sexes but normally function only in women.
> Milchdrüsen sind bei beiden Geschlechtern vorhanden, funktionieren aber gewöhnlich nur bei Frauen.

> Reproductive organs produce and transport gametes.
> Die Fortpflanzungsorgane produzieren und transportieren Gameten.

1 The human body › 1.6 Sexuality, human reproduction and life cycle

Male reproductive anatomy

testis, *pl* testes n	Hoden
seminiferous tubule [ˌsəmɪˈnɪfərəsˌtjuːbuːl] n	Hodenkanälchen
Leydig cell n	Leydig-Zelle
scrotum, *pl* scrota; scrotums n	Hodensack
duct n	Ductus
epididymis [ˌəpɪˈdɪdəmɪs] n	Nebenhoden
ejaculation [ɪˈdʒækjəleɪʃn] n	Ejakulation / Samenerguss
vas deferens [ˌvæsˈdefərenz] n	Vas deferens / Samenleiter
urethra [jʊəˈriːθrə] n	Harnröhre
semen [ˈsiːmən] n	Sperma
seminal vesicle n	Bläschendrüse / Samenblase
prostate gland n	Prostatadrüse
penis [ˈpiːnɪs], *pl* penises n	Penis
baculum n	Baculum *(Knochen, der die Erektion des Penis ermöglicht)*
glans penis n	Eichel
prepuce [ˈpriːpjus] n	Vorhaut / Präputium

» The male's external reproductive organs consist of the the penis and scrotum.
Die äußeren Fortpflanzungsorgane des Mannes bestehen aus Penis und Hodensack.

Human sexual response

life cycle n	Lebenszyklus
coitus [ˈkəʊɪtəs] n	Koitus
orgasm n	Orgasmus

The reproductive cycle of females

menstruation n	Menstruation
menstrual cycle n	Menstruationszyklus
oestrus n	Östrus
oestrous cycle	Östrischer Zyklus
gonadotropin-releasing hormone (GnRH) [gəʊnadətrɒːpin] n	gonadotropin-freisetzendes Hormon
follicle-stimulating hormone (FSH) n	follikelstimulierendes Hormon (FSH)
luteinising hormone (LH) n	luteinisierendes Hormon (LH)
menstrual cycle n	Menstruationszyklus

72

proliferative phase [prəʊˈlɪfəraɪtɪveˌfeɪs] n	Vermehrungsphase
endometrium [ˌendəʊˈmiːtrɪəm] n	Endometrium / Gebärmutterschleimhaut
ovarian cycle n	Ovarialzyklus
ovulation [ˌɒvjəˈleɪʃn] n	Ovulation
corpus luteum [ˌkɔːpəsˈluːtɪəm] n	Corpus luteum
progesterone [prəʊˈdʒestərəʊn] n	Progesteron
estrogen [ˈiːstrədʒn] n	Östrogen
menopause [ˈmenəpɔːz] n	Menopause
human oogenesis n	menschliche Oogenese
oogonium [ˌəʊəˈgəʊnɪəm], pl oogonia n	Oogonium
primary oocyte [ˌpraɪmrɪˈəʊəsaɪt] n	Oocyt I. Ordnung
secondary oocyte n	Oocyt II. Ordnung
ovum [ˈəʊvəm], pl ova n	Ovum

» Human females undergo menopause after about 450 cycles.
Weibliche Menschen unterliegen nach ungefähr 450 Zyklen einer Menopause.

The male reproductive system and its hormonal control

sex hormone n	Geschlechtshormon
androgen [ˈændrəʊdʒən] n	Androgen
testosterone [tesˈtɒstərəʊn] n	Testosteron
spermatogenesis [ˈspɜːmətəʊˌdʒenəsɪs] n	Spermatogenese
spermatogonium [ˈspɜːmətəʊˌgəʊnɪəm] n	Spermatogonium
primary spermatocyte [ˌpraɪmrɪˈspɜːmətəʊsaɪt] n	Spermatocyt I. Ordnung
secondary spermatocyte n	Spermatocyt II. Ordnung
sperm cell n	Samenzelle

» Androgens such as testosterone are directly responsible for the primary and secondary sex characteristics of the male.
Androgene wie Testosteron sind direkt für die primären und sekundären Geschlechtsmerkmale des Mannes verantwortlich.

Conception, embryonic development and birth

conception n	Empfängnis
cleavage [ˈkliːvɪdʒ] n	Aufspaltung / Furchung / Furchungsteilung

1 The human body › 1.6 Sexuality, human reproduction and life cycle

blastocyst [ˈblɑːstəˌsɪst] n	Blastocyste
chorionic gonadotropin [ˌkɔːriˈɒnɪkgoʊnædətrəʊpɪn] n	Choriongonadotropin
first trimester n	erstes Drittel *(einer Schwangerschaft)*
trophoblast [ˈtrɒfəblæst] n	Trophoblast
placenta [pləˈsentə] n	Plazenta
organogenesis [ˌɔːgənəʊˈdʒenəsɪs] n	Organogenese *(Anlagen der Organe)*
embryo n	Embryo
development n	Entwicklung
ontogeny [ɒnˈtɒdʒəni] n	Ontogenese *(Keimesentwicklung)*
foetus [ˈfiːtəs], *pl* foetuses / fetus *AE* n	Fetus *(Pl. Fetusse Feten)* / Fötus *(Pl. Föten)*
second trimester n	zweites Drittel (einer Schwangerschaft)
third trimester n	letztes Drittel (einer Schwangerschaft)
labour (pains) *BE* / labor *AE* / contractions n	Wehe
cervix [ˈsɜːvɪks], *pl* cervixes n	Gebärmuttermund / Zervix
childbirth / parturition / labour / delivery n	Entbindung
lactation n	Stillphase / Lactation
contraception n	Kontrazeption / Empfängnisverhütung
rhythm method n	Knaus-Ogino-Methode
natural family planning n	natürliche Familienplanung
barrier contraceptive n	Barriere-Verhütungsmittel
condom [ˈkɒndɒm] n	Kondom
diaphragm [ˈdaɪəfræm] n	Diaphragma
birth control pill n	Antibabypille
tubal ligation n	Eileiterabschnürung / Tubenligatur
vasectomy [vəˈsektəmi] n	Durchtrennung der Samenleiter / Vasektomie
abortion [əˈbɔːʃn] n	Abtreibung
modern reproductive technology n	moderne Reproduktionstechnik
in vitro fertilisation (IVF) n	künstliche Befruchtung

»
The three stages of labour:	Die drei Stadien der Wehen:
1. dilation of the cervix	1. Ausdehnung des Zervix
2. delivery of the infant by expulsion	2. Entbindung des Kindes durch Auspressen
3. delivery of the placenta	3. Entbindung der Plazenta

1.7 Food and diet

Food or "the need to feed"

food composition n	Nahrungszusammensetzung
water n	Wasser
fat n	Fett
protein n	Eiweiß / Protein
carbohydrate [ˌkɑːbəʊˈhaɪdreɪt] n	Kohlenhydrat
mineral n	Mineral
vitamin n	Vitamin
roughage [ˈrʌfɪʤ] / dietary fibre n	Ballaststoff
fruit n	Frucht / Obst
vegetable n	Gemüse
diet [daɪət] n	Ernährung
food pyramid n	Nahrungspyramide

Food pyramid »Abb. 36

fat and sugar	Fett und Zucker
fish, meat, eggs, pulses (legumes)	Fisch, Fleisch, Eier, Hülsenfrüchte
fruit	Frucht, Obst
bread and pastry	Brot und Feingebäck
vegetables	Gemüse
dairy products	Milchprodukte

energy balance n	Energiebilanz
energy content n	Energiegehalt
malnutrition n	Fehlernährung

» The daily requirement of a 14-year old youth is: 320 g carbohydrates, 85 g fat, 65 g proteins and 2.4 l water.
Der tägliche Bedarf eines 14-jährigen Jugendlichen ist: 320 g Kohlehydrate, 85 g Fett, 65 g Proteine und 2,4 l Wasser.
When planning your diet it is really important to remember vitamins and minerals. Do also not forget roughage!
Bei der Planung der Ernährung ist es wirklich wichtig auf Vitamine und Mineralien zu achten. Man sollte auch die Ballaststoffe nicht vergessen!
The food pyramid shows the recommended percentages of the different foods in a balanced diet.
Die Nahrungspyramide zeigt die empfohlenen Prozentanteile der unterschiedlichen Nahrungsmittel im Rahmen einer ausgewogenen Ernährung.

1.8 Digestion, absorption and use of food

Food processing: a closer look

omnivore ['ɒmnɪvɔː] n	Allesfresser / Omnivor
oral cavity n	Mundhöhle
dental structure n	Zahnstruktur
root n	Wurzel
neck n	Hals / Genick / Nacken
crown n	Zahnkrone
enamel [ɪ'næml] n	Zahnschmelz
dentine ['dentiːn] n	Dentin
pulp cavity n	Pulpahöhle / Zahnhöhle
gum n	Zahnfleisch
cement n	Zahnzement
dental root n	Zahnwurzel
blood vessel n	Blutgefäß
nerve n	Nerv
jaw bone n	Kieferknochen
ingestion [in'dʒestʃən] n	Nahrungsaufnahme
digestion [daɪ'dʒestʃən] n	Verdauung
digestive organ n	Verdauungsorgan
mouth n	Mund
swallowing n	Schlucken
nasopharynx [ˌneɪzəʊ'færɪŋks] n	Nasenrachen
soft palate n	weicher Gaumen
tongue n	Zunge
trachea [trə'kiːe] n	Trachea
salivary gland ['sælɪvərɪˌglænd] n	Speicheldrüse
pancreas ['pæŋkrɪəs] n	Bauchspeicheldrüse
appendix n	Appendix
liver n	Leber
gall bladder n	Gallenblase
intracellular digestion n	intrazelluläre Verdauung
extracellular digestion (in many animals) n	extrazelluläre Verdauung
digestive tract n	Verdauungstrakt
peristalsis [ˌperɪ'stælsɪs] n	Peristaltik
digestive juice n	Verdauungssaft
digestive gland n	Verdauungsdrüse
sphincter ['sfɪŋktə] n	Schließmuskel
enzymatic hydrolysis [ˌenzaɪ'mætiɪk haɪ'drɒləsɪs] n	enzymatische Hydrolyse

Stages of food processing

The main stages of food processing are: **ingestion, digestion, absorption and elimination (egestion).** **Ingestion**: the act of eating **Digestion**: food is broken down into molecules small enough for the body to absorb **Absorption**: the human's cell absorb small molecules such as simple sugars or amino acids from the digestive compartment **Elimination (egestion)**: undigested material passes out of the digestive system	Die Hauptstadien der Nahrungsverarbeitung sind: Nahrungsaufnahme, Verdauung, Absorption und Ausscheidung. **Nahrungsaufnahme**: der Essvorgang **Verdauung**: das Essen wird in Moleküle zerlegt, die klein genug sind, dass der Körper diese absorbieren kann **Absorption**: die Zellen des Menschen absorbieren kleine Moleküle, wie einfache Zucker oder Aminosäuren, vom Verdauungstrakt **Ausscheidung**: unverdautes Material wird dem Verdauungssystem entzogen

absorption n	Absorption

salivary amylase ['sælıvəriˌæmıleız] n	Pytalin
bolus ['bəʊləs] n	Bolus
pharynx ['færɒŋks] n	Pharynx / Rachen
epiglottis [ˌepɪ'glɒtɪs] n	Epiglottis / Kehldeckel
oesophagus [iː'sɒfəgəs], pl oesophagi / esophagus [iː'sɒfəgaɪ] AE n	Ösophagus

stomach ['stʌmək] n	Magen » Abb. 20
gastric juice n	Magensaft
pepsin n	Pepsin
pepsinogen [ˌpep'sɪnedʒən]	Pepsinogen
acid conditions n	saure Bedingungen
pyloric sphincter [paɪ'lɔːrɪk'sfɪŋktə] n	Schließmuskel des Magenpförtners

small intestine n	Dünndarm
duodenum [ˌdjuːə'diːnəm] n	Zwölffingerdarm
bile [baɪl] n	Galle
villus, pl villi ['vɪləs; 'vɪlaɪ] n	Zotte
microvilli n	Mikrovilli
lacteal ['læktɪəl] n	Lymphkapillare des Dünndarms
chylomicron [ˌkaɪləʊ'maɪkrɒn] n	Chylomikron (Lipidprotein Partikel)
hepatic portal vein [hɪˌpætɪkˌpɔːtl'veɪn] n	Leberpfortader

large intestine / colon ['kəʊlɒn] n	Dickdarm
caecum BE [siːkəm] / cecum AE n	Blinddarm / Caecum

1 The human body › 1.9 Blood circulatory system

faeces BE [ˈfiːsiːz] / feces AE n pl	Kot / Fäzes
rectum [ˈrektəm] n	Mastdarm / Rektum

1.9 Blood circulatory system

What is blood?

plasma n	(Blut-)Plasma
cellular element n	zelluläres Element
red blood cell n	rote Blutzelle / rotes Blutkörperchen
white blood cell n	weiße Blutzelle / weißes Blutkörperchen
platelet [ˈpleɪtlət] n	Blutplättchen
erythrocyte [ɪˈrɪθrəsaɪt] n	Erythrocyte
haemoglobin BE [ˌhiːməˈgləʊbɪn] / hemoglobin AE n	Hämoglobin
leucocyte [ˈljuːkəsaɪt] n	Leukocyt(e)
stem cell n	Stammzelle
erythropoietin (EPO) [ɪˌrɪθrəpɔɪˈetɪn] n	Erythropoietin (Epo)
blood clotting n	Blutgerinnung
fibrinogen [fɪˈbrɪnədʒn] n	Fibrinogen
fibrin [ˈfɪbrɪn] n	Fibrin
thrombus [ˈθrɒmbəs] n	Blutgerinnsel / Thrombus

» Blood is a connective tissue with cells suspended in plasma.
Blut ist ein Bindegewebe mit im Plasma gelösten Zellen.

The human heart

aorta [eɪˈɔːtə], pl aortas; aortae n	Aorta
artery [ˈɑːtəri], pl plateries n	Arterie
pulmonary artery [ˌpʌlmənriˈɑːtəri] n	Lungenarterie
left atrium [ˌleftˈeɪtriəm] n	linkes Atrium
vein [ˈveɪn] n	Vene
pulmonary vein [ˌpʌlmənriˈveɪn] n	Lungenvene
valve [vælv] n	Klappe
semilunar valve	Taschenklappe
ventricle [ˈventrɪkl] n	Ventrikel
left ventricle	linkes Ventrikel
right ventricle	rechtes Ventrikel

posterior vena cava [ˌpɒstɪərɪəˌviːnə'keɪvə] n	Vena cava posterior
right atrium n	Rechtes Atrium
anterior vena cava n	Vena cava anterior
cardiac cycle n	Herzzyklus
atrial and ventricular diastole [ˌeɪtrɪəlændven'trɪkjəledaɪ'æstəlɪ] n	Vorhof- und Kammerdiastole
ventricular systole [venˌtrɪkjəle'sɪstəlɪ] n	Kammersystole
heart rate n	Pulsfrequenz
cardiac output n	Herzzeitvolumen
stroke volume n	Schlagvolumen
atrioventricular valve n	Segelklappe
pulse n	Puls
heart disease n	Herzkrankheit
sinoatrial node [ˌsaɪnəʊeɪtrɪel'nəʊd] / pacemaker n	Sinusknoten
myogenic contraction [ˌmaɪədʒenɪkkən'trækʃn] n	spontane Muskelkontraktion
neurogenic [ˌnjʊərəʊ'dʒenɪk] adj	neurogen
atrioventricular node [ˌeɪtrɪəvənˌtrɪkjələ'nəʊd] n	Atrioventrikularknoten
electrocardiogram [ɪˌlektrəʊ'kɑːdiəgræm](ECG) n	Elektrokardiogramm (EKG)

» The valves prevent blood backflow within the heart.
Die Klappen verhindern den Rückfluss des Blutes in das Herz.

Principles of blood circulation

blood vessel n	Blutgefäß
endothelium [ˌendəʊ'θiːlɪəm] n	Endothelium
smooth muscle n	glatter Muskel
connective tissue n	Bindegewebe
artery ['ɑːtəri] n	Arterie
arteriole [ɑː'tɪərɪəʊl] n	Arteriole
venule ['venjuːl] n	Venule
vein ['veɪn] n	Vene
basement membrane n	Basalmembran
capillary [kə'pɪlri] n	Kapillare
blood flow velocity n	Geschwindigkeit des Blutstroms
blood pressure n	Blutdruck

1 The human body › 1.10 Lymphatic system

systolic pressure [sɪˈstɒlɪkˌpreʃə] n	systolischer Druck
diastolic pressure [ˌdaɪəˈstɒlɪkˌpreʃə] n	diastolischer Druck
capillary wall n	Kapillarwand

1.10 Lymphatic system » Abb. 21

Fluid return by the lymphatic system

lymph [lɪmf] n	Lymphe
lymphatic system [ˈlɪmfætɪkˌsɪstəm] n	lymphatisches System
palatine tonsil [ˌpælətaɪnˈtɒnsl] n	Gaumenmandel
thymus [ˈθaɪməs] n	Thymus
thoracic duct [θɔːˌræsɪkˈdʌkt] n	Brustlymphgang
spleen [spliːn] n	Milz
vermiform appendix [ˌvɜːmɪfɔːməˈpendɪks] n	Wurmfortsatz
red bone marrow n	rotes Knochenmark
lymphatic vessel [lɪmˌfætɪkˈvesl] n	Lymphkapillare
lymph node [ˈlɪmfˌnəʊd] n	Lymphknoten
interstitial fluid [ˌɪntəstɪʃlˈfluːɪd] n	interstitielle Flüssigkeit

» The lymphatic system drains into the circulatory system near the junction of the venae cavae with the right atrium.
Das Lymphsystem fließt in das Gefäßsystem nahe der Kreuzung der Hohlvene mit dem rechten Atrium ab.
It transports fats from the digestive tract to the circulatory system. The lymphatic system also maintains the volume and protein concentration of the blood. Finally, it helps defend against infection!
Es transportiert Fette vom Verdauungstrakt zum Gefäßsystem. Das lymphatische System erhält auch das Volumen und die Proteinkonzentration des Blutes. Schließlich hilft es bei Infektionen!

1.11 Respiratory system

Gas exchange

gas exchange n	Gasaustausch
metabolic rate n	Stoffwechselrate
respiratory substrate [rəˌspɪrətrɪˈsʌbstreɪt] n	Atmungssubstrat
respiratory surface n	respiratorische Oberfläche
lung n	Lunge

» The size and complexity of lungs are correlated with an animal's metabolic rate.
Die Größe und Komplexität der Lungen stehen im Verhältnis zum Stoffwechsel des Tieres.

thoracic cavity [θɔːˌræsɪkˈkævəti] / chest cavity n	Brusthöhle
air n	Luft
nostril n	Nasenloch
nasal cavity n	Nasenhöhle
pharynx [ˈfærɪŋks] n	Rachen / Pharynx
larynx [ˈlærɪŋks], pl larynxes [ˈlærɪŋksɪz] n	Kehlkopf / Larynx
epiglottis [ˌepɪˈɡlɒtɪs] n	Kehldeckel / Epiglottis
glottis n	Stimmritze / Glottis
vocal fold n	Stimmlippe
trachea [trəˈkiːe] n	Trachea
bronchus [ˈbrɒŋkəs], pl bronchi n	Bronchus / Bronchie
bronchioles [ˈbrɒŋkɪəʊlz] n pl	Bronchiolen (meist Pl)
epithelium [ˌepɪˈθiːliəm] n	Epithelium
mucus [ˈmjuːkəs] n	Schleim
mucous adj	schleimig
cilium [ˈsɪliəm], pl cilia n	Cilie / Wimper
alveolus [ˌælviˈəʊləs], pl alveoli n	Alveole

» The lung is an invaginated respiratory surface that connects to the atmosphere by narrow tubes.
Die Lunge is eine nach innen gewölbte respiratorische Oberfläche, die durch schmale Gänge mit der Atmosphäre verbunden ist.

How humans breathe

negative pressure breathing (air is pulled into the lungs instead of being pushed) n	Atmung via Unterdruck
suction pump n	Saugpumpe
rib cage n	Brustkorb
lung volume n	Lungenvolumen
air pressure n	Luftdruck
inhalation n	Einatmung
exhalation n	Ausatmung
contraction n	Kontraktion / Zusammenpressen
diaphragm [ˈdaɪəfræm] n	Zwerchfell

1 The human body › 1.11 Respiratory system

tidal volume n	Atemvolumen
vital capacity n	Vitalkapazität
residual volume [rɪˌzɪdjʊəlˈvɒljuːm] n	Restluftmenge
breath cycle n	Atmungszyklus
oxygen concentration n	Sauerstoffkonzentration

»

air inhaled	Luft eingeatmet
air exhaled	Luft ausgeatmet
rib cage expands as rib muscles contract	Brustkorb erweitert sich, während sich die Rippenmuskulatur zusammenzieht
diaphragm contracts (moves down)	Zwerchfell zieht sich zusammen (bewegt sich nach unten)
rib cage gets smaller as rib muscles relax	Brustkorb wird enger während Rippenmuskeln sich entspannen
diaphragm relaxes (moves up)	Zwerchfell entspannt sich (bewegt sich nach oben)

Respiratory pigments

respiratory pigment [rəˌspɪrətriˈpɪgmənt] n	Atmungspigment
partial pressure n	Partialdruck
oxygen transport n	Sauerstofftransport
haemoglobin BE [ˌhiːməˈgləʊbɪn] / hemoglobin AE n	Hämoglobin
dissociation curve [dɪˌsəʊʃɪˈeɪʃnˌkɜːv] n	Dissoziationskurve
erythrocyte [ɪˈrɪθrəsaɪt] n	Erythrocyte
Bohr effect [ˈbɔːrɪˌfekt] n	Bohr-Effekt
carbon dioxide transport [ˌkɑːbndaɪˈɒksaɪdˌtrænspɔːt] n	Kohlenstoffdioxid-Transport

Haemoglobin loads and unloads oxygen.
Hämoglobin lädt Sauerstoff auf und ab.
An effect called the *Bohr shift* means that a drop in pH lowers the affinity of haemoglobin for oxygen.
Ein Effekt, der als Bohr-Bewegung bezeichnet wird, beschreibt, dass eine Senkung des pH-Wertes die Affinität des Hämoglobins für Sauerstoff mindert.

1.12 Excretion and the kidneys

Osmoregulation and excretion in general

osmosis [ɒz'məʊsɪs] n	Osmose
osmolarity / osmotic pressure n	Osmolarität
isoosmotic [aɪ'sɒɒz‚mɒtɪk]	isoosmotisch
hyperosmotic	hyperosmotisch
hypoosmotic	hypoosmotisch
osmoregulation n	Osmoregulation
excretion [ɪk'skriːʃn] n	Exkretion / Ausscheidung
metabolism [mə'tæbəlɪzm] n	Stoffwechsel
nitrogen ['naɪtrədʒən] n	Stickstoff
ammonium [ə'məʊniəm], *pl* ammonia n	Ammonium
solute ['sɒljuːt] n	gelöste Substanz
waste product n	Abfallprodukt
physiological saline [‚fɪzɪəlɒdʒɪkl'seɪlaɪn] n	Kochsalzlösung

»
How do humans regulate solute concentrations and how do they balance the gain and loss of water?	Wie regulieren Menschen gelöste Konzentrationen und wie gleichen sie den Gewinn und Verlust von Wasser aus?
How do humans get rid of nitrogen containing the waste products of metabolism?	Wie werden Menschen die stickstoffhaltigen Abfallprodukte des Stoffwechsels los?

Water balance

Water gain	Water loss
ingested in liquid (1,500 ml)	**urine (1,500 ml)**
eingenommene Flüssigkeit	Urin / Harn
ingested in food (750 ml)	**evaporation (900 ml)**
durch Nahrung eingenommen	Evaporation / Verdunstung
derived from metabolic processes (250 ml)	**faeces (100 ml)**
aus Stoffwechselprozessen entstanden	Kot / Exkremente

Excretory system and process

filtration n	Filtration
filter v	filtrieren

1 The human body › 1.12 Excretion and the kidneys

semipermeable membrane [ˌsemɪpɜːmɪəblˈmembreɪn] n	semipermeable Membran (halbdurchlässig)
selective reabsorption [sɪˌlektɪvriːəbˈzɔːpʃn] n	selektive Rückresorption
secretion [sɪˈkriːʃn] n	Sekretion
kidney [ˈkɪdni] n	Niere
renal cortex [ˌriːnlˈkɔːteks] n	Nierenrinde
renal medulla [ˌriːnlmɪˈdʌlə] n	Nierenmark
nephron [ˈnefrɒn] n	Glomerulus
cortical nephron	Corticales Nephron
juxtamedullary nephron [ˌdʒʌkstəmɪˌdʌləriˈnefrɒn]	juxtamedullärer Glomerulus
proximal tubule [ˌprɒksɪmlˈtjuːbjuːl] n	proximaler Tubulus
loop of Henle n	Henlesche Schleife
distal tubule [ˌdɪstɪlˈtjuːbjuːl] n	distaler Tubulus
glomerulus [glɒˈmerʊləs] (a ball of capillaries) n	Glomerulus
Bowman's capsule n	Bowmannsche Kapsel
blood vessel n	Blutgefäß
afferent arteriole [ˈæfrntɑːˌtɪəriəʊl] n	afferente Arteriole
efferent arteriole [ˈefrntɑːˌtɪəriəʊl] n	efferente Arteriole
peritubular capillary [perɪˈtjuːbjeləkəˈpɪlri] n	peritubuläre Kapillare
collecting duct [kəˌlektɪŋˈdʌkt] n	Sammelrohr
vasa recta [ˌveɪsəˈrektə] n	Vasa recta
renal artery [ˌriːnlˈɑːtri] n	Arteria renalis / Nierenarterie
renal calyx [ˌriːnlˈkeɪlɪks] n	Nierenkelch
renal pelvis [ˌriːnlˈpelvɪs] n	Nierenbecken
renal vein [ˌriːnlˈveɪn] n	Vena renalis / Nierenvene
ureter [jʊəˈriːtə] n	Harnleiter
urinary bladder [ˌjʊərɪnəriˈblædə] n	Harnblase
urethra [jʊəˈriːθrə] n	Harnröhre
countercurrent multiplier system [ˌkaʊntəkʌrəntˈmʌltɪplaɪə] n	Gegenstromverstärker-System

» In humans, each kidney is bean-shaped and about 10 cm long.
The functional units of the human kidney are nephrons and associated blood vessels.
Each human kidney contains over 1 million tiny nephrons.
Bei Menschen ist jede Niere bohnenförmig und ca. 10 cm lang.
Die funktionellen Einheiten der menschlichen Niere sind Glomeruli und assoziierte Blutgefäße.
Jede menschliche Niere enthält über 1 Million winziger Glomeruli.

From blood filtrate to urine

The human kidney's ability to conserve water is a key terrestrial adaptation.
Die Fähigkeit der menschlichen Niere, Wasser für den Körper zurückzugewinnen, ist eine terrestrische Schlüsselanpassung.
The filtrate makes three trips between the medulla and cortex: first down, then up, and then down again in the collecting duct.
Das Filtrat macht drei Stationen zwischen dem Nierenmark und der Nierenrinde durch: erst runter, dann hoch und schließlich wieder in das Sammelrohr.

Regulation of kidney function

negative feedback circuit [negətɪvˈfiːdbækˌsɜːkɪt] n	negative Rückkopplung
antidiuretic hormone (ADH) [ˌæntɪdaɪjʊretɪkˈhɔːməʊn] n	antidiuretisches Hormon (ADH)
juxtaglomerular apparatus (JGA) [ˌdʒʌkstəgləˌmerəʃæpəˈreɪtəs] n	juxtamedullärer Apparat
angiotensin II [ˌændʒɪəˈtensɪn] n	Angiotensin II
aldosterone [ælˈdɒstərəʊn] n	Aldosteron
renin-angiotensin-aldosterone system (RAAS) [ˌriːnɪnˌændʒɪəʊtenʒɪn ˌældɒstərəʊnˈsɪstəm] n	Renin-Angiotensin-Aldosteron-System (RAAS)

» Antidiuretic hormone (ADH) enhances fluid retention by making the kidneys reclaim more water.
Das antidiuretische Hormon verstärkt die Zurückhaltung von Flüssigkeit, indem die Nieren mehr Wasser verlangen.
The renin-angiotensin-aldosterone system (RAAS) leads to an increase in blood volume and pressure.
Das Renin-Angiotensin-Aldosteron-System führt zu einem Ansteigen des Blutvolumens und des Druckes.

1.13 Immune system
Recognition and defence

microorganism [ˌmaɪkrəʊˈɔːgnɪzm] n	Mikroorganismus
bacteria	Bakterien
fungi	Fungi
protozoa [ˌprəʊtəˈzəʊə] n	Protozoa
infectious disease n	Infektionskrankheit

1 The human body › 1.13 Immune system

pathogen ['pæθədʒən] n	Pathogen (krankheitsauslösende Substanz)
external defence n	äußere Abwehr
acid mantle n	Säuremantel
lysozyme ['laɪsəzaɪm] n	Lysozym
innate immunity n	angeborene Immunität
macrophage ['mækrəfeɪdʒ] n	Makrophage
phagocyte ['fægəsaɪt] n	Phagocyt / Fresszelle
phagocytosis [ˌfægəʊsaɪ'təʊsɪs] n	Phagocytose / Zellfressen
complement system n	Komplementsystem
adaptive [ə'dæptɪv] (acquired immunity) adj	lernfähig / anpassungsfähig / adaptiv
antibody n	Antikörper
antigen ['æntɪdʒən] n	Antigen
memory cell n	Gedächtniszelle
secondary immune response n	sekundäre Immunantwort
vaccination [ˌvæksɪ'neɪʃn] n	Immunisierung / Impfung
vaccinate v	impfen
inoculation [ɪˌnɒkjə'leɪʃn] n	Impfung
inoculate v	impfen
inflammation n	Entzündung
infection [ɪn'fekʃn] n	Infektion
pus [pʌs] n	Eiter
immunisation BE / immunization AE n	Immunisierung
passive immunisation	passive Immunisierung
active immunisation	aktive Immunisierung
incubation period n	Inkubationszeit

» Describe the phenomenon of external defence!
Beschreibe(n Sie) das Phänomen der externen Abwehr!
The time interval that exists between the introduction of the pathogen and the occurence of the first clinical signs of disease is called *incubation period*.
Als Inkubationsphase wird das Zeitintervall bezeichnet, das zwischen der Einführung des Pathogens und dem Erscheinen der ersten Krankheitszeichen existiert, bezeichnet.

The immune response

lymphatic system [ˌlɪmfætɪk'sɪstəm] n	lymphatisches System
lymphatic organ n	lymphatisches Organ
thymus ['θaɪməs] n	Thymus
lymph node ['lɪmfˌnəʊd] n	Lymphknoten

thoracic duct [θɔːˌræsɪkˈdʌkt] n	Brustlymphgang
swollen [ˈsweʊlən] adj	angeschwollen

myeloid stem cell [ˌmaɪəlɔɪdˈstemsel] n	Blut-Stammzelle
phagocyte [ˈfægəsaɪt] n	Phagocyt / Fresszelle
monocyte [ˈmɒnəsaɪt] n	Monocyt
macrophage [ˈmækrəfeɪdʒ] n	Makrophage
granulocyte [ˈgrænjʊləsaɪt] n	Granulocyt
mast cell n	Mastzelle
lymphoid tissue n	Lymphgewebe
lymphocyte [ˈlɪmfəsaɪt] n	Lymphocyt
B cell n	B-Zelle
T cell n	T-Zelle
T cell receptor n	T-Zellrezeptor
helper T cell (T_H) n	T-Helferzelle
cytotoxic T cell (T_C) n	Cytotoxische T-Zelle
plasma cell n	Plasmazelle
lock-and-key principle n	Schlüssel-Schloss-Prinzip

antigen-antibody reaction n	Antigen-Antikörper-Reaktion
epitope [ˈepɪtəʊp] n	Epitop
blood group n	Blutgruppe
AB0 system n	AB0-System
rhesus system [ˈriːsəsˌsɪstəm] n	Rhesussystem
monoclonal antibody [ˌmɒnəkləʊnlˈæntɪbɒdiz] n	monoklonaler Antikörper
cell marker n	Zellmarker
ELISA [ɪˈlaɪsə] (Enzyme-Linked Immuno Sorbet Assay) n	ELISA-Test
clone [kləʊn] n	Klon
somatic recombination n	somatische Rekombination

» Antibodies are produced according to the building block principle.
Antikörper werden nach dem Baustein-Prinzip hergestellt.

adverse immune reaction [ˌædvɜːsɪˈmjuːnrɪækʃn] n	ungünstige Immunreaktion
allergy [ˈælədʒi] n	Allergie
allergen [ˈælədʒen] n	Allergen
hay fever n	Heuschnupfen
sensitisation BE / sensitization AE [ˌsensɪtaɪˈzeɪʃn] n	Sensibilisierung / Sensitivierung
IgE class n	IgE Klasse

1 The human body › 1.13 Immune system

histamine ['hɪstəmiːn] n	Histamin
allergic shock / anaphylactic shock [ˌænəfɪˌlæktɪk'ʃɒk] n	allergischer Schock / anaphylaktischer Schock
delayed hypersensitivity reaction type n	Spättyp
desensitisation *BE* [diːˌsensɪtaɪ'zeɪʃn] / desensitization *AE* n	Desensibilisierung
transplantation antigen n	Transplantationsantigen
immune suppression n	Immunsuppression
graft-versus-host disease n	Transplantat-gegen-Wirt-Reaktion
blood transfusion ['blʌdtrænsfˌfjuːʒn] n	Bluttransfusion
anti-A n	Anti-A
anti-B n	Anti-B
rhesus factor ['riːsəsˌfæktə] n	Rhesusfaktor
Rh-positive n	Rh-positiv
Rh-negative n	Rh-negativ
agglutination [əˌgluːtɪ'neɪʃn] n	Agglutination
IgG antibody n	IgG-Antikörper
autoimmune disease [ˌɔːtəʊɪ'mjuːndɪˌziːz] n	Autoimmunerkrankung
diabetes mellitus [daɪəbiːtiːz'melɪtəs] n	Diabetis mellitus
rheumatoid factor [ˌruːmətɔɪd'fæktə] n	Rheumafaktor

HLA system *(human leukocyte antigen)* n	HLA-System
organ donation n	Organspende
transplant rejection [ˌtrænsplɑːntrɪ'dʒekʃn] n	Transplantatablehnung

immunological tolerance n	immunologische Toleranz
autoimmunity [ˌɔːtəʊɪ'mjuːnəti] n	Autoimmunität
autoantibody [ˌɔːtəʊ'ænθɪbɒdɪ] n	Autoantikörper
inflammatory rheumatism [ɪn'flæmətriˌruːmətɪzm] n	entzündliches Rheuma

» The course of allergic reactions is complicated because of its various causes.
Aufgrund zahlreicher Ursachen wird der Verlauf allergischer Reaktionen komplizierter.

The ability of the immune system to distinguish self from nonself limits tissue transplantation.
Die Fähigkeit des Immunsystems, zwischen selbst und fremd zu erkennen, grenzt die Gewebe-Transplantation ein.

AIDS

AIDS / acquired immune deficiency syndrome n
HIV / human immunodeficiency virus n
retrovirus ['retrəʊvaɪrəs] n
viral envelope [ˌvaɪərəl'envələʊp] n
pin head / glycoprotein [ˌɡlaɪkəʊ'prəʊtiːn] n
capsid n
reverse transcriptase [rɪˌvɜːstræn'skrɪpteɪz] n
RNA (ribonucleic acid) n
reverse transcription [rɪˌvɜːstræn'skrɪpʃn] n
HIV-positive adj
therapeutic option [ˌθerəpjuːtɪk'ɒpʃnz] n
AZT / azidothymine n
host n

AIDS / erworbenes Immunschwäche-Syndrom
HIV / menschliches Immunschwäche-Virus
Retrovirus
Virushülle
Nadelkopf / Glykoproteine

Kapsid *(kapselartige Proteinstruktur)*
reverse Transkriptase

RNA / RNS (**R**ibo**n**uklein **S**äure)
reverse Transkription

HIV-positiv
therapeutische Alternative

Azidothymin
Wirt

» If the HIV RNA genome is reverse-transcribed inside a cell, the product DNA is integrated into the host cell's genome.
Das Produkt DNA wird in das Wirtszellengenom integriert, wenn das RNA-Genom innerhalb einer Zelle reversiv (umgekehrt) transkribiert wird.

Prion diseases

prion ['praɪɒn] *(proteinaceous infectious particle)* n
BSE [ˌbiːes'iː] *(bovine spongiform encephalopathy)* n
cow brain n

Prion *(Pl. Prione)*

BSE *(Hirnkrankheit bei Rindern)*

Gehirn einer Kuh

» Prions change the shape of normal proteins. Therefore, they can become infectious.
Prionen ändern die Form normaler Proteine. Deshalb können sie infektiös werden.

1.14 Health and disease

Global health

infectious disease n	Infektionskrankheit
epidemic n	Epidemie / Seuche
pandemic n	Pandemie *(örtlich nicht begrenzt; weltweit)*
malaria [məˈleərɪə] n	Malaria
plague [pleɪg] n	Pest
cholera [ˈkɒlrə] n	Cholera
World Health Organization *(WHO)* n	Weltgesundheitsorganisation
SARS [sɑːz] *(severe acute respiratory syndrome)* n	SARS
droplet infection n	Tröpfcheninfektion
flu / influenza [ˌɪnfluˈenzə] n	Grippe
bird flu n	Vogelgrippe
swine flu n	Schweinegrippe
Health Impact Assessment *(HIA)* n	Gesundheitsverträglichkeitsprüfung
health prevention n	Gesundheitsvorsorge
cow pox n	Kuhpocken
globalisation *BE* / globalization *AE* n	Globalisierung
travel advice n	Reisetipp
poverty n	Armut
developing country n	Entwicklungsland
newly industrialised country n	Schwellenland

> "Fear and the flu: The new age of pandemics" Newsweek headline, May 11 (2009)
> "Angst und die Grippe: Das neue Zeitalter der Pandemien" Newsweek-Überschrift, 11. März, 2009
>
> The WHO represents a special organization within the United Nations.
> Die WHO stellt eine spezielle Organisation innerhalb der Vereinten Nationen dar.

2 Plant families

2.1 Basic vocabulary: reproduction of plants in general

sexual reproduction n	geschlechtliche Fortpflanzung
division [dɪˈvɪʒn] n	Teilung
meiotic [maɪˈəʊtɪk] adj	meiotisch
undergo meiosis [ˌʌndəˈgəʊmaɪˈəʊsɪs]	Meiose durchlaufen
haploid [ˈhæplɔɪd] adj	haploid *(einfacher Chromosomensatz)*

gamete ['gæmiːt] n	Keimzelle / Gamet
male gamete	männliche Keimzelle
female gamete	weibliche Keimzelle
ovum ['əʊvəm], *pl* ova ['əʊvə] n	Eizelle
zygote ['zaɪgəʊt] n	Zygote
diploid ['dɪplɔɪd] adj	diploid *(doppelter Chromosomensatz)*
diploid zygote	diploide Zygote *(Zygote mit doppeltem Chromosomensatz)*
embryo n	Embryo
germinate ['dʒɜːmɪneɪt] / sprout v	keimen / auskeimen
germination [ˌdʒɜːmɪ'neɪʃn] / sprouting n	Keimung / Auskeimung
secrete [sɪ'kriːt] v	ausscheiden / absondern
chemotaxis [ˌkəməʊ'tæksɪs] n	Chemotaxis
bud [bʌd] n	Knospe
asexual reproduction n	ungeschlechtliche Fortpflanzung
cell division / mitotic division n	Zellteilung / Mitose
fragmentation n	Abbrechen *(Einschnürungen zwischen Zellgruppe)*
alternation of generations n	Generationswechsel
life cycle n	Lebenszyklus

2.2 Reproduction of green algae, bryophyta, and pteridophyta

isogamete [aɪ'sɒgəmiːt] n	Isogamet *(gleich große Gameten, Keimzellen)*
isogamous	Geschlechtszellen produzierend, die sich äußerlich nicht unterscheiden
plus gamete [ˌplʌs'gæmiːt] n	Plus Gamet *(positiv)* / männliche Keimzelle
minus gamete [ˌmaɪnəs'gæmiːt] n	Minus Gamet *(negativ)* / weibliche Keimzelle
thallus ['θæləs] n	Thallus *(vielzelliger Vegetationskörper bei Pflanzen, der nicht in Wurzel, Sprossachse und Blätter unterteilt werden kann und kein Stütz- und Leitgewebe hat)*
thallus plant	Lagerpflanze / Thalluspflanze
sporophyte ['spɒrəfaɪt] n	Sporophyt

2 Plant families › 2.2 Reproduction of green algae, bryophyta, and pteridophyta

gametophyte [gəˈmiːtəʊfaɪt] n sporophyte diploid generation [ˌspɒrəfaɪtˈdɪplɔɪdˌdʒenəˈreɪʃn] haploid gametophyte generation [ˈhæplɔɪdgəˈmiːtəʊfaɪtˌdʒenəˈreɪʃn] alternate with v	Gametophyt diploide Sporophyten Generation haploide Gametophyten Generation abwechseln mit
female organ n archegonium [ˌɑːkɪˈgəʊnɪəm], pl archegonia *(female)* n female gametophyte venter [ˈventə] n neck-canal cell n	weibliches Geschlechtsorgan Archegonium *(weibliches Geschlechtsorgan)* weiblicher Gametophyt Flaschenbauch Flaschenhalszelle
male organ n antheridium [ˌænθəˈrɪdɪəm] / antheridia *(male)* n sperm cell / spermatozoid [ˈspɜːmətəʊˌzəʊɪd] n sperm cell / spermatozoid [ˈspɜːmətəʊˌzəʊɪd] n sperm mother cell	männliches Geschlechtsorgan Antheridium / Antheridien *(männlich)* Schwärmer / Spermatozoid Schwärmer / Spermatozoid Schwärmermutterzelle
sporophyte [ˈspɒrəfaɪt] n spore [spɔː] n spore mother cell spore sac haploid spore	Sporophyt Spore Sporenmutterzelle Sporensack haploide Spore *(mit einfachem Chromosomensatz)*

Green algae » III. 10 Ecology – 10.1 Examples of aquatic ecosystems

alga [ˈælgə], *pl* algas; algae n
  green alga
phytoplankton [ˈfaɪtəʊˌplæŋktən] n
fresh water n
freshwater adj
chlamydomonas [ˌklæmɪdəˈməʊnəs] n
flagellum [fleˈdʒeləm], *pl* flagella n
vacuole [ˈvækjuəʊl] n
  contractile vacuole
  [kənˌtræktaɪlˈvækjuəʊl]
eye spot n
	Alge
	  Grünalge
	Phytoplankton / pflanzliches Plankton
	Süßwasser
	süßwasser~
	Chlamydomonas / Augentierchen
	Geißel
	Vakuole / Zellsaftraum
	  sich zusammenziehende Vakuole
	
	Augenfleck

pyrenoid ['paɪrənɔɪd] n	Pyrenoid *(Ort der Stärkesynthese)*
zoospore [ˌzuːəspɔː] *(haploid)* n	Zoospore *(haploid)*
zygospore ['zaɪgspɔː] n	Zygospore / Überdauerungsspore
autotrophic [ˌɔːtəˈtrɒfɪk] adj	autotroph / photosynthetisch aktiv

»
unicellular chlorophyll-containing organism	einzelliger chlorophyllenthaltender Organismus

Diatom

diatom ['daɪətəm] n	Kieselalge
salt water n	Salzwasser
shell n	Schale
pectin ['pɛktɪn] n	Pektin
impregnated ['ɪmprɛgneɪtɪd] adj	imprägniert / beschichtet
silica ['sɪlɪkə] n	Kieselsäure / Silizium
brittle ['brɪtl] adj	spröde
mask v	abdecken / verstecken / maskieren

»
impregnated with silica	mit Kieselsäure durchsetzt
masked by a pigment	durch ein Pigment abgedeckt

basic chain n	wesentliches Glied
food cycle n	Nahrungskreislauf
store oil n	Öl speichern
deposit [dɪˈpɒzɪt] n	Ablagerung
aid v	helfen
formation n	Entstehung / Bildung
petroleum [pəˈtrəʊliəm] n	Erdöl
diatomaceous earth [ˌdaɪətəmeɪʃəsˈɜːθ] n	Kieselgur

»
basic link in the food chain	wesentliches Glied in der Nahrungskette

Spirogyra

spirogyra [ˌspaɪərəˈdʒaɪərə] n	Schraubenalge
freshwater green alga n	Süßwasser Grünalge

2 Plant families › 2.2 Reproduction of green algae, bryophyta, and pteridophyta

multicellular [ˌmʌltɪˈseljʊlə] adj	vielzellig
unbranched adj	unverzweigt
filamentous [ˌfɪləˈmentəs] adj	fadenförmig
cytoplasmic strand [ˌsaɪtəʊplæzmɪkˈstrænd] n	Strang aus Cytoplasma
ribbon-like [ˈrɪbnlaɪk] adj	bandartig
conjugation [ˌkɒndʒʊˈgeɪʃn] n	Konjugation / Verbindung
tube n	Joch *(nur bei Spirogyra)*
conjugation tube	Jochbrücke *(nur bei Spirogyra)*
protrude [prəˈtruːd] v	herausragen

»

spiral ribbon-like chloroplast	schraubenförmig gewundener Chloroplast

Bryophyta » III. 10 Ecology – 10.7 Ecosystem forest

embryophyta [ˈembiəʊˌfaɪtə] / embryobionta n	Embryophyta / Embryobionta / Grüne Landpflanzen
bryophyta [braɪˈɒfaɪtə] n	Bryophyta / Moospflanzen
moss [mɒs] n	Laubmoos
liverwort [ˈlɪvəwɜːt] n	Lebermoos
conductive tissue [kənˈdʌktɪveˌtɪʃuː] n	Leitgefäße
rhizoid [ˈraɪzɔɪd] n	Rhizoid / Schweinwurzel
scale n	Schuppe
leaf-like scale	blattähnliche Schuppe

»

slender stem-like structure	schlanke stängelartige Struktur

gametophyte [gəˈmiːtəʊfaɪt] n	Gametophyt
dominant gametophyte plant	dominanter Gametophyt
club-shaped adj	keulenförmig
biflagellate [baɪˈflædʒleɪtɪd] adj	zweigeißelig
stalk [stɔːk] n	Stiel
bear (sth) v	(etw.) tragen

tip of shoot n	Sprossspitze
water-dependent adj	wasserabhängig
protonema [ˌprəʊtəʊˈniːmə] n	Protonema / Fadengeflecht

»

sugary chemical substance	zuckerhaltige chemische Substanz

capsule [ˈkæpsjuːl] n	Kapsel
calyptra [kəˈlɪptrə] n	Haube
capsule lid / operculum [əˈpɜːkjʊləm] n	Kapseldeckel
annulus cell [ˈænjələsel] n	Annulus Zelle *(bildet die Haut nach der Abdeckelung über der Kapsel)*
ring of teeth / peristome [ˈperɪstəʊm] n	Ring kleiner Zähnchen / Peristom
attached by its foot to the gametophyte	mit seinem Fuß mit dem Gametophyt verbunden
spores are dispersed by the wind	Sporen werden durch den Wind verbreitet

pioneer plant [ˌpaɪəniːəˈplɒːnt] n	Pionierpflanze
water storage n	Wasserspeicherung
soil amendment [ˈsɔɪləˈmenmənt] n	Verbesserung der Erde
erosion [ɪˈrəʊʒn] n	Erosion
rainwater n	Regenwasser
peat bog [ˈpiːtˌbɒg] n	Torfmoor
peat moss [ˈpiːtˌmɒs] n	Torfmoos
sphagnum peat moss [sfægnəmˈpiːtˌmɒs]	Torfmoos im Verrottungszustand
decaying matter [dɪˈkeɪɪŋˈmætə] n	verrottendes Material

Pteridophyta » III. 10 Ecology – 10.7 Ecosystem forest

fern [fɜːn] n	Farn
vascular [ˈvæskjələ] adj	Gefäß~
seedless vascular plants	samenlose Gefäßpflanze
cryptogam [ˈkrɪptəgræm] n	Kryptogam *(sich ohne Blüten vermehrende Pflanze)*
psilophyte [ˈsaɪləfaɪt] n	Psilophyt / Nacktfarn
club moss [ˈklʌbmɒs] n	Bärlapp
horsetail [ˈhɔːteɪl] n	Schachtelhalm
carboniferous era [ˌkɑːbəˈnɪfrəsˌɪərə] n	Karbonzeit
massive tree n	riesiger Baum
petrified fern forest [ˈpetrɪfaɪdfɜːnˈfɒrɪst]	versteinerter Farnwald
coal seam n	Kohlenflöz

2 Plant families › 2.2 Reproduction of green algae, bryophyta, and pteridophyta

»
dominant form of plant life	vorherrschende Pflanzenart
the sporophyte is the dominant phase	der Sporophyt ist die dominante Generation
the gametophyte is microscopic	der Gametophyt ist mikroskopisch

rhizome ['raɪzəʊm] n — Rhizom / Erdstamm / Wurzelstock
persistent leaf base n — überdauernde Stielreste / abgestorbener Blätter
terminal bud n — Endknospe
adventitious [ˌædvn'tɪʃəs] adj — sprossbürtige
  adventitious bud — sprossbürtige Knospe
  adventitious root — sprossbürtige Wurzel
underground storage stem n — unterirdischer Speicherstamm
tracheid ['treɪkiːɪd] n — Tracheide *(wasserführende Zelle)*
vascular system [ˌvæskjʊlə'sɪstəm] n — Gefäßsystem
divide vegetatively [dɪˌvaɪd'vedʒɪtətɪvli] n — (sich) vegetativ teilen *(ungeschlechtlich)*
frond [frɒnd] n — Wedel
watch spring n — Uhrfeder

»
| rolled up like a watch spring | wie eine Uhrfeder aufgerollt |

vein [veɪn] n — Blattader
sorus ['sɔːrəs], *pl* sori n — Sporenkapselhäufchen / Sorus
sporangium [spə'rændʒiəm], *pl* sporangia n — Sporenkapsel
stalked adj — gestielt
indusium [ɪn'duːzɪəm] n — Schleier *(nierenförmige Blättchen)*
placenta [plə'sentə] n *(with ferns only)* — Blatthöcker *(nur bei Farnen)*
annulus ['ænjələs] n — Ring *(leistenartige Erhebung)*
stomium ['stəʊmɪəm] n — Sollbruchstelle des Rings
sporophyll ['spɒrəfɪl] n — sporenkapseltragendes Blatt / Sporangium / tragendes Blatt

prothallus [prəʊ'θæləs] n — Vorkeim
gametophyte [gə'miːtəʊfaɪt] n — Gametophyt
  tailed sperm — mit Geißeln versehener Schwärmer

2.3 Common features of gymnosperms and angiosperms » III. 10 Ecology – 10.6 Terrestrial ecosystem

unisexual [ˌjuːnɪˈsekʃʊəl] adj	eingeschlechtlich
bisexual [baɪˈsekʃʊəl] adj	zweigeschlechtlich
hermaphrodite [hɜːˈmæfrədaɪt] / androgynous flower [ænˈdrɒdʒnəs] n	Zwitter / Zwitterblüte
hermaphrodite / androgynous adj	zwittrig
staminate [ˈstæmɪnət] / male flower	Staubblüte / männliche Blüte
pistillate [ˈpɪstɪleɪt] / female flower	Stempelblüte / weibliche Blüte
monoecious [məˈniːʃəs] adj	einhäusig
dioecious [daɪˈiːʃəs] / diecious adj	zweihäusig
pollen sac [ˈpɒlənˌsæk] / microsporangium [ˌmaɪkrəʊspɔːˈrændʒɪəm], *pl* microsporangia n	Pollensack / Mikrosporangium
microspore mother cell [ˌmaɪkrəʊˈspɔːmʌðəˌsel] n	Mikrosporenmutterzelle
haploid pollen grain / haploid microspore n	haploider Pollenkorn / haploide Mikrospore *(mit einfachem Chromosomensatz)*
male gametophyte	männlicher Gametophyt
covering n	Hülle
exine [eksaɪn] n	äußere Hüllschicht
intine [ɪntaɪn] n	innere Hüllschicht
air sac n	Luftsack

» The air sac is inflated with …. | Der Luftsack ist mit … aufgebläht.

pollination [ˌpɒləˈneɪʃn] n	Bestäubung
pollinate v	bestäuben
pollenise *BE* / pollenize *AE* v	bestäuben
pollinated / pollenised / pollenized adj	bestäubt
pollinator / pollination agent n	Bestäuber *(Überträger des Pollens)*
polleniser n	Bestäuber *(pollenspendende Pflanze)*
transference [trænsˈfɜːrns] n	Übertragung
transfer v	übertragen
anemophily [ˌænɪˈmɒfɪlɪ] / wind pollination n	Windbestäubung
shed v	ausschütten
wind-borne adj	durch Wind übertragen

2 Plant families › 2.4 Gymnosperms

» | shed in large quantities | in großen Mengen ausschütten

nucellus [njuːˈseləs] / macrosporangium / megasporangium, pl macro-/megasporangia n	Nucellus *(Gewebe in der Samenanlage, das sich in die Embryosackzellen entwickelt)*
diploid megaspore mother cell	diploide Embryosackmutterzelle
haploid megaspore / macrospore	haploide Embryosackzelle
ovule [ˈɒvjuːl] n	Samenanlage
micropyle [ˈmaɪkrəpaɪl] n	Micropyle *(Öffnung, an der die beiden Hüllen der Samenanlage zusammenstoßen)*
micropylar end n	an der Mikropyle
integument [ɪnˈtegjʊmənt] n	Hüllschicht / Integument / Hülle der Samenanlage
female gametophyte	weiblicher Gametophyt
differentiation [ˌdɪfrenʃiˈeɪʃn] n	Differenzierung
endosperm [ˈendəʊspɜːm] n	Endosperm
radical [ˈrædɪkl] n	Wurzel
plumule [ˈpluːmjuːl] n	Anlage des Stammes im Embryo
cotyledon [ˌkɒtɪˈliːdn] / seed leaf n	Keimblatt
testa [ˈtestə] n	Samenschale
wither [ˈwɪðə] v	verwelken / verdorren
seed n	Samen
mature seed	reifer Samen
wind dispersal [ˈwɪnddɪˌspɜːsl] n	Windverbreitung

2.4 Gymnosperms » III. 10 Ecology – 10.7 Ecosystem forest

phanerogam [ˈfænrəgæm] n	Blütenpflanze
vascular plant n	Gefäßpflanze
vascular seed-bearing plant	samentragende Gefäßpflanze
gymnosperm [ˈdʒɪmnəˌspɜːm] n	Nacktsamer / Gymnosperm
cone [kəʊn] n	Zapfen
conifer [ˈkɒnɪfə] *(cone-bearing tree)* n	Nadelbaum / Konifere *(zapfentragender Baum)*
ginkgo [ˈɡɪŋkəʊ] *(maidenhair tree)* n	Ginkgo
cycad [ˈsaɪkæd] n	Palmfarn
fossil remains n pl	fossiles Überbleibsel

tracheid ['treɪkiːɪd] n	Tracheide *(wasserführende Zelle)*
xylem vessel ['zaɪləm‚vesl] n	Xylem Gefäß *(Gefäß des Holzteils)*
vessel-less adj	ohne Tracheen
ovuliferous scale [‚ɒvjuː‚lɪfrəs'skeɪl] n	Fruchtschuppe / Fruchtblatt
woody ['wʊdi] adj	holzig
perennial [pə'reniəl] adj	mehrjährig
evergreen adj	immergrün
unisexual [‚juːnɪ'sekʃʊəl] adj	eingeschlechtlich

Example: fir tree

fir tree ['fɜː‚triː] n (*pinus sylvestris*)	Waldkiefer
tap-root ['tæpruːt] n	Pfahlwurzel
mycorrhiza fungus ['maɪkəraɪzə‚fʌŋgəs] n	Mykorrhizapilz
symbiosis [‚sɪmbaɪ'əʊsɪs] n	Symbiose
cylindrical [sə'lɪndrɪkl] adj	zylindrisch
rugged ['rʌgɪd] adj	zerfurcht
scaly ['skeɪli] adj	schuppig
bark [bɑːk] n	Borke
cork [kɔːk] n	Kork

elongated tap-root	tiefreichende Pfahlwurzel
strongly developed lateral root	stark ausgebildete Seitenwurzel
taper towards the apex	sich Richtung Baumspitze verjüngen

whorl [wɜːl] n	Wirtel
shoot n	Trieb / Spross
shoot of unlimited growth	Langtrieb
dwarf shoot of limited growth	Kurztrieb
axil ['æksɪl] n	Achsel
scale leaf n	Schuppe des Langtriebs
secondary growth n	Dickenwachstum
cambium ring ['kæmbɪəm‚rɪŋ] n	Kambiumring
ray n	Markstrahl
fibre *BE* ['faɪbə] / fiber *AE* n	Faser
resin ['rezɪn] n	Harz / Kunstharz
resin duct / resin canal	Harzkanal
secrete resin	Harz absondern

2 Plant families › 2.4 Gymnosperms

needle n	Nadel
stomatum, *pl* stomata n	Schließöffnung
cuticle [ˈkjuːtɪkl] n	Kutikula / Wachsschicht
thick waxy cuticle	dicke wächserne Kutikula
xerophytic [ˌzɪərəˈfaɪtɪk] adj	xerophytisch / Trockenheit überdauernd
male cone / microstrobilus n	Zapfenblüte
cluster n	Büschel
central axis n	zentrale Blütenachse
under side n	Unterseite

»

sunk beneath the level of the epidermis	bis unterhalb der Epidermisschicht versenkt
spirally arranged scale leaves / microsprophylls	schraubig angebrachte schuppenförmige Blättchen / Staubblätter

female cone / megastrobilus / macrostrobilus, *pl* strobili n	weibliche Zapfenblüte
bract scale [ˈbrækˌskeɪl] n	Deckschuppe
ovuliferous scale / carpellary scale n	Fruchtschuppe
upper surface n	Oberseite

primary endosperm [ˌpraɪməriˈendəʊspɜːm] n	Megaprothallium / primäres Endosperm
venter canal cell n	Bauchkanalzelle
mucilaginous secretion [ˌmjuːsɪˈlædʒɪnəs] n	Bestäubungstropfen
become entangled [bɪˈkʌmɪnˌtæŋɡld] v	(sich) verfangen
enlarge v	vergrößern
close up v	(ver-)schließen
seal v	versiegeln

rudimentary cell / prothallic cell [prəʊˈθælɪkˌsel] n	Mikroprothallium Zelle
antheridium mother cell [ˌænθəˈrɪdɪəmˌmʌðəsel] n	Antheridium Mutterzelle
pollen tube cell n	Pollenschlauchzelle
tube nucleus	Pollenschlauchzellkern
generative nucleus	generativer Zellkern
stalk cell n	Stielzelle
sperm cell n	Spermazelle

spermatogenous cell [ˌspɜːmətəˌdʒenəsˈsel]	spermatogene Zelle
split off v	abtrennen / absplittern
layer of tissue n	Gewebeschicht
wing n	Flügel

» the scales separate | die Zapfenschuppen spreizen sich

2.5 Angiosperm plant families: reproduction

reproductive apparatus [ˌriːprədʌktivæprˈeɪtəs] n	Fortpflanzungsapparat
flower n	Blüte
bud n	Knospe
floral organ n	Blütenorgan
leafy shoot [ˌliːfɪˈʃuːt] n	Laubspross
leafy shoot adapted	angepasster Laubspross
pedicel [ˈpedɪsel] / flower stalk n	Blütenstiel
receptacle [rɪˈseptəkl] n	Blütenboden
floral whorl n	Blattkreis
floral diagram n	Blütendiagramm
calyx [ˈkeɪlɪks] n	Kelch
sepal [ˈsepəl] n	Kelchblatt
corolla [kəˈrɒlə] n	Krone / Blütenkrone
petal n	Blütenblatt / Kronblatt
attract n	anlocken

»
ensure fertilisation	Befruchtung sicherstellen
ensure dispersal	Verbreitung sicherstellen
develop fruit containing seed	Früchte entwickeln, die Samen enthalten

incomplete flower n	unvollständige Blüte
complete flower n	vollständige Blüte
perianth [ˈperiænθ] n	Blütenhülle *(Kelch und Kronblätter unterschiedlich)*
perigone [ˌperɪˈɡəʊn] n	Perigon *(einfache Blütenhülle mit gleichaussehenden Blättern)*
tepal [ˈtiːpl]	Blatt des Perigon *(gleichartiges Blütenhüllblatt)*

2 Plant families › 2.5 Angiosperm plant families: reproduction

magnolia [mægˈnəʊliə] n	Magnolie
stamen [ˈsteɪmen] n	Staubblatt
androecium [ænˈdriːsiəm] n	Andrözeum / männliches Geschlechtsorgan
anther [ˈænθə] n	Staubbeutel
pollen lobe [ˈpɒlənˌləʊb] / locule [ˈlɒkjuːl] n	Theka (Pl. Theken)
bilocular	mit zwei Theken
connective tissue n	Konnektiv (Trennwand)
generative cell n	generative Zelle
tube cell n	Schlauchzelle
vegetative cell n	vegetative Zelle
filament [ˈfɪləmənt] n	Staubfaden
androecium [ænˈdriːsiəm] n	alle Staubblätter zusammen / Andrözeum (männliche Geschlechtsorgane)
dehiscence [dɪˈhɪsns] n (opening of the anther)	Aufplatzen des Staubbeutels
dehiscent [dɪˈhɪsnt] adj	aufplatzend
longitudinal slit [ˌlɒndʒɪˈtjuːdɪnlslɪt] n	länglicher Einriss / Schlitz
pore [pɔː] n	Pore
carpel [ˈkɑːpel] n	Fruchtblatt
pistil [ˈpɪstɪl] / gynoecium [ˌdʒaɪˈniːsiəm] / gynaeceum n	Stempel / Gynözeum / Gynäzeum / weibliches Geschlechtsorgan
innermost whorl n	innerster Kreis
stigma n	Narbe
hairy adj	haarig (haarförmige Papillen)
sticky adj	klebrig
feathery [ˈfeðri] adj	federig
globe shaped adj	knopfförmig
receive v	erhalten
adhere to [ədhɪətuː] v	festhalten an
distinguish [dɪˈstɪŋgwɪʃ] v	unterscheiden
reject v	verwerfen
style n	Griffel
ovary [ˈəʊvri] n	Fruchtknoten
carpel margin [ˈkɑːpelˌmɑːdʒɪn] n	Fruchtblattrand
enclose v	einschließen
cavity [ˈkævəti] n	Hohlraum

loculus ['lɒkjʊləs] n	Loculus *(Hohlraum, den das zusammengerollte Fruchtblatt um die Samenanlage bildet)*
funiculus ['fjuːnɪkjʊləs] n	Funiculus *(Stiel, der Samenanlage und Fruchtblattrand verbindet)*
placenta [plə'sentə] n	Plazenta *(Bereich, an dem die Samenanlage und Fruchtblatt verbunden sind)*
placentation [ˌplæsn'teɪʃn] n	Plazentation *(Art und Ort der Anlagerung der Samenanlage an das Fruchtblatt)*

megasporocyte [ˌmegəspɔːrəʊ'saɪt] n	Megasporenmutterzelle
degenerate v	verkümmern
megagametophyte [ˌmegəgæmi'təʊˌfaɪt] / embryo sac n	"weiblicher" Gametophyt / Megagametophyt / Embryosack
polar nucleus, *pl* nuclei n	Polkern
synergid cell [sɪ'nɜːdʒɪd] n	Synergid / Hilfszelle
antipodal cell [ænˌtɪpədl'sel] n	Antipod
chalaza [kə'leɪzə] n	Chalaza / „Nabelfleck" *(Übergang zwischen Stiel und Samenanlage)*
chalazal end	am Nabelfleck

nectary [ˌnektri], *pl* nectaries n	Nektarblatt / Nektardrüse / Nektarium
nectar ['nektə] n	Nektar
extrafloral nectarines	Nektarien *(außerhalb der eigentlichen Blüte, extraflorale Nektardrüsen)*
glandular ['glændjʊlə] adj	drüsig
nutrient source [ˌnjuːtriənt'sɔːs] n	Ernährungsquelle

》

sugar-rich liquid	zuckerreiche Lösung
sugar source for honey	Zuckerquelle für Honig
feed on nectar	sich von Nektar ernähren
fleshy glandular outgrowth	fleischiger drüsiger Auswuchs

Cross-pollination and how it is ensured

cross pollination / syngamy ['sɪŋɡəmi] n	Fremdbestäubung
cross pollenise *BE* / cross-pollenize *AE* v	fremdbestäuben

2 Plant families › 2.5 Angiosperm plant families: reproduction

crossbreed / hybridise BE / hybridize AE v	kreuzen
self-incompatible [ˌselfɪnkəmˈpætəbl] adj	unverträglich gegenüber dem eigenen Pollen
genetic variance [dʒəˌnetɪkˈveəriəns] n	genetische Vielfalt
proterandry [ˌprɒtəˈrændrɪ] n	Vormännlichkeit *Proterandrie*
proterandrous [ˌprɒtəˈrændrəs] adj	vorstäubend
proterogyny [prɒtəˈrɒdʒɪnɪ] n	Vorweiblichkeit *Proterogynie*
proterogynous [prɒtəˈrɒdʒɪnəs] adj	vorweiblich
dichogamy [daɪˈkɒgəmɪ] n	Dichogamie *(unterschiedliche Reifezeit der Staub- und Fruchtblätter)*
dichogamous adj	dichogam *(zu unterschiedlichen Zeit reif sein)*
heterostyly [ˈhetərəstaɪlɪ] n	Heterostylie *(Vorkommen unterschiedlicher Griffellängen an einer Pflanze)*
dimorphic flower n	zwei Blütenformen an einer Pflanze

> | | |
> |---|---|
> | self-pollenisation with a pollinator | Selbstbestäubung mit Hilfe eines Bestäubers |
> | similar stamen and carpel length | ähnliche Staub- und Fruchtblattlänge |
> | self-pollination without any pollinator | Selbstbestäubung ohne Fremdbestäuber |

cleistogamy [klaɪˈstɒgəmi] n	Kleistogamie *(Bestäubung vor Öffnung der Blüte)*
cleistogamous flower	kleistogame Blüte
chasmogamous flower	chasmogame Blüte *(öffnet sich im Normalfall vor der Bestäubung)*
self-compatible [ˌselfkəmˈpætəbl] adj	verträglich gegenüber dem eigenen Pollen
self-fertile plant [ˌselfˈfɜːtaɪlplɑːnt] n	selbstbefruchtende Pflanze

Abiotic pollination

abiotic pollination [ˌeɪbaɪˈɒtɪkpɒləˌneɪʃn] n	abiotische Bestäubung
wind-pollinated adj	windbestäubt
inconspicuous [ˌɪnkənˈspɪkjuəs] adj	unauffällig
degenerate adj	zurückgebildet
lacking adj	fehlend

loose adj	lose
dangle loosely	lose herunterhängen
hang out v	heraushängen
expose (sth to sth) v	(etw. etw.) aussetzen
light adj	leicht

»

| anthers loosely attached to filament | Staubbeutel lose am Staubfaden befestigt |
| enlarged sticky stigma | vergrößerte, klebrige Narbe |

catkin [ˈkætkɪn] / ament (male or female) n	Kätzchen (männlich oder weiblich)
petal n	Blütenblatt
bract [brækt] n	Schuppenblatt
bracteole [ˈbræktɪəʊl] n	Vorblatt
flower cluster [ˈflaʊəˌklʌstə] n	traubenartige Blütenbüschel
drooping [druːpɪŋ] adj	hängend

hydrophily (pollination by water) n	Hydrophilie / Hydrogamie (Bestäubung von Blüten durch Wasser)
hydrophilous species	Arten, die Bestäubung durch Wasser betreiben
surface hydrophily	Ephydrophilie (Bestäubung durch Verbreitung des Pollen über die Oberfläche des Wasser)

float [fləʊt] v	treiben / schwimmen
duckweed [ˈdʌkwiːd] n	Entengrütze
elodia canadensis [ɪˈləʊdɪə] n	Wasserpest
hornwort [ˈhɔːnwɜːt] n	Hornblatt
aerenchyma [eəˈreŋkɪmə] n	Luftgewebe
transitional phase [trænˌzɪʃənlˈfeɪz] n	Übergangsphase
distribute v	verbreiten
submerge v	untertauchen

»

distribute beneath the surface	unterhalb der Wasseroberfläche verbreiten
pollen submerged	unter Wasser getauchte Pollen
true submerged hydrophily	Hyphydrophilie, Bestäubung durch Verbreitung des Pollen unter der Oberfläche des Wassers

2 Plant families › 2.5 Angiosperm plant families: reproduction

Biotic pollination » III. 7 Evolution

biotic pollination [baɪˌɒtɪkpɒləˈneɪʃn] n	Bestäubung durch Lebewesen / biotische Bestäubung / Zoogamie / Zoophilie
bisexual / hermaphroditic [hɜːˌmæfrəˈdɪtɪk] / hermaprodite [hɜːˌmæfrəˈdaɪt] adj	zwittrig
brightly-coloured adj	leuchtend farbig
scented [sentɪd] adj	duftend
nutritional value [njuːˌtrɪʃnlˈvæljuː] n	Nährwert
resource n	Ressource / Quelle
spread v	verbreiten
spread inadvertently [spredˌɪnədˈvɜːtntli]	zufällig verbreiten

insect-pollinated adj	insektenbestäubt
pollination by insects / entomophily n	Bestäubung durch Insekten / Entomophilie
bee n	Biene
bumble bee	Hummel
bee pollination / melittophily	Bestäubung durch Bienen / Melittophilie
ultra-violet nectar guide n	ultraviolettes Blütenmal
sucrose-rich [ˌsuːkrəʊsˈrɪtʃ] n	reich an Rohrzucker / saccharosereich
buzz pollination [ˈbʌzpɒləˌneɪʃn] n	Bestäubung durch Brummen
vibrate v	vibrieren / in Schwingung geraten
vibration [ˌvaɪˈbreɪʃn] n	Erschütterung / Vibration / Schwingung
resonant vibration	Erschütterungen erzeugt durch die Schwingungen des Flügelschlags (das Brummen)
dislodge [dɪˈslɒdʒ] v	freisetzen

moth [mɒθ] n	Motte
moth pollination / phalaenophily	Bestäubung durch Motten / Phalaenophilie
hover [ˈhɒvə] v	schweben
nocturnal [nɒkˈtɜːnl] adj	nächtlich / nachtaktiv
tubular corolla [ˌtjuːbjələkəˈrɒlə] n	röhrenförmige Blütenkrone
butterfly n	Schmetterling
butterfly pollination / psychophily	Bestäugung durch Schmetterlinge / Psychophilie
narrow tube n	enge Röhre
spur [spɜː] n	Sporn

fly n	Fliege
fly pollination	Bestäubung durch Fliegen
open dish n	flacher Blütenboden
tube n	Röhre
pheromone ['ferəməʊn] n	Pheromon / Sexualhormon
precursor [priːˈkɜːsə] n	Vorstufe
booster [ˈbuːstə] n	Verstärker
mimic [ˈmɪmɪk] v	nachahmen
decay [dɪˈkeɪ] n	Fäulnis / Verwesung
decay v	verrotten
beetle n	Käfer
beetle pollination / cantharophily	Bestäubung durch Käfer / Cantharophilie

unpleasant odour (odor AE)	unangenehmer Geruch
odourless	geruchlos
heavily scented	stark duftend
flattened	abgeflacht
dish shaped	tellerartig

bird pollination / ornithophily [ˌɔːnɪˈθɒfəli] n	Bestäubung durch Vögel / Ornithophilie
hummingbird [ˈhʌmɪŋbɜːd] n	Kolibiri
nectarivore n	Nektarivor *(sich von Nektar ernährendes Tier)*
landing platform n	Landeplatz
bat pollination / chiropterophily n	Bestäubung durch Fledermäuse / Chiropterophilie
bell-shaped adj	glockenförmig
echolocation [ˌekəʊləˈkeɪʃn] n	Ortung durch Echolot

2.6 Fertilisation and development of embryo

generative cell n	generative Zelle
tube cell [ˈtjuːbˌsel] n	Schlauchzelle
vegetative cell n	vegetative Zelle
pollen tube n	Pollenschlauch
tube nucleus n	Schlauchnukleus
nutritive fluid [ˈnjuːtrətɪvˌfluːɪd] n	Nährflüssigkeit

2 Plant families › 2.6 Fertilisation and development of embryo

burst through ['bɜːstθruː] v   durchbrechen
generative nucleus   generativer Nukleus / Kern
penetrate ['penɪtreɪt] v   eindringen
disintegrate v   auflösen

» penetrate the micropyle | durch die Mikropyle eindringen

synergid cells assist | die Synergiden (Helferzellen) helfen

One male gamete fuses with the ovum = fertilisation.
Ein männlicher Gamet / eine männliche Keimzelle verschmilzt mit der Eizelle = Befruchtung.

The other male gamete fuses with the two polar nuclei of the endosperm nucleus = double fertilisation.
Der andere männliche Gamet, die andere männliche Keimzelle verschmilzt mit den Polkernen des Endospermkerns = doppelte Befruchtung.

The endosperm nucleus is triploid after fertilisation.
Der Endospermkern ist nach der Befruchtung triploid (hat einen dreifachen Chromosomensatz).

» endosperm nucleus → endosperm tissue | Endospermkern (Nukleus) → Endosperm Gewebe

integuments → seed coat / testa | Integumente → Samenschale

fertilised ovule ⇢ seed | befruchtete Samenanlage → Samen

matured ovary → fruit | reifer Fruchtknoten → Frucht

hypocotyl [ˌhaɪpəˈkɒtɪl] (*section of shoot below cotyledon*) n   Hypokotyl (*Abschnitt des Sprosses unterhalb des Keimblatts*)
epicotyl [ˈepɪkɒtɪl] n (*section of shoot above the cotyledon*)   Epikotyl (*Abschnitt des Sprosses oberhalb des Keimblatts*)
endospermous [ˈendəʊspɜːməs] / albuminous [ælˈbjuːmɪnes] adj   Endosperm erhaltend
exendospermous [ˈeksdəʊspɜːməs] / exalbuminous [ˌeksælˈbjuːmɪnes] adj   Endosperm verbrauchend

germ / sprout n   Keim
germinate ['dʒɜːmɪneɪt] / sprout v   keimen / auskeimen

germination [ˌdʒɜːmɪˈneɪʃn] / sprouting n — Keimung
  epigeous germination [epiˈdʒiːəsˌdʒɜːmɪneɪʃn] — epigäischen (überirdischen) Keimung
  hypogeous germination [haɪpəˈdʒiːəsˌdʒɜːmɪneɪʃn] — hypogäischen (unterirdischen) Keimung
  period of quiescence [ˌpɪərɪədəvkwiˈesns] n — Keimruhe

> | | |
> |---|---|
> | the hypocotyl elongates | der untere Sprossabschnitt streckt sich |
> | form a hook | einen Haken bilden |

2.7 Angiosperm plant families: recognizing angiosperms

root system n — Wurzelsystem
  adventitious root system [ˌædvntɪʃəsˈruːtˌsɪstəm] — Adventivwurzel / sprossbürtiges Wurzelsystem
  primary root / main root n — Hauptwurzel
  tap root system n — Pfahlwurzelsystem
  prop root / brace root n — sprossbürtige Stützwurzel
  fibrous root [ˌfaɪbrəsˈruːt] n — Faserwurzel
  lateral root [ˌlætrəlˈruːt] n — Nebenwurzel / Seitenwurzel

  tuberous root [ˌtjuːbərəsˈruːt] n — Wurzelknolle
  haustorium [hɔːˈstɔːrɪəm], pl haustuoria n — Saugwurzel
  anchoring root [ˌæŋkərɪŋˈruːt] n — Haftwurzel
  climbing root n — Kletterwurzel
  aerial root [eərɪəlˈruːt] n — Luftwurzel
  peg root [ˌpegˈruːt] n — Senkwurzel
  buttress [ˈbʌtrəs] / buttressed root n — Brettwurzel
  root stock n — Wurzelstock

shoot n — Spross / Trieb
  shoot system — Sprossachse
stem n — Stamm / Stängel
  aerial stem — oberirdischer Stamm
  subterranean stem [ˌsʌbtəˌreɪnɪənˈstem] — unterirdischer Stamm
  erect stem [ɪˌrektˈstem] — aufrechter Stamm
  prostrate stem [ˌprɒstreɪtˈstem] — liegender Stamm
  creeping stem — kriechender Stamm
  herbaceous stem [hɜːˌbeɪʃəsˈstem] — krautiger Stamm

2 Plant families › 2.7 Angiosperm plant families: recognizing angiosperms

> | woody stemmed plant | Pflanze mit verholztem Stamm |
> |---|---|
> | several stems of equal size | mehrstämmig / mehrere Stämme gleicher Größe |

annual [ˈænjuəl] adj	einjährig
tree n	Baum
main stem / trunk [trʌŋk] n	Hauptstamm
shrub [ʃrʌb] n	Strauch
woody plant n	verholzte Pflanze

lenticel [ˈlentɪsel] n	Lentizelle *(Atempore des Baumstamms)*
deciduous plant [dɪˌsɪdjuəsˈplɑːnt] n	sommergrüne Pflanze
bud [bʌd] n	Knospe
leaf, *pl* leaves n	Blatt
branch n	Ast
modified branch	angepasster Ast
twig n	Ast / Zweig
woody twig	hölzerner dünner Zweig
scar n	Narbe
twig scar	Astnarbe
bud scar	Knospennarbe
leaf scar	Blattnarbe

> | visible to the naked eye | mit dem bloßen Auge sichtbar |
> |---|---|

modified stem	modifizierter Stamm / angepasster Stamm
rhizome [ˈraɪzəʊm] n	Rhizom / Erdstamm / Wurzelstock
tuber [ˈtjuːbə] n	Knolle *(z. B. Kartoffel)*
corm [kɔːm] n	Kormus / flachkugelige Knolle *(z. B. Gladiole, Krokus)*
bulb [bʌlb] n	Zwiebel
twining stem [ˈtwaɪnɪŋˌstem] n	windender Spross
dextrorse twining [ˈdekstrəʊrsˌtwaɪnɪŋ] adj	linksdrehend *(z. B. Hopfen)*
sinistrorse twining adj	rechtsdrehend *(z. B. Bohnen)*
runner / stolon [ˈstəʊlɒn] n	Ausläufer
climbing stem n	Kletterstamm
stem tendril [ˈstemˌtendrl] n	Stammranke
thorn [θɔːn] n	Stammdornen

petiole ['petɪəʊl] n		Blattstiel	
leaf base n		Blattgrund	
flattened leaf base		abgeflachter Blattgrund	
sheath [ʃiːθ] n		Blattscheide	
sessile ['sesaɪl] / non-petiolate [ˌnɒn'petɪəʊl] adj		sitzend	
stipule ['stɪpjuːl] n		Nebenblatt / Stipel	
juncture ['dʒʌŋʃə] n		Verbindungsstelle	
juncture of petiole with stem		Verbindungsstelle von Blattstiel zum Stängel / Stamm	
Stipules can be	... leaf-like. ... scale-like. ... modified to form tendrils.	Nebenblätter können...	... blattähnlich sein. ... schuppenähnlich sein ... zu Ranken umgeformt sein.

leaf blade / lamina ['læmɪnə] n	Blattspreite
flat adj	flach
thin adj	dünn
broad adj	breit
system of veins n	Adersystem
xylem ['zaɪləm] n	Xylem / Holzteil
phloem ['fləʊem] n	Phloem / Siebteil
vascular bundle [ˌvæskjələ'bʌndl] n	Leitbündel
vein [veɪn] n	Ader
venation [viː'neɪʃn] n	Aderung
net-veined	netzadrig
pinnate venation [ˌpɪneɪtviː'neɪʃn]	fiederartige Blattaderung
pinnate-netted	fiedrig geadert
palmate venation [ˌpælmeɪtviː'neɪʃn]	fächerförmige Blattaderung
parallel-veined	paralleladrig

simple leaf n	einfaches Blatt
divided leaf n	geteiltes Blatt
indentation [ˌɪnden'teɪʃn] n	Einkerbung / Einschnitt
without indentation	ungekerbt
deep indentation	tief eingekerbt
compound leaf / pinnate leaf n	zusammengesetztes Blatt
palmately compound leaf	handförmig zusammengesetztes Blatt
pinnately compound leaf	fiedrig zusammengesetztes Blatt

2 Plant families › 2.7 Angiosperm plant families: recognizing angiosperms

trifoliate compound leaf [ˌtraɪˈfəʊlɪətˌkɒmpaʊndliːf] leaflet n	dreizählig gefingertes Blatt Blättchen / Fieder
margin [ˈmɑːdʒɪn] n	Rand
smooth adj	glatt
toothed adj	gezähnt
coarse toothed [ˌkɔːsˈtuːθt]	grob gezähnt
doubly toothed	doppelt gezähnt
lobed [ləʊbd] adj	gelappt
palmately lobed [ˌpælmətliˈləʊbd]	handförmig gelappt
serrated [sɪˈreɪtɪd] adj	gesägt
finely serrate	fein gesägt
doubly serrated	doppelt gesägt
undulated [ˈʌndjəleɪtɪd] adj	wellig
ciliate [ˈsɪlɪeɪt] adj	gewimpert
crenate [ˈkriːneɪt] adj	gekerbt
sinuate [ˈsɪnjʊət] adj	gebuchtet
spiny [ˈspaɪni] adj	dornig gezähnt
leaf shape n	Blattform
linear adj	linealisch
circular [ˈsɜːkjələ] adj	rundlich
heart-shaped adj	herzförmig
ovate [ˈəʊveɪt] / egg-shaped adj	eiförmig oval
oblong [ˈɒblɒŋ] adj	länglich
lance-shaped / lanceolate adj	lanzettlich
elliptic [ɪˈlɪptɪk] adj	elliptisch
digitate [ˈdɪdʒɪtət] (with finger-like lobes) adj	gefingert (handförmig zusammengesetztes Blatt)
pinnate [ˈpɪneɪt] adj	gefiedert
even pinnate	paarig gefiedert
odd pinnate	unpaarig gefiedert

»

arrangement of leaves on a stem	Blattstellung an der Sprossachse
one leaf at a node	ein Blatt pro Blattknoten
more than two leaves at a node	mehr als zwei Blätter pro Blattknoten

alternate [ɔːlˈtɜːnət] adj	wechselständig
opposite adj	gegenständig
decussate [dɪˈkʌseɪt] adj	kreuzgegenständig
distichous [ˈdɪstɪkəs] adj	zweizeilig

spiral adj	schraubig
whorled [wɜːld] adj	wirtelständig / quirlständig
rosulate ['rɒzjuːlət] adj	rosettig
basal rosulate ['beɪsl̩ˌrɒzjuːlet]	grundständig
dialypetal [dɪəli'petl] adj	mit doppelter Blütenhülle
sympetalous [sɪm'petləs] adj	verwachsenkronblättrig
petals are separate from each other	freikronblättrige Blüten
Anther is movable: versatile	Staubbeutel ist beweglich: beweglich vorstäubend

Anthers

basifixed anther: The filament and anther just continue in one line.	**basifixe Anthere**: Der Staubfaden setzt sich im Staubbeutel (der Anthere) fort.
dorsifixed anther: The filament is attached to the side of the anther facing the flower centre.	**dorsifixe Anthere**: Der Staubfaden ist an der Rückenseite des Staubbeutels angeheftet.
ventrifixed anther: The filament is attached to the side of the anther facing the perianth.	**ventrifixe Anthere**: Der Staubfaden ist der Bauchseite des Staubbeutels angeheftet.

monocarpellary [mɒneʊkɑː'pɪləri] adj	einfruchtblättrig
bicarpellary [baɪkɑː'pɪləri] adj	zweifruchtblättrig
tricarpellary [traɪkɑː'pɪləri] adj	dreifruchtblättrig
insertion point [ɪn'sɜːʃn] n	Ansatzpunkt
apocarpous [ˌæpəkɑːpəs] adj	Fruchtblätter nicht verwachsen / frei / apokarp
syncarpous [sɪn'kɑːpəs] adj	Fruchtblätter verwachsen / synkarp

Ovaries and flowers

inferior ovary → **epigynous flower**	unterständiger Fruchtknoten → epigyne Blüte
half-inferior ovary → **perigynous or half-epigynous flower**	mittelständiger Fruchtknoten → perigyne Blüte
superior ovary → **hypogynous flower**	oberständige Fruchtknoten → hypogyne Blüte

inflorescence [ˌɪnflɔː'resns] n	Blütenstand
peduncle [pɪ'dʌŋkl] n	Blütenstiel *(der die gesamte Blüte trägt)*

2 Plant families › 2.7 Angiosperm plant families: recognizing angiosperms

pedicel ['pedɪsel] n	Blütenstängel *(der einzelnen Blüte)*
solitary flower n	Einzelblüte
rachis ['reɪkɪs] n	Blütenspindel
infructescence n	Fruchtstand

spike n	Ähre
spadix ['speɪdɪks], *pl* spadices n	Kolben
umbel ['ʌmbəl] n	Dolde
corymb ['kɒrɪmb] n	Doldenrispe
racemose corymb ['ræsɪməʊzˌkɒrɪmb]	Scheindolde / Doldenrispe
panicle ['pænɪkl] n	Rispe
thyrsus [θərsɪs] n	Rispe *(mit Haupt- und verzweigten Nebenachsen)*

raceme ['ræsiːm] n	Traube
cyme [saɪm] n	Wickel
head / capitulum [kəˈpɪtjʊləm] n	Kopf *(Köpfchen)*
dichasium [daɪˈkeɪzɪəm] n	Dichasium
bostryx ['bɒstrɪks] n	Schraubel
pseudanthium [sjuːˈdænθɪəm] n	Scheinblüte / Pseudanthium

dehiscent [dɪˈɪsnt] adj	aufplatzend / aufspringend
dehiscent fruit	Streufrucht / Springfrucht / Öffnungsfrucht
follicle ['fɒlɪkl] n	Balgfrucht / Follikel
legume ['leɡjuːm] n	Hülsenfrucht
silique [sɪˈliːk] n	Schote
indehiscent [ɪnˈdəhɪsənt] adj	geschlossen
indehiscent fruit [ɪnˌdəhɪsəntˈfruːt]	Schließfrucht
achene [əˈkiːn] n	Achene / Schließfrucht
capsule ['kæpsjuːl] n	Kapsel
nut n	Nuss
samara [səˈmɑːrə] n *(e.g. maple)*	Flügelfrucht / Flügelnuss *(z. B. Ahorn)*
caryopsis [ˌkærɪˈɒpsɪs] n	Karyopse / Grasfrucht
dry fruit n	Trockenfrucht

schizocarp [skɪtseʊkɑːp] n	Klausenfrucht
lomentum [ləʊˈmentən] n	Gliederhülsen
silicule [sɪˈliːkjʊəl] n	Gliederschote

fleshy fruit n	Saftfrucht
berry n	Beere
drupe [druːp] n	Steinfrucht
aggregation of drupes	Sammelsteinfrucht
pome [pəʊm] n	Kernobst / Apfelfrucht

hesperidium [ˌhespəˈrɪdɪəm] n	Hesperidium / fleischige Beerenfrucht / Endokarpbeere
hep / hip [hɪp] n	Hagebutte
pseudocarp [ˌsjuːdəʊˈkɑːp] n	Scheinfrucht
pepo [ˌpiːpəʊ] n	Beerenfrucht der Kürbisfamilie
sorosis [səˈrəʊsɪs] n	Nussfruchtverband
syngonium n	Steinfruchtverband
coenocarpium [ˈsiːnəʊˌkɑːpɪəm] n	Beerenfruchtverband
fleshy adj	fleischig
spiny adj	stachelig
hooked adj	mit Häkchen versehen
winged adj	geflügelt
perennial plant [prˈenɪəlˌplɑːnt] n	mehrjährige Pflanze
annual plant n	einjährige Pflanze
biennial plant [baɪˈenɪəlˌplɑːnt] n	zweijährige Pflanze

2.8 Monocots

monocotyledons [ˌmɒnəˌkɒtɪˈliːdnz] / monocots [ˈmɒnəkɒts] n pl	Einkeimblätterige / Einkeimblättrige Süßgräser / Monocotyledoneae
monocotyledonous [ˌmɒnəkɒtɪˈliːdənəs] adj	einkeimblättrig
true grasses / poaceae *(formerly graminaeae)*	Poaceen *(früher Graminaceen)*
palm n	Palme
lily family / lilies / liliaceae [ˌlɪliːˈeɪsiːˌiː] n	Liliengewächse
amaryllis family [ˌæmrˈɪlɪs] / amaryllidaceae [ˌæməɪlɪˈdeɪsiːˌiː] n	Narzissengewächse
iris family / iridaceae n	Schwertlilien
banana family / musaceae n	Banangewächse
orchid family / orchidaceae n	Orchideen
one cotyledon / seed leaf / embryonic leaf n	ein Keimblatt
multiples of three adj	dreizählig
vascular bundle [ˌvæskjələˈbʌndl] adj	Leitbündel
scattered adj	verstreut
one furrow pollen / monosulcate pollen n	Einfurchenpollen
adventitious root n	sprossbürtige Wurzel

2 Plant families › 2.8 Monocots

| major leaf vein n | Hauptblattader |
| parallel adj | parallel |

» | rarely secondary growth | selten sekundäres Dickenwachstum |

True grasses

wheat n	Weizen
rye [raɪ] n	Roggen
barley ['bɑːli] n	Gerste
oats [əʊts] n pl	Hafer
millet ['mɪlɪt] n	Hirse
maize [meɪz] BE / corn AE n	Mais
rice n	Reis

hollow stem [ˌhɒləʊ'stem] n	hohler Stängel
culm [kʌlm] n	Halm
adventitious root n	sprossbürtige Wurzel
stem-clasping adj	stängelumfassend
leaf sheath n	Blattscheide
ligule ['lɪgjuːl] n	Blatthäutchen
parallel-veined blade n	parallelnervige Blattspreite
node [nəʊd] n	Stengelknoten
internode n	Internodie *(Abschnitt zwischen zwei Stengelknoten)*
nodal diaphragm [ˌnəʊdl'daɪəfræm]	Querwand
intercalary meristem [ɪn'tɜːklrɪˌmeristem] *(right above the node)*	Wachstumszone *(direkt über dem Knoten)*

» | leaves arranged alternately in two ranks | Blätter zweizeilig angeordnet |

panicle ['pænɪkl] n	Rispe
spikelet ['spaɪklɪt] n	Ährchen
bract [brækt] n	Tragblatt
glume [gluːm] n	Hüllspelze
lemma ['lemə] n	Deckspelze
palea ['peɪlɪə] n	Vorspelze
staminum ['stæmɪnəm], *pl* stamina n	Staubblatt
superior ovary n	oberständiger Fruchtknoten

feathery stigma n	federartiger Narbenast
lodicule n	Schwellkörper
awn n	Granne
fruit wall / pericarp ['perɪkɑːp] n	Fruchtwand
inseparable adj	untrennbar
caryopsis [ˌkærɪ'ɒpsɪs] n	Karyopse / einsamige Schließfrucht
vegetative propagation ['vedʒitətɪvˌprɒpə'geɪʃn]	vegetative Verbreitung
stolon ['stəʊlɒn] n	Ausläufer
tiller ['tɪlə] n	Trieb / Schössling
protein-rich adj	eiweißreich
aleurone layer [əˌljʊərəʊn'leɪə] n	Aleuronschicht
starchy nutritious tissue n	stärkehaltiges Nährgewebe
endosperm ['endəʊspɜːm] n	Endosperm
embryo / germ n	Samen / Sämling
cotyledon [ˌkɒtɪ'liːdn] / seed leaf n	Keimblatt
scutellum [ˌskjuː'teləm] n	Scutellum / Schildchen
coleoptile [ˌkɒlɪ'ɒptaɪl] n	Blattscheide des Keimblattes
coleorhiza [kɒlɪə'raizə] n	Wurzelscheide
degradation n	Verkümmerung / Verkümmern
saccharose ['sækərəʊz] / sucrose ['suːkrəʊz] n	Saccharose / Sukrose / Haushaltszucker
fructan (plant sugar) n	Fruktan (Pflanzenzucker)
glutenin ['ɡlʊtənɪn] n	Gluten
globulin ['ɡlɒbjʊlɪn] n	Globulin
albumin ['ælbjʊmɪn] n	Albumin
bran [bræn] n	Kleie
essential oils n pl	ätherische Öle
forage ['fɒrɪdʒ] n	Grünfutter / Viehfutter
fodder ['fɒdə] n	Trockenfutter / Viehfutter
cereal ['sɪərɪəl] n	Getreide
major source n	Hauptquelle
carbohydrate [ˌkɑːbəʊ'haɪdreɪt] n	Kohlenhydrat
sugar n	Zucker
sugarcane n	Zuckerrohr

wetland habitat preservation	Erhalt von Feuchtgebieten
land reclamation	Landrückgewinnung / Bodensanierung
erosion control	Eindämmung der Erosion

2.9 Dicotyledons

General characteristics: Examples of families and their general characteristics

dicotyledons [ˌdaɪkɒtɪˈliːdnz] n	Dikotylen / Zweikeimblättrige
net-veined adj	netznervig
reticulate [rɪˈtɪkjələt] adj	netzartig
multiples of four / multiples of five adj	vierzählig / fünfzählig
three furrow pollen / trisulcate pollen n	Dreifurchenpollen
vascular bundle [ˌvæskjələˈbʌndl] n	Leitbündel
woody tissue n	Holzgewebe / verholztes Gewebe
secondary growth n	sekundäres Dickenwachstum

»

contain endosperm	Endosperm enthalten
roots grow from the radicle	Wurzeln entwickeln sich aus der Keimwurzel
arranged in a ring	ringförmig angeordnet

rose family / rosaceae [rəʊˌzeɪsiːˌiː]	Familie der Rosengewächse

»

many spirally arranged stamen	viele spiralförmig angeordnete Staubblätter

buttercup family / ranunculaceae [rəˌnʌnkjʊˈleɪsiːˌiː]	Familie der Hahnenfußgewächse
radially symmetrical adj	radiärsymmetrisch
regular / actinomorphic [ˌæktɪnəˈmɔːfɪk] adj	radiärsymmetrisch

daisy family / asteraceae [ˌæstəˈreɪsiːˌiː] (formerly compositae)	Familie der Korbblütler / Asterngewächse
composite flower n	zusammengesetzte Blüte
disc floret n	Röhrenblüte
ray floret [ˈreɪˌflɒrɪt] n	Zungenblüte

zygomorphic [ˌzaɪgəˈmɔːfɪk] adj	zygomorph (zweiseitig symmetrisch)
regular flowers n	röhrenblütige Korbblütler / zungenblütige Korbblütler
irregular flowers n	strahlenblütige Korbblütler (mit beiden Blütenformen)
bract [brækt] n	Hüllblatt
achene [əˈkiːn] n	einsamiges Nüsschen / Schließfrucht

celery family [ˌselrif'fæmlɪ] / carrot family / apiaceae ['apɪəsɪə] (formerly umbelliferae)	Familie der Doldengewächse
hollow stem	hohler Stängel
umbel ['ʌmbel] n	Dolde
compound umbel	Scheindolde
seed capsule n	Samenkapsel

»

bracts surrounding the umbel	die Dolde umgebende Hüllblätter

legume family / bean family / leguminosae [lɪˌgjuːmɪ'nəʊsiː] n	Familie der Hülsenfrüchtler
caesalpiniaceae n	Johannisbrotgewächse
papilionaceae [pəˌpɪlɪə'neɪsiːˌiː] n	Schmetterlingsblütler
mimosaceae n	Mimosengewächse

tap root system n	Pfahlwurzelsystem
bacterial nodule [bæk'tɪərɪəlˌnɒdjuːl] n	Wurzelknöllchen durch Knöllchenbakterien

zygomorphic flower [ˌzaɪgəmɔːfɪk'flaʊə] n	zweiseitig symmetrisch Blüte
persistent calyx [pə'sɪstntˌkeɪlɪks] n	überdauernder Kelch (bleibt bis zur Fruchtbildung erhalten)
standard / banner n	Fahne
wing petal n	Flügel
keel petal n	Schiffchen
monocarpellary [mɒneʊkɑː'pɪləri] adj	einfruchtblättrig
bent stile [bent'staɪl] n	gebogener Griffel
terminal stigma n	endständige Narbe

»

one standard / one banner	eine Fahne
two wing petals	zwei Flügel
one keel petal	ein Schiffchen
calyx joined	Kelch verwachsen
fused at the apex	an der Spitze zusammengewachsen
sticky receptive stigmatic surface	klebrige Narbenoberfläche

marginal ['mɑːdʒɪnl] adj	wandständige
marginal placentation ['mɑːdʒɪnlˌplæsn'teɪʃn]	wandständige Plazentation
marginal ovule ['mɑːdʒɪnl'ɒvjuːl]	wandständige Samenanlagen (am Rand des Fruchtblattes angeordnet)

2 Plant families › 2.9 Dicotyledons

stamen ['steɪmen] n	Staubblatt
stamen tube	Staubblattröhre
free stamen	freies Staubblatt
snap mechanism n	Hebelmechanismus
jolt up [dʒəʊlt'ʌp] v	hochschnellen

»   depress the keel   das Schiffchen herunterdrücken

cabbage family / brassicaceae	Familie der Kreuzblütler /
(formerly cruciferae)	Brasscicaceen (früher Kruziferen)
seedpod / pod n	Samenhülse / Schote
silique [sɪ'liːk] n	Schote (Bezeichnung der Fruchtform)
silicle ['sɪlɪkl] n	Schötchen
carpel ['kɑːpel]	Fruchtblatt
two-chamber adj	zweikammerig
membrane ['membreɪn] n	Scheidewand
thin membrane	dünne Scheidewand
persistant membrane	Scheidewand bleibt stehen

»   two fused carpels   zwei zusammengewachsene Fruchtblätter
    open from the bottom   von unten nach oben aufspringen

labiate family [ˌleɪbiəɪt'fæmlɪ] / Lamiaceae n	Familie der Lippenblütler / Lamiaceen
bilaterally symmetrical [baɪ'lætrlɪsɪˌmetrɪkl] adj	bilateral symmetrisch
tubular calyx ['tjuːbjələˌkeɪlɪks]	röhrenförmiger Blütenkelch
upper lip n	Oberlippe
helmet-shaped adj	helmförmig
lower lip n	Unterlippe
three-lobed adj	3-lippig
square stems	viereckiger Stamm
decussate [dɪ'kʌseɪt] adj	kreuzgegenständig
achene [ə'kiːn] n	Schließfrucht / einsamiges Nüsschen

bellflower family / campanulaceae n	Glockenblumengewächse / Campanulaceen

poppy family / papaveraceae [pəˌpeɪveˈreɪsiːˌiː] n	Mohngewächse / Papaveraceae
potato family / nightshade family / solanaceae [ˌsɒləˈneɪsiːˌiː] n	Nachtschattengewächse / Solanaceae
potato n	Kartoffel
staple diet n	Grundnahrung
carbohydrate-rich adj	kohlenhydrathaltig
poisonous [ˈpɔɪznəs] adj	giftig
alkaloid [ˈælklɔɪd] n	Alkaloid
borage family [ˌbɒrɪdʒˈfæmlɪ] / forget-me-not family / boraginaceae n	Raublattgewächse / Borretschgewächs / Boraginaceae
carnation family / pink family / caryophyllaceae n	Nelkengewächse / Caryophyllaceae
figwort family / snapdragon family / scrophulariaceae n	Braunwurzgewächse / Rachenblütengewächse / Scrophulariaceae
cranesbill family / geranium family / geraniaceae [dʒɪˌreɪniːˈeɪsiːˌiː] n	Storchenschnabelgewächse / Geraniengewächse / Geranieceen
heath family / ericaceae [ˌerɪˈkeɪsiːˌiː] n	Heidekrautfamilie / Ericaceen
periwinkle family / apocynaceae n	Hundsgiftgewächse
mallow family / malvaceae n	Malvengewächse / Malvaceae
mallow [ˌmæləʊ] n	Malve
lime tree BE / linden tree AE n	Linde
food plant n	Futterpflanze
honey plant	Futterpflanze für Bienen
herbal tea [ˈhɜːblˌtiː] n	Kräutertee
soft wood n	Weichholz
ornamental tree n	Parkbaum
heart-shaped adj	herzförmig
symmetrical adj	regelmäßig
nutlet [ˈnʌtlɪt] n	Nüsschen
winged [wɪŋd] adj	geflügelt
bract [brækt] n	Hochblatt
wind-dispersed [ˈwɪnddɪˌpɜːst] adj	durch den Wind verbreitet
pollinated by insects	Bestäubung durch Insekten

2 Plant families › 2.10 Deciduous tree families

More families

wood sorrel family / oxalidaceae n	Sauerkleegewächse / Oxalidaceae
saxifrage family / saxifragaceae [ˌsæksɪfrəˈgeɪsiːˌiː] n	Steinbrechgewächse / Saxifragaceae
hydrangea [haɪˈdreɪndʒə] n	Hortensie
primrose family / primulaceae n	Primelgewächse / Primulaceae
leadwort family / plumbaginaceae n	Grasnelkengewächse / Plumbaginaceae
sea thrift [ˈsiːˌθrɪft] n	Grasnelke
sea lavender [ˈsiːˌlævndə] n	Halligflieder
phlox family [ˌflɒksˈfæmli] / polemoniaceae n	Sperrkrautgewächse / Himmelsleitergewächse Polemoniaceae
garden phlox n	Phlox
bedstraw family / rubiaceae [ˌruːbɪˈeɪsiːˌiː] n	Rötegewächse / Rubiaceae
woodruff [ˈwʊdrʌf] n	Waldmeister
sedge family [ˌsædʒˈfæmli] / Cyperaceae [ˌsɪpəˈreɪsiːˌiː] n	Familie der Sauergräser
sedge [sedʒ] n	Segge

2.10 Deciduous tree families » III. 10 Ecology – 10.7 Ecosystem forest: Reproduction

The birch family

birch family [ˌbɜːtʃˈfæmli] / betulaceae [ˌbetʃəˈleɪsiːˌiː] n	Birkengewächse / Betulaceae
alder [ˈɔːldə] n	Erle
hornbeam [ˈhɔːnbiːm] n	Hainbuche
hazel [ˈheɪzl] n	Hasel
monoecious [məˈniːʃəs] adj	einhäusig
staminate / male flower n	Staubblüte / männliche Blüte
pistillate [ˈpɪstɪleɪt] / female flower n	Stempelblüte / weibliche Blüte
one-seeded adj	einsamig
indehiscent fruit [ɪnˌdəhɪsəntˈfruːt] n	Schließfrucht

cupule [ˈkjuːpjuːl] n	Fruchtbecher
cobnut [ˈkɒbnʌt] n	Haselnuss
husk [hʌsk] n	Schale
outer fibrous husk	äußere, faserige Schale
shell n	Hülle
smooth shell	weiche Hülle

kernel ['kɜːnl] n	Samenkern
protein-rich adj	eiweißreich
unsaturated fat [ˌʌnˌsætʃreɪtɪd'fæt] n	ungesättigte Fettsäure

The beech family

beech family / fagaceae n	Buchengewächse / Fagaceen
bark [baːk] n	Rinde
smooth bark	glatte Rinde
sparsely toothed [ˌspɑːsli'tuːθt] adj	leicht gesägt
monoecious [mə'niːʃəs] adj	einhäusig
male catkins n	männliche Kätzchen
three-angled nut n	dreikantige Nüsse
edible adj	essbar
soft-spined husk n	weichstachelige Hülle
cupule ['kjuːpjul] n	Fruchtbecher
dense leaf litter n	dichter Laubabfall

»
female flowers are borne in pairs	weibliche Blüten werden paarweise getragen

oak n	Eiche
furrowed bark	gefurchte Rinde
lobed margin n	gelappter Rand
unisexual catkins n	eingeschlechtliche Kätzchen
nut n	Nussfrucht
acorn ['eɪkɔːn] n	Eichel
one-seeded adj	einsamig
tannin content ['tænɪnˌkɒntənt] n	Tanningehalt
cork oak n	Korkeiche

»
spirally arranged leaves	spiralig angeordnete Blätter

The willow family

willow family n	Weidengewächse / Salicaceae
willow ['wɪləʊ] n	Weide
weeping willow	Trauerweide
sallow ['sæləʊ]	Salweide
poplar ['pɒplə] n	Pappel

dioecious [daɪˈiːʃəs] adj	zweihäusig
catkin n	Kätzchen
staminate (male) flower n	Staubkätzchen / männliche Blüte
calyx [ˈkeɪlɪks] n	Kelch
nectariferous gland [ˈnektərəfərəsˌglænd] n	Nektardrüse
rachis [ˈreɪkɪs] n	Blütenspindel
drooping raceme [ˈdruːpɪŋˌræsiːm] n	hängende Traube
pistillate [ˈpɪstɪleɪt] / female flower n	Stempelkätzchen / weibliche Blüte
single ovary	ein Fruchtknoten
two-lobed style	zweilappige Narbe
one-celled ovule	einzellige Samenanlage
two-valved capsule [ˈtuːvælvtˌkæpsjuːl]	zweischalige Kapsel

»

at the base of a scale	in der Achsel einer (Kätzchen)Schuppe

The seeds are furnished with long, silky, white hairs.
Die Samen sind mit einem langen, seidig-weißen Haarschopf ausgestattet.

mulberry family / moraceae n	Maulbeerbaumgewächse / Moraceen
silkworm n	Seidenraupe

3 Metabolism

3.1 Physical principles of biological energy transformation

metabolism [məˈtæbəlɪzm] n	Metabolismus / Stoffwechsel (Aufnahme, Umbau und Abbau von Stoffen)
metabolise [məˈtæbəlaɪz] BE / metabolize AE v	Stoffwechsel haben / Stoffwechsel betreiben
convert v	umwandeln
conversion [kənˈvɜːʃn] n	Umwandlung
interconvert v	sich gegenseitig umwandeln (wechselseitig)
interconversion n	wechselseitige Umwandlung
anabolism [əˈnæbəlɪzm] n	Anabolismus / aufbauender Stoffwechsel
anabolic reaction	anabolische Reaktion / aufbauende Reaktion
require energy v	Energie benötigen

consume energy v		Energie verbrauchen
molecule n		Molekül
simple molecule		einfaches Molekül
complex molecule		komplexes Molekül
low energy molecule		energiearmes Molekül

		complexity	Komplexität
	increase	order	Ordnung erhöhen
		disorder	Unordnung
capture energy in the chemical bonds			Energie in den chemischen Bindungen binden

catabolism [kə'tæbəlɪzm] n	Katabolismus / abbauender Stoffwechsel
catabolic reaction	katabolische Reaktion / abbauende Reaktion
release energy v	Energie freisetzen
energy conversion / transformation of energy n	Energie-Umwandlung
living system n	lebendes System

When energy-rich molecules like glucose are broken down into low energy molecules like H_2O and CO_2, the free energy released is trapped in ATP.
Wenn energiereiche Moleküle wie Glukose in energiearme Moleküle, wie H_2O und CO_2 abgebaut werden, wird die freigesetzte Energie in Form von ATP gespeichert.

Energy is the capacity of a system to do work.
Energie ist die Fähigkeit eines Systems, Arbeit zu verrichten.

create v	erzeugen / produzieren
Forms of energy	
kinetic energy	kinetische Energie
potential energy	potenzielle Energie / Lageenergie
electric energy	elektrische Energie
chemical energy	chemische Energie
internal energy	innere Energie

destroy v	zerstören
reactant [ri'æktənt] n	Ausgangsstoff / Edukt

3 Metabolism › 3.1 Physical principles of biological energy transformation

product n | Produkt / Reaktionsprodukt / Endstoff
low-energy reactant | energiearmer Ausgangsstoff
energy-rich reactant | energiereicher Ausgangsstoff
energy-rich product | energiereiches Reaktionsprodukt
low-energy product | energiearmes Reaktionsprodukt

» In any conversion of energy from one form to another, it is neither created nor destroyed.
Bei der Umwandlung von Energie von einer Form in die andere, wird weder Energie erzeugt noch zerstört.
In any conversion of energy from one form to another, the total energy before and after the conversion is the same.
Bei der Umwandlung von Energie von einer Form in die andere, ist die Gesamtmenge an Energie vor und nach der Umwandlung gleich.

total energy n | Gesamtenergiemenge *(Energieinhalt eines chemischen Systems)*
usuable energy | für Arbeitsvorgänge in der Zelle nutzbarer Energiebetrag
thermal energy n | Wärmeenergie
unusable energy n | Wärmeenergie
friction ['frɪkʃn] n | Reibung
radiation n | Strahlung
heat n | Wärme

» exchange heat | Wärme austauschen

enthalpy [ɪn'θɔːlpɪ] n | Enthalpie *(Bezeichnung für die abgegebene bzw. aufgenommene Wärmemenge einer Reaktion, Energiemaß)*
overall enthalpy change ΔH | gesamte freigesetzte Reaktionsenergie ΔH
reaction enthalpy (H) | Reaktionsenthalpie
free energy (G) n | freie Energie
change in free energy (ΔG) | Änderung der freien Enthalpie
constant pressure n | konstanter Druck

» absolute temperature (T) in Kelvin | absolute Temperatur in Kelvin
ΔH = total amount of energy added or released | ΔH = gesamter Energiebetrag, der dem System zugefügt oder entzogen wird

endothermic reaction [ˌendəʊˈθɜːmɪkriˌækʃn] n	endotherme Reaktion *(die reagierenden Ausgangsstoffe (Edukte) nehmen Energie von außen auf)*
exothermic reaction [ˌeksəʊˈθɜːmɪkriˌækʃn] n	exotherme Reaktion *(Energie wird an die Umwelt abgegeben)*

»

fraction of energy	Anteil der Energie
decrease in energy	Abnahme der Energie
return to the low-energy initial state	Rückkehr in einen energiearmen Grundzustand

order n	Ordnung
disorder n	Unordnung
entropy [ˈentrəpi] n	Entropie *(Maß der Unordnung)*
randomness [ˈrændəmnəs] n	Zufälligkeit / Wahllosigkeit
randomly adv	wahllos
complexity n	Komplexität *(Maß der Ordnung)*

»

tendency for disorder	Zunahme der Entropie (Tendenz zur Unordnung)
restrained in movement	in der Bewegung gehemmt

forward and reverse reaction n	Umkehrreaktion
equilibrium [ˌiːkwɪˈlɪbriəm] n	Gleichgewicht
chemical equilibrium	chemisches Gleichgewicht
equilibrium point	Gleichgewichtszustand *(Endzustand)*
static state [ˈstætɪkˌsteɪt] n	„Stillstand" *(Gleichgewichtslage bleibt konstant)*
observable [əbˈzɜːvəbl] adj	beobachtbar

»

take place at the same rate	mit der selben Geschwindigkeit ablaufen
under specific conditions	unter bestimmten Bedingungen
product-to-reactant ratio	Verhältnis zwischen Ausgangsstoff und Endprodukt
proceed to … / go the way to … completion	*(Ablauf der Reaktion)* bis zur vollständigen Umsetzung der Ausgangsstoffe durchführen

3 Metabolism › 3.2 Role of ATP

| directly related to the point of equilibrium | direkt mit dem Gleichgewichtszustand zusammenhängend |

Most chemical reactions run both forward and backward.
Die meisten chemischen Reaktionen sind umkehrbar.

3.2 Role of ATP

ATP (adenosine triphosphate) [æd'enəʊsiːnˌtraɪ'fɒsfeɪt] n	ATP *(Adenosintriphosphat)*
ADP (adenosine diphosphate) n	ADP *(Adenosindiphosphat)*
nitrogenous base adenine [naɪ'trɒdʒɪnəsˌbeɪs'ædəˌnɪn] n	stickstoffhaltige (organische) Base Adenin
bonded to adj	verbunden mit
ribose ['raɪbəʊs] n	Ribose / Zucker
energy currency n	Energiewährung
nucleotide ['njuːkliətaɪd] n	Nukleotid
property n	Eigenschaft
loss (of) n	Verlust (von)
building block n	Baustein

»

building block for nucleic acids	Baustein für Nukleinsäuren
repel each other	sich gegenseitig abstoßen

hydrolyse ['haɪdrəlaɪz] *BE* / hydrolize *AE* v	hydrolysieren
hydrolysis [haɪ'drɒləsɪs] n	Hydrolyse
phosphorylate [ˌfɒsfərə'leɪt] v	phosphorylieren
phosphorylation n	Phosphorylierung

bioluminescence [baɪəʊˌluːmɪ'nesnts] n	Biolumineszenz *(Fähigkeit von Organismen zu leuchten)*
luminescent [ˌluːmɪ'nesnt] adj	luminiszent / leuchtend
luciferin [luː'sɪfərən] n	Luciferin *(Sammelbegriff für alle Leuchtstoffe)*
luciferase ['luːsɪfəreɪs] n	Luziferase (Enzym)
firefly n	Glühwürmchen / Leuchtkäfer
bacterial contamination n	bakterielle Verunreinigung
marine organism n	Meereslebewesen
predator ['predətə] n	Fressfeind
mate n	Sexualpartner

avoid predators	Fressfeinde vermeiden
signal to mates	Sexualpartner anlocken

couple v	koppeln
energy-coupling n	energetische Kopplung
intermediate n	Zwischenprodukt
fuel molecule n	Molekül, das Energie liefert (z. B. Glukose)
coupled reaction n	gekoppelte Reaktion

3.3 Enzymes

Definition, location and identification, examples of enzymes

enzyme ['enzaɪm] n	Enzym
catalyst ['kætəlɪst] n	Katalysator
catalyse BE / catalyze AE v	katalysieren
biological catalyst [baɪəˌlɒdʒɪkl'kætərɪst]	Biokatalysator (Reaktionsbeschleuniger)
catalytic action [ˌkætə'lɪtɪkækʃn]	katalysierte Reaktion
enzyme-catalysed reaction	enzymatisch katalysierte Reaktion
organic adj	organisch
inorganic adj	anorganisch

starch [stɑːtʃ] n	Stärke
suspension [sə'spenʃn] n	Suspension / Auflösung / Aufschwemmung
starch suspenison n	Stärkeaufschwemmung
disaccharide [daɪ'sækəraɪd] n	Disaccharid (auch: Zweifachzucker)
monosaccharide [mɒnəʊ'sækəraɪd] n	Monosaccharid (auch: Einfachzucker)
electrophoresis [ɪˌlektrəfə'riːsɪs] n	Elektrophorese
amylase ['æmɪleɪz] n	Amylase
chymotrypsin [ˌkaɪmə'trɪpsɪn] n	Chymotrypsin
trypsin ['trɪpsɪn] n	Trypsin
protease ['prəʊtieɪz] n	Protease (proteinspaltende Enzyme)
catalase ['kætəleɪs] n	Katalase
digestive juice [daɪ'dʒestɪvˌdʒuːs] n	Verdauungssäfte
pancreas ['pæŋkriəs] n	Bauchspeicheldrüse
duodenum [ˌdjuːə'diːnəm] n	Zwölffingerdarm
small intestine n	Dünndarm

3 Metabolism › 3.3 Enzymes

Enzyme shape and reactivity

macromolecule [ˌmækrəˈmɒlɪkjuːl] n	Makromolekül
protein n	Protein / Eiweiß
quaternary structure [kwəˈtɜːnri] n	Quartärstruktur
subunit	Untereinheiten
polypeptide [ˌpɒlɪˈpeptaɪd] n	Polypeptid / Aminosäurekette
polypeptide subunits [ˌpɒlɪˈpeptaɪd]	Peptidketten
catalytic subunit	katalytische Untereinheit *(eine der Peptidketten bildet das aktive Zentrum)*

»
Enzymes are …	… protein in nature. … water-soluble. … globular.	Enzyme sind	… primär Proteine. … wasserlöslich. … globular, rundlich.

apoenzyme [ˌæpəˈenzaɪm] *(protein component of enzyme)* n	Apoenzym *(Proteinanteil des Enzyms)*
non-protein molecular partners of enzymes n	Wirkgruppen
prosthetic group [prɒsˈθetɪkˌɡruːp] n	prostethische Gruppe

»
tightly bound to sth permanently attached to sth	fest verbunden mit etw. auf Dauer verbunden mit etw.

The prosthetic group is permanently bound to the apoenzyme.
Die prosthetische Gruppe ist auf Dauer mit dem Apoenzym verbunden.

retinal [ˈretɪnəl] n	Retinal
haem *BE* / heme *AE* [hiːm] n	Häme
cofactor n	Kofaktor
coenzyme n	Koenzym *(auch: Coenzym)*
inorganic ion coenzyme [ˌɪnɒːˈɡænɪkˈaɪənkəʊˌenzaɪm]	anorganisches Ion *(z. B. Cu, Zn, Fe)* Koenzym

Examples of prosthetic groups and coenzymes

Prosthetic groups retinal – converts light energy haem – binds O_2, and electrons; contains iron cofactor Coenzymes NAD, FAD, ATP, coenzyme A	Prosthetische Gruppen Retinal – wandelt Lichtenergie um Häme – bindet O_2 und Elektronen; enthält den Kofaktor Eisen Koenzyme NAD, FAD, ATP, Koenzym A

» | The cofactor | Der Kofaktor
| ... is essential to the enzyme's function. | ... ist wichtig für die Enzymfunktion.
| ... is an inorganic ion. | ... ist ein anorganisches Ion (z. B. Cu, Zn, Fe).
| The coenzyme | Das Koenzym
| ... is a carbon-containing molecule. | ... ist ein kohlenstoffhaltiges Molekül.
| ... binds temporarily. | ... kann sich wieder vom Apoenzym trennen (abdissoziieren).

How do enzymes function?

initiate v	auslösen
accelerate [ək'seləreɪt] v	beschleunigen
alter v	verändern
activation energy (Ea) n	Aktivierungsenergie (Ea)

» | rate of a reaction | Reaktionsgeschwindigkeit
| crossing of the activation energy threshold | Überschreiten des Schwellenwerts der Aktivierungsenergie

lower (sth) v	(etw.) herabsetzen / (etw.) senken
lower adj	geringer / niedriger
reversible reaction n	Hin- und Rückreaktion
reverse reaction n	Rückreaktion
approach v	erreichen / (an)nähern
equilibrium [ˌiːkwɪ'lɪbriəm] n	Gleichgewicht
chemical equilibrium	chemischer Gleichgewichtszustand

» Equilibrium is approached more rapidly.
Der Gleichgewichtszustand wird schneller erreicht.
Enzymes initiate or speed up a reaction by lowering the activation energy.
Enzyme lösen eine Reaktion aus oder beschleunigen diese durch das Herabsetzen der Aktivierungsenergie.

energy profile n	Energiediagramm
amount of energy n	Energiebetrag
overall energy relief n	Gesamtmenge der freigesetzten Energie

3 Metabolism › 3.3 Enzymes

energy barrier n	Energieschwelle *(Energiebetrag, der als Aktivierungsenergie eingespeist werden muss, um eine Reaktion auszulösen)*
enthalpy [ɪnˈθɔːlpɪ] n	Enthalpie *(Bezeichnung für die abgegebene bzw. aufgenommene Wärmemenge einer Reaktion, Energiemaß)*
overall enthalpy change ΔH	gesamte freigesetzte Reaktionsenergie ΔH
substrate [ˈsʌbstreɪt] n	Substrat / Ausgangsstoff / Edukt
reactant [riˈæktnt] n	Edukt / Ausgangsstoff
interaction [ˌɪntəˈækʃn] n	Wechselwirkung
product n	Produkt / Endstoff
stable adj	stabil / fest
unstable adj	instabil / schnell zerfallend

» Activation energy (Ea) initiates a reaction.
Die Aktivierungsenergie (Ea) löst eine Reaktion aus.
Ea is needed to change reactants into unstable molecular forms.
Ea wird benötigt, um in den Ausgangsstoffen Bindungen aufzubrechen.
Lowering activation energy brings reactants into close proximity to each other.
Die Herabsetzung der Aktivierungsenergie bringt die Ausgangsstoffe (Edukte) in räumliche Nähe zueinander.

On an energy profile, the enthalpy change is measured from the energy of the reactants to the energy of the products.
Bei einem Energiediagramm wird die Freisetzung von Reaktionsenergie über den Vergleich des Energiegehalts der Ausgangsstoffe (Edukte) und des Energiegehalts der Produkte (Endstoffe) ermittelt.

Functioning: the specificity of enzymes

active site n	aktives Zentrum *(oder: katalytisches Zentrum)*
tertiary structure [ˌtɜːʃriˈstrʌktʃə] n	Tertiärstruktur
surface n	Oberfläche
specificity n	Spezifität
specificity of an enzyme	Enzymspezifität
specifity of action	Wirkungsspezifität
substrate specificity	Substratspezifität
fit v	entsprechen / (in etw.) passen
bind (to) v	binden (an)

shape n three dimensional shape	Form / Passform dreidimensionale (Pass-)Form

» The tertiary structure shows specific "clefts" or "crevices" on the surface of the enzyme.
Die Tertiärstruktur weist ganz bestimmte „Vertiefungen" oder „Spalten" an der Oberfläche des Enzyms auf.

Models explaining the functioning of enzymes

lock-and-key model n	Schlüssel-Schloss-Modell » Abb. 41–42
lock (enzyme) n	Schloss(-Enzym)
key (substrate) n	Schüssel(-Substrat)
key hole *(active site)* n	Schlüsselloch
induced fit n	Hand-im-Handschuh-Prinzip *(modernere Modellvorstellung, die den chemischen Reaktionen Rechnung trägt – das aktive Zentrum wird durch das Anlagern des Substrats verändert)*
substrate-binding region [sʌbstreɪtˌbaɪndɪŋˈriːdʒn] n	Bindungszentrum

»
change shape temporarily	die Gestalt kurzfristig verändern
return to the initial state	zum Ursprungszustand zurückkehren

dissociate [dɪˈsəʊʃieɪt] v	trennen
enzyme-substrate complex (ES) n	Enzym-Substrat-Komplex
bond n	Bindung / Verbindung
bonding n	Binden / Verbinden

»
restore sth to its initial form	etw. zur ursprünglichen Form zurückführen
An enzyme – substrate complex is held together by …	Ein Enzym-Substrat-Komplex wird zusammengehalten durch …
… hydrogen bonds.	… Wasserstoffbrückenbindung.
… Van der Waals interactions / Van der Waals attractions (attraction or repulsion of electrically charged groups).	… Van der Waals'sche Interaktionen (unspezifische Anziehungen oder unspezifisches Abstoßen zweier Atome, die nahe beieinander liegen).

3 Metabolism › 3.3 Enzymes

... hydrophobic interaction.	... hydrophobe (wasserabstoßende) Kräfte.
... covalent bonding.	... kovalente Bindungen (durch ein gemeinsames Elektronenpaar zwischen zwei in einem Molekül benachbarten Atomen gekennzeichnet).

Types of enzymes

oxidoreductase e.g. redox reaction (such as removal of hydrogen by catalase)	Oxidoreduktase z. B. Redox-Reaktion (wie Abspalten von Wasserstoff durch Katalase)
transferase	Transferase
hydrolase	Hydrolase
lyase	Lyase
isomerase	Isomerase
ligase	Ligase

The names of enzymes reflect the specificity of their functions and often end with the suffix "ase".
Die Namen der Enzyme spiegeln ihre Wirkungsspezifität wider und enden oft mit der Nachsilbe "ase".

Factors influencing enzyme activity: enzyme / substance concentration

progress of reaction n	Reaktionsverlauf
progress curve n	Sättigungskurve / asymptotische Kurve (sich einem Sättigungswert annähernde Kurve)
level off v	abflachen
flatten out v	abflachen / sich verlangsamen (z.B. der Anstieg)

»

plot against sth	in Abhängigkeit von etw. aufzeichnen (z. B. in Abhängigkeit von bestimmten Daten)
saturate sth with sth	etw. mit etw. sättigen
directly proportional to sth	direkt proportional zu etw.

Michaelis-Menten constant n	Michaelis-Menten Konstante
substrate concentration n	Substratkonzentration
enzyme concentration n	Enzymkonzentration
maximum rate n	maximal mögliche Rate

maximum value n	maximal möglicher Wert *(z. B. Umsetzungsrate, Geschwindigkeit etc.)*
turnover number (TON) n	Wechselzahl
excess of substrate n	Überschuss an Substraten *(Substratmolekülen)*

» The initial rate of an enzyme-catalysed reaction plotted against enzyme concentration (substrate concentration) shows that …
Die Reaktionsgeschwindigkeit einer enzymatisch katalysierten Reaktion in Abhängigkeit von der Enzymkonzentration (Substratkonzentration) zeigt, dass …
The reaction is carried out at various different enzyme concentrations.
Die Reaktion wird mit verschiedenen Enzymkonzentrationen durchgeführt.

Factors influencing enzyme activity: temperature

three-dimensional adj	dreidimensional
the effect of sth n	der Einfluss von etw.
the effect on sth n	der Einfluss auf etw.
affect sth v	sich auf etw. auswirken / etw. beeinflussen

»
be dependent on sth	von etw. abhängig sein
the effect of temperature	der Einfluss der Temperatur
to affect the tertiary structure of the enzyme molecule	sich auf die Tertiärstruktur des Enzymmoleküls auswirken

van't Hoff's rule n	RGT-Regel *(Reaktions-Geschwindigkeits-Temperatur Regel; auch: das Van't Hoffsche Gesetz)*
increase exponentially v	(sich) exponentiell erhöhen
double v	(sich) verdoppeln
quadruple [ˈkwɒdrʊpl] v	(sich) vervierfachen
collide [kəˈlaɪd] v	aufeinander stoßen

»
	frequently	häufig	
collide	more frequently	häufiger	aufeinander stoßen
	rarely	selten	

3 Metabolism › 3.3 Enzymes

move	slowly / fast	sich langsam / sich schnell bewegen

denature [ˌdiːˈneɪtʃə] v	denaturieren
progressively adv	Schritt für Schritt *sukzessiv*
retain (sth) v	(etw.) behalten / (etw.) bewahren
retain activity	Aktivität behalten
adaptation (to sth) n	Anpassung (an etw.)

»

adaptation to	Anpassung an
… hot springs	… heiße Quellen
… deep-sea thermal vents	… hydrothermale Schlote (Risse in der Nähe von Vulkanen unterhalb des Meeres)

Factors influencing enzyme activity: pH Value

pH value n	pH-Wert
depend on v	abhängig sein von
acidity [əˈsɪdəti] n	Azidität *(Säuregehalt)*
alkalinity [ˌælkəlˈɪnəti] n	Basizität / Alkalinität *(Basengehalt Alkalität)*
disrupt [dɪsˈrʌpt] v	unterbrechen / zerstören

»

the effect of pH changes	der Einfluss von pH Veränderungen
high / low acidity / alkalinity	hohe / niedrige Azidität / Basizität / Alkalinität
disrupt the precise three-dimensional arrangement of the protein chains	die bestimmte (spezifische) dreidimensionale Anordnung der Proteinketten unterbrechen

ionisation [ˌaɪənaɪˈseɪʃn] n	Ladungsverhältnis
charge n	Ladung
proton donor [ˈprəʊtɒnˌdəʊnə] n *(loses protons)*	Protonenspender *(Molekül, das Protonen abgibt)*
proton acceptor [ˈprəʊtɒnækˈseptə] n *(gains protons)*	Protonenrezeptor *(Molekül, das Protonen aufnimmt)*
folding n	Faltung
alter v	(ver)ändern

» | affect the ionisation | sich auf das Ladungsverhältnis auswirken
| ionisation may change | das Ladungsverhältnis kann sich ändern

The folding of the protein may be altered.
Die Faltung des Proteins kann sich ändern.

| activity of an enzyme n | Enzymaktivität |
| range of pH n | pH-Toleranz |

» | reduce the activity of an enzyme | Enzymaktivität reduzieren / drosseln / mindern |
| act over a narrow range of pH | eine geringe pH-Toleranz haben |

distinct optimum pH [dɪˌstɪnt'ɒptɪməmˌpiː'eɪtʃ] n — spezifisches pH Optimum
alkaline conditions ['ælkəlaɪn] n — basisches Milieu
acidic conditions [ə'sɪdɪk] n — saures Milieu
saliva [sə'laɪvə] n — Speichel
starch [stɑːtʃ] n — Stärke

» | hydrolyse starch | Stärke aufschließen

Saliva is approximately neutral.
Speichel ist ungefähr neutral.

Enzymes are sensitive to their environment.
Enzyme reagieren sensibel auf ihre Umwelt.

3.4 Regulation of enzyme activities

inhibitor [ɪn'hɪbɪtə] n — Hemmstoff / Inhibitor
inhibition [ˌɪnɪ'bɪʃn] n — Hemmung
toxin ['tɒksɪn] n — Gift
inactivate v — inaktivieren / funktionslos machen
irreversible [ˌɪrɪ'vɜːsəbl] adj — irreversibel *(nicht mehr rückgängig zu machen)*

reversible adj — reversibel *(rückgängig zu machen)*
  reversible inhibition — reversible Hemmung *(Hemmstoffe lösen sich wieder)*

3 Metabolism › 3.4 Regulation of enzyme activities

irreversible inhibition	irreversible Hemmung (Hemmstoffe lösen sich nicht mehr)
interact (with sth) v	(mit etw.) interagieren

» | the capacity to interact with sth | die Fähigkeit mit etw. zu interagieren |

competitive inhibitor n	kompetitive Hemmstoffe (konkurrierende Hemmstoffe, die Substrate verdrängen)
competitive inhibition n	kompetitive Hemmung
non-competitive inhibitor	nicht-kompetitive Hemmstoffe
non-competitive inhibition	nicht-kompetitve Hemmung

»

Competitive inhibitors	Kompetitive Hemmstoffe
… cannot participate in the catalysed reaction.	… können nicht vom Enzym umgesetzt werden.
… structurally resemble the substrate.	… ähneln strukturell dem Substrat.
… can be overcome by adding more substrate.	… können durch Hinzufügen von mehr Substrat wirkungslos gemacht werden.

allosteric inhibition [ˌæləˈsterɪk] n	allosterische Hemmung (eine Art nicht kompetitiver Hemmung)
allosteric enzyme n	allosterisches Enzym
regulatory subunit n	allosterisches Zentrum
metabolic pathway [ˌmetəbɒlɪkˈpɑːθweɪ] n	Stoffwechselprozess / Stoffwechselkette
starting material n	Ausgangsprodukt
intermediate product n	Zwischenprodukt
end product n	Endprodukt
commitment step n	Stoffwechselkette auslösende Reaktion
energetically wasteful adj	energetisch verschwenderisch / energetisch nicht sinnvoll
feedback inhibition / end-product inhibition n	„feed-back"-Hemmung / Endprodukt-Hemmung
non-allosteric enzyme n	nicht allosterisches Enzym (Enzym, das keine allosterische Bindungsstelle hat)

| active inactive | form of an enzyme | aktivierte / aktive inaktivierte / passive / gehemmte | Form des Enzyms |

The final product allosterically inhibits the enzyme that catalyses the commitment step.
Das Endprodukt hemmt allosterisch das Enzym, das die erste Reaktion am Beginn der Stoffwechselkette auslöst.

3.5 Industrial and commercial uses of enzymes

commercial adj	wirtschaftlich
the use (of sth) n	die Nutzung (von etw.)
commercial use (of sth)	wirtschaftliche Nutzung (von etw.)
commercial importance [kə'mɜːʃˌɪm'pɔːtns]	wirtschaftliche Bedeutung
advantage n	Vorteil
the advantage (of sth)	der Vorteil (von etw.)

aqueous solution ['eɪkwɪəs] n	wässerige Lösung
detergent [dɪ'tɜːdʒnt] n	Detergenz / Waschmittel / Fettlöser
food industry n	Lebensmittelindustrie
medical research n	medizinische Forschung
application n	Anwendung
diagnosis [ˌdaɪəɡ'nəʊsɪs] n	Diagnose
treatment n	Behandlung
extract v	extrahieren / herauslösen
purify v	reinigen
immobilise BE / immobilize AE [ɪ'məʊblaɪz] v	unbeweglich machen / fixieren
immobilisation BE / immobilization AE [ɪˌməʊblaɪ'zeɪʃn] n	Fixierung

Immobilisation by	Fixierung durch
... adsorption onto an insoluble matrix.	... Anlagerung an ein nicht-lösliches Fixierungsmittel.
... covalent binding onto a solid support.	... kovalente Bindung an ein festes Gerüst.
... entrapment within a gel.	... Einlagerung in ein Gel.
... encapsulation behind a selectively permeable membrane.	... Einkapselung mithilfe einer selektiv permeablen / durchlässigen Membran.

3 Metabolism › 3.6 Aerobic pathways of glucose metabolism

surface n	Oberfläche
solid surface	feste Oberfläche
toxicity [tɒkˈsɪsəti] n	Toxizität
toxicity testing	Toxizitätsprüfung
in vitro toxicity testing	in-vitro-Toxizitätsprüfung
test strip n	Teststäbchen
glucose oxidase test strip	Teststäbchen zur Überprüfung von Glukose *(im Harn)*
hydrogen peroxide [ˈhaɪdrədʒən pəˈrɒksaɪd] n	Wasserstoffperoxid
dye [daɪ] n	Farbstoff
coronary vessel [ˈkɒrənri ˈvesl] n	Herzkranzgefäß
stroke n	Schlaganfall
heart attack n	Herzinfarkt
(blood) clot n	(Blut-)Gerinnsel
scaffolding of fibrin [ˈskæfldɪŋ əv ˈfɪbrɪn] n	Fibringerüst
biosensor [ˈbaɪəʊsensə] n	Biosensor
tumour marker n	Tumormarker
antibody [ˈæntɪˌbɒdi], *pl* antibodies n	Antikörper
detection [dɪˈtekʃn] n	Entdeckung / Erkennung / Nachweis / Ermittlung
early detection / early diagnosis n	Früherkennung
intercellular space n	Zellzwischenraum
buffered solution / buffer solution n	Pufferlösung
loading solution n	Stammlösung

3.6 Aerobic pathways of glucose metabolism

harvesting of energy / generation of energy n	Energiegewinnung
starch [stɑːtʃ] n	Stärke *(ein Speicherstoff der Glukose bei Pflanzen)*
glycogen [ˈɡlaɪkədʒən] n	Glykogen *(ein Speicherstoff der Glukose bei Tieren)*
energy-investing reaction n	Energie bindende Reaktion *(z.B. Photosynthese)*
energy-harvesting reaction n	Energie freisetzende Reaktionen *(z.B. Zellatmung)*

» the harvesting of energy from glucose | der Energiegewinn aus Glukose

multistep metabolic pathway n	mehrschrittiger Stoffwechselweg
respiration [ˌrespɪrˈeɪʃn] n	Atmung
external respiration n *(exchange of oxygen / carbon dioxide between environment and organism)*	äußere Atmung *(Sauerstoff bzw. Kohlenstoffdioxidaustausch zwischen Umwelt und Organismus)*
internal respiration n *(gaseous exchange between body fluids – e.g. blood – and cells)*	innere Atmung *(Gasaustausch zwischen den Körperflüssigkeiten – z.B. Blut – und den Zellen)*
cellular respiration n	Zellatmung
balanced (reaction) equation [ɪˈkweɪʒn] n	Summengleichung
oxygen supply n	Sauerstoffversorgung
earthworm n	Regenwurm

» | ventilation of the ground | Durchlüftung des Erdreiches |

aerenchymatous tissue	Gewebe mit luftgefülltem Hohlraum *(im Inneren von Stängeln und Wurzeln)*
aerenchyma [eəˈreŋkɪmə] n	Atemwurzel *(bei Sumpfpflanzen)*
intensity of respiration n	Atmungsintensität
heat of respiration n	Atmungswärme
temperature-depending adj	temperaturabhängig
combustion [kəmˈbʌstʃn] n	Verbrennung

» | a process is compartmentalised | ein Vorgang findet in Kompartimenten statt |

glycolysis [ɡlaɪˈkɒːləsɪs] n	Glykolyse
cytosol *(plasma and organelles)* n	Cytosol *(Plasma and Organellen)*
generate v	generieren / herstellen / bilden
aerobic [eəˈrəʊbɪk] adj	aerob
oxidation n	Veratmung / Oxidation / Stoffabbau
complete oxidation	vollständige Veratmung (Oxidation) / vollständiger Stoffabbau

» | external to mitochondrion | außerhalb des Mitochondriums |
| | in the presence of oxygen | in Anwesenheit von Sauerstoff |

pyruvate [paɪˈruːveɪt] n	Brenztraubensäure / Pyruvat
glycolytic [ɡlaɪˈkɒlɪtɪk] adj	glykolytisch
cleavage [ˈkliːvɪdʒ] n	Spaltung

3 Metabolism › 3.6 Aerobic pathways of glucose metabolism

»

| glycolytic cleavage of glucose to two molecules of pyruvate | glykolytische Spaltung von Glukose in zwei Moleküle Brenztraubensäure |

Oxidative decarboxylation reaction

Bei der oxidative Decarboxilierung der Brenztraubensäure (die zur Bildung von Acetyl-CoA führt) verwendet man diverse Begriffe, um den „Verbindungsschritt" zwischen Glykolyse und Zitronensäurezyklus zu beschreiben:
pyruvate decarboxylation reaction
oxidative decarboxylation **of** *pyruvate*
pyruvate oxidation
the transition reaction
the link reaction
the oxidative decarboxylation reaction

acetyl¯CoA ['æsɪtaɪl] n	Acetyl¯CoA *(aktivierte Essigsäure)*
NAD⁺ nicotinamide adenine dinucleotide n	NAD⁺ Nicotinamidadenindinukleotid
NADH¯ electron donor n	NADH¯ Elektronendonator / Elektronenspender
hydrogen ion (H⁺) ['haɪdrədʒən'aɪən] n	Wasserstoffion
proton ['prəʊtɒn] n	Proton
electron [ɪ'lektrɒn] n	Elektron

»

| universal energy intermediary | universelles energiereiches Zwischenprodukt |

waste product n	Abfallprodukt
net energy n	Nutzenergie / Arbeitsenergie
net energy trapped	gebundene Nutzenergie (Arbeitsenergie)

citric acid [ˌsɪtrɪk'æsɪd] n	Zitronensäure
citric acid cycle n	Zitronensäurezyklus
Krebs cycle n	Krebszyklus
tricarboxylic acid cycle (TCC) ['traɪˌkɑːbɒksɪlɪksaɪkl] n	Tricarbonsäurezyklus (TCC)
oxaloacetate [ˌɒksələʊ'æsəteɪt] n	Oxalessigsäure / Oxalacetat
regenerate v	regenerieren
FAD (flavin adenine dinucleotide) n	FAD Flavin-Adenin-Dinukleotid

chain n		Kette
respiratory chain		Atmungskette
electron transport chain		Elektronentransportkette

»

inside the mitochondrion	im Mitochondrion
inside the matrix	in der Matrix
inner membrane of mitochondrion	innere Mitochondrienmembran

cytochrome [saɪtə'krəʊm] n	Cytochrom
electron carrier n	Elektronenträger

»

accept electrons	Elektronen aufnehmen

redox reaction n *(oxidation-reduction reaction)*	Redoxreaktion
reduction [rɪ'dʌkʃn] n *(gain of one or more electrons by an atom, ion, or molecule)*	Reduktion *(Aufnahme eines oder mehrerer Elektronen)*
oxidation [ˌɒksɪ'deɪʃn] n *(loss of one or more electrons)*	Oxidation *(Abgabe eines oder mehrerer Elektronen)*
oxidising agent ['ɒksɪdaɪzɪŋˌeɪdʒnt] n *(reactant that becomes reduced)*	Oxidationsmittel *(der Ausgangsstoff, der reduziert wird)*
reducing agent n *(reactant that becomes oxidised)*	Reduktionsmittel *(das oxidiert wird)*
potential n	Ladung
difference of potential	Ladungsdifferenz

»

intermembrane space / inner mitochondrial membrane	Raum zwischen den beiden Mitochodrien-Membranen

difference in pH value n	Unterschied im pH-Wert
proton concentration gradient ['prəʊtɒnˌkɒnsntreɪʃn'greɪdiənt] n	Protonengradient

»

establish	a gradient	einen Gradienten	aufbauen
maintain			aufrechterhalten

143

3 Metabolism › 3.7 Anaerobic pathways of glucose metabolism

electronegative adj	elektronegativ
proton pump n	Protonenpumpe
proton motive force n	Protonen bewegende Kraft
key reaction n	Schlüsselreaktion
oxyhydrogen [ˌɒksiˈhaɪdrədʒən] n	Knallgas
hydrogen-oxygen reaction / Knallgas reaction n	Knallgasreaktion
energy efficiency n	energetischer Wirkungsgrad

»
controlled release of energy	stufenweise Energiefreisetzung
chemiosmotic mechanism for ATP synthesis	chemiosmotischer Mechanismus der ATP Synthese (Bewegung der Wassterstoffionen über eine Membran während der Atmungskette)

3.7 Anaerobic pathways of glucose metabolism

anaerobic adj	anaerob
anaerobe [ˈænərəʊb] n	Anaerobier
obligate anaerobic bacteria	obligatorisch anaerobe Bakterien *(können sowohl unter anaeroben wie aeroben Bedingungen leben)*
fermentation [ˌfɜːmenˈteɪʃn] n	Gärung
alcoholic fermentation	alkoholische Gärung
ethyl alcohol / ethanol n	Ethanol (Alkohol)
yeast [jiːst] n	Hefe
ethanal [əθɜrˈnɒl] / acetaldehyde n [ˌæsɪˈtældɪhaɪd]	Ethanal / Acetaldehyd
final electron acceptor n	terminaler (endgültiger) Elektronenakzeptor

»
in the absence of oxygen	unter Sauerstoffausschluss
exceed the concentration of sth	Konzentration von etw. überschreiten

lactic acid n	Milchsäure / Laktat
lactate fermentation [ˈlækteɪt] n	Milchsäuregärung
oxygen debt n	„Sauerstoffschuld" *(Sauerstoffmenge, die für die Umwandlung von Laktat in ungiftige Brenztraubensäure benötigt wird)*

pant v	hecheln / keuchen / nach Luft schnappen

»
pay one's oxygen debt	Sauerstoffdefizit auffüllen

"Oxygen debt" describes the oxygen needed to convert toxic lactic acid to pyruvate.
Die „Sauerstoffschuld" beschreibt die für die Umwandlung von Laktat in ungiftige Brenztraubensäure benötigte Sauerstoffmenge.

butyric acid [bjuːˌtɪrɪkˈæsɪd] / butanoic acid n	Buttersäure / Butanol
butanoate-producing bacterium n	Buttersäurebakterie
putrefaction [ˌpjuːtrɪˈfækʃn] n	Fäulnis / Verwesung (Zersetzung unter Sauerstoffausschluss)
putrefying bacteria [ˈpjuːtrɪfaɪɪŋ] n	Fäulniserreger
decompose v	verwesen / verrotten
incomplete oxidation n	unvollständige Veratmung / unvollständiger Stoffabbau
energy yield n	Energieausbeute

»
decomposition of animal proteins	Zersetzung tierischer Eiweiße

Because the breakdown of glucose is incomplete, much less energy is released than during aerobic respiration.
Da der Abbau von Glukose unvollständig ist, wird viel weniger Energie freigesetzt als während der aeroben Atmung.

3.8 Photosynthesis

photosynthesis [ˌfəʊtəʊˈsɪnθəsɪs] n	Fotosynthese
photosynthetic [ˌfəʊtəʊsɪnˈθetɪk] adj	fotosynthetisch
photosynthetic active	fotosynthetisch wirksam
biomass n	Biomasse
molecular formula n	Summenformel
equation [ɪˈkweɪʒn] n	Gleichung
balanced equation	Reaktionsgleichung / Reaktionsschema

3 Metabolism › 3.8 Photosynthesis

»
convert light energy into chemical energy	Lichtenergie in chemische Energie umwandeln
produced in abundance	im Überfluss produziert
proceed within the chloroplast	in den Chloroplasten ablaufen
reduce CO_2 to carbohydrates	Kohlenstoffdioxid zu Kohlenhydraten reduzieren

Photosynthesis comprises two pathways.
Die Fotosynthese setzt sich aus zwei Reaktionsfolgen zusammen.

Photosynthesis resides in different parts of the organelle.
Die Fotosynthese findet an verschiedenen Orten des Organells statt.

light reaction / photosynthesis light phase n	Primärprozess
light-dependent reaction n	lichtabhängige Reaktion
light-independent reaction / the Calvin cycle n	Sekundärprozess / lichtunabhängige Reaktion / der Calvin-Zyklus
behave v	sich verhalten
inversely proportional adj	umgekehrt proportional

Light

Light behaves both as electromagnetic waves as well as energy-rich particles (photons).
Licht lässt sich sowohl als eine Menge elektromagnetischer Wellen als auch als Strom winziger Energieteilchen verstehen.
The energy of light is inversely proportional to the wavelength.
Die Energie des Lichtes ist umgekehrt proportional zu seiner Wellenlänge (*d.h. die Quanten des kurzwelligen Lichtes sind energiereicher als die langwelligen Lichtes*).

radiation n	Strahlung
electromagnetic wave n	elektromagnetische Welle
prism ['prɪzm] n	Prisma
visible spectrum n	sichtbares Licht
wavelength	Wellenlänge
photon ['fəʊtɒn] n	Photon / Lichtquant / Energieteilchen

»
propagated by waves	über Wellen verbreitet

Where does photosynthesis take place and how can light be absorbed?

chloroplast ['klɒrəplɑːst] n	Chloroplast
matrix n	Matrix
intermembrane space n	Zwischenmembranraum *(zwischen Innen- und Außenmembran)*
stroma n *(area outside the thylakoid membranes)*	Stroma *(Reaktionsraum außerhalb der Thylakoid Membrane)*
granum ['grænəm], *pl* grana / stack of thylakoids n	Granum / Thylakoidstapel *(Pl. Grana)*
starch grain n	Stärkekorn
pigment n	Pigment / Blattfarbstoff
purified pigment	Blattfarbstoffe in reiner Form
isolated pigment	isolierte Blattfarbstoffe
plastidial DNA n	Plastiden DNA
plastoglobule / drop of lipids n	Lipidtröpfchen

thin-layer chromatography n	Dünnschichtchromatografie
chlorophyll ['klɔːrəfɪl] n *(chlorophylls a and b)*	Chlorophyll *(Chlorophyll a und b)*
complex ring structure n	komplexe Ringstruktur *(Porphyrinring)*
magnesium atom n	Magnesiumatom
long hydrocarbon "tail" n	lange Kohlenwasserstoffkette
thylakoid membrane [ˌθaɪləˈkɔɪd] n	Thylakoidmembran
methyl group ['meθl] n *(chlorophyll a)*	Methylgruppe *(Kennzeichen v. Chlorophyll a)*
aldehyde group ['ældɪhaɪd] n *(chlorophyll b)*	Aldehydgruppe *(Kennzeichen v. Chlorophyll b)*
carotenoid [ˌkərotəˈnɔɪd] n	Carotinoid
xantophyll [ˌzænθeˈfɪl] n	Xantophyll *(Untergruppe der Carotinoide)*
lutein ['luːtiːn] n	Lutein *(ein Farbstoff der Xantophylle)*
carotene n	Carotin

» The long tails anchor the chlorophyll molecules to integral proteins in the thylakoid membrane.
Die langen Kohlenwasserstoffketten der Chlorophyllmoleküle verankern diese mit den integralen Membranproteinen der Thylakoidmembran.
Thin layer chromatography is used to separate and determine …
Dünnschichtchromatografie wird zum Trennen und Bestimmen von … eingesetzt.
A sheet of glass is coated with an adsorbent material.
Eine Trägerplatte wird mit einem adsorbierenden Material beschichtet.

3 Metabolism › 3.8 Photosynthesis

stationary phase n	stationäre Phase
mobile phase n	mobile Phase
solvent / solvent mixture n	Laufmittel / Fließmittel
capillary action [kəˈpɪlrɪˌækʃn] n	Kapillarkraft

» During the stationary phase the solvent is drawn up the plate via capillary action.
Das Fließmittel saugt sich über Kapillarkräfte in der stationären Phase nach oben.

absorb v	absorbieren
absorption spectrum	Absorptionsspektrum
absorption property	Absorptionseigenschaft
action spectrum n	Wirkungsspektrum

» | | |
|---|---|
| break light up into its constituent spectral colours | Licht spektral zerlegen |

reflect v	reflektieren
oxygen-dependent bacterium n	sauerstoffliebende Bakterie
green alga Spirogyra [ˌspaɪərəˈdʒaɪərə] n	Grünalge Spirogyra (Algenfaden, den Engelmann benutzte)
accumulate v	ansammeln
accumulation n	Ansammlung
overlap n	überlappen / überschneiden

» | | |
|---|---|
| release oxygen | Sauerstoff abgeben |
| with peaks for | mit Höchstwerten bei |
| light of a certain wavelength | Licht einer gewissen Wellenlänge |

light-harvesting complex n	Lichtsammelkomplex
adjacent antenna pigments [əˈdʒeɪsntænˈtenəˌpɪgmənts] n	benachbarte Antennenpigmente
energy-absorbing antenna system	Energie absorbierende Lichtsammelfalle
accessory pigment n	akzessorisches Pigment / Hilfspigment / Antennenpigment (Carotinoide, Chlorophyll b etc.)
photosynthetic reaction centre n	Reaktionszentrum des Lichtsammelkomplexes

> There is a chlorophyll a molecule at the core of the photo system reaction centre.
> Ein Chlorophyll a Molekül befindet sich in der Mitte des Reaktionszentrums des Photosystems.

excitation n	Anregung
ground state n *(with lower energy)*	Grundzustand *(mit geringerer Energie)*
excited state n *(with higher energy)*	Anregungszustand *(mit höherer Energie)*
fluorescence [flɔː'resns] n	Fluoreszenz / Fluoreszenzstrahlung

> | lose as fluorescence | als Fluoreszenzstrahlung verlieren |
> |---|---|
> | Photons may … | (Licht)quanten können … |
> | … bounce off the chlorophyll a molecule. | … vom Chlorophyll a Molekül abprallen. |
> | … be scattered. | … verstreut werden. |
> | … be reflected. | … reflektiert werden. |
> | … be transmitted. | … übertragen werden. |
> | … be absorbed. | … absorbiert werden. |
> | … be raised from … to … | … angehoben werden von … auf …. |
>
> An electron is boosted into a shell farther from its nucleus.
> Ein Elektron wird auf eine vom Kern weiter entfernte Schale übertragen.
>
> An electron is held less firmly.
> Ein Elektron wird weniger fest gehalten.
>
> A molecule is made more chemically reactive.
> Ein Molekül wird in einen energiereicheren angeregten Zustand versetzt.

electron [ɪ'lektrɒn] n	Elektron
energised electron	angeregtes Elektron *(Elektron auf einem höheren Energieniveau)*
electron deficit *(oxidised)*	Elektronenentzug *(oxidiert)*
electron carrier	Elektronenüberträger
reducing agent n *(electron donor)*	Elektronen liefernder Stoff / Reduktionsmittel *(Elektronendonator)*

> An electron is displaced from the photo system.
> Das Photosystem gibt ein Elektron ab.

3 Metabolism › 3.8 Photosynthesis

What happens after light has been absorbed by chlorophyll?

electron transport chain n
photophosphorylation / electron flow
 [ˌfəʊtəʊˌfɒsfəriˈleɪʃn] n
cyclic electron flow n
non-cyclic electron flow n
ATP synthase n

Elektronentransportkette
Fotophosphorylierung

zyklische Fotophosphorylierung
nicht zyklische Fotophosphorylierung
ATP Synthase *(Enzym)*

» | harvest chemical energy | ATP (chemische Energie) bilden

An electron is passed on in a redox reaction to an oxidizing agent.
Ein Elektron wird über eine Redoxreaktion an einen Elektronenakzeptor abgegeben.

photolysis [fəʊˈtɒləsɪs] n

proton [ˈprəʊtɒn] n
hydrogen ion n
waste product n
isotope [ˈaɪsətəʊp] n
radioisotope [ˌreɪdiəʊˈaɪsətəʊp] n
Hill reaction n

Photolyse *(Spaltung des Wassers in Protonen, Elektronen und Sauerstoff)*
Proton
H+
Abfallprodukt
Isotop
Radioisotop *(radioaktives Isotop)*
Hill-Reaktion

» | source of oxygen | Quelle des Sauerstoffs
| split water | Wasser spalten
| trace the flow of oxygen | den Weg des Sauerstoff verfolgen
| ^{18}O-labelled water | Wasser mit dem schweren Sauerstoffisotop ^{18}O
| in molecular terms | als chemische Formel

proton gradient n

proton motive force n

Protonengradient
 (Konzentrationsunterschied an Protonen)
Protonen bewegende Kraft
 (gerichtete Protonenwanderung)

» | generate a chemiosmotic potential across the membrane | ein chemiosmotisches Potential auf beiden Seiten der Biomembran aufbauen (durch Protonengradient, pH- und Ladungsunterschied)
| provide enough energy | genügend Energie liefern

radioisotope labelling experiments	Isotopen Markierungsversuche
tracer method n	Tracermethode *(Methode, die mit Markierungsstoffen arbeitet)*
X-ray film n	Röntgenfilm
chromatogram ['krəʊmətəgræm] n	Chromatogramm
fluorescent dye [flɔː'resnt͵daɪ] n	Fluoreszenzfarbstoff

identify the sequence of reactions	die Abfolge der Reaktionen aufklären
expose cultures to sth	die Kulturen etwas aussetzen (mit etwas „füttern")
extract organic compounds	organische Verbindungen extrahieren / entnehmen
establish … / provide … / furnish … proof / evidence	einen Nachweis erbringen

CO_2 fixation [fɪk'seɪʃn] n	CO_2-Fixierung
ribulose 1,5-bisphosphate (RuBP) n	Ribulose-(1,5)-bisphosphat
RuBisCo (ribulose bisphosphate carboxylase) n	RubisCo (Ribulosebisphosphat-Carboxylase)
carbon dioxide acceptor [͵kɑːbndaɪ'ɒksaɪdək͵septə] n	CO_2 Akzeptor *(bindet CO_2)*
glyceraldehyde 3-phosphate (G3P) n	3-Phosphoglycerat(3-PG) / Glycersinsäurephosphat / Glycerinaldehyd-3-phosphat (GAP)
3-carbon sugar phosphate ['fɒsfeɪt] n	Triosephosphat
disaccharide sucrose [daɪ'sækraɪd͵suːkrəʊs] n	Disaccharid Saccharose *(Zweifachzucker Rohrzucker)*
constituent monosaccharides [kən'stɪtjuənt͵mɒnə'sækraɪdz] n	anteilige Monosaccharide *(Einfachzucker)*

What happens to the products of photosynthesis?

insoluble starch [ɪn'sɒljəbl͵stɑːtʃ] n	unlösliche Stärke
storage organ *(e.g. root, tuber, fruit, seed)* n	Speicherorgan *(z.B. Wurzel, Knolle, Frucht, Samen)*
raw material n	Ausgangsstoff
nutrient ['njuːtrɪənt] n	Baustoff / Nährstoff
energy source / source of energy n	Energieträger / Nährstoff

3 Metabolism › 3.8 Photosynthesis

cellulose [ˈseljələʊs] n	Zellulose
oil n	Öl
essential oils	ätherische Öle
fat n	Fett
signal molecule n	Signalstoff
fragrance molecule n	Duftstoff
flavour molecule n	Geschmacksstoff
bitter constituent [ˌbɪtərˈkənstɪtjuənt] n	Bitterstoff

root nodule / root tubercle n	Wurzelknöllchen
root tubercle bacterium n	Knöllchenbakterie
free nitrogen of the air n	Luftstickstoff
leguminous plant [lɪˈgjuːmɪnəsˌplænt] n	Hülsenfrüchtler *(Leguminose)*
subfamily n	Unterfamilie
pea plants / papilionoid n	Schmetterlingsblütler
subfamily n	Unterfamilie
subfamily Papilionoideae	Unterfamilie Schmetterlingsblütler
runner bean n	Stangenbohne

How do plants cope with adverse conditions?

C4 photosynthesis n	von C4- Pflanzen betriebene Photosynthese
graminaceae [grəˈmɪnəˌkɪə] n	Gräser (Süßgräser)
sedge [sedʒ] n	Segge
maize [meɪz] *BE* / corn *AE* n	Mais
sugar cane n	Zuckerrohr
sorghum [ˈsɔːgəm] n	Hirse

peroxisome [pəˈrɒksɪˌsəʊm] n	Peroxisom *(Organell der Zelle)*
intense sun n	starke Sonneneinstrahlung
solar radiation n	Sonneneinstrahlung
arid [ˈærɪd] adj	wasserarm

»

water-use-efficiency	ökonomische Nutzung von Wasser
adaptations to arid conditions	Anpassungen an Trockenheit

This is an adaptive mechanism for minimizing the loss of photosynthetic carbon.
Dies ist ein Anpassungsmechanismus, der die Minderung der Fotosyntheseleistung verhindert.

photorespiration [ˌfəʊtəʊˌrəspərˈeɪʃn] n	Lichtatmung / Fotorespiration

photorespire [ˌfəʊtəʊˌrɪ'spaɪə] n	Lichtatmung betreiben
intermediate compound n	Zwischenprodukt
HATCH-SLACK-cycle [ˌhætʃ ˌslæk'saɪkl] / the C4 cycle n	Hatch-Slack-Zyklus / C4 Zyklus
oxaloacetate [ˌɒkseləʊ'æsəteɪt] n	Oxalacetat / Oxalessigsäure
malate [meɪleɪt] n	Malat / Apfelsäure

» | (ring of) bundle-sheath cells | (Kranz von) Bündelscheidenzellen |

crassulacean acid metabolism / CAM photosynthesis [ˌfəʊtə'sɪnθəsɪs] n	Crassulaceen *(Dickblattgewächse)* Säurestoffwechsel / CAM-Mechnismus
succulent ['sʌkjələnt] n	Sukkulente / sukkulente Pflanze
leave n	Blatt
fleshy leaves	fleischige Blätter
swollen leaves	verdickte Blätter
stem n	Sprossachse
stomatum, *pl* stomata n	Spaltöffnung

phosphoenolpyruvate (PEP) [ˌfɒsfəʊˌiːnɒlpaɪ'ruːveɪt] n	Phosphoenolpyruvat (PEP)
hydronium ion ['haɪˌdreʊnɪəmˌaɪən] n	Oxonium-Ionen (H_3O^+) / Hydroxonium
acidification [əˌsɪdɪfɪkeɪʃn] n	Ansäuerung / Versauerung
deacidification n	Entsäuerung
diurnal acid rhythm [ˌdaɪ'ɜːnlˌæsɪdˌrɪðm] n	diurnaler Säurerhythmus
evolve [ɪ'vɒlv] v	sich herausbilden
evolve convergently	konvergent entstehen *(konvergent [unabhängig voneinander] während der Evolution entstehen)*

» | separated in time | zeitlich getrennt |
| separated spatially | räumlich getrennt |

How do prokaryotes harvest energy?

chemosynthesis [kiːməʊˌsɪnθəsɪs] n	Chemosynthese
chemosynthesiser n	Chemosynthese betreibender Mikroorganismus
chemosynthetic active bacteria	chemosynthetisch tätige Bakterien

3 Metabolism › 3.8 Photosynthesis

> | Nitrifying organisms | Nitrifizierende Organismen |
> | --- | --- |
> | ... are chemoautotrophic. | ... sind chemoautotroph. |
> | ... produce energy to be coupled to ATP synthesis. | ... gewinnen Energie, die für die ATP-Synthese verwendet wird. |
> | ... use carbon dioxide as their carbon source for growth. | ... benutzen CO_2 als ihre Kohlenstoffquelle für das Wachstum. |

nitrogen n	Stickstoff
nitrogen cycle	Stickstoffkreislauf
ammonium ion (NH_4^+) [əˈməʊniəmˌaɪən] n	Ammoniumion
ammonia / **ammonia hydroxide** (NH_3) n	Ammoniak
ammonia salt n	Ammoniumsalze
culture medium / **nutrient solution** n	Nährlösung
nitrate ion (NO_3^-) n	Nitrationen
nitrite ion / (NO_2^-) n	Nitritionen
nitrification [ˌnaɪtrɪfɪˈkeɪʃn] ($NH_3 \rightarrow NO_2^- \rightarrow NO_3^-$) n	Nitrifikation
nitrifiying bacteria n	nitrifizierende Bakterien
nitrosomonas n	Nitrosomonas *(Bakteriengattung der Nitritbakterien, Nitrosofizierer)*
oxidise ammonia [ˈɒksɪdaɪzˌəməʊniə] n	Ammonium oxidieren
nitrite-oxidizing bacteria n *(oxidation of nitrite into nitrate)*	Nitratbakterien / Nitritoxidierer *(Sammelbegriff von Bakterien, die $NO_2^- + \tfrac{1}{2} O_2 \rightarrow NO_3^-$ verwandeln)*
nitrobacter [ˌnaɪtrəʊˈbæktr] n	Nitrobakter *(Bakteriengattung der Nitratbakterien)*

> | convert sth into nitrite | etw. in Nitrit verwandeln |
> | --- | --- |
> | degredation of proteins | Eiweißzersetzung |

denitrification n ($NO_3^- \rightarrow NO_2^- \rightarrow NO \rightarrow N_2O \rightarrow N_2$ gas)	Denitrifikation
sewage plant [ˈsuːɪdʒˌplaːnt] n	Kläranlage
municipal wastewater n	kommunale Abwässer

»   intermediate gaseous nitrogen oxide products   gasförmige Stick(stoff)oxid Zwischenprodukte

conversion of nitrate into finally molecular nitrogen (N_2)   Umwandlung von Nitrat in letztendlich molekularen Stickstoff

replenishes the nitrogen cycle   den Stickstoffzyklus wieder aufstocken

ammonification [ə̩ˌməʊnɪfɪˈkeɪʃn] n   Ammonifikation *(Bildung von Ammoniak und seinen Salzen: $NH_4^+ X^-$)*

mineralisation n   Mineralisierung
microbial [maɪkrəʊbɪəl] adj   mikrobiell
urea [jʊˈriːə] n   Harnstoff
uric acid [ˌjʊərɪkˈæsɪd] n   Harnsäure
organic nitrogen n   organischer Stickstoff
faeces *BE* [ˈfiːsiːz] / feces *AE* n pl   Kot / Fäzes
microbial ammonification n   mikrobielle Ammonifikation

»   Mineralisation is the conversion of organically bound nitrogen into inorganic forms.
Mineralisierung ist die Umwandlung von organisch gebundenem Stickstoff in anorganische Stickstoffformen.
Nitrification is part of the mineralisation process.
Nitrifikation ist Teil des Mineralisierungsprozesses.
Urea, uric acid and organic nitrogen of feces are substrates for microbial ammonification.
Harnstoff, Harnsäure und im Kot gebundener organischer Stickstoff sind Substrate für die mikrobielle Ammonifikation.

sulphur *BE* / sulfur *AE* n [ˈsʌlfə]   Schwefel
   elementary sulphur   elementarer Schwefel
sulphide *BE* / sulfide *AE* adj [ˈsʌlfaɪd]   sulfidisch
sulphide *BE* / sulfide *AE* n   Sulfit
hydrogen sulphide n   Schwefelwasserstoff (H_2S)
   sulphur spring   Schwefelquelle
   sulphur bacteria   Schwefelbakterien
   colourless sulphur bacteria   farblose Schwefelbakterien
protein decomposition n   Fäulnis von Eiweißen

3 Metabolism › 3.8 Photosynthesis

» By oxidizing hydrogen sulphide to elementary sulphur, energy is obtained by certain chemoautotrophic, aerobic sulphide oxidizing bacteria (colourless sulphur bacteria).
Durch die Oxidation von Schwefelwasserstoff zu elementarem Schwefel gewinnen bestimmte, chemoautotrophe, aerobe, sulfid-oxidierende Bakterien (farblose Schwefelbakterien) Energie.
This energy (generated in this reaction) is used to synthesise organic compounds from inorganic carbon dioxide.
Die bei diesen Reaktionen frei werdende Energie wird zur Synthese organischer Verbindungen aus anorganischem Kohlenstoffdioxid genutzt.
Chemotrophic, aerobic and anaerobic bacteria are used in the treatment of waste water. They remove nutrients such as nitrogen and phosphorous causing eutrophication.
Aerobe wie auch anaerobe chemotrophe Bakterien werden bei der Abwasserklärung eingesetzt. Sie entfernen Nährsalze wie Stickstoff und Phosphate, die eine Eutrophierung der Gewässer hervorrufen würden.

hydrogen oxidizing bacteria n	Knallgasbakterien
methane (CH_4) n	Methangas
methane-forming bacteria / methanogens n	Methanbildner
biogas [ˈbaɪəʊˌɡæs] n	Biogas
combustion of methane [kəmˈbʌstʃnəvˈmiːθeɪn] n	Verbrennung von Methan
deep sea vent n	Tiefseeschlote
Archaea [əˈkiːə] n	Archaea
hot volcanic spring n	heiße vulkanische Quelle

»
methane rich	reich an Methan
carbon dioxide rich	reich an Kohlenstoffdioxid

Methanogens produce a methane and carbon dioxide rich biogas which can be fed into the gas distribution system.
Methanbildner stellen ein Biogas her, das reich an Methan und Kohlenstoffdioxid ist. Dies kann in das Gasnetz eingespeist werden.

ore [ɔː] n	Erz
sulphide ore	sulfidische Erze
heavy metal sulphide n	Schwermetallsulfid
sulphate BE / sulfate AE n	Sulfat *(Salze der Schwefelsäure H_2SO_4)*
sulphate-reducing bacteria n	sulfatreduzierende Bakterien
iron n	Eisen
ferro-oxidizing bacteria n	Eisenbakterien

microbial mats n	Bakterienrasen
bog iron ore [ˌbɒgˈaɪənɔː] n	Raseneisenerz
biometallurgy [ˌbaɪəʊmetˈælədʒi] n	Metallgewinnung durch Mikroben
heavy metal sulphate n	Schwermetallsulfat
soluble heavy metal sulphate	lösliches Schwermetallsulfat
bioleaching [ˌbaɪəʊˈliːtsɪŋ] n	Erzlaugung

» | extraction of specific metals | Herauslösen spezifischer Metalle |

iron sulphide / iron mineral n	Eisensulfid
sulphur removal / desulphurisation n	Entschwefelung
sulphuric *BE* / sulfuric *AE* adj	Schwefel~
sulphuric acid (H_2SO_4) n	Schwefelsäure
sulphur trioxide gas (SO_3) n	Sulfitgas
sulphite *BE* / sulfite *AE* n	Sulfit *(Salz der schwefeligen Säure H_2SO_3)*
sulphide *BE* / sulfide *AE* n	Sulfidschwefel
thiosulphate *BE* / thiosulfate *AE* n	Thiosulfat *(Derivat der Thioschwefelsäure $H_2S_2O_3$)*
inorganic sulphur / sulphur compounds n	anorganische Schwefelverbindungen
desulphurisation *BE* / desulfurization *AE* n	Entschwefelung
microbial coal desulphurisation	Entschwefelung von Kohle durch Bakterien

salinity [səˈlɪnəti] n	Salzgehalt
high salinity	hohe Salzkonzentration
halobacteria / haloarchaea n	Halobakterien
halorhodopsin	Bakteriorhodopsin

» | hostile condition | lebensfeindliche Bedingung |

4 Cell biology – Cytology

4.1 Eukaryotic cells

Cell types

cell n	Zelle
animal cell n	tierische Zelle / Tierzelle » Abb. 39
nerve cell	Nervenzelle
cartilage cell [ˈkɑːtɪlɪdʒsel]	Knorpelzelle
glandular cell [ˈglændjʊləsel]	Drüsenzelle
secretory cell [ˈsekrətrisel]	sekretorische Zelle
bone cell	Knochenzelle
body cell	Körperzelle
somatic cell [səˈmætɪksel]	somatische Zelle
embryonic cell [ˌembrɪˈɒnɪksel]	Embryozelle
reproductive cell / germline cell [ˈdʒɜːmlainsel]	Fortpflanzungszelle / Keimbahnzelle
stem cell	Stammzelle
oral mucosa cell [ˌɔːrlmjuːˈkəʊsəsel]	Mundschleimhautzelle
cheek cell	Wangenzelle
plant cell n	pflanzliche Zelle / Pflanzenzelle » Abb. 38
cork cell	Korkzelle
elodea cell [ɪˈləʊdɪəsel]	Elodeazelle
waterweed / pondweed [ˈpɒndwiːd] / elodea	Wasserpest / Elodea
onion cell	Zwiebelzelle
meristematic cell [ˌmerɪstɪˈmætɪksel]	Meristemzelle
stone cell	Steinzelle
sclerenchyma fibre cell [ˌsklɪəˈreŋkɪməfaɪbəsel]	Sklerenchymzelle

» Describe the form of the cell and make a sketch/drawing.
Beschreibe(n Sie) die Form der Zelle und fertige(n Sie) ein Skizze/Zeichnung an.

Compare the animal cell to/with a plant cell.
Vergleiche(n Sie) die tierische Zelle mit einer Pflanzenzelle.

This plant cell / animal cell is ... spherical.	Diese pflanzliche / tierische Zelle ist ... kugelig / kugelförmig.
... cubic.	... würfelartig / würfelförmig.
... oblong.	... länglich.
... cylindrical.	... zylindrisch.
... gelatinous.	... gallertartig.
... lenticular.	... linsenförmig.
... tubular.	... röhrenförmig.
... filamentous / thread-like.	... fadenförmig.
... irregular.	... unregelmäßig.
sth exhibits particular characteristics	etw. zeigt besondere Merkmale
sth exhibits anomalies / characteristics	etw. weist Besonderheiten auf
The particular structure shows / reveals / indicates that ...	Die besondere Struktur zeigt / macht deutlich / deutet darauf hin, dass ...
From the particular structure one can conclude that ...	Aus der besonderen Struktur kann man schließen, dass ...

cell theory n
organelle [ˌɔːgn'el], pl organelles n
cytoplasm ['saɪtəʊplæzm] n
eukaryote [juːˈkærɪɒt] n
eukaryotic cell [juːkærɪɒtɪk'sel] n

layer of cells n

Zelltheorie
Organell *(Pl. Organellen)*
Zellplasma / Cytoplasma
Eukaryo(n)t
eukaryo(n)tische Zelle *(Zelle mit echtem Zellkern)*

Zellschicht

» Cells containing a nucleus are called eukaryotic (cells). » Abb. 37–39
Zellen, die einen Zellkern besitzen, werden als eukaryotische Zellen bezeichnet.
Cells without a nucleus are called prokaryotic (cells).
Zellen, die keinen Zellkern besitzen, werden als prokaryotische Zellen bezeichnet.

Tissues   » Abb. 40

tissue ['tɪʃuː] n
epidermis [ˌepɪˈdɜːmɪs] n
cuticle ['kjuːtɪkl] n
waxy adj
secrete [sɪˈkriːt] v
palisade layer ['pælɪˌseɪdleɪə] n
mesophyll ['mesəʊfɪl] n

Gewebe
Epidermis
Kutikula / Wachsschicht
wachsartig
ausscheiden / absondern
Palisadenschicht
Mesophyll *(photosnthetisch aktives Gewebe)*

4 Cell biology – Cytology › 4.1 Eukaryotic cells

spongy mesophyll n	Schwammschicht
meristem ['merɪstem] n	Meristem (undifferenziertes mitotisch aktives Gewebe bei Pflanzen)
bone marrow ['bəʊnˌmærəʊ] n	Knochenmark
blood n	Blut
bone tissue / osseous tissue ['ɒsɪəsˌtɪʃuː] n	Knochengewebe
connective tissue n	Bindegewebe
epithelial tissue [epɪ'θɪlɪəlˌtɪʃuː] n	Epithel
keratinised BE / keratinized [ˌkerətɪnaɪzd] adj	verhornt
parenchyma [pə'reŋkɪmə] (functional parts of an organ in the body) n	Parenchym (Funktionsgewebe eines Organs)
cartilage tissue ['kɑːtɪlɪdʒˌtɪʃuː] / chondroid tissue n	Knorpelgewebe
muscle tissue ['mʌslˌtɪʃuː] n	Muskelgewebe

» In a cross section of a leaf several different layers can be identified, e.g. the cuticule, the upper and the lower epidermis, the palisade layer, and the spongy layer.
In einem Blattquerschnitt können unterschiedliche Schichten identifiziert werden, z. B. die Kutikula, die obere und untere Epidermis, die Palisadenschicht und die Schwammschicht.

The cuticle is not cellular, hence is is not regarded as a tissue.
Die Kutikula besteht nicht aus Zellen und wird daher nicht als Gewebe angesehen.

A tissue is defined as a group of similar and differentiated cells that act in concert to fulfil a particular function.
Ein Gewebe wird als eine Gruppe von ähnlichen, differenzierten Zellen definiert, die zusammenarbeiten, um eine bestimmte Funktion zu erfüllen.

Cell differentiation

totipotent [təʊ'tɪpətnt] adj	totipotent (Zelle die sich noch zu allen Zelltypen entwickeln kann)
differentiation [ˌdɪfrenʃi'eɪʃn] n	Differenzierung
determination [dɪˌtɜːmɪ'neɪʃn] n	Determination
protist ['prəʊtɪst] n	Einzeller
multicellular organism [ˌmʌltiseljələ'ɔːgnɪzm] n	Vielzeller
flagellum [flə'dʒeləm], pl flagella n	Geißel / Flagellum
flagellar pocket	Geißelsäckchen
long flagellum	lange Geißel

cilium ['sɪliəm], *pl* cilia n	Wimper / Cilie
oral groove n	Mundfeld
cytostome ['saɪtəʊstəʊm] n	Zellmund / Cytostom
cytopyge ['saɪtəʊˌpaɪdʒ] n	Zellafter / Cytopyge
vacuole ['vækjuəʊl] n	Zellsaftraum / Vakuole
food vacuole	Nahrungsvakuole
pulsating vacuole	pulsierende Vakuole
protein vacuole	Eiweißvakuole
central vacuole	Zentralvakuole
extraplasmic space n	extraplasmatischer Raum
extracellular space n	extrazellulärer Raum
cell wall n	Zellwand
primary cell wall	primäre Zellwand
secondary cell wall	sekundäre Zellwand
cellulose ['seljələʊs] n	Zellulose
lignin ['lɪgnɪn] n	Lignin
pit [pɪt] n	Tüpfel
plasmodesmata n pl	Plasmodesmata / Plasmodesmen (*Zell-Zell-Verbindung; Sg. Plasmodesmos ungebräuchlich*)
Casparian strip [kæˌspeərɪənˈstrɪp] n	Kasparischer Streifen

» Cells are the fundamental, structural, and functional units of living organisms.
Zellen sind die grundlegenden, strukturellen und funktionellen Einheiten von Lebewesen.
There are more than 100 different cell types in the human body.
Es gibt mehr als 100 verschiedene Zelltypen im menschlichen Körper.
All creatures are made up of cells.
Alle Lebewesen sind aus Zellen aufgebaut. (Schleiden und Schwann)

Determination is a process by which cells become progressively restricted in their potency (potential) to differentiate into various cell types.
Determination ist ein Prozess, bei dem die Zellen immer mehr in ihrer Möglichkeit, sich in verschiedene Zelltypen entwickeln bzw. differenzieren zu können, eingeschränkt werden.

4.2 Prokaryotic cells » Abb. 37

prokaryotic cell [proʊˈkærɪotɪkˈsel] n	prokaryo(n)tische Zelle / Procyte (*Zelle ohne echten Zellkern*)
bacterium [bækˈtɪərɪəm], *pl* bacteria n	Bakterium
cyanobacteria [ˌsaɪənəʊbækˈtɪərɪə] n	Cyanobakterien

4 Cell biology – Cytology › 4.3 Organelles

blue-green alga ['ælgə] n	Blaualge
archaebacteria [ˌɑːkɪbæk'tɪərɪə] n	Archebakterien
virus ['vaɪrəs], *pl* viruses n	Virus *(Pl. Viren)*
phage [feɪdʒ] n	Phage
flagellum [flə'dʒeləm], *pl* flagella n	Geißel / Bakteriengeißel / Flagellum
bacterial cell wall n	Bakterienzellwand
murein ['mjʊəriːn] n	Murein
peptidoglycan [pepˌtaɪdəʊ'glaɪkæn] n	Peptidoglykan
gram-positive [ˌgræm'pɒzɪtɪv] adj	gram positiv / gram-negativ
slime layer ['slaɪmˌleɪə] n	Schleimkapsel
vesicle ['vesɪkl] n	Vesikel / Bläschen
cell membrane n	Zellmembran
thylakoid ['θaɪləkɔɪd] n	Thylakoid
cytoplasm ['saɪtəʊplæzm] n	Cytoplasma
nucleoid ['njuːklɪətaɪd] n	Kernäquivalent
annular DNA ['ænjələˌdiːen'eɪ] / circular DNA / ring-shaped DNA n	ringförmige DNA-Struktur
plasmid n	Plasmid
70S ribosome ['raɪbəsəʊm] n	70S Ribosom

» Compare the prokaryotic cell to/with a eukaryotic cell.
Vergleiche(n Sie) die prokaryo(n)tische Zelle mit einer eukaryo(n)tischen Zelle.

Compare the bacterial flagellum to/with a eukaryotic flagellum.
Vergleiche(n Sie) die Bakteriengeißel mit einem eukaryo(n)tischen Flagellum.

Bacteria are prokaryotes. Since viruses are not cellular and do not exhibit metabolism on their own, they cannot be regarded as living organisms.
Bakterien sind Prokaryo(n)ten. Da Viren nicht zellulär sind und keinen eigenen Stoffwechsel aufweisen, können sie nicht als Lebwesen angesehen werden.

4.3 Organelles

organelle [ˌɔːgn'el], *pl* organelles n	Organelle *(Pl. Organellen)*
sub unit n	Untereinheit
organ n	Organ
organism n	Organismus

» Organelles are specialised subunits of a cell that have a specific function. They can be compared to organs of an organism.
Organellen sind spezialisierte Untereinheiten einer Zelle, die eine bestimmte Funktion haben. Man kann sie mit Organen in einem Organismus vergleichen.

Organelles with one or two membranes   » Abb. 38-39

nucleus ['nju:kliəs], *pl* nuclei n	Zellkern / Nukleus
macronucleus [ˌmækrəʊ 'nju:kliəs]	Großkern / Macronukleus
micronucleus [ˌmaɪkrəʊ 'nju:kliːs]	Kleinkern / Micronukleus
nucleolus [njuː'kliːələs], *pl* nucleoli n	Kernkörperchen / Nukleolus *(Pl. Nukleoli)*

mitochondrion [ˌmaɪtə'kɒndriən], *pl* mitochondria n	Mitochondrium *(Pl. Mitochondrien)*
chloroplast ['klɒrəplɑːst] n	Chloroplast
chlorophyll ['klɔːrəfɪl] n	Chlorophyll
chromoplast ['krəʊməplæst] n	Chromoplast
carotenoid ['kærətɪnɔɪd] n	Carotinoid / Karotinoid *(Pl. Carotinoide)*
leucoplast ['luːkəplæst] n	Leukoplast
unpigmented [ˌʌnpɪg'mentɪd] adj	unpigmentiert
plastid ['plæstɪd] n	Plastid *(Pl. Plastiden)*

peroxisome [pə'rɒksɪsəʊm] n	Peroxisom
lysosome ['laɪsəsəʊm] n	Lysosom
liposome ['lɪpəsəʊm] n	Liposom

golgi apparatus ['gɒldʒɪæpəˌreɪtəs] n	Golgi-Apparat
dictyosome [dɪktɪəsəʊm] n	Diktyosom
trans region n	Trans-Seite / Sekretionsseite
cis region n	Cis-Seite / Bildungsseite
golgi vesicle ['gɒldʒɪˌvesɪkl] n	Golgi-Vesikel
membranous cisterna [ˌmembrənəsɪ'stɜːnə], *pl* cisternae n	Membranzisterne *(Pl. -zisternen)*

synthesis ['sɪnθəsɪs] n	Synthese
synthesise *BE* / **synthesize** ['sɪnθəsaɪz] v	synthetisieren
vacuole ['vækjʊəʊl] n	Vakuole / Zellsaftraum
cell sap n	Zellsaft
anthocyanin *pl* , anthocyanins [ˌænθə'saɪən] n	Anthocyan *(Pl. Anthocyane)*

endoplasmic reticulum (ER) [ˌendəʊplæzmɪkrɪ'tɪkjʊləm] n	endoplasmatisches Retikulum (ER)
rough endoplasmic reticulum	raues endoplasmatisches Retikulum
smooth endoplasmic reticulum	glattes endoplasmatisches Retikulum

4 Cell biology – Cytology › 4.4 Chemical content of a cell

> The organelles of plant and animal cells fulfil specific functions in the cells' metabolism.
> Die Organellen von Pflanzen- und Tierzellen erfüllen spezifische Funktionen im Zellstoffwechsel.
>
> When analysing the microstructure of the organelles it can be noticed that some are separated from the cytoplasm by one or two membranes whereas other organelles do not have a membrane.
> Wenn man die Feinstruktur der Organellen analysiert, findet man einige durch eine oder zwei Membranen vom Cytoplasma abgetrennte Organellen, während andere Organellen keine Membran besitzen.

Organelles without membranes

centrosome [ˈsentrəʊsəʊm] n	Zentrosom
centriole [ˈsentriəʊl] n	Zentriole
flagellum [fləˈdʒeləm], *pl* flagella n	Geißel / Flagellum
ribosome [ˈraɪbəsəʊm] n	Ribosom
80S ribosome	80S Ribosom
cytoskeleton [ˌsaɪtəʊˈskelɪtn] n	Cytoskelett
microtubule [ˌmaɪkrəʊˈtjuːb juːl], *pl* microtubules n	Mikrotubulus *(Pl. Mikrotubuli)*
α- and β-tubulin dimer [ˈælfə] [ˈbiːtə]	α- und β-Tubulin-Dimere
microfilament [ˌmaɪkrəʊˈfɪləmənt] / actin filament [ˌæktənˈfɪləmənt] n	Mikrofilament / Aktinfilament
actin [ˈæktɪn] n	Actin
myosin [ˈmaɪəsɪn] n	Myosin
dynein [ˈdaɪniːn] n	Dynein
proteasome [ˈprəʊtɪəsəʊm] n	Proteasom
nine-plus-two pattern n	9+2-Muster

> Depending on the function of a cell the types and numbers of organelles can vary greatly.
> Abhängig von der Funktion einer Zelle kann sich die Art und Anzahl von Organellen deutlich unterscheiden.

4.4 Chemical content of a cell

Molecules and reactions

carbohydrate [ˌkɑːbəʊˈhaɪdreɪt] n	Kohlenhydrat
lipid [ˈlɪpɪd] / fat n	Lipid / Fett

Four classes of biomolecules in living organisms

Structural elements of living organisms are composed of:	Strukturelle Bestandteile von Lebewesen setzen sich zusammen aus:
Nucleic acids (DNA, RNAs)	Nukleinsäuren (DNS, RNS)
Proteins	Proteinen
Lipids	Lipiden
Carbohydrates	Kohlenhydraten

They are mainly made up of the elements carbon, hydrogen, oxygen, nitrogen, phosphorus, and a bit of sulphur.
Sie bestehen hauptsächlich aus den Elementen Kohlenstoff, Wasserstoff, Sauerstoff, Stickstoff, Phosphor und ein bisschen Schwefel.

Structural elements	Elements contained
Carbohydrates	C, H, O
Fats	C, H, O
Proteins	C, H, N, O, S
Nucleic acids	C, H, O, P

protein n	Protein / Eiweiß
nucleic acid n	Nukleinsäure
DNA n *(Deoxyribo Nucleic Acid)*	DNA / DNS *(**D**esoxyribo**n**uklein **S**äure)*
RNA *(Ribonucleic Acid)* n	RNA / RNS *(**R**ibo**n**uklein **S**äure)*
substance n	Stoff / Substanz
organic substances	organische Stoffe / organische Substanzen
salt n	Salz
ion ['aɪən] n	Ion
living thing n	Lebewesen

make up living things	Lebewesen ausmachen
classes of living things	Klassen von Lebewesen
negatively / positively charged ions	positiv / negativ geladenen Ionen

component n	Bestandteil
metabolic reaction [ˌmetəˌbɒlɪkriˈækʃn] n	Stoffwechselreaktion
molecular formula [məˈlekjələˈfɔːmjələ] n	Summenformel
structural formula n	Strukturformel

water molecule (H_2O) n	Wassermolekül
atom [ˈætəm] n	Atom
oxygen atom	Sauerstoffatom

4 Cell biology – Cytology › 4.4 Chemical content of a cell

hydrogen ['haɪdrədʒən] n	Wasserstoff
hydrogen atom	Wasserstoffatom
electron [ɪ'lektrɒn] n	Elektron
electron pair	Elektronenpaar

»
chemical and physical properties	chemische und physikalische Eigenschaften
distribution of charge	Verteilung der Ladung

bond v	verbinden
hydrogen bond [ˌhaɪdrədʒən'bɒnd]	Wasserstoffbrückenbindung
V-shaped structure n	V-förmige Struktur
electronegativity [ɪˌlektrəʊˌnegə'tɪvɪti] n	Elektronegativität
attract v	anziehen / anlocken
polar molecule n	polares Molekül
electrostatic interaction [ɪˌlektrəʊstætɪkə'trækʃn] n	elektrostatische Wechselwirkung
occur [ə'kɜː] v	auftreten
interact v	einander beeinflussen / wechselwirken
dipole ['daɪpəʊl] n	Dipol
hydration [haɪ'dreɪʃn] n	Hydration
universal solvent n	universales Lösungsmittel
compound ['kɒmpaʊnd] n	Verbindung
carbon compound	Kohlenstoffverbindung
organic compound	organische Verbindung
saturated ['sætʃəreɪtɪd] adj	gesättigt
saturated carbon compound [ˌsætʃəreɪtɪd'kɑːbnˌkɒmpaʊnd]	gesättigte Kohlenstoffverbindung
unsaturated carbon compound	ungesättigte Kohlenstoffverbindung

Chemical elements of biomolecules

carbon (C)	Kohlenstoff
hydrogen (H)	Wasserstoff
hydrocarbon (CH)	Kohlenwasserstoff
oxygen (O)	Sauerstoff
nitrogen (N)	Stickstoff
sulphur (S)	Schwefel
phosphorus, phosphor (P)	Phosphor

alcohol n	Alkohol
alkanol ['ælkənɒl] n	Alkanol
ethanol ['eθənɒl] n	Ethanol / Äthanol
glycerine ['glɪsriːn] n	Glycerin
hydroxyl group (-OH) [haɪ'drɒksaɪl,gruːp] n	Hydroxylgruppe / OH-Gruppe
oxygen atom ['ɒksɪdʒən,ætəm] n	Sauerstoffatom
residue ['rezɪdjuː] n	Rest
non-polar residue	unpolarer Rest
carbonyl compound ['kɑːbənaɪl,kɒmpaʊnd] n	Karbonylverbindung
carbonyl group (-CO) n	Karbonylgruppe
aldehyde ['ældɪhaɪd] n	Aldehyd
ketone ['kiːtəʊn] n	Keton

»

be polarised	gepolt sein
be polar	polar sein
be reactive	reagierend sein / reaktiv sein

carboxylic acid [,kɑːbɒk,sɪlɪk'æsɪd] n	Karboxylsäure
carboxyl group (-COOH) n	Karboxylgruppe
acetic acid [ə'siːtɪk'æsɪd] n	Essigsäure
citric acid [,sɪtrɪk'æsɪd] n	Zitronensäure
butyric acid [bjuː,tɪrɪk'æsɪd] n	Buttersäure
hydrocarbon tail ['haɪdrəkɑːbn,teɪl] n	Kohlenwasserstoff-Schwänzchen
palmitic acid [pæl,mɪtɪk'æsɪd] n	Palmitinsäure
fatty acid n	Fettsäure
amine ['æmiːn] n	Amin
amino group (-NH$_2$) [ə'miːnəʊ,gruːp] n	Aminogruppe

»

component of fats	Baustein von Fetten
act as a base	als Base fungieren
component of amino acids	Bestandteil von Aminosäuren

carbon atom n	Kohlenstoffatom
building block of proteins n	Baustein der Proteine / Baustein der Eiweiße
linking reaction n	Verbindungsreaktion

link sth	etw. verbinden
react with sth	mit etw. reagieren
release a water molecule	ein Wassermolekül freisetzen
reverse a reaction	eine Reaktion rückgängig machen / eine Reaktion umkehren
break down sth/cleave sth	etw. aufspalten
release sth	etw. freisetzen

A condensation reaction is a chemical reaction in which two molecules combine to form one single molecule, together with the loss of a small molecule, mostly water.
Eine Kondensation ist eine chemische Reaktion, bei der sich zwei Moleküle zu einem Molekül verbinden, wobei ein kleines Molekül, meistens Wasser, freigesetzt wird.

Hydrolysis is a chemical process in which a molecule is cleaved/broken down into two parts by the addition of a molecule of water.
Eine Hydrolyse ist ein chemischer Prozess, bei dem ein Molekül durch das Hinzufügen eines Wassermoleküls in zwei Teile gespalten wird.

Proteins » Abb. 43

amino acid [əˌmiːnəʊˈæsɪd] n	Aminosäure
essential amino acid	essentielle Aminosäure
building block n	Baustein
building block of proteins	Baustein der Eiweiße (Proteine)
property n	Eigenschaft
residual group / R-group n	Restgruppe / Rest
side chain n	Seitenkette
peptide [ˈpeptaɪd] n	Peptid
peptide bond	Peptidbindung
dipeptide [daɪˈpeptaɪd] n	Dipeptid
oligopeptide [ˌɒlɪɡəˈpeptaɪd] n	Oligopeptid
polypeptide [ˌpɒlɪˈpeptaɪd] n	Polypeptid
extension n	Ausdehnung
extend v	(sich) ausdehnen
spatial adj	räumlich
three-dimensional adj	dreidimensional

structure n
  primary structure
  secondary structure
  tertiary structure [ˌtɜːʃriˈstrʌktʃə]
  quaternary structure
  [kwəˈtɜːnriˈstrʌktʃə]
sequence n
condensation [ˌkɒndenˈseɪʃn] n
condense v
amphoteric [ˌæmfəˈterɪk] adj

lipophilic [ˌlɪpəˈfɪlɪk] adj
hydrophilic adj
lipophobic adj
hydrophobic [ˌhaɪdrəˈfəʊbɪk] adj

Struktur
  Primärstruktur
  Sekundärstruktur
  Tertiärstruktur
  Quaternärstruktur

Reihenfolge / Sequenz
Kondensation
kondensieren
amphoter *(kann als Säure oder Base reagieren)*

lipophil / fettliebend
hydrophil / wasserliebend
lipophob / fettunlöslich
hydrophob / wasserunlöslich

Classification of amino acids

amino acid	Aminosäure	3-letter code	1-letter code	Polarity, side chain charge at pH 7, other properties	essential
Alanine	Alanin	Ala	A	non-polar, neutral, aliphatic	
Arginine	Arginin	Arg	R	polar, positive, aliphatic	yes
Asparagine	Asparagin	Asn	N	polar, neutral, aliphatic	
Aspartic acid	Asparaginsäure	Asp	D	polar, negative, aliphatic	
Cysteine	Cystein	Cys	C	non-p., neutr., aliph., contains S	
Glutamic acid	Glutaminsäure	Glu	E	polar, negative, aliphatic	
Glutamine	Glutamin	Gln	Q	polar, neutral, aliphatic	
Glycine	Glycin	Gly	G	non-polar, neutral, aliphatic	
Histidine	Histidin	His	H	polar, positive, aliphatic	yes
Isoleucine	Isoleucin	Ile	I	non-polar, neutral, aliphatic	yes
Leucine	Leucin	Leu	L	non-polar, neutral, aliphatic	yes
Lysine	Lysin	Lys	K	polar, positive, aliphatic	yes
Methionine	Methionin	Met	M	non-polar, neutral, contains S	yes
Phenylalanine	Phenylalanin	Phe	F	non-polar, neutral, aromatic	
Proline	Prolin	Pro	P	non-polar, neutral, aliphatic	
Serine	Serin	Ser	S	polar, neutral, aliphatic	
Threonine	Threonin	Thr	T	polar, neutral, aliphatic	yes
Tryptophan	Tryptophan	Trp	W	non-polar, neutral, aromatic	
Tyrosine	Tyrosin	Tyr	Y	polar, neutral, aromatic	
Valine	Valin	Val	V	non-polar, neutral, aliphatic	yes

4 Cell biology – Cytology › 4.4 Chemical content of a cell

» Different amino acids have different poperties depending on their residual group.
Verschiedene Aminosäuren haben abhängig von ihrer Restgruppe verschiedene Eigenschaften.
There are four different classes of amino acids determined by different side chains: non-polar and neutral, polar and neutral, acidic and polar (negatively charged), and basic (positively charged).
Es gibt, bestimmt durch die unterschiedlichen Seitenketten, vier verschiedene Klassen von Aminosäuren: unpolare neutrale, polare neutrale, saure polare (negativ geladene) und basische (positiv geladene).

» The primary structure of a protein is defined by the amiono acid sequence; the secondary, tertiary and quaternary structure are determined largely by the primary structure.
Die Primärstruktur eines Proteins wird als Aminosäuresequenz definiert; die Sekundär-, Tertiär- und Quaternärstruktur werden größtenteils durch die Primärstruktur bestimmt.

Carbohydrates (Saccharides)

carbohydrate [ˌkɑːbəʊˈhaɪdreɪt] n	Kohlenhydrat
open chain form n	Kettenform
open-chain adj	offenkettig
ring form n	Ringform
cyclic adj	zyklisch / ringförmig
chemical composition n	chemischer Aufbau
monosaccharide [ˌmɒnəˈsæraɪd] / simple sugar n	Monosaccharid / Einfachzucker
glucose [ˈgluːkəʊs] n	Glukose / Traubenzucker
fructose [ˈfrʌktəʊs] n	Fruktose / Fruchtzucker
ribose [ˈraɪbəʊz] n	Ribose
disaccharide [dɪˈsækəraɪd] n	Disaccharid / Zweifachzucker
maltose [ˈmɔːltəʊz] n	Maltose / Malzzucker
cellobiose [ˌseləˈbaɪəʊs] n	Cellobiose / Zellobiose
saccharose [ˈsækərəʊz] / sucrose [ˈsuːkrəʊz] n	Saccharose / Sukrose / Haushaltszucker / Kristallzucker
lactose [ˈlæktəʊz] / milk sugar n	Laktose / Milchzucker
polysaccharide [ˌpɒlɪˈsækəraɪd] n	Polysaccharide / Mehrfachzucker
polymers of monosaccharides [ˈpɒlɪməzɒvˌsækəraɪd]	Polymere von Monosacchariden (chemische Verbindungen)
α-amylose [ˈælfəˌæmɪləʊz] n	α-Amylose
cellulose [ˈseljələʊs] n	Zellulose
starch [stɑːtʃ] n	Stärke (pflanzliche Stärke)

| glycogen ['glaɪkədʒən] n | Glykogen *(tierische Stärke)* |
| macromolecule [ˌmækrə'mɒlɪkjuːl] n | Makromolekül |

link (sth) v	(etw.) verbinden
linking reaction n	Verbindungsreaktion
react (with sth) v	(mit etw.) reagieren
add water v	Wasser hinzufügen
break down (sth) v	(etw.) aufspalten

» | release a water molecule | ein Wassermolekül freisetzen |
| reverse a reaction | eine Reaktion rückgängig machen / eine Reaktion umkehren |

Lipids

lipid ['lɪpɪd], *pl* lipids n	Lipid *(Pl. Lipide)*
fat n	Fett
oil n	Öl
fatty acid n	Fettsäure
saturated fatty acid	gesättigte Fettsäure
unsaturated fatty acid	ungesättigte Fettsäure
polyunsaturated fatty acid [ˌpɒlɪʌn'sætʃəreɪtɪdˌfæti'æsɪd]	mehrfach ungesättigte Fettsäure
essential fatty acid	essentielle Fettäure
palmitic acid [pælˌmɪtɪk'æsɪd] n	Palmitinsäure
stearic acid [stɪˌærɪk'æsɪd] n	Stearinsäure
oleic acid [əʊˌliːɪk'æsɪd] n	Ölsäure
linoleic acid [ˌlɪnəliːɪk'æsɪd] n	Linolsäure
linolenic acid [ˌlɪnəlenɪk'æsɪd] n	Linolensäure
neutral fat n	Neutralfett
triglyceride [traɪ'glɪsəraɪd] n	Triglycerid
diglyceride [dɪ'glɪsəraɪd] n	Diglyderid
monoglyceride [mɒnəʊ'glɪsəraɪd] n	Monoclycerid
metabolic intermediate [ˌmetəbɒlɪkɪntə'miːdiət] n	Stoffwechselzwischenprodukt
glycerol ['glɪsrɒl] n	Glycerin
ester bond ['estəˌbɒnd] n	Esterbindung
emulsify [ɪ'mʌlsɪfaɪ] v	emulgieren
steroid ['sterɔɪd], *pl* steroids n	Steroid *(Pl. Steroide)*
cholesterol [kə'lestrɒl] n	Cholesterol
phospholipid [ˌfɒsfə'lɪpɪd] n	Phospholipid
lecithine ['lesɪθin] n	Lecitin

4 Cell biology – Cytology › 4.4 Chemical content of a cell

sphingolipid [ˌsfɪŋeʊˈlɪpɪd] n
Sphingolipide *(Baustein der Zellmembran)*

sphingosine [ˌsfɪŋeʊsaɪn] n *(amino alcohol with an unsaturated hydrocarbon chain)*
Sphingosin *(ungesättigter Aminoalkohol)*

amphipatic [ˌæmfɪˈpæθɪk] adj — amphipatisch
lipophilic [ˌlɪpəˈfɪlɪk] adj — lipophil / fettliebend
hydrophilic adj — hydrophil / wasserliebend
lipophobic adj — lipophob / fettunlöslich
hydrophobic [ˌhaɪdrəˈfəʊbɪk] adj — hydrophob / wasserunlöslich

Lipids

Lipids are a very diverse molecular group; they are broadly defined as lipophilic, naturally-occurring molecules.
Lipide stellen eine sehr breit gefächertet Molekülgruppe dar. Sie werden allgemein als lipophile, natürlich auftretende Moleküle definiert.

They can be classified in several groups, of which the fatty acids, glycerides, phospholipids, sphingolipids, steroids are the most important.
Sie können in verschiedene Guppen eingeordnet werden, von denen die Fettsäuren, Glyzeride, Phospholipide, Sphingolipide und Steroide die wichtigsten sind.

Class	Chemical compounds	Main function
fatty acids	fatty acids	metabolic intermediates
glycerides	glycerol + one to three fatty acids	
monoglycerides	glycerol + one fatty acid	metabolic intermediates
diglycerides	glycerol + two fatty acids	metabolic intermediates
triglycerides = neutral fats	glycerol + three fatty acids	energy storage
phospholipids (e.g. lecitine)	glycerol + phosphat + two fatty acids	building block of biomembranes
sphingolipids (e.g. sphingomyeline)	sphingosin + fatty acid	signal transmission, cell recognition, neural tissue
steroids (e.g. cholesterin)	fused 4 ring-structure	building block of biomembranes, precursor of steroid-hormons

Fatty acids

Common name	Chemical structure
Saturated fatty acids:	
Palmitic acid	$C_{15}H_{31}COOH$
Stearic acid	$C_{17}H_{35}COOH$
Unsaturated fatty acids:	
Oleic acid	$CH_3(CH_2)_7CH=CH(CH_2)_7COOH$
Linoleic acid	$CH_3(CH_2)_4CH=CHCH_2CH=CH(CH_2)_7COOH$
α-Linolenic acid	$CH_3CH_2CH=CHCH_2CH=CHCH_2CH=CH(CH_2)_7COOH$

> Bio-membranes are composed of several classes of lipids (phospholipids, steroids, sphingolipids, glycolipids), and proteins.
> Biomembranen bestehen aus verschiedenen Lipidklassen (Phospholipiden, Steroiden, Sphingolipiden, Glykolipiden) und Proteinen.
> Amphipathic molecules are molecules that have both a hydrophobic and a hydrophilic region.
> Amphipatische Moleküle haben beides, eine hydrophobe (unpolare, wasserabstoßende) und eine hydrophile (polare, wasserliebende) Region.

4.5 Biomembrane   » Abb. 44

Organisation of Biomembranes / Aufbau der Biomembranen

lipid mebrane / lipid bilayer / bio-membrane [ˌbaɪəʊˈmembreɪn] n	Biomembran
monolayer [ˈmɒnəˌleɪə] n	Einzelschicht
bilayer [ˈbaɪˌleɪə] n	Doppelschicht
barrier n	Barriere / Grenzschicht
surface n	Oberfläche

> | separate from sth by sth | von etw. durch etw. trennen |

micelle [maɪˈsel] n	Mizelle
liposome [ˈlɪpəsəʊm] n	Liposom
membrane [ˈmembreɪn] n	Membran
inner membrane	innere Membran
outer membrane	äußere Membran
membrane protein n	Membranprotein
integral membrane protein [ˈɪntɪgrlˌmembreɪnprəʊtiːɪn]	integrales Membranprotein
peripheral membrane protein [pəˈrɪfrəlˌmembreɪnprəʊtiːɪn]	peripheres Membranprotein
transmembrane protein [ˈtrænsmembreɪnprəʊtiːɪn]	Transmembranprotein
glycocalyx [ˈglaɪkəʊkeɪlɪks] n	Glycokalyx
glycoprotein n *(protein with carbohydrate chain)*	Glycoprotein *(Potein mit Kohlenhydratgruppe)*

extracellular matrix (ECM) [ˌekstrəˌseljʊləˈmeɪtrɪks] n	extrazelluläre Matrix
compartment [kəmˈpɑːmənt] n	Kompartiment

4 Cell biology – Cytology › 4.5 Biomembrane

membrane model n	Membranmodell
fluid mosaic model [ˌfluːɪdməʊˌzeɪɪkˈmɒdl] n	Flüssig-Mosaik-Modell
Brownian motion [ˌbraʊnjənˈməʊʃn] n	Brown'sche Molekularbewegung
horizontal movement n	horizontale Bewegung
vertical movement n	vertikale Bewegung
flip over v	sich überschlagen
fusion n	Fusion
fuse v	fusionieren / vereinigen
membrane flow n	Membranfluss
raft n	Floß

» Biomembranes are composed of … | Biomembranen bestehen aus …
The cytoplasma is separated from the extracellular matrix by a membrane.
Das Cytoplasma ist durch eine Membran von der extrazellulären Matrix getrennt.

Transport of molecules within the cell and through biomembranes

diffusion [dɪˈfjuːʒn] n	Diffusion
concentration gradient n	Konzentrationsgradient
osmosis [ˌɒzˈməʊsɪs] n	Osmose
permeable [ˈpɜːmiəbl] adj	durchlässig
impermeable [ɪmˈpɜːmiəbl] adj	undurchlässig
semipermeable [semɪˈpɜːmiəbl] adj	semipermeabel / halb durchlässig
selectively permeable [sɪˈlektɪvliˌpɜːmiəbl]	selektiv permeabel

turgid [ˈtɜːdʒɪd] adj	turgeszent
turgor pressure [ˈtɜːgəˌpreʃə] n	Turgor
hydrostatic pressure [ˌhaɪdrəstætɪkˌpreʃə] n	hydrostatischer Druck
isotonic [ˌaɪsəˈtɒnɪk] adj	isoton
physiological salt solution n	physiologische Kochsalzlösung
hypotonic [haɪpəˈtɒnɪk] adj	hypoton
hypertonic [ˌhaɪpəˈtɒnɪk] adj	hyperton

plasmolysis [plæz'mɒləsɪs] n	Plasmolyse
deplasmolysis [ˌdiːplæz'mɒləsɪs] n	Deplasmolyse
osmotic equation [ɒzˌmɒtɪkɪ'kweɪʒn] n	osmotische Zustandsgleichung / Saugkraftgleichung
osmotic phase diagram n	osmotisches Zustandsdiagramm
wilted [wɪltɪd] adj	welk
red cabbage n	Rotkohl / Blaukraut
kidney ['kɪdni] n	Niere
renal function [ˌriːnl'fʌŋʃn] n	Nierenfunktion
channel protein n	Kanalprotein / Tunnelprotein
carrier protein n	Carrier-Protein / Carrier
facilitated diffusion [fəˌsɪlɪteɪtɪddɪ'fjuːʒn] n	erleichterte Diffusion
active transport n	aktiver Transport
secondary active transport	sekundär aktiver Transport
passive transport n	passiver Transport
symport ['sɪmpɔːt] n	Symport
antiport ['æntɪpɔːt] n	Antiport
direction n	Richtung
energy consumption n	Energieverbrauch
energy independent adj	energieunabhängig
pinocytosis [ˌpaɪnə'saɪteʊsɪs] n	Pinocytose
phagocytosis [ˌfagə'saɪteʊsɪs] n	Phagocytose / Zellfressen
exocytosis [ˌeksəʊ'saɪteʊsɪs] n	Exocytose
endocytosis [ˌendəʊ'saɪteʊsɪs] n	Endocytose
uptake ['ʌpteɪk] n	Aufnahme
take up v	aufnehmen
excretion [ɪk'skriːʃn] n	Exkretion / Ausscheidung
excrete v	ausscheiden
ion pump n	Ionenpumpe
sodium-potassium pump (Na^+/K^+ pump) n	Natrium-Kalium-Pumpe

» Different substances pass through biomembranes by means of different transport mechanisms.
Verschiedene Stoffe passieren die Biomembranen mittels verschiedener Transportmechanismen.

4.6 Analysis of cells

Electron Microscopy » Abb. 8

electron microscope (EM) n	Elektronenmikroskop (EM)
transmission electron microscope (TEM) n	Transmissionselektronenmikroskop (TEM)
scanning electron microscope (SEM) n	Rasterelektronenmikroskop (REM)
scanning tunneling microscope n	Tunnelelektronenmikroskop

fix v	fixieren
dehydrate ['diːhaɪdreɪt] v	entwässern
heavy metal ion n	Schwermetall-Ion
embed [ɪm'bed] v	einbetten
resin ['rezɪn] n	Kunstharz / Harz
paraffine [ˌpærə'fiːn] n	Paraffin
metal grid ['metlˌgrɪd] n	Metallnetz (Objektträger für EM)
freeze-fracturing [ˌfriːz'fræktʃərɪŋ] n	Gefrierbruch
freeze-etching [ˌfriːzetʃɪŋ] n	Gefrierätzen
freeze-etching technique n	Gefrierätztechnik
metallisation BE ['metəlaɪzeɪʃn] / metallization AE n	Metallisierung / Bedampfung mit Metall
metallise BE / metallize AE v	metallisieren / mit Metall bedampfen
magnetic lens [mægˌnetɪk'lenz] n	magnetische Linse
antibody ['æntɪbɒdi] n	Antikörper
ultra-thin section [ˌʌltrəθɪn'sekʃn] n	Ultradünnschnitt
ultramicrotome [ˌʌltrə'maɪkrəʊˌtoʊm] n	Ultramikrotom

» Specimens to be analysed by electron microscopy must be fixed, dehydrated, and "stained".
Proben, die mittels Elektronenmikroskopie untersucht werden sollen, müssen fixiert, dehydriert und "gefärbt" werden.

Cytological methods for research and analysis: centrifugation

centrifugation ['sentrɪfjuːgeɪʃn] n	Zentrifugation
zonal centrifugation	Zonalzentrifugation
centrifuge ['sentrɪfjuːdʒ] v	zentrifugieren
spin down (colloquial) v	abzentrifugieren

» spin at 1200 rpm (revolutions per minute) | mit 1200 U/min (Umdrehungen pro Minute) zentrifugieren

specific gravity n	Dichte
buoyant density [ˌbɔɪənt'densɪti] n	Schwebedichte
buoyant density centrifugation	Dichtegradientenzentrifugation
sedimentation [ˌsedɪmən'teɪʃn] n	Sedimentation / Ablagerung
resuspend [riːsə'spend] v	resuspendieren / wieder aufschlämmen
homogenise BE / homogenize AE [hə'mɒdʒənaɪz] v	homogenisieren
cell debris / debris [sel'deɪbriːs] n	Trümmer
solve v	lösen
decant v	dekantieren / abgießen

> Spin down the debris at 2000 rpm and decant the supernatant into a fresh tube.
> Zentrifugiere(n Sie) die Trümmer bei 2000 U/min ab und dekantiere(n Sie) den Überstand in ein frisches Röhrchen.
> Organells or molecules can be separated by buoyant density centrifugation because of their different sepecific gravities.
> Organellen oder Moleküle können durch Dichtegradientenzentrifugation getrennt werden, weil sie unterschiedliche Dichte besitzen.

Cell culture and cytometry

cell culture n	Zellkultur
incubator ['ɪŋkjʊbeɪtə] n	Inkubator / Brutschrank
suspension culture n	Suspensionskultur
cell suspension n	Zellsuspension
adhesion culture [əd'hiːʒən] n	Adhäsionskultur
monolayer n	Ein-Zellschicht
supernatant [ˌsuːpə'neɪtnt] n	Überstand
sediment ['sedɪmənt] n	Sediment / Ablagerung
pellet ['pelɪt] n	Pellet
homogenate [hɒ'mɒdʒɪnɪt] n	Homogenat
homogenise BE / homogenize AE [hə'mɒdʒənaɪz] v	homogenisieren
homogeneous [ˌhɒmə'dʒiːnɪəs] adj	homogen
growth medium, pl growth media n	Kulturmedium / Nährflüssigkeit
petri dish ['petriˌdɪʃ] n	Petrischale
coating ['kəʊtɪŋ] n	Beschichtung
cytometer [saɪte'mitə] n	Cytometer
flow cytometry	Durchflusscytometrie
cell sorter n	Zellsortierer / Zellsorter

4 Cell biology – Cytology › 4.6 Analysis of cells

FACS (fluorecence activated cell sorter) n
fraction ['frækʃn] n

FACS (Fluoreszensaktivierter Zellsortierer)
Fraktion

» Different types of cells have specific growth media requirements.
Verschiedene Zelltypen haben unterschiedliche Ansprüche an das Kulturmedium.
A cytometer is used to analyse cells or other microscopic particles suspended in a stream of fluid.
Man verwendet ein Cytometer, um Zellen oder andere mikroskopische Partikel, die in einem Flüssigkeitsstrom suspendiert sind, zu analysieren.

Autoradiography, in situ methods, and immunostaining

autoradiography n
radioactivity n
radioactive adj
uptake n
take up v
accumulation [əˌkjuːmjə'leɪʃn] n
accumulate v
locate v
photographic emulsion
 [ˌfəʊtəgræfɪkɪ'mʌlʃn] / film n
silver bromide [ˌsɪlvə'brəʊmaɪd] n
silver grain n

Autoradiografie
Radioaktivität
radioaktiv
Aufnahme
aufnehmen
Anreicherung
anreichern
lokalisieren
fotografische Emulsion / Film

Silberbromid
Silberkorn / Silberkörnchen

» develop a film | einen Film entwickeln

expose (sth to sth) v
exposition n
antibody n
 secondary antibody
specific adj
link (with) v
fluorescent dye [flɔː'resntˌdaɪ] n
detection n
in situ [ˌɪn'sɪtjuː] adv (lit.: in place)

enzyme ['enzaɪm] n
substrate ['sʌbstreɪt] n

(etw. etw.) aussetzen
Exposition
Antikörper
 Zweit-Antikörper
spezifisch
koppeln (an)
fluoreszierender Farbstoff
Nachweis
in situ (wörtlich: an Ort und Stelle, am Platz)

Enzym
Substrat

Electophoresis

electrophoresis [ˌɪlektrəfə'riːsɪs] n	Elektrophorese
electrophoresis buffer n	Elektrophoresepuffer
gel electrophoresis	Gel-Elektrophorese
paper electrophoresis	Papier-Elektrophorese
matrix n	Matrix
pore [pɔː] n	Pore
gel pocket [ˈdʒelˈpɒkɪt] n	Auftragstasche
lane [leɪn] n	Spur
band n	Bande
electrode [ɪˈlektrəʊd] n	Elektrode
anode [ˈænəʊd] n	Anode
cathode [ˈkæθəʊd] n	Kathode
anion [ˈænaɪən] n	Anion
cation [ˈkætaɪən] n	Kation
electric(al) field n	elektrisches Feld
migrate [maɪˈgreɪt] v	wandern
separate v	trennen
charge [ˈtʃɑːdʒ] n	Ladung
size n	Größe
shape n	Form
denature [ˌdiːˈneɪtʃə] v	denaturieren
detergent [dɪˈtɜːdʒnt] n	Detergenz

» Molecules can be separated by electrophoresis as they migrate at different speed in the electric field, depending on their size, shape, and charge.
Moleküle können durch Elektrophorese getrennt werden, da sie abhängig von ihrer Größe, Form und Ladung unterschiedlich schnell im elektrischen Feld wandern.

5 Genetics

5.1 Mendelian and Classical Genetics

Mendelian Genetics

gene [dʒiːn] n	Gen
genetic adj	genetisch
genetic trait	genetisches Merkmal
genetically adv	genetisch
character n	Merkmal
phenotype [ˈfiːnətaɪp] n	Phänotyp

5 Genetics › 5.1 Mendelian and Classical Genetics

variation n	Variation / Abweichung
vary ['veəri] v	variieren / abweichen / schwanken
modify v	modifizieren
environment n	Umwelt
environmental adj	umweltbedingt
environmental factor	Umweltfaktor

round (R) adj	rund (R)
wrinkled (r) ['rɪŋkld] adj	runzlig (r)
capital letter / capital / upper case letter n	Großbuchstabe
lower case letter / minuscule ['mɪnəskjuːl] / lower case character n	Kleinbuchstabe
genotype ['dʒiːnətaɪp] n	Genotyp
dominant adj	dominant
recessive adj	rezessiv
intermediate adj	intermediär
polygenic [ˌpɒlɪ'dʒiːnɪk] adj *(several genes influence one trait)*	polygen *(mehrere Gene sind für ein Merkmal verantwortlich)*
heterozygous [ˌhetrə'zaɪgəs] adj	heterozygot / mischerbig
homozygous [ˌhɒmə'zaɪgəs] adj	homozygot / reinerbig
true breeding adj	reinerbig
mixed breeding adj	mischerbig
hybrid ['haɪbrɪd] n	Hybride / Mischling

》 Dominant genes are represented by capital letters.
Dominante Gene werden mit Großbuchstaben gekennzeichnet.

stem n	Stiel / Stängel
pod [pɒd] n	Hülse
narrowed ['nærəʊd] adj	eingeengt / eingeschnürt
stamen ['steɪmən] n	Staubblatt
pollen ['pɒlən] n	Pollen
pollination n	Bestäubung
self pollination	Selbstbestäubung
cross pollination	Fremdbestäubung
pollinate v	bestäuben
carpel ['kɑːpel] n	Fruchtblatt
stigma n	Narbe
style n	Griffel
ovary ['əʊvri] n	Fruchtknoten
pistil ['pɪstɪl] n	Stempel

Mendelian laws / Mendel's laws	Mendelsche Regeln / Mendelsche Gesetze
1st / 2nd / 3rd Mendelian law/principle	1. / 2. / 3. Mendelsche Regel/Gesetz

principle of uniformity / law of uniformity / principle of dominance / law of dominance n
    Uniformitätsregel / Uniformitätsgesetz

law of segregation n
    Spaltungsregel

law of independent assortment [ˌlɔːəvɪndɪˌpendəntəˈsɔːtmənt]
    Unabhängigkeitsregel

Punnet square [ˈpʌnɪtˌskweə] n
    Punnet-Quadrat / Rekombinationsquadrat

cross / cross-breeding n   Kreuzung
crossbreed v   kreuzen
crossing scheme n   Kreuzungsschema
  monohybrid cross [ˌmɒnəʊhaɪbrɪdˈkrɒs]
    monohybride Kreuzung
  dihybrid cross [ˌdaɪhaɪbrɪdˈkrɒs]
    dihybride Kreuzung
  backcross
    Rückkreuzung *(Kreuzung von heterozygoten Nachkommen mit dem homozygot rezessiven Elternteil)*

intercross n
    Geschwisterkreuzung *(Kreuzung von heterozygoten Geschwistern untereinander)*

incross n   Inzucht

offspring, *pl* offspring n   Nachkomme(n)
sibling, *pl* siblings n   Geschwister
ancestor [ˈænsestə] n   Vorfahr
parents n pl   Eltern
parental generation (P) n   Elterngeneration (P)
filial generation [ˌfɪliəldʒenəˈreɪʃn] n   Filialgeneration
  first filial generation (F1)   erste Filialgeneration (F1)
  second filial generation (F2)   zweite Filialgeneration (F2)
hybrid n   Hybride / Mischling

allele [əˈliːl] n   Allel
  dominant allele   dominantes Allel
  recessive allele   rezessives Allel
meiosis [maɪˈəʊsɪs] n   Meiose

5 Genetics › 5.1 Mendelian and Classical Genetics

gamete ['gæmiːt] / germ cell n	Gamet (Pl. Gameten) / Geschlechtszellen / Keimzellen
zygote ['zaɪgəʊt] n	Zygote
radish ['rædɪʃ] n	Radieschen
Marvel of Peru n	Wunderblume
petunia [pɪ'tjuːnɪə] n	Petunie
crown n	Kamm *(bei Vögeln)*
feathers / plumage ['pluːmɪdʒ] n	Gefieder
mane [meɪn] n	Mähne
coat [kəʊt] n	Fell
coat colour	Fellfarbe
spotted adj	gefleckt
mottled ['mɒtld] adj	gesprenkelt
agouti [ə'guːti] adj	agouti *(farblich gebänderte Haare)*
albino [æl'biːnəʊ] adj	albino
albino n	Albino
wildtype adj	wildtyp(artig)
wildtype n	Wildtyp
horn n	Horn

»
Genetic traits can be classified as …	Genetische Merkmale können als …
… dominant (the dominant allele is always expressed).	… dominant (werden immer sichtbar) …
…recessive (the recessive trait is subordinate to the dominant trait).	… rezessiv (das rezessive Merkmal wird vom dominanten Allel unterdrückt)
… intermediate (a mixed phenotype becomes visible).	… intermediär (ein gemischter Phänotyp wird sichtbar) …
	… klassifiziert werden.

Extrachromosomal inheritance

plastid ['plæstɪd] n	Plastid (Pl. Plastiden)
chloroplast ['klɒrəplɑːst] n	Chloroplast
maternal [mə'tɜːnl] adj	maternell / maternal / mütterlich
paternal [pə'tɜːnl] adj	paternell / paternal / väterlich
green-white mottled adj	grün-weiß panaschiert
pollinate v	bestäuben
chromosome ['krəʊməsəʊm] n	Chromosom
extrachromosomal adj	extrachromosomal
extranuclear adj	außerhalb des Zellkerns

inheritance [ɪnˈherɪtns] n	Vererbung
plasmatic inheritance	plasmatische Vererbung

Genetic recombination in prokaryotes

recombination n	Rekombination / Neukombination
genetic recombination	genetische Rekombination
prokaryote [prəʊˈkærɪɒt] n	Prokaryot / Prokaryont
conjugation [ˌkɒndʒʊˈgeɪʃn] n (direct transfer of DNA from one bacterium into another)	Konjugation (direkter DNA-Transfer von einem Bakterium in ein anderes)
fertility factor [fəˈtɪlətɪˌfæktə] n	Fertilitätsfaktor
F-plasmid (F$^+$) n	F-Plasmid (F$^+$)
donor [ˈdəʊnə] n	Donor / Spender
recipient n	Empfänger / Rezipient
cytoplasmic channel [ˌsaɪtəplæzmɪkˈtʃænl] n	Cytoplasmabrücke
disrupt [dɪsˈrʌpt] v	abbrechen / unterbrechen

» | high frequency of recombination (Hfr) | hohe Rekombinationsfrequenz (Hfr) |

transformation n (uptake of DNA)	Transformation (Aufnahme von DNA)
uptake n	Aufnahme
take up v	aufnehmen
integrate v	integrieren
incorporate v	einbauen
temporary adj	vorübergehend
transduction [trænsˈdʌkʃn] n (DNA-transfer through viruses)	Transduktion (DNA-Transfer durch Viren)
phage [feɪdʒ] n (viruses that attack bacteria)	Phage (Viren, die Bakterien angreifen)
bacteriophage [bækˈtɪəriəfeɪdʒ] n	Bakteriophage

Sex determination

sex n	Geschlecht
sex determination n	Geschlechtsbestimmung / Geschlechtsdetermination
male adj	männlich
female adj	weiblich
sex chromosome n	Geschlechtschromosom

5 Genetics › 5.1 Mendelian and Classical Genetics

SRY gene (sex determing region on the Y-chromosome) n
TDF (testis determining factor) n
heterogametic [ˌhetrəʊgəˈmetɪk] adj
homogametic [ˌhɒməgəˈmetɪk] adj
temperature dependent adj
social adj
haplodiploid system [ˌhæpləˈdɪplɔɪdˌsɪstəm] n
hymenoptera [ˌhaɪmɪˈnɒptrə] n (bees, wasps, ants)
XX-X0 system n
hermaphrodite [hɜːˈmæfrədaɪt] n
sexually mature adj
proboscis [prəˈbɒsɪs] n

SRY-Gen (Geschlechtsbestimmende Region auf dem Y-Chromosom)
TDF (Tesitis [Hoden] bestimmender Faktor)
heterogametisch (XY)
homogametisch (XX)
temperaturabhängig
sozial
Diplo-Haplo-Mechanismus

Hautflügler (Bienen, Wespen, Ameisen)
XX-X0-System
Hermaphrodit / Zwitter
geschlechtsreif
Rüssel

Sex determination

System	Charakteristics	Organism
XX/XY	female (f): XX male (m): XY	**mammals, drosophila** Säugetiere, Drosophila
XX/X0	female (f): XX male (m): X0	**crickets, grasshoppers and some other insects** Grillen, Grashüpfer und einige andere Insekten
haplo-diploid	f: diploid m: haploid	**bees, ants, wasps** Bienen, Ameisen, Wespen
temperature	f: egg incubation below and above a critical teperature m: egg incubation within a critical teperature	**alligators, snapping turtles** Alligatoren, Schnappschildkröten
	f: egg incubation above 30°C m: egg incubation below 25°C	**European pond turtle** Europäische Teichschildkröte
social	f: free living larvae m: larvae living on the proboscis of a female	**Bonellia (an echiuroid worm)** Bonellia (Echiura, Igelwurm)

» In most cases sex determination is genetic: Males and females have different alleles or different genes (often located on sex chromosomes) that specify their sexual development.
In den meisten Fällen ist die Geschlechtsdetermination genetisch: Männchen und Weibchen haben unterschiedliche Allele oder unterschiedliche Gene (oft auf Geschlechtschromosomen), die ihre geschlechtliche Entwicklung bestimmen.

In mammals, including humans, males are heterogametic (XY), whereas females are the homogametic sex (XX).
Bei Säugetieren, inklusive der Menschen, sind die Männchen heterogametisch (XY), während Weibchen das homogametische Geschlecht (XX) darstellen.
In birds and butterflies and many reptiles females are heterogametic (ZW) and males are homogametic (ZZ).
Bei Vögeln, Schmetterlingen und vielen Reptilienarten sind die Weibchen heterogametisch (ZW) und die Männchen homogametisch (ZZ).
In some cases environmental factors (e.g. temperature) or social factors (e.g. relative body size) are sex determining.
In einigen Fällen sind Umweltfaktoren (z.B. Temperatur) oder soziale Faktoren (z.B. relative Körpergröße) geschlechtsbestimmend.

Genetic mapping

genetic map n	genetische Karte
linkage analysis n	Kopplungsanalyse
fruit fly n	Fruchtfliege
Drosophila melanogaster [drəˈsɒfɪləmelənəˌgæstə] n	Drosophila melanogaster
linkage group n	Kopplungsgruppe
chiasma [kaɪˈæzmə], *pl* chiasmata [kaɪˈæzmətə] n	Chiasma *(Pl. Chiasmata)*
chiasmatic adj	chiasmatisch
crossing-over n	Überkreuzung
crossover value n	Austauschwert
centiMorgan (cM) [ˈsentɪˌmɔːgn] n	CentiMorgan (cM)
genetic distance n	genetische Entfernung
genetic map n	genetische Karte
coupled / linked adj	gekoppelt
sex-linked adj	geschlechtsgekoppelt
three-point analysis n	Dreipunktanalyse / Dreifaktor(en)kreuzung
complementation analysis n	Komplementationsanalyse
bristle [ˈbrɪsl] n	Borste
wing n	Flügel
curled / curly adj	gelockt
ebony [ˈebni] n	Ebenholz
claret [ˈklærət] adj	weinrot
dachshund [ˈdæksnd] n	Dackel
hump backed / humpy [ˈhʌmpi] adj	buckelig

5 Genetics › 5.1 Mendelian and Classical Genetics

bar n
shaven, shaved adj
cinnabar (red) ['sɪnəbɑː] n
vermil(l)ion [vəˈmɪljən] adj
lobe [ləʊb] n *(lobe shaped eyes of Drosophila)*
lethal [ˈliːθl] adj
lethal factor n

Stab / Stange
rasiert
Zinnober(rot)
zinnoberrot
Lappen *(gelappte Augen bei Drosophila)*
tödlich
Letalfaktor *(Allel, das bei homozygotem Vorliegen den Organismus nicht überlebensfähig macht)*

» A linkage group equates to / represents a chromosome.
Eine Kopplungsgruppe entspricht einem Chromosom.

Commonly used mutations in Drosophila Genetics

Mutation and abbreviation	Chromosome	Description	Beschreibung
Bar (B)	I	bar shaped eyes	stabförmige Augen
black (b)	II	black body colour	schwarz (Körperfarbe)
bobbed (bb)	I	shorter bristles	kürzere Borsten
brown (bw)	II	brown eyes	braun (Augenfarbe)
cinnabar (cn)	II	eyes like cinnabar	Zinnoberrot (Augenfarbe)
curled (cu)	III	curled wings	nach oben gebogene (wörtlich: gelockte) Flügel
Curly (Cy)	II	curled wings	nach oben gebogene (wörtlich: gelockte) Flügel
dachs (d)	II	shorter legs, like a dachshund	kurze Beine, wie ein Dackel
ebony (e)	III	darker, ebony-like body colour	dunkler, ebenholzfarbener Körper
eyeless (ey)	IV	missing eyes	fehlende Augen
Lobe (L)	II	lobed eyes	gelappte Augen
roughoid (ru)	III	rough eyes	raue Augen
sepia (se)	III	sepia eyes	sepia (dunkle Augenfarbe)
shaven (sv)	IV	without bristles	rasiert, fehlende Borsten
vermillion (v)	I	light red eyes	hellrote, zinnoberrote Augen
vestigial (vg)	II	short wings	stummelflügelig (Flügelmutante)
white (w)	I	white eyes	weiß (Augenfarbe)
yellow (y)	I	yellow body colour	Gelber Körper

Dominant genes are represented by capital letters.
Dominante Gene werden mit Großbuchstaben gekennzeichnet.

Breeding

breeding n	Zucht / Züchtung
animal breeding	Tierzucht
plant breeding	Pflanzenzucht
agriculture n	Landwirtschaft
harvest n	Ernte
harvest v	ernten
yield n	Ertrag

animal husbandry [ˌænɪməlˈhʌzbəndrɪ] n	Tierhaltung
selection n	Auswahl / Selektion
select v	auswählen
cross v	kreuzen
half-breed / hybrid / mongrel [ˈmʌŋgrl] n	Mischling
domestication [dəˌmestɪˈkeɪʃn] n	Domestizierung / Domestikation
domesticate v	domestizieren
livestock n	Vieh / Nutztiere
cattle n pl	Rinder / Vieh
poultry [ˈpəʊltri] n	Geflügel
rear [rɪə] v	aufziehen / züchten
fibre *BE* [ˈfaɪbə] / fiber *AE* n	Faser
dairy n	Molkerei
dairy product n	Molkereiprodukt

horticulture [ˈhɔːtɪkʌltʃə] n	Gartenbau
mildew resistance [ˈmɪldjuːrɪˌzɪstns] n	Mehltau-Resistenz
tolerance n	Toleranz
arid-tolerant [ˈærɪdˌtɒlrnt] adj	trockentolerant
frost-tolerant adj	frosttolerant
hardy [ˈhɑːdi] adj	winterhart
high-yielding adj	ertragsreich
trait n	Eigenschaft
desirable trait	erwünschte Eigenschaft
adverse trait	unerwünschte Eigenschaft

cultivate v	anbauen
crop n	Feldfrucht / Kulturpflanze
cereal [ˈsɪəriəl] n	Getreide
legume [ˈlegjuːm] n	Hülsenfrucht

crop wild relative (CWR) n	wild wachsende Verwandte *(von domestizierten Pflanzen)*

5 Genetics › 5.2 Cytogenetics

gene pool n
landrace ['lænd‚reɪs] n

cultigen ['kʌltɪdʒen] n

GMO (genetically modified organism) n

Genpool
Landrasse *(besondere Anpassung durch natürlichen Selektionsdruck)*
Züchtung *(durch züchterische Selektion entstanden)*
GMO (genetisch modifizierter Organismus)

»	tolerance to	... aridity ... humidity ... high temperature ... frost	Toleranz gegen- über	... Trockenheit ... Feuchtigkeit ... hohen Temperaturen ... Frost

5.2 Cytogenetics

Mitosis » Abb. 45

cytogenetics n
cell n
  cell cycle
cytokinesis [‚saɪtəkaɪ'niːsɪs] / cell division n
mitosis [maɪ'təʊsɪs] n
mitotic adj
stage n
phase n

Cytogenetik / Zellgenetik
Zelle
  Zellzyklus
Cytokinese / Zellteilung

Mitose
mitotisch
Stadium
Phase

prophase ['prəʊfeɪz] n
metaphase ['metəfeɪz] n
anaphase ['ænəfeɪz] n
telophase ['teləfeɪz] n
interphase ['ɪntəfeɪz] n
G_1-Phase n
S-phase n
G_2-Phase n
G_0-Phase n

Prophase
Metaphase
Anaphase
Telophase
Interphase
G_1-Phase
S-Phase
G_2-Phase
G_0-Phase

replicate v
duplicate v
DNA synthesis n
condense [kən'dens] v
visible adj

replizieren
duplizieren
DNA-Synthese
kondensieren
sichtbar

nuclear envelope [ˌnjuːklɪərˈenvələʊp] n	Kernhülle
disintegrate v	auflösen
spindle apparatus / mitotic spindle n	Spindelapparat
mitotic spindle	Spindelapparat *(während einer Mitose)*
meiotic spindle	Spindelapparat *(während einer Meiose)*
equatorial plate / equatorial plane n	Äquatorialplatte / Äquatorialebene
chromatin [ˈkrəʊmətɪn] n	Chromatin
chromosome [ˈkrəʊməsəʊm] n	Chromosom
chromatid [ˈkrəʊmətɪd] n	Chromatid *(Pl. Chromatiden)*
sister chromatid	Schwesterchromatid
2n n *(diploid)*	2n *(diploid)*
2C n *(chromosome with two sister chromatids)*	2C *(Chromosom mit zwei Schwesterchromatiden)*
centromere [ˈsentrəmɪə] n	Zentromer / Centromer
kinetochore [kɪˈnetəkɔː] n	Kinetochor *(Spindelfaseransatzstelle)*
pole n	Pol
daughter cell n	Tochterzelle
cleavage furrow n	Teilungsfurche

Cell cycle » Abb. 45–46

Stage / Phase	Description	Beschreibung
Interphase		
G1-phase	Cells grow.	Zellen wachsen.
S-phase	DNA replicates.	DNA wird repliziert (verdoppelt sich).
G2-phase	Cells grow further and prepare for mitosis.	Zellen wachsen weiter und bereiten sich auf die Mitose vor.
Mitosis		
prophase	The chromatin is condensed and the chromosomes become visible.	Das Chromatin verdichtet sich und die Chromosomen werden sichtbar.
metaphase	The spindle apparatus pulls the chromosomes into the equatorial plane.	Der Spindelapparat zieht die Chromosomen in die Äquatorialebene.
anaphase	The chromatids are separated and pulled to the poles.	Die Chromatiden werden getrennt und zu den Polen gezogen.
telophase	The mitotic spindle breaks down, chromatin decondenses, the new nuclei reassemble and the cells divide.	Der Spindelapparat löst sich auf, das Chromatin dekondensiert, die neuen Kerne bilden sich und die Zellen teilen sich.
G0-phase	Cells that do not divide further, differentiate into a permanent tissue cell.	Zellen, die sich nicht weiter teilen, bilden sich in eine Dauergewebezelle um.

5 Genetics › 5.2 Cytogenetics

cell plate n	Zellplatte
differentiate [ˌdɪfˈrenʃieɪt] v	differenzieren
permanent tissue cell n	Dauergewebezelle

Analysis of a karyogram

centromeric adj	zentromerisch
metacentric [ˌmetəˈsentrɪk] adj	metazentrisch
submetacentric	submetazentrisch
acrocentric [ˌækrəʊˈsentrɪk] adj	akrozentrisch
telomere [ˈteləˌmɜː] n	Telomer
telomeric adj	telomerisch

karyotype [ˈkærɪətaɪp] n	Karyotyp
karyogram [ˈkærɪəgræm] n	Karyogramm
colchicine [ˈkɒltʃɪsiːn] n	Colchizin
microtubule [ˌmaɪkrəʊˈtjuːbjuːl] n	Mikrotubulus
tubulin [ˈtjuːbʊlɪn] n	Tubulin
spindle apparatus / mitotic spindle n	Spindelapparat
spindle fibre n	Spindelfaser
arrest (sth) v	(etw.) anhalten
hypotonic [haɪpəˈtɒnɪk] adj	hypoton
distilled water [dɪˌstɪldˈwɔːtə] n	destilliertes Wasser
swell v	schwellen / quellen
centrifuge [ˈsentrɪfjuːdʒ] v	zentrifugieren
fix v	fixieren
glacial acetic acid [ˌgleɪʃləˌsiːtɪkˈæsɪd] n	Eisessig
methanol [ˈmeθənɒl] n	Methanol
burst v	aufplatzen
stain v	färben
Giemsa-staining [giːˈemzəˌsteɪnɪŋ] n	Giemsa-Färbung
G-banding n	G-Bänderung
R-banding n	R-Bänderung
FISH n (fluorescence "in situ" hybridisation)	FISH (Fluoreszenz „in situ" Hybridisierung)

autosome [ˈɔːtəsəʊm] n	Autosom (alle Chromosomen, die nicht zu den Geschlechtschromosomen zählen)
sex-chromosome / gonosome [ˈgɒnəsəʊm] n	Geschlechtschromosom / Gonosom
sex-linked adj	geschlechtsgekoppelt
homologous [həˈmɒləgəs] adj	homolog

size n	Größe
shape n	Form
pattern n	Muster
banding pattern	Bandenmuster
classify n	klassifizieren / sortieren
NOR (nucleolus organizing region)	NOR (Nukleolus organisierende Region)
haploid ['hæplɔɪd] adj	haploid
diploid ['dɪplɔɪd] adj	diploid
polyploid adj	polyploid
aberration [ˌæbəˈreɪʃn] n	Abweichung / Aberration
numerical aberration	numerische Aberration
aneuploidy [ˌænjuːplɔɪdi] n	Aneuploidie *(einzelne Chromosomen zuviel/zuwenig)*
trisomy ['trɪsəmɪ] n	Trisomie *(XXX)*
monosomy [məˈnɒsəmɪ] n	Monosomie *(XO)*
translocation n	Translokation

Analysis of polytene chromosomes

polytene chromosome [ˌpɒlitiːnˈkrəʊməsəʊm] n	Polytänchromosom
giant chromosome n	Riesenchromosom
salivary gland [sæˈlɪvrɪˌglænd] n	Speicheldrüse
chironomid [kaɪˈrɒnəmɪd] n	Chironomus / Chironomide / Zuckmücke
replication n	Replikation
round of replication	Replikationsrunde
subsequent adj	folgend
band n	Bande
banding pattern	Bandenmuster
puff [pʌf] n	Puff *(wörtl. Bausch; wird im Deutschen um Verwechselungen mit „Bordell" zu vermeiden auch [paff] ausgesprochen)*
puff up v	aufbauschen
developmental stage n	Entwicklungsstadium *(Pl. –stadien)*
^{3}H n *(tritium, a radioactive hydrogene isotope)*	^{3}H *(Tritium, ein radioaktives Wasserstoffisotop)*
radioactively marked / radioactively labelled	radioaktiv markiert
(r)NTP (ribonucleotide triphosphate) [ˌraɪbəˌnjuːklɪətaɪdtraɪˈfɒsfeɪt] n	(r)NPT (Ribonukleotid-Triphosphat)

5 Genetics › 5.2 Cytogenetics

adenosine triphosphate (ATP) [əˌdenəsiːntraɪˈfɒsfeɪt] n	Adenosin-Triphosphat (ATP)
cytidine triphosphate (CTP) [ˌsaɪtɪdiːntraɪˈfɒsfeɪt] n	Cytidin-Triphosphat (CTP)
guanosine triphosphate (GTP) [ˌgwɑːnəsiːnˈtraɪfɒsfeɪt] n	Guanosin-Triphosphat (GTP)
uridine triphosphate (UTP) [ˌjʊərɪdiːntraɪˈfɒsfeɪt] n	Uridin-Triphosphat (UTP)
autoradiography n	Autoradiografie
transcriptional adj	transkriptionell / Transkriptions-
condense v	kondensieren
condensed adj	kondensiert

Meiosis » Abb. 46

meiosis [maɪˈəʊsɪs] n	Meiose
meiosis I	erste meiotische Teilung / Reifeteilung I
meiosis II	zweite meiotische Teilung / Reifeteilung II
reductional division n	Reduktionsteilung
separation step n	Reduktionsschritt / Trennstufe
germline [ˈdʒɜːmˌlaɪn] n	Keimbahn
reproductive cell / germline cell	Fortpflanzungszelle / Keimbahnzelle
gamete / germ cell	Gamete / Keimzelle
halve (sth) [hɑːv] v	(etw.) halbieren
half, pl halves n	Hälfte
haploid [ˈhæplɔɪd] adj	haploid
diploid [ˈdɪplɔɪd] adj	diploid
heterozygous [ˌhetrəˈzaɪgəs] adj	heterozygot / mischerbig
homozygous [ˌhɒməˈzaɪgəs] adj	homozygot / reinerbig
hemizygous [ˌhemɪˈzaɪgəs] adj	hemizygot

crossing over n	Überkreuzung
chiasma, pl chiasmata n	Chiasma (Pl. Chiasmata)
recombination n	Rekombination
recombine v	rekombinieren
recombination nodule n	Rekombinationsknoten
exchange v	austauschen
swap [swɒp] v	tauschen
genetic material n	Erbgut
tetrad [ˈtetræd] n	Tetrade
sever [ˈsevə] v	sich trennen

shuffle v	mischen
disintegrate v	desintegrieren / auflösen
divide v	(sich) teilen
cytokinesis [ˌsaɪtəkaɪˈniːsɪs] / cell division n	Cytokinese / Zellteilung

sexual reproduction n	geschlechtliche Fortpflanzung
asexual reproduction n	ungeschlechtliche Fortpflanzung
copulation [ˌkɒpjəˈleɪʃn] / mating [ˈmeɪtɪŋ] n	Kopulation / Begattung
copulate / mate v	kopulieren / begatten
gonad [ˈgəʊnæd] n	Gonade / Keimdrüse
ovary, pl ovaries n	Eierstock / Ovar
testicle [ˈtestɪkl], pl testicles, testes n	Hoden
spore [spɔː] n	Spore
oocyte [ˈəʊəsaɪt], pl oocytes n	Oocyte
ovum [ˈəʊvəm], pl ova / egg cell n	Eizelle / Ei
spermatozoa [ˌspɜːmətəˈzəʊə] / sperm / sperm cell n	Spermatoza (Pl.) / Spermium / Sperminenzelle
sperm head n	Spermienkopf
sperm tail n	Spermienschwanz
acrosome [ˈækrəsəʊm] n (part of the sperm head)	Akrosom (Teil des Spermiumkopfes)
insemination [ɪnˌsemɪˈneɪʃn] n	Insemination / Befruchtung / Besamung

fertilise BE / fertilize AE n	befruchten
fertilisation BE / fertilization AE n	Befruchtung
internal fertilisation n	innere Befruchtung
external fertilisation n	äußere Befruchtung
zygote [ˈzaɪgəʊt] n	Zygote
cortical reaction [ˌkɔːtɪklriˈækʃn] / zona reaction [ˌzəʊnəriˈækʃn] n	Rindenreaktion
impermeable [ɪmˈpɜːmiəbl] adj	undurchlässig
inhibit v	unterdrücken / verhindern

gametangium [ˌgæmɪˈtændʒɪəm], pl gametangia n	Gametangium (Pl. Gametangia)
alternation of generations n	Generationswechsel
hydrozoan [ˌhaɪdrəˈzəʊən] n	Hydrozoe (Pl. Hydrozoen)
cnidarian [naɪˈdeərɪən] n	Cnidarie (Pl. Cnidarien) / Nesseltier
jellyfish / medusa [mɪˈdjuːzə] n	Qualle / Meduse
polyp [ˈpɒlɪp] n	Polyp
sporophyte [ˈspɒrəfaɪt] n	Sporophyt
sporangium [spəˈrændʒɪəm], pl sporangia n	Sproangium

5 Genetics › 5.2 Cytogenetics

sorus [ˈsɔːrəs], *pl* sori n	Sorus *(Pl. Sori)* / Sporenkapselhäufchen
prothallium [prəʊˈθælɪəm] n	Prothallium
gametophyte [gəˈmiːtəʊfaɪt] n	Gametophyt
fern [fɜːn] n	Farn
gymnosperm [ˈdʒɪmnəˌspɜːm] n	Gymnosperme / Nacktsamer
conifer [ˈkɒnɪfə] n	Konifere / Nadelbaum
cone [kəʊn] n	Zapfen
angiosperm [ˈændʒɪəˌspɜːm] n	Angiosperme / Bedecktsamer
embryo sac cell n	Embryosackzelle
stamen n	Staubblatt
carpel n	Fruchtblatt
seedling n	Keimling
diplophase (2n) [ˈdɪpləʊfeɪz] / diploid phase n	Diplophase (2n)
haplophase (1n) [ˈhæpləfeɪz] / haploid phase n	Haplophase (1n)

Meiosis I

Stage / Phase Meiosis I	Description	Beschreibung
prophase I	Chromatin begins to condense and the homologous chromosomes consisting of two chromatids each begin to pair, thus forming tetrads. Crossing over occurs and chromatids swap genetic material.	Das Chromatin verdichtet sich und die homologen Chromosomen, die aus je zwei Chromatiden bestehen, beginnen sich zu paaren und formen so Tetraden. Crossing over findet statt und die Chromatiden tauschen genetisches Material aus.
metaphase I	The meiotic spindle pulls the tetrads into the equatorial plane. Crossing over becomes visible as chiasmata or recombination nodules.	Der Spindelapparat zieht die Tetraden in die Äquatorialebene. Crossing-over werden als Chiasmata oder Rekombinationsknoten sichtbar.
anaphase I	Chiasmata are severed. Chromosome pairs are separated and whole chromosomes are pulled to the opposite poles. This way the genetic information is distributed by chance to the two daughter cells.	Die Chiasmata werden getrennt. Die homologen Chromosomenpaare trennen sich und ganze Chromosomen werden zu den gegenüberliegenden Polen gezogen. Auf diese Weise wird das Genom zufällig auf die beiden Tochterzellen verteilt.
telophase I	Two new nuclear envelopes form around the chromosomes. The cells which are now haploid (1n) but still have two chromatids (2c) per chromosome divide.	Zwei neue Kernhüllen bilden sich um die Chromosomen. Die Zellen, die nun haploid (1n) sind, aber immer noch noch zwei Chromatiden (2c) pro Chromosom haben, teilen sich.

Meiosis II

prophase II	The chromosomes condense again and the nuclear envelope disintegrates.	Die Chromosomen kondensieren nochmals und die Kernhülle löst sich auf.
metaphase II	The chromosomes arrange in the equatorial plane with the help of the spindle apparatus.	Die Chromosomen arrangieren sich mit Hilfe des Spindelapparats in der Äquatorialebene.
anaphase II	The sister chromatids detach from each other at the centromer and are pulled towards the opposite cell poles.	Die Schwesterchromatiden lösen sich von einander und werden zu den gegenüberliegenden Zellpolen gezogen.
telophase II	New nuclear envelopes form around the chromatids (1n, 1c). Cytokinesis follows.	Die Kernhüllen bilden sich um die Chromatiden (1n, 1c). Die Cytokinese erfolgt.

» Without meiosis there would be no sexual reproduction.
Ohne Meiose gäbe es keine geschlechtliche Fortpflanzung.
Meiosis is indispensable to halve the number of chromosomes in a diploid organism, to recombine genetic information, and to produce germ cells.
Die Meiose is unabdingbar, um die Anzahl der Chromosomen eines diploiden Organismus zu halbieren, die genetische Information zu durchmischen und um Keimzellen zu bilden.
Meiosis takes place in two major separation steps, called Meiosis I and Meiosis II.
Die Meiose besteht aus zwei bedeutenden Reduktionsschritten, die als 1. und 2. meiotische Teilung bezeichnet werden.

Subdivision of prophase I

Prophase I is subdivided into …
Leptotene (chromosomes start to condense)
Zygotene (chromosomes pair)
Pachytene (crossing over takes place)
Diplotene (homologous chromosomes separate a bit, but remain attached to each other at the sites of crossing over)
Diakinesis (nuclear envelope disintegrates)

Prophase I wird unterteilt in …
Leptotän (Chromosomen kondensieren)
Zygotän (Chromosomen paaren sich)
Pachytän (Crossing over finden statt)
Diplotän (homologe Chromosomen trennen sich ein bisschen, bleiben aber noch an den Stellen der Crossing over zusammen)
Diakinese (Kernhülle löst sich auf)

5.3 Human genetics

Inheritable traits and diseases

inheritable adj	vererbbar
hereditary disease [hɪˌredɪtrɪdɪ'ziːz] n	Erbkrankheit
trait n	Merkmal
congenital disease [kənˌdʒenɪtldɪ'ziːz] n	angeborene Krankheit
congenital disorder n	angeborene Störung
family tree / pedigree ['pedɪgriː] n	Stammbaum
pedigree analysis	Stammbaumanalyse
X-chromosome-linked adj	X-chromosomal(-gekoppelt)
autosome n	Autosom
gonosome n	Gonosom
autosomal adj	autosomal
gonosomal adj	gonosomal
recessive adj	rezessiv
dominant adj	dominant

> located on chromosome 11 — auf Chromosom 11 liegend

genetic association n	genetische Assoziation
pattern of inheritance / mode of inheritance n	Erbgang / Vererbungsmuster
conductor n	Überträger
carrier n	Träger
affected adj	betroffen
unaffected adj	nicht betroffen
polygenetic / polygenic adj	polygenetisch / polygenisch
continuous variation n	kontinuierliche Variabilität
gene-environment interaction n	Gen-Umwelt-Interaktion
multifactorial inheritance n	multifaktorielle Vererbung
skin colour n	Hautfarbe
body length n	Körpergröße
body mass n	Körpermasse
diabetes mellitus [ˌdaɪəbiːtiːz'melɪtəs] n	Diabetes mellitus / Zuckerkrankheit
tongue n	Zunge
tongue roller n	Roller *(Fähigkeit die Zunge aufzurollen)*
PTC taster n	PTH-Schmecker
Phenylthiocarbamide (PTC)	Phenylthioharnstoff (PTH)

earlobe n	Ohrläppchen
free earlobe	freies Ohrläppchen
attached earlobe	angewachsenes Ohrläppchen

haemophilia BE [ˌhiːməˈfɪliə] / hemophilia AE n	Hämophilie / Bluterkrankheit
royal adj	königlich / Königs~
blood clotting n	Blutgerinnung
blood clotting cascade	Blutgerinnungskaskade
factor VIII n	Faktor VIII
glycoprotein n	Glykoprotein
plasma n	(Blut-)Plasma
blood donor n	Blutspender
occur v	stattfinden

albinism [ˈælbɪnɪzm] n	Albinismus
red-green colour blindness n	Rot-Grün-Blindheit
brachydactyly [ˌbrækɪˈdæktɪlɪ] n	Kurzfingrigkeit
Chorea Huntington [kɒrˌɪəˈhʌntɪŋtən] / Huntington's disease n	Chorea Huntington / Veitstanz
movement disorder n	Bewegungsstörung
Tay-Sachs disease [ˌteɪˈsæksdɪˌziːz] n	Tay-Sachs-Syndrom
rickets [ˈrɪkɪts] n	Rachitis
hypophosphatemic rickets [haɪpəfɒsˌfætəmɪkˈrɪkɪts] / vitamin D resistant rickets	hypophosphatämische Rachitis / Vitamin D resistente Rachitis
phenylketonuria (PKU) [ˌfiːnaɪlkiːtəˈnjʊərɪə] n	Phenylketonurie (PKU)
amino acid metabolism [əˌmiːnəʊæsɪdmeˈtæblɪzm] n	Aminosäurestoffwechsel
phenylalanine [ˌfiːnaɪlˈæləniːn]	Phenylalanin
tyrosine [ˈtaɪrəsiːn]	Tyrosin
diet low in phenylalanine	phenylalaninarme Diät
toxic adj	toxisch / giftig
toxic metabolite [ˌtɒksɪkməˈtæbəlaɪt] n	toxisches Stoffwechselprodukt
myelin sheath [ˈmaɪəlɪnˌʃiːθ] n	Myelinscheide

disability n	Behinderung
mental disability	geistige Behinderung
mentally disabled	geistig behindert
Marfan's syndrome [ˈmɑːfənzˌsɪndrəʊm] / arachnodactyly [ˌəræknəˈdæktɪlɪ] n	Marfan-Syndrom / Spinnenfingrigkeit
fibrilline [ˈfaɪbrɪliːn] n	Fibrillin

5 Genetics › 5.3 Human genetics

connective tissue n — Bindegewebe
joint n — Gelenk
flexible adj — beweglich / flexibel
spine n — Rückgrat
chest n — Brustkorb
arm span n — Armspanne
cystic fibrosis (CF) / mucoviscidosis [ˌmjuːkəʊvɪsiːˈdəʊsɪs] n — cystische Fibrose / Mucoviszidose
CFTR gene n *(cystic fibrosis transmembrane conductance regulator)* — CFTR-Gen *(cystische Fibrose Transmembran-Leitfähigkeitsregulator)*
transmembrane proteine n — Transmembranprotein
channel for chloride ions / chloride ion channel n — Kanal für Chlorid-Ionen / Chloridionenkanal
faulty adj — fehlerhaft
mucus [ˈmjuːkəs] n — Schleim
cough n — Husten
life expectancy n — Lebenserwartung
Duchenne muscular dystrophy [duːˈʃenˌmʌskjʊləˈdɪstrəfi] n — Dychennsche Muskeldystrophie
muscle n — Muskel
progressive adj — fortschreitend / progressiv
neuro-degenerative [ˌnjʊərəʊdɪˈdʒenrətɪv] adj — neurodegenerativ *(nervenzellenzersetzend)*
psychological adj — psychologisch
Rett syndrome [ˈretˌsɪndrəʊm] n — Rettsyndrom

SNP / single nucleotide polymorphism [ˌsnɪp] n — SNP *(Polymorphismus der ein einzelnes Nukleotid betrifft)*
trinucleotide expansion [traɪˌnjuːkliətaɪdɪkˈspænʃn] n — Trinukleotid-Expansion
fragile X syndrome n — Fragiles-X-Syndrom
CpG-island n *(small genomic regions with increased CpG content, often located upstream of promoters)* — CpG-Insel *(kleine genomische Abschnitte mit erhöhtem CpG-Gehalt, die sich oft vor Promotoren befinden)*
house keeping gene n — Haushaltsgen
methylation [ˌmeθɪˈleɪʃn] n — Methylierung
gene activitiy n — Genaktivität
imprinting [ɪmˈprɪntɪŋ] n *(parent-of-origin-specific gene expression)* — Imprinting *(elternspezifische Genexpression)*
Angelman syndrome n — Angelman-Syndrom
Prader-Willi syndrome n — Prader-Willi-Syndrom
maternal adj — maternal / maternell / mütterlich
paternal adj — paternal / paternell / väterlcih

epigenetics [ˌepɪdʒɪ'netɪks] n *(changes in phenotype caused by DNA-modifications and not by DNA sequence)*
haplotype ['hæpləˌtaɪp] n

Epigenetik *(DNA-Modifikationen und nicht die Basenabfolge ist für einen geänderten Phänotyp verantwortlich)*
Haplotyp

Examples of different patterns of inheritance in humans

Pattern of inheritance Erbmuster	Syndrome Syndrom	Genetic cause Genetische Ursache
autosomal recessive	cystic fibrosis	mutation of the CFTR-gene on the long arm of chromosome 7
	sickle cell anemia	point mutation of the beta-globin gene located on chromosome 11
	phenylketonuria (PKU)	mutation of the phenylalanine hydroxylase located on the short arm of chromosome 12
autosomal dominant	Chorea Huntington / Huntington's chorea	trinucleotide expansion in the huntington-gene on chromosome 4, neuro-degenerative disorder, psychological effects, movement disorder
gonosmal recessive	Duchenne muscular dystrophy	mutation of the dystrophin gene
	Haemophilia A	mutation in the factor VIII gene, blood clotting does not occur
gonosmal dominant	Rett syndrome	mutation of the MECP2 gene

Blood group systems

blood group n
blood group system n
AB0 system n
codominant [kəʊ'dɒmɪnənt] adj
red blood cell n
surface antigen n
glycolipid [ˌɡlaɪkəʊ'lɪpɪd] n
protein n
rhesus system ['riːsəsˌsɪstəm] n
  rhesus antigens (C, c, D, E, e)
  main antigen (D)
RhD positive adj
RhD negative adj
anti-D prophylaxis [ˌæntiˈdiːprɒfɪˌlæksɪs] n
placenta [pləˈsentə] n
prevent v

Blutgruppe
Blutgruppensystem
AB0-System
kodominant
rotes Blutkörperchen / rote Blutzelle
Oberflächenantigen
Glykolipid
Protein
Rhesussystem
  Rhesusfaktor-Antigene (C, c, D, E, e)
  Haupt-Antigen (D)
Rhesus-positiv / Rh(D)+ / Rh+ / Rh
Rhesus-negativ / Rh(D)- / Rh- / rh
anti-D-Prophylaxe
Plazenta
verhindern

5 Genetics › 5.3 Human genetics

suffer v	leiden
antibody production n	Antikörperbildung
anti-D antibody n	anti-D-Antikörper
injection n	Injektion
blood exchange n	Blutaustausch
newborn n	Neugeborenes

Genetic counselling

genetic counselling n	genetische Beratung

»
genetic counselling is advised	genetische Beratung wird empfohlen

expecting parents n	werdende Eltern
expecting mother n	werdende Mutter
abortion [ə'bɔːʃn] n	Schwangerschaftsabbruch / Fehlgeburt / Abort
spontaneous abortion	Fehlgeburt
induced abortion	Abtreibung / eingeleiteter Abort
induce abortion	eine Fehlgeburt einleiten
legal abortion	legale Abtreibung
miscarriage ['mɪsˌkærɪdʒ] n	Fehlgeburt
miscarry v	eine Fehlgeburt haben
abort [ə'bɔːt] v	als Abort abgehen / abstoßen / abtreiben

»
carry out an abortion	einen Schwangerschaftsabbruch durchführen
procurement of miscarriage	Herbeiführung einer Fehlgeburt
exempt of punishment / unpunished	straffrei

indication rule n	Indikationslösung
period rule n	Fristenlösung
conscience ['kɒnʃns] n	Gewissen
ethical values [ˌeθɪkl'væljuːz] n	ethische Werte / ethische Wertvorstellungen
religious values n	religiöse Werte / ethische Wertvorstellungen
decision n	Entscheidung
decide v	entscheiden
pro-choice [ˌprəʊ'tʃɔɪs] n	„für-die-Wahl" (Abtreibungsbefürworter)

pro-life n			„für-das-Leben" (Abtreibungsgegner)
disability / handicap n			Behinderung
support v			unterstützen
disabled adj			behindert

cope with sth		mit etwas zurechtkommen
supportive environment		unterstützendes Umfeld
decide	in favour of sth	sich für etw.
	against sth	sich gegen etw.	entscheiden

embryo n — Embryo
fetus ['fi:təs] n — Fötus / Fetus
pregnancy n — Schwangerschaft
live birth n — Lebendgeburt
lethal ['li:θl] adj — letal / tödlich
family tree n — Familienstammbaum
pedigree ['pedɪgri:] n — Stammbaum

prenatal diagnosis — Pränataldiagnostik
 [pri:ˌneɪtldaɪəg'nəʊsɪs] n
preimplantation genetic diagnosis — Präimplantationsdiagnostik (PID)
 (PGD) [pri:ˌɪmplɑ:nteɪʃndʒəˌnetɪk
 daɪə'gnəʊsɪs] n
ultrasound examination n — Ultraschalluntersuchung
triple test n — Tripeltest
cleft lip n — Lippenspalte
cleft jaw n — Kieferspalte
cleft palate [ˌkleft'pælət] n — Gaumenspalte
surgery n — Operation / Chirurgie
avoid v — vermeiden
consequence n — Folge / Konsequenz
increase v — erhöhen
 increased risk — erhöhtes Risiko
amniocentesis [ˌæmnɪəʊsen'ti:sɪs] n — Amniozentese
chorionic villus sampling — Chorionzottenbiopsie
 [kɔ:rɪˌɒnɪk'vɪləsˌsɑ:mplɪŋ] n
placenta [plə'sentə] n — Plazenta
uterus ['ju:trəs], pl uteruses; uteri n — Gebärmutter / Uterus
umbilical cord [ʌmˌbɪlɪkl'kɔ:d] n — Nabelschnur
 umbilical cord vein — Nabelschnurvene

5 Genetics › 5.3 Human genetics

Examples of different mutations affecting humans

Chromosomal aberrations
Chromosomale Abweichungen
- **Numerical aberrations of autosomes** Numerische Abweichungen von Autosomen
- **Numerical aberrations of gonosomes** Numerische Abweichungen von Gonosomen
- **Structural aberrations** Strukturelle Abweichungen

Trisomie 21 / trisomy 21 (Down syndrome)
Trisomie 18 / trisomy 18 (Edwards syndrome)
Trisomie 13 / trisomy 13 (Pateau syndrome)
Trisomie X / trisomy X (Poly-X-female syndrome)
Monosomie X / monosomy X (Turner syndrome)
XXY (Klinefelter syndrome)

5p- (five p *minus* = deletion at the short arm of chromosome 5, Cri-du-chat syndrome)
4p- (deletion at the short arm of chromosome 4) (Wolf-Hirschhorn syndrome)
Deletion of some bands of the long arm of chromosome 15
- Prader-Willi syndrome if the paternal chromosome is affected
- Angelman syndrome if the maternal chromosome is affected

Trinucleotide expansions
Trinukleotid-Expansionen
- **Non-poly-glutamine-disease** Nicht-Polyglutaminerkrankung
- **Poly-glutamine-disease** Polyglutaminerkrankung

CGG-repeat expansion of the X-chromosome from 20–30 repeats to more than 200 repeats; fragile-X-syndrome
CAG-repeat expansion of the short arm of chromosome 4 from <27 repeats to more than 36 repeats; Huntington's disease / Chorea Huntington

Small deletion
Kleine Deletion
- **deletion of 3 nucleotides** Deletion von 3 Nukleotiden
- **deletion of 1 nucleotide** Deletion von einem Nukleotid

amino acid 508 of the CFTR-gene is deleted; cystic fibrosis
single nucleotide deletion in codon 44 leads to frame shift and stop codon at postion 60 of the β-Globin gene; β-thalassemia

Point mutations (SNPs)
Punktmutationen
- **transversion** Transversion

- **transition** Transition

A to T transversion in the hemoglobinA gene (short arm of chromsome 11) resulting in an amino acid exchange at position 6 of the protein from glutamate to valine resulting in the HgbS (sickle cell anemia)
G to A transition of postion 1376 of the GPDH-gene results in an amino acid exchange at postion 459 of arginine to proline which results in a decreased funktion of GP6D (glucose-6-phosphate dehydrogenase)

5.4 Population genetics   » III. 7. Evolution – 7.1 Population genetics

gene pool n	Genpool
population n	Population
allele frequency [əˈliːlˌfriːkwənsi] n	Allelfrequenz
distribution of allele frequencies	Verteilung von Allelfrequenzen
natural selection n	natürliche Selektion
genetic drift n	Gendrift
founder effect n	Gründereffekt
gene flow n	Genfluss
migration n	Migration
isolation [ˌaɪslˈeɪʃn] n	Isolation
isolate v	isolieren
probability n	Wahrscheinlichkeit
prerequisite [ˌpriːˈrekwɪzɪt] n	Voraussetzung
panmixia [pænˈmɪksɪə] n	Panmixie
sickle cell anemia [ˌsɪklseləˈniːmɪə] / sickle cell disease n	Sichelzellanämie
peppered moth [ˌpepədˈmɒθ] n	Birkenspanner
pollution n	Umweltverschmutzung
polluted adj	verschmutzt
soot n	Ruß
birch tree [ˈbɜːtʃˌtriː] n	Birke
lichen [ˈlaɪkən] n	Flechte
Hardy-Weinberg principle n	Hardy-Weinberg-Gesetz
fitness n	Fitness
reproductive fitness	reproduktive Fitness
advantage of heterozygosity n	Heterozygotenvorteil
population bottleneck [ˌpɒpjəˈleɪʃn̩ˌbɒtlnek] n	Flaschenhalseffekt
ethnical group n	ethnische Gruppe

» In an ideal population (i.e. all individuals have the same reproductive fitness, all individuals can breed with all individuals of the opposite sex) the allele frequencies remain constant.
In einer idealen Population (d.h. alle Individuen haben die gleiche reproduktive Fitness, alle Individuen können sich mit allen Individuen des anderen Geschlechts paaren) bleiben die Allelfrequenzen konstant.

genetic association n	genetische Assoziation
population based genetic association study	populationsbasierte genetische Assoziationsstudie

5 Genetics › 5.5 Molecular genetics

family based genetic association study	familienbasierte genetische Assoziationsstudie
linkage disequilibrium [ˌlɪŋkɪdʒˌdɪsekwɪˈlɪbriəm] n	Kopplungs-Ungleichgewicht
χ-square / chi-square n	χ-Quadrat / Chi-Quadrat
Pearson's chi-square test	Pearsons χ^2-Test
statistical significance n	statistische Signifikanz
gene lethality [ˈdʒiːnliːˌθæləti] n	Letalität aufgrund eines genetischen Defekts
lethal factor n	Letalfaktor
lethal allele n	letales Allel

5.5 Molecular genetics

DNA – the carrier of hereditary information

nucleic acid n	Nukleinsäure
protein n	Protein
genetic adj	genetisch
genetic information	genetische Information
hereditary adj	Erb~ / angeboren / erblich
hereditary information	Erbinformation
evidence n	Hinweis / Indiz
proof n	Beweis
prove v	beweisen

pneumonia [njuːˈməʊniə] n	Lungenentzündung
bacterial strain	Bakterienstamm
colony, pl colonies n	Kolonie
rough adj	rau / uneben
smooth adj	glatt
R cells n	R-Zellen
S cells n (cells of rough and smooth colonies, respectively)	S-Zellen (Zellen von rauen bzw. glatten Kolonien)
capsule [ˈkæpsjuːl] n	Kapsel
slimy capsule	Schleimkapsel
polysaccharide capsule [ˌpɒlɪˈsækraɪdˌkæpsjuːl]	Polysaccharidkapsel
virulent [ˈvɪrʊlnt] adj	virulent / schädigend
harmless adj	unschädlich

killed [ˈdednd] adj	abgetötet

heat-inactivation n	Hitzeinaktivierung
heat-inactivated adj	hitzeinaktiviert
transformation n	Transformation
transforming agent n	transformierender Stoff / transformierendes Agens
transfer v	übertragen
incubate ['ɪŋkjʊbeɪt] v	inkubieren
mix v	mischen
enable v	befähigen
uptake n	Aufnahme
take up v	aufnehmen
cleave, cleft, cleft v	spalten
protein cleaving adj	proteinspaltend
protease ['prəʊtieɪz] (protein cleaving enzyme)	Protease (proteinspaltendes Enzym)
DNase [ˌdiːen'eɪz] (DNA cleaving enzyme)	DNase (DNAspaltendes Enzym)
interfere with [ˌɪntə'fɪəwɪð] v	wechselwirken mit
inhibit v	unterdrücken / verhindern
separate v	trennen

» DNA is the transforming agent, altering the properties of a bacterial strain.
Die DNA ist das transformierende Agens, welches die Eigenschaften eines Bakterienstammes ändert.

DNA structure » Abb. 47

DNA n (Deoxyribo Nucleic Acid)	DNA / DNS (Desoxyribonuklein Säure)
deoxyribose [diːˌɒksɪ'raɪbəʊz] n	Desoxyribose
pentose ['pentəʊz] n	Pentose (Fünffachzucker)
phosphate n	Phosphat
backbone n	Rückgrat
sugar phosphate ester ['ʃʊgəˌfɒsfeɪtˌestə] n	Zucker-Phosphat-Ester
nucleotide ['njuːklɪətaɪd] n (nitrogenous base + sugar + phosphate)	Nukleotid (stickstoffhaltige Base + Zucker + Phosphat)
nucleoside n (base + sugar)	Nukleosid (Base + Zucker)
nitrogenous base [naɪˌtrɒdʒɪnəs'beɪs] n	stickstoffhaltige Base
adenine ['ædɪnɪn] n	Adenin
cytosine ['saɪtəsiːn] n	Cytosin
guanine ['gwɑːniːn] n	Guanin

5 Genetics › 5.5 Molecular genetics

thymine ['θaɪmiːn] n	Thymin
uracil ['jʊərəsɪl] n *(substitutes thymine in RNAs)*	Uracil *(ersetzt Thymin in RNAs)*
purine (G, A) ['pjʊəriːn] n	Purin (G, A)
pyrimidine (C, T, U) [pɪ'rɪmɪdiːn] n	Pyrimidin (C, T, U)
base pair (bp) n	Basenpaar
Chargaff's rule n	Chargaff-Regel

double helix ['dʌbl‚hiːlɪks] n	Doppelhelix
helical ['helɪkl] adj	helikal / schraubenförmig
double helical	doppelhelikal
twisted rope ladder n	verdrillte Strickleiter
strand n	Strang
antiparallel adj	antiparallel
rung [rʌŋ] / step n	Leitersprosse / Stufe
bond n	Bindung
hydrogene bond	Wasserstoffbrückenbindung
stacking interaction n	Stapel-Wechselwirkung
sterical / steric adj	sterische / räumliche
complementary adj	komplementär
X-ray n	Röntgenstrahl
X-ray crystallography [krɪstl'ɒɡrəfi]	Röntgen-Kristallografie
X-ray examination	Röntgenuntersuchung
propose v	vorschlagen

The double-helical DNA consists of two long polymers of simple units called nucleotides.
Die doppelhelikale DNA besteht aus zwei langen Polymeren, die aus einfachen Bausteinen, die Nukleotide genannt werden, zusammengesetzt sind.
It looks like a twisted rope ladder whose rungs are made of base pairs and the sugar phophate esters form the upright sides.
Sie sieht aus wie eine verdrillte Strickleiter, deren Sprossen aus Basenpaaren zusammengesetzt sind, und die Zucker-Phosphat-Ester bilden die Seiten.
For sterical reasons the rungs always consist of a big (purine) base and a small (pyrimidine) base.
Aus räumlichen Gründen besteht eine Sprosse immer aus einer großen (Purin-) Base und einer kleinen (Pyrimidin-) Base.

package v	verpacken
histone ['hɪstəʊn] n	Histon
pin curler n	Lockenwickler
nucleosome ['njuːklɪəsəʊm] n	Nukleosom
bead [biːd] / pearl n	Perle
string n	Schnur

coil v	aufwinden / spulen
wrap v	wickeln
wrapped (around sth)	(um etw.) gewickelt
ratio n	Verhältnis

»
at a ratio of 1:1	im Verhältnis 1:1

chromatin ['krəʊmətɪn] n	Chromatin
heterochromatin [ˌhetrəʊ'krəʊmətɪn] n	Heterochromatin
euchromatin ['juːkrəʊmətɪn] n	Euchromatin
spatial adj	räumlich
temporal adj	zeitlich
30 nm chromatine fibre n	30-nm-Chromatinfaser

»
The DNA of eukaryotes is coiled twice around a histone complex to form a nucleosome.
Die DNA der Eukaryoten ist zweimal um einen Histon-Komplex gewickelt, um so ein Nukleosom zu bilden.
This way the histone complexes function as pin curlers and the DNA is shortened at a ratio of 6:1.
Auf diese Weise fungieren die Histon-Komplexe als „Lockenwickler" und die DNA wird auf ein Sechstel gekürzt.
In an electron microscope image the nucleosomes look like beads on a string.
In einem elektronenmikroskopischen Bild sehen die Nukleosomen wie Perlen auf einer Schnur aus.

Extracting DNA

DNA n *(Deoxyribo Nucleic Acid)*	DNA / DNS *(Desoxyribonuklein Säure)*
extract from v	extrahieren aus
isolate v	isolieren
cell n	Zelle
tissue ['tɪʃuː] n	Gewebe
plant tissue	pflanzliches Gewebe
animal tissue	tierisches Gewebe
homogenate [hə'mɒdʒɪnɪt] n	Homogenat
homogenise *BE* [hə'mɒdʒɪnaɪz] / homogenize *AE* v	homogenisieren
mortar ['mɔːtə] n	Mörser / Reibschale
pestle ['pesl] n	Pistill / Stößel
stick blender n	Pürierstab

5 Genetics › 5.5 Molecular genetics

debris [ˈdeɪbriː] n	Debris / Zelltrümmer
precipitation [prɪˌsɪpɪˈteɪʃn] n	Fällung
precipitate n	Präzipitat
precipitate v	ausfällen
centrifuge [ˈsentrɪfjuːdʒ] n	Zentrifuge
centrifuge v	zentrifugieren
sediment n	Sediment / Ablagerung
supernatant n	Überstand
filter n	Filter
filter v	filtrieren
washing-up liquid n	Spülmittel
washing powder / laundry detergent n	Waschpulver
deep frozen adj	tiefgefroren
ethanol [ˈeθənɒl] n	Ethanol
spool (sth) v	(etw.) aufwickeln / (etw.) aufspulen
wind v	winden / wickeln
stir v	rühren
glass rod n	Glasstab
glass stirrer n	Glasrührer
thread-like adj	fädig

DNA Replication

replication n	Replikation
replicate v	replizieren
duplicate v	duplizieren
replication fork	Replikationsgabel
replication bubble	Replikationsblase
replication mechanism	Replikationsmechanismus
DNA polymerase n	DNA-Polymerase
helicase [ˈhelɪkeɪs] n	Helicase
zipper n	Reißverschluss
slide n	Schieber *(am Reißverschluss)*
origin of replication (ori) n	Replikationsursprung
strand n	Strang
leading strand	führender Strang / kontinuierlicher Strang
lagging strand	nachfolgender Strang / diskontinuierlicher Strang
forward strand	Vorwärtsstrang
reverse strand	Gegenstrang
template n	Template / Matrize

primer ['praɪmə] n	Primer
loop n	Schlaufe / Schleife
Okazaki fragment n	Okazaki-Fragment
ligase ['lɪgeɪz] n	Ligase
unwind v	entwinden / entdrillen
terminate v	beenden / abbrechen
semi-conservative adj	semikonservativ
conservative adj	konservativ
dispersed [dɪ'spɜːst] adj	verteilt / dispers
CsCl-gradient n	CsCl-Gradient
density n	Dichte
density gradient n	Dichtegradient
buoyant density gradient centrifugation	Dichtegradientenzentrifugation
increasing density	zunehmende Dichte
decreasing density	abnehmende Dichte
centrifugation tube n	Zentrifugationsröhrchen
isotope ['aɪsətəʊp] n	Isotop
^{14}N (normal nitrogen isotope)	^{14}N (normales Stickstoffisotop)
^{15}N (heavy nitrogen isotope)	^{15}N (schweres Stickstoffisotop)
culture medium n	Kulturmedium
heavy DNA n	schwere DNA

Gene expression – transcription

genetic information n	Erbinformation
gene expression n	Genexpression
express v	exprimieren
gain access v	Zugang bekommen
movable adj	beweglich
nucleus ['njuːklɪəs], *pl* nuclei n	Nukleus / Zellkern
transcription n	Transkiption *(Umschreiben von DNA auf RNA)*
transcribe v	transkribieren / umschreiben
RNA polymerase n	RNA-Polymerase
RNA n *(ribonucleic acid)*	RNA / RNS (**R**ibo**n**uklein **S**äure)
hnRNA n *(pre-mRNA)*	hnRNA *(heteronukleäre RNA / prä-mRNA; Vorstufe der mRNA)*
mRNA n *(messenger RNA)*	mRNA *(Boten-RNA)*

5 Genetics › 5.5 Molecular genetics

RNA polymerase

RNA polymerase I (makes rRNA in eukaryotes)	RNA-Polymerase I (produziert rRNA in Eukaryoten)
RNA polymerase II (makes mRNA in eukaryotes)	RNA-Polymerase II (produziert mRNA in Eukaryoten)
RNA polymerase III (makes tRNA in eukaryotes)	RNA-Polymerase III (produziert tRNA in Eukaryoten)

tRNA n *(transfer RNA)*	tRNA *(RNA, die die Aminosäuren transportiert)*
rRNA n *(ribosomal RNA)*	rRNA *(ribosomale RNA)*
uracil [ˈjʊərəsɪl] n *(base)*	Uracil *(Base)*
uridine [ˈjʊərɪdiːn] n *(nucleoside)*	Uridin *(Nukleosid)*
UTP n *(Uridine triphosphate)*	UTP / Uridin-Triphosphat
5' *(five prime)*	5' *(fünf Strich)*
3' *(three prime)*	3' *(drei Strich)*
coding strand / codogenic strand / template strand *(in the doublehelical DNA the coding strand serves as template)*	codogener Strang / Matrizen-Strang *(der codogene Strang ist der Strang der Doppelhelix, der als Matrize dient)*
non-coding strand / reverse strand	nicht codogener Strang / „reverse"-Strang
process v	prozessieren
edit v	editieren
cap n	Cap *(5' Ende einer mRNA)*
capping v	„capping" / „cappen" *(mit einem Cap versehen)*
capping process	Prozess des „Cappings"
poly-A tail n	poly-A-Schwanz *(3' Ende einer mRNA)*
polyadenylation [ˌpɒliædɪnɪˈleɪʃn̩] n	Polyadenylierung
splicing n	Spleißen / Splicing *(Ausschneiden der Introns und Zusammenfügen der Exons einer m-RNA)*
splice (sth) v	*(etw.)* zusammenkleben / *(etw.)* verbinden
alternative splicing	alternatives Spleißen / alternatives Splicing
intron [ˈɪntrɒn] n	Intron
exon [ˈeksɒn] n	Exon
polycistronic [ˌpɒlɪsɪsˈtrɒnɪk] adj *(contains more than one gene)*	polycistronisch *(enthält mehr als ein Gen)*

gene regulation n	Genregulation
promoter [prə'məʊtə] n	Promotor
transcription factor n	Transkriptionsfaktor
repressor n	Repressor
activator n	Aktivator
terminator n	Terminator *(Abbruchsequenz für die Transkription)*
terminate v	abbrechen
antisense technique [ˌæntɪsenstek'niːk] n	Antisense-Technik / Gegenstrang-Technik
RNAi n *(RNA interference)*	RNAi *(RNA-Interferenz)*
siRNA *(small interfering RNA)*	kleine, störende RNA
post-transcriptional gene silencing (PTGS)	post-transkriptionelles Gene Silencing *(Ausschalten bereits transkribierter Gene)*

Differences between DNA and RNA

DNA
- The sugar is deoxyribose.
- Most DNAs are double stranded (double helix).
- The bases are ACGT.
- DNAs are synthesised by a DNA polymerase.
- DNAs are usually very long molecules which contain the whole genome or a large fraction of it (one chromosome).

RNA
- The sugar is ribose.
- Most RNAs are single stranded.
- The bases are ACGU.
- RNAs are synthesised by RNA polymerases.
- RNAs are usually relatively short molecules, containing one or few genes (mRNAs), linking the DNA-information to protein-information (tRNAs), or being a compound of the ribosome (rRNAs).

- Der Zucker ist Desoxyribose.
- Die meisten DNAs sind doppelsträngig (Doppelhelix).
- Die Basen sind ACGT.
- DNAs werden von einer DNA-Polymerase synthetisert.
- DNAs sind für gewöhnlich relativ lange Moleküle, die das ganze Genom oder einen großen Teil davon enthalten.

- Der Zucker ist Ribose.
- Die meisten RNAs sind einzelsträngig.
- Die Basen sind ACGU.
- RNAs werden durch RNA-Polymerasen synthetisiert.
- RNAs sind für gewöhnlich relativ kurze Moleküle, die ein oder wenige Gene beinhalten (mRNAs), die ein Verbindungsglied zwischen der DNA-Information und der Protein-Information darstellen (tRNAs), oder einen Baustein der Ribosomen darstellen (rRNAs).

5 Genetics › 5.5 Molecular genetics

Differences between procaryotic and eucaryotic mRNAs

Prokaryotic mRNAs...	Eukaryotic mRNAs...
... can be polycistronic (i.e. can contain more than one gene).	... are always monocistronic (i.e. contain only one gene).
... can be translated while being still transcribed.	... need to be transported through the nuclear pores in order to be translated.
... contain no introns.	... contain almost always introns.
... do not need to be processed.	... need to be processed (i.e. capped, spliced, and polyadenylated).
... are degraded rapidly.	... can be edited.
	... have a longer life span (half life).
... können polycistronisch sein (d.h. können mehr als ein Gen enthalten).	... sind immer monocistronisch (d.h. enthalten nur ein Gen).
... können translatiert werden, während sie noch transkribiert werden.	... müssen durch die Kernporen geschleust werden, um tranlatiert zu werden.
... enthalten keine Introns.	... enthalten fast immer Introns.
... müssen nicht prozessiert werden.	... müssen prozessiert werden (d.h. gecappt, gespleißt und polyadenyliert).
... werden schnell degradiert (abgebaut).	... können editiert werden.
	... haben eine längere Lebensspanne (Halbwertszeit).

» RNA synthesis takes place from 5' to 3', which means that the RNA polymerase moves along the template strand of the DNA in 3' to 5' direction.
Die RNA-Synthese findet von 5' zu 3' statt, was bedeutet, dass die RNA-Polymerase den Template-Strang der DNA von 3' nach 5' abliest.
The processing of eukaryotic mRNAs comprises capping (adding a 5' cap), splicing (removing of introns) and polyadenylation (adding of a 3'polyA-tail).
Das Prozessieren der eukaryotischen mRNA umfasst das „Capping" (Versehen mit einem 5' Cap), das Spleißen (Entfernung der Introns) und die Polyadenylierung (Hinzufügen eines 3' polyA-Schwanzes).

Gene expression – translation

translation n	Translation / Übersetzung
translate v	translatieren / übersetzen
DNA sequence n	DNA-Sequenz
amino acid sequence [əˌmiːnəʊˈæsɪdˌsiːkwəns] n	Aminosäure-Sequenz
amino acid chain n	Aminosäure-Kette
genetic code n	genetischer Code
crack [kræk] v	knacken

resolve v	lösen
degenerate adj	degeneriert
redundant [rɪˈdʌndənt] adj	redundant
universal adj	universell
triplet n	Triplett / Dreiergruppe
codon [ˈkəʊdɒn] n	Codon » Abb. 48
start codon (AUG)	Startcodon (AUG)
stop codon (UAG UAA UGA)	Stoppcodon (UAG UAA UGA)
anticodon [ˌæntiˈkəʊdɒn] n	Anticodon
mRNA / messenger RNA	mRNA / Boten-RNA
poly-A tail n	Poly-A-Schwanz (3' Ende der mRNA)
cap n	Cap / Kappe

ribosome [ˈraɪbəsəʊm] n	Ribosom
70S ribosome n (prokaryotic ribosome)	70S Ribosom (Prokaryoten-Ribosom)
50S subunit (large subunit of a prokaryotic ribosome)	50S Untereinheit (große Untereinheit eines Prokaryonten-Ribosoms)
30S subunit (small subunit of a prokaryotic ribosome)	30S Untereinheit (kleine Untereinheit eines Prokaryonten-Ribosoms)
80S ribosome n (eukaryotic ribosome)	80S Ribosom (Eukaryoten-Ribosom)
60S subunit (large subunit of a eukaryotic ribosome)	60S Untereinheit (große Untereinheit eines Eukaryoten-Ribosoms)
40S subunit (small subunit of a eukaryotic ribosome)	40S Untereinheit (kleine Untereinheit eines Eukaryoten-Ribosoms)

endoplasmic reticulum (ER) [ˌendəʊplæzmɪkrɪˈtɪkjʊləm] n	endoplasmatisches Retikulum
rough endoplasmic reticulum	raues Endoplasmatisches Retikulum
smooth endoplasmic reticulum	glattes Endoplasmatisches Retikulum

P-site n	P-Stelle / P-Region (Peptidyl-Ort)
A-site n	A-Stelle / A-Region (Aminoacyl-Ort)
vacant [ˈveɪknt] adj	frei / vacant
initiation [ɪˌnɪʃiˈeɪʃn] n	Initiation / Anfang
initiation complex	Initiationskomplex (kleine ribosomale UE fMet-tRNA mRNA)
initiation factor (IF)	Initiationsfaktor (IF)
start methionine [ˌstɑːtmɪˈθaɪəniːn] n	Startmethionin
formyl-methionine [ˌfɔːmɪlmɪˈθaɪəniːn] n	N-Formyl-Methionin (in Prokaryonten)
elongation [ˌiːlɒŋˈɡeɪʃn] n	Verlängerung
elongation process	Verlängerungsvorgang
loaded t-RNA	beladene t-RNA

complementary adj	komplementär

5 Genetics › 5.5 Molecular genetics

respective adj	entsprechend
detach v	ablösen
attach v	anlagern
link v	verknüpfen
pair v	paaren
peptide bond [ˌpeptaɪdˈbɒnd] n	Peptidbindung
repeat v	wiederholen
termination n	Abbruch
tRNA n *(transfer RNA)*	tRNA *(RNA, die die Aminosäure transportiert)*
cloverleaf [ˈkləʊvəliːf] n	Kleeblatt
cloverleaf structure	Kleeblattstruktur
cloverleaf-shaped	kleeblattförmig
amino acid binding site (3') n	Aminosäurebindungsstelle
ribosome attachment site n	Ribosomenbindungsstelle
load v	laden / beladen
aminoacyl-tRNA synthetase [əˌmiːnəʊˌæsɪlˌtiːɑːrenˌeɪˈsɪnθəteɪz] n	Aminoacyl-tRNA-Synthetase *(Enzym, das die tRNA belädt)*
wobble hypothesis [ˌwɒblhaɪˈpɒθəsɪs] n	Wobbelhypothese
preference n	Vorzug / Bevorzugung
codon preference	Codon-Präferenz / Codon-Bevorzugung
genetic dialect n	genetischer Dialekt
open reading frame (ORF) n	offenes Leseraster
untranslated region (UTR) n	untranslatierte Region
frame shift mutation n	Leserastermutation
nonsense mutation n	Unsinnsmutation *(vorzeitiges Stoppcodon)*

» Nirenberg and Lederer resolved / cracked the genetic code.
Nirenberg und Lederer "knackten" den genetischen Code.
The genetic code is degenerate, i.e. in most cases there is more than one codon for a specific amino acid, e.g. Alanine is coded by GCA, GCC, GCG and GCU.
Der genetische Code ist degeneriert, d.h. in den meisten Fällen gibt es mehr als ein Codon für eine spezifische Aminosäure, z. B. Alanin wird von GCA, GCC, GCG und GCU kodiert.
The genetic code is almost universal, i.e. a specific codon codes in nearly all species for the same amino acid.
Der genetische Code ist fast universell, das bedeutet, dass in nahezu allen Spezies ein spezifisches Codon für die gleiche Aminosäure kodiert.

» Vokabular zu den chemischen Eigenschaften von Aminosäuren: III. 4 Cytology 4.4 Chemical content of a cell

Gene expression – gene regulation

gene expression n	Genexpression
gene regulation n	Genregulation
constitutive adj	konstitutiv *(immer exprimiert)*
facultative ['fækltətɪv] adj	fakultativ / reguliert *(bei Bedarf exprimiert)*
metabolism [mə'tæblɪzm] n	Stoffwechsel / Metabolismus
metabolite [mə'tæbəlaɪt] n	Stoffwechselprodukt / Metabolit
degrade [dɪ'greɪd] v	abbauen
lactose ['læktəʊz] / milk sugar n	Laktose / Milchzucker
operon ['ɒpərɒn] n	Operon
operon model n	Operon-Modell
Lac-operon	Lac-Operon
Trp-operon	Trp-Operon
polycistronic messenger [pɒlɪsɪsˌtrɒnɪk'mesɪndʒə] n	polycistronische mRNA
promoter n	Promotor / Promoter
operator n	Operator
structural gene n	Strukturgen
regulatory gene n	Regulatorgen
terminator n	Terminator
repressor n	Repressor
holo-repressor	Holo-Repressor
apo-repressor	Apo-Repressor
obstruction n	Behinderung
block v	blockieren
detachment n	Ablösung
detach v	ablösen
effector [ɪ'fektə] n	Effektor
induction n	Induktion
substrate induction n	Substratinduktion
induce v	induzieren / einschalten
activator n	Aktivator
activated adj	aktiviert
inactivated adj	deaktiviert / inaktiviert
state n	Zustand / Status
increase (sth) v	(etw.) erhöhen
end product repression n	Endprodukthemmung
repress v	reprimieren / unterdrücken
switch off v	ausschalten / abschalten
feedback n	Rückkopplung
adapt v	(sich) adaptieren / (sich) anpassen

5 Genetics › 5.5 Molecular genetics

» Genes only expressed when needed are called facultatively expressed or regulated genes.
Gene, die nur exprimiert werden, wenn sie gebraucht werden, werden fakultativ exprimierte oder regulierte Gene genannt.
They can be either induced by a substrate or repressed by an end product.
Sie können entweder durch ein Substrat induziert werden oder durch ein Endprodukt abgeschaltet werden.

yeast cell n	Hefezelle
heavy metal n	Schwermetall
trace element n	Spurenelement
copper ['kɒpə] n	Kupfer
protective adj	schützend
dispose v	entsorgen
bind (to sth) v	(an etw.) binden
metal transcription factor (MTF) n	Metall-Transkriptionsfaktor
metal response element (MRE) n	metallresponsives Element
respond (to sth) v	antworten (auf etw.) / reagieren (auf etw.)
responsive adj	reagierend
hormone n	Hormon
phyto hormone [ˌfaɪtəʊˈhɔːməʊn] n	Phytohormon / Pflanzenhormon
gibberelin [ˌdʒɪbəˈrelɪn] n	Gibberelin (ein Pflanzenhormon)
seed n	Samen
seedling n	Keimling
cotyledon [ˌkɒtɪˈliːdn] n	Keimblatt (botanisch)
aleurone layer [əˌljʊərəʊnˈleɪə] n	Aleuronschicht
endosperm [ˈendəʊspɜːm] n	Endosperm / Mehlkörper
starch [stɑːtʃ] n	Stärke
swell v	schwellen / quellen
longitudinal section n	Längsschnitt
transversal section / transverse section n	Querschnitt
cross section n	Querschnitt
half, pl halves n	Hälfte
destaining / decolouration BE / decoloration AE n	Entfärbung
iodine-potassium solution [ˌaɪədiːnpəˌtæsɪəmsəˈluːʃn] n	Jod-Kaliumiodid-Lösung
expression profile n	Expressionsprofil
microarray [ˌmaɪkrəəˈreɪ] n	Mikroarray
DNA chip n	DNA-Chip

hybridisation *BE* / hybridization *AE* [ˌhaɪbrɪdaɪˈzeɪʃn] n	Hybridisierung
fluorescent [flɔːˌresnt] adj	fluoreszierend
fluorescently labelled probe n	fluoreszierend markiert Probe / Sonde
scanner n	Skanner
detection n	Detektion
detect v	erkennen

From genotype to phenotype

genotype [ˈdʒiːnətaɪp] n	Genotyp
phenotype [ˈfiːnətaɪp] n	Phänotyp
characteristic / trait / feature n	Merkmal
polygenic inheritance [ˌpɒlɪdʒiːnɪkɪnˈherɪtəns] n *(several genes influence one characteristic)*	Polygenie *(mehrere Gene sind an der Ausprägung eines Merkmals beteiligt)*
polygenic adj	polygen
pleiotropy [plaɪˈɒtrəpi] n *(one gene influences several features)*	Polyphänie *(ein Gen ist an der Ausprägung mehrerer Merkmale beteiligt)*
pleiotrop adj	polyphänisch
appearance n	Erscheinung(sform)
appear v	erscheinen
determine v	festlegen / determinieren
coding adj	kodierend
non-coding adj	nicht kodierend
linear adj	linear / gradlinig
soft wired adj	weich verdrahtet

mould [məʊld] n	Schimmelpilz
Neuraspora n	Neuraspora
deficiency mutant n	Mangelmutante
minimal medium n	Minimalmedium
complete medium n	Vollmedium

one gene – one enzyme hypothesis	ein Gen – ein Enzyme Hypothese
one gene – one polypeptide hypothesis	ein Gen – ein Polypeptid Hypothese

lack v	ermangeln / fehlen
enzymatic defect n	Enzymdefekt

Definitions: Gene, genotype, genome and others

Term	Definition	Fachwort	Definition
genotype	all genes of an organism	Genotyp	alle Gene eines Organismus
phenotype	appearance of an organism; all characteristics of an organism	Phänotyp	Erscheinungsbild eines Organismus; alle Merkmale eines Organismus
gene	DNA segment coding for an RNA	Gen	DNA-Abschnitt, der für eine RNA codiert
genome	entire genetic information of an organism, including genes and non-coding DNA	Genom	gesamte genetische Information eines Organismus, einschließlich der nicht kodierenden DNA
haplotype	inherited unit of all variations of one chromosomal segment	Haplotyp	vererbte Einheit von allen Variationen eines chromosomalen Abschnitts
transcriptome	all mRNAs of a cell	Transkriptom	alle mRNAs einer Zelle
proteome	all proteins of a cell	Proteom	alle Proteine einer Zelle

metabolic intermediate [ˌmetəbɒlɪkɪntəˈmiːdiət] n — Stoffwechselzwischenprodukt
metabolic pathway [ˌmetəbɒlɪkˈpɑːθweɪ] n — Stoffwechselprozess / Stoffwechselkette
precursor [priːˈkɜːsə] n — Vorstufe
tryptophan synthesis [ˌtrɪptəfænˈsɪnθəsɪs] n — Tryptophan-Synthese
shikimic acid n — Shikimisäure
chorismic acid n — Chorisminsäure
anthranilic acid [ˌænθrəˈnɪlɪkˌæsɪd] n — Anthranilsäure
indole [ˈɪnˌdəʊl] n — Indol
arginin synthesis [ˈɑːdʒɪniːnˌsɪnθəsɪs] n — Arginin-Synthese
ornithine [ˈɔːnɪθiːn] n — Ornithin
citrulline [ˈsɪtrəˌliːn] n — Citrullin

splicing n — Spleißen / Splicing (Ausschneiden der Introns und Zusammenfügen der Exons einer m-RNA)
 alternative splicing — alternatives Spleißen
 cell-type-specific splicing — zelltypspezifisches Spleißen
 tissue-specific splicing — gewebespezifisches Spleißen
 alternative exon usage n — alternativer Exongebrauch
 calcitonin gene [kælsɪˈtəʊnɪnˌdʒiːn] n — Calcitonin-Gen
  calcitonin n — Calcitoin (Peptidhormon)

neuropeptide CGRP [njʊərə'peptaɪdsiːdʒiːɑːˌpiː] (calcitonin gene related protein) n	Neuropeptid CGRP (Calcitonin-Gen verwandtes Protein)
parathyroid (gland) [ˌpærəˌθaɪrɔɪd'glænd] n	Nebenschilddrüse

RNA editing n (changes in the base sequence of the later translated RNA)	RNA-Editing / RNA-Edition (Änderung der Basensequenz der später translatierten RNA)
lipid catabolism n	Fettabbau
apolipoprotein B [ˌæpəˌlaɪpə'prəʊtiːn] n	Apolipoprotein B
ApoB-100 n (larger variant)	ApoB-100 (größere Variante)
binding partner n	Bindungsparter
ApoB-48 n (smaller variant)	ApoB-48 (kleinere Variante)
premature ['prematʃə] adj	vorzeitig
sense codon n	Sinncodon
stop codon n	Stopcodon

proteasome ['prəʊtɪəsəʊm] n	Proteasom
degradation n	Abbau / Degradation
degrade v	abbauen
mark v	markieren
recognize v	erkennen
superior [suː'pɪərɪə] adj	übergeordnet
cylindrical [sə'lɪndrɪkl] adj	zylindrisch
canal n	Kanal
ubiquitin [juː'bɪkwɪtɪn] n (protein that lables other proteins which are to be degraded)	Ubiquitin (Protein, das andere abzubauende Proteine markiert)
unfold v	auffalten / entfalten
protease ['prəʊtieɪz] n (protein cleaving enzyme)	Protease (proteinspaltendes Enzym)
reuse / recycle v	wiederverwenden / recyclen

Mutagens and Mutations   » III. 5.3 Human genetics

mutation n	Mutation
mutagen ['mjuːtədʒən] n	Mutagen
mutate v	mutieren
mutagenesis [ˌmjuːtə'dʒenəsɪs] n	Mutagenese
random mutagenesis	zufällige Mutagenese
directed mutagenesis / targeted mutagenesis	gerichtete Mutagenese / gezielte Mutagenese

5 Genetics › 5.5 Molecular genetics

chemical mutagen n	chemisches Mutagen
base analogue, *pl* analogues n	Basenanalogon *(Pl. -analoga)*
5-bromouracil (5BU)	5-Brom(o)uracil (5BU)
[ˌfaivˌbrəʊməʊˈjʊərəsɪl] n	
ethidium bromide (EB)	Ethidiumbromid (EtBr)
[eˈθɪdiːəmˌbrəʊmaɪd] n	
benzanthracene [benˈzænθrəˌsiːn] n	Benzanthrazen
intercalating [ɪnˈtɜːkəleɪtɪŋ] adj	interkalierend / dazwischenlagernd
ENU (N-ethyl-N-nitrosourea) n	N-Ethyl-N-nitrosoharnstoff / Ethylnitrosoharnstoff
EMS (ethyl methanesulfonate) n	Ethyl-Methyl-Sulfonat
methylating [ˈmeθleɪtɪŋ] adj	methylierend
psoralene n	Psoralen
cross-linking adj	quervernetzend
physical mutagen n	physikalisches Mutagen
raditation n	Strahlung
irradiation [ɪˌreɪdiˈeɪʃn] n	Bestrahlung
UV irradiation	UV-Bestrahlung
gamma radiation [ˈgæməreɪdiˌeɪʃn]	Gammastrahlung
ionising [ˈaɪənaɪzɪŋ] adj	ionisierend
X-ray n	Röntgenstrahl
corpuscular ray [kɔːˈpʌskjələˌreɪ]	Teilchenstrahl
hydroxyl radical [haɪˈdrɒksɪlˌrædɪkl] n	Hydroxyl-Radikal
8-oxoguanine (8-OxoG) n	8-Oxoguanin (8-OxoG)
keto-enol-tautomerism n	Keto-Enol-Tautomerie
Ames test [ˈeɪmztest] n	Ames-Test
mutagenic potential [ˌmjuːtədʒenɪkpəˈtenʃl] n	mutagenes Potential / Mutagenität
point mutation n	Punktmutation
SNP / single nucleotide polymorphism [ˌsnɪp] n	SNP *(Polymorphismus, der ein einzelnes Nukleotid betrifft)*
frame shift mutation n	Leserastermutation
nonsense mutation n	Unsinnsmutation
silent mutation n	stille Mutation
back mutation n	Rückmutation
transversion [trænzˈvɜːʃn] n	Transversion *(Austausch: Purin gegen Pyrimidin oder umgekehrt)*
transition [trænˈzɪʃn] n	Transition *(Austausch: Purin gegen Purin Pyrimidin gegen Pyrimidin)*
deletion [dɪˈliːʃn] n *(shortform: del)*	Deletion *(kurz: Del)*
insertion [ɪnˈsɜːʃn] n *(shortform: in)*	Insertion *(kurz: In)*
chromosomal mutation n	Chromosomenmutation

translocation n	Translokation
balanced translocation	balancierte Translokation
imbalanced translocation	unbalancierte Translokation
inversion n	Inversion

> breakage and fusion | Bruch und Fusion

genomic mutation n	Genommutation
polypoloidisation *BE* / polypoloidization *AE* n	Polyploidisierung
UV irradiation n	UV-Bestrahlung
thymine dimer / thymidine dimer [ˈθaɪmɪdiːnˌdaɪmə] n	Thymin-Dimer / Thymidin-Dimer
excision repair [ekˌsɪʒnrɪˈpeə] n	Exzisionsreparatur *(Reparatur durch Ausschneiden)*

> Mutagens are sometimes employed to investigate gene functions.
> Mutagene werden manchmal verwendet, um Genfunktionen zu untersuchen.

5.6 Developmental genetics

Normal development

development n	Entwicklung
developmental genetics n	Entwicklungsgenetik
sexual reproduction n	geschlechtliche Fortpflanzung
asexual reproduction n	ungeschlechtliche Fortpflanzung
parthenogenesis [ˌpɑːθənəʊˈdʒenɪsɪs] n	Parthenogenese / Jungfernzeugung
fertilisation *BE* / fertilization *AE* n	Befruchtung
acrosome reaction [ˈækrəʊsəʊriˌækʃn] n	Akrosomen-Reaktion
oocyte [əʊəsaɪt], *pl* oocytes n	Oocyte
ovum [ˈəʊvəm], *pl* ova / egg cell n	Eizelle / Ei
spermatozoa [ˌspɜːmətəʊˈzəʊɒn] / sperm / sperm cell n	Spermatoza *(Pl.)* / Spermium / Spermienzelle

egg n	Ei
egg shell	Schale
egg integument [ˈegɪnˌtegjəmənt]	Eihülle
oogenesis [ˈəʊəˌdʒenəsɪs] n	Oogenese
ovary [ˈəʊvri], *pl* ovaries n	Eierstock
follicle cell n	Follikelzelle

5 Genetics › 5.6 Developmental genetics

nurse cell n	Nährzelle
surround v	umgeben
yolk [jəʊk] n	Dotter
rich in yolk	dotterreich
little yolk	dotterarm
brood care n	Brutpflege
genetic brood care n	genetische Brutpflege
mass reproduction n	Massenreproduktion
nutritive [ˈnjuːtrətɪv] adj	ernährend
nutrient [ˈnjuːtriənt] n	Nährstoff
egg white / albumen [ˈælbjʊmən] n	Eiweiß *(im Vogelei)* / Albumin

model organism n	Modellorganismus
sea urchin [ˈsiːˌɜːtʃɪn] *(Strongyluscentrotus)* n	Seeigel
fruit fly *(Drosphila melanogaster)* n	Fruchtfliege
nematode [ˈnemətəʊd] / round worm *(Caenorhabditis elegans)* n	Nematode / Fadenwurm
amphibian [æmˈfɪbiən] n	Amphibie
clawed frog *(Xenopus)* n	Krallenfrosch
zebrafish [ˈzebrəfɪʃ] n	Zebrafisch
mouse n	Maus
mammal [ˈmæml] n	Säugetier
mammalian adj	Säugetier~

zygote [zaɪɡəʊt] n	Zygote
species-specific adj	artspezifisch
determine v	festlegen / determinieren
maternal adj	mütterlich / maternal
blastomere [ˈblæstəʊmɜː] n	Blastomere *(Produkt der ersten Furchungsteilungen)*
micromere [ˈmaɪkrəʊmɜː] n	Mikromere *(die kleinsten Zellen bei inequaler Furchung)*
morula [mɔjulə] n	Morula
blastula [ˈblæstjulə] n	Blastula
blastocoel [ˈblæstəʊsiːl] n	Blastocoel *(Hohlraum der Blastula)*
gastrula [ˈɡæstrʊlə] n	Gastrula
primitive gut / archenteron [ɑːˈkæntərɒn] n	Urdarm
blastopore [ˈblæstəpɔː] n	Blastopore / Urmund
neurula [ˈnʊrələ] n	Neurula
solid adj	kompakt / fest
hollow adj	hohl
cavity [ˈkævəti] n	Hohlraum

larva ['lɑːvə], *pl* larvae n	Larve
pluteus [plutɪəs] n	Pluteus(-larve)
metamorphosis [ˌmetə'mɔːfəsɪs] n	Metamorphose
germ layer n	Keimblatt
ectoderm ['ektəʊˌdɜːm] n	Ektoderm
endoderm ['endəʊˌdɜːm] n	Entoderm
mesoderm ['mesəʊˌdɜːm] n	Mesoderm
precursor [priː'kɜːsə] n	Vorläufer
migrate v	wandern
invaginate [ɪn'vəˌʤɪneɪt] n	invaginieren / einstülpen
converge n	konvergieren / zusammenlaufen
prospective adj	prospektiv
fate n	Schicksal
exoskeleton [ˌeksəʊ'skelɪtn] n	Außenskelett / Exoskelett
endoskeleton [ˌendəʊ'skelɪtn] n	inneres Skelett / Endoskelett
corda (dorsalis) ['kɔːdə] n	Corda (dorsalis)
back bone n	Rückgrat
gonad ['gəʊnæd] n	Gonade / Keimdrüse
sex organ n	Geschlechtsorgan / Sexualorgan
excretion [ɪk'skriːʃn] n	Ausscheidung / Exkretion

Prospective fate of the germ layers

germ layer	prospective fate	Keimblatt	Voraussichtliches Schicksal
ectoderm	skin with glands and nails, nervous system with sensory cells, exoskeleton	Ektoderm	Haut mit Drüsen und Nägeln, Nervensystem mit Sinneszellen, Exoskelett
endoderm	gut, liver, pancreas, swim bladder, lung, gills, thyroid, thymus	Entoderm	Darm, Leber, Bauchspeicheldrüse, Schwimmblase, Lunge, Kiemen, Schilddrüse, Thymus
mesoderm	endoskeleton, muscles, blood and lymph systems, heart, excretional organs, gonads	Mesoderm	Innenskelett, Muskeln, Blut- und Lymphgefäße, Herz, Ausscheidungsorgane, Gonaden

egg type n	Eityp
isolecital [ˌaɪsəʊˌlesɪθəl] adj	isolecital *(Dotter gleichmäßig verteilt)*
anisolecital adj	anisolecital *(Dotter ungleichmäßig verteilt)*
vegetal pole n	vegetativer Pol
animal pole n	animaler Pol
cleavage type ['kliːvɪʤtaɪp] n	Furchungstyp
complete cleavage	totale Furchung

complete-equal / holoblastic [ˌhɒləblæstɪk]	total-äqual
complete-inequal	total-inäqual
spiral cleavage	Spiralfurchung
radial cleavage	Radiärfurchung
bilateral cleavage [baɪˌlætrl'kliːvɪdʒ]	Bilateralfurchung
partial cleavage	partielle Furchung
superficial cleavage	superfizielle Furchung
discoidal cleavage [dɪsˌkɔɪdl'kliːvɪdʒ]	discoidale Furchung
periphery [pəˈrɪfri] n	Peripherie
germinal disc [ˈdʒɜmɪnlˌdɪsk] n	Keimscheibe
blastodisc [ˈblæstəʊˌdɪsk] n	Discoblastula *(Blastomeren am animalen Pol auf dem Dotter)*

determination [dɪˌtɜːmɪ'neɪʃn] n	Determinierung / Festlegung
determine v	determinieren / festlegen
differentiation [ˌdɪfrenʃz'eɪʃn] n	Differenzierung
differentiate v	differenzieren
stem cell n	Stammzelle
omnipotent adj *(can produce a complete organism)*	omnipotent *(kann einen ganzen Organismus hervorbringen)*
pluripotent adj *(can produce all cell types)*	pluripotent *(kann alle Zelltypen hervorbringen)*
multipotent adj *(can produce the cell types of the surrounding tissue)*	multipotent *(kann die Zelltypen des umgebenden Gewebes hervorbringen)*
germ line n	Keimbahn
soma [ˈsəʊmə], *pl* somas; somata n	Zellkörper / Soma

tying experiment n	Schnürungsexperiment
transplantation experiment n	Transplantationsexperiment
undisturbed adj	ungestört
meridional [məˈrɪdiənl] adj	meridional *(den Längenkreis betreffend)*
equatorial [ˌekwəˈtɔːriəl] adj	äquatorial
ventral [ˈventrl] adj	ventral *(bauchseitig)*
dorsal [ˈdɔːsl] adj	dorsal *(rückenseitig)*
anterior [ænˈtɪəriə] adj	anterior / vorne
posterior [pɒsˈtɪəriə] adj	posterior / hinten
body axes n	Körperachse
grey crescent [greɪˈkresnt] / animal hemisphere [ˌænɪməl'hemɪsfɪə] n *(dark pigmented)*	grauer Halbmond
pigmented adj	pigmentiert
organiser n	Organisator

Spemann's organiser n	Spemannscher Organisator
induction n	Induktion
induce v	induzieren / einschalten
nematode ['nemətəʊd] / round worm (Caenorhabditis elegans) n	Nematode / Fadenwurm
regulative development n	Regulationsentwicklung
mosaic development n	Mosaikentwicklung

according to the origin	herkunftsgemäß
according to the new location	ortsgemäß

Gene regulation during development

full-grown adj	erwachsen / ausgewachsen
embryogenesis [ˌembrɪ'ɒˌdʒenɪsɪs] n	Embryogenese
predetermine [ˌpriːdɪ'tɜːmɪn] v	festlegen / vorherbestimmen
maternal effect n	maternaler Effekt / materneller Effekt
maternal gene n	maternales Gen / maternelles Gen
zygotic gene [zaɪ'ɡɒtɪkˌdʒiːn] n	zygotisches Gen
deposit v	deponieren / ablegen
concentration gradient n	Konzentrationsgradient
morphogen ['mɒfəʊˌdʒen] n	Morphogen / Signalmolekül
morphogenic adj	morphogen
diffuse [dɪ'fjuːs] v	diffundieren
gap gene n	Lückengen
segmentation gene n	Segmentierungsgen
pair rule gene	Paarregelgen
segment polarity gene	Segmentpolaritätsgen
segment boundary	Segmentgrenze
homoeotic gene BE / homeotic gene AE [ˌhəʊmɪɒtɪk'dʒiːn]	homöotisches Gen
antennapedia [ænˌtenə'piːdiə] n	Antennapedia
homoeobox BE / homeobox AE ['həʊmɪəbɒks] n (DNA-sequence coding for the homeodomain)	Homöobox (DNA-Sequenz, die für die Homöodomäne codiert)
homoeodomain BE / homeodomain AE [ˌhəʊmɪədə'meɪn] n	Homöodomäne
hox gene ['hɒksˌdʒiːn] n	Hox-Gen (homöotisches Gen im Wirbeltier)
hox cluster n	Hox-Cluster

5 Genetics › 5.6 Developmental genetics

cascade [kæs'keɪd] n	Kaskade
subordinated n	untergeordnet
interference n	Interferenz / Beeinflussung
artificial interference	künstliche Beeinflussung
re-establish v	wiederherstellen
inject v	injizieren

RNA of maternal effect genes such as *bicoid* is deposited by maternal cells into the anterior pole of the egg. When its translation starts, the respective protein (Bicoid protein) forms a concentration gradient.
Die RNA maternaler Effekt-Gene, wie z.B. *bicoid*, wird von mütterlichen Zellen in dem vorderen Pol des Eis abgelegt. Wenn ihre Translation beginnt, formt das entsprechende Protein (Bicoid-Protein) einen Konzentrations-Gradienten.
This gradient has a morphogenic effect on the activation of specific zygotic genes.
Dieser Gradient wirkt sich auf die Aktivierung von spezifischen zygotischen Genen aus, die für die Gewebeausbildung und damit die spätere Gestalt bedeutend sind.

Methods used in developmental biology and genetics

observation n	Beobachtung
time-lapse microscopy n	Zeitraffer-Mikroskopie
lineage tracing ['lɪniɪʤˌtreɪsɪŋ] n	Verfolgung einer Zelllinie
immuno-staining [ˌɪmjənəʊ'steɪnɪŋ] n	Immunfärbung
specific antibody n	spezifische Antikörper
enzyme-linked [ˌenzaɪm'lɪŋkt] adj	Enzym-verknüpft
artifical interference n	künstliche Interferenz
in situ hybridisation [ɪnˌsaɪtuˌhaɪbrɪdaɪ'zeɪʃn] n	In-situ-Hybridisierung
screen n	Screen / Durchmusterung / Filter
mutagenesis [ˌmjutə'ʤenəsɪs] n	Mutagenese
mutagenesis screen	Mutagenese-Screen
saturation mutagenesis screen	Sättigungs-Mutagenese-Screen
chemical mutagenesis	chemische Mutagenese
X-ray n	Röntgenstrahlen
X-ray mutagenesis	Mutagenese durch Röntgenstrahlen
knock out n	Knock-out *(ein Gen wird ausgeschaltet)*
knock in n	Knock-in *(ein normalerweise ausgeschaltetes Gen wird eingeschaltet)*
RNAi n *(RNA interference)*	RNAi / inhibitorische RNA
morpholino [mɔːfɒlaɪnəʊ] n	Morpholino
expression profile n	Expressionsprofil

»	fluorescent dye injection	Injektion eines fluoreszierenden Farbstoffes
	fate mapping	Kartierung des „Schicksals" bestimmter Zellen/Kartierung der „Entwicklungsgeschichte einer Zelle"

Aging and death

age n	Alter
age v	altern
death n	Tod
die v	sterben
life expectancy n	Lebenserwartung
Werner syndrome n	Werner-Syndrom
fast motion n	Schnelldurchlauf / Zeitraffer
replication-enzyme complex n	Replikations-Enzym-Komplex
genetic programme n	genetisches Programm
deterioration [dɪˌtɪərɪəˈreɪʃn] n	Verfall / Verschleiß
deteriorate [dɪˈtɪərɪreɪt] v	verfallen
long-lived adj	langlebig
perish [ˈperɪʃ] v	vergehen / zugrunde gehen
counting mechanism n	Zählwerk
telomere [ˈteləˌmɜː] n	Telomer
apoptosis [ˌæpɒptəʊsɪs] n (programmed cell death)	Apoptose (programmierter Zelltod)
course of apoptosis	Apoptoseverlauf
apoptotic programme	Apoptoseprogramm
accumulation n	Anhäufung
pollutant n	Schadstoff
oxygen radical [ˌɒksɪdʒənˈrædɪkl] n	Sauerstoffradikal
cellular respiration n	Zellatmung
metabolic [ˌmetəˈbɒlɪk] adj	Stoffwechsel~
metabolically active	stoffwechselaktiv

»	programmed cell death	programmierter Zelltod

tadpole [ˈtædpəʊl] n	Kaulquappe
drop off v	abfallen
degenerate v	degenerieren / zurückbilden

5 Genetics › 5.6 Developmental genetics

surplus ['sɜːpləs] adj	überflüssig
stroke n	Schlaganfall
heart failure n	Herzinsuffizienz
limit n	Grenze
without limits	unbegrenzt
necrosis [nek'rəʊsɪs] n	Nekrose *(Zell- oder Gewebetod durch äußere Faktoren)*

regulator protein n	Kontrollprotein / Regulationsprotein
p53 n	P53 *(Kontrollprotein der Apoptose)*
bud off [ˌbʌd'ɒf] v	abschnüren / knospen
degrade v	abbauen
death sentence n	Todesurteil
membranous ['membrənəs] adj	membranumschlossen
vesicle ['vesɪkl] n	Vesikel / Bläschen
tumour suppressor gene [ˌtjuːməsə'presədʒiːn] / antioncogene [ˌæntɪ'ɒŋkəʊdʒiːn] n	Tumor-Unterdrücker-Gen / Tumor-Suppressor-Gen

Cancer – development out of control

cancer ['kænsə] n	Krebs
tumour BE / tumor AE ['tjuːmə] n	Tumor
benign [bɪ'naɪn] adj	gutartig
malignant [mə'lɪgnənt] adj	bösartig
myoma [maɪ'əʊmə] n	Myom
polyp ['pɒlɪp] n	Polyp
carcinoma [ˌkɑːsɪ'nəʊmə] n	Karzinom
blastoma [blæs'təʊmə] n	Blastom
sarcoma [sɑː'kəʊmə] n	Sarkom
infiltrate ['ɪnfɪltreɪt] v	infiltrieren / eindringen
daughter tumour / metastasis [met'æstəsɪs] n	Tochtergeschwulst / Metastase

misdirect v	fehlsteuern
oncogene ['ɒŋkədʒiːn] n	Onkogen / krebserregendes Gen
proto-oncogene n	Proto-Onkogen
growth factor n	Wachstumsfaktor
receptor molecule n	Rezeptormolekül / Rezeptor
transcription factor n	Transkriptionsfaktor
chimney sweeper ['tʃɪmnɪˌswiːpə] n	Schornsteinfeger
carcinogenic [ˌkɑːsɪnə'dʒenɪk] / cancer-causing adj	karzinogen / krebs-verursachend

carcinogen n	Karzinogen
mutagenic [ˌmjuːtəˈdʒenɪk] adj	mutagen
mutagen n	Mutagen
tar [tɑː] n	Teer
carbon particle n	Kohlenstoffpartikel
soot n	Ruß
high energy rays n	energiereiche Strahlung
UV rays [juːviːˈreɪz] n	UV-Strahlung
X-rays [ˈeksreɪz] n	Röntgenstrahlung
initiate v	auslösen
virus [ˈvaɪrəs], pl viruses n	Virus (Pl. Viren)
resemble v	ähneln
cell division control gene n	Zellteilungskontrollgen
retinoblastoma [ˌretənəʊblæsˈtəʊmə] n	Netzhautkrebs
predisposition n	Prädisposition
predisposed adj	prädisponiert
germline mutation n	Keimbahnmutation
somatic mutation [səˌmætɪkmjuːˈteɪʃn] n	somatische Mutation
colon cancer n	Dickdarmkrebs
two-hit hypothesis n	Zwei-Treffer-Theorie
membrane-bound adj	membrangebunden
receptor protein n	Rezeptorprotein

> | loss of function | Funktionsverlust |
> |---|---|
> | gain of function | Funktionsgewinn / Funktionserlangung |

cancer therapy n	Krebsbehandlung / Krebstherapie
cytostatic [ˌsaɪtəʊˈstætɪk], pl cytostatics n	Cytostatikum (Pl. Cytostatika)
(radioactive) radiation n	(radioaktive) Bestrahlung
risk analysis n	Risikoanalyse
immunological [ˌɪmjənəˈlɒdʒɪkl] adj	immunologisch
surface marker n	Oberflächenmarker / Oberflächenmerkmal

> | preventive medical check-up | Vorsorgeuntersuchung |
> |---|---|
>
> Cancer is often associated with a loss of function in a tumour suppressor gene.
> Krebs ist oft mit einem Funktionsverlust eines Tumor-Suppressorgens verbunden.

5.7 Immunogenetics

Immune system

immunology n	Immunologie
recoginition n	Erkennen / Erkennung
pathogen [ˈpæθədʒən] n	Pathogen *(krankheitsauslösende Substanz)*
pathogenic adj	pathogen
pathogenic organismen	krankheitsauslösender Organismus
microorganism [ˌmaɪkrəʊˈɔːgnɪzm] n	Mikroorganismus / Mikrobe / Kleinstlebewesen
bacterium [bækˈtɪərɪəm], *pl* bacteria n	Bakterie *(Pl. Bakterien)*
fungus [ˈfʌŋgəs], *pl* fungi [ˈfʌŋgaɪ] n	Pilz
protozoan [ˌprəʊtəʊˈzəʊn], *pl* protozoa *(sg unusal)* n	Protozoon *(Pl. Protozoa; Einzeller)*
virus [ˈvaɪrəs], *pl* viruses n	Virus *(Pl. Viren)*
parasite [ˈpærəsaɪt] n	Parasit *(Pl. Parasiten)*
internal parasite	Endoparasit
intestinal parasite [ɪnˌtestɪnlˈpærəsaɪt]	Darmparasit
worm n	Wurm
parasitic worm	parasitierender Wurm

overcome v	bezwingen / durchdringen
invade v	eindringen
invader n	Eindringling
outer barrier n	äußere Barriere
defence *BE* / defense *AE* n	Verteidigung
defend v	verteidigen
distinguish v	unterscheiden
self n	Selbst
non-self n	Nicht-selbst / körperfremd
foreign invader n	körperfremder Eindringling
internal defence system n	inneres Abwehrsystem
immune system n	Immunsystem
innate immune system	angeborenes Immunsystem
aquired immune system	erworbenes Immunsystem
jawed vertebrates [ˌdʒɔːdˈvɜːtɪbreɪts] / gnathostomata [ˌneɪθəʊˈstəʊmətə] n pl	Kiefermäuler *(Wirbeltiere ohne Rundmäuler)* / Gnathostomata
cyclostomata [ˌsaɪkləˈstəʊmətə] n pl	Rundmäuler / Cyclostomata

> body's own material | körpereigenes Material
>
> The ability to distinguish between self and non-self is the basis of the immune system.
> Die Fähigkeit zwischen "Selbst" und "Nicht-selbst" zu unterscheiden, ist die Basis des Immunsystems.

response n	Antwort
respond v	antworten
lag time [ˈlæɡˌtaɪm] n	Verzögerung
macrophage [ˈmækrəfeɪdʒ] n	Makrophage
phagocyte [ˈfæɡəsaɪt] n	Phagocyte / Fresszelle
scavenge [ˌskævɪndʒ] v	reinigen / beseitigen
phagocytosis [ˌfæɡəsaɪˈtəʊsɪs] n	Zellfressen / Phagocytose *(Aufnahme fester Bestandteile in die Zelle)*
ingest [ɪnˈdʒest] v	aufnehmen / (Nahrung) zu sich nehmen
surface n	Oberfläche
attach v	anlagern
absorption n	Absorption
absorb v	aufsaugen / aufnehmen
degradation n	Abbau
degrade v	abbauen
digestion [daɪˈdʒestʃn] n	Verdauung
digest [ˈdaɪdʒest] v	verdauen
vesicle [ˈvesɪkl] n	Vesikel / Bläschen
membranous vesicle n	Membranvesikel
lysosome [ˈlaɪsəsəʊm] n	Lysosom
fuse v	fusionieren / vereinigen
complement system n	Komplementsystem *(Komponente des unspezifischen Immunsystems bei Säugetieren)*
adhere [ədˈhɪə] v	anheften
enhance [ɪnˈhɑːns] v	verstärken
lable v	markieren / etikettieren
lable n	Etikett
recognize v	erkennen
receptor molecule n	Rezeptormolekül / Rezeptor
receptor mediated phagocytosis n	rezeptorvermittelte Phagocytose
adaptive immune system n	spezifisches Immunsystem
adaptor molecule n	Brückenmolekül / Zwischenmolekül
surface molecule n	Oberflächenmolekül
antibody n	Antikörper

5 Genetics › 5.7 Immunogenetics

antigen n	Antigen
antigen binding site	Antigenbindungsstelle
receptor binding site	Rezeptorbindungsstelle
epitope ['epɪtəʊp] n	Epitop
white blood cell n	weißes Blutkörperchen
memory cell n	Gedächtniszelle
immunisation BE / immunization AE [ˌɪmjənaɪ'zeɪʃn] n	Immunisierung
passive immunisation	passive Immunisierung
active immunisation	aktive Immunisierung
incubation period n	Inkubationszeit
vaccination [ˌvæksɪ'neɪʃn] n	Impfung
vaccinate v	impfen
inoculation [ɪˌnɒkjə'leɪʃn] n	Impfung
inoculate v	impfen

》

secondary immune response	sekundäre Immunantwort

inflammation n	Entzündung
infection n	Infektion
source of infection	Infektionsherd
pus [pʌs] n	Eiter

The innate and the aquired immune system

innate immune system angeborenes Immunsystem	**aquired immune system** erworbenes Immunsystem
non-specific response unspezifische Antwort	**specific response to(wards) pathogens and antigens** spezifische Antwort auf Pathogene und Antigene
immidate maximal response sofortige maximale Antwort	**lag time between contact and maximal response** „Lag-time" zwischen Kontakt und maximaler Antwort
no memory kein Gedächtnis	**immunological memory** immunologisches Gedächtnis
cell mediated and humoral components zellvermittelte und humorale Komponenten	
can be found in nearly all life forms kann in fast allen Lebewesen gefunden werden	**is found in jawed vertebrates only** kommt nur in höheren Lebewesen vor

swell v	anschwellen
permeability n	Durchlässigkeit
capillary [kəˈpɪlri], *pl* capillaries n	Kapillare

immune response n	Immunantwort
phylogenetic [ˌfaɪləʊdʒəˌnetɪk] adj	entwicklungsgeschichtlich / phylogenetisch
lymphatic system [ˌlɪmfætɪkˈsɪstəm] n	Lymphsystem
lymph [lɪmf] n	Lymphe
lymph vessle	Lymphgefäß
lymph node	Lymphknoten
palatine [ˈpælətaɪn] n	Gaumen
palatine tonsil [ˌpælətaɪnˈtɒnsl]	Gaumenmandel
spleen [spliːn] n	Milz
vermiform appendix [ˌvɜːmɪfɔːməˈpendɪks] n	Wurmfortsatz
thymus [ˈθaɪməs] n	Thymus

leucocyte [ˈljuːkəsaɪt] n	Leukocyt(e)
origin n	Ursprung / Herkunft
bone marrow n	Knochenmark
lymphocyte [ˈlɪmfəsaɪt] n	Lymphocyt
lymphoid lineage [ˌlɪmfɔɪdˈlɪnɪdʒ] n	lymphoide Zelllinie
myeloid lineage [ˌmaɪəlɔɪdˈlɪnɪdʒ] n	myeloide Zelllinie / myeloische Zelllinie
myelocyte [ˈmaɪələˌsaɪt] n	Myelocyt
progenitor [prəˈdʒenɪtə] n	Vorläufer
maturation n	Reifung
mature v	reifen
mature adj	reif
differentiate [ˌdɪfˈrenʃieɪt] v	(aus-)differenzieren
bursa of Fabricius [ˌbɜːsəəvfəˈbrɪʃəs] n	Bursa Fabricii *(Lymphatisches Organ zur Reifung von B-Zellen in Vögeln)*

lymphoid progenitor n	lymphoide Vorläuferzelle
lymphoid lineage n	lymphoide Linie
helper T cell (T$_H$) n	T-Helfer-Zelle
cytotoxic T cell (T$_C$) [ˌsaɪtəʊtɒksɪk] n	T-Killerzelle / cytotoxische T-Zelle
B cell n	B-Zelle / B-Lymphocyt
plasma cell n	Plasmazelle
myeloid progenitor n	myeloide Vorläuferzelle / myeloische Vorläuferzelle
granulocyte [ˈgrænjʊləsaɪt] n	Granulocyt
basophil granulocyte / basophil [ˈbeɪsəfɪl]	basophiler Granolocyt / Basophiler

5 Genetics › 5.7 Immunogenetics

neutrophil granolocyte / neutrophil [ˈnjuːtrəˌfɪl]	neutrophiler Granolocyt / Neutrophiler
eosinophil granolocyte / eosinophil [ˌiːəˈsɪnəfɪl]	eosinophiler Granolocyt / Eosinophiler
monocyte [ˈmɒnəsaɪt] n	Monocyt
macrophage [ˈmækrəfeɪdʒ] n	Makrophage
mast cell n	Mastzelle

» For maturation T-cell progenitors migrate from the bone marrow to the thymus; B-cells mature in the bursa of Fabricius (in birds) or in the spleen and in the bone marrow (in mammals).
Um zu reifen, wandern T-Zellvorläufer vom Knochenmark zum Thymus; B-Zellen reifen in der Bursa Fabricii (bei Vögeln) bzw. in der Milz und im Knochenmark (bei Säugetieren).

White blood cells

Lymphoid lineage	Myeloid Lineage
Lymphocytes: • B lymphocytes (B cells), plasma cells • T lymphocytes, helper T cells (T_H), cytotoxic T cells Natural killer cells (NK-cells)	• Monocytes (makrophage progenitor) • Dendritic cells • Mast cells • Granulocytes (basophils, neutrophils, eosinophils)

antibody production n	Antikörperproduktion
immunoglobulin [ˌɪmjʊnəʊˈɡlɒbjʊlɪn] n	Immunoglobulin
penetrate [ˈpenɪtreɪt] v	eindringen
bacterium [bækˈtɪərɪəm], *pl* bacteria n	Bakterium
bacterial protein fragments n	bakterielle Proteinfragmente
antigen [ˈæntɪdʒən] n	Antigen
antigen presenting cell	antigen präsentierende Zelle
T cell receptor n	T-Zellrezeptor
recognize v	erkennen
present v	präsentieren
attach v	anheften / anlagern
activate v	aktivieren
stimulate v	stimulieren
hormone n	Hormon
hormonal adj	hormonell
cytokine [ˈsaɪtəkaɪn] n	Cytokin
antigen receptor n	Antigenrezeptor
lock-and-key principle n	Schlüssel-Schloss-Prinzip

antibody producing adj	Antikörper produzierend
secrete [sɪˈkriːt] v	sezernieren / ausscheiden
humoral [ˈhjuːmrl] adj	humoral
memory cell n	Gedächtniszelle
multiply v	vervielfachen
agglutinate [əˈgluːtɪnət] v	agglutinieren / verklumpen
agglutination n	Agglutination

> After having ingested a bacterium, macrophages present fragments of its proteins on their surface.
> Nachdem Makrophagen ein Bakterium phagocytiert haben, präsentieren sie Bruchstücke seiner Proteine auf ihrer Oberfläche.
> Helper T cells recognise the fragments with their T-cell receptor and activate B cells.
> T-Helfer-Zellen erkennen diese Fragmente mit ihrem T-Zellrezeptor und aktivieren B-Zellen.

Antibody diversity

antibody diversity n	Antikörpervielfalt
Y-shaped adj	Y-förmig / ypsilonförmig
heavy chain (hc) n	schwere Kette
light chain (lc) n	leichte Kette
disulphide bond [daɪˌsʌlfaɪdˈbɒnd] n	Disulfidbrücke
constant region n	konstante Region
variable region n	variable Region
antibody class n	Antikörperklasse
IgG *(monomer)* n	IgG / Immunoglobulin G *(Monomer)*
IgM *(pentamer)* n	IgM / Immunoglobulin M *(Pentamer)*
IgD *(monomer)* n	IgD / Immunoglobulin D *(Monomer)*
IgE *(monomer)* n	IgE / Immunoglobulin E *(Monomer)*
IgA *(dimer)* n	IgA / Immunoglobulin A *(Dimer)*
building block principle n	Baukastenprinzip
somatic recombination n	somatische Rekombination
rearrangement n	Umlagerung
VJ recombination n	VJ-Rekombination *(für die leichte Kette)*
VDJ recombination n	VDJ-Rekombination *(für die schwere Kette)*
V segment / variable segment n	V-Region *(Exons für den variablen Teil der leichten bzw. schweren Kette des Antikörpers)*

5 Genetics › 5.7 Immunogenetics

J segment / joint region n	J-Region *(Exons für den Verbindungsteil der leichten bzw. schweren Kette des Antikörpers)*
C segment / constant segment n	C-Region *(Exons für den konstanten Teil der leichten bzw. schweren Kette des Antikörpers)*
D segment / diversity segment n	D-Region *(Exons für den diversen Teil der schweren Kette des Antikörpers)*
alternative splicing n	alternatives Spleißen
class switching n	Klassenwechsel

»
The large variety of antibodies is caused by several factors: somatic recombination alternative splicing mutations	Die große Antikörpervielfalt wird durch verschiedene Faktoren verursacht: somatische Rekombination alternatives Spleißen Mutationen

Monoclonal antibodies

monoclonal antibody (mAb) [ˌmɒnəkləʊnlˈæntɪbɒdi] n	monoklonaler Antikörper (MAK)
immunise *BE* / immunize *AE* v	immunisieren
myeloma cell [maɪəˈləʊməˌsel] n	Myelomazelle
cancer cell n	Krebszelle
lymphocyte [ˈlɪmfəsaɪt] n	Lymphocyt
spleen [spliːn] n	Milz
fuse v	fusionieren / vereinigen
hybridoma cell [ˌhaɪbrɪˈdəʊmə] n	Hybridomazelle
clone [kləʊn] n	Klon *(Gruppe genetisch identischer Zellen bzw. Organismen)*
separate v	trennen

»
separate into single cells	Zellen vereinzeln
culture separately	einzeln kultivieren / getrennt in Kultur nehmen

immortal adj	unsterblich
immortalise *BE* / immortalize *AE* v	immortalisieren
secrete [sɪˈkriːt] v	ausscheiden / absondern
culture supernatant [ˈkʌltʃəˌsuːpəˈneɪtnt] n	Kulturüberstand

ELISA [ɪˈlaɪsə] n (Enzyme-linked Immuno Sorbent Assay)	ELISA (enzymgekoppelter Immuno-Assay)
coat n	Beschichtung
coat v	beschichten
purify v	reinigen / aufreinigen
(af)fixed adj	befestigt
primary antibody n	Primär-Antikörper / primärer Antikörper
secondary antibody n	Sekundär-Antikörper / sekundärer Antikörper
enzyme-linked adj	mit einem Enzym gekoppelt / verknüpft
test tube n	Reagenzglas / Reaktionsgefäß
microtitre plate [ˈmaɪkrətaɪtrəˌpleɪt] n	Mikrotiterplatte / Lochplatte
colourless adj	farblos
stain n	Farbstoff
stain v	färben
cell type n	Zelltyp
distinguish v	unterscheiden
discriminate v	unterscheiden / diskriminieren
surface molecule n	Oberflächenmolekül
common adj	gemeinsam
identification n	Identifizierung
fluorescent dye [flɔːˈresntˌdaɪ] n	Fluoreszenzfarbstoff

Adverse immune reactions

adverse adj	unerwünscht
allergy [ˈælədʒi] n	Allergie
allergen [ˈælədʒen] n	Allergen
immediate type n	Soforttyp
hay fever n	Heuschnupfen
allergic (bronchial) asthma n	allergisches (Bronchial-)asthma
reddening [ˈrednɪŋ] n	Rötung
sneezing n	Niesen / Niesreiz
life-threatening adj	lebensbedrohlich
anaphylactic [ˌænəfɪˌlæktɪk] adj	anaphylaktisch
shock n	Schock
contact allergy n	Kontaktallergie
eczema [ˈeksɪmə] n	Ekzem
neurodermatitis [ˌnjʊərədɜːməˈtaɪtɪs] n	Neurodermitis

5 Genetics › 5.7 Immunogenetics

delayed (hypersensitivity reaction) type n	verzögerter (Hypersensitivitätsreaktions-)Typ
mediate v	vermitteln
treatment n	Behandlung
treat v	behandeln
avoid v	vermeiden
increasing adj	steigend
desensitisation BE [diːˌsensɪtaɪˈzeɪʃn] / desensitization AE n	Desensibilisierung / Hyposensibilisierung
sublingual immunotherapy (SLIT) n	sublinguale Immuntherapie (SLIT)
histamine [ˈhɪstəmiːn] n	Histamin
release v	freilassen / freisetzen
dilation [daɪˈleɪʃn] n	Erweiterung
drug intolerance n	Arzneimittelunverträglichkeit
cramp n	Krampf
blood pressure n	Blutdruck
transplantation n	Transplantation
transplantate v	transplantieren
transfusion n	Transfusion
transfuse n	transfundieren
rejection n	Ablehnung / Abstoßung
graft / transplant n	Transplantat
transplantation antigen n	Transplantationsantigen
donor [ˈdəʊnə] n	Spender / Donor
recipient n	Empfänger
compatibility n	Kompatibilität / Übereinstimmung
human leucocyte antigen (HLA) n	humanes Leukocyten-Antigen (HLA)
major histocompatibility complex (MHC) [ˌmeɪdʒəˌhɪstəʊkəmpætɪˈbɪlətɪˌkɒmpleks] n	Haupt-Histokompatibilitätskomplex (MHC)
MHC-protein n	MHC-Protein
antigen presenting protein n	Antigen-präsentierendes Protein
immune suppression n	Immunsuppression
immunosuppressed [ˌɪmjuːnəsəˈprest] adj	immunsupprimiert

» | graft-versus-host reaction | Transplantat-gegen-Empfänger-Reaktion (auch: „graft-versus-host"-Reaktion) |

kidney [ˈkɪdni] n	Niere
cornea [ˈkɔːniə] n	Hornhaut
pancreas [ˈpæŋkriəs] n	Bauchspeicheldrüse / Pankreas

bone marrow n	Knochenmark
heart n	Herz
liver n	Leber
blood transfusion n	Bluttransfusion
red blood cell / erythrocyte [ɪ'rɪθrəsaɪt] n	rotes Blutkörperchen / Erythrocyte
IgM (immunoglobuline M) n	IgM (Immunoglobulin M)
blood group system n	Blutgruppensystem
AB0 system n	AB0-System
rhesus system ['riːsəsˌsɪstəm] n	Rhesussystem
blood goup A/B/AB/0 n	Blutgruppe A/B/AB/0
prior [praɪə] adv	vorherig
intestinal [ɪn'testɪnl] adj	Darm~ / intestinal
blood exchange n	Blutaustausch
placenta [plə'sentə] n	Plazenta / Mutterkuchen
placental barrier	Plazentaschranke
pass through v	durchsickern / durchgehen
incompatibility n	Unverträglichkeit / Inkompatibilität

»
anti-B, anti body against blood group antigen B	Anti-B, Antikörper gegen das Blutgruppenantigen B

autoimmune deficiency [ˌɔːtəʊɪˌmjuːndɪ'fɪʃnsi] n	Autoimmungstörung
autoimmune disease n	Autoimmunerkrankung
islet of Langerhans [ˌaɪlɪtəv'læŋəhæns] n	Langerhans'sche Insel
diabetes mellitus type 1 [ˌdaɪəbiːtiːz'melɪtəs] n	Diabetes mellitus Typ 1
chronic inflammatory rheumatism [ˌkrɒnɪkɪn'flæmətriˌruːmətɪzm] n	chronischer entzündlicher Rheumatismus
joint inflammation n	Gelenkentzündung
rheumatoid factor [ˌruːmətɔɪd'fæktə] n	Rheumafaktor
insulin production n	Insulinproduktion / Insulinbildung
thyroid ['θaɪrɔɪd] n	Schilddrüse
thyroid hyperfunction ['θaɪrɔɪdˌhaɪpə'fʌŋkʃn] n	Schilddrüsenüberfunktion
autoantibody n	Autoantikörper
pernicious anaemia [pəˌnɪʃəsə'niːmɪə] n	perniziöse Anämie
immunological tolerance n	immunologische Toleranz
self tolerance n	Selbsttoleranz

5 Genetics › 5.7 Immunogenetics

AIDS » Abb. 51

AIDS / acquired immune deficiency syndrome	AIDS / erworbenes Immundefizienzsyndrom
HIV (human immunodeficiency virus) n	HIV
envelope n	Virushülle / Envelop
glycoprotein [ˌglaɪkəʊˈprəʊtiːn] n	Glycoprotein
pin head n	Nadelkopf
capsid [ˈkæpsɪd] n	Kapsid *(kapselartige Proteinstruktur)*
helper T cell (T$_H$) n	T-Helfer-Zelle
cell surface molecule CD4 n	Zelloberflächenmolekül CD4
retrovirus [ˈretrəvaɪrəs] n	Retrovirus
reverse transcriptase [rɪˌvɜːstrænˈskrɪpteɪz] n	reverse Transkriptase
reverse transcription n	reverse Transkription
integrase n	Integrase
protease [ˈprəʊtieɪz] n	Protease
pro-virus n	Provirus
burst v	platzen
release v	freisetzen

course of disease n	Krankheitsverlauf
HIV-positive adj	HIV-positiv
symptom [ˈsɪmtəm] n	Symptom
final stage n	letztes Stadium
pneumonia [njuːˈmeʊniə] n	Lungenentzündung
toxoplasmosis [ˌtɒksəplæzˈməʊsɪs] n	Toxoplasmose
tumour *BE* [ˈtjuːmə] / tumor *AE* n	Tumor
Kaposi's-sarcoma [kəˈpəʊsɪzsɑːˌkəʊmə] n	Kaposi-Sarkom
lymphoma [lɪmˈfəʊmə] n	Lymphom

therapeutic option n	Behandlungsmöglichkeit
reverse transcriptase inhibitor n	Reverse Transkriptase-Inhibitor
base analogue, *pl* base analogues n	Basenanalogon *(Pl. Basenanaloga)*
azidothymindine (AZT) n	Azidothymin
unborn adj	ungeboren
vaccine [ˈvæksiːn] / serum n	Impfstoff
variable adj	variabel / veränderlich
mutate v	mutieren
camouflage [ˈkæməflɑːʒ] n	Tarnung
camouflaged adj	getarnt

protection n	Schutz
condom n	Kondom
unprotected sex n	ungeschützter Geschlechtsverkehr
body fluid n	Körperflüssigkeit
semen ['siːmən] n	Sperma
lymph [lɪmf] n	Lymphe
breast milk n	Muttermilch
vaginal secretion n	Scheidensekret
drug addict n	Drogenabhängiger
addicted to drugs	drogenabhängig
trace of blood n	Blutspur
transmission n	Weitergabe / Verbreitung / Ansteckung

risk of infection	Infektionsrisiko
risk of transmission	Ansteckungsgefahr

Prion diseases

infectious [ɪnˈfekʃəs] adj	infektiös
prion [ˈpraɪɒn] n	Prion (Pl. Prione)
proteinaceous infectious particle [prəʊtəˌneɪʃəsɪnˌfekʃəsˈpɑːtɪkl] n	proteinöser infektiöser Partikel
PrP^c n (harmless form of the prion protein)	PrP^c (celluläre Form des Prion-Proteins; damit harmlos)
PrP^{sc} n (infectious form of the prion-protein)	PrP^{sc} (Scrapieform des Prion-Proteins)
glycoprotein n	Glycoprotein
BSE (bovine spongiforme encephalopathy) [ˌbəʊvaɪnˌspʌndʒɪfɔːmˌenkefəˈlɒpəθi] n	BSE
bovine adj	Rinder-betreffend / Rinder~
spongiform adj	schwammförmig
encephalopathy n	Enzephalopathie / Gehirnkrankheit
mad cow disease n	Rinderwahnsinn
cattle n pl	Rinder / Vieh
scrapie [ˈskreɪpi] n (prion disease in sheep)	Skrapie / Traberkrankheit (Prionen-Krankheit bei Schafen)
scrape v	kratzen

Creutzfeldt-Jakob disease (CJD) / kuru n — Creutzfeldt-Jakob-Krankheit / Kuru *(Prionen-Krankheit bei Menschen)*
spatial structure n — räumliche Struktur
proteinase resistant ['prəʊtɪneɪzrɪˌzɪstnt] adj — resistent gegenüber Proteinase
X-ray resistant adj — resistent gegenüber Röntgenstrahlen
cease v — einstellen / vergehen
domino effect n — Dominoeffekt / Kettenreaktion
cross species v — Art(en)grenzen überwinden

5.8 Methods of DNA analysis and more applied genetics

thread-like adj — fädig
fragment n — Fragment / Bruchstück
fragment v — fragmentieren
restriction enzyme n — Restriktionsenzym
restriction fragment n — Restriktionsfragment
  restriction fragment length polymorphism (RFLP) — Restriktionsfragmentlängenpolymorphismus (RFLP)
restriction site n — Restriktionsschnittstelle

> recognition site of a restriction enzyme — Erkennungssequenz eines Restriktionsenzyms
> employ a restriction enzyme — ein Restriktionsenzym verwenden
> cut/cleave with a restriction enzyme — mit einem Restriktionsenzym schneiden/spalten

recognize v — erkennen
specific adj — spezifisch
palindromic [ˌpælɪn'drɒmɪk] adj — palindromisch *(von vorne und hinten zu lesen)*

defined adj — definiert
protruding [prə'truːdɪŋ] adj — überhängend
sticky end n — klebriges Ende *(„sticky end" ist auch im Deutschen gebräuchlich)*

overhang n — Überhang
compatible adj — kompatibel

> Restriction enzymes cleave DNA at specific DNA-sequences so-called restriction sites.
> Restriktionsenzyme schneiden die DNA an spezifschen Sequenzen, den sogenannten Restriktionsstellen.
>
> Restriction sites are often palindromic which means that the sequence is the same, regardless whether one reads the forward or reverse strand.
> Restriktionsstellen sind oft palindromisch (rückwärts laufend), was bedeutet, dass die Erkennungssequenz die gleiche ist, unabhängig davon, ob man den Vorwärts- oder den Rückwärtsstrang liest.
> *Bam*HI and *Sau*3A produce compatible ends in having the same overhang.
> *Bam*HI und *Sau*3A produzieren kompatible Enden mit dem gleichen Überhang.

separate v	trennen / auftrennen / separieren
separation n	Auftrennung
migrate v	wandern
charge n	Ladung
charge v	laden
negatively charged adj	negativ geladen
positively charged adj	positiv geladen
electrophoresis [ɪˌlektrəfəˈriːsɪs] n	Elektrophorese
gel-electrophoresis n	Gel-Elektrophorese
paper-electrophoresis n	Papier-Elektrophorese
capillary-electrophoresis n	Kapillar-Elektrophorese
electrophoresis chamber / electrophoresis apparatus [ɪˌlektrəfəˈriːsɪs ˌæprˈeɪtəs]	Elektrophorese-Kammer / -Apparatur
electrophoresis buffer	Elektrophorese-Puffer
electrical field n	elektrisches Feld
gel [dʒəl] n	Gel
agarose gel [ˌægərəʊzˈdʒəl]	Agarose-Gel
polyacrylamide gel [ˌpɒliəˈkrɪləmaɪdˈdʒəl]	Polyacrylamid-Gel
gel tray	Gel-Träger
slot n	„Slot" / Langloch / Geltasche
comb n	Kamm
band n	Bande
molecular weight standard n	Molekulargewichtsstandard / Größenmarker
base pair (bp) n	Basenpaar
dye n	Farbstoff
stain v	färben

5 Genetics › 5.8 Methods of DNA analysis and more applied genetics

» The fragments migrate during gel-electrophoresis according to their size and charge.
Die Fragmente wandern während der Gel-Elektrophorese in Abhängigkeit von ihrer Größe und Ladung.

transfer v	transferieren / übertragen
blot v	„blotten" / aufsaugen
blot n *(membrane with the transferred material: DNA, RNA or proteine)*	„Blot" *(Membran mit dem transferierten Material: DNA, RNA oder Protein)*
capillary transfer [kəˌpɪləriˈtrænsfɜː] n	Kapillartransfer
nylon membrane n	Nylonmembran
blotting paper n	Löschpapier
paper towel n	Papierhandtuch
Southern blot n *(named after Prof. Ed Southern, who invented this technique)*	„Southern-Blot" / transferiertes DNA-Gel *(nach Prof. Ed Southern benannt)*
Northern blot n	„Northern-Blot" *(transferiertes RNA-Gel)*
Western blot n	„Western-Blot" *(transferiertes Protein-Gel)*

» To detect individual DNA-fragments with a radioactively labelled probe, at first the fragments are transferred to a nylon membrane by means of capilliary transfer (Southern blot).
Um einzelne DNA-Fragmente mit einer radioaktiv-markierten Probe aufzuspüren, werden zunächst die Fragmente mittels Kapillartransfer auf eine Nylon-Membran übertragen.

hybridisation BE / hybridization AE [ˌhaɪbrɪdaɪˈzeɪʃn] n	Hybridisierung
hybridise BE / hybridize AE n	hybridisieren
radioactive adj	radioaktiv
probe n	Probe / Sonde
label n	Etikett
label (sth) v	(etw.) markieren / (etw.) kennzeichnen / (etw.) beschriften
complementary adj	komplementär
autoradiograph n	Autoradiografie
X-ray film n	Röntgenfilm
develop (sth) v	(etw.) entwickeln
visible adj	sichtbar
blacken [ˈblækn] v	schwärzen
blackening n	Schwärzung
blackened bands	geschwärzte Banden
blackened spots	geschwärzte Punkte

| label a probe radioactively | eine Probe radioaktiv markieren |

melt v	schmelzen
melting curve n	Schmelzkurve
melting point n	Schmelzpunkt
AT-rich region n	AT-reiche Region
GC-rich region n	GC-reiche Region
denature [ˌdiː'neɪtʃə] v	denaturieren
denaturing / denaturation n	Denaturierung
strand n	Strang
single-strand(ed) DNA	Einzelstrang-DNA
double-strand(ed) DNA	Doppelstrang-DNA
renature v	renaturieren
renaturing / renaturation n	Renaturierung
reanneal [ˌriːə'niːl] v	bei niedrigerer Temperatur wieder aneinander lagern *(wörtl. abkühlen, ausglühen)*
mismatch n	Fehlpaarung / falsche Paarung
close match	gute Entsprechung
perfect match	perfekte Entsprechung / perfekte Paarung
degree of relationship n	Verwandtschaftsgrad

C_0t–curve n	C_0t-Kurve
reassociation study n	Reassoziationsstudie
reassociation kinetics n	Reassoziationskinetik
complexity n	Komplexität
repetitive DNA [rɪ'petətɪv] n	repetitive DNA
satellite DNA n *(DNA forming satellite bands during buoyant density centrifugation)*	Satelliten-DNA *(DNA, die bei Dichtegradientenzentrifugation Satellitenbanden bildet)*
tandem repeat ['tændəmrɪˌpiːt] n	Tandem-Wiederholung
short tandem repeats (STRs)	kurze Tandem-Wiederholungen
alphoid DNA n	a-Satelliten-DNA / Alphoid-DNA
transposable element / transposon [træns'pəʊzɒn] n	transponierbares Element / Transposon
retroviral insertion [ˌretrəvaɪrlɪn'sɜːʃn] n	retrovirale Insertion
jumping gene n	springendes Gen
single copy DNA n	single-copy-DNA *(DNA, die im Genom als einzelne Kopie vorliegt)*

5 Genetics › 5.8 Methods of DNA analysis and more applied genetics

UV spectrometer [juːviːspekˈtrɒmɪtə] n	UV-Spektrometer
spectrometrically adj	spektrometrisch
wavelength n	Wellenlänge
absorption n	Absorption
absorb v	absorbieren

» Double stranded DNA melts into two single strands when the temperature is increased above 80–90°C.
Doppelsträngige DNA schmilzt in zwei Einzelstränge, wenn die Temperatur auf über 80–90°C erhöht wird.

isolate v	isolieren
isolation n	Isolierung / Isolation
amplify [ˈæmplɪfaɪ] v	amplifizieren / vermehren
amplification n	Amplifikation / Vermehrung
cut v	schneiden
sequence v	sequenzieren
sequence n	Sequenz
sequencing n	Sequenzierung

PCR » Abb. 49

PCR (polymerase chain reaction) n	PCR (Polymerase-Kettenreaktion)
generate v	herstellen / generieren
DNA replicated	vervielfältigte DNA
generate DNA	DNA herstellen
test tube n	Reagenzglas / Reaktionsgefäß
reaction volume n	Reaktionsvolumen
thermocycler [ˈθɜːməˌsaɪklə] n	Thermocycler / PCR-Maschine
(thermal) block n	(Thermo-)Block
heated lid n	beheizter Deckel
silicone oil [ˈsɪlɪkəʊnˌɔɪl] n	Silikonöl
primer [ˈpraɪmə] n	Primer
oligonucleotide [ˌɒlɪgəˈnjuːkliətaɪd] n	Oligonukleotid *(DNA-Fragment aus wenigen Nukleotiden bestehend)*
reverse adj	rückwärts
forward adj	vorwärts
dNTP (deoxyNucleotideTriphosphate) n	dNTP (desoxyNukleotidtriphosphat)
DNA polymerase	DNA-Polymerase
Taq polymerase n	Taq-Polymerase

heat-stable / temperature resistant adj	hitzestabil / temperaturesistent
melting temperature	Schmelztemperatur
hot spring n	heiße Quelle
thermophilus aquaticus n	thermophiles Bakterium

cycle n	Zyklus
repeat v	wiederholen
PCR-step n	PCR-Schritt
thermal cycling steps ['θɜːmlˌsaɪklɪŋsteps] n	Verdopplungszyklus *(Prozess des schrittweisen Erhitzens und Abkühlens)*
annealing n	Anlagerung *(wörtl. Ausglühen, Abkühlen)*
anneal v	anlagern / annealen
extension n	Verlängerung
extend v	verlängern
DNA melting n	Aufschmelzen der DNA *(Zerlegung in Einzelstränge)*

»

heating of the sample	Erhitzen der Probe
cooling of the sample	Abkühlen der Probe

single-stranded DNA n	DNA Einzelstrang
double-stranded DNA n	DNA Doppelstrang
complement ['kɒmplɪmənt] v	vervollständigen
template n	Template / Matritze
exponential adj	exponentiell

»

copy a billion times / billionfold	milliardenfach kopieren

»

A heat-stable DNA polymerase is the prerequisit for PCR.
Eine hitzestabile DNA-Polymerase ist die Vorraussetzung für die PCR.
DNA is repeatedly denatured, primers are annealed and extended. Thus a specific DNA segment which is located beween the two primer binding sites is exponentially amplified.
DNA wird wiederholt denaturiert, Primer werden angelagert (annealed) und verlängert. So wird ein spezifisches DNA-Segment, was zwischen den beiden Primerbindungsstellen liegt, exponentiell amplifiziert.

Chain termination method

sequencing n	Sequenzierung
sequencing reaction n	Sequenzier(ungs)reaktion
modified adj	modifiziert
modify v	modifizieren
ddNTP (dideoxynucleotide triphosphate) n	Didesoxynukleotid-Triphosphat
sequencing primer n	Sequenzier(ungs)primer
chain termination method n	Kettenabbruchmethode

> | | |
> |---|---|
> | chain termination method by Sanger | Kettenabbruchverfahren von Sanger |
> | cut at random | willkürlich zerschneiden |

continue v	fortsetzen
incorporate v	einbauen
radioactive nucleotide n	radioaktives Nukleotid
fluorescence dye-linked nucleotide n	Fluoreszenzfarbstoff-gekoppeltes Nukleotid
DNA polymerase n	DNA-Polymerase
electrophoresis [ɪˌlektrəfə'riːsɪs] n	Elektrophorese
pherograph ['ferəgrɑːf] v (separate by electorphoresis)	pherografieren (trennen durch Elektrophorese)
electric(al) field n	elektrisches Feld
separate v	trennen
fragment n	Fragment / Bruchstück
migrate v	wandern
fluorescence detector n	Fluoreszenz-Detektor
recorder n	Rekorder / Schreiber
printout n	Ausdruck
autoradiography n	Autoradiografie

> The most commonly used sequencing method for DNA is the chain termination method.
> Die gebräuchlichste DNA-Sequenzierungsmethode ist die Kettenabbruchmethode.
> DNA is denatured, a sequencing primer is annealed and extended.
> DNA wird denaturiert, ein Sequenzierprimer wird angelagert (annealed) und verlängert.
> The extension reaction is terminated by incorporation of ddNTPs.
> Die Verlängerung wird durch den Einbau von ddNTPs abgebrochen.

In case of using fluorescently labelled ddNTPs, all termination reactions be can carried out in one reaction tube, because each of the ddNTPs (A, C, G, T) is linked to a differently coloured dye.
Benutzt man fluoreszenzmarkierte ddNTPs könnnen alle Terminationsreaktionen in einem Reaktionsgefäß durchgeführt werden, weil jedes der ddNTP (A, C, G, T) mit einem unterschiedlichen Farbstoff verknüpft ist.
After having denatured the mixture again, fragments of different legth are separated electrophoretically with short fragments migrating the fastest.
Nach erneuter Denaturierung können die Fragmente unterschiedlicher Länge elektrophoretisch aufgetrennt werden, wobei die kurzen Fragmente am schnellsten wandern.

DNA fingerprinting and more research methods

criminology n	Kriminalistik
suspect n	Verdächtiger
establish sb's guilt v	(jmd. einer Schuld) überführen
sample n	Probe
saliva sample	Speichelprobe
sample material	Probenmaterial
distinctive [dɪˈstɪŋtɪv] adj	unverwechselbar
tamper-proof [ˈtæmpəpruːf] adj	fälschungssicher
genetic fingerprint n	genetischer Fingerabdruck
forensic scientist [fəˈrensɪkˌsaɪəntɪst] n	Forensiker
scene of crime n	Tatort
allocate [ˈæləkeɪt] v	zuordnen
fingerprinting [ˈfɪŋɡəprɪntɪŋ] n	Identifizierung durch Fingerabdruck
genetic fingerprint	genetischer Fingerabdruck
DNA analysis n	DNA-Analyse
identification n	Identifizierung

Terminology: Genetic fingerpriting

Genetic fingerpriting is also known as:
DNA profiling – DNA testing – DNA typing

amplify v	amplifizieren / vermehren
code v	kodieren
coding DNA n	kodierende DNA
non-coding DNA n	nichtkodierende DNA
selection-neutral adj	selektionsneutral
accumulate v	anhäufen
evolution n	Evolution

5 Genetics › 5.8 Methods of DNA analysis and more applied genetics

repetitive sequence [rɪˌpetətɪv'siːkwəns] n	repetitive DNA-Sequenz
short tandem repeats (STRs) n	sich wiederholende Abschnitte im Erbgut *(kürzer als VNTRs)*
variable number tandem repeats (VNTRs) n	Minisatelliten DNA / Minisatellit / sich wiederholende Abschnitte im Erbgut
protein-coding gene n *(non-coding gene)*	für Protein codierendes Gen *(nicht codierendes Gen)*
single nucleotide polymorphism (SNP) ['sɪŋgl'njuːkliətaɪdˌpɒlɪ'mɔːfɪzm] n	SNP *(Punktmutationen, in denen sich zwei Allele unterschieden)*
detect v	entdecken / aufspüren
easily detectable	leicht zu entdecken
probability n	Wahrscheinlichkeit

microsatellite [ˌmaɪkrə'sætlaɪt] n	Mikrosatellit
restriction fragment n	Restriktionsfragment
fragment length n	Fragmentlänge
RFLP (restriction fragment length polymorphism) [rɪˌstrɪkʃn'frægməntˌleŋθpɒlɪ'mɔːfɪzm]	RFLP (Restriktionsfragment-Längen-Polymorphismus)
restriction enzyme n	Restriktionsenzym
cutting site / restriction site n	Schnittstelle / Restriktionsschnittstelle
restriction endonuclease [rɪ'strɪkʃnˌendəʊ'njuːklɪeɪz] n	Restriktionsendonuklease

gel electrophoresis n	Gelelektrophorese
gel [dʒel] n	Gel
agarose gel ['ægərəʊzˌdʒel]	Agarose-Gel
polyacrylamide gel [ˌpɒliə'krɪləmaɪdˌdʒəl]	Polyacrylamid-Gel

» determination of fragment length in comparison
Ermittlung der Länge der Fragmente im Vergleich

denaturing / denaturation n	Denaturierung
denaturate v	denaturieren
alkaline solution n	alkalische Lösung
sodium hydroxide (NaOH) [ˌsəʊdɪəmhaɪ'drɒksaɪd] n	Natriumhydroxid (NaOH)
blot v	ablöschen / aufsaugen / „blotten"

Southern blot n *(named after Prof. Ed Southern, who invented this technique)*	„Southern-Blot" / transferiertes DNA-Gel *(nach Prof. Ed Southern benannt)*
nylon membrane n	Nylonmembran
fixation n	Fixierung
fix v	fixieren

probe n	Probe / Sonde
radioactive adj	radioaktiv
radioactive-sensitive adj	radioaktiv empfindlich
X-ray film n	Röntgenfilm
label / mark v	markieren
hybridise *BE* [ˈhaɪbrɪdaɪz] / hybridize *AE* n	hybridisieren
band n	Bande
blacken [ˈblækn] v	schwärzen
pattern n	Muster

fatherhood / paternity n	Vaterschaft
exclude v	ausschließen
eliminate v	eliminieren / ausscheiden
compare v	vergleichen

Gene mapping and the human genome project

human genome project (HGP) n	Humangenomprojekt
HUGO (human genome organization) n	HUGO (Human-Genom-Organisation)
map n	Karte
map v	kartografieren / kartieren
topographical map [tɒpəˈgræfɪklˌmæp] n *(banding pattern of the chromosome)*	topografische Karte *(Bandenmuster des Chromosoms)*
genetic map n *(recombination frequency)*	genetische Karte *(Rekombinationshäufigkeit)*
physical map n *(distance in bp, kbp or Mbp)*	physikalische Karte *(Abstände in bp, kbp oder Mbp)*
transcript map n *(localisation of cDNAs on the physical map)*	Transkriptionskarte *(Lage der cDNAs auf der physikalischen Karte)*

sequencing n	Sequenzbildung / Sequenzierung
hierarchical sequencing [ˌhaɪˈrɑːkɪklˌsiːkwənsɪŋ]	hierarchische Sequenzierung *(Sequenzierung überlappender Klone)*

shotgun sequencing	Shotgun-Sequenzierung *(Aneinanderreihung von DNA-Sequenzen auf Grundlage von überlappenden Basenfolgen des gesamten Genoms)*
sequencing by hybridisation n	Hybridsequenzierung
genomic library n	Genom-Bibliothek
large insert library	Genombibliothek mit großen Inserts
clone [kləʊn] n	Klon
overlapping fragment n	überlappendes Fragment
chromosomal walking n	„Chromosomal-Walking"
YAC (yeast artificial chromosome) n	YAC *(künstliches Hefechromosom)*
PAC (P1 derived artificial chromosome) n	PAC *(künstliches Bakterienchromosom das vom P1-Phagen her abgeleitet wurde)*
BAC (bacterial artificial chromosome) n	BAC *(künstliches Bakterienchromosom)*
cosmid ['kɒzmɪd] n *(artificial bacterial plasmid that is transfected via lambda phage extract)*	Cosmid *(künstliches Bakterienplasmid, das über Lambda Phagen Extrakte transfiziert wird)*
lambda phage ['læmdə,feɪdʒ]	Lambda-Phage *(Bakteriophage, bei dem ein Teil des Genoms durch Fremd-Inserts ersetzt werden kann)*
lambda library n	Lambda-Bibliothek

» | minimal tiling path | minimaler Weg mit überlappenden Klonen |

colony hybridisation n	Koloniehybridisierung *(Hybridisierung auf Nylonfilter, auf denen zuvor die DNA von Bakterien- oder Hefezellen fixiert wurde)*
colony lift n	„Kolonielift" *(eine Nylonmembran wird vorsichtig auf eine Agar-Platte mit Bakterienkolonien gelegt; beim Abziehen bleibt ein Teil der Kolonie an der Membran haften)*
lyse [laɪz] v	lysieren
insert preparation n	Insert-Herstellung / Insert-Vorbereitung
partially digested adj	teilweise verdaut *(mit Restriktionsenzymen)*
random adj	zufällig / zufalls~

shear [ʃɪə] v	scheren *(durch Scherkräfte zerkleinern)*
ligate v	ligieren

> | ligate to the vector | mit dem Vektor ligieren |

subcloning n	„Subcloning"
shotgun library n	Schrotschuss-Bibliothek
select v	auswählen

> Normally, for sequencing a whole genome, at first large insert libraries are constructed.
> Um ein ganzes Genom zu sequenzieren werden normalerweise zuerst Genbibliotheken mit großem Insert hergestellt.
> Then a minimal tiling path is established.
> Dann wird ein „minimal tiling path", d.h. ein minimaler Weg mit überlappenden Klonen festgelegt.
> The inserts of the selected clones are subcloned by making a small insert shotgun library.
> Die Inserts der ausgewählten Klone werden subkloniert, indem eine Schrotschuss-Bibliothek mit kleineren Inserts hergestellt wird.
> The clones of the shotgun library are sequenced, and the sequence reads are assembled to represent the sequence of the whole "large insert" clone.
> Die Klone der Schrotschuss-Bibliothek werden sequenziert und Sequenzen werden zusammengesetzt, um die Sequenz des ganzen „Large Insert"-Klons zu erhalten.

exon ['eksɒn] n	Exon
exon prediction program	Exonvorhersageprogramm
exon-intron boundaries	Exon-Intron-Grenzen
ORF (open reading frame) n	offenes Leseraster
cDNA (complementary DNA) n	cDNA *(komplementäre DNA zur RNA)*
mRNA (messenger RNA) n	mRNA (Boten-RNA)
align [ə'laɪn] v	anlegen / ausrichten
annotate ['ænəteɪt] v	annotieren / mit Kommentaren versehen
consensus [kən'sensəs] n	Konsensus / Konsens

> After sequencing a genome the sequence needs to get analysed and annotated.
> Nach dem Sequenzieren eines Genoms, muss die Sequenz noch analysiert und mit Kommentaren versehen werden.
> Exon prediction programs search for open reading frames, exon-intron boundaries, start-codons and consensus promoter sequences.
> Exonvorhersageprogramme suchen nach offenen Leserastern, Exon-Intron-Grenzen, Startcondons und Konsensus-Promotor-Sequenzen.

5 Genetics › 5.8 Methods of DNA analysis and more applied genetics

> The sequences of known cDNAs are aligned with the genomic sequence.
> Die Sequenzen von bekannten cDNAs werden an der genomischen Sequenz ausgerichtet.

Applied genetics in medicine

diagnosis [ˌdaɪəɡˈnəʊsɪs] n	Diagnostik / Diagnose
diagnose v	diagnostizieren
diagnostic adj	diagnostisch
risk n	Risiko
risk estimation	Risikoabschätzung
relief n	Erleichterung
suffer v	leiden
lower (sth) v	(etw.) vermindern / herabsetzen
elevate [ˈelɪveɪt] v	erhöhen
elevated risk n	erhöhtes Risiko
DNA chip n	DNA-Chip
array [əˈreɪ] n	Anordnung / Datenfeld
DNA microarray [ˌdiːenˈeɪmaɪkrəʊəˈreɪ] / gene chip n	DNA-Chip
monitor v	beobachten / kontrollieren
splice variants n	Spleißvarianten
expression level n	Genexpression
genotyping [ˈdʒenəʊtaɪpɪŋ] n	Genotypisierung

> The microarray format has the abilitiy to identify splice variants of the same gene
> Das DNA Chip-Format ermöglicht es, die Spleißvarianten des gleichen Gens zu ermitteln.
> Comparing expression levels in general one variant is most abundantly expressed.
> Der Vergleich der Genexpressionen ergibt, dass eine Variante am häufigsten auftriff.

artificially synthesised adj	künstlich hergestellt
silicon [ˈsɪlɪkən] n	Silizium
dot matrix [ˌdɒtˈmeɪtrɪks] n	Punktraster
variant n	Variante
attach v	befestigen
fluorescently labelled adj	fluoreszenz-markiert
hybridise BE / hybridize AE n	hybridisieren
patient sample n	Patientenprobe
competition n	Konkurrenz
competitive adj	kompetitiv / konkurrierend
scanner n	Scanner

scan v   "scannen" / abrastern
mass screen n   Massenscreen

» A DNA chip ususally consists of several thousand different DNA oligonucleotides which are attached to a glass or silicone surface in a defined dot matrix.
Ein DNA-Chip besteht aus einigen tausend verschieden DNA-Oligonukleotiden, die an eine Glas- oder Silikonoberfläche in Form einer definierten Punktmatrix gebunden sind.
Fluorescently labelled patient DNA is hybridised to the chip.
Fluoreszenzmarkierte Patienten-DNA wird mit den Chip hybridisiert.

6 Biotechnology » III. 3.5 Industrial and commercial uses of enzymes; 5.7. Immunogenetics; 10.12 River and stream ecosystem: sewage water treatment; drinking water treatment

6.1 Keywords

biotechnology n	Biotechnologie
bacterium [bæk'tɪərɪəm], pl bacteria n	Bakterium
yeast cell n	Hefezelle
baker's yeast	Bäckerhefe
brewer's yeast	Bierhefe
microorganism [ˌmaɪkrəʊ'ɔːɡnɪzm] n	Mikroorganismus / Mikrobe / Kleinstlebewesen
cultivate v	kultivieren
culture n	Kultur
active substance / agent n	Wirkstoff
penicillin [ˌpenɪ'sɪlɪn] n	Penicillin
incorporate v	einbauen
transgenic adj	transgen
genetically modified organism (GMO) n	genetisch modifizierter Organismus (GMO)
large scale adj	in großem Maßstab / in großem Umfang
large scale production n	Massenproduktion / Massenfertigung
batch culture n	Batch-Kultur *(statische Kultur in geschlossenem System)*
large batch production n	Großserienfertigung
fermentation [ˌfɜːmen'teɪʃn] n	Gärung
fermenter n	Fermenter *(Gärbottich, Rührkessel etc.)*
closed vessel n	geschlossener Behälter
steam sterilised n	durch Dampf sterilisiert

6 Biotechnology › 6.1 Keywords

sterile nutrient n	steriler Nährstoff
maximum level of product n	höchste Produktmenge
yield of product n	Produktertrag / Produktausbeute
harvest v	ernten
product removal n	Entfernen des Produkts
waste substance n	Abfallstoff
decrease of product	Verminderung des Produkts *(der Produktionsrate)*
contaminate v	verunreinigen / kontaminieren
contaminant n	verunreinigende Substanz / Schadstoff

»
harvesting time is critical	die Erntezeit ist wesentlich
shut down	Herunterfahren (z. B. einer Anlage)
vessels need to be cleaned and resterilised	Gefäße müssen gesäubert und neu sterilisiert werden

continuous fermentation n	Durchlaufgäranlage
open fermenter n	offener Fermenter *(z.B. Gärbottich)*
regular sampling n	regelmäßige Probeentnahme
in equilibrium adj	im Gleichgewicht
input n	Zugabe
output n	Entnahme
regular input	regelmäßige Zugabe
regular output	regelmäßige Entnahme

mycoprotein n	Mycoprotein *(Pilzprotein)*
airlift fermenter / bioreactor n	Airlift Reaktor *(Umwälzung der Inhaltsstoffe erfolgt über das Einblasen von Luft)*
stirrer n	Rührer
sparger n	Strömungsleitrohr
gas outlet n	Gasaustritt
monitor v	kontrollieren / beobachten
flavour n	Geschmacksstoff

Commercial production of cheese

pasteurise v	pasteurisieren *(Erhitzen unter 100 °C von z.B. verderblichen Lebensmitteln zwecks Haltbarmachung)*
texture n	Beschaffenheit

flavour n	Geschmack
raw milk n	Rohmilch
cream n	Rahm
coagulate / clot v	gerinnen / koagulieren
lactic acid n	Milchsäure / Laktat
casein n *(milk protein)*	Kasein / Casein *(Milchprotein)*
curd n	Käsebruch
whey n	Molke / Käsewasser
rennet n	Lab / Chymosin
mould n	Form
ripening n	Reifung
rind n	Rinde
press sth into a mould	etw. in eine Form pressen

Commercial production of beer

barley ['bɑːli] n	Gerste
hop n	Hopfen
brewer's yeast n *(Saccharomyces cerevisiae)*	Brauhefe
malting n	Mälzen
malt n	Malz
germinate ['dʒɜːmɪneɪt] v	keimen / ankeimen
seed embryo n	Keimling
amylase n	Amylase *(spaltet Stärke in Maltose bzw. Glukose)*
milling n	Mahlen
grist n	Mahlgut
mash n	Maische
wort n	Bierwürze / Stammwürze
finings n	Klärmittel
filtration n	Filtration / Filtrierung

Food additives made by yeast

yeast [jiːst] n	Hefe(-pilz)
self-digestion / autolysis n	Selbstverdauung / Autolyse
breakdown product / autolysate n	Abbauprodukt *(Produkt das durch die Selbstauflösung entsteht)*

centrifugation ['sentrɪfjuːgeɪʃn] n	Zentrifugation
dehydration n	Dehydration / Entwässern / Trocknung
food additive n	Lebensmittelzusatzstoff / Lebensmittelzusatz

6.2 Gene transfer

gene [dʒiːn] n	Gen
genetic adj	genetisch
geneticist [dʒən'netɪsɪst] n	Genetiker
genetic engineering n	Gentechnologie / Gentechnik / Genmanipulation
gene transfer n	Gentransfer
genome ['dʒiːnəʊm] n	Erbgut
transformation n	Transformation
transform v	transformieren
recombination n	Rekombination
recombine v	rekombinieren / neu kombinieren

»
uptake of naked DNA	Aufnahme von reiner DNA
transfer of genetic material	Übertragung von Erbmaterial
natural gene transfer is the basis of …	natürlicher Gentransfer bildet die Grundlage für …

Conjugation

auxotroph ['ɔːksətrɒf] adj	auxotroph (einen Stoff nicht bilden könnend)
strain n	Stamm / Bakterienstamm
vitamin Biotin [ˌvɪtəmɪn'baɪətɪn] / vitamin B7 n	Vitamin B7 / Biotin
minimal nutrient medium [ˌmɪnɪmlnjuːtriənt'miːdiəm] n	Minimalnährmedium
agar ['eɪgɑː] n	Agar
solid nutrient medium agar n	festes Agarnährmedium

»
| spread sth on the medium | etw. auf das (Nähr-)Medium auftragen |

Amino acids

Methionine	Methionin
Leucine	Leucin
Threonine	Threonin
(Three out of 20 canonical amino acids)	(Drei von 20 kanonischen Aminosäuren)

bacterial colony n | Bakterienkolonie
centrifuge ['sentrɪfjuːdʒ] n | Zentrifuge
supernatant fluid [suːpəˈneɪtnt͵fluːɪd] n | Überstand
gradient [ˈɡreɪdiənt] n | (Dichte-)Gradient

remove by centrifugation	durch Zentrifugation trennen
form a gradient	einen (Dichte-)gradienten bilden

pellet [ˈpelɪt] n | Rückstand
supplement [ˈsʌplɪmənt] n | Ergänzung / Zugabe
bacterial lawn [bækˈtɪərɪəl͵lɔːn] n | Bakterienrasen

fertility factor [fəˈtɪləti͵fæktə] / f-factor / sex factor n | Fertilitätsfaktor
sex pilus [ˈseks͵paɪləs], *pl* pili n | Sexpilus
surface appendage [ˈsɜːfɪsə͵pendɪdʒ] n | Plasmafortsatz
circular DNA [ˈsɜːkld͵diːenˈeɪ] n | DNA-Ring / ringförmige DNA
plasmid n | Plasmid
 circular plasmid | Plasmidring
resistance gene [rɪˈzɪstəns͵dʒiːn] n | Resistenzgen
HFR strain (*high frequency of recombination*) n | Bakterienstämme mit Fertilitätsfaktor
donor [ˈdəʊnə] n | Donor / Spender
recipient n | Rezipient / Empfänger
transfer n | Übertragung
replication n | Replikation
origin n | Ursprung / Ausgangspunkt
 oriT (origin of transfer) site | Startbereich des Transfers *(und Replikation)*
coding region n | kodierender Bereich / kodierende Region
inducible promoter [ɪn͵djuːsɪblprəˈməʊtə] n | induzierbarer Promotor *(ein Bereich, der angeschaltet und abgeschaltet werden)*

6 Biotechnology › 6.2 Gene transfer

sensitive adj	empfindlich
insensitive adj	unempfindlich
resistant adj	restistent
ampicillin-sensitive [æmpɪˈsɪlɪˌsensitive]	Ampicillin-sensitiv
ampicillin-resitant [æmpɪˈsɪlɪnrˌzɪstnt]	Ampicillin-resistent
replicate v	replizieren
autonomous [ɔːˈtɒnəməs] adj	autonom
antibiotic [ˌæntɪbaɪˈɒtɪk] n	Antibiotikum
colon bacterium [ˈkəʊlɒnbækˌtɪəriəm] n	Darmbakterium
diarrhoea BE [ˌdaɪəˈrɪə] / diarrhea AE [ˌdaɪəˈriːə] n	Durchfallerkrankung

»

be sensitive to a certain antibiotic	empfindlich gegen ein bestimmtes Antibiotikum sein
rapid increase of resistant bacteria	rasche Zunahme resistenter Bakterien
application of antibiotics	Einsatz von Antibiotika
without consulting a doctor	ohne Beratung mit einem Arzt / einer Ärztin
terminate a therapy	eine Therapie beenden

Transduction

lactose [ˈlæktəʊs] / milk sugar n	Laktose / Milchzucker
lac⁺-strain [ˈlækˌstreɪn] n	lac⁺-Stamm
bacteria culture / bacteriological culture n	Bakterienkultur
phage [feɪdʒ] n	Phage
infect / contaminate [kənˈtæmɪneɪt] v	infizieren

»

transfer of DNA by viruses	Übertragung von DNA mithilfe von Viren
construction of a phage with a fragment of the bacterial genome	Bildung eines Phagen mit einem Anteil des Bakterien-Chromosomes
attachment of a lac⁺ transducing phage	Anheftung eines lac⁺ transduzierenden Phagen

Transfection

carcinogen [kɑːˈsɪnədʒn] adj	karzinogen
carcinogen n	Karzinogen
extract n	Extrakt
extract v	extrahieren / herauslösen
tumour BE [ˈtjuːmə] / tumor AE n	Tumor
oncogene [ˈɒŋkədʒiːn] n	krebserregendes Gen / Onkogen

treatment n	Behandlung
treat v	behandeln
calcium phosphate [ˌkælsɪəmˈfɒsfeɪt] n	Calcium-Phosphat

particle gun [ˈpɑːtɪkl ˌgʌn] n	Particle-Gun / Partikelbeschuss-Gun
tungsten [ˈtʌŋstən] n	Wolfram
lipofection [lɪpəˈfekʃn] n	Lipofektion *(DNA-Aufnahme durch Liposomen)*
electroporation [ɪˌlektrəpɔːrˈeɪʃn] n *(high voltage treatment)*	Elektroporation *(Behandlung mit hoher Spannung)*
electric pulse n	elektrischer Puls
permeable [ˈpɜːmiəbl] adj	durchlässig
coated particle n	beschichteter Partikel
liposome [ˈlɪpəsəʊm] n	Liposom
foreign DNA n	Fremd-DNA

6.3 Techniques used to generate recombinant DNA

How are DNA fragments generated?

genetic tool n	genetisches Werkzeug
isolate v	isolieren
restriction enzyme n	Restriktionsenzym
chemical scissors [ˌkemɪklˈsɪzəz] n	genetische Scheren
dispose of [dɪˈspəʊzɒv] v	unschädlich machen
cleavage [ˈkliːvɪdʒ] / cut n	Schnitt
cleave, cleft, cleft / cut (up sth), cut, cut v	(etw.) zerschneiden
fragment n	Schnittstück / Fragment
arbitrary [ˈɑːbɪtrri] adj	beliebig / arbiträr
random adj	zufällig / zufalls~
recognition sequence [rekəgˈnɪʃnˌsiːkwəns] n	Erkennungssequenz

6 Biotechnology › 6.3 Techniques used to generate recombinant DNA

»
cut DNA fragments at specific sequences	DNA Fragmente an einer ganz bestimmten Basenfolge zerschneiden
targeted cleavage of	gezieltes Zerschneiden von

restriction site / cleavage site n	Schnittstelle
cut / section n	Schnitt
blunt cut	glatter Schnitt
staggered cut [ˌstæɡədˈkʌt]	versetzter Schnitt
end n	Ende
blunt end [ˌblʌntˈend]	glattes Ende
overlapping end / overhang	überlappendes Ende
sticky ends [ˌstɪkiˈendz]	klebrige Enden / sticky ends
protruding [prəˈtruːdɪŋ] / overhanging adj	überhängend / vorstehend
overhang n	Überhang
3′ overhang n	3′-Überhang
5′ overhang n	5′-Überhang
average fragment length n	durchschnittliche Fragmentlänge

» The recognition sequence of most restriction enzymes is palindromic.
Die Erkennungssequenz der meisten Restriktionsenzyme ist palindromisch.
The restriction enzyme EcoRI generates 3′ protruding ends.
Das Restriktionsenzym EcoRI erzeugt 3′ überhängende Enden.
The restriction enzyme HaeIII cuts at the recognition sequence GGCC and generates blunt ends.
Das Restriktionsenzym HaeIII schneidet bei der Erkennungssequenz GGCC und erzeugt stumpfe Enden.
The average fragment length of a restriction enzyme digest depends on the length of the recognition sequence.
Die durchschnittliche Fragmentlänge eines Restriktionsverdaus hängt von der Länge der Erkennungssequenz ab.

base pair (bp) n	Basenpaar
palindromic [ˌpælɪnˈdrɒmɪk] adj	palindromisch *(von vorne und hinten zu lesen)*
restriction digestion [rɪˈstrɪkʃndaɪˌdʒestʃn] n	Restriktionsverdau

»
fragments with complementary ends	Schnittstücke mit komplementären Enden
attach DNA fragments	DNA Stücke aneinander lagern
rejoin DNA fragments	DNA Stücke wieder miteinander verknüpfen

How are the DNA fragments separated and identified?

interval n	Abstand
regular intervals	regelmäßige Abstände
irregular intervals	unregelmäßige Abstände
gel electrophoresis n	Gelelektrophorese
purify n	aufreinigen
fluorescent dye ['flɔː'resnt‚daɪ] n	Fluoreszenzfarbstoff

»

purify / separate an individual fragment	ein bestimmtes DNA Fragment aufreinigen
identify a fragment	ein DNA Fragment bestimmen, identifizieren
the desired fragment	das gewünschte DNA Fragment
stain with fluorescent dye	mit Fluoreszenzfarbstoff markieren

DNA probe [‚diːen'eɪprəʊb] / probe n	Gensonde
single-stranded DNA n	Einzelstrang DNA
single-stranded DNA probe	einzelsträngige Gensonde
sample DNA ['sɑːmpl‚diːen'eɪ] n	DNA Probe
Southern Blotting [‚sʌðən'blɒtɪŋ] n	Southern Blotting *(Technik, DNA von einem Gel auf eine Membran zu übertragen, um damit bestimmte DNA Sequenzen zu ermitteln)*
alkaline solution [‚ælkəlaɪnsə'luːʃn] n	alkalische Lösung
denature [‚diː'neɪtʃə] v	spalten / denaturieren
nylon membrane n	Nylonmembran
transfer v	übertragen
hybridisation probe [‚haɪbrɪdaɪ'zeɪʃn‚prəʊb]	Gensonde *(die Basenpaarungen ausbildet)*
binding [baɪndɪŋ] n	Fixierung / Bindung
non-specific binding	unspezifische Bindung

»

fragment bound to membrane	fixiertes Fragment

unbound probe [ʌn'baʊnd‚prəʊb] n	Gensonde *(die keine DNA binden konnte)*
wash v	reinigen
substrate ['sʌbstreɪt] n	Trägermaterial
pattern ['pætn] n	Muster

6 Biotechnology › 6.3 Techniques used to generate recombinant DNA

banding pattern ['bændɪŋˌpætn] n
characteristic banding pattern

Bandenmuster
charakteristisches Bandenmuster

» The pattern of hybridisation is visualised by …
… X-ray film.
… exposure to UV radiation for detection of fluorecently labelled probes.
…development of colour on the membrane.

Das Ausmaß der Hybridisierung wird sichtbar gemacht durch …
… einen Röntgenfilm.
… Bestrahlung mit UV-Licht, um fluoreszenzmarkierte Proben zu detektieren.
… Entwicklung von Farben auf der Membran.

How can genes be inserted into prokaryotic or eukaryotic cells?

gene shuttle / carrier agent n
vector ['vektə] n
intron ['ɪntrɒn] n
excise [ek'saɪz] v
splicing machinery [ˌsplaɪsɪŋməˈʃiːnri] n

Genfähre
Vektor
Intron
herausschneiden
Spleißmechanismus

» Bacteria lack the splicing machinery to excise introns.
Bakterien fehlt der Spleißmechanismus, um die Introns herauszuschneiden.

yeast [jiːst] n
  expression vector n
replication n
replication complex n

Hefe(-pilz)
  Expressionvektor
Replikation
Replikationskomplex

» Totipotency is a property that makes plants a good host.
Totipotenz ist eine Eigenschaft, die pflanzliche Zellen zu guten Wirtszellen macht.

origin of replication / replicon / replication unit (ORI)

Startpunkt für die Replikation

leading strand n
foreign gene / transgene ['trænsˌdʒiːn] n
foreign DNA n
foreign protein [ˌfɒrɪn'prəʊtiːn] n

durchgehender DNA-Strang
Fremdgen
Fremd-DNA
Fremdprotein

insert [ɪn'sɜːt] / transfect [ˌtrænsˈfekt] v
insertion [ɪn'sɜːʃn] n

einfügen / einschleusen
Einschleusung

clone [kləʊn] n	Klon *(Gruppe genetisch identischer Zellen bzw. Organismen)*
clone v	klonieren
DNA ligase [ˌdiːenerˈlaɪgeɪz] n	DNA-Ligase
paste [peɪst] / glue v	kleben
ligate v	verknüpfen
ATP dependent adj	ATP-abhängig
link v	verbinden / verknüpfen
compatible adj	kompatibel
complementary adj	komplementär
phosphatase [ˈfɒsfəteɪz] n	Phosphatase
shrimp alkaline phosphatase (SAP) n	alkalische Phosphatase aus Shrimp (SAP)
remove v	entfernen
phosphate group n	Phosphat-Gruppe
prevent v	verhindern

» The DNA ligase links two DNA fragments in an ATP dependent reaction.
Die DNA-Ligase verbindet zwei DNA-Fragmente in einer ATP-abhängigen Reaktion.
The reaction works better for compatible (complementary protruding) ends than for blunt ends.
Die Reaktion erfolgt leichter für kompatible (komplementär überhängende) Enden als für stumpfe Enden.
To prevent self-ligation of the vector its ends are dephosphorylated, i.e the 5′ phosphate groups are removed by a phosphatase.
Um eine Selbstligation des Vektors zu verhindern, werden seine Enden dephosphoryliert, d.h. die 5′ Phosphatgruppen werden durch eine Phosphatase entfernt.

splicing n	Spleißen / Überlaschung / Verbindung
splice (sth) v	spleißen / überlaschen / verbinden

plasmid n	Plasmid
hybrid plasmid [ˈhaɪbrɪdˌplæzmɪd]	Hybridplasmid
recombinant plasmid [ˌriːˈkɒmbɪnənt] / transformed plasmid	rekombinantes Plasmid / transformiertes Plasmid

» insert the desired gene into the gap — das gewünschte Gen in die Lücke einfügen
plasmid spliced with the isolated gene — Plasmid mit eingeschleustem Fremdgen

incorporate (into sth) v	einpflanzen (in etw.)
reprogramming [ˌriːˈprəʊɡræmɪŋ] n	Umprogrammierung
host cell n	Empfängerzelle

6 Biotechnology › 6.3 Techniques used to generate recombinant DNA

replacement n	Austausch
tag (with sth) [ˈtægˌwɪð] / label with [ˈleɪblˌwɪð] v	markieren (mit etw.)
reporter gene / genetic markers n	Reportergene *(zur Identifikation einer gelungenen Einschleusung von Fremd-DNA)*
selectable marker n	selektierbarer Marker
metabolic marker n	metabolischer Marker
resistance n	Resistenz
antibiotic [ˌæntɪbaɪˈɒtɪk], *pl* antibiotics n	Antibiotikum *(Pl. Antibiotika)*
antibiotic resistance n	Antibiotikaresistenz
provide with v	versorgen mit / versehen mit
resistance gene [rɪˈzɪstnsˌdʒiːn] n	Resistenzgen
streptomycin [ˌstreptəˈmaɪsɪn] n	Streptomycin
velvet stamp [ˈvelvɪtˌstæmp] n	Stempel / Samtstempel
duplicating stamp / duplicating pad n	Duplizier-Stempel
selection medium n	Selektionsnährboden *(der bestimmte Stoffe enthält)*
supplement n	Ergänzung
supplement v	ergänzen
culture medium n	Kulturmedium
agar plate [ˈeɪgəˌpleɪt] n	Agar-Platte
petri dish [ˈpetriˌdɪʃ] n	Petrischale
transformation n	Transformation
plate out v	ausplatieren
plate [pleɪt] v	Platte
colour change *BE* / color change *AE* n	Farbumschlag
become visible [bɪˌkʌmˈvɪzəbl] v	sichtbar werden
promoter [prəˈməʊtə] n	Promotor
activated promoter	aktiver Promotor
operon [ˈɒpərɒn] n	Operon
link to / bind to v	koppeln
effector [ɪˈfektə] n	Effektor
proliferation [prəˌlɪfrˈeɪʃn] n	starke Zunahme
proliferation of cells	Zellvermehrung
colony, *pl* colonies n	Kolonie
construct n *(plasmid with an insert)*	Konstrukt *(Plasmid mit einem Insert)*
survive v	überleben

DNA of different origin	DNA unterschiedlicher Herkunft
switch on of foreign DNA	Einschalten des Fremdgens

In transformation experiments, antibiotic resistance genes or metabolic markers are used for selection.
Bei Transformationsexperimenten werden Antibiotikaresistenzgene oder metabolische Marker zur Selektion benutzt.
A gene of interest is inserted into a vector and then transferred (transformed) into bacteria.
Das Gen von Interesse wird in einen Vektor eingefügt und dann in Bakterien geschleust.

Reverse transcriptase and cDNA production

reverse transcription n	reverse Transkription
reverse transcriptase n	reverse Transkriptase
reverse transcribe v	revers transkribieren
cDNA (complementary DNA) n	cDNA *(komplementär DNA zur mRNA)*
full length cDNA n	Volllängen-cDNA
oligo(dT) primer n	oligo(dT)-Primer
degrade v	abbauen
1st / 2nd strand synthesis n	Erststrangsynthese / Zweitstrangsynthese

Expression of a foreign gene and the extraction of the gene product

expression vector n *(vector with a promoter adjacent to the insertion site of the gene)*	Expressionsvektor *(Vektor, mit einem Promotor neben der Insertionsstelle des Gens)*
shuttle vector n *(vector with an insert that can be expressed and/or propagated in pro- and eukaryotic cells)*	Shuttle-Vektor *(Vektor, dessen Insert sowohl in eu- als auch in prokaryotischen Zellen vermehrt und/oder exprimiert werden kann)*
bacterial plasmid n	bakterielles Plasmid
prokaryotic promoter [ˌprəʊkærɪˈɒtɪkprəˈməʊtə] n	prokaryotischer Promotor
inducible promoter [ɪnˌdjuːsɪblprəˈməʊtə] n	induzierbarer (aktivierbarer) Promotor
cultivate v	kultivieren
propagate [ˈprɒpəɡeɪt] v	vermehren / fortpflanzen

6 Biotechnology › 6.3 Techniques used to generate recombinant DNA

suitable condition n	geeignete Bedingung
tag n	Markierung / Etikett / „tag"
His-tag	His-Tag (Markierung bestehend aus 6 Histidinen)
beta-galactosidase [ˌbiːtəɡəˈlæktəʊsɪdeɪz] n	Beta-Galactosidase
fusion protein n (protein of interest plus tag)	Fusionsprotein (Protein von Interesse plus „tag")
cleave off v	abspalten
affinity chromatography [əˌfɪnətɪkrəʊməˈtɒɡrəfi] n	Affinitätschromatografie
purification [ˌpjʊərɪfɪˈkeɪʃn] n	Reinigung / Aufreinigung
posttranslational modification n	posttranslationale Modifikation
glycoprotein n	Glycoprotein
glycosylation [ˌɡlaɪkəʊsəˈleɪʃn] n	Glycosylierung
disulphide bridge [daɪˌsʌlfaɪdˈbrɪdʒ] n	Disulfidbrücke
CHO cell (chinese hamster ovary cell)	CHO-Zelle (Zellen, die aus einem Eierstocktumor eines Hamsters isoliert wurden)
yeast cell n	Hefezelle

» genetically engineered drug | gentechnisch hergestelltes Medikament

Where do the DNA fragments come from? » 5.8 Methods of DNA analysis and more applied genetics

gene library n	Genbibliothek / Genbank

» A genomic gene library contains the complete genomic DNA of an organism.
Eine gemischte Genbibliothek enthält die DNA des gesamten Genoms.

A single clone of the gene library harbours a single fragment of DNA.
Ein einzelner Klon der Genbank beherbergt ein einziges DNA-Fragment.

cDNA library n	cDNA Bibliothek / cDNA Bank
synthetic gene [sɪnˈθetɪkdʒiːn] n	künstliches Gen
flanking sequence [ˈflæŋkɪŋˌsiːkwəns] n (e.g. sequence for transcription initiation)	flankierende Sequenz (z. B. die Basensequenz für den Startpunkt)

mutagenesis [ˌmjuːtə'dʒenəsɪs] n   künstliche Mutation / Mutagenese
mutagenesis techniques   Methoden, künstlich Mutationen zu erzeugen

> Complementary DNA (cDNA) is obtained by reverse transcription from mRNA.
> Durch reverse Transkription der mRNA erhält man die cDNA.

6.4 More applications of genetic engineering techniques

detection [dɪ'tekʃn] n	Nachweis / Entdeckung
diagnosis [ˌdaɪəg'nəʊsɪs] n	Diagnose / Diagnostik
hereditary [hɪ'redɪtri] adj	angeboren / erblich / Erb~
inherit [ɪn'herɪt] v	erben
hereditary disease	Erbkrankheit
infectious disease [ɪn'fekʃəsdɪˌziːz]	ansteckende Krankheit
human genome project (HGP) n	Humangenomprojekt *(der HUGO = Human-Genom-Organisation)*
monitoring ['mɒnɪtərɪŋ] n	Überwachung
environmental monitoring	Überwachung des Naturschutzes
genetic marker n	genetische Marker
paternity testing [pə'tɜːnətiˌtestɪŋ] n	Vaterschaftsgutachten
prenatal diagnostic [priːneɪtlˌdaɪəg'nɒstɪk] n	pränatale Diagnostik
heterozygosity testing / heterozygous testing [ˌhetrə'zaɪgəsˌtestɪŋ] n	Heterozygotentest
screen (sb for sth) v	(jmd. auf etw.) untersuchen / überprüfen
track down v	aufspüren

> | | |
> |---|---|
> | existence of specific mutations | Vorliegen bestimmter Mutationen |
> | screen for the presence of inherited abnormalities | Vorsorgeuntersuchung zur Feststellung ererbter Missbildungen / Abnormitäten durchführen |
> | analyse patterns of migration | Wanderbewegungsmuster analysieren |
> | analyse claims of ethnicity / relatedness | Ethnizitäts- / Verwandtschaftsansprüche analysieren |
> | replace more forgeable forms of identification | leichter zu fälschende Identifikationsformen ersetzen |
> | track down the genetic basis of inherited diseases | genetischen Grundlage von Erbkrankheiten aufspüren |

6 Biotechnology › 6.4 More applications of genetic engineering techniques

Genetic tests	
paternity testing	Vaterschaftstest
prenatal diagnostic	pränatale Diagnostik
heterozygosity testing / heterozygous testing	Heterozygotentest (zur Ermittlung rezessiver Erbkrankheiten)

cancer [ˈkænsə] n Krebs
  cancer research Krebsforschung
radiation n Strahlung
  level of radiation Strahlungsdosis
significant [sɪgˈnɪfɪkənt] adj beträchtlich / signifikant

»   expose to a significant level of radiation einer signifikanten (beträchtlichen) Bestrahlungsdosis aussetzen

  be a boon to cancer research ein Segen für die Krebsforschung sein

diversity of proteins n Vielfalt der Proteine
transcription n Transkription
  posttranscriptional [ˌpoʊsttrænˈskrɪpʃnl] nach der Transkription
translation n Translation / Übersetzung
  posttranslational nach der Translation
homogeneity [ˌhəʊmədʒəˈneɪəti] n Homogenität
functional (coding) sequences n funktionale (kodierende) Sequenzen
ENCODE *(abbreviation: ENCyclopedia Of DNA Elements)* n ENCODE *(Projekt zur Erforschung des nicht-kodierenden Anteils des Erbguts)*

proteome [ˈprəʊtiˌəʊm] n Proteom *(Gesamtheit aller Protein z.B. eines Organismus)*

two dimensional electrophoresis n 2D-Gelelektrophorese *(zur Trennung von Proteinen eingesetzt)*

mass spectrometry [ˌmæsˈspekˈtɒmɪtri] n Massenspektrometer *(Verfahren zum Messen des Masse-zu-Ladungs-Verhältnisses)*

electromagnet [ɪˌlektrəˈmægnɪt] n Elektromagnet

Applied genetics in agriculture

agriculture n	Landwirtschaft
crop n	Nutzpflanze
breed v	züchten
species difference / species boundary n	Artengrenze

desired feature	erwünschte Eigenschaft
undesired feature	unerwünschte Eigenschaft

Agrobacterium tumefaciens [ˌægrɒbæk'tɪərɪəmtjuːmɪˌfeɪʃns] n	Agrobacterium tumefaciens
enter v	eindringen
selectable marker n	selektionierbarer Marker
regenerate v	regenerieren

manipulation n	Manipulation
manipulate v	manipulieren
control v	steuern
gene vehicle ['dʒiːnˌvɪəkl] n	Gentaxi

soil bacteria ['sɔɪlbækˌtɪərɪə] n	Bodenbakterium
wound / injury n	Verletzung
growth n	Wachstum
uncontrolled growth	unkontrolliertes Wachstum
crown gall [ˌkraʊn'gɔːl] n	Galle / Wurzelhalsgallentumor
secrete [sɪ'kriːt] v	absondern / ausscheiden
secrete nutrients [sɪˌkriːt'njuːtrɪənts]	Nährstoffe absondern
tumour-inducing ['tjuːməɪnˌdjuːsɪŋ] adj	tumorerregend
tumour-inducing regions of plasmid (Ti)	tumorerregende Teile des Plasmids (Ti)
Ti plasmid n	Ti Plasmid
protoplast ['prəʊtəplæst] n	Protoplast *(Pflanzenzelle ohne Zellwand)*
induce (sth) [ɪn'djuːs] v	(etw.) anregen / (etw.) einleiten / (etw.) hervrufen
induce mitosis [ɪnˌdjuːsmaɪ'təʊsɪs] / cell division	Zellteilung anregen
callus (tissues) culture ['kæləsˌkʌltʃə] n	Kalluskultur

6 Biotechnology › 6.4 More applications of genetic engineering techniques

cotton boll worm / boll weevil [ˌbəʊl'wiːvl] n	Baumwollkapselwurm
weevil ['wiːvl] n	Rüsselkäfer
pest n	Schädling
cotton pest	Baumwollschädling
insecticide [ɪn'sektɪsaɪd] n	Insektenvernichtungsmittel / Insektizid
crop n	Nutzpflanze
genetically modified crop	genetisch manipulierte Nutzpflanzen

maize BE / corn AE n	Mais
rape / rapeseed n	Raps
fungus ['fʌŋɡəs], pl fungi ['fʌŋɡaɪ] n	Pilz
resistance n	Resistenz
herbicide resistance ['hɜːbɪsaɪdrɪˌzɪstns]	Herbizidresistenz
increased resistance	erhöhte Resistenz
herbicide / weed killer n	Unkrautvernichtungsmittel

sugar beet n	Zuckerrübe
rhizomania [ˌraɪsəʊmeɪniə] n	Wurzelbärtigkeit
rhizobial bacterium [ˌraɪsəʊbɪəlb'æktɪəriəm] n	Wurzelbakterie
N fertilizer [en'fɜːtəlaɪzə] n	Stickstoffdünger
generate v	generieren / herstellen
nodule ['nɒdjuːl] n	(Wurzel)Knöllchen
nodulation ['nɒdjuːleɪʃn] n	Knöllchenbildung

»

induce the formation of nodules	die Bildung von Wurzelknöllchen induzieren / einleiten
generate nodulation in non-legumes	die Bildung von Knöllchen bei Pflanzen, die nicht zu den Hülsenfrüchtlern gehören, hervorrufen
replace N-fertilizer	Stickstoffdünger ersetzen

Brazil nut n	Paranuss
allergy ['ælədʒi] n	Allergie
allergic (to sth) adj	(gegen etw.) allergisch
allergenic [ælə'dʒenɪk] n	allergen
allergenic trait	Allergie hervorrufendes Merkmal *(hier: Sequenz)*

provoke allergies	Allergien hervorrufen
have an allergenic effect	allergen wirken
show allergic reactions in …	allergische Reaktion bei … zeigen

soybean n	Sojabohne
genetically modified / genetically engineered adj	genetisch manipuliert / genmanipuliert
genetically modified food	genetisch manipulierte Lebensmittel
nutrient risk analysis n	lebensmittelchemische Risikountersuchung

block v	blockieren
pectinase ['pektɪneɪz] n	Pektinase
pectin ['pektɪn] n	Pektin
degrade (sth) v	(etw.) abbauen
maturation (of fruit) [ˌmætjrˈeɪʃn] n	Reifung (der Frucht) *(Prozess)*
maturity (of fruit) n	Reifegrad (der Frucht) *(Zustand)*

pectin degrading enzyme	Pektin abbauendes Enzym
degrade the cell wall	die Zellwand abbauen
tomatoes mature off the vine	Tomaten reifen nach der Ernte (d.h. sie werden grün geerntet)
tomatoes mature on the vine	Tomaten reifen an der Pflanze

ripening ['raɪpnɪŋ] n	Reifen / Reifung
ripen v	reifen
Flavr Savr tomato / anti-squishy tomato n	Anti-Matsch-Tomate
polygalacturonase n	Polygalacturonase
inverse adj	entgegengesetzt

soft / squishy adj	matschig
firm adj	haltbar
firmness [fɜːmnəs] n	Festigkeit
decay [dɪˈkeɪ] n	Verwesung(-sprozess) / Fäulnis
shelf life n	Haltbarkeit
have a certain shelf life	begrenzt haltbar sein
aromatic adj	aromatisch

6 Biotechnology › 6.4 More applications of genetic engineering techniques

aroma n	Aroma
full aroma	volles Aroma
antisense technology n	Antisense-Technik / Gegenstrang-methode
gene-silencing n	Geninaktivierung
method of gene-silencing	Methode der Geninaktivierung

» | prevent protein production from a targeted gene | die Proteinsynthese eines speziellen Gens verhindern |

vitamin A rice / golden rice n	Vitamin A-Reis
attributable adj	zuordenbar / zuschreibbar
beta-carotene [ˌbiːtəˈkærətiːn] n	Beta-Carotin
precursor [priːˈkɜːsə] n	Vorstufe / Vorläufer
availability n	Verfügbarkeit
availability of iron n	Eisenverfügbarkeit
nutrient condition n	Ernährungsbedingung
developing country n	Entwicklungsland

Genetically engineered animals

growth hormone n	Wachstumshormon
giant mouse n	Riesenmaus
wild-type mice n	Mäusestamm *(genetisch nicht manipuliert)*
increase n	Steigerung / Zunahme
rapid increase in weight	schnelle Gewichtszunahme
stress n	Überlastung
stress on joints	Überlastung der Gelenke
carp, *pl* carps; carp n	Karpfen
trout [traʊt], *pl* trouts; trout n	Forelle
slaughter weight n	Schlachtgewicht
molecular pharming / gene pharming n	Gen-Pharming
gene pharming n	Gen-Pharming
farming n	Landwirtschaft
pharmaceutical [ˌfɑːməˈsjuːtɪkl] adj	pharmazeutisch
wordplay n	Wortspiel
livestock n	Nutztiere
pharmaceutics [ˌfɑːməˈsjuːtɪks] n pl	Arzneimittelherstellung
drug n	Medikament

factor VIII n	Faktor VIII
haemophilia BE [ˌhiːməˈfɪliə] / hemophilia AE n	Hämophilie / Bluterkrankheit
lactose [ˈlæktəʊz] / milk sugar n	Laktose / Milchzucker
lactalbumine n	Laktalbumin
mammary gland [ˌmæmriˈglænd] / lactiferous gland [lækˈtɪferəsˌglænd] n	Milchdrüse / Brustdrüse

»
release in the milk / secrete in the milk	in die Milch ausscheiden

tissue-plasminogen-activator (tPA) [ˈtɪʃuːplæzˌmɪnədʒənˈæktɪveɪtə] n	Gewebe-Plasminogen-Aktivator
blood clots [ˈblʌdˌklɒts] n	Blutgerinnsel
dissolution of blood clots [ˌdɪsəˈluːʃn]	Auflösung von Blutgerinseln
channel protein n	Kanalprotein
cystic fibrosis (CF) / mucoviscidosis [ˌmjuːkəʊvɪsɪːˈdəʊsɪs] n	Mukoviszidose / cystische Fibrose
cystic fibrosis patient	Mukoviszidosepatient(in)

»
switch off / turn off / silence	a specific gene	bestimmtes Gen ausschalten

knockout animal n	Knockout-Tier
carcinogen-mouse [kɑːˈsɪnədʒnˌmaʊs] n	Krebsmaus
patent [ˈpeɪtnt] v	patentieren
patented adj	patentiert
have sth patented	etw. patentieren lassen
patented animal	patentiertes Tier
research n	Forschung

»
testing of new therapies	Erprobung von neuen Therapien

Applications in medical sciences

medical science n	Medizin
inherited disease [ɪnˈherɪtɪddɪˌziːz] n	Erbkrankheit
acquired disease [əˈkwaɪərəddɪˌziːz] n	erworbene Krankheit / spontan auftretende Krankheit

6 Biotechnology › 6.4 More applications of genetic engineering techniques

sickle cell anemia [ˌsɪklseləˈniːmɪə] n	Sichelzellanämie
cystic fibrosis (CF) [ˌsɪstɪkfaɪˈbrəʊsɪs] / mucoviscidosis n	cystische Fibrose / Mukovsizidose
diabetes [ˌdaɪəˈbiːtiːz] n	Diabetes
diabetic n	Diabetiker(in) / Zuckerkranke(r)
have diabetes	an Diabetes erkrankt sein
insulin [ˈɪnsjəlɪn] n	Insulin » Abb. 50
genetically engineered insulin	gentechnisch hergestelltes Insulin
mass production n	Massenproduktion
synthesise artificially [sɪnθəsaɪzˌɑːtɪˈfɪʃli] v	künstlich herstellen
synthesise adequately [sɪnθəsaɪzˈædɪkwətli] v	in ausreichenden Mengen synthetisieren / in ausreichenden Mengen produzieren
affordable adj	bezahlbar / erschwinglich
fermenter [fɜːˈmentə] n	Fermenter / Gärbottich
haemophilia [ˌhiːməˈfɪliə] BE / hemophilia AE n	Bluterkrankheit / Hämophilie
haemophile [ˌhiːməˈfɪliæk] / haemophiliac BE / hemophile / hemophiliac AE n	Bluter(in)
impaired [ɪmˈpeəd] adj	geschädigt
impaired ability	eingeschränkte Fähigkeit
glutamic acid [gluːˌtæmɪkˈæsɪd] n	Glutaminsäure
lysine [ˈlaɪsiːn] n	Lysin
blood clotting factor n	Blutgerinnungsfaktor
erythropoietin (EPO) [ɪˌrɪθrəpɔɪˈetɪn] n	Erythropoietin (EPO)
red blood cell / corpuscle n	rotes Blutkörperchen / rote Blutzelle
hemoglobin [ˌhiːməˈgləʊbɪn] / haemoglobin n	Hämoglobin

»
prime regulator of red blood cell production	primärer Blutbildungsfaktor
promote the differentiation and development of red blood cells	Differenzierung und Entwicklung der roten Blutkörperchen vorantreiben
initiate the production of hemoglobin	die Produktion von Hämoglobin auslösen

performance-enhancing drug [pəˈfɔːmənsɪnˈhɑːsɪŋˌdrʌg] n	leistungssteigernde Droge
viscosity n	Viscosität / Zähflüssigkeit
viscosity of the blood	Flüssigkeitgrad des Blutes (hier: Zähflüssigkeit)

dysfunctional enzyme [dɪsˌfʌŋʃnl'enzaɪm] n	unzureichendes Enzym / nicht funktionstüchtiges Enzym
phenylketonuria (PKU) [ˌfiːnaɪlkiːtə'njʊərɪə] n	Phenylketonurie (PKU)
phenylalanine [ˌfiːnaɪl'æləniːn] n	Phenylalanin
phenylalanine hydroxylase	Phenylalanin Hydroxylase
tyrosine ['taɪrəsiːn] n	Tyrosin
tryptophan ['trɪptəfæn] n	Tryptophan
arginine ['ɑːdʒiniːn] n	Arginin
melanin ['melənɪn] n	Melanin
mental retardation ['mentlˌriːtɑː'deɪʃn] n	geistige Behinderung
premature death [ˌpremətʃə'deθ] n	vorzeitiges Ableben / frühzeitiger Tod
therapeutic adj	therapeutisch
gene therapy n	Gentherapie
somatic gene therapy	somatische Gentherapie
in-vivo gene transfer [ɪnˌviːvəʊ'dʒiːnˌtrænsfɜː] n	In-vivo-Gentransfer *(Gentransfer am Lebewesen)*
ex-vivo gene transfer n	Ex-vivo-Gentransfer *(Gentransfer außerhalb des Lebewesens z.B. in Zellkultur)*
intact [ɪn'tækt] adj	intakt / funktionierend
somatic cell n	somatische Zelle
epithelial cell [ˌepɪθiːlɪəl'sel] n	Epithelzelle
liposome ['lɪpəʊsəʊm] n	Liposom
viral vector [ˌvaɪrl'vektə] n	viraler Vektor / Virus-Vektor
therapeutic benefit [θerəˌpjuːtɪk'benɪfɪt] n	therapeutischer Nutzen
clinical trials ['klɪnɪklˌtraɪəlz] n	klinische Versuchsreihen
stem cell n	Stammzelle
bone marrow stem cell ['bəʊnˌmærəʊ'stemsel] n	Knochenmarksstammzelle
embryonic stem cell	embryonale Stammzelle
reintroduce n	wieder einschleusen
aerosol ['eərəsɒl] n	Spray / Aerosol
viral particle n	viraler Partikel / Viruspartikel
inhale v	inhalieren
preliminary level [prɪ'lɪmɪnrɪˌlevl] n	Versuchsstadium
toxicity [tɒk'sɪsəti] n	Giftigkeit
allele [ə'liːl] n	Allel

6 Biotechnology › 6.5 Genetic engineering: hopes and fears

tumour suppressor gene [ˌtjuːməsəˈpresədʒiːn] / antioncogene [ˌæntɪˈɒŋkəʊdʒiːn] n	Tumor-Unterdrücker-Gen / Tumor-Suppressor-Gen
» functional alleles of the tumour suppressor gene	aktive Allelen eines Tumor Unterdrücker / Suppressor Gens

pharmacogenomics [ˌfɑːməkəʊdʒɪˈnɒmɪks] n	Pharmakogenomik *(erforscht die Bedeutung der Erbanlagen auf die Wirkung von Arzneimitteln)*
gene pharming n	Gen-Pharming
transgenic adj	transgen
mammary gland n	Milchdrüse
green gene technology n	grüne Gentechnologie *(transgene Pflanzen)*
red gene technology n	rote Gentechnologie *(transgene Tiere)*
white gene technology n	weiße Gentechnologie *(gentechnologische Arzneimittelherstellung)*
predispose (sth to sth) [ˌpriːdɪˈspəʊz] v	(etw. eine) Veranlagung vorgeben / (etw.) prädisponieren / (etw.) a priori festlegen
disposition [ˌdɪspəˈzɪʃn] n	Veranlagung
obesity [əˈbiːsəti] n	Fettleibigkeit

» For somatic gene therapy differentiated cells or somatic stemcells are manipulated in a way that they contain a functional copy of the defect gene.
Für somatische Gentherapie werden differenzierte Zellen oder somatische Stammzellen so manipuliert, dass sie eine funktionierende Kopie des defekten Gens enthalten.

6.5 Genetic engineering: hopes and fears

germline gene therapy [ˌdʒɜːmlaɪnˈdʒiːnˌθerəpi] n	keimbahnbetreffende Gentherapie
microinjection [ˌmaɪkrəʊɪnˈdʒekʃn] n	Mikroinjektion
micropipette n	Mikropipette
micromanipulator n	Mikromanipulator
fertilise *BE* / fertilize *AE* n	befruchten
prohibit v	verbieten
uterus [ˈjuːtrəs], *pl* uteruses; uteri n	Uterus / Gebärmutter

unintentional adj	unbeabsichtigt
incalculable [ɪnˈkælkjələbl] adj	unkalkulierbar / unberechenbar

> Gene therapy in the human germline is prohibited in Germany and many other countries because of incalculable risks.
> Gentherapie der menschlichen Keimbahn ist in Deutschland und vielen anderen Ländern wegen unkalkulierbarer Risiken verboten.

rate of yield n	Ertragsrate
double the rate of yield	Dopplung der Ertragsrate
stress tolerance n	Stresstoleranz

nutrient use efficiency	verbesserte Ausbeute der Nährsalze im Boden
crop productivity	Ertragssteigerung
sustainable food security	nachhaltige Absicherung der Nahrungsversorgung

boost [buːst] v	steigern
concern n	Bedenken
long term adj	langfristig
health risk n	Gesundheitsrisiko

pass on accidentally	versehentlich weitergeben
long term health risk	langfristiges Gesundheitsrisiko
have a significant impact on sth	eine bedeutende Auswirkung auf etw. haben
have an impact on biodiversity	eine Auswirkung auf die Artenvielfalt haben
upset the balance of nature	das natürliche Gleichgewicht durcheinander bringen

exploitation [ˌeksplɔɪˈteɪʃn] n	Ausbeutung
commercialisation [kəˌmɜːʃəlaɪˈzeɪʃn] n	Kommerzialisierung / Vermarktung
property (of) n	Besitz (von)
genealogy database [ˌdʒiːniˈælədʒiˌdeɪtəbeɪs] n	Datenbank der Genealogie / Ahnenforschung / Familienforschung
descend from [dɪˈsendˌfrɒm] v	abstammen von
founder n	Gründer~

7 Evolution

evolution [ˌiːvəˈluːʃn] n
  transspecific evolution
  biochemical evolution
  molecular evolution
  cultural evolution
  human evolution n
  coevolution n
theory of evolution, *pl* theories n
rate of evolution n
evolutionary [ˌiːvəˈluːʃnri] adj
  evolutionary lineage
  evolutionary process

Evolution
  transspezifische Evolution
  chemische Evolution
  molekulare Evolution
  kulturelle Evolution
  Evolution des Menschen
  Coevolution
Evolutionstheorie
Evolutionsrate
evolutionär / die Evolution betreffend
  Evolutionslinie
  Evolutionsvorgang

---

evolutionary synthesis n
Catastrophism [kəˈtæstrəfɪzm] n

Lamarckism [ləˈmɑːkɪzm] n
Darwinism [ˈdɑːwɪnɪzm] n
Creationism [kriˈeɪʃnɪzm] n
Intelligent Design n

synthetische Evolutionstheorie
Katastrophentheorie / Kataklysmen-
  theorie
Lamarckismus
Darwinismus
Kreationismus
Intelligent Design

7.1 Population genetics

population n
  initial population
individual n
gene [dʒiːn] n
genetic adj
allele [əˈliːl] n
recombination n
mutation [mjuːˈteɪʃn] n
modification [ˌmɒdɪfɪˈkeɪʃn] n
gene frequency, *pl* frequencies n
  [ˈdʒiːnˌfriːkwənsi] n
gene pool n
gene flow n
genetic drift n
founder effect n
population bottleneck n
extinction [ɪkˈstɪŋkʃn] n

Population
  Ausgangspopulation
Individuum
Gen
genetisch
Allel
Rekombination
Mutation
Modifikation
Genhäufigkeit / Genfrequenz

Genpool
Genfluss
Gendrift
Gründereffekt
Flaschenhalseffekt
Extinktion / (Massen-)Aussterben

> A gene pool is the total number of alleles within a population.
> Ein Genpool ist die Gesamtheit aller Allele in einer Population.
> Gene flow is the exchange of alleles between populations.
> Der Genfluss ist der Austausch von Allelen zwischen Populationen.
> Genetic drift is a change in the gene pool by random influences, e.g. volcanic eruption.
> Die Gendrift ist eine Änderung des Genpools durch zufällige Einflüsse, z.B. Vulkanausbruch.

7.2 Adaptation

ecological niche [ˌiːkəˈlɒdʒɪklˌniːʃ] n	ökologische Nische
abiotic factor [ˌeɪbaɪˈɒtɪkˈfæktə] n	abiotischer Faktor
biotic factor n	biotischer Faktor
predator [ˈpredətə] n	Fressfeind
prey [preɪ] n	Beute
territory, pl territories [ˈterɪtri] n	Revier
competition n	Wettbewerb / Konkurrenz
interspecific competition	zwischenartliche Konkurrenz
intraspecific competition	innerartliche Konkurrenz

> | occupy an ecological niche | eine ökologische Nische besetzen |
> |---|---|

adaptation [ˌædæpˈteɪʃn] n	Anpassung
fitness n	Fitness *(Bedeutung: Angepasstheit Tauglichkeit)*
reproductive fitness	reproduktive Fitness
generation n	Generation
reproduction n	Fortpflanzung
reproductive success n	Fortpflanzungserfolg
offspring, pl offspring n	Nachkomme(n)

> | struggle for life | Kampf ums Dasein |
> |---|---|
> | survival of the fittest | Überleben der am besten Angepassten |

selection n	Selektion / Auswahl
natural selection	natürliche Selektion / natürliche Auslese
sexual selection	sexuelle Selektion
intraspecific selection	innerartliche Selektion
interspecific selection	zwischenartliche Selektion

7 Evolution › 7.2 Adaptation

stabilizing selection	stabilisierende Selektion
directional selection	gerichtete Selektion / transformierende Selektion
disruptive selection	aufspaltende Selektion
selection pressure n	Selektionsdruck
artificial selection [ɑːtɪˌfɪʃlsɪˈlekʃn] n	künstliche Selektion
breeding n	Zucht
domestication [dəˌmestɪˈkeɪʃn] n	Domestizierung / Domestikation

» Stabilizing selection occurs in well adapted populations. Selection eliminates extreme variants.
Stabilisierende Selektion tritt in gut angepassten Populationen auf. Die Selektion wirkt gegen extreme Varianten.
Directional selection occurs when environmental factors change.
Gerichtete Selektion tritt auf, wenn sich Umwelteinflüsse ändern.
Disruptive selection has an effect on the most frequent variants. It can be caused by parasites.
Aufspaltende Selektion richtet sich gegen die häufigsten Formen. Sie kann durch Parasiten ausgelöst werden.

camouflage [ˈkæməflɑːʒ] n	Tarnung
camouflage	tarnen
cryptic coloration [ˈkrɪptɪkˌkʌləˈreɪʃn] n	Tarnfärbung / Schutzfärbung
warning n	Warnung
warn v	warnen
warning colour BE / color AE n	Warnfärbung
mimicry [ˈmɪmɪkri] n	Mimikry
hoverfly, pl flies [ˈhɒvəflaɪ] n	Schwebfliege
mimesis [mɪˈmiːsɪs] n	Mimese

» In mimicry the animal resembles another, venomous or otherwise harmful animal.
Bei der Mimikry gleicht das Tier einem anderen, giftigen oder anderweitig gefährlichen Tier.
In mimesis the animal resembles a thing or part of a plant that the predator is indifferent about, e.g. a leaf.
Bei der Mimese gleicht das Tier einem Gegenstand oder Pflanzenteil, der dem Fressfeind gleichgültig ist, z. B. einem Blatt.

predisposition [ˌpriːdɪspəˈzɪʃn] n	Prädisposition
predispositioned	prädisponiert
preadaptation [ˌpriːædæpˈteɪʃn] n	Präadaptation
industrial melanism [ɪnˌdʌstriəlˈmelənɪzm] n	Industriemelanismus
melanin [ˈmelənɪn] n	Melanin

peppered moth [ˌpepəd'mɒθ] n	Birkenspanner
soot n	Ruß
blackened by soot	rußgeschwärzt

7.3 Species

species ['spiːʃiːz], *pl* species n	Art
subspecies	Unterart
original species	Ausgangsart
species concept	Artbegriff
morphological species [ˌmɔːfə'lɒdʒɪkl]	morphologischer Artbegriff
genetic species	genetischer Artbegriff
typological species [taɪpəlɒdʒikl]	klassischer Artbegriff
ecological species	ökologischer Artbegriff
palaeontological species [ˌpæliɒntə'lɒdʒɪkl] / paleontologic species *AE*	paläontologischer Artbegriff
speciation ['spesɪeɪʃn] n	Artbildung / Speziation
allopatric speciation	allopatrische Artbildung
sympatric speciation	sympatrische Artbildung
variability [ˌveərɪə'bɪləti] n	Variabilität
formation n	Entstehung / Bildung
biodiversity [ˌbaɪəʊdaɪ'vɜːsəti] n	Artenvielfalt

»

diverge into	sich auftrennen in
… two genera	… zwei Gattungen
… several species	… mehrere Arten
… different races	… verschiedene Rassen

isolation n	Isolation
reproductive isolation *(prezygotic, postzygotic)*	Fortpflanzungsisolation *(präzygote, postzygote)*
geographic isolation	geographische Isolation
ecological isolation	ökologische Isolation
ethological isolation	ethologische Isolation

7.4 Homology, analogy and rudiments

divergence [daɪ'vɜːdʒəns] n	Divergenz
divergent adj	divergent

convergence [kən'vɜːdʒns] n	Konvergenz
convergent adj	konvergent
analogy [ə'nælədʒi] n	Analogie
analogous [ə'næləgəs] adj	analog
homology [hə'mɒlədʒi] n	Homologie
anatomical homology	anatomische Homologie
biochemical homology	biochemische Homologie
molecular homology	molekulare Homologie
homologous structure [hə'mɒləgəs]	homologe Struktur
homologous organ	homologes Organ
homology criterion, pl criteria / criterion for homology [kraɪ'tɪərɪən] n	Homologiekriterium
criterion of relative position	Kriterim der Lage
criterion of special quality	Kriterium der spezifischen Qualität
criterion of series of intermediates	Kriterium der Stetigkeit
line of regression n	Regressionsreihe
line of progression n	Progressionsreihe
ontogeny [ɒn'tɒdʒəni] n	Ontogenese *(Keimesentwicklung)*
phylogeny [faɪ'lɒdʒəni] n	Phylogenese

Anatomical homology

anatomic structure n	anatomischer Bau
front limbs n pl	Vordergliedmaßen
notochord ['nəʊtəkɔːd] / chorda dorsalis n	Notochord / Chorda dorsalis *(Vorstufe der Wirbelsäule)*
gill arch ['gɪlˌɑːtʃ] n	Kiemenbogen
gill slit n	Kiemenspalte
gill pouch ['gɪlˌpaʊtʃ] n	Kiementasche
jaw joint ['dʒɔːˌdʒɔɪnt] n	Kiefergelenk
auditory ossicle [ˌɔːdɪtri'ɒsɪkl] n	Gehörknöchelchen
malleus ['mælɪəs] n	Hammer
anvil ['ænvɪl] n	Amboss
stapes ['steɪpiːz] n	Steigbügel
circulation system n	Herzkreislaufsystem
eye n	Auge
pigment n	Pigmentschicht
photoreceptor cell [ˌfəʊtəʊrɪ'septəˌsel] n	Lichtsinneszelle
pit eye n	Grubenauge

pinhole eye [ˌpɪnhəʊl'aɪ] n	Blasenauge
lens eye [ˌlenz'aɪ] n	Linsenauge
rudimentary [ˌruːdɪ'mentri] adj	rudimentär
rudimentary organ / vestigial organ n	Rudiment / Rudimentärorgan
vestigial [ves'tɪdʒiəl] adj	verkümmert
atavism ['ætəvɪzm] n	Atavismus
atavistic adj	atavistisch

Rudimentary organs

pelvic girdle [ˌpelvɪk'gɜːdl] n *(whale)*	Beckengürtel *(Wal)*
rudimentary metacarpals [ˌmetə'kɑːpl] n *(horse)*	Griffelbeine *(Pferd)*
pelvic girdle / shoulder girdle n *(slowworm)*	Schulter- und Beckengürtel *(Blindschleiche)*
coccyx ['kɒksɪks], *pl* coccyxes; coccyges n *(humans)*	Steißbein *(Mensch)*
ear muscles n *(humans)*	Ohrmuskeln *(Mensch)*
green petals [ˌgriːn'petlz] n *(tulip)*	grüne Blütenblätter *(Tulpe)*

7.5 Genealogy

genealogy, *pl* genealogies [ˌdʒiːni'ælədʒi] n	Abstammung / Stammbaum
molecular genealogy	molekularbiologischer Stammbaum
DNA genealogy	DNA Stammbaum
palaeontologic genealogy [ˌpæliˌɒntə'lɒdʒɪkˌdʒiːni'ælədʒi] / paleontologic genealogy *AE*	paläontologischer Stammbaum
phylogenetic tree [faɪləʊdʒəˌnetɪk'triː] n	Stammbaum
monophyletic group [mɒneʊfi'letɪkˌgruːp] n	monophyletische Gruppe *(geschlossene Abstammungsgemeinschaft)*

» A monophyletic group is a group of all the descendants of a common ancestor.
Eine monophyletische Gruppe ist eine Gruppe aller Nachkommen eines gemeinsamen Vorfahren.

lineage n	Abstammungslinie
cytochrome C [saɪtəˌkrəʊm'siː] n	Cytochrom C

7 Evolution › 7.6 Early Earth

mutation [mjuːˈteɪʃn] n	Mutation
mutation rate	Mutationsrate
mutation event	Mutationsschritt
number of mutations	Anzahl der Mutationsschritte
rate of evolution n	Evolutionsrate
hyracotherium [haɪrəkəˈθɪrɪəm] n	Urpferdchen

» The rate of evolution is the number of amino acid changes per unit of time.
Die Evolutionsrate ist die Zahl der Aminosäureaustausche je Zeiteinheit.

7.6 Early Earth

Pangaea [ˈpændʒɪə] n	Pangäa
Gondwana [gɒndˈwɑːnə] n	Gondwana
Laurasia [lɔːˈreɪʒə] n	Laurasia

Chemical evolution

chemical evolution n	chemische Evolution
lithosphere [ˈlɪθəsfɪə] n	Erdkruste / Lithosphäre
early atmosphere n	Uratmosphäre

Early atmosphere

Gases of the early atmosphere	Gase der Uratmosphäre
N_2 nitrogen	Stickstoff
CO_2 carbon dioxide	Kohlenstoffdioxid
H_2O water	Wasserdampf
CH_4 methane	Methan
H_2S hydrogen sulphide	Schwefelwasserstoff

volcano, *pl* volcanoes [vɒlˈkeɪnəʊ] n	Vulkan
magma [ˈmæɡmə] n	Magma
black smoker n	schwarzer Raucher
mineral n	Mineral
energy n	Energie
lightning n	Blitz
radioactivity n	Radioaktivität
UV radiation / ultraviolet radiation [ˌʌltrəˈvaɪələt] n	UV-Strahlung

> In 1953, Stanley Miller exposed a mixture of gases of the early atmosphere to electrical sparks. This produced organic compounds such as amino acids and nucleotides.
> 1953 setzte Stanley Miller ein Gemisch aus Gasen der Uratmosphäre elektrischen Lichtbögen aus. Dies schuf organische Verbindungen wie Aminosäuren und Nukleotide.

membrane ['membreɪn] n	Membran
double-membrane	Doppelmembran
phospholipid layer [ˌfɒsfəʊ'lɪpɪd] n	Phospholipidschicht
metabolic compartment [ˌmetə'bɒlɪkkəm'pɑːtmənt] n	Reaktionsraum
protobiont [ˌprəʊtəʊ'baɪɒnt] n	Protobiont
eukaryote [juː'kærɪɒt] n	Eukaryo(n)t
eukaryotic cell n	Eucyte / eukaryo(n)tische Zelle
prokaryote [prəʊ'kærɪɒt] n	Prokaryo(n)t
prokaryotic cell n	Procyte / prokaryo(n)tische Zelle
endosymbiotic theory [endəʊˌsɪmbaɪ'ɒtɪkθɪəri] n	Endosymbiontenhypothese / Endosymbiontentheorie
endocytosis [endəʊ'saɪtəʊsɪs] n	Endocytose
bacterium [bæk'tɪərɪəm], pl bacteria n	Bakterium
alga ['ælgə], pl algas; algae n	Alge
mitochondrion [ˌmaɪtə'kɒndrɪən], pl mitochondria n	Mitochondrium
plastid ['plæstɪd] n	Plastid *(Pl. Plastiden)*
symbiont ['sɪmbaɪɒnt] n	Symbiont
cell organelle n	Zellorganelle
chromosome ['krəʊməsəʊm] n	Chromosom
histone ['hɪstəʊn] n	Histon
circular DNA n	ringförmige DNA

Palaeontology

palaeontology / paleontology *AE* [ˌpælɪɒn'tɒlədʒi] n	Paläontologie
eon ['iːɒn] / aeon n	Zeitalter

7 Evolution › 7.6 Early Earth

Eon		
Precambrian = Archean + Proterozoic Phanerozoic = Paleozoic + Mesozoic + Cenozoic Paleozoic = Cambrian + Ordovician + Silurian + Devonian + Carboniferous + Permian Mesozoic = Triassic + Jurassic + Cretaceous Cenozoic = Tertiary + Quaternary **Precambrian** chemical evolution, photosynthesis, bacteria, respiration, eukaryotes (cyanobacteria), multicellular organisms, ediacara biota **Cambrian** invertebrates, trilobites , shell, conodonts **Ordovician** molluscs, bivalves, cephalopods, Nautilus, fish, seaweed **Silurian** fern, stomata, transport tissue, myriapods, scorpions, fresh water fish **Devonian** lycopodium, equisetum, roots, insects, bony fish, coelacanths, amphibs (ichthyostega) **Carboniferous** coal forests, tree fern, seed fern, giant insects **Permian** gymnosperms, ginkgo, conifers, reptiles, pterosaurs, mass extinction of marine animals **Triassic** many reptile species, dinosaurs, mammals **Jurassic** ammonites, ichthyosaurs, giant dinosaurs (Brontosaurus), Archaeopteryx **Cretaceous** Triceratops, Tyrannosaurus, angiosperms, many forms of insects, birds; by the end of the cretaceous many groups of reptiles become extinct **Cenozoic** mammals spread; first species of homo	Präkambrium = Archaikum + Proterozoikum Phanerozoikum = Paläozoikum + Mesozoikum + Känozoikum Paläozoikum = Kambrium + Ordivizium + Silur + Devon + Karbon + Perm Mesozoikum = Trias + Jura + Kreide Känozoikum = Tertiär + Quartär **Präkambrium** chemische Evolution, Photosynthese, Bakterien, Atmung, Eukaryoten (Cyanobakterien), Vielzeller, Ediacara-Fauna **Kambrium** Wirbellose, Trilobiten, Schale, Conodonten-Tiere **Ordovizium** Weichtiere, Schnecke, Muscheln, Nautilus, Fische, Tange **Silur** Nacktfarne, Spaltöffnung, Leitgewebe, Tausendfüßer, Skorpione, Süßwasserfische **Devon** Bärlapp-Gewächse, Schachtelhalm, Wurzeln, Insekten, Knochenfische, Quastenflosser, Amphibien (Ichthyostega) **Karbon** Steinkohlewälder, Baumfarn, Samenfarn, riesige Insekten **Perm** Nacktsamer, Ginkgo, Nadelhölzer, Reptilien, Flugsaurier, Massenaussterben von Meerestieren **Trias** viele Reptilienarten, Dinosaurier, Säuger **Jura** Ammoniten, Fischsaurier (Ichthyosaurus), Riesenformen (Brontosaurus), Archaeopteryx **Kreide** Triceratops, Tyrannosaurus, bedecktsamige Blütenpflanzen, viele Insektenarten, Vögel; am Ende der Kreidezeit sind viele Reptiliengruppen ausgestorben **Känozoikum** Ausbreitung der Säugetiere, erste Menschenart	

„Living fossils"

living fossil n	„lebendes Fossil"
limulus n	Pfeilschwanzkrebs
nautilus [ˈnɔːtɪləs] n	Nautilus
coelacanth [ˈsiːləkænθ] n	Quastenflosser
triops / tadpole shrimp n	Triops
ginkgo [ˈgɪŋkəʊ] n	Ginkgo
sequoia [sɪˈkwɔɪə] n	Mammutbaum

Transitional fossils

transitional fossil [trænˈzɪʃnəl] n	Brückentier
fossil intermediary [ˌɪntəˈmiːdiəri] n	Übergangsform
missing link n	„Missing Link" *(fehlendes Bindeglied)*
platypus [ˈplætɪpəs] n	Schnabeltier
peripatus [pəˈrɪpətəs] n	Peripatus
seymuria [ˈsiːmjuːria] n	Seymuria

» Transitional fossils are evidence for transspecific evolution.
Brückentiere sind Indizien für transspezifische Evolution.

Archaeopteryx

archaeopteryx [ˌɑːkiˈɒptrɪks] n	Archäopteryx / Urvogel *(wörtlich aus dem Griechischen: archaios = uralt / pteryx = Flügel)*

bird characteristic n	Vogelmerkmal
birdlike adj	vogelähnlich
birdlike skull	vogelähnlicher Schädel
birdlike pelvis	Vogelbecken
birdlike hindlimbs	Beinskelett
birdlike forelimbs	vogelähnliches Armskelett
feather n	Feder
feathers / plumage [ˈpluːmɪdʒ] n	Gefieder
wishbone n	Gabelbein

»
wings with birdlike forelimbs	Flügel mit vogelähnlichem Armskelett
first toe pointing backwards	erste Zehe gegenübergestellt

7 Evolution › 7.6 Early Earth

reptile characteristic ['reptaɪlˌkærəktə'rɪstɪks] n	Reptilienmerkmal
rib n	Rippe
jaw [dʒɔː] n	Kiefer
sternum n	Brustbein
digit n	Finger
claw n	Kralle

ribs without backward enforcement	Rippen ohne Versteifungsfortsätze
jaws with teeth	Kiefer mit Zähnen
small and flat sternum	kleines flaches Brustbein
three free digits with claws	drei freie Finger mit Krallen
long tail	lange Schwanzwirbelsäule

Ichthyostega

ichthyostega ['ɪkθiəstɪgə] n	Ichthyostega *(wörtlich aus dem Griechischen: ichthys = Fisch / stega = Dach; Schädel)*

fish characteristic n	Merkmal der Fische
fin n	Flosse
dorsal fin ['dɔːslˌfɪn]	Rückenflosse
caudal fin ['kɔːdlˌfɪn]	Schwanzflosse
fishlike adj	fischähnlich
fishlike skull	fischähnlicher Schädel
fishlike teeth	fischähnliches Gebiss

amphibian n	Amphibie
amphibian characteristic	Merkmal der Amphibien
limbs n pl	Extremitäten / Gliedmaßen
four limbs	vier Extremitäten
shoulder girdle n	Schultergürtel
pelvic girdle [ˌpelvik'gɜːdl] n	Beckengürtel

7.7 Human evolution

Human ancestors

ancestor ['ænsestə] n	Vorfahr
line of descent [ˌlaɪnəvdɪ'sent] n	Vorfahrenreihe
hominisation n	Menschwerdung / Hominisation
primate ['praɪmeɪt] n	Primat
monkey / ape n	Affe
new world monkey	Neuweltaffe
old world monkey	Altweltaffe
great ape / hominid	Menschenaffe
hominid ['hɒmɪnɪd] n	Menschenaffe / Hominidae
hominoid ['hɒmɪnɔɪd] n	Menschenartiger / Hominoidae
prehominid n	Vormensch / Prähominidae
Australopithecus afarensis [ˌɒstrələ'pɪθɪkəs] n	Australopithecus afarensis
euhominid n	Euhominidae („echte" Menschen)
Homo habilis n	Homo habilis
Homo erectus n	Homo erectus
Java man ['dʒɑːvəˌmæn] / Pithecanthropus [ˌpɪθɪ'kænθrəpəs] n	Javamensch / Pithecanthropus
Neanderthal [ni'ændətɑːl] / Homo neanderthalensis n	Neandertaler / Homo neanderthalensis
Homo sapiens [ˌhəʊməʊ'sæpiənz] n	Homo sapiens
Cro-Magnon [ˌkrəʊ'mænjɒn] n	Cromagnonmensch
Homo sapiens sapiens n	Homo sapiens sapiens

Bipedalism

upright adj	aufrecht
biped ['baɪped] n	Aufrechtgänger
bipedal [baɪ'piːdl]	zweibeinig
bipedalism [baɪ'piːdlɪzm]	Zweibeinigkeit / Bipedie
quadruped ['kwɒdrəped] n	Vierbeiner
spine / vertebral column [ˌvɜːtɪbrl'kɒləm] n	Wirbelsäule
double-s-shaped adj	doppelt S-förmig
arched adj	einfach gekrümmt

7 Evolution › 7.7 Human evolution

pelvis ['pelvɪs] n	Becken
wide adj	breit
narrow ['nærəʊ] adj	schmal
bowl shaped adj	schüsselförmig
strong adj	stark
weak adj	schwach
gluteal muscle ['gluːtɪəlˌmʌsl] / buttock muscle ['bʌtəkˌmʌsl] n	Gesäßmuskulatur
neck muscles n	Nackenmuskulatur
foramen magnum [fəˈreɪmenˌmægnəm] n	Foramen magnum / Hirnhauptloch (Unterstützungspunkt des Schädels)

> | | |
> |---|---|
> | in the bottom of the skull | unten am Schädel |
> | at the back of the skull | hinten am Schädel |

precision grip n	Präzisionsgriff
grip v	greifen
gripping hand	Greifhand
gripping foot	Greiffuß
thumb n	Daumen
opposable thumb [əˌpəʊzəblˈθʌm]	opponierbarer Daumen
knuckle-walking ['nʌklˌwɔːkɪŋ] n	Knöchelgang
arch (of foot) n	Fußgewölbe

Head and skull

cerebrum [səˈriːbrəm] n	Großhirn
skull n	Schädel
brain skull n	Hirnschädel
neurocranium [ˌnjʊərəʊˈkreɪnɪəm] n	Hirnschädel
facial bone / viscerocranium n	Gesichtsschädel
flat adj	flach
large adj	groß
front / forehead n	Stirn
brow ridge ['braʊˌrɪdʒ] n	Überaugenwulst
nose n	Nase
chin n	Kinn
muzzle ['mʌzl] n	Schnauze
jaw [dʒɔː] n	Kiefer
dental arcade [ˌdentlɑːˈkeɪd] n	Zahnbogen

parabolic [ˌpærəˈbɒlɪk] adj parabolisch
U-shaped adj U-förmig

Cultural evolution

cultural evolution n kulturelle Evolution
opposable thumb n opponierbarer Daumen
language n Sprache
communication n Kommunikation
exchange of information n Informationsaustausch

communication by	gestures facial expressions sounds language	Kommunikation durch	Gestik Mimik Laute Sprache

tool n Werkzeug
  make tools Werkzeuge herstellen
  use of tools Werkzeugbenutzung
stone n Stein
  stone tool Steinwerkzeug
bronze n Bronze
iron n Eisen

shape a stone	einen Stein behauen
grind a stone	einen Stein schleifen

flint [flɪnt] / flint stone n Feuerstein
chopper [ˈtʃɒpə] n Faustkeil
bone n Knochen
bow and arrow n Pfeil und Bogen
fire n Feuer

use of fire	Nutzung des Feuers
to make fire	Feuer machen

hunter-gatherer [ˌhʌntəˈgæðrə] n Jäger und Sammler
nomad [ˈnəʊmæd] n Nomade

sedentism n	Sesshaftigkeit
sedentary ['sedntri] adj	sesshaft
Neolithic Revolution [ˌniːəˈlɪθɪk] n	Neolithische Revolution
agriculture n	Ackerbau
domestication of animals [dəˌmestɪˈkeɪʃn] n	Domestikation von Tieren *(aus Wildtieren Haus-, Nutztiere machen)*
tent n	Zelt
cave [keɪv] n	Höhle
cave dweller [ˈkeɪvˌdwelə]	Höhlenbewohner
settlement n	Siedlung
town n	Stadt
art n	Kunst
sculpture n	Plastik
Venus of Willendorf n	Venus von Willendorf
cave painting n	Höhlenmalerei
religion n	Religion
funeral rites [ˈfjuːnrəlˌraɪts] n	Totenkult

8 Ethology

8.1 Topics and methods of ethology

Topics and problems

ethology [iːˈɒlədʒi] n	Verhaltensforschung / Ethologie
ethologist n	Verhaltensforscher(in)
behaviour *BE* / behavior *AE* [bɪˈheɪvjə] n	Verhalten
behavioural *BE* / behavioral *AE* [bɪˈheɪvjərəl] adj	Verhaltens~
animal behaviour	tierisches Verhalten
zoology [zuˈɒlədʒi] n	Zoologie
animal communication n	tierische Kommunikation
animal emotions n	tierische Emotionen
learning n	Lernen
imprinting [ɪmˈprɪntɪŋ] n	Prägung
imitation n	Nachahmung
instinct [ˈɪnstɪŋt] n	Instinktverhalten / Instinkt
sexual conduct [ˌsekʃʊəlˌkɒndʌkt] n	sexuelles Verhalten

»

the development	of behaviour	Entwicklung von Verhalten
the control		Verhaltenskontrolle
the organisation		Steuerung von Verhalten
the behavioural adaption for survival		Verhaltensanpassung zur Überlebenssicherung

benefits of behaviour n	Nutzen des Verhaltens
neural mechanism [ˌnjʊərlˈmekənɪzm] n	neuronale Kontrolle
neuron [ˈnjʊərɒn] n	Neuron / Nervenzelle
hormone [ˈhɔːməʊn] n	Hormon
neurons and hormons	Nerven und Hormone

habitat [ˈhæbɪtæt] n	Habitat / Lebensraum
habitat selection [ˌhæbɪtætsɪˈlekʃn]	Wahl des Lebensraums
living in groups	das Leben in Gruppen

»

the evolution of	parental care	Entwicklung	der elterlichen Fürsorge
	social behaviour		des Sozialverhaltens
	human behaviour		des menschlichen Verhaltens

8 Ethology › 8.1 Topics and methods of ethology

Ethology describes the scientific study of animal behaviour and is a subject area of zoology.
Die Verhaltensforschung (Ethologie) beschreibt die wissenschaftliche Untersuchung von tierischem Verhalten und ist eine Fachrichtung der Zoologie.

Ethology has the desire to understand animals by studying for example their communication, their emotions, their social behaviour and their choice of habitats.
Die Verhaltensforschung (Ethology) beabsichtigt, Tiere zu verstehen, indem sie beispielsweise ihre Kommunikation, ihre Gefühlsregungen, ihr Sozialverhalten und ihre Wahl der Lebensräume untersucht.

Methods

field research n	Freilandbeobachtung
ethogram [iːˈθegræm] n	Ethogramm / Aktionskatalog
biological research centre n	Forschungsstation
laboratory experiment n	Laborexperiment
Skinner box n	Skinner Box
deprivation [ˌdeprɪˈveɪʃn] n	Entbehrung
deprivation experiment / Kasper – Hauser experiment	Isolierungsexperiment / Kasper-Hauser Experiment
sensory deprivation [ˌsensri deprɪˈveɪʃn]	sensorische Deprivation / Reizentzug

facilities [fəˈsɪlətiz] n pl	technische Hilfsmittel
shot n	Filmaufnahme
slow motion picture n	Zeitlupenaufnahme
time-lapse shot / undercranking [ˌʌndəˈkræŋkɪŋ] n	Zeitrafferaufnahme
lightning n	Beleuchtung
shadow box n	Schaukasten
identification marking n	Markierung *(von Tieren)*
transmitter [trænzˈmɪtə] n	Sender

observation n	Beobachtung
observe (sb / sth) v	(jmd. / etw.) beobachten
observer n	Beobachter
description [dɪˈskrɪpʃn] n	Beschreibung
describe (sb / sth) v	(jmd. / etw.) beschreiben
measuring [ˈmeʒərɪŋ] n	Messen
measure (sth) v	(etw.) messen
evaluation [ɪˌvæljuˈeɪʃn] n	Auswertung
evaluate (sth) v	(etw.) auswerten

interpretation n	Interpretation
interpret (sth) v	(etw.) interpretieren
analysis [əˈnæləsɪs] n	Analyse
analyse (sth) BE [ˈænlaɪz] / analyze AE v	(etw.) analysieren
analyst n	Analyst / Analytiker(in)

» If you want to study animal behaviour, it is important not only to use one method but to employ different methods that complement each other.
Wenn man tierisches Verhalten untersuchen möchte, ist es wichtig, nicht nur eine Untersuchungsmethode zu verwenden, sondern verschiedene Methoden, die sich gegenseitig ergänzen.

8.2 Instinct

behavioural pattern [bɪˌheɪvjərəlˈpætn] n	Verhaltensmuster
fixed action pattern (FAP) n	Erbkoordination *(auch: Instinkt)*
stimulus [ˈstɪmjələs], *pl* stimuli [ˈstɪmjəlaɪ] n	Reiz
sign stimulus	Schlüsselreiz
sensory stimulus	Sinnesreiz
sensory adj	Sinnes~
sensory perception [ˌsensrɪpəˈsepʃn]	Sinneswahrnehmung
sensory message	Sinnesmitteilung
releaser [rɪˈliːsə] n	Auslöser
motivation n	innerer Antrieb

»
innate releasing mechanism	angeborener Auslösemechanismus
preprogrammed series of movement	vorprogrammierte Reihe von Bewegungen
adaptive reaction	adaptive Reaktion
activate (sth) release (sth) stimulate (sth)	(etw.) auslösen
process (sth)	(etw.) verarbeiten
control (sth)	(etw.) kontrollieren
highlight (sth)	(etw.) verdeutlichen

8 Ethology › 8.3 Learning

Simple stimuli can activate complex behaviours.
The red dot on a parent gull's bill, for example, releases the gull chick's begging behaviour.
Einfache Reize können komplexe Verhaltensmuster auslösen.
Der rote Punkt auf dem Schnabel einer elterlichen Möwe löst beispielsweise das Bettelverhalten einer Jungmöwe aus.

8.3 Learning

learning n	Lernen
learning mechanism	Lernmechanismus
modification [ˈmɒdɪfɪˈkeɪʃn] n	Veränderung
adaptive modification [əˌdæptɪvmɒdɪfɪˈkeɪʃn]	anpassende Veränderung
modification of behaviour	Veränderung des Verhaltens
experience n	Erfahrung
benefit [ˈbenɪfɪt] n	Nutzen
counterbalancing benefits [ˌkaʊntəˈbælənsɪŋˈbenefɪts]	ausgleichender Nutzen
based on adj	basierend auf

» Learning describes the adaptive modification of behaviour based on experience.
Lernen beschreibt die anpassende Veränderung des Verhaltens basierend auf Erfahrung.
Learning only occurs if learning mechanisms are not too costly and if there are some major counterbalancing benefits.
Lernen findet nur statt, falls die Lernmechanismen nicht zu aufwendig sind und es einen bedeutenden ausgleichenden Nutzen gibt.

Operant Conditioning

condition v	konditionieren / bedingen / festsetzen
operant conditioning [ˌɒprnt kənˈdɪʃnɪŋ] n	operante Konditionierung / Lernen am Erfolg (Lernform, die auf Versuch und Irrtum basiert und bei der eine Handlung öfter ausgeführt wird, wenn sie belohnt wird)
operant conditioning chamber n	Raum für operante Konditionierung
instrumental conditioning n	instrumentelle Konditionierung
trial-and-error learning n	Lernen durch Versuch und Irrtum

Skinner box n	Skinner Box
modification n	Veränderung / Modifizierung
modify ['mɒdɪfaɪ] v	verändern / modifizieren
rat chow pellet ['rættʃaʊˌpelɪt] n	Rattenfutter-Pellet
cage n	Käfig
bar n	Hebel
bar-pressing behaviour	Verhalten des Hebeldrückens
food hopper ['fuːdˌhɒpə] n	Futterschale / Futterschacht

approach a bar	sich einem Hebel nähern
press a bar	einen Hebel drücken
await the arrival of a pellet of rat chow	das Erscheinen des Rattenfutter-Pellets erwarten
pop into a food hopper	in einen Futterschacht fallen
associate a particular activity with food	eine besondere Aktivität mit Futter assoziieren
receive rewards	Belohnungen erhalten
increase / decrease a consequence	eine Konsequenz steigern / mindern

inhibition [ˌɪnɪ'bɪʃn] n	Hemmung
inhibit (sth) [ɪn'hɪbɪt] v	(etw.) hemmen
avoidance [ə'vɔɪdns] n	Vermeidung
avoid (sth) v	(etw.) vermeiden
refuse to do (sth) v	sich weigern etw. zu tun
positive reinforcement [ˌpɒzətɪvriːɪn'fɔːsmənt] n	positive Verstärkung *(Positiv: Darbietung einer positiven Konsequenz)*
negative reinforcement n	negative Verstärkung *(Negativ: Entzug einer aversiven Konsequenz)*
reinforce (sth) positively v	(etw.) positiv verstärken
punishment ['pʌnɪʃmənt] n	Bestrafung
punish (sb) v	(jmd.) bestrafen
extinction [ɪk'stɪŋkʃn] n	Löschung

8 Ethology › 8.3 Learning

> Operant conditioning is that an animal learns to associate a voluntary action with a consequence that follows from that action.
> Beim operanten Konditionieren lernen Tiere eine freiwillige Handlung mit einer daraus folgenden Konsequenz zu assoziieren.

Associative Learning: classical and operant conditioning

associative learning [əˈsəʊʃɪətɪvˌlɜːnɪŋ] n	assoziatives Lernen
classical conditioning n	klassische Konditionierung
Pavlovian conditioning [pævˌləʊvɪənkənˈdɪʃnɪŋ]	Pawlowische Konditionierung
respondent conditioning [rɪˌspɒndəntkənˈdɪʃnɪŋ]	respondente Konditionierung
stimulus, *pl* stimuli n	Reiz
neutral stimulus	neutraler Reiz
unconditioned stimulus (US)	unkonditionierter / angeborener Reiz
unconditioned response (UR)	unkonditionierte / angeborene Reaktion
conditioned stimulus (CS)	konditionierter / bedingter Reiz
conditioned response (CR)	konditionierte / bedingte Reaktion
reflex [ˈriːfleks] n	Reflex
conditional reflex	bedingter Reflex
trigger n	Auslöser
stimulus-response theory [stɪmjələsrɪˈspɒnsˌθɪəri] n	Reiz-Reaktionstheorie
involuntary reflex action [ɪnˌvɒləntˌrɪriːfleksˈækʃn] n	unwillkürliche Reflexhandlung

> | | |
> |---:|---|
> | salivary conditioning of Pavlov's dog | Speichelkonditionierung beim Pawlowschen Hund |
> | salivate in the presence of (sb / sth) | speicheln in Anwesenheit von (jmd. / etw.) |
> | cause salivation | Speichelfluss verursachen |
> | measure salivation | Speichelfluss messen |
> | salivate in response to (sb / sth) | speicheln als Antwort auf (jmd. / etw.) |
> | be associated with food | mit Essen verbunden sein |

metronome ['metrənəʊm] n	Taktmesser
implanted cannula [ɪmˈplɑːntɪdˌkænjələ] n	eingepflanzte Kanüle
interval between (sth) [ˌɪntəvlbɪˈtwiːn] n	Zeitabstand zwischen (etw.)
counterconditioning [ˈkaʊntəkənˌdɪʃnɪŋ] n	Gegenkonditionierung
desensitisation *BE* [diːˌsensɪtaɪˈzeɪʃn] / desensitization *AE* n	Desensibilisierung *(Methode der Verhaltenstherapie, die erlerntes Verhalten wieder verlernen lässt)*

replace sth by sth	etw. durch etw. ersetzen
expose sb to sth	jmd. etw. aussetzen

Learning by association means that a stimulus, based on experience, is linked to another one that does not have anything to do with the first stimulus.
Lernen durch Assoziation bedeutet, dass ein auf Erfahrung basierender Reiz mit einem weiteren Reiz verknüpft wird, der nichts mit dem ersten Reiz zu tun hat.

Imprinting

imprinting [ɪmˈprɪntɪŋ] n	Prägung
filial imprinting [ˌfɪliəlɪmˈprɪntɪŋ] n	Nachfolgeprägung *(Kinder lernen das Verhalten ihrer Eltern)*
mis-imprinting n	Fehlprägung
sensitive phase n	sensible (Lebens-)Phase
learned attachment (to sb / sth) [ˈlɜːndəˌtætʃmənttuː] n	Bindung (zu jmd. / etw.)

greylag (goose) [ˈɡreɪlæɡˌɡuːs], *pl* geese [ɡiːs] n	Graugans
greylag gosling [ˈɡreɪlæɡˌɡɒzlɪŋ]	Graugansküken
gaggle of geese [ˈɡæɡləvˌɡiːs] n	Gänseschar
nidifugous bird [nɪˌdɪfjʊɡəsˈbɜːd] n	Nestflüchter

incubator [ˈɪŋkjʊbeɪtə] n	Brutschrank / Inkubator
hatch [hætʃ] v	schlüpfen
imprint v	prägen
follow (sb) v	(jmd.) folgen
reach adulthood v	Erwachsenenalter erreichen
prefer (sb) [prɪˈfɜː] v	(jmd.) bevorzugen

8 Ethology › 8.3 Learning

have a preference for (sb / sth)	eine Vorliebe für (jmd. / etw.) haben
innate / inherited behaviour	angeborenes Verhalten
imprint sth / sb on an animal	ein Tier auf etw./ jmd. prägen
hereditary basis of the imprinting mechanisms	erbliche Grundlage für die Imprinting-Mechanismen

Konrad Lorenz demonstrated how incubator-hatched geese had imprinted on the first moving stimulus they had seen within the critical period after hatching.
Konrad Lorenz demonstrierte wie im Brutschrank geschlüpfte Gänse auf den ersten Bewegungsreiz, den sie innerhalb der sensiblen Phase nach ihrem Schlüpfen sahen, geprägt waren.

Imitation

imitation n	Nachahmung
model ['mɒdl] n	Vorbild
observer n	Beobachter
matching degree n	Anpassungsgrad

observe sb / sth	jmd. / etw. beobachten
imitate sb / sth	jmd. / etw. nachahmen
replicate sb / sth	jmd. / etw. nachbilden
copy sb / sth	jmd. / etw. imitieren
match the demonstration	der Darstellung entsprechen
learn by imitation	durch Nachahmung lernen
be modelled on sb / sth	jmd. / etw. zum Vorbild haben

Imitation describes a behaviour modelled on the behaviour of someone else.
Nachahmung beschreibt ein Verhalten, das das Verhalten eines anderen zum Vorbild hat.

8.4 Behavioural ethology

Animal communication

interspecific communication [ˌɪntəspəˌsɪfɪkkəmjuːnɪˈkeɪʃn] n	zwischenartliche Kommunikation
intraspecific communication [ˌɪntrəspəsɪfɪkkəmjuːnɪˈkeɪʃn] n	innerartliche Kommunikation
exchange of information n	Informationsaustausch
signal n	Signal
sender n	Sender
recipient n	Empfänger
information transfer n	Informationsübertragung
sender recipient relationship n	Sender-Empfänger-Beziehung

> | | |
> |---|---|
> | influence sb / sth | jmd. / etw. beeinflussen |
> | be performed by sb | durchgeführt werden von jmd. |
> | to transfer sth | etw. übertragen |
>
> A sender recipient relationship contains a sender of the information, an information transfer and a recipient of the information.
> Eine Sender-Empfänger-Beziehung beinhaltet einen Sender der Information, eine Informationsübertragung und einen Empfänger der Information.
>
> An animal can influence a different animal by signals transferred.
> Ein Tier kann ein anderes Tier durch die übertragenen Signale beeinflussen.

vocal communication [ˌvəʊklkəmjuːnɪˈkeɪʃn] n	Verständigung durch Laute
bird song n	Vogellied
sing in alternation [ˌsɪŋɪnɔːltəˈneɪʃn] / duetting v	abwechselnd singen *(im Duett singen)*
warning cry, *pl* warning cries n *(e.g. of monkeys)*	Warnschrei *(z. B. von Affen)*
territorial call [terɪˈtɔːriəlˌkɔːl] n *(e.g. of gibbons)*	Revierruf *(z. B. von Gibbons)*
mating call [ˈmeɪtɪŋˌkɔːl] n *(e.g. of frogs)*	Paarungsruf *(z. B. von Fröschen)*

chemical communication n	chemische Kommunikation
olfactory communication [ɒlˌfæktri kəmjuːnɪˈkeɪʃn] n	Verständigung durch Gerüche
pheromone [ˈferəməʊn] n	Pheromon / Sexualhormon *(chemisches Signal)*

8 Ethology › 8.4 Behavioural ethology

attractant [əˈtræktənt] n	Lockstoff
scent [sent] n	Duftstoff
absorb (sth) v	(etw.) aufnehmen

visual communication n	optische Kommunikation
non-verbal communication n	nonverbale Kommunikation
warning colouration n (e.g. of wasps)	Warnfärbung (z. B. von Wespen)
mimicry [ˈmɪmɪkri] n (e.g. of a hoverfly)	Mimikry (z. B. einer Schwebefliege) (Nachahmungsverhalten zum eigenen Vorteil)
posture [ˈpɒstʃə] n	Körperhaltung
gesture [ˈdʒestʃə] n	Gestik / Gebärde

»
growl with teeth bared	zähnefletschend knurren
rattle with sth	mit etw. rasseln
warn sb of sth	jmd. vor etw. warnen

predator [ˈpredətə] n	Räuber / Fressfeind
prey [preɪ] n	Beute
predator-prey relationship	Räuber-Beute Beziehung
enemy n	Feind

Function

agonistic behaviour [ˌægənɪstɪkbɪˈheɪvjə] n	Kampfverhalten
courtship ritual [ˈkɔːtʃɪpˌrɪtjuəl] n	Balzritual

»
attract / maintain the attention of sb	Aufmerksamkeit von jmd. wecken / aufrechterhalten
mating	Paarung

food call n	Nahrungsruf
food-related signal n	nahrungsbezogenes Signal
alarm call n	Warnruf

»
attract sb to a food source	jmd. zu einer Futterquelle locken
feed sb	jmd. füttern

reduce the risk of an attack	die Gefahr eines Angriffs minimieren
run for cover	Schutz suchen
become immobile	unbeweglich werden
gather into a group	sich zu einer Gruppe zusammenschließen

dance language of honey bees n	Tanzsprache der Honigbienen
waggle dance [ˈwæglˌdɑːns] n	Schwänzeltanz *(zeigt, dass die Nahrungsquelle weiter vom Bienenstock entfernt ist)*
zig-zag pattern [ˈzɪgzægˌpætn] n	Zick-Zack-Muster
waggle pattern n	Schwänzelmuster
round dance n	Rundtanz *(zeigt, dass sich die Nahrungsquelle in nächster Umgebung befindet)*
circular pattern [ˈsɜːkjələˌpætn] n	kreisförmiges Muster

comb [kəʊm] / honeycomb n	Wabe
beehive [ˈbiːhaɪv] n	Bienenstock
forager (bee) [ˈfɒrɪdʒə] n	Wildbeuter / Sammlerin
worker (bee) n	Arbeiterin
queen bee n	Bienenkönigin
wag [wæg] v	schwänzeln
forage [ˈfɒrɪdʒ] v	nach Futter suchen
food source n	Futterquelle

food source towards the sun	Futterquelle in Richtung Sonne
food source in the opposite direction of the sun	Futterquelle in entgegengesetzter Richtung zur Sonne

Successfully foraging honey bees use two forms of dances to communicate about food sources.
Erfolgreich sammelnde Honigbienen benutzen zwei Tanzformen, um über Futterquellen zu kommunizieren.

The waggle dance indicates that food is farther away from the beehive.
Der Schwänzeltanz zeigt an, dass sich die Nahrung weiter weg vom Bienenstock befindet.

Interpretation

excitement n	Aufregung
anticipation [æn͵tɪsɪˈpeɪʃn] n	Vorfreude
playfulness n	Verspieltheit
enjoyment n	Freude
relaxation [͵riːlækˈseɪʃn] n	Enspannung
anxiety [æŋˈzaɪəti] n	Ängstlichkeit
statement of interest n	Bekundung von Interesse
uncertainty [ʌnˈsɜːtnti] n	Unsicherheit
apprehension [͵æprɪˈhenʃn] n	Besorgnis / dunkle Vorahnung

Postures and gestures of animals can have several meanings, for example excitement, enjoyment, anxiety or uncertainty.
Körperhaltungen und Gestiken von Tieren können verschiedene Bedeutungen haben, wie beispielsweise Aufregung, Freude, Ängstlichkeit oder Unsicherheit.

Living in groups

society [səˈsaɪəti] n	Gesellschaft
social relationship n	soziale Beziehung
strong company n	enger Zusammenhalt
association [ə͵səʊʃiˈeɪʃn] n	Verband
individualised association [͵ɪndɪˈvɪdʒuəlaɪzdəsəʊʃi͵eɪʃn]	individualisierter Verband
open anonymous association [͵əʊpn əˈnɒnɪməs əsəʊʃi͵eɪʃn]	offener anonymer Verband
closed anonymous association	geschlossener anonymer Verband
proprietary company [prə͵praɪətriˈkʌmpəni] n	Privatgesellschaft
hierarchy [ˈhaɪrɑːki] / precedence [ˈpresɪdns] n	Rangordnung
specific order of precedence	bestimmte Rangordnung
dioecious [daɪˈiːʃəs] adj	getrenntgeschlechtlich
hierarchically classified adj	hierarchisch geordnet
rank below v	im Rang niedriger sein
rank before v	im Rang höher sein
social position n	soziale Stellung
group member n	Gruppenmitglied

> Birds live in open anonymous associations because they can change their flocks and do not have a specific order of precedence.
> Vögel leben in offenen anonymen Verbänden, weil sie ihre Schwärme wechseln können und keine spezifische Rangordnung haben.
> Insects in colonies do not know each other, but they are connected by one collective feature, for example the same smell, so that they live in a closed anonymous association.
> Insekten in Kolonien bzw. Staaten kennen sich untereinander nicht, sind aber durch ein gemeinsames Merkmal, wie beispielsweise den Geruch, miteinander verbunden, so dass sie in einem geschlossenen anonymen Verband leben.

herd [hɜːd] n	Herde
flock n	Herde / Schar / Schwarm
pack [pæk] n	Rudel
shoal [ʃəʊl] n	Schwarm
colony, pl colonies n	Kolonie / Staat
wolf pack / pack of wolves	Wolfsrudel
buffalo herd	Büffelherde
flock of sheep	Schafsherde
ant colony	Ameisenkolonie
wasp colony	Wespenkolonie
shoal of fish	Fischschwarm
flock of birds	Vogelschwarm
comment fighting [ˈkɒmentˌfaɪtɪŋ] n	Kommentkampf
damaging fight n	Beschädigungskampf
hunting ground n	Jagdrevier
territory [ˈterɪtri] n	Territorium / Revier
feeding territory	Nahrungsrevier
reproduction territory [ˌriːprəˈdʌkʃnˌterɪtri]	Fortpflanzungsrevier
nesting territory [ˈnestɪŋˌterɪtri]	Brutrevier
courtship district / courtship ground	Balzrevier

> intimidating and threatening behaviour — Imponier- und Drohverhalten

		acoustically	ein Revier … markieren	akustisch
mark one's	territory	olfactorily		olfaktorisch / geruchlich
		electrically		elektrisch
		visually		optisch
	keep sb off one's patch		sein Revier gegen jmd. verteidigen	

8 Ethology › 8.4 Behavioural ethology

In comment fightings rivals do not hurt each other.
In Komment- oder Tunierkämpfen verletzten sich die Kontrahenten nicht.

A territory ensures that an individual, a couple or a group has lots of options for searching food, mating or raising the offspring without being disturbed by conspecifics.
Ein Revier stellt sicher, dass ein Individuum, ein Paar oder eine Gruppe viele Möglichkeiten für die Futtersuche, für das Paaren oder das Aufziehen der Jungen hat, ohne von den Artgenossen gestört zu werden.

altruism ['æltruɪzm] n	Altruismus
altruistic behaviour [ˌæltru'ɪstɪkbɪˌheɪvjə] n	altruistisches Verhalten / uneigennütziges Verhalten
backer ['bækə] n	Helfer / Unterstützer
feeding n	Fütterung
defence of a nest n	Nestverteidigung

»

warn sb against sth	jmd. vor etw. warnen
help sb with sth	jmd. mit etw. helfen
support sb	jmd. unterstützen
take advantage of sth	einen Vorteil aus etw. ziehen

genetic egoism [dʒəˌnetɪk'iːgəʊɪzm] n	genetischer Egoismus (zusammenarbeitende Individuen suchen letztendlich ihren eigenen Vorteil)
reciprocal altruism [reˌsɪprəʊkl'æltruɪzm] n	reziproker Altruismus (Nächstenliebe zwischen Nichtverwandten)
reproductive behaviour n	Fortpflanzungsverhalten
individual fitness n	individuelle Fitness
offspring, pl offspring n	Nachkomme(n)
pairing / mating n	Paarung
copulation [ˌkɒpjə'leɪʃn] n	Paarungsakt
visual attraction n	optische Anlockung
acoustic attraction [əˌkuːstɪk'ətrækʃn] n	akustische Anlockung
attraction by scents n	Anlockung mittels Duftstoffen

intrasexual competition [ˌɪntrəˌsekʃʊəlˌkɒmpə'tɪʃn] n	innergeschlechtliche Konkurrenz
partner choice n	Partnerwahl
male n	Männchen

female n	Weibchen
cock [kɒk] n	Vogelmännchen
sexual selection n	sexuelle Selektion / sexuelle Auslese
selection pressure [sɪˈlekʃnˌpreʃə] n	Selektionsdruck
mating system n	Paarungssystem
mating ritual n	Paarungsritual
fixed action pattern (FAP) n	festes Handlungsmuster
monogamy [məˈnɒɡəmi] n	Monogamie *(sexuelle Beziehung mit einem Männchen oder Weibchen für mindestens eine Fortpflanzungsperiode)*
polygyny [pəˈlɪdʒɪni] n	Polygynie *(Vielweiberei)*
polyandry [ˈpɒliændri] n	Ployandrie *(Vielmännerei)*

attract sb	jmd. anziehen / anlocken
compete against sb / sth	mit jmd. / etw. konkurrieren
choose sb as a partner	jmd. als Partner wählen
assume sb as a partner	jmd. als Partner annehmen
display	balzen
propagate reproduce breed	sich vermehren / sich fortpflanzen

Behaviour of primates

primate [ˈpraɪmeɪt] n	Primat
mammal [ˈmæml] n	Säugetier
strepsirrhini [ˌstrepsəˈraɪni] n	Feuchtnasenaffe / Strepsirrhini
monkey n	Affe
tarsier [ˈtɑːsɪər] n	Koboldmaki
ape *(e.g. chimpanzee)* n	Menschenaffe *(z. B. Schimpanse)*
human n	Mensch
haplorrhini [ˌhæpləˈraɪni] n	Trockennasenaffe / Haplorrhini
lemur [ˈliːmə] n	Lemur
loris [ˈlɔːrɪs] n	Faulaffe
galago [ɡəˈleɪɡɔː] / bush baby n	Galago / Buschbaby
aye-aye [ˈaɪaɪ] n	Aye-Aye / Fingertier
relationship n	Verwandtschaft
be related (to sb) v	(mit jmd.) verwandt sein

8 Ethology › 8.4 Behavioural ethology

> Primates are subdivided into the "wet-nosed" and "dry-nosed" primates.
> Primaten werden in die Feuchtnasenaffen und Trockennasenaffen untergliedert.
> The Strepsirrhini cover apes and humans whereas the Haplorrhini include lemurs and galagos, for example.
> Die Strepsirrhini umfassen die Menschenaffen und die Menschen wohingegen die Haplorrhini beispielsweise die Lemuren und Galagos einschließen.

cognitive ability [ˌkɒgnətɪvəˈbɪleti], pl abilities / cognitive skill n	kognitive Fähigkeit
self-knowledge / self-perception [ˌselfpəˈsepʃn] n	Selbstkenntnis
self-awareness [ˌselfəˈweənəs] / consciousness of self [ˈkɒnʃəsnəsəvˌself] n	Ich-Bewusstsein
imagination n	Vorstellungsvermögen
conspecific [ˌkɒnspɪˈsɪfɪk] n	Artgenosse
conspecific adj	zur selben Art gehörend
understand (sb / sth) v	(jmd. / etw.) verstehen
creating traditions n	Traditionsbildung
learn (sth) v	(etw.) erlernen
imitation n	Nachahmung
copy (sb / sth) v	(jmd. / etw.) nachahmen
culture n	Kultur

> | | |
> |---|---|
> | put oneself in sb's position | sich in (jmd.) hineinversetzen |
> | catch one's own reflexion | sich im Spiegel selbst erkennen |

Apes are able to catch their own reflexion.
Menschenaffen sind in der Lage, sich im Spiegel selbst zu erkennen.

make use of tools	von Werkzeugen Gebrauch machen
sit on leaves	auf Blättern sitzen
avoid a wet ground	einen feuchten Boden meiden
have a scratch with a stone or a stick	sich mit einem Stein oder Stock kratzen
swab a wound with leaves	eine Wunde mit Blättern betupfen
examine a wound	eine Wunde untersuchen
crack nuts	Nüsse knacken
smash nuts with a stone as a hammer and a root or a flat stone as an anvil	Nüsse mit einem Stein als Hammer und einer Wurzel oder einem flachen Stein als Amboss zerschlagen

fish for termites	nach Termiten angeln / suchen
gain bone marrow out of a hollow bone of a hunted down monkey	Knochenmark aus einem Röhrenknochen eines erjagten Affens gewinnen

8.5 Ethology of human behaviour

Skills of a baby

suck	saugen
sucking reflex [ˈsʌkɪŋˌriːfleks] n	Saugreflex

nurse a baby / breast-feed a baby	einen Säugling stillen

palmar grasp [ˈpælməˌgrɑːsp] n	Greifreflex
crawling motion [ˌkrɔːlɪŋˈməʊʃn] n	Kriechbewegung
step v	schreiten
intense crying n	Schreiweinen
embody [ɪmˈbɒdi] / express v	zum Ausdruck bringen
contact behaviour n	Kontaktverhalten
reference person [ˈrefrnsˌpɜːsn] n	Bezugsperson
mutual trust [ˈmjuːtʃuəlˌtrʌst] n	Vertrauensverhältnis

The sucking reflex, the palmar grasp, the crawling motion, the intense crying and the contact behaviour are behavioural patterns of a baby which are inborn.
Der Saugreflex, der Greifreflex, die Kriechbewegung, das Schreiweinen und das Kontaktverhalten sind Verhaltensweisen eines Säuglings, die angeboren sind.
When a baby is breast-fed for the first time, it is able to coordinate the muscles of the tongue, mouth and neck from the beginning to act out the sucking reflex.
Wenn ein Säugling das erste Mal gestillt wird, ist er in der Lage die Muskeln der Zunge, des Mundes und des Halses von Anfang an zu koordinieren, um den Saugreflex ausführen zu können.

Learning for life

curiosity behaviour n	Neugierverhalten
play behaviour n	Spielverhalten

get to know the environment	die Umwelt kennenlernen

8 Ethology › 8.5 Ethology of human behaviour

| explore the environment | die Umwelt entdecken |

Babys discover their environment by the innate curiosity and play behaviour.
Säuglinge erkunden ihre Umwelt durch das angeborene Neugier- und Spielverhalten.

trial-and-error learning n	Lernen durch Versuch und Irrtum
operant learning [ˈɒprnt ˌlɜːnɪŋ] n	Lernen am Erfolg
learning by imitation n	Lernen durch Nachahmung
insight learning [ˈɪnsaɪt ˌlɜːnɪŋ] n	Lernen duch Einsicht
type of learner n	Lerntyp
multichannel learning [ˌmʌltiˈtʃænl ˌlɜːnɪŋ] n	mehrkanaliges Lernen

sense organ n	Sinnesorgan
eye	Auge
ear	Ohr
skin	Haut
tongue [tʌŋ]	Zunge
nose	Nase

memory n	Gedächtnis
autobiographical memory [ˌɔːtəbaɪəgræfɪklˈmemri]	autobiographisches Gedächtnis
photographic memory	photographisches Gedächtnis
eye memory	visuelles Gedächtnis

short-term memory n	Kurzzeitspeicher
middle-term memory n	mittelfristiger Gedächtnisspeicher
long-term memory n	Langzeitgedächtnis / Langzeitspeichers

»

keep sth / sb in mind	jmd. / etw. im Gedächtnis behalten
recall sth	sich etw. ins Gedächtnis rufen
memorise sth	etw. abspeichern
store sth	etw. speichern
remember sb / sth	sich an jmd. / etw. erinnern
filter sth	etw. filtern, aussondern
combine sth with sth link sth with sth connect sth with sth	etw. mit etw. verknüpfen

The short-term memory stores information for only 10–20 seconds and filters important pieces of information that go into the middle-term memory. Unimportant pieces of information get lost.
Das Kurzzeitgedächtnis speichert Informationen für nur 10–20 Sekunden und sondert wichtige Informationen aus, die in den mittelfristigen Gedächtnisspeicher gelangen. Unwichtige Informationen gehen verloren.

Living together

social life n	soziales Zusammenleben
social contact n	sozialer Kontakt
family n	Familie
circle of friends n	Freundeskreis
companionship [kəmˈpænjənʃɪp] n	Kameradschaft

» The human being lives a social life and is closely connected to his family, his circle of friends or further companionships.
Der Mensch lebt ein soziales Leben und ist eng verbunden mit seiner Familie, seinem Freundeskreis oder weiteren Kameradschaften.

elevator effect n	Fahrstuhleffekt
individual distance n	Individualdistanz
wall contact behaviour n	Wandkontaktverhalten

»
not tolerate strangers	Fremde nicht dulden
avoid eye-contact	Blickkontakt meiden
prefer a seat near a wall	einen Platz in Wandnähe bevorzugen

When individuals who do not know each other meet in an elevator, on a bench or at a station, they aim to have their own space where they do not tolerate any strangers.
Wenn Individuen, die sich nicht kennen, im Fahrstuhl, auf einer Parkbank oder an einer Haltestelle aufeinandertreffen, sind sie bemüht, ihren eigenen Raum zu haben, in dem sie keine Fremden dulden.

captivity [kæpˈtɪvəti] n	Gefangenschaft
territorial behaviour n	Territorialverhalten

»
set the boundaries of sth	etw. abgrenzen

8 Ethology › 8.5 Ethology of human behaviour

keep distance	Abstand einhalten
occupy a territory	ein Territorium / Revier in Anspruch nehmen

social position n	soziale Stellung
rank before v	höher im Rang sein
rank below v	im Rang nachstehen
change the social position v	die soziale Stellung wechseln
attract attention v	Aufmerksamkeit auf sich ziehen
aggressive behaviour n	Aggressionsverhalten
imposing behaviour n	Imponierverhalten
display (sth) v	(etw.) zur Schau stellen
brawn [brɔːn] n	Muskelkraft
award n	Auszeichnung
luxury item [ˌlʌkʃri'aɪtem] n	Luxusartikel

»

call sb's attention to sth	jmd. auf etw. aufmerksam machen

frightening behaviour n	Drohverhalten
rival ['raɪvl] n	Rivale
physical attack n	körperlicher Angriff
submissive behaviour n	Demutsverhalten
inferiority [ɪnˌfɪəri'ɒrəti] n	Unterlegenheit
superiority n	Überlegenheit
conciliation [kənˌsɪli'eɪʃn] n	Beschwichtigung

»

intimidate sb	jmd. einschüchtern
threaten sb	jmd. bedrohen
be in an inferior position	unterlegen sein
bow and scrape	sich unterwürfig verhalten
conciliate sb	jmd. beschwichtigen

outsider n	Außenseiter
bullying ['bʊliɪŋ] n	Mobbing
discrimination [dɪˌskrɪmɪ'neɪʃn] n	Diskriminierung
tension n	Spannung
frustration n	Frust

become a vicitim of sb / sth	Opfer von jmd. / etw. werden
bully sb	jmd. mobben
relieve sth	etw. abbauen
calm down	abreagieren

A conflict can be solved without physical violence, but with words, gestures and mimics.
Ein Konflikt kann ohne körperliche Gewalt, aber mit Worten, Gestik und Mimik gelöst werden.

9 Neurobiology

9.1 Stimulation and conduction

Neurons » Abb. 33

neurobiology [ˌnjʊərəbaɪˈɒlədʒi] n	Neurobiologie
nervous system n	Nervensystem
neuron [ˈnjʊərɒn] n	Neuron / Nervenzelle
electrical impulse n	elektrischer Impuls
soma [ˈsəʊmə], pl somas; somata / cell body n	Soma / Zellkörper
nucleus [ˈnjuːkliəs], pl nuclei n	Zellkern / Nukleus
cell(ular) extension [ˌseljələɪkˈstenʃn] n	Zellfortsatz
branched adj	verästelt
dendrite [ˈdendraɪt] n	Dendrit
axon [ˈæksɒn] n	Axon
axon hillock [ˈæksɒnˌhɪlək]	Axonhügel
giant axon [ˈdʒaɪentˌæksɒn]	Riesenaxon
synaptic knob [sɪˈnæptɪˌknɒb] n	Endknöpfchen
synapse [ˈsaɪnæps] n	Synapse
glial cell [ˈglɪəlˌsel] n	Gliazelle
myelin [ˈmɪəlɪn] n	Myelin
myelin sheath [ˈmɪələnˌʃiːθ]	Markscheide / Myelinscheide
node of Ranvier [ˌnəʊdɒvˈrɒnvɪeɑ] n	Ranvier-Schnürring
nerve [nɜːv] n	Nerv
nerve fibre	Nervenfaser
incoming signal n	eintreffendes Signal

9 Neurobiology › 9.1 Stimulation and conduction

» The neuron is divided into a cell body (soma) and cellular extensions. The soma contains, amongst other things, the nucleus.
Das Neuron ist einen Zellkörper (Soma) und in Zellfortsätze unterteilt. Das Soma enthält, neben anderen Dingen, den Zellkern.
A nerve fibre is defined by an axon and its surrounding sheath cells. Bundles of many of these fibres are enclosed by connective tissue and form a thick nerve.
Eine Nervenfaser wird durch ein Axon und dessen umgebende Hüllzellen definiert. Bündel vieler dieser Fasern werden durch Bindegewebe eingeschlossen und bilden einen dicken Nerv.

Neurobiology: practicals

slaughtered animal	Schlachttier	**Petri dish(es)**	Petrischale(n)
spinal cord	Rückenmark	**microscope**	Mikroskop
white matter	weiße Substanz	**microscope slide**	Objektträger
grey matter	graue Substanz	**stained sample**	angefärbtes Präparat
slightly frozen	leicht angefroren	**Golgi stain**	Golgi-Färbung
razor blade	Rasierklinge	**equipment**	Ausrüstung
scalpel	Skalpell	**Giemsa solution**	Giemsa-Lösung
scissors	Schere	**distilled water**	destilliertes Wasser
tweezers with sharp points	spitze Pinzette		

» Compare the two figures (micro and drawing) with regard to their information value.
Vergleiche die beiden Abbildungen (Mikroskop und Zeichnung) hinsichtlich ihres Informationsgehalts.

The resting potential » Abb. 35

nerve-muscle tissue n	Nerv-Muskel-Gewebe
frog n	Frosch
voltage ['vəʊltɪdʒ] n	Spannung
current n	Strom
measurement n	Messung
perform (sth) v	(etw.) ausführen
electrode [ɪ'lektrəʊd] n	Elektrode
oscilloscope [ə'sɪləskəʊp] n	Oszilloskop
hard glass capillary n	hartes Glaskapillar
salt solution / saline solution n	Salzlösung

conduct v	führen / leiten
extracellular body fluid [ˌekstrəseljələ'bɒdiˌfluːɪd] n	extrazelluläre Körperflüssigkeit / Extrazellulärflüssigkeit
extracellular recording [ˌekstrəseljələ'rɪ'kɔːdɪŋ] n	extrazelluläre Ableitung
axon membrane [ˌæksɒn'membrən] n	Axonmembran
membrane potential ['membrənpəˌtenʃl] n	Membranpotential
resting potential [ˌrestɪŋpə'tenʃl] n	Ruhepotential
resting adj	ruhend
K^+ ions n	K^+ Ionen
Na^+ ions n	Na^+ Ionen
Cl^- ions n	Cl^- Ionen
KCl solution n	KCl-Lösung
ion concentration [aɪənˌkɒnsn'treɪʃn] n	Ionenkonzentration
selective ion channel [sɪˌlektɪv'aɪəntʃænl] n	selektiver Ionenkanal

» The membrane is selectively permeable. | Die Membran ist selektiv permeabel.

lipid bilayer / double layer of lipids n	Lipid-Doppelschicht
dissolved ions [dɪˌzɒlvd'aɪənz] n	gelöste Ionen
positive charge [ˌpɒzɪtɪv'tʃɑːdʒ] n	positive Ladung
accumulate [ə'kjuːmjəleɪt] v	anhäufen / akkumulieren
concentration gradient n	Konzentrationsgradient
electric(al) field [ɪˌlektrɪk'fiːld] n	elektrisches Feld
equilibrium [ˌiːkwɪ'lɪbriəm] n	Gleichgewicht
potassium equilibrium potential [pəˌtæsɪəmiːkwɪ'lɪbriəmpəˌtenʃl] n	Kalium-Gleichgewichtspotential
ATP (adenosine triphosphate) [əˌdenəsiːntraɪ'fɒsfeɪt] n	Adenosintriphosphat
sodium-potassium pump (Na^+/ K^+ pump)	Natrium-Kalium-Pumpe
membrane protein ['membreɪnˌprəʊtiːn] n	Membranprotein
electrogenic pump n	elektrogene Pumpe
influx ['ɪnflʌks] n	Einstrom

> Various channel proteins have been discovered that are located within the lipid layer of the cell membrane. They only let one type of ion pass, e.g. K⁺ions.
> Man hat verschiedene Tunnelproteine entdeckt, die innerhalb der Lipidschicht der Zellmembran lokalisiert sind. Sie lassen nur einen Ionentyp passieren, z. B. K⁺Ionen.
> The potassium equilibrium potential is the basis for the membrane potential; it is present in a non-stimulated or resting neuron. This voltage is therefore called the *resting potential*.
> Das Kalium-Gleichgewichtspotential ist die Basis des Membranpotentials; es ist in einem nicht-stimulierten oder ruhenden Neuron vorhanden. Diese Spannung wird daher Ruhepotential genannt.

Action potential

action potential n	Aktionspotential
stimulation n	Stimulation
stimulus ['stɪmjələɪ], *pl* stimuli ['stɪmjəliː] n	Reiz
electrical impulse n	elektrischer Impuls
sensory cell n	Sinneszelle
transmit [trænz'mɪt] v	übermitteln
brain n	Gehirn
motor nerve cell n	Motoneuron
short-term change n	kurzfristige Veränderung
Loligo n *(a squid)*	Loligo *(ein Tintenfisch)*
application point [ˌæplɪ'keɪʃnpɔɪnt] n	Ansatzpunkt
recording site n	Messstelle
decrease [dɪ'kriːs] v	abnehmen
increase ['ɪnkriːs] v	vergrößern / verstärken
hyperpolarisation [ˌhaɪpəˌpəʊlərɑɪ'zeɪʃn] n	Hyperpolarisation
depolarisation [diːˌpəʊlɑɪ'zeɪʃn] n	Depolarisation
threshold voltage ['θreʃəʊldˌvəʊltɪdʒ] n	Schwellenspannung
rising phase n	Aufstrich
depolarisation phase	Depolarisationsphase
repolarisation [ˌriːpəʊlərɑɪ'zeɪʃn] n	Repolarisation
overshoot ['əʊvəʃuːt] n	Überschuss
all-or-nothing principle n	Alles-oder-Nichts-Gesetz
ion theory of excitation n	Ionentheorie der Erregung
voltage-gated channels [ˌvɒltɪdʒgeɪtɪd'tʃænl] n	spannungsabhängige Kanäle
refractory period [rɪˌfræktərɪ'pɪərɪəd] n	Refraktärzeit
stimulating current n	stimulierende Strömung

stimulation electrode n	Reizelektrode
recording electrode n	Messelektrode

» The axons of Loligo are especially large in diameter (up to 1 mm) and therefore are highly suitable for measurements.
Die Axone von Loligo sind vor allem im Durchmesser (bis zu 1mm) groß und sind daher besonders für Messungen geeignet.

electrotonic conduction n	elektrotonische Leitung
continuous conduction n	kontinuierliche Leitung
sodium channel n	Natriumkanal

» Are axons "one-way streets"? | Sind Axone "Einbahnstraßen"?

Saltatory conduction »Abb. 34

saltatory conduction [ˌsæltətrɪkən'dʌkʃn] n	saltatorische Erregungsleitung
myelinated axons ['maɪəlɪneɪtɪdˌæksɒnz] n	myelinisierte Axone
node of Ranvier [ˌnəʊdɒv'rɒnveɑ] n	Ranvier-Schnürring

» The nodes of Ranvier lie about 2 mm apart. | Die Ranvier-Schnürringe liegen etwa 2 mm auseinander.

The receptor potential

receptor cell n	Rezeptorzelle
primary sensory cell n	primäre Sinneszelle
muscle spindle n	Muskelspindel
receptor potential n	Rezeptorpotential

9 Neurobiology › 9.2 Connecting neurons

» The receptor potential works as follows: The muscle spindles are stretched if the muscle fibre is stretched.
Das Rezeptorpotential arbeitet folgendermaßen: Die Muskelspindeln werden gedehnt, wenn die Muskelfaser gedehnt wird.
Na^+ ion channels in the sensory neuron are opened.
Na^+Ionenkanäle werden im sensorischen Neuron geöffnet.
The membrane is depolarised via the diffusion of Na^+ ions into the axon; the membrane is depolarised.
Die Membran wird durch die Na^+Ionendiffusion in das Axon depolarisiert; die Membran ist depolarisiert.

9.2 Connecting neurons

Synapses

synapse ['saɪnæps] n	Synapse
synaptic knob n	Endknöpfchen
synaptic cleft [sɪˌnæptɪk'kleft]	synaptische Spalte
synaptic vesicle	synaptisches Bläschen
presynaptic [ˌpriːsɪ'næptɪk] adj	präsynaptisch
postsynaptic [ˌpəʊstsɪ'næptɪk] adj	postsynaptisch
neurotransmitter [ˌnjʊərəʊtrænz'mɪtə] n	Neurotransmitter
transmitting substance n	Überträgerstoff
acetylcholine [ˌæsɪtaɪl'kəʊliːn] n	Acetylcholin
excitatory postsynaptic potential (EPSP)	erregendes postsynaptisches Potential
frequency code ['friːkwənsiˌkəʊd] n	Frequenzcode
amplitude code ['æmplɪtjuːdˌkəʊd] n	Amplituden-Code
information flow [ˌɪnfəˌmeɪʃn'fləʊ] n	Informationsfluss

» Compare the synaptic cleft to the sodium ion channels in the axon membrane.
Vergleiche(n Sie) den synaptischen Spalt mit Natrium-Ionenkanälen in der Axonmembran.

Neurotransmitter molecules are released into the synaptic cleft if an action potential reaches the synaptic cleft; the postsynaptic cell becomes depolarised.
Neurotransmitter-Moleküle werden in den synaptischen Spalt freigelassen, wenn ein Aktionspotential die synaptische Spalte erreicht; die postsynaptische Zelle wird depolarisiert.

Motor end plate and neurotoxins

motor end plate n	motorische Endplatte
neuromuscular junction [ˌnjʊərəʊmʌskjʊləˈdʒʌŋkʃn] n	neuromuskuläre Endplatte
myosin [ˈmaɪəsɪn] n	Myosin
actin [ˈæktɪn] n	Aktin
neurotoxin [ˌnjʊərəʊˈtɒksɪn] n	Neurotoxin
botulinum toxin [ˌbɒtjʊˈlaɪnəmˌtɒksɪn] n	Botulinum-Toxin
black widow n	Schwarze Witwe
coniine [ˈkəʊnɪɪn] n	Coniin
hemlock [ˈhɛmlɒk] n	Schierling
cup of hemlock	Schierlingsbecher
nightshade n	Nachtschattengewächs
deadly nightshade	tödliches Nachtschattengewächs
cramp n	Krampf
paralysis [pəˈrælɔsɪs] n	Paralyse

» The muscle contracts if a motor neuron transmits action potentials to the muscle.
Der Muskel kontrahiert, wenn der Motoneuron zum Muskel Aktionspotentiale überträgt.
Motor end plates are larger than synaptic clefts. However, they have the same basic structure.
Motorische Endplatten sind größer als synaptische Spalten. Sie haben jedoch die gleiche grundlegende Struktur.

Summation

summation [sʌmˈeɪʃn] n	Summation
spatial summation [ˌspeɪʃlsʌˈmeɪʃn]	räumliche Summation
temporal summation [ˌtemprəlsʌˈmeɪʃn]	zeitliche Summation
soma [ˈsəʊmə], pl somas; somata / cell body n	Soma / Zellkörper
excitatory synapses [ɪkˌsaɪtətrɪsɪˈnæpsiːz] n	erregende Synapsen
inhibitory synapses [ɪnˌhɪbɪtrɪsɪˈnæpsiːz] n	hemmende Synapsen
hyperpolarisation [ˌhaɪpəˌpəʊləraɪˈzeɪʃn] n	Hyperpolarisation
inhibitory postsynaptic potential (IPSP) [ɪnˌhɪbətrɪˌpəʊstsaɪnæptɪkpəˈtenʃl] n	inhibitorisches postsynaptisches Potential

presynaptic inhibition [ˌpriːsɪnæptɪkɪnɪˈbɪʃn] n	präsynaptische Hemmung
trigger v	auslösen

Reflexes » Abb. 31–32

reflex [ˈriːfleks] n	Reflex
reflex arc	Reflexbogen
knee joint n	Kniegelenk
knee jerk reflex	Kniesehnenreflex
muscle spindle n	Muskelspindel
spinal cord n	Rückenmark
sensory nerve n	sensorischer Nerv
motor nerve n	motorischer Nerv
monosynaptic n	monosynaptisch
monosynaptic reflex	monosynaptsicher Reflex
polysynaptic [ˈpɒlɪsɪˌnæptɪk] adj	polysynaptisch
polysynaptic reflex	polysynaptischer Reflex
effector [ɪˈfektə] n	Effektor
reacting organ n	reagierendes Organ
blink reflex n	Lidschlagreflex
cough [kɒf] n	husten

9.3 Sensory organs of the nervous system

Receptors and stimulation

receptor [rɪˈseptə] n	Rezeptor
chemoreceptor [ˌkeməʊrɪˈseptə]	Chemorezeptor
mechanoreceptor [ˌmekənəʊrɪˈseptə]	Mechanorezeptor
photoreceptor	Photorezeptor
thermoreceptor	Thermorezeptor
electroreceptor	Elektrorezeptor
stimulus, *pl* stimuli n	Reiz
chemical n	Chemikalie
light n	Licht
sound waves n	Schallwellen
sensory organ n	Sinnesorgan
ear n	Ohr
eye n	Auge
nose n	Nase
tongue n	Zunge

skin n	Haut
transduction [trænsˈdʌkʃn] n	Transduktion
process v	verarbeiten
reference value n	Sollwert
input n	Eingabe des Sollwerts
output n	Istwert
controller n	Regler
sensor n	Fühler
error n	Regelgröße *(Differenz zwischen Ist- und Sollwert)*

> Sensory organs translate the stimuli of the environment into the language of the nervous system.
> Sinnesorgane übersetzen die Umweltreize in die Sprache des Nervensystems.

A sensory system I: the eye »Abb. 27

light receptor cell n	Lichtrezeptorzelle
sensory cell n	Sinneszelle
retina [ˈretɪnə] n	Retina / Netzhaut
cone [kəʊn] n	Zapfen
rod [rɒd] n	Stäbchen
membranous disk n	Membranscheibchen
decomposition n	Zerfall
chain n	Kette
spatial adj	räumlich
fovea [ˈfɒvɪə] / central pit n	Fovea / Sehgrube
blind spot n	Blinder Fleck
optic nerve n	Sehnerv
horizontal cell n	Horizontalzelle
amacrine cell [æməˈkaɪnˌsel] n	Amakrinzelle
ganglion cell [ˈgæŋgɪənˌsel] n	Ganglionzelle
visual field n	Gesichtsfeld
monocular visual field [məˈnɒkjʊləvɪdʒʊəlˈfiːld]	monokulares Gesichtsfeld
binocluar visual field [bɪˈnɒkjʊləvɪdʒʊəlˈfiːld]	binokulares Gesichtsfeld
compound eye n	Komplexauge / Facettenauge »Abb. 29

9 Neurobiology › 9.3 Sensory organs of the nervous system

> polarisation of light | Polarisation des Lichts
>
> The direct adequate physical stimulus of light is represented by electromagnetic waves of wavelengths between 400 and 750 nm.
> Der direkte adäquate physikalische Reiz des Lichts wird durch elektromagnetische Wellen mit Wellenlängen zwischen 400 und 750 nm repräsentiert.

rhodopsin [rəˈdɒpsɪn] n | Rhodopsin
opsin [ˈɒpsɪn] n | Opsin
retinal [ˈretɪnəl] n | Retinal
  11-cis retinal | 11-cis-Retinal
  all-trans-retinal | all-trans-Retinal
night blindness n | Nachtblindheit
second messenger molecules (cGMP) [ˌsekəndmesɪndʒəˈmɒlɪkjuːlz] n | sekundäre Botenstoffe
light quantum [ˌlaɪtkwantəmˈfəʊtɒn] / photon n | Lichtquant / Photon
bipolar cell [ˌbaɪpəʊləˈsel] n | bipolare Zelle

> Compare a primary sensory cell to a light sensory cell.
> Vergleiche(n Sie) eine primäre Sinneszelle mit einer Lichtsinneszelle.

adaptation n | Anpassung
adapt v | (sich) adaptieren / (sich) anpassen
adjustment [əˈdʒʌsmənt] n | Einstellung

> Leaving a highly illuminated room and going out into the night …
> Beim Verlassen eines hell erleuchteten Raumes und beim Hinausgehen in die Nacht …

spectral range n | Spektralbereich
primary colour n | Grundfarbe / Primärfarbe
colour triangle n | Farbdreieck
  | (gleichschenklig) » Abb. 30
additive colour mixing n | additive Farbmischung
subtractive colour mixing n | subtraktive Farbmischung
contrast n | Kontrast
receptive field n | rezeptives Feld
lightness value n | Lichtwert
brightness value n | Helligkeitswert
twilight n | Dämmerung
lateral inhibition n | laterale Inhibition

perception [pəˈsepʃn] n Wahrnehmung / Perzeption
optic chiasma [ˌɒptɪkkaɪˈæzmə] n optisches Chiasma / Sehnervenkreuzung
cognition [kɒɡˈnɪʃn] n Erkennen / Kognition

> **trichromatic colour theory** | **trichromatische Farbenlehre**
>
> The processing of stimulations in the eye is adjusted to recognize changes and contrasts. This includes differences in movements, brightness and colour contrasts.
> Die Erregungsverbreitung im Auge ist darauf ausgerichtet, Veränderungen und Kontraste zu erkennen.
> Dies beinhaltet Differenzen bei Bewegungen, Helligkeit und Farbkontrasten.

Sensory system II: mechanoreceptors

Merkel nerve ending n Merkel-Zelle
Merkel's disc n Tastscheibe
Meissner's corpuscle [ˈmaɪsnəzˌkɔːpʌsl] n Meissner-Körperchen
hair follicle receptor [ˈheəˌfɒlɪklrɪˈseptəz] n Haarfollikel-Rezeptor
Pacinian corpuscle [pəˈsɪnɪənˌkɔːpʌsl] n Pacini-Körperchen
detect v entdecken
vibration n Vibration / Schwingung / Erschütterung

Sensory system III: sensory organs of the inner ear

cupula [ˈkjuːpjuːlə] n Cupula *(Gallertkegel, in dem Sinneshaarzellen für das Gleichgewichtsorgan liegen)*
calcium carbonate crystals [ˌkælsɪəmkɑːbəneɪtˈkrɪstlz] n Kalkkristalle
otolith [ˈəʊtəlɪθ] / statolith [ˈstætəʊlɪθ] n Otolith / Statolith
sensor for rotation n Drehsinnesorgan
labyrinth [ˈlæbrɪnθ] n Labyrinth
cochlea [ˈkɒklɪə] n Cochlea / Schnecke
basilar membrane n Basilarmembran
cochlear duct [ˈkɒklɪəˌdʌkt] n häutiger Schneckengang
tympanic canal [tɪmˈpænɪkkənæl] n Paukentreppe
organ of Corti n cortisches Organ / Corti-Organ

9 Neurobiology › 9.4 Nervous system

Sensory system IV: chemical senses

papillae [pəˈpɪlə] n	Geschmackspapillen
taste bud n	Geschmacksknospe
odour [ˈəʊdə] / odor AE n	Geruchsstoff
olfactory sensory neuron [ɒlˌfæktrɪˈsensriˈnjʊərɒn] n	Riechsinneszelle
receptor molecule n	Rezeptormolekül

9.4 Nervous system » III. 1 Human Body – 1.4 Nervous system

neuron [ˈnjʊərɒn] n	Neuron / Nervenzelle
interneuron	Interneuron
sensory neuron	Sensoneuron
motor neuron	Motoneuron

information processing circuits	informationsverabeitende Kreisläufe

axon [ˈæksɒn] n	Axon
extracellular body fluid n	Extrazellulärflüssigkeit / extrazelluläre Körperflüssigkeit
central nervous system (CNS) n	zentrales Nervensystem
brain n	Gehirn
limbic system n	limbisches System
spine n	Rückgrat / Stachel
spinal cord n	Rückenmark
spinal ganglion [ˈspaɪnlˌgæŋgliən] n	Spinalganglion
spinal nerve n	Spinalnerv
white matter n	weiße Substanz
grey matter n	graue Substanz
bipolar nerve cell n	bipolare Nervenzelle
anterior horn [ænˌtɪrɪəˈhɔːnz] n	Vorderhorn
posterior horn n	Hinterhorn
dorsal root [ˈdɔːslˌruːt] n	Dorsalwurzel
ventral root [ˈventrlˌruːt] n	Ventralwurzel
peripheral nervous system (PNS) n	peripheres Nervensystem
autonomic nervous system / vegetative nervous system n	autonomes Nervensystem / vegetatives Nervensystem
parasympathetic [ˌpærəsɪmpəθetɪk] adj	parasympathisch
acetylcholine [ˌæsɪtaɪlˈkəʊliːn] n	Acetylcholin
sympathetic adj	sympathisch
hormone n	Hormon

adrenalin / epinephrine *AE* [ˌepɪˈnefrɪn]　Adrenalin
n
noradrenalin [ˌnɔːrəˈdrenlɪn] *BE* /　Noradrenalin
norepinephrine [ˌnɔːrəˌepɪˈnefrɪn] *AE* n

> The brain and spinal cord together are called the *central nervous system* (CNS).
> Gehirn und Rückenmark werden zusammen als Zentrales Nervensystem (ZNS) bezeichnet.
> The autonomic nervous system is divided into two functional subsystems: the parasympathetic and sympathetic nervous system.
> Das autonome Nervensystem ist in zwei funktionelle Untersysteme unterteilt: das parsympathische und das sympathische Nervensystem.
> Feelings such as fear, anger and happiness are accompanied by typical body reactions that are initiated by the autonomic nervous system.
> Gefühle wie Angst, Zorn und Glück werden von typischen körperlichen Reaktionen begleitet, die vom autonomen Nervensystem begonnen wurden.

Parasympathetic nervous system

eyes	**pupil constriction, lacrimal gland/tear-producing gland**
Augen	Pupillenkontration, Tränendrüse
glands	**mucus secretion**(large amount / low viscosity)
Drüsen	Schleimabsonderung (große Menge / niedrige Zähflüssigkeit)
heart	**frequency, blood pressure**
Herz	Frequenz, Blutdruck
bronchi	**constriction, secretion**
Bronchien	Konstriktion, Sekretion
blood vessels	**in the muscles, in the digestive organs**
Blutgefäße	in den Muskeln, in den Verdauungsorganen
gastrointestinal tract	**secretion, peristalsis, sphincter**
Magen-Darm-Trakt	Sekretion, Peristaltik, Schließmuskel
genitals	**erection**
Genitalien	Erektion
urinary bladder	**bladder muscle, sphincter**
Harnblase	Muskel, der für die Blase zuständig ist; Schließmuskel

cerebrum [səˈriːbrəm] n　　　　　　　Großhirn
cerebral cortex [ˌsərəbrlˈkɔːteks] n　　Großhirnrinde
hippocampus [ˌhɪpəʊˈkæmpəs] n　　　Hippocampus
cerebral hemisphere [ˌsərəbrlˈhemɪsfɪə]　Großhirnhemisphäre
n
　right and left hemisphere　　　　　　rechte und linke Hemisphäre
corpus callosum [ˌkɔːpəskəˈləʊsəm] n　Balken / Corpus callosum

Sympathetic nervous system

eyes / Augen	**pupil dilation** / Pupillenerweiterung
salivary glands / Speicheldrüsen	**mucous secretion (small amount / high viscosity)** / Schleimsekretion (kleine Menge / hohe Viskosität)
heart / Herz	**frequency, stroke volume** / Frequenz, Schlagvolumen
bronchi / Bronchien	**dilation** / Erweiterung
blood vessels / Blutgefäße	**in the muscles, in the digestive organs** / in den Muskeln, in den Verdauungsorganen
liver, pancreas / Leber, Bauchspeicheldrüse	**glycogen breakdown** / Glykogenabbau
fat cells / Fettzellen	**release of fatty acids** / Freisetzung der Fettsäuren
gastrointestinal tract / Magen-Darm-Trakt	**peristalsis, sphincter** / Peristaltik, Schließmuskel
sweat glands / Schweißdrüse	**secretion** / Sekretion
adrenal medulla / Nebennierenmark	**secretion (adrenalin / noradrenaline)** / Sekretion (Adreanlin, Noradrenalin)
genitals / Gentialien	**ejaculation, contraction** / Ejakulation, Kontraktion
urinary bladder / Harnblase	**urination, sphincter** / Harnentleerung, Schließmuskel

diencephalon [daɪenˈsəfəˌlɒn] / interbrain n — Diencephalon
thalamus [ˌθæləməs] n — Thalamus / Receptaculum
epiphysis [ˈepɪphəsɪs] / pineal gland n — Epiphyse
hypothalamus [ˌhaɪpəˈθæləməs] n — Hypothalamus
hypophysis [haɪˈpəfesɪs] n — Hirnanhangdrüse
follicle-stimulating hormone (FSH) n — follikelstimulierendes Hormon (FSH)
midbrain n — Mesencephalon / Mittelhirn *(liegt zwischen Pons und Cerebellum)*

cerebellum [ˌserɪˈbeləm] n — Cerebellum / Kleinhirn
pons [pɒnz] n — Brücke
medulla oblongata [medˈʌləɒblɒŋgətə] *(elongation of the spinal cord)* n — verlängertes Mark
brainstem n — Hirnstamm / Stammhirn

10 Ecology

ecology n	Ökologie
ecological adj	ökologisch
ecosystem n	Ökosystem
abiotic [ˌeɪbaɪˈɒtɪk] adj	abiotisch / unbelebt
biotic [baɪˈɒtɪk] / biological adj	biotisch / lebend
biotope [ˈbaɪətəʊp] / habitat [ˈhæbɪtæt] n	Biotop
biocoenosis [ˌbaɪəsɪˈnəʊsɪs] n	Biozönose
autecological [ɔːtˌiːkəˈlɒdʒɪkl] adj	autökologisch
autecology / population ecology n	Autökologie *(Ökologie einer Art)*
community n	Lebensgemeinschaft
community ecology n	Populationsökologie *(Wechselbeziehungen innerhalb der Gesamtheit aller Individuen einer Art in einem Ökosysytem und ihrer speziellen Umwelt)*
synecology [ˌsɪnɪˈkɒlədʒɪ] n	Synökologie *(Ökologie der Lebensgemeinschaften untereinander und zu ihrer Umwelt)*
synecological adj	synökologisch
purview [ˈpɜːvjuː] n	Bereich
population n	Population
component n	Bestandteil
factor n	Faktor

chemical and physical components	chemische und physikalische Faktoren

expose (sth to sth) v	(etw. etw.) aussetzen
survival strategy n	Überlebensstrategie
adaptation n	Anpassung
adjustment n	Anpassung
withstand [wɪðˈstænd] v	widerstehen / aushalten / ertragen
tolerance n	Toleranz » Abb. 52
range of tolerance	Toleranzbereich
zone of intolerance	Pessimum *(Grenzwert: Maximum oder Minimum)*

10 Ecology

upper limit of tolerance / lower limit of tolerance	Pessimum *(ab diesem Bereich ist der Organismus zwar noch überlebens- aber nicht mehr fortfähigpflanzungsfähig)*
law of tolerance	Wirkungsgesetz der Umweltfaktoren
optimum level / optimum range n	Optimum *(Bereich in dem sich Organismus am besten entwickelt)*
vitality n	Vitalität / Lebenskraft
existence n	Bestehen / Überleben
abundance [ə'bʌndəns] n	Häufigkeit
distribution (of) n	Verbreitung (von)
distribution of organisms	Verbreitung der Lebewesen

> | | |
> |---|---|
> | in relation to abiotic factors | in Bezug auf abiotische Faktoren |
> | be determined by sth | von etw. bestimmt sein |

eurypotent [jʊə'rɪpətnt] n *(wide range of tolerance)*	euryök / eurypotent
stenopotent ['stenəʊpətnt] n *(narrow range of tolerance)*	stenök / stenopotent
acclimatisation [əˌklaɪmətaɪ'zeɪʃn] n	Akklimatisierung / Anpassung
ecological niche n	ökologische Nische
threshold effect ['θreʃəʊldɪˌfekt] n	Schwellenwerteffekt
limiting factor n	begrenzender Faktor
outweigh [ˌaʊt'weɪ] v	ausschlaggebend sein

Law of tolerance

The existence, abundance, and distribution of a species in an ecosystem are determined by whether the levels of one or more physical or chemical factors fall within the range tolerated by that species.
Das Überleben, die Häufigkeit und Verbreitung einer Art wird durch die Umweltfaktoren bestimmt, die innerhalb des Toleranzbereiches einer Art liegen.
The limiting factor (farthest from the optimum), outweighs the rest and limits or prevents the growth of a population, even if all the other factors are at or near the optimum range of tolerance.
Der limitierende Faktor (am weitesten vom Optimum entfernt), ist ausschlaggebend und begrenzt bzw. verhindert das Wachstum einer Population, auch wenn alle anderen Faktoren im Optimumsbereich liegen.

10.1 Abiotic factors affecting all populations » III. 10.7 Ecosystem Forest – Interaction within the biocenosis of a forest

Light

light dependence n	Lichtabhängigkeit
light intensity n	Beleuchtungsstärke
periodicity [ˌpɪərɪəˈdɪsəti] n	Periodizität
solar irradiation [ˌsəʊləɪreɪdiˈeɪʃn] n	Sonneneinstrahlung
irradiance [ɪˈreɪdiəns] n	Bestrahlungsstärke
heat radiation n	Wärmestrahlung

» | annual mean daily insolation | Jahresmittel der täglichen Sonneneinstrahlung |

biological clock n	innere Uhr
biorhythm [ˈbaɪəˌrɪðm] n	Biorhythmus
diurnal [ˌdaɪˈɜːnl] adj	Tages~ / täglich wiederkehrend
diurnal rhythm	tageszeitlicher Rhythmus
seasonal adj	jahreszeitlich bedingt
seasonal rhythm n	jahreszeitlicher Rhythmus

» | sleep-wake cycle / sleep-wake rhythm | Wach-Schlaf-Zyklus / Wach-Schlaf-Rhythmus |

reproductive cycle n	Fortpflanzungszyklus
courtship [ˈkɔːtʃɪp] n	Balz
nesting behaviour n	Brutverhalten
migration [maɪˈgreɪʃn] n	Wanderbewegung / Wanderung
migratory [ˈmaɪgrətri] adj	migratorisch / wandernd / Wander~
migratory behaviour	Zugverhalten
migratory direction	Zugrichtung

photomorphogenesis [foʊtoʊˌmɔːfəʊˈgenəsis] n	Fotomorphose
node [nəʊd] n	Sprossknoten / Nodie
internode	Internodie *(Sprossabschnitt zwischen zwei Sprossknoten)*
elongate [ˈiːlɒŋgeɪt] v	verlängern
etiolation [ˌiːtɪəˈleɪʃn] n	Etoilement / Vergeilung
chlorotic [ˈklɔːrɒtɪk] adj	Chlorophyllmangel

photoperiodism [ˌfəʊtəʊˈpɪərɪədɪzm] n	Photoperiodismus
long-day plant (LDP) n	Langtagspflanze

10 Ecology › 10.1 Abiotic factors affecting all populations

short-day plant (SDP) n	Kurztagspflanze
day-neutral plant n	tagneutrale Pflanze

Temperature

metabolic [ˌmetəˈbɒlɪk] adj	stoffwechselgesteuert
range of temperature / fluctuation of temperature n	Temperaturschwankung(en)
homoiothermic [həˌmɔɪəˈθɜːmɪk] / homeothermic adj	gleichwarm / homöotherm
homoiotherms [həˌmɔɪəθɜːm] / homeotherms n	Gleichwarme / Homöotherme / Warmblüter
warm-blooded adj	warmblütig
heterothermic / poikilothermic [ˌpɔɪkɪləʊˈθɜːmɪk] (colloquial also: cold-blooded) adj	wechselwarm / poikilotherm
poikilotherm [ˌpɔɪkɪləʊθɜːm] / ectotherm [ˈektəʊθɜːm] n	Wechselwarmer (Tier)
eurytherm [ˈjʊərɪθɜːm] (can withstand a high range of temperatures)	eurytherm (kann große Temperaturschwankungen ertragen)
stenotherm [ˌstenəθɜːm] (can withstand a low range of temperatures)	stenotherm (kann nur geringe Temperaturschwankungen ertragen)
core body temperature n	Körperkerntemperatur

»

metabolic heat regulation	stoffwechselgesteuerte Wärmeregulation
hypothalamus thermoreceptor	Wärmerezeptor des Hypothalamus (Teil des Zwischenhirns)

cooling n	Abkühlen
evaporate [ɪˈvæpreɪt] v	verdunsten
sweat v	schwitzen
pant v	hecheln
fan v	fächeln
heat conduction n	Wärmeleitung
blood vessel n	Blutgefäß
shunting vessels	Blutgefäße, die gegenläufig angeordnet sind
dilate [daɪˈleɪt] v	sich weiten
constrict [kənˈstrɪkt] v	sich zusammenziehen / kontrahieren

countercurrent heat exchange system n	Gegenstrom-Wärmeaustausch-System
extremities [ɪkˈstremətiz] n pl	Gliedmaßen / Extremitäten
nonessential [ˌnɒnɪˈsentʃl] adj	unwichtig / lebensunwichtig
heat dissipation [ˈhiːtdɪsɪˌpeɪʃn] n	Wärmeabstrahlung
torpor [ˈtɔːpə] n	Kältestarre *(auch: Wärmestarre)*
nocturnal [nɒkˈtɜːnl] adj	nachtaktiv / nächtlich
burrow [ˈbʌrəʊ] n	Erdhöhle

evaporative cooling	Abkühlen durch Verdunstungskälte
conductional heat loss	Wärmeverlust durch Wärmeabgabe
blood vessels to the skin	Blutgefäße zur Haut hinführend
splay out extremities	Abspreizen von Extremitäten
bask (in the sun)	sich sonnen / sich in der Sonne aufwärmen

behavioural thermoregulation [bɪˌheɪvjərəlˈθɜːməregjəˌleɪʃn] n	thermoregulatorische Verhaltensweise
posture [ˈpɒstʃə] n	Körperhaltung
huddle [ˈhʌdl] v	sich zusammendrängen / sich aneinander schmiegen
cluster [ˈklʌstə] v	eine Traube bilden
shiver [ˈʃɪvə] v	zittern
insulation [ˌɪnsjəˈleɪʃn] n	Isolation
insulate v	isolieren
winter fur n	Winterfell
downy hair [daʊniˈheə] n	Wollhaar
preen [priːn] / groom [gruːm] v	putzen
spread by grooming	durch Feder- und Fellpflege verteilen
preen oil [priːnˈɔɪl] n	Bürzeldrüsenfett
preen gland n	Bürzeldrüse
blubber [ˈblʌbə] v	Fettschicht *(z. B. bei Walen und Robben)*
layer of fat v	Fettschicht
adipose tissue n	Fettgewebe
fat cell n	Fettzelle
brown fat cells	braune Fettzellen
white fat cells	weiße Fettzellen
hibernation [ˌhaɪbəˈneɪʃn] n	Winterschlaf / Überwinterung
bouts of hibernation	Winterruhephasen
hibernate v	Winterschlaf halten / überwintern
hibernator n	Winterschläfer

10 Ecology › 10.1 Abiotic factors affecting all populations

trigger off metabolism	den Stoffwechsel erhöhen
reduce heat loss	den Wärmeverlust verringern
conserve heat	Wärme erhalten / Wärme sparen
generate metabolic heat	Stoffwechselwärme erzeugen
shivering heat production	Erzeugung von Stoffwechselwärme durch Kältezittern
elevate / rise body temperature	die Körpertemperatur erhöhen
trap a layer of warm air	eine warme Luftschicht einschließen
orient to the sun / shade	sich nach der Sonne / dem Schatten richten

ecogeographic rule n   ökogeografische Regel
Bergmann's rule n   Bergmann-Regel
correlate v   korrelieren / in Wechselbeziehung stehen

latitude n   Breitengrad
body mass n   Körpermasse

closely related species	nahe verwandte Arten
surface area-to-volume ratio	Verhältnis von Volumen zu Oberfläche

Allen's rule n   Allen-Regel
appendage [əˈpendɪdʒ] n   Körperanhang / Körpergliedmaß
body proportion n   Körperproportion

Temperature and plant

van't Hoff equation n   RGT-Regel
temperature dependence *(of enzyme reactions)*   Temperaturabhängigkeit *(von Enzymenreaktionen)*
rate of photosynthesis n   Photosyntheseleistung
water balance n   Wasserhaushalt
vegetation period n   Vegetationsperiode
growing season n   Wachstumsperiode
hair-covered plants n   Pflanzen mit Behaarung
thorn / spine n   Dorn / Stachel
stunted growth n   niedriger Wuchs

| cushion plant n | Polsterpflanze |
| rosette plant n | Rosette |

Water and salt balance » Siehe auch entsprechende Ökosysteme

store v	speichern
storage n	Speicherung
water storage	Wasserspeicherung
loss n	Verlust
loss of water / water loss	Wasserverlust
cutaneous loss [kjuːˈteɪnɪəsˌlɒs]	Verlust über die Haut
excretory loss	Verlust über Ausscheidungen
respiratory loss	Verlust über die Atmung
fatty deposit / layer of fat n	Fettschicht
outer covering n	Außenschicht
urine [ˈjʊərɪn]	Urin
concentrate urine	konzentrierter Urin
dilute urine [daɪˈluːtˌjʊərɪn]	verdünnter Urin
faeces BE / feces AE [ˈfiːsiːz] n	Kot / Fäzes
dew [djuː] n	Tau

| | body's temperature fluctuates | die Körpertemperatur schwankt |

osmoregulation n	Osmoregulation (Regulation des osmotischen Drucks im Körper) »Abb. 53
homeostasis [ˌhəʊmɪəˈsteɪsɪs] n	Homeostase (Gleichgewicht der Körperfunktionen)
contractile vacuole [kənˌtræktaɪlˈvækjʊəʊl] n	pulsierende Vakuole
osmoconformer [ˌɒsməkəˈfɔːmə] n	Osmokonformer (passen die Osmolarität ihrer Körperflüssigkeiten der Umgebung an)
poikilosmotic adj	poikilosmotisch (Adj. zu Osmokonformer) »Abb. 54
osmoregulator n	Osmoregulierer
excretion [ɪkˈskriːʃn] n	Ausscheidung / Exkretion
gill [ɡɪl] n	Kieme
stenohaline [ˈstenəʊheɪlaɪn] adj	stenohalin (mit geringer Salztoleranz)
euryhaline [jʊəˈrɪheɪlaɪn] adj	euryhalin (mit großer Salztoleranz)
nephron [ˈnefrɒn] n	Nephron
kidney [ˈkɪdni] n	Niere

10 Ecology › 10.1 Abiotic factors affecting all populations

» | excretion via gills | Ausscheidung über die Kiemen

water shortage n Wassermangel
arid region n Trockengebiete
xerophyte ['zɪərəfaɪt] n Xerophyt *(Pflanze, die an trockene Standorte angepasst ist)*
perennial [pə'reniəl] adj mehrjährig / überdauernd
annual adj einjährig *(Pflanzen, die nur über ihre Samen überdauern)*
bulb n (Blatt-/Stamm-)Knolle / Zwiebel
rhizome ['raɪzəʊm] n Wurzelstock / Rhizom / Wurzelstamm
tuber ['tjuːbə] n Wurzelknolle
taproot n Pfahlwurzel
  extensive shallow roots weites flaches Wurzelgeflecht *(Flachwurzler)*

thick cuticle n dicke Kutikula
waxy layer n Wachsschicht
stoma, *pl* stomata n Schließzelle / Stoma *(Pl. Stomata)*
succulent n Sukkulente / Fleischpflanze / Saftpflanze
succulent ['sʌkjələnt] adj fleischig / saftig / sukkulent

»
sunken into cavity		in Hohlraum eingesenkt	
fleshy		fleischiger	
succulent	stem	sukkulenter	Stamm
succulent	leaves	sukkulente	Blätter
	roots		Wurzeln

shed leaves n Blätter abwerfen
spine / thorn n Dorn

» | leaves in drooping / vertical position | Blätter am Stamm herabhängend

aquatic plant / hydrophyte n Wasserpflanze / Hydrophyt
hydrophytic adj hydrophytisch *(z. B. Eigenschaft)*
air spaces / aerenchyma cell n Aerenchym / Durchlüftungsgewebe
swollen leaf stalk *(petiole)* aufgeblasener Blattstiel
submerged adj unter Wasser *(unter Wasser liegend lebend; untergetaucht lebend)*

floating leaf n	Schwimmblatt
divided feathery leaf n	fädig zerschlitztes Blatt
reduced root system n	zurückgebildetes Wurzelwerk
less vascular tissue n	zurückgebildetes Leitbündelgewebe
less supportive tissue n	zurückgebildetes Stützgewebe

»
keep the leaves afloat	die Blätter über Wasser halten, freischwimmend
are coated with a smooth, waxy cuticle	bedeckt von einer glatten, wächsernen Kultikula
to be buoyed by water	Auftrieb durch Wasser haben

clay soil n	Lehmboden
humus n	Humus
halophyte ['hæləfaɪt] n	Salzpflanze / Halophyt
halophytic adj	halophytisch *(z.B. Eigenschaften)*
high soil salinity n	hoher Salzgehalt des Bodens
salinity n	Salzgehalt
salt excretion n	Salzausscheidung

hygrophyte n	Hygrophyt
moisture-loving adj	feuchtigkeitsliebend
anchoring n	Verankerung / das Verankern
soft ground n	weicher Untergrund
waterlogged adj	dauerfeucht / sumpfig
pliable adj	biegsam

»
extensive root systems for anchoring to soft ground	stark ausgebildetes Wurzelwerk zum Verankern in weichem Untergrund
weak, pliable stems that can stand the current's ebb and flow	schwache, biegsame Stengel, die das Auf und Ab der Strömung aushalten

mesophyte n	Mesophyt
mesophytic adj	mesophytisch *(z.B. Eigenschaft, gemäßigtes Klima zu ertragen)*

10.2 Population ecology

Competiton and niches » Siehe auch entsprechende Ökosysteme » Abb. 55

competition n	Konkurrenz / Wettbewerb
compete (for sth) v	(um etw.) konkurrieren
habitat ['hæbɪtæt] n	Lebensraum / Habitat

10 Ecology › 10.2 Population ecology

interaction n	Wechselwirkung
interrelation [ˌɪntərɪˈleɪʃn] n	Wechselbeziehung / wechselseitige Beziehung
conspecies [kɒnˈspiːʃiːz] n pl	Artgenosse
coexist [ˌkəʊɪɡˈzɪst] v	koexistieren / zusammenleben
principle of competition exclusion	Konkurrenzausschlussprinzip

> | | |
> |---|---|
> | member of the same species | Artgenosse |
> | interrelation between organisms | Wechselbeziehung zwischen Organismen |

niche n	Nische
ecological niche	ökologische Nische
fundamental niche	Nische, die dem ökologischen Optimum entspricht
realized niche	Nische, die dem natürlichen Vorkommen entspricht, aber kaum dem Optimum entspricht
vacant niche / empty niche	unbesetzte Nische
crowded niche	besetzte Nische
nutritional niche / feeding niche / feeding-niche	Nahrungsnische

> | | |
> |---|---|
> | occupy a niche | eine Nische besetzen |
> | fill a niche | eine Nische füllen |
> | exploit a slightly different niche | eine etwas andere Nische nutzen |

limiting resource n	Umweltfaktor, der am weitesten vom Optimum entfernt ist
vie (for sth) [vaɪ] / compete (for sth) n	(um etw.) buhlen
demand / requirement n	Anspruch
environmental requirement	Anspruch an die Umwelt

> | | |
> |---|---|
> | nutritional niche separation in coexisting species in the same habitat | Aufteilung in unterschiedliche Nahrungsnischen bei nebeneinander lebenden Arten im gleichen Lebensraum |

development stage / stage of development n	Entwicklungsstadium
brood [bruːd] / offspring n	Brut

breeding n	Aufzucht
breeding season	Brutzeit
hatch [hætʃ] v	schlüpfen

indigenous [ɪnˈdɪdʒɪnəs] adj	heimisch
non-indigenous species	nicht heimische Art *(bewusst oder unbewusst eingeschleppt)*
neophyte [ˈniːəfaɪt] n	Neophyt *(nicht heimische Pflanze)*
neozoen [ˌniːəʊˈzəʊɒn] n	Neozoen *(nicht heimisches Tier)*
invasive species	sich schnell verbreitende, gebietsfremde Art *(aus Sicht von Naturschützern problematisch)*
non-native habitat n	nicht heimischer Lebensraum

Interspecific competition

intraspecific adj	innerartlich / intraspezifisch
interspecific adj	zwischenartlich / interspezifisch
intraspecific competition	innerartliche Konkurrenz / intraspezifische Konkurrenz
interspecific competition	zwischenartliche Konkurrenz / interspezifische Konkurrenz
overlap v	überschneiden / übereinstimmen

physiological optimum n	physiologisches Optimum
ecological optimum n	ökologisches Optimum
resource n	Ressource
species' range / range of species	Verbreitung der Art(en)
differ v	sich unterscheiden
spatially [ˈspeɪʃli] adv	räumlich

»

interference competition	konkurrierende Ansprüche bezüglich des Lebensraums
exploitation competition	konkurrierende Ansprüche bezüglich gemeinsam genutzter Ressourcen
compete for resources	um Ressourcen konkurrieren
shortage of resources	Verknappung der Ressourcen
differ spatially	sich „räumlich" unterscheiden (z. B. Nistplätze an verschiedenen Orten)
differ temporally	sich „zeitlich" unterscheiden (z. B. verschiedene Blühzeiten, verschiedene Jagdzeiten)

10 Ecology › 10.2 Population ecology

Further interrelations and answers to competition

predator ['predətə] n	Räuber / Fressfeind
predatory adj	räuberisch / Raub~
prey [preɪ] n	Beute / Beutetier
predator-prey relationship	Räuber-Beute-Verhältnis
advantage n	Vorteil
disadvantage n	Nachteil / Schaden

predate on sth	etw. jagen / etw. fressen / etw. erbeuten
be prey to	Beute sein von
prey on sth	auf etwas Jagd machen, Beute machen
do damage to sth	etw. Schaden zufügen

camouflage ['kæməflɑːʒ] n	Tarnung
camouflage v	tarnen
aposematic colouration [ˌæpɒsɪmætɪkˌkʌləˈreɪʃn] n	Warnfärbung
mimicry ['mɪmɪkri] n	Mimikry *(harmlose Art ahmt wehrhafte nach)*
mimic, mimicked v	nachahmen
protective mimicry	Tarnfarbe / Schutzfärbung
mimesis [mɪˈmiːsɪs] n	Mimese *(Nachahmung eines Teils des Lebensraums, z. B. ein Blatt)*

parabiosis [ˌpærəbaɪˈəʊsɪs] n	Parabiose
commensalism [kəˈmensəlɪzm] n	Kommensalismus
commensal [kəˈmensl] n	Nutznießer
commensal relationship	Beziehung, bei der es nur einen Nutznießer gibt

flock n	Schwarm / Schar / Herde
colony, *pl* colonies n	Kolonie

Parabiosis – commensialism

The living together of two or more different species, as in mixed flocks of birds or in mixed colonies of ants. One member draws a benefit from it, the other member is not affected in either a positive or negative way.
Das Zusammenleben zweier oder mehrer verschiedener Arten, wie bei gemischten Vogelschwärmen oder Ameisenkolonien. Der eine Partner zieht einen Nutzen aus der Beziehung, der andere hat weder einen Vor- noch einen Nachteil.

Alliance

Community of species that do not really need one another but draw advantages from each other when together: giraffe → wildebeest / gnu → gazelle
Interessensgemeinschaft von Arten, die einander nicht wirklich benötigen, jedoch gemeinsam Vorteile voneinander haben: Giraffe → Gnu → Gazelle

symbiosis [ˌsɪmbaɪˈəʊsɪs] n	Symbiose
parasitism [ˈpærəsɪtɪzm] n	Parasitismus
parasite [ˈpærəsaɪt] n	Parasit / Schmarotzer
ectoparasite [ˌektəʊˈpærəsaɪt] n	Ektoparasit *(der auf der Hautoberfläche verbleibt)*
infestation [ˌɪnfesˈteɪʃn] n	Befall
infested (with sth) v	(von etw.) befallen
tick [tɪk] n	Zecke
tick infested	Zecken befallen
arachnid [əˈræknɪd] n	Spinnentier
feed on blood	sich von Blut ernähren
vector [ˈvektə] n	Überträger / Vektor
transmit [trænzˈmɪt] v	übertragen
disease transmission	Krankheitsübertragung
Lyme disease [ˈlaɪmdɪˌziːz]	Borreliose
influenza [ˌɪnfluˈenzə] / flu *(umgangssprachlich)* n	Grippe
influenza-like adj	grippeähnlich
vaccine [ˈvæksiːn] / serum n	Impfstoff
penicillin [ˌpenɪˈsɪlɪn] n	Penicillin
penicillin treatment	Penicillinbehandlung
anti-inflammatory drug [ˌæntiɪŋˈflæmətəriˌdrʌg] n	entzündungshemmendes Mittel
tick-borne encephalitis virus / TBE virus	TBE Virus
tick-borne meningoencephalitis (FSME)	Frühsommermeningoencephalitis (FSME)
tick-borne influenza-like virus	Virus, der grippeähnliches Krankheitsbild hervorruft und von Zecken übertragen wird
endoparasite [ˌendueˈpærəsaɪt] n	Endoparasit *(der in den Wirt eindringt)*

10 Ecology › 10.2 Population ecology

tapeworm ['teɪpwɜːm] n	Bandwurm
fox tapeworm	Fuchsbandwurm
host n	Wirt
primary host / final host / definite host	Endwirt
intermediate host	Zwischenwirt
rodent ['rəʊdnt] n	Nagetier
heteroecism [hetə'rɪʃɪsm] n	Wirtswechsel
heteroecious [hetə'rɪʃɪs] adj	Wirtswechsel betreibend
heterogenesis [ˌhetrə'dʒenəsɪs] n	Generationswechsel

Symbiotic relationship

The nature of a symbiotic relationship can change as circumstances change, e.g. useful bacteria living in a mutualistic relationship with man can turn parasitic.
Die wechselseitige Beziehung zweier Arten kann sich je nach Umständen verändern, z. B. nützliche Bakterien, die in einer mutualistischen (symbiotischen) Beziehung mit uns Menschen leben, können parasitisch werden.

Unrelated but coping with similar habitats

convergence [kən'vɜːdʒns] n	Konvergenz
convergent evolution	konvergente Evolution
related adj	verwandt
unrelated adj	nicht verwandt
analogous structure [ə'næləgəsˌstrʌktʃə] n	analoge Struktur *(ähnliche Struktur nicht verwandter Arten)*
analogy [ə'nælədʒi] n	Analogie
biological traits n	biologischer Merkmale
select v	selektieren / auswählen
selected adj	selektiert / ausgewählt
optimise *BE* / optimize *AE* v	optimieren
selective pressure n	Selektionsbedingung / Selektionsdruck
living conditions n pl	Lebensbedingungen
ecological equivalence n	Stellenäquivalenz
concurrence [kən'kʌrns] n	Übereinstimmung
evidence n	Indiz / Hinweis

» acquisition of similar biological traits in unrelated species due to similar ecological niches
Entwicklung ähnlicher biologischer Merkmale bei nicht verwandten Arten auf Grund ähnlicher ökologischer Nischen

10.3 Population dynamics

Population density

population ecology n	Populationsökologie
population size n	Populationsgröße
population density n	Populationsdichte
average population density	durchschnittliche Populationsdichte
density dependent factor	dichteabhängiger Faktor
density independent factor	dichteunabhängige Faktor *(z.B. Klima)*
sexual reproduction pattern n	Fortpflanzungsmuster / Fortpflanzungsart
per capita [pəˈkæpɪtə]	Pro-Kopf *(hier: pro Individuum)*
birth rate n	Geburtenrate
mortality rate n	Sterberate
growth rate / rate of growth n	Zuwachsrate
crowding n	soziale Enge
alter v	ändern
hormonal balance n	hormonelles Gleichgewicht
resorption [rɪˈsɔːpʃn] n	Auflösung
resorption of the embryo	Auflösung des Embryos
infertility [ˌɪnfəˈtɪləti] n	Unfruchtbarkeit
fecundity [fɪˈkʌndəti] n	Fruchtbarkeit
aggressiveness n	Aggressivität
cannibalism [ˈkænɪblɪzm] n	Kannibalismus
predation [prɪˈdeɪʃn] n	Räuber-Beute-Beziehung
hiding place n	Versteck
disease n	Krankheit
infectious disease	ansteckende Krankheit
non-infectious disease	nicht ansteckende Krankheit
carrying capacity n	Umweltkapazität
migration n	Wanderung
emigration n	Auswanderung
mass emigration	Massenauswanderung
mass migration	Massenwanderbewegung
at random adj	willkürlich
earth slide n	Erdrutsch
flood / flooding / inundation [ˌɪnʌnˈdeɪʃn] n	Überschwemmung
natural catastrophe / natural disaster [ˌnætʃrldɪˈzɑːstə] n	Naturkatastrophe

10 Ecology › 10.3 Population dynamics

pesticide n	Pestizid
toxin ['tɒksɪn] n	Gift
accumulate [əˈkjuːmjəleɪt] v	anreichern / speichern / sammeln / akkumulieren
accumulation n	Anreicherung / Ansammlung / Anhäufung

Population growth models

growth n	Wachstum
grow v	wachsen
exponential growth	exponentielles Wachstum
grow exponentially	exponentiell wachsen
grow indefinitely	unendlich wachsen
lag phase ['læɡˌfeɪz] n	Lagphase / Anlaufphase
S-shaped curve	logistische Kurve *(Sigmoid Kurve)*
asymptotic [ˌæsɪmˈtɒtɪk] / asymptotical adj	asymptotisch / allmählich
oscillate ['ɒsɪleɪt] v	pendeln
periodic cycle n	periodische Schwankungen
fluctuation [ˌflʌktʃuˈeɪʃn] n	Schwankung
constant adj	konstant
even out (sth) / balance (sth) v	(etw.) ausgleichen
simplify v	vereinfachen
simplification n	Vereinfachung
carrying capacity (K) / point of stabilisation n	Kapazitätsgrenze (K)
zero growth rate n	Nullwachstumsrate
saturation value n	Sättigungspunkt
crash n	Zusammenbruch
crash v	zusammenbrechen
population crash / population die back	Zusammenbruch einer Population
exceed [ɪkˈsiːd] / overshoot v	überschreiten
variable n	Variable
boom-bust cycle n	Aufschaukelungskreis
cyclic curve n	zyklische Schwankungen
fitness n	Fortpflanzungspotential

» | reproductive time lag | Verzögerungsphase durch die Zeit zwischen Befruchtung und tatsächlichem Auftreten von Nachkommen

| resource fluctuations | Schwankungen bei den Ressourcen verursachen |
| generate consumer fluctuations | Schwankungen bei den Konsumenten der Ressourcen |

Competitive exclusion is predicted by a number of mathematical and theoretical models.
Das Konkurrenzausschlussprinzip wird durch etliche mathematische und theoretische Modelle vorhergesagt.

Lottka-Voltera equations n	Lottka-Voltera Regeln
Lottka-Voltera models n	Lottka-Voltera Modelle
mathematical model n	mathematisches Modell
approximation [əˌprɒksɪˈmeɪʃn] n	Annäherung
mutual dependency [ˌmjuːtʃuəldɪˈpendənsi] n	gegenseitige Abhängigkeit
plot (against sth) v	darstellen (in Abhängigkeit von etw.)

»
| plot the density of the predator population against the density of prey population | die Populationsdichte der Räuberpopulation in Abhängigkeit von der Populationsdichte der Beute darstellen |

ecological potential n	ökologische Potenz
r-selected species / r-strategist n	r-Stratege
opportunistic adj	opportunistisch / jede Gelegenheit ergreifend
short-lived species n	kurzlebige Art
early maturity onset n	frühe Geschlechtsreife
parthenogenetic [ˌpɑːθənəˈdʒenetɪk] adj	parthenogenetisch
viviparous [vɪˈvɪpərəs] adj	lebend gebärend
oviparous [əʊˈvɪpərəs] adj	Eier legend / ovipar

»
| unstable / unpredictable environment | sich schnell verändernder Lebensraum |

K-selected species / K- strategist n	K-Strategen
lifespan n	Lebensdauer
longevity [lɒnˈdʒevəti] n	Langlebigkeit
long-lived adj	langlebig
long generation time n	lange Generationszeit
number of offspring n	Nachkommenzahl
parental care n	Brutpflege

10 Ecology › 10.4 Feeding relationships

10.4 Feeding relationships

feeding relationship n	Nahrungsbeziehung
producer n	Produzent
consumer n	Konsument
herbivore ['hɜːbɪvɔː] n	Pflanzenfresser / Herbivor
herbivorous [hɜːˈbɪvrəs] adj	pflanzenfressend
carnivore [ˈkɑːnɪvɔː] n	Fleischfresser / Carnivor
carnivorous [kɑːˈnɪvrəs] adj	fleischfressend
omnivore [ˈɒmnɪvɔː] n	Allesfresser / Omnivor
omnivorous [ɒmˈnɪvrəs] adj	allesfressend

> 1st / 2nd / 3rd level consumer | Konsument 1. / 2. / 3. Ordnung

plant tissue feeder n	Gewebefresser
organic detritus feeder / detritivore [dɪˈtrɪtɪvɔː] n	Detritivor / Detritusfresser / Schwebstofffresser
detritivorous [ˈdɪtrɪtɪvrəs] adj	Abfall fressend
destruent n	Destruent / Zersetzer
scavenger [ˈskævɪndʒə] n	Aasfresser
blood-feeding insect n	blutsaugendes Insekt
plant juice sucker n	Pflanzensauger
saprophyte [ˈsæprəfaɪt] n	Saprophyt / Fäulnisbewohner *(ernähren sich von totem Material)*
saprophytic [ˈsæprəfɪtɪk] adj	saprophytisch

> | | |
> |---|---|
> | feed on blood | sich von Blut ernähren |
> | feed on plant juices | sich von Pflanzensäften ernähren |

decomposer [ˌdiːkəmˈpəʊzə] n	Zersetzer
matter n	Material / Substanzen / Bestandteile
dead plant matter	totes Pflanzenmaterial
organic matter	organisches Material / organische Substanzen / organische Bestandteile
mineralise BE / mineralize AE v	mineralisieren
mineralisation BE / mineralization AE n	Mineralisierung
detritus mineralisation	Mineralisierung des Detritus

> | | |
> |---|---|
> | biologically induced mineralisation (BIM) | durch Mineralisierer (Bakterien) herbeigeführte Mineralisierung organischer Stoffe |

| food chain n | Nahrungskette |
| food web n | Nahrungsnetz |

> | sth is eaten by sth | etw. wird gefressen von |

arrow n	Pfeil
trophic level [ˌtrɒfɪkˈlevl] n	Trophieebene
autotrophic level [ˌɔːtəˈtrɒfɪk]	Trophieebene der Produzenten
pyramid of net production n	Nahrungspyramide »Abb. 56
gross primary production (GPP) n	Bruttoprimärproduktion
net primary production (NPP) n	Nettoprimärproduktion
net ecosystem productivity n	Netto-Ökosystem-Produktivität

pyramid of numbers / ecological pyramid n	Zahlenpyramide *(Anzahl der Organismen auf der Trophieebene)*
biomass n	Biomasse
biomass pyramid	Biomassenpyramide
energy flow n	Energiefluss
pyramid of energy flow	Energieflusspyramide
efficient [ɪˈfɪʃnt] adj	effizient / rationell / wirtschaftlich
pass on v	weitergeben

> | be available for the next trophic level | der nächsten Trophieebene zur Verfügung stehen |

10.5 Environmental cycles

cycle of matter compounds	Kreislauf der Stoffe
nutrient cycle n	Nährstoffkreislauf
lithosphere [ˈlɪθəsfɪə] n	Erdkruste / Lithosphäre
hydrosphere [ˈhaɪdrəʊsfɪə] n	Hydrosphäre *(Hydro = Wasser)*
atmosphere [ˈætməsfɪə] n	Atmosphäre
biosphere [ˈbaɪəsfɪə] n	Biosphäre
geosphere [ˈdʒiːɒsfɪə] n	Geosphäre / Erdhülle
pedosphere [pɪˈdɒsfɪə] n	Pedosphäre *(Lithosphäre, Hydrosphäre, Atmosphäre und Biosphäre)*

| anthropogenic [ˌænθrəpəʊˈdʒenɪk] adj | menschlich bedingt / anthropogen / von Menschen verursacht |

imbalance n	Ungleichgewicht
balanced adj	ausgeglichen
disrupted adj	gestört

10 Ecology › 10.5 Environmental cycles

| » | have an impact on sth | sich auf etwas auswirken |

incorporate v	einbauen
reincorporate v	zurückeinbauen
interconnect v	miteinander verwoben sein
exchange n	Austausch
exchange v	austauschen
transform / convert v	umwandeln
transformation / conversion n	Umwandlung
dissolve v	(sich) lösen
be taken up (by) v	aufgenommen werden (von)
break down v	abbauen / zersetzen
degrade v	abbauen / zersetzen
consume v	verbrauchen

oxidise BE [ˈɒksɪdaɪz] / oxidize AE v	oxidieren
reduce v	reduzieren
leach (sth) v	(etw.) auslaugen / ausschwemmen
replenish [rɪˈplenɪʃ] v	auffüllen / regenerieren / aufstocken / ergänzen
accumulate v	anreichern / ablagern / ansammeln
accumulation n	Anreicherung / Ablagerung / Ansammlung
wash into v	einschwemmen
overload v	überfrachten

| » | be washed away | ausgeschwemmt werden, ausgewaschen werden |
| | escape into the atmosphere | in die Atmosphäre entweichen |

Water cycle

ground water n	Grundwasser
drain away v	versickern
water reservoir [ˈwɔːtəˌrezəvwɑː] n	Wasserspeicher
transpiration n	Transpiration *(Verdunstung über einen Organismus)*
transpire v	transpirieren / verdunsten
evaporation [ɪˌvæpəˈreɪʃn] n	Verdunstung *(über abiotische Flächen)*

348

evaporate [ɪˈvæpəreɪt] v	verdunsten
respiration [ˌrespɪˈreɪʃn] n	Atmung
sweating n	Schwitzen
panting n	Hecheln
humidity [hjuːˈmɪdəti] n	Feuchtigkeit

draining away of underground water	Versickern von Grundwasser
washing out of mineral salts	das Herauswaschen von Mineralsalzen
taking in of water via roots	Aufnahme von Wasser über die Wurzeln
distribution throughout the plant	Verteilung durch die ganze Pflanze

atmospheric water n	atmosphärisches Wasser
condense [kənˈdens] v	kondensieren / niederschlagen *(von gasförmig zu flüssig)*
precipitation [prɪˌsɪpɪˈteɪʃn] n	Niederschlag
runoff [ˈrʌnɒf] n	Abfluss
assimilate [əˈsɪmɪleɪt] v	assimilieren / verarbeiten

Biogeochemical cycles: Carbon cycle » Abb. 57

biogeochemical cycle n	biogeochemischer Kreislauf
reservoir [ˈrezəvwɑː] n	Reservoir / Lagerstätte
deposit n	Lagerstätte / Ablagerung
exchange pool n	Ort des Austauschs von Stoffen
residence n	Verweildauer / Verweilzeit
steady state n	Gleichgewichtszustand

carbon n	Kohlenstoff
carbon cycle	Kreislauf des Kohlenstoffs
inorganic carbon	anorganischer Kohlenstoff
carbon reservoir	Kohlenstoffreservoir
source n	Quelle
decay [dɪˈkeɪ] n	Zerfallsprozesse / Verrottungsprozesse

respiration [ˌrespɪˈreɪʃn] n	Atmung
combustion [kəmˈbʌstʃn] n	Verbrennung(-sprozesse)
fossil fuel burning	Verbrennen fossiler Brennstoffe
land use n	Bodennutzung
agriculture n	Landwirtschaft
deforestation n	Entwaldung / Abholzung

10 Ecology › 10.5 Environmental cycles

(CO_2^-) sink n	(CO_2^-) Falle
ocean n	Ozean
reforestation n	Wiederaufforstung
photosynthesis [ˌfəʊtə'sɪnθəsɪs] n	Fotosynthese
limestone n	Kalkstein
closed system n	geschlossenes System
carbon monoxide [ˌkɑːbnmə'nɒksaɪd] n	Kohlenstoffmonoxid
carbon dioxide [ˌkɑːbndaɪ'ɒksaɪd] n	Kohlenstoffdioxid
carbonate n	Carbonat
bicarbonate [ˌbaɪ'kɑːbnət]	Bicarbonat
low solubility adj	schwerlöslich
hydrocarbon [ˌhaɪdrə'kɑːbn] n	Kohlenwasserstoff

Nitrogen cycle » Abb. 58

nitrogen n	Stickstoff
nitrogen cycle	Stickstoffkreislauf
ammonium ion (NH_4^+) [ə'məʊniəmˌaɪən] n	Ammoniumion
ammonia / ammonia hydroxide (NH_3) n	Ammoniak
ammonia salt n	Ammoniumsalze
culture medium / nutrient solution n	Nährlösung
nitrate ion (NO_3^-) n	Nitrationen
nitrite ion (NO_2^-) n	Nitritionen

nitrification [ˌnaɪtrɪfɪ'keɪʃn] n ($NH_3 \rightarrow NO_2^- \rightarrow NO_3^-$)	Nitrifikation
nitrifiying bacteria n	nitrifizierende Bakterien
nitrosomonas n	Nitrosomonas *(Bakteriengattung der Nitritbakterien, Nitrosofizierer)*
nitrite-oxidizing bacteria n *(oxidation of nitrite into nitrate)*	Nitratbakterien / Nitritoxidierer *(Sammelbegriff von Bakterien die $NO_2^- + \frac{1}{2} O_2 \rightarrow NO_3^-$ verwandeln)*
nitrobacter [ˌnaɪtrəʊ'bæktr] n	Nitrobakter *(Bakteriengattung der Nitratbakterien)*

»		
	oxidize ammonia	Ammonium oxidieren
	convert sth into nitrite	in Nitrit verwandeln
	degredation of proteins	Eiweißzersetzung

denitrification ($NO_3^- \rightarrow NO_2^- \rightarrow NO \rightarrow N_2O \rightarrow N_2$ gas) n	Denitrifikation
sewage plant [ˈsuːɪdʒˌplɑːnt] n	Kläranlage
municipal wastewater n	kommunale Abwässer

intermediate gaseous nitrogen oxide products	gasförmige Stick(stoff)oxide (Zwischenprodukte)
conversion of nitrate into molecular nitrogen (N_2)	Umwandlung von Nitrat in letztendlich molekularen Stickstoff
replenish the nitrogen cycle	den Stickstoffzyklus wieder aufstocken

ammonification [əˌməʊnɪfɪˈkeɪʃn] n	Ammonifikation *(Bildung von Ammoniak und seinen Salzen (NH_4^+X)*
mineralisation *BE* / mineralization *AE* n	Mineralisierung
microbial [maɪkrəʊbɪəl] adj	mikrobiell
urea [jʊˈriːə] n	Harnstoff
uric acid [ˌjʊərɪkˈæsɪd] n	Harnsäure
organic nitrogen n	organischer Stickstoff
faeces *BE* / feces *AE* [ˈfiːsiːz] n pl	Kot / Fäzes
microbial ammonification n	mikrobielle Ammonifikation

Sulphur cycle

sulphur *BE* / sulfur *AE* [ˈsʌlfə] n	Schwefel
sulphur cycle n	Schwefelkreislauf
stored adj	gespeichert
underground adj	unterirdisch
sulphate *BE* / sulfate *AE* n	Sulfat *(Salze der Schwefelsäure H_2SO_4)*
sulphate salt	Sulfat Salz
weathering n	Verwitterung
weather v	verwittern
natural source n	natürliche Quelle
emit v	ausstoßen / abgeben
volcanic eruption n	Vulkanausbruch

release stored sulphur	gespeicherten Schwefel freisetzen
convert into sulphate	in Sulfate umwandeln

tidal flats / mudflats n pl — Watt
ferrous sulphide ['ferəsˌsʌlfaɪd] n — Eisensulfat
sulphur dioxide n — Schwefeldioxid (SO_2)
hydrogen sulphide gas (H_2S) n — Schwefelwasserstoff
sulphuric acid n — Schwefelsäure
  sulphuric acid particles — Schwefelsäurepartikel
rainfall n — Regen / Niederschlag
acid rain n — saurer Regen
perturbed [pə'tɜːbd] adj — gestört
  heavily perturbed — schwer gestört
sulphate aerosol ['sʌlfeɪtˌeərəsɒl] n — Sulfat Aerosol

plants incorporate sulphates into their tissues	Pflanzen bauen Sulphate in ihre Gewebe ein
rate of denitrification	Geschwindigkeit der Denitrifikation

Phosphorous cycle

phosphorous cycle n — Stoffkreislauf des Phosphors
nutrient ['njuːtrɪənt] n — Nährsalz
  essential nutrient — lebensnotwendiges Nährsalz
  limiting nutrient — begrenzendes / limitierendes Nährsalz

phosphate n — Phosphat
  phosphate salt — Phosphatsalz
  phosphoric acid — Phosphorsäure
  dilute phosphoric acid [daɪ'luːtfɒs'fɒrɪkˌæsɪd] — gelöste Phosphorsäure
mycorrhiza fungus [ˌmaɪkə'raɪzəˌfʌŋgəs] n — Mykorrhizapilz

building block of cell membranes, DNA, RNA, and ATP	Baustein von Zellmembranen, DNA, RNA und ATP
excel at taking up phosphate salts	unübertroffen sein in der Aufnahme von Phosphaten

10.6 Terrestrial ecosystems » II. 1. Plants; 2. Animals

terrestrial ecosystem [təˌrestrɪəlˈiːkəʊˌsɪstəm] n	terrestrisches Ökosystem / Landökosystem
biome [ˈbaɪəʊm] n	Biom / Vegetationszone *(weitgefasste Pflanzengesellschaft)*
tundra / Arctic tundra [ˌɑːktɪkˈtʌndrə] n	Tundra
alpine tundra	Alpine Tundra
taiga [ˈtaɪgə] n	Taiga
forest n	Wald
boreal forest [ˈbɔːrɪəlˌfɒrɪst]	nördlicher Nadelwaldgürtel
temperate deciduous forest	sommergrüner Laub- und Mischwald der gemäßigten Zonen
temperate evergreen forest	Nadelwald der gemäßigten Zonen
tropical rain forest	tropischer Regenwald
thorn forest	Buschlandschaft *(weder Steppe noch Wüste)*
chaparral [ʃæpəˈræl] n	mediterranes Biom
maquis [mækˈiː] n	Macchie
desert n	Wüste
savanna [səˈvænə] n	Savanne
grassland n	Graslandschaft
temperate grassland	Steppe der gemäßigten Zone
steppe [step] n	Steppe
sclerophyllous vegetation [sklɪəˌrɒfɪləsvedʒɪˈteɪʃn] n	Hartlaubzone

10.7 Ecosystem forest

deciduous forest [dɪˌsɪdjʊəsˈfɒrɪst] n	Laubwald
oak forest [ˈəʊkˌfɒrɪst] n	Eichenwald
birch forest [ˈbɜːtʃˌfɒrɪst] n	Birkenwald
mixed deciduous forest n	Laubmischwald
mixed oak forest n	Eichenmischwald
mixed beech forest n	Buchenmischwald
woodrush beech forest n	Hainsimsen-Buchenwald
riparian forest [raɪˈpeərɪənˌfɒrɪst] / alluvial forest [əˈluːvɪəlˌfɒrɪst] / floodplain forest n	Auwald

10 Ecology › 10.7 Ecosystem forest

old growth forest / primeval forest / virgin forest n	Urwald *(von Menschen unberührt)*
dry forest n	Trockenwald
mangrove forest [ˈmaŋgrəʊvˌfɒrɪst] n	Mangrovenwald
bog forest [ˈbɒgˌfɒrɪst] n	Hochmoorwald
high forest n	Hochwald
coniferous forest [kəˈnɪfrəsˌfɒrɪst] n	Nadelwald
fir forest [ˈfɜːˌfɒrɪst] n	Tannenwald
tree limit n	Baumgrenze
elevational [ˌelɪˈveɪʃnl] adj	höhenbedingt
working forest n	Wirtschaftswald
forest cultivation n	Waldbewirtschaftung
forest industry n	Holzverarbeitungsindustrie
monoculture n	Monokultur
forest stand n	Waldbestand

»

data on forest yields	ertragskundliche Walddaten
forest management measures	forstwirtschaftliche Maßnahmen
large scale forest conversion	großflächiger Waldumbau
dwindling forest resources	abnehmende Waldbestände

acid rain n	saurer Regen
forest damage n	Forstschaden
forest decline / forest die back n	Waldsterben
forest use plan n	Waldfunktionsplan
pastoral forest [ˈpɑːstrlˌfɒrɪst] n	Hutewald
avalanche forest [ˈævlɑːnʃˌfɒrɪst] n	Bannwald
protection forest n	Schutzwald
recreational forest n	Erholungswald
city forest / municipal forest [mjuːˈnɪsɪplˌfɒrɪst] n	Stadtwald

»

classification of forest soils	Gütebestimmung des Waldbodens

forest area n	Waldfläche
edge of the woods n	Waldrand
forest clearing n	Kahlfläche / Lichtung
forest clearance n	Rodung
dominance n	Deckungsgrad

Layers of the forest

stratification [ˌstrætɪfɪˈkeɪʃn] n	Gliederung / Stratifikation
layer n	Stockwerk
forest soil n	Walderde
forest floor n	Waldboden
litter layer / foerna / förna n	Förna / Laubschicht / Laubstreu / Bestandsabfall
forest floor organic layer / humus [ˈhjuːməs] n	Humus
root layer n	Wurzelschicht
rooting system n	Wurzelwerk
root free soil core n	Unterboden (B-Horizont)
shallow root tree	Flachwurzler
deep root tree	Tiefwurzler
taproot [ˈtæpruːt]	Pfahlwurzel
shallow rooting plant	flach wurzelnde Pflanze
moss layer n	Moosschicht
common moss	Gemeines Laubmoos
liverwort	Lebermoos
blueberry / bilberry n	Heidelbeere
lignonberry n	Preiselbeere
lichen [ˈlaɪkən] n	Flechte
crustose lichen	Krustenflechte
foliose lichen	Blattflechte / Laubflechte
fruticose lichen	Strauchflechte
bolete [ˈbəʊliːt] / tubed fungus n	Röhrling / Röhrenpilz
edible boletus [ˌedɪblbəʊˈliːtəs]	Steinpilz
edible adj	essbar
poisonous [ˈpɔɪznəs] / adj	giftig
cap n	Hut
gill [gɪl] n	Lamelle
agaric [ˈægərɪk] / gill fungus n	Blätterpilz
rusella [ruːˈselə] n	Täubling
volva [ˈvɒlvə] n	Knolle / Scheide
chanterelle [ˌʃɑːtəˈrel] n	Leistenpilz
chanterelle *(chantarellus cibarius)*	Pfifferling
coral fungus n	Korallenpilz
puffball / puff-ball n	Bovist

10 Ecology › 10.7 Ecosystem forest

morel [mɒrˈel] n	Morchel
polypore [ˌpɒlɪˈpɔː] n	Porling
teeth fungus n	Stachelpilz
herb layer n	Krautschicht
grasses n	Gräser
great wood rush n	Wald-Hainsimse
spring snowflake n	Märzenbecher
bulb n	Zwiebel
lily-of-the-valley n	Maiglöckchen
shoot n	Pflanzenspross / Trieb
rhizome [ˈraɪzəʊm] n	Rhizom / Wurzelstock / Erdstamm
bulbous corydalis [ˈbʌlbəskərɪˌdəlɪs] n	Lerchensporn
tuber [ˈtjuːbə] n	Knolle *(Erdstamm zur Knolle ausgebildet)*
seedling n	Keimling
fern [fɜːn] n	Farn
frond [frɒnd] n	Wedel
horsetail [ˈhɔːsteɪl] n	Schachtelhalm
lycopodium [ˌlaɪkəˈpəʊdiəm] n	Bärlappgewächs
hygrophyte [ˈhaɪgrəfaɪt] n	Hygrophyt *(Pflanzen typischer Feuchtbiotope)*
moisture-loving adj	feuchtigkeitsliebend

» | rolled up in a spiral | zu einer Spirale aufgerollt |

shrub layer n	Strauchschicht
field maple n	Feldahorn
hawthorn [ˈhɔːθɔːn] / whitethorn [ˈwaɪtθɔːn] n	Weißdorn
hazel n	Hasel
hazelnut n	Haselnuss
blackthorn n	Schlehdorn
sweet cherry n	Vogelkirsche
woodbine / honeysuckle n	Geißblatt
European spindletree n	Pfaffenhütchen
elder [ˈeldə] n	Holunder
tree layer n	Baumschicht
trunk n	Stamm
canopy [ˈkænəpi] n	Krone
canopy layer	Kronenschicht

oak n	Eiche
pendunculate oak	Stieleiche
sessile oak ['sesaɪl͵əʊk]	Traubeneiche
acorn ['eɪkɔːn] n	Eichel *(Frucht der Eichen)*
maple (tree) n	Ahorn
sycamore ['sɪkəmɔː]	Bergahorn
Norway maple	Spitzahorn
elm (tree) n	Ulme
whych-elm	Bergulme
lime (tree) n	Linde
small-leaved lime	Winterlinde
willow ['wɪləʊ] n	Weide
goat willow	Salweide

Neophytes

maidenhair tree n	Ginkgo / Frauenhaarbaum / Mädchenhaarbaum
northern red oak n	Amerikanische Roteiche
silver maple n	Silberahorn
box elder n	Eschenahorn
black locust [͵blæk'ləʊkəst] n	Gemeiner Schotendorn / Robinie
tree of heaven n	Götterbaum
redwood n	Mammutbaum

Animals of the forest » II. 1 Plants

red deer n	Rotwild
roe deer n	Rehwild
hare [heə] n	Hase
mouse n	Maus
common dormouse	Haselmaus
edible dormouse / fat dormouse	Siebenschläfer
badger ['bædʒə] n	Dachs
wild boar [waɪld'bɔː] n	Wildschwein
squirrel ['skwɪrl] n	Eichhörnchen
racoon [rə'kuːn] n	Waschbär
brown bear n	Braunbär
wildcat n	Wildkatze
lynx [lɪŋks], *pl* lynxes n	Luchs
weasel ['wiːzl] n	Wiesel

10 Ecology › 10.7 Ecosystem forest

stoat [stəʊt] n	Hermelin
ferret ['ferɪt] n	Frettchen
fox, *pl* foxes n	Fuchs
wolf n	Wolf
common noctule [ˌkɒmən'nɒktjuːl] n (bat)	Großer Abendsegler *(Fledermaus)*
hedgehog ['hedʒhɒg] n	Igel
buzzard ['bʌzəd] n	Bussard
red kite n	Rotmilan
goshawk ['gɒshɔːk] n	Habicht
sparrow hawk n	Sperber
owl n	Eule
barn owl	Schleiereule
long-eared owl	Waldohreule
wood grouse ['wʊdˌgraʊs] n	Auerhahn
pigeon ['pɪdʒən] n	Taube
wood pigeon	Ringeltaube
tit n	Meise
blue tit	Blaumeise
marsh tit	Sumpfmeise
great tit	Kohlmeise
coal tit	Tannenmeise
woodpecker ['wʊdˌpekə] n	Specht
green woodpecker	Grünspecht
black woodpecker	Schwarzspecht
great spotted woodpecker	Buntspecht
nuthatch ['nʌthætʃ] n	Kleiber
bluejay ['bluːdʒeɪ] / jaybird / Eurasian jay n	Eichelhäher
golden oriole [ˌgəʊldn'ɔːrɪəl] n	Pirol
wren [ren] n	Zaunkönig
robin n	Rotkehlchen
chaffinch ['tʃæfɪnʃ] n	Buchfink
blackbird n	Amsel
toad [təʊd] n	Kröte
snake n	Schlange
European adder / common viper / crossed viper n	Kreuzotter
bark beetle n	Borkenkäfer

spruce moth ['spruːsˌmɒθ] n	Fichtenspanner
ant n	Ameise
hornet ['hɔːnɪt] n	Hornisse
ladybird n	Marienkäfer
wolf spider n	Wolfsspinne
tick n	Zecke
slug [slʌg] n	Nacktschnecke
snail [sneɪl] n	Schnecke *(mit Gehäuse)*
worm n	Wurm
earthworm	Regenwurm
nematode ['nemətəʊd] n	Nematode / Rundwurm
millipede ['mɪlɪpiːd] n	Doppelfüßer / Tausendfüßer
centipede ['sentɪpiːd] n	Hundertfüßer
mite [maɪt] / acarian n	Milbe
pseudoscorpion [ˌsjuːdəʊ'skɔːpiən] n	Pseudoskorpion
springtail / collembolan [kə'lembələn] n	Springschwanz
bristletail ['brɪsəlteɪl] / silverfish n	Silberfisch
campodea [kæm'pədɪə] n	Doppelschwanz
earwig n	Ohrwurm
wireworm n	Drahtwurm *(Larve des Schnellkäfers)*
grub [grʌb] n	Engerling
amoeba [ə'miːbə] n	Amöbe
ciliate ['sɪlɪeɪt] n	Wimpertierchen
blue alga, *pl* algae n	Blaualge
bacterium [bæk'tɪərɪəm], *pl* bacteria n	Bakterie

Interactions within the biocenosis of a forest

spring forest geophyte [ˌsprɪŋ'fɒrɪst'dʒiːəʊfaɪt] n	Waldfrühblüher
blossoming time n	Blütezeit
period of growth / growth period n	Wachstumsperiode
dormancy ['dɔːmensi] n	Keimruhe / Samenruhe / Knospenruhe / Ruhezustand
germination [ˌdʒɜːmɪ'neɪʃn] n	Keimung / Keimen / Sprießen
blossom v	Blüten treiben
shade plant n	Schattenpflanze
shade leaf n	Schattenblatt
partial-shade plant n	Halbschattenpflanze

light compensation point n	Lichtkompensationspunkt
light saturation n	Lichtsättigung
sun leaf n	Lichtblatt

»
multilayered palisade parenchyma tissue	mehrschichtiges Palisadengewebe

pollinator / pollination agent n	Bestäuber
frugivorous [fruːˈdʒɪvrəs] adj	Früchte fressend
dispersal [dɪˈspɜːsl] n	Verbreitung
period of frost n	Frostperiode
overwintering plant n	überwinternde Pflanze
(winter) hardiness n	Winterhärte
freeze tolerant adj	frosttolerant
antifreeze n	Frostschutzmittel
antifreeze protein	Anti-Frost Protein / Frostschutzprotein

leaf browser n	Laubfresser
gall former [ˈgɔːlˌfɔːmə] n	Gallbildner
leaf miner n	Blattminierer
litter decomposing animal n	Streuzersetzer
sap feeder n	Säftesauger

wood-boring insect n	Holzbohrer
bark-boring insect n	Rindenbohrer
seed predator n	Samenfresser
ground breeder n	Bodenbrüter
hole-nesting bird n	Höhlenbrüter

Forest floor ecosystem

forest floor n	Waldboden
A-horizon n	A-Horizont
foerna / förna / litter layer n	Förna / Laubschicht / Laubstreu / Bestandsabfall
organic layer n	organische Auflage
leaf litter n	Blattlaubfall
woody debris [ˌwʊdiˈdeɪbriː] n	Holzabfall

»
rate of decomposition	Abbaugeschwindigkeit

topsoil ['tɒpsɔɪl] n	Oberboden
aeration [eə'reɪʃn] n	Durchlüftung
rooting n	Verwurzelung
water holding capacity (WHC) n	Wasserspeicherfähigkeit
earthworm burrow n	Regenwurmfraßgang
clay-humus complex [kleɪ'hjuːməsˌkɒmpleks] n	Ton-Humus Komplex
mycorrhiza [ˌmaɪkə'raɪzə] n	Mykorrhiza
mycorrhizal plant	Pflanze, die in Symbiose mit Mykorrhiza lebt
mycorrhizal fungus [maɪkə'raɪzlˌfʌŋgəs]	Mycorrhizapilz in Symbiose mit einem Baum
mycelium [maɪ'siːliəm] n	Pilzgeflecht
penetrate ['penɪtreɪt] v	eindringen
root tissue n	Wurzelgewebe
phosphorus source n	Phosphorquelle
stunted growth n	Krüppelwuchs

» | access phosphorus sources | Phosphorquellen zugänglich machen

B-Horizon n	B-Horizont / Unterboden
broken down rocks n	Gesteinssplitter
weathered stones n	verwittertes Gestein
iron salt n	Eisen-Salz

» | washed out minerals and nutrient salts | herausgewaschene Mineralstoffe und Nährsalze

C-horizon n	C- Horizont / Untergrundboden
partially broken-down rock n	Felstrümmer
bedrock ['bedrɒk] n	anstehendes Gestein
clay n	Ton
sand n	Sand
lime n	Kalk
granite ['grænɪt] n	Granit
capillary force n	Kapillarkraft
water holding capacity (WHC) n	Wasserspeicherkapazität
soil texture n	Bodenbeschaffenheit
grain size n	Korngröße
soil density n	Bodendichte

10 Ecology › 10.7 Ecosystem forest

» | susceptible to leaching (of e.g. essential nutrient salts) | anfällig für Versickerung (z. B. wertvoller Nährsalze) |

Endangered forest » III. 10.5 Environmental cycles – Water cycle » Abb. 59

rain forest n	Regenwald
primeval forest n	Urwald
timber ['tɪmbə] n	Holz
tropical wood n	tropisches Holz
native wood n	einheimisches Holz
spruce [spruːs] n	Fichte
fir (tree) [fɜː] n	Tanne
cut down v	abholzen
slash burning / fire clearing n	Brandrodung
reforestation n	Wiederaufforstung

buffer ['bʌfə] n	Puffer
buffer v	puffern
buffer acidity	Säure abpuffern
soil buffering capacity	Pufferkapazität des Bodens
tinsel syndrome ['tɪnsl͵sɪndrəʊm] n	Lamettasyndrom
bastard branch n	Seitentrieb
stork's nest n	Storchennest

» | loss of needles | Verlust an Nadeln |
| premature autumn / fall discoloration | frühzeitige Herbstverfärbung |
| drooping branches | hängende Zweige |

nutrient leaching n	Auswaschen der Nährsalze
clay mineral n	Tonmineral
tree ring analysis n	Baumringanalyse
slowed growth n	verlangsamtes Wachstum
stunted growth n	Krüppelwuchs
foliage ['fəʊliːdʒ] n	Blattwerk

» | increase in toxic aluminium | Zunahme an giftigem Aluminium |
| waxy coating on needles and leaves | Wachsschicht auf Nadeln und Blättern |

10.8 Meadow ecosystem »II. 1 Plants

meadow ['medəʊ] n	Wiese
hay meadow	Heuwiese
wet meadow	Nasswiese
water logged adj	wassergesättigt
cocksfoot ['kɒksfʊt]	Knäulgrass
timothy ['tɪməθi]	Wiesen-Lieschgras
common bent	Rotes Straußgras
sweet vernal-grass	Gemeines Ruchgras
crested dog's-tail	Kammgras
meadow foxtail n	Wiesenfuchsschwanz
yellow oatgrass n	Glatthafer
Italian ryegrass n	Weidelgras
smooth meadow-grass n	Wiesenrispengras
creeping soft grass n	Weiches Honiggras
meadow fescue [ˌmedəʊˈfeskjuː] n	Wiesenschwingel
soft brome [sɒftˈbrəʊm] n	Weiche Trespe
meadow melick n	Perlgras
common quaking grass n	Zittergras
redtop / meadow bent n	(weißes) Straußgras
buttercup n	Butterblume / Hahnenfuß
vetch [vetʃ] n	Wicke
clover n	Klee
red clover	Rotklee
dandelion ['dændɪlaɪən] n	Löwenzahn
knapweed n	Flockenblume
field scabious [ˈfiːldˌskeɪbiəs] n	Ackerwitwenblume
hawkbit n	Herbstlöwenzahn
ox-eye daisy n	Margerite
cowslip n	Schlüsselblume
bluebell n	Glockenblume
cow parsley n	Wiesenkerbel
cuckoo flower ['kʊkuːflaʊə] n	Wiesenschaumkraut
yarrow ['jærəʊ] n	Schafgarbe
plantain n	Wegerich
dock n	Ampfer
nettle n	Nessel
selfheal n	Braunelle
thistle n	Distel
bugle ['bjuːgl] n	Kriechender Günsel

daisy n	Gänseblümchen
common bedstraw [ˌkɒmən'bedstrɔː] n	Gemeines Labkraut

orchid ['ɔːkɪd] n	Orchidee
common spotted orchid	Geflecktes Knabenkraut
green-winged orchid	Kleines Knabenkraut
twayblade orchid [ˌtweɪbleɪd'ɔːkɪd] n	Nestwurz
yellow-rattle n	Kleiner Klappertopf
annual species n	einjährige Art
semi-parasite n	Halbschmarotzer

legume ['legjuːm] n	Leguminose / Hülsenfrüchtler
nodule ['nɒdjuːl] n	Knöllchen
protein-rich *(e.g. foliage)* n	eiweißreich *(z.B. Blattgrün)*

> | | |
> |---|---|
> | able to fix atmospheric nitrogen | in der Lage, Luftstickstoff zu binden |
> | adds nitrogen to the soil | reichert den Boden mit Stickstoff an |

Food plants and the effect of cultivation » II. 1 Plants

stinging nettle n	Brennnessel
food plant n	Futterpflanze
butterfly n	Schmetterling
caterpillar ['kætəpɪlə] n	Raupe
meadow brown butterfly n	Großes Ochsenauge
marbled white butterfly n	Schachbrett / Damenbrett
large skipper n	Rostfarbiger Dickkopffalter

perennial [pə'renɪəl] adj	mehrjährig
tussock ['tʌsək] n	Grashorst
base of grass n	Grund des Grases
silage ['saɪlɪdʒ] n	Silage
pasture field n	Weide
grazing regime n	Beweidungsverlauf

> | | |
> |---|---|
> | intensively cultivated | intensiv bewirtschaftet |
> | intensive cutting | intensiver Beschnitt |
> | preclude to complete one's life cycle | die Vollendung des Lebenszyklus verhindern |

Examples of animal species

glow-worm n	Glühwürmchen
grasshopper n	Grashüpfer
bush-cricket n	Heupferd
froghopper / spittlebug n	Schaumzikade
'cuckoo spit' n	Kuckucksspeichel
nymphs n	Nymphen
foam surrounding nymphs	Schaum, der die Nymphen umgibt
hoverfly ['hɒvəflaɪ] n	Schwebfliege
long horned beetle / longhorn beetle n	Bockkäfer
rove beetle ['rəʊvˌbiːtl] n	Kurzflügler
ladybird n	Marienkäfer
larva of ladybird	Marienkäferlarven
green fly / aphid ['eɪfɪd] n	Blattlaus
ground beetle n	Laufkäfer
grub [grʌb] n	Engerling
weevil ['wiːvl] n	Rüsselkäfer

small tortoiseshell [ˌsmɔːl'tɔːtəʃel] n	Kleiner Fuchs
map butterfly n	Landkärtchen
painted lady n	Distelfalter
crane fly n	Wiesenschnake
harvestman, pl harvestmen / daddy longlegs AE n	Weberknecht
arachnid [ə'ræknɪd] n	Spinnentier
crab spider n	Krabbenspinne
garden spider n	Kreuzspinne

meadow ant n	Gelbe Wiesenameise / Gelbe Wegameise
leatherjacket n	Schnakenlarve
crane fly n	Erdschnake
wireworm n	Drahtwurm *(Larve des Schnellkäfers)*
click beetle n	Schnellkäfer

»

root-feeding aphid	sich von Wurzelsäften ernährende Blattlaus
break down and recycle the dung	Dung abbauen und wiederverwerten

10 Ecology › 10.9 Man-made ecosystems

10.9 Man-made ecosystems

Hedge

cultural landscape n	Kulturlandschaft
hedge n	Hecke
sloe [sləʊ] / blackthorn n	Schlehe
privet ['prɪvɪt] n	Liguster
dog rose n	Heckenrose

Dry stone wall

dry stone wall n	Trockenmauer
vineyard ['vɪnjəd] n	Weinberg
terrace n	Terrasse
lizard ['lɪzəd] n	Zauneidechse
crevice ['krevɪs] n	Mauerritze
weasel n	Mauswiesel

stonecrop n	Scharfer Mauerpfeffer
succulent ['sʌkjələnt] n	Sukkulente / Fleischpflanze / Saftpflanze
succulent adj	fleischig / saftig / sukkulent

xerophyte ['zɪərəfaɪt] n	Xerophyt / Trockenpflanze
spine / thorn n	Dorn
hens and chicks plant / common houseleek n	Dach-Hauswurz
leaf rosette n	Blattrosette
outlast v	überdauern

»
leaves in drooping / vertical position	Blätter am Stamm herabhängend
roots firmly planted in the soil	Wurzeln fest im Erdreich verankert
shed leaves	Blätter abwerfen
dry up temporarily	vorübergehend austrocknen

Meadow orchard

meadow orchard n	Streuobstwiese
table apple / dessert apple n	Tafelapfel

apple with storage quality n	Lagerapfel
windfall n	Fallobst
cider ['saɪdə] n	Most
pasture n	Weide / Weideland
use as pastures	beweiden
sheep pasture	Schafweide
scythe [saɪð] n	Sense
hoopoe ['huːpuː] n	Wiedehopf
red-backed shrike n	Neuntöter
shelter n	Unterschlupf

Waste ground – common plants

common evening primrose n	Gemeine Nachtkerze
wild carrot n	Wilde Möhre
Canada goldenrod n	Goldraute
yellow chamomile n	Färberhundskamille
tansy ['tænzi] n	Rainfarn
gallant soldier n	Knopfkraut
groundsel ['graʊnsl] n	Kreuzkraut
garlic mustard n	Knoblauchrauke
field bindweed n	Ackerwinde

Town ecosystem

urbanophobic [ˌɜːbeɪnəˈfəʊbɪk] adj	Arten, die Verstädterung vermeiden
urbanophil [ˌɜːbeɪnəfaɪl] adj	Arten, die verstädtern

nest in	… caves	in Höhlen	… nisten
	… crevices in rocks	in Felsspalten	
	… bushes and trees	in Büschen und Bäumen	
	… undergrowth	in Unterholz / Gestrüpp	
	… holes of a lamp	in Löchern von Lampen	
	… traffic light posts	in in / auf Verkehrsampeln	

kestrel ['kestrl] n	Turmfalke
swift n	Schwalbe
starling n	Star
sparrow n	Spatz
black redstart n	Hausrotschwanz
common pigeon n	Straßentaube

10 Ecology › 10.9 Man-made ecosystems

song thrush n
dunnock ['dʌnək] n
chaffinch ['tʃæfɪnʃ] n
chiffchaff ['tʃɪftʃæf] n

Singdrossel
Heckenbraunelle
Buchfink
Zilpzalp

Heather

slash burning / fire clearing n
heather ['heðə] n
heath ['hi:θ] / moorland n
  Luneburg Heath
juniper heathland ['dʒu:nɪpəˌhi:θlænd] n
fieldfare n
Swabian highlands n
juniper bush / juniper shrub ['dʒu:nɪpəˌʃrʌb] n
broom / gorse [gɔ:s] n
carline thistle [kɑ:laɪn'θɪsl] n
gentian [-dʒenʃn] n

Brandrodung
Heide *(Pflanze)*
Heide *(Landschaft)*
  Lüneburger Heide
Wacholderheide

Wacholderdrossel
Schwäbische Alb
Wacholderbusch

Ginster
Silberdistel
Enzian

poor soil n
carnivorous plant [kɑ:ˌnɪvrəs'plɑ:nt] n
insectivorous plant [ˌɪnsek'tɪvrəs] n

mineralstoffarmer Boden
Carnivore / fleischfressende Pflanze
Insektivore / insektenfressende Pflanze

boggy ['bɒgi] adj
peat soil n
nitrogen-poor adj
  lack nitrogen
trap n
pitcher plant n
sundews ['sʌndju:z] n
sticky hair n
Venus flytrap n
snap shut v
leaf blade / lamina ['læmɪnə] n

sumpfig
Torfboden
stickstoffarm
  stickstoffarm sein
Falle
Kannenpflanze
Sonnentau
klebrige Haare
Venusfliegenfalle
zuschnappen
Blattspreite

From heath to forest

growth stage n
pioneer stage n
building stage n

Wachstumsphase
Initialstadium
Aufbaustadium

	heather shoot n	Heideschössling
	grazing n	Beweidung
	moor burning n	Moorbrand / Abbrennen von Heideflächen
»	plagioclimax community	durch menschliche Eingriffe herbeigeführte scheinbare Klimaxgesellschaft
	mature stage n	Klimaxphase
	degenerative stage n	Zerfallsphase
	overgrazing n	Überweidung
	low-lying land n	Sumpfland
	reforestation n	Wiederaufforstung
»	heather becomes woody	die Heide verholzt
	reclamation of low-lying land	Rückgewinnung von Sumpfland

10.10 Examples of aquatic ecosystems

aquatic ecosystem n	aquatisches Ökosystem
fresh water n	Süßwasser
glacier ['glæsiə] n	Gletscher
aquifer ['ækwɪfə] n	(grund-)wasserführende Schicht
freshwater ecosystem n	Ökosystem der Binnengewässer / Süßwasserökosysteme
brook n	Bach
river n	Fluss
stream n	Strom
canal n	Kanal
lake n	See
reservoir ['rezəvwɑː] / artificial lake n	Stausee
dam n	Staudamm
pond n	Teich
seasonal pond n	temporärer Teich *(trocknet jahreszeitlich bedingt aus)*
spring n	Quelle
wetland n	Feuchtgebiet / Feuchtbiotop
ground water n	Grundwasser

10 Ecology › 10.10 Examples of aquatic ecosystems

marine ecosystem n	marines Ökosystem *(Ökosystem des Meers)*
ocean n	Meer
salt marsh n	Salzmarsch
intertidal ecosystem [ˌɪntətaɪdl'iːkəʊsɪstəm] n	Ökosystem Wattenmeer / Gezeitenökosystem
estuary ['estjʊəri] n	Mündungsgebiet / Flussmündungsgebiet / Meeresarm
lagoon [lə'guːn] n	Lagune
mangrove ['mæŋgrəʊv] n	Mangrove
coral reef n	Korallenriff
deep sea n	Tiefsee
sea floor n	Meeresboden

Animals in freshwater ecosystems » II. 2 Animals

dichotomous key [daɪ'kɒtəməsˌkiː] n	Bestimmungsschlüssel
zooplankton [ˌzuːə'plæŋktən] n	Plankton / Zooplankton / tierische Kleinstlebewesen
ciliate ['sɪlɪeɪt] n	Wimpertierchen
paramecium [ˌpærə'miːsiəm] n	Pantoffeltierchen / Paramecium
cnidarian [naɪ'deərɪən] n	Nesseltier *(z. B. Süßwasserpolyp)*
polychaeta ['pɒlɪkiːt], *pl* polychaetae n	Polychaeta / Borstenwurm
chaetognath ['kiːtənæθ] *(arrow worm)*	Pfeilwurm
larva ['lɑːvə], *pl* larvae n	Larve
mayfly n	Eintagsfliege
blackfly larva n	Kriebelmückenlarve
spotted sedge / hydropsyche ['haɪdrəʊsaɪki] / net spinning caddis n	Wasserseelchen
caddisfly n	Köcherfliege
dragon fly n	Libelle
snipe fly n	Ibisfliege
alderfly ['ɔːldəˌflaɪ] n	Schlammfliege
stonefly n	Steinfliege
chironimid [kaɪ'rəʊnəmɪd] / non-biting midge n	Zuckmücke
phantom midge n	Büschelmücke
hyphydrus ovatus [haɪfaɪdrəs'əʊveɪtəs] n	Kugelschwimmer
backswimmer n	Rückenschwimmer *(räuberisch)*

water boatman n	Rückenschwimmer *(saugt Pflanzensäfte)*
pond skater / water strider n	Wasserläufer
toe biter / (creeping) water bug n	Schwimmwanze
marsh beetle larva (Scirtidae spec) n	Jochkäferlarve
long-toed water beetle n	Hakenkäferlarve
water tiger n	Gelbrandkäfer
crustacean [krʌˈsteɪʃn] n	Krebstier
copepod [ˈkəʊpɪpɒd] n	Copepode *(Kleinkrebs spec)*
calanoida [kəlænɒɑɪdə] n	Ruderfußkrebs
cyclops [ˈsaɪklɒps] n	Hüpferling
krill [krɪl] n	Krill *(Kleinkrebs)*
daphnia [ˈdæfnɪə] n	Blattfußkrebs *(z. B. Wasserfloh)*
waterlouse, *pl* waterlice n	Wasserassel
ostracod [ˈɒstrəkɒd] n	Muschelkrebs
water flea / daphnia [ˈdæfnɪə] n	Wasserfloh / Daphnia
mollusc [ˈmɒləsk] n	Weichtier *(z. B. Schnecke)*
pond snail n	Schlammschnecke
amber snail n	Bernsteinschnecke
ramshorn snail n	Posthornschnecke
ferrissia wautieri [fɜːrɪʃiəwəʊtɪəri] n	Mützenschnecke
mussel [ˈmʌsl] n	Muschel
swan mussel	Große Teichmuschel
freshwater leech n	Süßwasseregel
mudworm / tubifex worm / sewage worm n	Schlammröhrenwurm

Vertebrates

vertebrate [ˈvɜːtɪbreɪt] n	Wirbeltier / Vertebrat
fish n	Fisch
eel n	Aal
carp n	Karpfen
perch n	Barsch
loach n	Schmerle
sculpin [ˈskʌlpɪn] n	Groppe
rudd [rʌd] n	Rotfeder

10 Ecology › 10.11 Lake ecosystem

roach [rəʊtʃ] n	Rotauge
pike [paɪk], *pl* pikes; pike n	Hecht
predatory fish n	Raubfisch
non-predatory fish	Friedfisch

dipper / white throated dipper n	Wasseramsel
great crested grebe n	Haubentaucher
great reed warbler n	Rohrsänger
little bittern n	Zwergdommel
heron n	Graureiher
white swan n	Höckerschwan
Eurasian coot n	Blässhuhn / Bläßralle
common moorhen n	Teichralle
mallard [ˈmælɑːd] n	Stockente

duck bird n	Entenvogel
tufted duck n	Reiherente
Northern Shoveler n	Löffelente
diving duck	Tauchente
dabbling duck / pond duck / freshwater duck	Schwimmente
duckling	Entenküken
chick, *pl* chicks n	Küken

tadpole n	Kaulquappe
frog n	Frosch
toad n	Kröte
newt n	Molch
grass snake / ringed snake / water snake n	Ringelnatter

10.11 Lake ecosystem »Abb. 60

A structured body

zoning [ˈzəʊnɪŋ] n	Zonierung *(Aufteilung des Sees in bestimmte Bereiche)*
benthic zone [ˌbenθɪkˈzəʊn]	Benthal *(Seeboden)*
profundal zone [prəʊˌfʌndlˈzəʊn]	Profundal *(Tiefenseeboden)*
littoral zone [ˌlɪtrəlˈzəʊn]	Litoral *(Uferzone)*
shallow transition zone	flache Übergangszone
limnetic zone [lɪmˌnetɪkˈzəʊn]	Pelagial *(Freiwasserzone)*

euphotic zone [juːˌfɒtɪk'zəʊn] / trophogene zone [trɒfəˌdʒiːn'zəʊn]	Nährschicht
tropholytic zone [trəfəˌlɪtɪk'zəʊn]	Zehrschicht
sediment n	Ablagerung / Sediment
penetrate ['penɪtreɪt] v	durchdringen
turbid ['tɜːbɪd] adj	trübe
suspended particle n	gelöstes Teilchen
compensation depth n	Tiefe der Kompensationsebene
compensation level n	Kompensationsebene
detritus rain [dɪ'traɪtəsˌreɪn] n	Detritusregen / Detritussedimentation *(Absinken organischer Teilchen auf den Grund)*

swamp n	Sumpf
reed swamp	Sumpfschilfgürtel
swamp moors	Sumpfmoor
bog [bɒg] n	Sumpf / Moor
marsh n	Sumpf / Moor / Marsch
marsh swamp forest	Moorwald

swamp thicket n	sumpfiges Dickicht
sphagnum moss [ˌsfægnəm'mɒs] n	Torfmoos
alder marsh ['ɔːldəˌmɑːʃ] / marshland forest n	Bruchwald / Erlenbruchwald
shoreline n	Uferzone
swamp zone n	Schilfrohrzone
emergent plant n	Sumpfpflanze
emergent	aufragend
anchor (sth) ['æŋkə] v	(etw.) verankern

» extensive root systems for anchoring to soft ground
stark ausgebildetes Wurzelwerk zum Verankern in weichem Untergrund

reed [riːd] n	Schilfrohr
common reed	Gemeines Schilfrohr
pliable adj	biegsam
hollow adj	hohl
air-passage n	luftführendes Stängelteil
aeration [eə'reɪʃn] n	Belüftung
aerenchyma [eə'reŋkɪmə] / air spaces n	Aerenchym / Durchlüftungsgewebe
rush n	Binse
common rush	Flatterbinse

Ecology › 10.11 Lake ecosystem

hydrophyte ['haɪdrəfaɪt] n	Hydrophyt
hydrophytic	hydrophytisch
aquatic plant / hydrophyte n	Wasserpflanze / Hydrophyt
submerged adj	unter Wasser *(unter Wasser liegend lebend; untergetaucht lebend)*
floating leaf n	Schwimmblatt
buoyancy ['bɔɪənsi] n	Auftrieb

»
reduced	root system	zurückgebildetes	Wurzelwerk
less	vascular tissue supportive tissue	zurückgebildetes	Leitbündelgewebe Stützgewebe
keep the leaves afloat		die Blätter über Wasser halten (freischwimmend)	
be buoyed by water		Auftrieb durch Wasser haben	

rooted floating-leaved plant zone n	Schwimmblattpflanzenzone
water smart weed n	Wasserknöterich
white water lily n	Seerose
free-floating plant zone n	Schwimmpflanzenzone
duckweed ['dʌkwiːd] / lemna minor n	Entengrütze / kleine Wasserlinse
Canadian pond weed n	Kanadische Wasserpest
water milfoil ['wɔːtəˌmɪlfɔɪl] n	Tausendblatt
curled pond weed n	Krauses Laichkraut
hornwort n	Hornkraut

submergent plant n	Tauchpflanze
totally submerged rooted plant n	Unterwasserpflanze
stonewort [stəʊnwɜːt] n	Armleuchteralge
aquatic moss n	Quellmoos
alga ['ælgə], *pl* algas; algae n	Alge

nekton ['nektən] n	Nekton *(freischwebender, freischwimmender Organismus)*
pleuston [plʊəstən] n	Pleuston *(Sammelbegriff: größere Tiere und Pflanzen, deren Lebensraum das Oberflächenhäutchen des Wassers ist)*
neuston ['njuːstən] n	Neuston *(Sammelbegriff: Mikroorganismen deren Lebensraum das Oberflächenhäutchen des Wassers ist)*

plankton ['plæŋktən] n	Plankton *(schwebende Mikroorganismen)*
planktonic	als Plankton
phytoplankton [ˌfaɪtəʊ'plæŋktən]	pflanzliche Kleinstlebewesen / Phytoplankton
surface skin n	Oberflächenhäutchen *(des Wassers)*

Animal adaptaptations to aquatic life

filter feeder n	Filtrierer
appendage [ə'pendɪdʒ] n	Fortsatz
descend v	absinken
impede [ɪm'piːd] v	erschweren
antenna, *pl* antennae n	Antenne
peraeopod [pə'raɪəˌpɒd] *(swimming leg)* n	Blattfuß
water current n	Wasserstrom
second pair of antennae	zweites Antennenpaar

bell animacule / vorticella [ˌvɔːtɪ'selə] n	Glockentierchen
stalk [stɔːk]	Stiel
contractile stalk	zusammenziehbarer Stiel
circle of cilia ['sɜːkləʊˌsɪliə]	Wimpernkranz

hydra ['haɪdrə] n	Süßwasserpolyp
tentacle n	Fangarm
thread cell / cnidia / nematocyst [nəmətəsɪst] / stinging cell n	Nesselzelle
paralyse *BE* / paralyze *AE* v	lähmen

oar [ɔː] n	Ruder
oarlike hindlegs	ruderähnliche Hinterbeine
breathing tube n	Schnorchel / Atemröhre
abdomen ['æbdəmən] n	Hinterleib
abdominal pocket	„Lufttaschen" *(auf der Bauchseite des Hinterleibs, eigentlich ein Haarfilz)*
air sac n	Lufttaschen
hydrostatic function [haɪdrəʊˌstætɪk'fʌŋʃn] n	auftriebgebende Funktion

nutritional niche [njuː'trɪʃnlˌniːʃ] n	Nahrungsnische

limiting resource n	Umweltfaktor, der am weitesten vom Optimum entfernt ist
buoyancy ['bɔɪənsi] n	Auftrieb
dive n	Tauchgang

> | | |
> |---|---|
> | nutritional niche separation in coexisting species in the same habitat | Aufteilung in unterschiedliche Nahrungsnischen bei nebeneinander lebenden Arten im gleichen Lebensraum |
> | vie for sth | um etwas buhlen |

school of fish / shoal of fish / swarm of fish n	Fischschwarm
flock of birds n	Vogelschwarm
assemble in swarms / gather in swarms n	Schwärme bilden

sediment of the lake n	Seebodenschlamm
bottom-dwelling animal n	Bodentier
benthos ['benθɒs] n	am Boden eines Sees lebende Tiere
hemoglobin-rich tail end [ˌhiːməˈgləʊbɪnrɪtʃ] n *(also: haemoglobin-rich)*	Hinterende mit hoher Hämoglobinkonzentration
wave v	hin- und herschwingen / pendeln / undulierende Bewegung machen

The seasons of the lake

seasonal phase n	jahreszeitlich bedingte Phase
anomaly [əˈnɒməli] n	Unregelmäßigkeit / Anomalie
anomaly of water density n	Anomalie des Wassers Dichte
anomalous density [əˌnɒmələsˈdensɪti]	Dichteanomalie
state of aggregation n	Aggregatzustand
solid adj	fest
liquid adj	flüssig
melt v	schmelzen
ice cover / sheet of ice n	Eisdecke
solubility [ˌsɒljəˈbɪləti] n	Löslichkeit
gas solubility	Löslichkeit von Gas
saturation n	Sättigung
saturation value	Sättigungswert

thermal stratification n Temperaturschichtung
epilimnion [ˌepɪˈlɪmnɪən] / surface water n Epilimnion / Oberflächenwasser
hypolimnion [ˌhaɪpəˈlɪmɪən] / deepwater n Hypolimnion / Tiefenwasser
metalimnion [ˌmetəˈlɪmnɪən] n Metalimnion
thermocline [ˈθɜːməklaɪn] / discontinuity layer n Sprungschicht
solar radiation n Sonneneinstrahlung
convection n Konvektion
uniform adj einheitlich
  uniform temperatures einheitliche Temperaturen
mix v durchmischen
  lake mixing Durchmischen des Sees
  thorough mixing gründliches Durchmischen
  contribute to mixing zur Durchmischung beitragen

circulate v umwälzen / zirkulieren
circulation n Zirkulation
  partial circulation Teilzirkulation
enrich v anreichern
exchange n Austausch
replenish [rɪˈplenɪʃ] v regenerieren / auffüllen / ergänzen
overturn v umwälzen
overturn n Umwälzung
  autumn overturn BE / fall overturn AE Herbstzirkulation
  spring overturn Frühlingszirkulation

» wind circulates | der Wind wälzt um
enrich in oxygen | mit Sauerstoff anreichern
ecosystem substrate exchange | Stoffaustausch im Ökosystem
replenishment of oxygen | Sauerstoffergänzung

stagnation [stæɡˈneɪʃn] n Stagnation / Stillstand
  summer stagnation Sommerstagnation
  winter stagnation Winterstagnation
devoid (of sth) adj ohne (etw.) sein
  water devoid of oxygen sauerstoffarmes Wasser
  deoxygenated water [diːˈɒksɪdʒəneɪtɪdˌwɔːtə] sauerstoffarmes Wasser

10 Ecology › 10.11 Lake ecosystem

anoxic conditions [æn'ɒksɪkkən͵dɪʃnz] n pl	anaerobe Bedingungen
cyclic pattern n	wiederkehrendes Muster |("
»
deprive of oxygen	Sauerstoff entziehen
accelerate the depletion of dissolved oxygen	die Abnahme des gelösten Sauerstoffs beschleunigen

Water quality of a lake

inflow n	Zufluss
outflow n	Abfluss
water income n	Wasserzufluss / Wassereinspeisung
feeder river ['fiːdə͵rɪvə] n	Zufluss *(durch einen Fluss, Nebenfluss)*
surface influents n	Oberflächenzufluss / oberirdischer Zufluss
surface effluent n	Oberflächenabfluss / oberirdischer Abfluss
seepage ['siːpɪdʒ] / leaching [liːtʃɪŋ] n	Versickerung
seep v	versickern
evapotranspiration [ɪ͵væpəʊ͵trænspə'reɪʃn] n	Evapotranspiration *(Verdunstung – abiotisch und biotisch)*
drainage basin n	Niederschlagsgebiet / Wassereinzugsgebiet
watershed / catchment area n	Wassereinzugsgebiet
oligotrophic [͵ɒlɪgə'trɒfɪk] adj	oligotroph
water clarity n	Trübungsgrad des Wassers
water transparency / Secchi depth ['sekɪ͵depθ] n	Sichttiefe *(Sichttiefe nach Secchi)*
sandy adj	sandig
rocky adj	felsig
bedrock ['bedrɒk] n	Grundgestein
lake basin n	Seebecken
lake bottom n	Seeboden
loading n	Belastung / Befrachtung
loading capacity	Belastbarkeit
nutrient loading	Nährstoffbelastung / Nährstofffracht
mesotrophic [͵mesə'trɒfɪk] adj	mesotroph
eutrophic [juː'trɒfɪk] adj	eutroph

shallow adj	flach
strata ['strɑːtə] n pl	Schichten
leaching n	Versickerung
shoreline erosion n	Infererosion
flow characteristic n	Fließeigenschaft
blanket of algae / carpet of algae n	Algenrasen
cover over v	verlanden

»
block the sunlight	das Sonnenlicht blockieren
the lake has covered over	der See ist verlandet

oxygen deficiency n	Sauerstoffmangel
oxygen depletion [ˌɒksɪdʒndɪˈpliːʃn] n	Sauerstoffzehrung / Sauerstoffverbrauch
biological oxygen demand (BOD)	biologischer Sauerstoffbedarf (BSB)
die v	umkippen

»
biologic death of a lake	biologischer Tod des Sees

The lake will die within a year or two.
Der See wird innerhalb von ein oder zwei Jahren umkippen.

Field work at a lake

water quality assessment n	Wassergütebestimmung
field work n	Arbeit vor Ort
Niskin bottle n	Schöpfflasche
sample jar ['sɑːmplˌdʒɑː] n	Probenglas
light meter n	Luxmeter
Secchi disc ['sekɪˌdɪsk] n	Secchi-Scheibe *(Sichttiefenmessung)*
turbidity [tɜːˈbɪdəti] / cloudiness n	Wassertrübung
phytoplankton net n	Phytoplanktonnetz
zooplankton net n	Zooplanktonnetz
water column [ˈwɔːtəˌkɒləm] n	Wasserkörper
epibiotic organism [ˌepiˈbaɪɒtɪkˌɔːgnɪzm] n	Aufwuchsorganismus / Aufsitzer

»
bug survey / macro invertebrates' study	Untersuchung mit dem Auge erkennbarer Wirbelloser

Silting and desilting of a lake

genesis n	Entstehungsgeschichte
glacial ['gleɪsɪəl] adj	eiszeitlich
glacial period / ice age	Eiszeit
post-glacial period	Nacheiszeit
glacier ['glæsɪə] n	Gletscher
glacier movement	Gletscherbewegung
alpine glacier	Alpengletscher
meltwater n	Schmelzwasser
river depression n	Flusssenke
moraine [mɒˈreɪn] n	Moräne
rock flour n	Gesteinsmehl
clay mud [ˈkleɪˌmʌd]	Tonmudde
shoreline forest	Uferbewaldung
humic acid n	Humussäure
limestone n	Kalk
lime-free	kalkfrei
lime mud	Kalkmudde
glacial rubble n	Moränenschotter
fen peat [ˈfɛnpiːt] / reed peat n	Riedtorf / Schilftorf
rannoch-rush / scheuchzeria n	Blumenbinsen
Scheuchzeria peat	Blumenbinsentorf
sphagnum [ˈsfægnəm] n	Torfmoos
sphagnum peat	Torfmoostorf
silt up v	verlanden
silting / silting up / siltation n	Verlandung
alder swamp n	Erlenbruchwald
raised bog n	Hochmoor
raised bog peat	Hochmoortorf
heather / heath / erica n	Heidekraut
purple moorgrass n	Pfeifengras
common lizard n	Bergeidechse
adder / European adder / crossed viper / northern viper n	Kreuzotter
dredging [drɛdʒɪŋ] n	Ausbaggern
slurry [ˈslʌri] n	Flüssigschlamm
slurry pipeline	Rohrleitung für Flüssigschlamm
velocity [vɪˈlɒsəti] n	Geschwindigkeit

aeration [eəˈreɪʃn] n	Belüftung
hypolimnetic aeration	Belüftung der Tiefenschicht
aerator [eəˈreɪtə] n	Belüfter
stirrer n	Luft-Wasser-Gemisch Rührer
diffuser [dɪˈfjuːzə] n	Belüfter
submerged diffuser	Unterwasser-Belüfter
bubbler [ˈbʌble] n	Blasdüsenrohr
bubble plume	Blasenfahne
restoration n	Sanierung
succession [səkˈseʃn] n	Sukzession / Entwicklungsabfolge
hay infusion n	Heuaufguss
white film n	Kahmhaut
primary succession n	primäre Sukzession
primary coloniser n	Pionierorganismus
pioneer species n pl	Pionierart(en)
seral stage n pl	Stufe der Sukzession
seral stage 1	erste Sukzessionsstufe
succession process n	sukzessiver Prozess
climax community n	Klimaxgesellschaft(en)
climax succession n	Klimaxstadium

»
alter deposition patterns	die Art der Sedimentation ändern
deflect succession	eine Entwicklungsabfolge ändern, verfälschen

10.12 River and stream ecosystem

lotic systems [ˌləʊtɪkˈsɪstəmz] n pl	Fließgewässer
river n	Fluss
creek [kriːk] n	Bach
rivulet [ˈrɪvjələt] n	Bächlein
stream n	Bach / Flüsschen
river bed n	Flussbett
river bottom	Flussgrund
river bed's gradient	Gefälle / Neigung des Flussbetts
steepness n	Steilheit / Gefälle
course gradient n	Gefälle des Flussverlaufs
current n	Strom / Strömung
current velocity	Fließgeschwindigkeit

10 Ecology › 10.12 River and stream ecosystem

flow rate n	Durchflussmenge / Fließgeschwindigkeit
modest flow rate	schwache Strömung
turbulence ['tɜːbjələns]	Verwirbelung / Turbulenz
drainage basin n	Niederschlagsgebiet / Wassereinzugsgebiet
river basin n	Flussbecken / Flusseinzugsgebiet / Flussgebiet
roughness *(of the stream bed)* n	Unebenheit / Oberflächenkörnung *(des Strombetts)*
depth n	Breite
deep adj	breit
width [wɪtθ] n	Weite
wide adj	weit
tributary ['trɪbjətri] n	Nebenfluss / Zufluss
confluence n	Zusammenfluss / Einmündung *(eines Nebenflusses)*
source n	Quelle
headwaters n pl	Quellgebiet
watershed / catchment area n	Wassereinzugsgebiet
upper reaches n pl	Oberlauf
trout [traʊt], *pl* trouts; trout n	Forelle
trout zone	Forellenregion
brown trout	Bachforelle
greyling *BE* / grayling *AE* n	Äsche
greyling zone *BE* / grayling zone *AE*	Äschenregion
salmonidae / salmon family *(pl)* n	Salmoniden
deepening n	Vertiefung
rebedding n	Veränderung des Bachbetts
middle reaches n pl	Mittellauf
meandering [mi'ændərɪŋ] adj	meandrierend / gewunden
lateral erosion n	Erosion an den Uferböschungen
gravel / pebbles n	Kies
leafy canopy n	Blätterdach
day-night oxygen fluctuation n	Tag-Nacht-Sauerstoffschwankungen
barb [bɑːb] / barbel ['bɑːbəl] n	Barbe
barbel zone	Barbenregion
lower reaches n pl	Unterlauf

bream [briːm] n	Brachse
bream zone	Brachsenregion
stagnant ['stægnənt] adj	stillstehend / unbewegt / stagnierend
shallow water zone n	Flachwasserzone
alluvium [ə'luːviəm] n	Schlick / Schlamm
silt [sɪlt] n	Schlick / Schlamm
alluvium n	Schwemmland
mouth of a river / delta / estuary n	Mündungsbereich
basin n	Becken
flounder n	Flunder
brackish water n	Brackwasser
salt water / sea water / marine water n	Salzwasser
fresh water n	Süßwasser
spring-fed brook n	Quellbach
meltwater n	Schmelzwasser
spring runoff n	Schneeschmelze
flood / flooding / inundation [ˌɪnʌn'deɪʃn] n	Überschwemmung
dry season n	Trockenzeit
water level n	Wasserstand

a streams' flooding cycles	periodisch auftretende Flussüberflutungen
annual spring flood	jährliche Frühlingsüberschwemmung

bedload n	Geschiebe
boulder ['bəʊldə]	Geröll
boulder bedload	Geröll / Geschiebe
current-induced adj	strömungsbedingt
stream pool / riffle ['rɪfl] n	Bereich mit geringer Strömung
stagnant water zone n	Stillwasserzone
mud bottom n	Weichboden
turbidity [tɜː'bɪdəti] n	Wassertrübung
rock bottom n	Hartboden
torrent ['tɒrnt] n	Sturzbach / reißender Strom
mountain torrent	Gebirgsbach
cataract ['kætrækt] / rapid n	Stromschnelle
cascade / waterfall n	Wasserfall
gorge [gɔːdʒ] n	Schlucht
dissolved organic matter (DOM) n	gelöstes organisches Material *(Grad der Trübung)*

10 Ecology › 10.12 River and stream ecosystem

Adaptations

adaptation n	Anpassung
current-resisting property n	Eigenschaft, die hilft, der Wasserströmung Widerstand zu leisten
clinging property n	Eigenschaft, die ein Verdriften verhindert
gill appendage [gɪləˈpendɪʤ] n	Kiemenanhang
river limpet n	Flussmützenschnecke
lung-breathing snail n	lungenatmende Schnecken
thin wall of the mantle cavity	dünne Wand der Mantelhöhle, Lungenhöhle
suck to the rock	an Gestein festsaugen
case n	Köcher
case-less	köcherlos
spotted sedge / hydropsyche [haɪdrəʊˈsaɪk] / net spinning caddis n	Wasserseelchen
net / web n	Netz
net spinner	Netzspinner
spinneret n	Spinndrüsen
thread	Faden
sticky thread	klebriger Faden
fixed retreat n	festgeheftete Wohnröhre
crevice [ˈkrevɪs] n	Spalte
crevice of rocks	Felsspalte
pupal enclosure [ˈpjuːpəlɪnˈkləʊʒə] n	Puppenhülle
safety cord n	Sicherheitsleine
anchor [ˈæŋkə] v	verankern
drift n	Verdriftung
net to filter drifting plankton	Fangnetz um Schwebplankton herauszufiltern
camouflage with	tarnen mit
dorso-ventral flattening of the body	abgeflachter Körper
smooth surface n	glatte Oberfläche
shelter n	Schutz
cavity [ˈkævəti] n	Hohlraum

air siphoning [eəˈsaɪfnɪŋ] n	Ansaugen von Luft
water surface tension n	Wasseroberflächenspannung

limnetic zone [lɪmˌnetɪkˌzəʊn] n	freie Wasserzone
body shape n	Körperform
organ structure n	Organstruktur
function n	Funktion
correlate v	korrelieren / entsprechen *(in Wechselbeziehung stehen)*

Man-made problems

riparian zone [raɪˈpeərɪənˌzəʊn] n	Uferzone
riparian deforestation	Entwaldung der Uferzone
riverine vegetation n	Uferbewuchs / Ufervegetation
building density n	Bebauungsdichte
surface sealing n	Oberflächenversiegelung
soil sealing n	Erdversiegelung
compaction [kəmˈpækʃn] n	Verdichtung
riverine traffic n	Flussverkehr
riverine zone n	Fließgewässerraum

meander straightening / river straightening n	Flussbegradigung
straight ditch / straight canal n	gerader Graben / gerader Kanal
river bed structure n	Flussbettstruktur
river bed composition n	Flussbettzusammensetzung
stream narrowing n	Verengung des Strombetts
flood protection n	Hochwasserschutz
fine grain sediment n	feinkörniges Sediment
coarse grain sediment n	grobkörniges Sediment

reservoir [ˈrezəvwɑː] / artificial lake n	Stausee
dam n	Staudamm
dam up v	aufstauen
drinking water reservoir n	Trinkwasserspeicher
lock n	Schleuse
fish pass / fish passage / fish ladder n	Fischtreppe
fish elevator n	Fischaufzug
leap up v	heraufspringen
migratory fish [ˈmaɪgrətəriˌfɪʃ] n	Wanderfisch

dredge [dredʒ] v	ausbaggern

Ecology › 10.12 River and stream ecosystem

aggradation [ˌægrəˈdeɪʃn] n	Abtragung
degradation [ˌdegrəˈdeɪʃn] n	Anschwemmung / Verlandung
water discharge n	Ablaufwasser
toxic load n	Giftstoffbelastung
wash out v	herauspülen
leaching of nutrients n	Nährsalzauswaschung
waste water n	Abwasser
air pollution n	Luftverschmutzung
run-off rainwater n	Regenwasser, das in Fluss gelangt
acidity / acid content n	Säuregehalt
renaturalise *BE* / renaturalize *AE* n	renaturieren
renaturalisation *BE* / renaturalization *AE*	Renaturalisierung

Overloading and self purification of lotic systems

outfall n	Einleitung
sewage [ˈsuːɪdʒ] n	Abwasser
sewage outfall	Abwassereinleitungsstelle
raw domestic sewage	Haushaltsabwasser
faeces *BE* / feces *AE* [ˈfiːsiːz] n pl	Fäkalien
industrial waste water n	Industrieabwasser
chemical n	Chemikalie
fertiliser *BE* / fertilizer *AE* n	Düngemittel
health hazard n	Gesundheitsgefährdung
deoxygenation n	Sauerstoffzehrung
aerobic biodegradation process n	aerober Abbauprozess
anaerobic biodegradation process n	anaerober Abbauprozess
anaerobic digestion / rotting / putrefaction [ˌpjuːtrɪˈfækʃn] n	Fäulnisprozess
rotting mud / sludge [slʌdʒ] n	Faulschlamm
overload n	Überlastung / zu große Belastung
self-purification n	Selbstreinigung
self-purification capacity	Selbstreinigungskraft
dilution [daɪˈluːʃn] n	Verdünnung
aeration [eəˈreɪʃn] n	Belüftung
dissolved oxygen (DO) n	gelöster Sauerstoff
sedimentation n	Ablagerung / Absetzen / Sedimentation
adsorption n	Anlagerung / Adsorption
phyto-remediation [ˈfaɪtərɪˌmiːdiˈeɪʃn] n	Sanierung durch Pflanzen

floatation [fləˈteɪʃn] / flotation [fləʊˈteɪʃn] n	Schwimmaufbereitung
floating solid n	Schwimmstoff
flock n	Flocke
flocculation [ˌflɒkjəˈleɪʃn] n	Ausflockung
microbial degradation n	Abbau durch Mikroorganismen

Water quality indicators

biochemical oxygen demand (BOD) n	Biologischer Sauerstoffbedarf (BSB)
bioindicator n	Bioindikator
plant indicator n	pflanzlicher Leitorganismus
animal indicator n	tierischer Leitorganismus
microbial indicator [maɪˈkrəʊbjəlˌɪndɪkeɪtə]	Mikroorganismen als Leitorganismen
accumulation potential n	Schadstoffanreicherung
cumulative [ˈkjuːmjələtɪv] adj	Gesamt~ / kumulativ
pollutant n	Schadstoff *(hier: wassergefährdender Stoff)*
contaminant n	Schadstoff
contamination n	Verunreinigung / Kontamination
sampling n	Probenentnahme
population count n	Ermittlung der Zahl der Individuen einer Population

Water quality testing

chemical testing: pH, BOD, COD; nitrate, phosphorous compounds; metals such as copper, zinc, cadmium, lead, mercury; oil, grease, petrol, hydrocarbons and pesticides **physical testing:** temperature, solid concentration, turbidity	**chemische Untersuchungen:** pH, BSB, CSB; Nitrat, Phosphatverbindungen; Metalle wie Kupfer, Zink, Cadmium, Blei, Quecksilber; Öl, Schmierstoffe, Benzin, Kohlenwasserstoffe und Pestizide **physikalische Untersuchung:** Temperatur, Konzentration der Feststoffe, Trübungsgrad

Water sources and use

ground water / underground water n	Grundwasser
spring water n	Quellwasser
surface water n	Oberflächenwasser

10 Ecology › 10.12 River and stream ecosystem

running water n	Fließgewässer / fließendes Gewässer
standing water n	stehendes Gewässer
drinking water n	Trinkwasser
cooling agent n	Kühlwasser
hydro-electric power station n	Wasserkraftwerk
thermal power station [ˌθɜːmlˈpaʊəˌsteɪʃn] n	Wärmekraftwerk
household n	Haushalt
agriculture n	Landwirtschaft
irrigation [ˌɪrɪˈɡeɪʃn] n	Bewässerung

Stormwater treatment – sewage treatment

separate sewage system n	Trennkanalisation
stormwater *(rainwater plus anything the rain carries along with it)*	Regenwasser *(Regenwasser und alles was der Regen wegschwemmt)*
storm sewage / combined wastewater n	Mischwasser
stormwater holding tank	Regenrückhaltebecken

sewage plant [ˈsuːɪdʒˌplɑːnt] n	Kläranlage
screening n	mechanische 1. Stufe einer Kläranlage

primary clarifier / primary sedimentation tank n	Absetz- oder Vorklärbecken
sludge n	Schlamm
settling sediment n	Sinkstoff
sludge trap n	Schlammfang
floating material *(e.g. oil grease etc)* n	Schwebstoffe *(z. B. Öl, Schmierstoff etc.)*
oil separator n	Ölabscheider
skim off v	abschöpfen

biological treatment n	biologische Klärstufe
aeration tank n	Belebungstank
surface aerated basin n	Belebtschlammbecken

carbon reduction n	Abbau von Kohlenstoffverbindungen zu Kohlenstoffdioxid
nitrification [ˌnaɪtrɪfɪˈkeɪʃn] n	Nitrifizierung
denitrification	Denitrifizierung
humus tank n	Nachklärbecken
return activated sludge n	Rücklaufschlamm

sludge bulking n	Blähschlammbildung
receiving water n	Vorfluter
chemical treatment n	chemische Verfahren 3. Klärstufe
precipitation agent dispensing installation n	Fällmittellöseanlage
digester ['daɪdʒestə] / digestion tank n	Faulbehälter / Faulraum
sludge tower n	Faulturm
sludge tank n	Schlammbecken
digestion [daɪ'dʒestʃn] n	Ausfaulung
sludge digestion n	Schlammfaulung
digested sludge n	Faulschlamm
aerobic sludge digestion n	aerobe Schlammbehandlung
anaerobic sludge digestion n	anaerobe Schlammbehandlung
thermophilic digestion ['θɜːməfaɪlɪkdaɪ'dʒəstʃn] n	thermophile Faulung
digester gas ['daɪdʒestəˌgæs] n	Faulgas
gasometer n	Gasometer / Gasbehälter
sludge disposal n	Schlammbeseitigung
mechanical small sewage treatment plant n	mechanische Kleinkläranlage
soakaway n	Sickeranlage

Drinking water treatment

potable ['pəʊtəbl] adj	trinkbar
potable water n	Trinkwasser
purification [ˌpjʊərɪfɪ'keɪʃn] n	Reinigung / Klärung
purify v	reinigen / klären
water purification	Trinkwasseraufbereitung
drinking water treatment n	Trinkwasseraufbereitung
drinking water treatment plant	Trinkwasseraufbereitungsanlage
water quality n	Wasserqualität

high bacteriological quality	hohe Qualität mit geringer bakterieller Verseuchung
rich in dissolved solids	reich an gelösten Stoffen
low pH value	niedriger pH Wert

raw water n	Rohwasser
bankside reservoir ['bæŋksaɪd,rezəvwɑː] n	Uferfiltration
biological purification n	biologische Reinigung
screening n	Filterung
screen filter	Grob- und Feinfilter
sand filter	Sandfilter, durch den das Wasser tröpfelt
gravel filter	Kiesfilter
suspended solid n	Schwebstoff
activated charcoal / carbon n	Aktivkohle
activated charcoal / carbon filter	Aktivkohlefilter
flocculation basin ['flɒkjəleɪʃn,beɪsn] n	Flockungsbecken
flocculation ['flɒkjəleɪʃn]	Ausflockung / Flockenbildung
flocculating agent	Flockungsmittel
coagulation [kəʊ,ægjə'leɪʃn] n	Koagulation / Flockung / Ausfällung / Gerinnung
coagulant (agent) [kəʊ'ægjʊlənt,eɪdʒənt]	Fällmittel
clarify v	reinigen
turbidity [tɜː'bɪdəti] n	Trübung
polymer ['pɒlɪmə] n	Polymer
ion exchange n	Ionenaustausch
electrodialysis n	Elektrodialyse
reverse osmosis n	Umkehrosmose
sedimentation basin / clarifier basin / settling basin n	Sedimentationsbecken
clarifier retention time n	Rückhaltezeit
residence time n	Aufenthaltszeit
weir [wɪə] n	Reuse
mechanical cleaning device n	mechanische Säuberungseinrichtung
rapid sand filter n	schneller Sandfilter
taste n	Geschmack
odour ['əʊdə] / odor AE n	Geruch
disinfection n	Desinfektion
anti-biological agent n	Desinfektionsmittel
chlorination [,klɔːrɪ'neɪʃn] n	Chlorierung
protozoan [,prəʊtəʊ'zəʊn], pl protozoa (sg unusal) n	Protozoon (Pl. Protozoa; Einzeller)

cyst [sɪst] n	Cyste *(Überdauerungsform)*
ozone n	Ozon
ozonation [ˌəʊzəʊˈneɪʃn] n	Ozonisierung
UV radiation n	UV-Bestrahlung
residual disinfectant n	Rückstände des Desinfektionsmittels
hydrogen peroxide [ˌhaɪdrədʒənpəˈrɒksaɪd] n	Wasserstoffperoxid
solar water disinfection n	Wasserdesinfektion durch Sonnenbestrahlung
water fluoridation n	Fluoridierung des Wassers
water conditioning n	Wasseraufbereitung *(in Bezug auf Einstellen des Härtegrades)*
degree of hardness n	Härtegrad
lava filter n	Lava-Filter
nutrient-free soil n	nährsalzfreie Erde
water-purifying plant n	wasserreinigende Pflanze
boiling n	Kochen
distillation n	Destillation *(über Wasserverdampfung)*
desalination [diːsælɪˈneɪʃn] n	Entsalzung
water consumption / consumption of water n	Wasserverbrauch
water shortage n	Wassermangel
virtual water / embedded water / embodied water n	virtuelles Wasser

Virtual water content and water footprint

Virtual water content of a product volume of water used to produce a product	**Virtueller Wassergehalt eines Produktes** Wassermenge, die verbraucht wird, um ein Produkt herzustellen
Water footprint water contained in a product, including the volume of water used to produce the product.	**Wasserfußabdruck** im Produkt enthaltenes Wasser, mit Angabe zur Wassermenge, die gebraucht wird, um das Produkt herzustellen

10.13 Wetland ecosystems

wetland n	Feuchtbiotop / Feuchtgebiet
waterlogged soil n	wassergesättigter Boden
saturated [ˈsatʃəreɪtɪd] adj	gesättigt
saturated with moisture	wassergesättigt / staunass

saturation n — Sättigung *(hier: Stau)*
flood / flooding / inundation — Überschwemmung / Überflutung
[ˌɪnʌnˈdeɪʃn] n
permanently adv — permanent / immer / ganzjährig
temporarily adv — zeitweilig
ponding n — Pfützenbildung

Water can be	... saltwater. ... freshwater. ... brackwater. ... brackish.	Wasser kann ...	Salzwasser sein. Süßwasser sein. Brackwasser sein. brackig sein.

salinity [səˈlɪnəti] n — Salzgehalt
  salt avoiding species — salzvermeidende Art
  salt sensitive species — Salz-intolerante Art

swamp n — Sumpf / Flachmoor
  freshwater swamp forest / flooded forest — Sumpfwald
  peat swamp forest — Bruchwald
woody debris [ˌwʊdiˈdeɪbriː] n — Holzabfall
spruce swamp n — Bruchmoor
bog [bɒg] n — Moor / Sumpf
  peat bog — Torfmoor
  raised bog — Hochmoor
sphagnum moss [ˌsfægnəmˈmɒs] n — Torfmoos
  bog forest — Hochmoorwald / Moorwald / Sumpfwald
  quaking bog — Schwingrasenmoor
acidic peat [əˌsɪdɪkˈpiːt] n — saurer Torf

The German Wadden Sea

Wadden Sea / North Sea mudflats — Wattenmeer
[ˌnɔːθˈsiːˌmʌdflæts] n
tidal flats / mudflats n pl — Wattfläche
marsh n — Marsch
  salt marsh — Salzwiese
  salt marsh cliff — Salzwiesenkliff
  pioneer zone n — Pionierzone
tidal creek / tide way / tideway n — Priel

dune [djuːn] n	Düne
landslide of dunes	dem Land zugewandte Dünenzone
summer polder ['sʌməˌpɒldə] n	Sommerpolder
dike [daɪk] n	Deich
transition zone n	Übergangszone
feeding ground n	Nahrungsbereich
migratory bird n	Zugvogel
roosting site ['ruːstɪŋˌsaɪt] n	Rastplatz
breeding site / nesting site n	Nistplatz
breeding bird n	Brutvogel
spawning ground ['spɔːnɪŋˌgraʊnd] n	Laichplatz
hydrophyte ['haɪdrəfaɪt] n	Hydrophyt / Wasserpflanze
hygrophyte ['haɪgrəfaɪt] n	Hygrophyt *(Pflanzen typischer Feuchtbiotope)*
halophyte ['hæləfaɪt] *(salt tolerant species)* n	Halophyt *(salztolerante Arten)*
optional halophyte	fakultativer Halophyt
obligatory halophyte	Eu-Halophyt *(obligat)*
halophytic adj	halophytisch
salinity n	Salzgehalt *(des Bodens)*
salt indifferent adj	Salz-indifferent
salt exclusion n	Salzausschluss *(Aufnahme über die Wurzeln erfolgt nicht)*
elymus ['elɪməs] n	Quecke
elymus athericus [ˌelɪməs'æθɜːrɪkəs] n	Dünenquecke

» | cellular osmotic adjustment | osmotische Anpassung

sea purslane ['siːˌpɜːslɪn] n	Portulak-Salzmelde
salt bladder n	Salzblase
sea thrift (armeria maritima) n	Strand-Grasnelke
sea lavender (limonium vulgare) n	Strandflieder
salt gland n	Salzdrüse
salt excretion n	Salzausscheidung

» | intraplant salt translocation | Salz wird in spezialisierten Zellen gespeichert und als Blasen abgegeben

European spoonbill n	Löffler
common eiders [ˌkɒmən'aɪdəz] n	Eiderente

10 Ecology › 10.14 Endangered marine ecosystems

Indigenous Wadden Sea species	
The **common seal**, the **grey seal** and the **harbour porpoise** are indigenous Wadden Sea species.	Der **Gemeine Seehund**, die **Kegelrobbe** und der **Schweinswal** sind im Wattenmeer heimische Arten.

shellfish-eating bird species n	schalentierfressende Vogelart
hen harrier ['hen,hæriə] n	Kornweihe
short-eared owl n	Sumpfohreule
wader species ['weɪdəˌspiːʃiːz] n	Wattvogelart
common redshank [ˌkɒmən'redʃæŋk] n	Rotschenkel
great ringed plover n	Sandregenpfeifer
Kentish plover [ˌkentɪʃ'plʌvə] n	Seeregenpfeifer
northern lapwing n	Kiebitz
oystercatcher ['ɔɪstəˌkætʃə] n	Austernfischer
curlew ['kɜːljuː] n	Großer Brachvogel
tern [tɜːn] n	Seeschwalbe
lugworm ['lʌɡwɜːm] n	Wattwurm
U- or J-shaped-burrow n	U- oder J-förmige Röhre
tail end n	Hinterende
bristle ['brɪsl] n	Borste
bushy gills n	Außenkiemen
bait n	Köder
acorn barnacle [ˌeɪkɔːn'bɑːnəkl]	Gemeine Seepocke / Gezeitenseepocke
sessile ['sesaɪl] adj	festgewachsen
common hermit crab n	Einsiedlerkrebs
carapace ['kærəpeɪs] n	Schale
whelk [welk] n	Wellhornschnecke

»

cast of coiled defecated sediment	Kothaufen in Form von Sandschnüren
adopt an empty shell	ein leeres Gehäuse annehmen (besetzen)

10.14 Endangered marine ecosystems

coastal waters n pl	Küstengewässer
oil spill n	Ölpest
pipeline n	Pipeline / Rohrleitung

oil platform n	Ölplattform
oil rig n	Ölbohrplattform / Ölbohrinsel
cleaning of tanks n	Säubern von Tanks
ocean dumping n	Verklappung
overfishing n	Überfischung
school of fish / shoal of fish / swarm of fish n	Fischschwarm
fish stock n	Fischbestand
fishing quota ['fɪʃɪŋˌkwəʊtə] n	Fangquote
bycatch n	Beifang
trawl net ['trɔːlˌnet] n	Schleppnetz
sonar ['səʊnɑː] n	Echolot

change in species composition	Veränderung in der Zusammensetzung der Fischbestände

tuna ['tjuːnə] n	Tunfisch
swordfish n	Schwertfisch
marlin ['mɑːlɪn] n	Marlin / Speerfisch
cod [kɒd] n	Dorsch / Kabeljau
halibut ['hælɪbət] n	Heilbutt
skate n	Rochen
flounder n	Flunder
salmon n	Lachs
shrimp n	Garnele / Krabbe
aquaculture ['ækwəˌkʌltʃə] n	Aquakultur
marine adj	Meeres~
marine life n	Meereslebewesen
microorganism n	Mikroorganismen
mass reproduction n	Massenvermehrung
mass blossoming n	Massenauftreten
algae bloom / algae blossoming ['ældʒiːˌblɒsmɪŋ] n	Algenblüte

10.15 Perils threatening our environment

General phrases

environment n	Umwelt
environmentalist n	Umweltschützer

10 Ecology › 10.15 Perils threatening our environment

environmental adj	die Umwelt betreffend / ökologisch
environmental studies	Umweltstudien
environmentally aware	umweltbewusst
conservation n	Erhaltung / Bewahrung
preservation n	Erhaltung
sustainable adj	nachhaltig / zukunftsträchtig
sustainable development	nachhaltige Entwicklung
sustainability n	Nachhaltigkeit
ecologically beneficial / environment saving adj	umweltschonend
environmentally friendly adj	umweltfreundlich
environmentally-friendly measure / environmentally sound measure	umweltfreundliche Maßnahme
environment compatible / ecologically sound adj	umweltverträglich
environmental stress n	Umweltbelastung
damage limitation n	Schadensbegrenzung
curtail [kɜːˈteɪl] v	begrenzen / eindämmen
protection n	Schutz
protect v	schützen
prevent v	verhindern
prevention n	Verhinderung
preventative adj	vorbeugend / vorsorglich
preventative measure	Präventivmaßnahme
restore v	wiederherstellen
quality of life n	Lebensqualität
resource n	Ressource / Mittel
wildlife activist n	Naturschützer
habitable [ˈhæbɪtəbl] adj	bewohnbar
inhabitable adj	unbewohnbar
extinction [ɪkˈstɪŋkʃn] n	Aussterben / Extinktion
extinction of species	Aussterben von Spezies / Artensterben
extinct adj	ausgestorben *(auf der ganzen Welt)*
biodiversity [ˌbaɪəʊdaɪˈvɜːsəti] n	Artenvielfalt / Biodiversität
extirpate [ˈekstɜːpeɪt] v	ausrotten
extirpated	ausgerottet *(in einem speziellen Ökosystem)*

biologically impoverished	verarmt (an Arten- und Lebensraumvielfalt)
do nothing about a problem	nichts gegen ein Problem unternehmen
do something about it	etwas dagegen unternehmen
examination of currently available details / data	Untersuchung gegenwärtig vorliegender Einzelheiten / Daten
prediction / forecast / prognosis for sth	Voraussage / Prognose für etw.
call for / demand for sth	Forderung nach etw.

pollution [pəˈluːʃn] n	Verschmutzung
pollutant n	Schadstoff
pollute v	verschmutzen
polluting adj	umweltschädlich / umweltverschmutzend
polluted adj	umweltverschmutzt / verunreinigt / verschmutzt
contaminate v	verseuchen / verunreinigen
contamination n	Verseuchung
load n	Last
load v	belasten

equilibrium [ˌiːkwɪˈlɪbriəm] n	Equilibrium / Gleichgewicht
balance n	Balance / Gleichgewicht
fragile [ˈfrædʒaɪl] adj	anfällig / zerbrechlich
sensitive adj	empfindlich
feeble [ˈfiːbl] adj	schwach / unwirksam
delicate [ˈdelɪkət] adj	empfindlich
imbalance n	Ungleichgewicht
imminent [ˈɪmɪnənt] adj	bevorstehend
impact n	Auswirkung / Einfluss / Einwirkung
vicious circle [ˌvɪʃəsˈsɜːkl] n	Teufelskreis

have an impact on sth	Auswirkung haben auf etw. / sich auf etw. auswirken / etw. beeinflussen
upset the delicate balance	das empfindliche Gleichgewicht stören

danger n	Gefahr
endanger v	bedrohen / gefährden
peril [ˈperɪl] n	Gefährdung / Gefahr / Risiko / Risiken

10 Ecology › 10.15 Perils threatening our environment

imperil [ɪmˈperl] v	gefährden
imperilled adj	gefährdet
threat n	Bedrohung / Gefährdung / Gefahr
threaten v	bedrohen / drohen
menace [ˈmenɪs] n	Androhung / Drohung / Bedrohung / Plage / Landplage / drohende Gefahr
hazard [ˈhæzəd] n	Gefährdung
risk n	Risiko
risky adj	riskant
devastate [ˈdevəsteɪt] v	zerstören
ravage [ˈrævɪdʒ] v	verwüsten
poison v	vergiften
poisonous [ˈpɔɪznəs] adj	giftig
toxic adj	giftig
harmful adj	schädlich
noxious [ˈnɒkʃəs] adj	schädlich / ungesund
lethal [ˈliːθl] adj	tödlich

Biomagnification

insidious [ɪnˈsɪdiəs] adj	schleichend / heimtückisch
insidious poisoning	schleichende Vergiftung
pest n	Schädling
chemical pest control	chemische Schädlingsbekämpfung
pesticide n	Schädlingsbekämpfungsmittel / Pestizid
herbicide n	Unkrautvernichtungsmittel / Herbizid
fungicide n	Pilzvernichtungsmittel / Fungizid
insecticide [ɪnˈsektɪsaɪd] n	Insektenvernichtungsmittel / Insektizid
accumulate [əˈkjuːmjəleɪt] v	anreichern
accumulation of	Anreicherung von
biomagnification [ˌbaɪəʊmægnɪfɪˈkeɪʃn] / bioamplification [ˌbaɪəʊæmplɪfɪˈkeɪʃn] / bioaccumulation [ˌbaɪəʊəˌkjuːmjʊˈleɪʃn] n (the progressive build up of persistent substances by successive trophic levels such as DDT)	Anreicherung eines schwer bis nicht abbaubaren Stoffes (durch sein Durchlaufen der auf einanderfolgenden Nahrungsebenen wie z.B. DDT)

DDT n	DDT (Insektizid)
malaria [məˈleəriə] n	Malaria

mosquito [mɒsˈkiːtəʊ] n	Stechmücke
Anopheles [əˈnɒfɪliːz] n	Anopheles *(Stechmückengattung)*
vector [ˈvektə] n	Überträger / Vektor
ornithologist [ˌɔːnɪˈθɒlədʒɪst] n	Vogelkundler / Ornithologe
eggshell n	Eischale
bird of prey n	Raubvogel
bald eagle n	Weißkopf-Seeadler
sea eagle n	Seeadler
extinction n	Aussterben / Extinktion
threatened by extinction	vom Aussterben bedroht
food chain n	Nahrungskette
zooplankton n	Zooplankton / tierische Kleinstlebewesen
phytoplankton [ˈfaɪtəʊˌplæŋktən] n	Phytoplankton / pflanzliche Kleinstlebewesen
body fat n	Körperfett

Endangered species and nature conservancy

nature conservancy [ˈneɪtʃəkɒnˌsɜːvnsi] n	Naturschutz
habitat map n	Biotopkarte / Biotopkartierung
biotope order [ˈbaɪətəʊpˌɔːdə] n	Biotopordnung
biotope protection n	Biotopschutz
habitat system	Biotopverbundsystem
habitat network n	Biotopverbundnetz
biotope network n	Biotopvernetzung
beaver [ˈbiːvə] n	Biber
American beaver	Nordamerikanischer Biber
European beaver	Europäischer Biber
Red List n	Rote Liste
extinction risk n	Gefährdungsgrad
reserve / sanctuary [ˈsæŋtʃʊəri] n	Schutzgebiet
protective measure n	Schutzmaßnahme
juniper heathland / juniper heath [ˈdʒuːnɪpəˌhiːθlænd] n	Wacholderheide
sheep grazing n	Schafbeweidung
tending strategy n	Pflegemaßnahme
scythe (sth) [saɪð] v	(etw.) mähen *(mit der Sense)*

10 Ecology › 10.15 Perils threatening our environment

conservation of nature	Erhaltung der natürlichen Lebensgrundlage

natural monument / natural landmark n	Naturdenkmal
ineffective adj	wirkungslos
nature reserve / conservation area n	Landschaftsschutzgebiet
buffer zone n	Pufferzone
biosphere reserve n	Biosphärenreservat
forest reserve n	Bannwald im Sinne von Schonwald
forest management n	forstliche Bewirtschaftung
forest area n	Waldfläche
Wadden Sea n	Wattenmeer
Bavarian Forest National Park n	Nationalpark Bayerischer Wald
Swabian mountains / Swabian highlands n pl	Schwäbische Alb

Invasive alien species

indigenous species [ɪnˌdɪdʒɪnəsˈspiːʃɪz] n	heimische Art
introduced species n	eingeschleppte Art
invasive species [ɪnˌveɪsɪvˈspiːʃɪz] n	invasive Art *(die sich selbstständig im neu eingeführten Ökosystem ausbreitet)*
introduce v	aussetzen / einschleppen
knowingly adj	bewusst
unknowingly adj	unbewusst
stowaway [ˈstəʊəˌweɪ] n	blinder Passagier
import (of) n	Einfuhr (von)

on the verge of extinction	am Rand des Aussterbens
patch habitat	inselartiger Lebensraum
economic damage	wirtschaftlicher Schaden

Varroa mite [ˈværəʊəˌmaɪt] n	Varroa Milbe
grape phylloxera [ˈgreɪpfɪˌlɒksrə] n	Reblaus
giant hogweed [ˌdʒaɪəntˈhɒgwiːd] n	Riesenbärenklau

Industrial farming versus ecological farming

industrial farming n	industrielle Landwirtschaft
monoculture n	Monokultur
monocultural farming n	Anbau in Monokulturen
crops n pl	Feldfrüchte / Saat / Gesamternte
soil exhaustion n	Auslaugen des Bodens
soil erosion n	Bodenerosion / Bodenabtragung
soil fertility n	Bodenfruchtbarkeit
desertification n	Versteppung / Wüstwerdung
infertile adj	unfruchtbar
genetic diversity n	Artenvielfalt
paddy field ['pædiˌfiːld] n	Reisfeld

husbandry / animal husbandry n	Viehhaltung / Viehzucht
mass animal farming / mass livestock farming / intensive animal husbandry	Massentierhaltung
manure [məˈnjʊə] / dung [dʌŋ] n	Dung / Mist
liquid manure	Gülle
farm slurry [ˈfɑːmˌslʌri]	Jauche
fertilizer n	Düngemittel / Dünger
dairy produce n	Molkereiprodukte / Milchprodukte
cattle n pl	Rinder / Vieh
bowl n	Eingeweide / Darm
methane (CH$_4$) n	Methan

»
mineral salts seep into ground water	Mineralsalze sickern in das Grundwasser

ecological farming n	ökologische Landwirtschaft
humane husbandry / species appropriate husbandry n	artgerechte Tierhaltung
chemical-free adj	ohne chemische Stoffe / Chemie-frei
compost [ˈkɒmpɒst] n	Kompost
repress v	unterdrücken
weed n	Unkraut
mixed cultivation n	Mischkulturen
outdoor cultivation n	Freilandhaltung

»
repression of weeds by sowing in between	Unterdrückung des Unkrauts durch Zwischenpflanzung

The "waste-problem"

rubbish *BE* / garbage *AE* / refuse / trash / litter / junk n	Abfall / Müll
waste management n	Müllbeseitigung
disposal [dɪˈspəʊzl] n	Beseitigung
degradable [dɪɡreɪdəbl] adj	abbaubar
biodegradable [ˌbaɪədɪˈɡreɪdəbl] adj	biologisch abbaubar
recycling n	Wiederverwertung
recycle v	wiederverwerten

»

reprocessing plant	Wiederaufbereitungsanlage
reprocess raw materials	Rohstoffe wiederaufbereiten

throw-away adj	Wegwerf-
disposable bottle / non-returnable bottle n	Einwegflasche
returnable bottle n	Mehrwegflasche
bottle bank n	Altglascontainer / Flaschencontainer
convenience packaging [kənˈviːniənsˌpækɪdʒɪŋ] n	verbraucherfreundliche Verpackung / benutzerfreundliche Verpackung
scrap iron [ˈskræpˌaɪən] n	Alteisen
scrap yard n	Schrottplatz

»

built-in obsolescence / planned obsolescence	geplanter Verschleiß

drain pipe [ˈdreɪnˌpaɪp] / waste pipe n	Abflussrohr *(im Gebäude)*
sewer [sʊə] n	Abflussrohr *(unterirdisch)*
dump [dʌmp] / tip / refuse dump n	Müllhalde
dumping ground	Müllhalde / Müllkippe
dump v	wegwerfen
compost heap n	Komposthaufen
special waste n	Sondermüll
high-level radioactive waste	hochradioaktiver Müll

incinerating plant [ɪnˈsɪnreɪtɪŋˌplɑːnt] n	Müllverbrennungsanlage
incinerator	Verbrennungsofen
grille [ɡrɪl] n	Rost
clinker [ˈklɪŋkə] n	Schlacke
steam turbine [ˈstiːmˌtɜːbaɪn] n	Dampfturbine

filtering facilities n pl	Filteranlagen
scrubber ['skrʌbə] n	Filteranlage *(zur Gasreinigung)*
exhaust n	Abgase
dioxin [daɪˈɒksɪn] n	Dioxin

clean the exhausts	Abgase reinigen
particulate screening device	Ruß- / Staubfilter

Air pollution

air pollution n	Luftverschmutzung
energy consumption n	Energieverbrauch
emission n	Ausstoß / Emission
emit v	ausstoßen
industrial plant n	Fabrik / Fabrikanlage
immission n	Immission *(Niederschlag des Ausstoßes/der Emission)*
immit v	ablagern / aufnehmen

emissions from industrial plants	Emissionen von Industrieanlagen

fossil fuel n *(oil, coal)*	fossiler Brennstoff
renewable [rɪˈnjuːəbl] adj	erneuerbar
carbon monoxide n	Kohlenmonoxid
carbon dioxide n	Kohlenstoffdioxid
hydrocarbon [ˌhaɪdrəˈkɑːbn] n	Kohlenwasserstoff
nitrous oxide [ˌnaɪtrəsˈɒksaɪd] n	Stickstoffoxid
acid rain n	saurer Regen

increase in CO_2 levels	CO_2-Anstieg

chimney n	Kamin / Schornstein *(z. B. bei einem Haus)*
furnace / stack [stæk] n	Industrieschornstein
further afield [ˌfɜːðəəˈfiːld] adj	weiter weg
vicinity [vɪˈsɪnəti] n	Nachbarschaft
respiratory disorder n	Erkrankung der Atemwege
asthma [ˈæsθmə] n	Asthma

10 Ecology › 10.15 Perils threatening our environment

bronchitis [brɒŋ'kaɪtɪs] n	Bronchitis
stonework n	Mauerwerk

» „high stacks" policy | Politik der „hohen Schornsteine"

emission filter n	Emissionsfilter
curb [kɜːb] v	eindämmen / verringern
combat ['kɒmbæt] v	bekämpfen

»
reduce emissions of toxic / harmful substances / pollutants	Ausstoß von Schadstoffen verringern
command-and-control strategies	Zwangsmaßnahmen / ordnungsrechtliche Maßnahmen

combustion [kəm'bʌstʃn] n	Verbrennung
combustion engines	Verbrennungsmotoren
lean-burn engine n	Magermotor
catalytic converter n	Katalysator
exhaust fumes n pl	Auspuffgase / Abgase
lead n	Blei
unleaded	bleifrei
fuel efficiency n	Energieeinsparung

smog n *(smoke together with fog)*	Smog
inversion [ɪn'vɜːʃn] n *(weather condition)*	austauscharme Wetterlage
atmospheric inversion	atmosphärische Inversion
atmospheric layering	atmosphärische Schichtung
atmospheric circulation	atmosphärische Zirkulation
atmospheric particulate	atmosphärischer Schwebstoff
domestic coal fire n	Hausbrand
power station n	Kraftwerk
lighting n	Beleuchtung
suffocate ['sʌfəkeɪt] v	ersticken
public transport n	öffentlicher Verkehr

CFCs (chlorofluorocarbons) n	FCKWs
aerosol can ['eərəsɒl,kæn] n	Spraydose
refrigerant [rɪ'frɪdʒrənt] n	Kühlmittel
insulation [,ɪnsjə'leɪʃn] n	Isolierung

foam n	Schaumstoff
solvent ['sɒlvənt] n	Lösungsmittel
chlorine ['klɔːriːn] n	Chlor
appliance / gadget ['gædʒɪt] / apparatus [ˌæprˈeɪtəs] / device n	(Haushalts-)Gerät

Climate

Climate

climate record	Klimabeobachtung
climate change	Klimaveränderung
climate controlling factors	auf das Klima einwirkende Faktoren
stable climatic conditions	stabile Klimaverhältnisse
temperate climate	gemäßigtes Klima
continental climate	Kontinentalklima
marine climate	Seeklima

atmospheric monitoring n	atmosphärische Überwachung
atmospheric composition n	atmosphärische Zusammensetzung

》

cooler / warmer than mean / average temperature	kälter / wärmer als die Durchschnittstemperatur
a winter warmer than usual	ein zu warmer Winter

atmospheric aerosol n	atmosphärisches Aerosol
atmospheric ozone n	atmosphärisches Ozon
ozone layer n	Ozonschicht
deplete [dɪˈpliːt] v	verringern
depletion n	Verringerung / Schwund
ozone depletion	Ozonschwund
ozone hole n	Ozonloch
greenhouse / hothouse ['hɒthaʊs] n	Treibhaus
greenhouse effect / hothouse effect	Treibhauseffekt
natural greenhouse effect	natürlicher Treibhauseffekt
anthropogenic greenhouse effect [ˌænθrəpəʊdʒenɪkˈgriːnhaʊsɪˌfekt] / man-made greenhouse effect	anthropogener Treibhauseffekt
greenhouse gas	Treibhausgas
ozone-oxygen cycle n	Ozon-Sauerstoff Kreislauf

10 Ecology › 10.15 Perils threatening our environment

triatomic ozone molecule [ˌtraɪəˈtɒmɪkˌəʊzəʊnˌmɒlɪkjuːl] n	dreiatomiges Ozonmolekül
diatomic molecular oxygen [ˈdaɪəˌtɒmɪkməˈlekjələˌɒksɪdʒən] n	zweiatmiges molekulares Sauerstoffmolekül
free oxygen atom n	freies Sauerstoffatom
"M" = third body n	M = „dritter Stoßpartner"

ozone molecules absorb ultraviolet radiation	Ozonmoleküle absorbieren UV Strahlung
atomic oxygen reacts with other oxygen molecules to reform ozone	atomarer Sauerstoff verbindet sich mit anderen Sauerstoffmolekülen, um Ozon zu regenerieren
carry off excess reaction energy	überschüssige Reaktionsenergie abtransportieren
ozone removal	Ozonzerfall
kinetic energy of molecular motion	kinetische Energie der Molekularbewegung

free radical n	freies Radikal
hydroxyl [haɪˈdrɒksɪl](OH) n	Hydroxyl
nitric oxide [ˌnaɪtrɪkˈɒksaɪd](NO) n	Nitroxyl
chlorine [ˈklɔːriːn](Cl) n	Chloratom
bromide [ˈbrəʊmaɪd](Br) n	Bromatom
catalyse [ˈkætəlaɪz] v	katalysieren
recombination reaction n	Rekombinationsreaktion
decomposition reaction [ˌdiːkɒmpəˈzɪʃnriˌækʃn] n	Zerfallsereignis
tens of thousands n	zehntausende

stable balance of ozone production by solar radiation and removal by recombination	stabiles Gleichgewicht zwischen Ozonproduktion durch UV-Strahlung und Ozonzerfall durch Rekombination
overall amount of ozone	Gesamtmenge an Ozon

thermal radiation n	Wärmestrahlung
intensify [ɪnˈtensɪfaɪ] v	verstärken / intensivieren
global warming n	Erderwärmung
radiation n	Strahlung
ultra-violet radiation	UV-Strahlung
waste heat n	Abwärme

cloud cover n	Wolkendecke
evaporation [ˌɪvæpəˈreɪʃn] n	Verdunstung
drought [draʊt] n	Dürre
biosphere [ˈbaɪəsfɪə] n	Biosphäre / Lebensraum
skin cancer n	Hautkrebs

> | | |
> |---|---|
> | be reflected by | reflektiert werden von |

fermentation process [fɜːmenˈteɪʃnˌprəʊses] n	Gärungsprozess
methane (CH_4) n	Methan
digestive process n	Verdauungsprozess
cellulose [ˈseljələʊs] n	Zellulose

global warming potential (GWP) n	Klimawirksamkeit eines Gases
retention period [dɪˈtenʃnˌpɪərɪəd] n	Verweildauer
sea level n	Meeresspiegel
flood / flooding / inundation [ˌɪnʌnˈdeɪʃn] n	Überflutung / Überschwemmung
glacier [ˈglæsɪə] n	Gletscher
gulf stream [ˈgʌlfˌstriːm] n	Golfstrom
coral n	Koralle
coral reef	Korallenriff
bleach v	ausbleichen
feedback n	Rückkopplung
positive feedback	positive Rückkopplung
negative feedback	negative Rückkopplung
unprecedented [ʌnˈpresɪdntɪd] adj	noch nie da gewesen / beispiellos
unpredictable adj	nicht voraussagbar / nicht vorhersehbar / schwer einschätzbar / unberechenbar
living space n	Lebensraum
surface of the earth n	Erdoberfläche

Nuclear power

nuclear power plant n	Atomkraftwerk
fallout n	radioaktiver Niederschlag
cancer [ˈkænsə] n	Krebs
caesium *BE* / cesium *AE* [ˈsiːzɪəm] n	Caesium
irradiate [ɪˈreɪdieɪt] v	verstrahlen

10 Ecology › 10.15 Perils threatening our environment

reprocessing plant n	Wiederaufbereitungsanlage
nuclear waste n	Atommüll

> phasing out of nuclear energy | Ausstieg aus der Kernenergie

Population dynamics

developed country n	Industriestaat
transition country / newly industrialized country / threshold country n	Schwellenstaat
developing country n	Entwicklungsland
divide n	Kluft / Spalt
disparity [dɪˈspærəti] n	Ungleichheit / Verschiedenheit
stage n	Stadium / Stufe
feature n	Merkmal
deficiency [dɪˈfɪʃnsi] n	Unzulänglichkeit
scarcity [ˈskeəsəti] n	Mangel
urbanise BE [ˈɜːbnaɪz] / urbanize AE v	verstädtern
urbanisation BE / urbanization AE n	Verstädterung

population growth n	Bevölkerungswachstum
overpopulation n	Überbevölkerung
family planning n	Familienplanung
birth rate n	Geburtenrate
survival n	Überleben
survive v	überleben
infant mortality n	Kindersterblichkeit
life expectancy n	Lebenserwartung
poverty n	Armut

contraceptive [ˌkɒntrəˈseptɪv] n	Verhütungsmittel
income n	Einkommen
higher income	besseres (höheres) Einkommen
social benefits n pl	Sozialleistungen
social security n	Sozialversicherungssystem / soziale Sicherheit

education n	Bildung
level of education	Bildungsniveau
infant marriage n	Kinderehe
sex education n	sexuelle Aufklärung

» to become economically independent | wirtschaftlich unabhängig werden

hygiene ['haɪdʒiːn] n	Hygiene
hygienic adj	hygienisch
sanitation [ˌsænɪ'teɪʃn] n	Sanitäreinrichtungen / sanitäre Anlagen
epidemic [ˌepɪ'demɪk] n	Seuche / Epidemie
epidemic adj	ansteckend / epidemisch
typhoid ['taɪfɔɪd] n	Typhus
dysentery ['dɪsntri] n	Ruhr
measles ['miːzlz] n	Masern
whooping cough n	Keuchhusten
tuberculosis [tjuːˌbɜːkjə'leʊsɪs] n	Tuberkulose
AIDS n	AIDS

vaccine ['væksiːn] / serum n	Impfstoff
vaccination [ˌvæksɪ'neɪʃn] n	Impfung
inoculation [ɪˌnɒkjə'leɪʃn] n	Impfung
inoculate v	impfen
disinfectant [ˌdɪsɪn'fektənt] n	Desinfektionsmittel

diet n	Kost / Nahrung
malnutrition n	Mangelernährung
nutritious [njuː'trɪʃəs] adj	nahrhaft
exploit v	ausbeuten / ausschöpfen / zunutze machen
refine [rɪ'faɪn] v	veredeln
process v	weiterverarbeiten
cocoa ['kəʊkəʊ] n	Kakao
soybean n	Sojabohne
sorghum ['sɔːɡəm] / mille n	Hirse
locust infestation ['ləʊkəstˌɪnfes'teɪʃn] n	Heuschreckenbefall
parched [pɑːtʃt] adj	verdörrt / versengt

»

cash crop	für den Verkauf bestimmte Anbaufrucht
combat desertification	das Vordringen von Wüsten bekämpfen / der Versteppung Einhalt gebieten
development aid / foreign aid n	Entwicklungshilfe
GNP (Gross National Product) n	Bruttosozialeinkommen

11 Reproduction, growth and development › 11.1 Asexual reproduction

> **Agenda 21**
>
> | | |
> |---|---|
> | local Agenda 21 | lokale Agenda 21 |
> | 21 stands for the 21st century | 21 steht für das 21. Jahrhundert |
> | think globally – act nationally | global denken – national handeln |
> | act locally | lokal, vor Ort handeln |
> | plan of action | Aktionsprogramm |
> | sustainable development | nachhaltige Entwicklung |

energy demand n	Energiebedarf
energy balance n	Energiebilanz
energy consumption n	Energieverbrauch
total final energy consumption (tfec)	Endenergieverbrauch
Energy Conservation Act n	Energieeinsparungsgesetz
energy conservation / energy saving	Energieeinsparung
turn of energy policies n	Energiewende

11 Reproduction, growth and development

11.1 Asexual reproduction

reproduction n	Vermehrung *(für alles Lebendige)*
propagation [ˌprɒpəˈgeɪʃn] n	Vermehrung *(Pflanzen)*
proliferation [prəˌlɪfrˈeɪʃn] n	Vermehrung *(Tiere)*
asexual reproduction	ungeschlechtliche Fortpflanzung
vegetative reproduction	vegetative Fortpflanzung
mitotic division [maɪˈtɒtɪkdɪˌvɪʒn] n	mitotische Teilung / Kernteilung
totipotency [ˌtəʊtɪˈpəʊtənsi] / totipotence n	Totipotenz
stable habitat n	stabiler Lebensraum
living conditions n	Lebensbedingungen
favourable / favorable *AE* adj	günstig
unfavourable adj	ungünstig
rapid adj	schnell
rapid distribution	schnelle Ausbreitung
offspring, *pl* offspring n	Nachkomme(n)
characteristic / trait / quality n	Eigenschaft
maintain v	erhalten
maintain a characteristic	eine Eigenschaft erhalten

hereditary [hɪˈredɪtri] adj	erb~
hereditary identical	erbgleich
hereditary information	Erbinformation
clone [kləʊn] n	Klon
genetic variability n	genetische Vielfalt
variance [ˈveərɪəns] n	Verschiedenheit / Streuung
regeneration n	Regeneration
unicellular organism [ˌjuːnɪseljələˈɔːgənɪzm] n	einzelliger Organismus
bisection [baɪˈsekʃn] / binary fission [ˌbaɪnriˈfɪʃn] n	Zweiteilung
longitudinal [ˌlɒndʒɪˈtjuːdɪnl] adj	längs
transverse adj	quer
fission / section n	Teilung
transverse fission / transverse section	Querteilung
multiple fission	Vielfachteilung
budding [ˈbʌdɪŋ] n	Sprossung
pinch off v	abschnüren
baker's yeast n	Bäckerhefe
brewer's yeast n	Bierhefe
hyphen [ˈhaɪfn] n	Hyphen *(Pilzfäden aus denen sich Fruchtkörper entwickeln)*
fungus [ˈfʌŋgəs], *pl* fungi [ˈfʌŋgaɪ] n	Pilz
mold [məʊld] n	Schimmelpilz
mildew [ˈmɪldjuː] n	Mehltaupilz
spore [spɔː] n	Spore
mito-spore [ˈmaɪtəʊspɔː]	Mito-Spore *(durch Mitose entstandene Spore)*
alga [ˈælgə], *pl* algas; algae n	Alge
fern [fɜːn] n	Farn
moss n	Moos
reproductive unit n	Fortpflanzungszelle
basic food resource n	Nahrungsgrundlage
suitable adj	geeignet
vegetative reproduction n	vegetative Fortpflanzung
parent n	Eltern
multicellular parent organism	vielzelliger Elternorganismus
lesser calendine [ˌleseˈkæləndaɪn] n	Scharbockskraut
leaf axil [ˈliːfˌæksɪl] n	Blattachsel
leaf bud n	Blattknospe

11 Reproduction, growth and development › 11.1 Asexual reproduction

cell tissue n	Zellgewebe
callus ['kæləs] n	Kallus
runner n	Ausläufer
aerial runner	oberirdischer Ausläufer
subterranean runner [ˌsʌbtəˌreɪnɪənˈrʌnə]	unterirdischer Ausläufer
strawberry n	Erdbeere
creeping buttercup *(ranunculus repens)* n	Kriechender Hahnenfuß
quack grass / couch grass n	Quecke
deadnettle ['dednetl] n	Taubnessel
root tuber n	Wurzelknolle
dahlia ['deɪlɪə] n	Dahlie
stem tuber n	Sprossknolle
potato n	Kartoffel
bulb n	Zwiebel
bulblet n	Brutzwiebel
cutting n	Steckling
graft [grɑːft] v	pfropfen
grafting n	Propfung
scion [saɪən] n	Edelreiser
rootstock ['ruːtstɒk] n	Unterlage
fuse [fjuːz] v	verwachsen
vascular cambium [ˌvæskjʊləˈkæmbɪəm] n	Kambium der Leitbündel / Leitbündelkambium

> | | |
> |---|---|
> | susceptible to diseases | Anfällig für Krankheiten |
> | less / more susceptible to diseases | weniger / mehr krankheitsanfällig |

daughter cell n	Tochterindividuum
multicellular daughter cell	vielzelliges Tochterindividuum
separate v	ablösen
hydra ['haɪdrə] n	Süßwasserpolyp
coral species n	Korallenart
reef-building adj	Riff aufbauend
intra-tentacular budding [ˌɪntrətenˈtækjələˌbʌdɪŋ] / gemmation [dʒeˈmeɪʃn] n	Knospung im Fangarmbereich *(Bildung von Dauerknospen vielzelligen Dauerstadien)*
gemmule ['dʒemjuːl] n	Dauerknospe
oral disc n	Mundöffnung

extratentacular budding n	Knospung *(in der Nähe der Fußscheibe)*
bryozoan [ˌbraɪəˈzəʊən] / moss animals n	Moostierchen / Bryozoen
colony, *pl* colonies n	Tierstock / Kolonie

pinch off n	Abschnürung
fragmentation n	Abbrechen *(von Körpersegmenten)*
flatworm n	Plattwurm
echinoderm [ɪˈkaɪnədɜːm] n	Stachelhäuter
sea anemone [ˈsiːəˌneməni] n	Seestern

11.2 Sexual reproduction » III. 1 Human body – 1.6 Sexuality, human reproduction and life cycle

Basics

gamete [ˈɡæmiːt] n	Gamet / Keimzelle
diploid [ˈdɪplɔɪd] adj	diploid *(doppelter Chromosomensatz)*
meiosis [maɪˈəʊsɪs] n	Meiose
haploid [ˈhæplɔɪd] adj	haploid *(einfacher Chromosomensatz)*
isogamy [aɪˈsɒɡəmi] n	Isogameie *(Gameten sind gleicher Größe)*
anisogamy [ˌænaɪˈsɒɡəmi] n	Anisogamie *(Gameten ungleicher Größe)*
oogamy [əʊˈɡəmi] n	Oogamie *(die unbewegliche Eizelle ist größer als die männlichen Gameten)*
attractant [əˈtræktənt] n	Lockstoff
insemination [ɪnˌsemɪˈneɪʃn] n	Besamung
fertilisation *BE* / fertilization *AE* n	Befruchtung
zygote [ˈzaɪɡəʊt] n	Zygote

oviparous [əʊˈvɪpərəs] adj	Eier legend / ovipar
ovoviparous [ˌəʊvəʊvɪˈvɪpərəs] adj	ovovivipar *(„Ei-lebend geboren" – Eier werden im Leib ausgebrütet Jungtiere schlüpfen noch vor Eiablage im Leib)*
viviparous [vɪˈvɪpərəs] adj	lebend gebärend

The process of fertilisation – animals

jelly coat n	Gallerthülle
oocyte [ˈəʊəsaɪt], *pl* oocytes n	Eizelle / Oocyte

413

acrosome ['ækrəsəʊm] n	Akrosom
acrosome filament ['ækrəsəʊmˌfɪləmənt]	Akrosomfaden
acrosome reaction	Lockerung des Eirindengewebes am Befruchtungshügel
vitelline layer [vɪˌtelɪn'leɪə] n	Eirinde
sperm [spɜːm], *pl* sperms; spermatozoa [ˌspɜːmətə'zəʊɒn] n	Spermium *(Pl. Spermien)*
head n	Kopf
middle piece n	Mittelstück
tail n	Schwanzteil
fertilisation membrane n	Befruchtungsmembran
centriole ['sentriəʊl] n	Centriol
mitochondrion [ˌmaɪtə'kɒndrɪɒn], *pl* mitochondria n	Mitochondrium
digest ['daɪdʒest] v	abbauen
enlarge v	vergrößern
fuse v	vereinigen
first division n	erste Teilung
fallopian tube [fəˌləʊpiən'tjuːb] / oviduct ['əʊvɪdʌkt] n	Eileiter

parthogenesis [ˌpɑːθɪnə'dʒenɪsɪs] n	Parthenogenese / Jungfernzeugung
parthenogenetic adj	parthenogenetisch
special case n	Sonderfall
fertilised *BE* / fertilized *AE* n	befruchtet
fertilised egg	befruchtetes Ei
unfertilised egg	unbefruchtetes Ei
stick insect / walking sticle n	Stabheuschrecke
rotifer ['rəʊtɪfə] n	Rädertierchen
aphid ['eɪfɪd] n	Blattlaus
drone [drəʊn] n	Drohne
queen bee n	Königin
worker (bee) n	Arbeiterin

Alternation of generations – animals

medusa [mɪ'djuːzə], *pl* medusae [mɪ'djuːziː] n	Meduse
jellyfish, *pl* jellyfish n	Qualle
larval form [ˌlɑːvl'fɔːm] n	Larvenform
sessile polyp [ˌsesaɪl'pɒlɪp] n	festsitzender Polyp
winter egg n	Wintereier *(Wasserfloh)*
summer egg n	Sommereier

Seed development: Germination and growth

germination [ˌdʒɜːmɪˈneɪʃn] n	Keimung
germinable adj	keimfähig
seed dormancy [ˈsiːdˌdɔːmənsi] n	Keimruhe
vernalisation *BE* / vernalization *AE* [ˌvɜːnəlaɪˈzeɪʃm] n	Keimung nach einer Frostperiode
induce v	induzieren / einleiten / hervorrufen / veranlassen
cell division region / growing point / growth region n	Zellteilungszone
apical meristem [ˌæpɪklˈmerɪstem] n	Apikalmeristem / Wachstumskegel
cell elongation region [ˈseliːlɒŋɡeɪʃnˌriːdʒn] n	Zellstreckungszone
cell differentiation region n	Differenzierungszone
root cap / calyptra [kəˈlɒptrə] n	Wurzelhaube

Ontogeny – mammals » III. 1 Human body – 1.6 Sexuality, human reproduction and life cycle

ontogeny [ɒnˈtɒdʒəni] n	Ontogenese *(Keimesentwicklung)*
undifferentiated cell n	undifferenzierte Zelle
animal pole n	animaler Pol
vegetal pole n	vegetativer Pol
marginal zone n	Randzone
cleavage [ˈkliːvɪdʒ] n	Furchung
cleave, cleft, cleft v	furchen
cleavage furrow [ˈkliːvɪdʒˌfʌrəʊ]	Furche
morula [ˈmɔːrʊlə] n	Maulbeerkeim / Morula
blastomere [ˈblæstəʊmɜː] n	Blastomere
blastocyst [ˈblæstəˌsɪst] n	Blastocyste
blastocoel [ˈblæstəʊsiːl] n	Keimhöhle
embryoblast [ˈembrɪəʊˌblɑːst] n	Embryoblast
trophoblast [ˈtrɒfəblæst] n	Trophoblast
chorionic villus [kɔːrɪˌɒnɪkˈvɪləs] n	Chorionzotten
human chorionic gonadotropin hormone (HCG / hCG) [ˌhjuːmən kɔːrɪˌɒnɪk ˌɡɒnədəʊˈtrəʊpɪn ˈhɔːməʊn] n	Human choriongonadotropin (HCG) *(Trophoblastenhormon)*
pregnancy test n	Schwangerschaftstest
embedding [ɪmˈbedɪŋ] n	Einnistung
embed v	einnisten

11 Reproduction, growth and development › 11.2 Sexual reproduction

placenta [pləˈsentə] n	Plazenta
placental barrier	Plazentaschranke

gastrulation [ˌgæstrʊˈleɪʃn] n	Gastrulation
gastrula [ˈgæstrʊlə] n	Gastrula
germ layer n	Keimblatt
developmental fate n	Grundmuster
anlage [ˈʌnlɑːgə] n	Anlage
organ anlage	Organanlage

ectoderm [ˈektəʊˌdɜːm] n	Ektoderm
mesoderm [ˈmesəʊˌdɜːm] n	Mesoderm
endoderm [ˈendəʊˌdɜːm] n	Endoderm
organogenesis [ˌɔːgnəʊˈdʒenɪsɪs] n	Organogenese *(Anlage der Organe)* / Ontogenese
somitogenesis n	Differenzierung des dorsalen Mesodermstreifens Somit *(Ursegment)*
somitomere n	Entstehung der Körpergestalt
neurulation [ˌnjʊərəˈleɪʃn] n	Neurulation
neural crest [ˌnjʊərəlˈkrest] n	Neuralwulst
neural plate n	Neuralplatte
neural tube n	Neuralrohr
notochord [ˈnəʊtəkɔːd] / chorda dorsalis [ˌkɔːdədɔːˈseɪlɪs] n	Notochord / Chorda dorsalis *(Vorstufe der Wirbelsäule)*

primitive gut / archenteron [ɑːˈkentərɒn] n	Urdarm
primitive gut / coelom [ˈsiːləm] n	Urdarmhöhle
blastopore [ˈblæstəʊpɔː] / primitive mouth n	Urmund
secondary coelom n	sekundäre Leibeshöhle / Coelom
morphogenesis [ˌmɔːfəˈdʒenɪsɪs] n	Morphogenese *(Entwicklung der Körpergestalt Neumundtier: Deuterostomier)*
deuterostome [ˈdjuːtərəstəʊm] n	Altmundtiere
protostome [ˈprəʊtəstəʊm] n	Protostomier

optic vesicle n	Augenblase
rudiment n	Rudiment
pharyngeal arch [fəˌrɪndʒɪəlˈɑːtʃ] n	Kiemenbogen
pharyngeal pouch [fəˌrɪndʒɪəlˈpaʊtʃ] n	Kiementasche
pharyngeal cleft [fəˌrɪndʒɪəlˈkleft] n	Kiemenspalt
fetus [ˈfiːtəs] n	Fötus / Fetus

amniotic fluid [ˌæmnɪɒtɪkˈfluːɪd] n Fruchtwasser
premature birth [ˌpremətʃəˈbɜːθ] n Frühgeburt

Ontogeny – amphibians

unequal adj inäqual
micromere n Mikromer
macromere n Makromer
pigmented adj pigmentiert
  dark pigmented   dunkel pigmentiert
blastula stage [ˌblæstjʊləˈsteɪdʒ] n Blasenkeim / Blastula
yolk [jəʊk] n Dotter
metamorphosis [ˌmetəˈmɔːfəsɪs] n Metamorphose
tadpole [ˈtædpəʊl] n Kaulquappe
respiration by gills n Kiemenatmung

Ontogeny – birds and reptiles

yolk sac [jəʊkˈsæk] n Dottersack
blastula [ˌblæstjʊlə] n Blastula
neural groove n Neuralrinne
amnion [ˈæmnɪən] n Amnion
allantois [əˈlæntəʊɪs] n Allantois *(embryonaler Harnsack)*
serosa [sɪˈrəʊsə] n Serosa *(äußere embryonale Membran, Chorion)*

air cell n Luftkammer
albumen [ˈælbjʊmən] n Eiweiß
chalaza [kəˈleɪzə], *pl* chalazae n Hagelschnur

> blastula forms a flattend disc | Blastula bildet eine flache Scheibe

Determination and differentiation

self-assembly n Selbstkonstruktion
self-organisation n Selbstorganisation
regulation n Regulation
regulate v regulieren
determination [dɪˌtɜːmɪˈneɪʃn] n Determination
determine v determinieren / bestimmen / festlegen

11 Reproduction, growth and development › 11.2 Sexual reproduction

prospective potency n	prospektive Potenz
prospective fate n	prospektive Bedeutung
developmental disturbance n	Störung der Entwicklung
mosaic embryo [məˌzeɪkˈembrɪəʊ] n	Mosaiktyp *(Zellen z. T. bereits nach 1. Teilung determiniert)*
regulative embryo [ˌregjələtɪvˈembrɪəʊ] n	Regulationstyp *("Schicksal" der Zellen wird schrittweise bestimmt)*
map v	kartieren / kartografieren

» | migration of cells | Wanderbewegung der Zellen |

isolation experiment n	Isolationsversuch
ovum of newt [ˈəʊvəməvˌnjuːt] n	Molchei
grey crescent [greɪˈkresnt] / animal hemisphere [ˌænɪməlˈhemɪsfɪə] n *(dark pigmented)*	grauer Halbmond
tissue transplantation n	Gewebetransplantation
induction n	Induktion
induce v	auslösen

» | organisational determinant of the local environment | ortsgemäße Determination (Bestimmung) |
| determination by site | herkunftsgemäße Determination (Bestimmung) |

abnormal development n	abweichende Entwicklung
host n	Wirt
host tissue	Wirtsgewebe
host cell	Wirtszelle
donor [ˈdəʊnə] n	Spender / Donor
donor tissue	Spendergewebe
organiser (region) n	Organisator
interaction n	Wechselwirkung / Wechselbeziehung
adjacent cell [əˈdʒeɪsntˌsel] n	benachbarte Zelle
detect v	erkennen
respond (to sth) v	(auf etw.) reagieren
re-orient v	neu orientieren
irreversibility [ˌɪrɪˌvɜːsəˈbɪləti] n	Unabänderlichkeit
irreversible adj	unabänderlich / irreversibel *(nicht mehr rückgängig zu machen)*

gene regulation n	Genregulation
blastopore ['blæstəʊpɔː] n	Urmund
dorsal lip of blastopore	dorsale Urmundlippe
molecular cue [məˌlekjələ'kjuː] n	Signalstoff
transcription factor n	Transkriptionsfaktor
regulatory protein n	regulatorisches Protein / Regulatorprotein
cascade [kæs'keɪd] n	Kaskade

pattern formation n	Musterbildung
concentration gradient n	Konzentrationsgradient
anterior-posterior axis n	Körperachse
morphogen gene ['mɔːfədʒnˌdʒiːn] n	Morphogen
regulatory gene n	Regulatorgen
segmentation gene n	Segmentierungsgen
homoeotic gene BE / homeotic gene AE [ˌhəʊmɪɒtɪk'dʒiːn]	homöotisches Gen
homoeobox BE / homeobox AE ['hɒmɪəbɒks]	Homöobox
concur (with) [kən'kɜː] v	übereinstimmen (mit)
in-line / post~ adj	nachgeschaltet
transcriptional regulatory factor	Transkriptionsregulationsfaktor
similar sequence	ähnliche Reihenfolge

»   in early evolution | zu einem frühen Zeitpunkt der Evolution

Historic experiments

developmental regulation n	Entwicklungssteuerung
acetabularia [ˌæsɪtæbjə'eərɪə] (unicelluar green alga) n	Acetabularia *(einzellige Grünalge)*
cap n	Schirm
graft onto [grɑːft] v	aufpropfen
knockout method n	Knock-out Verfahren
targeted knock out	gezieltes Ausschalten
loss n	Ausfall
deduce [dɪ'djuːs] v	rückschließen
nuclear transplantation n	Kerntransplantation
xenopus [zenəʊ'pʌs] / African clawed frog n	Xenopus / Krallenfrosch
differentiated cell n	ausdifferenzierte Zelle

419

denucleate oocyte entkernte Eizelle / kernloses Ei
  [dɪˌnjuːklɪeɪtˈəʊəʊsaɪt] n
clone v klonieren
udder cell [ˈʌdəˌsel] n Euterzelle

Englisches Stichwortregister

A-horizon 360
A-site 213
AB0 system 87, 199, 239
abdomen 53, 375
aberration 191
abiotic 329
abiotic factor 281
abiotic pollination 104
abnormal development 418
abort 200
abortion 74, 200
abscissa 41
absorb 148, 231, 246, 304
absorption 77, 231, 246
abundance 330
accelerate 131
accessory pigment 148
acclimatisation 330
accommodate 67
accumulate 148, 178, 249, 317, 344, 348, 398
accumulation 148, 178, 227, 344, 348
accumulation potential 387
acetabularia 419
acetic acid 167
acetyl 142
acetylcholine 68, 320, 326
achene 114, 118, 120
acid conditions 77
acid mantle 86
acid rain 352, 354, 403
acidic 21
acidic conditions 137
acidic peat 392
acidification 153
acidity 21, 136, 386
acknowledgements 36
acorn 123, 357
acoustic attraction 308
acquired disease 275
acrocentric 190
acrosome 193, 414
acrosome reaction 221
actin 164, 321
actin filament 63
action potential 318
action spectrum 148
activate 234
activated 215
activated charcoal 390
activation energy 131

activator 211, 215
active site 132
active substance 255
active transport 175
activity of an enzyme 137
adapt 215, 324
adaptation 136, 281, 324, 329, 384
adaptive 86
adaptive immune system 231
adaptor molecule 231
add water 171
adder 380
additive colour mixing 324
adenine 205
adenosine triphosphate 192
adhere 231
adhere to 102
adhesion culture 177
adipose tissue 61, 333
adjacent antenna pigments 148
adjacent cell 418
adjustment 324, 329
ADP 128
adrenalin 68, 327
adsorption 386
advantage 139, 340
advantage of heterozygosity 203
adventitious 96
adventitious root 115, 116
adverse 237
adverse immune reaction 87
aeration 361, 373, 381, 386
aeration tank 388
aerator 381
aerenchyma 105, 141, 373
aerenchymatous tissue 141
aerial root 109
aerobic 141
aerobic biodegradation process 386
aerobic sludge digestion 389
aerosol 277
aerosol can 404
affect sth 135
affected 196
afferent arteriole 84
affinity chromatography 268
affordable 276
agar 258
agar plate 266

agaric 355
age 227
agglutinate 235
agglutination 88, 235
aggradation 386
aggressive behaviour 314
aggressiveness 343
agitate 20
agonistic behaviour 304
agouti 182
agriculture 187, 271, 294, 349, 388
Agrobacterium tumefaciens 271
aid 93
AIDS 89, 240, 409
aim 34
air 81
air cell 417
air pollution 386, 403
air pressure 81
air sac 97, 375
air siphoning 385
air spaces 336
air-passage 373
airlift fermenter / bioreactor 256
alarm call 304
albinism 197
albino 182
albumen 417
albumin 117
alcohol 29, 167
aldehyde 167
aldehyde group 147
alder 48, 122
alder marsh 373
alder swamp 380
alderfly 370
aldosterone 85
aleurone layer 117, 216
alga 17, 92, 287, 374, 411
algae bloom 395
align 253
alkaline 21
alkaline conditions 137
alkaline solution 250, 263
alkalinity 136
alkaloid 121
alkanol 167
all-or-nothing principle 318
allantois 417

421

allele 181, 277, 280
allele frequency 203
Allen's rule 334
allergen 87, 237
allergenic 272
allergic 272
allergic asthma 237
allergic shock 88
allergy 87, 237, 272
allocate 249
allosteric enzyme 138
allosteric inhibition 138
alluvium 383
α-amylose 170
alphoid DNA 245
alter 131, 136, 343
alternate 112
alternate with 92
alternation of generations 91, 193
alternative exon usage 218
alternative splicing 236
altruism 308
altruistic behaviour 308
alveolus 54, 81
amacrine cell 323
amaryllis family 115
amber snail 371
Ames test 220
amine 167
amino acid 168
amino acid binding site 214
amino acid chain 212
amino acid metabolism 197
amino acid sequence 212
amino group 167
aminoacyl-tRNA synthetase 214
ammonia 154, 350
ammonia salt 154, 350
ammonification 155, 351
ammonium ion 154, 350
ammonium 83
amniocentesis 201
amnion 417
amniotic fluid 417
amoeba 26, 359
amount of energy 131
amphibian 17, 222, 290
amphipatic 172
amphoteric 169
amplification 246
amplify 65, 246, 249
amplitude 64
amplitude code 320

ampulla 65
amylase 129, 257
anabolism 124
anaerobe 144
anaerobic 144
anaerobic biodegradation process 386
anaerobic digestion 386
anaerobic sludge digestion 389
analogous 284
analogous structure 342
analogy 284, 342
analyse 12, 297
analysis 297
analyst 297
anaphase 188
anaphylactic 237
anatomic structure 284
anatomy 15, 53
ancestor 181, 291
anchor 373, 384
anchoring 337
anchoring root 109
androecium 102
androgen 73
anemone 49
anemophily 97
aneuploidy 191
Angelman syndrome 198
angiosperm 194
angiotensin II 85
animal 17
animal cell 158
animal communication 295
animal emotions 295
animal husbandry 187
animal indicator 387
animal pole 223, 415
anion 179
anisogamy 413
anisolecital 223
anlage 416
anneal 247
annealing 247
annotate 253
annual 110, 336
annual plant 115
annual species 364
annular DNA 162
annulus 96
annulus cell 95
anode 179
anomaly 376
Anopheles 399

anoxic conditions 378
ant 52, 359
antagonist 63
antenna 375
antennapedia 225
anterior 224
anterior horn 68, 326
anterior vena cava 79
anterior-posterior axis 419
anther 102
antheridium 92
antheridium mother cell 100
anthocyanin 163
anthranilic acid 218
anthropogenic 347
anthropology 15
anti-A 88
anti-B 88
anti-biological agent 390
anti-D antibody 200
anti-D prophylaxis 199
anti-inflammatory drug 341
antibiotic 260, 266
antibody 86, 140, 176, 178, 231
antibody class 235
antibody diversity 235
antibody producing 235
antibody production 200, 234
anticipation 306
antidiuretic hormone 85
antifreeze 360
antigen 86, 232, 234
antigen receptor 234
antigen presenting protein 238
antigen-antibody reaction 87
antiparallel 206
antipodal cell 103
antiport 175
antisense technique 211
antisense technology 274
anus 53
anvil 65, 284
anxiety 306
aorta 54, 78
ape 309
apex 66
aphid 414
apical meristem 415
apocarpous 113
apocynous 113
apoenzyme 130
apolipoprotein B 219
apoptosis 227
aposematic colouration 340
appear 217

appearance 217
appendage 334, 375
appendix 76
apple 48
apple with storage quality 367
appliance 405
application 139
application point 318
apply 12
apprehension 306
approach 131
approximation 345
aquaculture 395
aquatic ecosystem 369
aquatic moss 374
aquatic plant 336, 374
aqueous solution 139
aquifer 369
arachnid 17, 341, 365
arbitrary 261
arch 292
Archaea 156
archaebacteria 162
archaeopteryx 289
arched 291
archegonium 92
arginin synthesis 218
arginine 277
arid 152
arid region 336
arid-tolerant 187
arm bone 62
arm span 198
aroma 274
aromatic 273
array 254
arrest 190
arrow 347
art 294
arteriole 79
artery 54, 78, 79
arthropod 17
artifical interference 226
artificial selection 282
artificially synthesised 254
asexual reproduction 91, 193, 221
ash 48
assemble in swarms 376
assimilate 349
association 306
associative learning 300
asterisk 36
asthma 403

asymmetrical 44
asymptotic 344
at random 343
AT-rich region 245
atavism 285
atavistic 285
atmosphere 347
atmospheric aerosol 405
atmospheric composition 405
atmospheric monitoring 405
atmospheric ozone 405
atmospheric water 349
atom 165
ATP 128, 317
ATP dependent 265
ATP synthase 150
atrial and ventricular diastole 79
atrioventricular node 79
atrioventricular valve 79
atrium 54
attach 214, 231, 234, 254
attract 101, 166
attract attention 314
attractant 304, 413
attraction by scents 308
attributable 274
auditory nerve 65
auditory ossicle 284
Australopithecus afarensi 291
autecological 329
autecology 329
autoantibody 88, 239
autoimmune deficiency 239
autoimmune disease 88, 239
autoimmunity 88
autonomic nervous system 68, 326
autonomous 260
autoradiograph 244
autoradiography 178, 192, 248
autosomal 196
autosome 190, 196
autotrophic 93
auxotroph 258
availability 274
avalanche forest 354
average 39
average fragment length 262
avoid 201, 238, 299
avoidance 299
award 314
awn 117
axil 99

axis 41
axon 68, 315, 326
axon membrane 317
aye-aye 309
azidothymindine 240
AZT 89
B cell 87, 233
B-Horizon 361
BAC 252
back bone 223
back mutation 220
backbone 205
backer 308
backswimmer 370
bacteria culture 260
bacterial cell wall 162
bacterial colony 259
bacterial contamination 128
bacterial lawn 259
bacterial nodule 119
bacterial plasmid 267
bacterial protein fragments 234
bacterial strain 204
bacterium 17, 161, 230, 234, 255, 287, 359
baculum 72
badger 50, 357
bait 394
baker's yeast 411
balance 64, 397
balanced 347
balanced equation 141
bald eagle 399
banana family 115
band 179, 191, 243, 251
banding pattern 264
bankside reservoir 390
bar 186, 299
barb 382
bark 99, 123
bark beetle 358
bark-boring insect 360
barley 49, 116, 257
barnacle 52
barrier 173
barrier contraceptive 74
Bartholin's gland 71
basal layer 61
base 66
base analogue 220, 240
base of grass 364
base pair 206, 243, 262
based on 298
basement membrane 79

basic chain 93
basic food resource 411
basilar membrane 325
basin 383
basswood 48
bastard branch 362
bat 50
bat pollination 107
batch culture 255
Bavarian Forest National Park 400
be related 309
be taken up 348
bead 206
beaker 28
bear 49, 94
beaver 50, 399
become entangled 100
become visible 266
bedload 383
bedrock 361, 378
bedstraw family 122
bee 53, 106
beech 48
beech family 123
beehive 305
beetle 53, 107
behave 146
behaviour 70, 295
behavioural 295
behavioural pattern 297
behavioural sciences 15
behavioural thermoregulation 333
bell animacule 375
bell curve 42
bell-shaped 107
bellflower family 120
benefit 298
benefits of behaviour 295
benign 228
bent stile 119
benthos 376
benzanthracene 220
Bergmann's rule 334
berry 114
beta-carotene 274
beta-galactosidase 268
biflagellate 94
bicarpellary 113
biennial plant 115
bilaterally symmetrical 120
bilayer 173
bilberry 48

bile 77
bind 132, 216
binding 263
binding partner 219
binocular microscope 24
binoculars 31
biochemical oxygen demand 387
biochemistry 15
biocoenosis 329
biodiversity 283, 396
bioethics 15
biogas 156
biogeochemical cycle 349
bioindicator 387
bioleaching 157
biological 15
biological clock 331
biological oxygen demand 379
biological purification 390
biological research centre 296
biological traits 342
biological treatment 388
biologist 15
biology 15
biology store 27
bioluminescence 128
biomagnification 398
biomass 145, 347
biome 353
biometallurgy 157
biorhythm 331
biosensor 140
biosphere 347, 407
biosphere reserve 400
biotechnology 15, 255
biotic 329
biotic factor 281
biotic pollination 106
biotope 329
biotope network 399
biotope order 399
biotope protection 399
bio~ 15
biped 291
bipedalism 61
bipolar cell 324
bipolar nerve cell 68, 326
birch 48
birch family 122
birch forest 353
birch tree 203
bird 17
bird characteristic 289

bird flu 90
bird of prey 51, 399
bird pollination 107
bird song 303
birdlike 289
birth control pill 74
birth rate 343, 408
bisection 411
bisexual 97, 106
bitter constituent 152
biuret reaction 29
biuret test 29
bivalve 52
black locust 357
black redstart 367
black smoker 286
black widow 321
blackberry 48
blackbird 50, 358
blacken 244, 251
blackfly larva 370
blackthorn 356
bladder 54
blanket of algae 379
blastocoel 222, 415
blastocyst 74, 415
blastodisc 224
blastoma 228
blastomere 222, 415
blastopore 222, 416, 419
blastula 222, 417
blastula stage 417
bleach 407
blind spot 67, 323
blindworm 51
blink reflex 322
block 215, 246, 273
blood 54, 59, 160
blood cell 58
blood circulatory system 70
blood clots 275
blood clotting 78, 197
blood clotting factor 276
blood donor 197
blood exchange 200, 239
blood flow velocity 79
blood goup A/B/AB/0 239
blood group 87, 199
blood group system 199, 239
blood pressure 79, 238
blood transfusion 88, 239
blood vessel 54, 62, 67, 76, 79, 84, 332
blood-feeding insect 346

blossom 359
blossoming time 359
blot 244, 250
blotting paper 244
blubber 333
blue alga 359
blue-green alga 162
bluebell 363
blueberry 355
bluejay 358
body axes 224
body cell 58
body defence mechanism 61
body fat 399
body fluid 241
body length 196
body mass 196, 334
body proportion 334
body shape 385
bog 373, 392
bog forest 354
bog iron ore 157
boggy 368
Bohr effect 82
boil 22
boiling 391
boiling point 22
bolete 355
bolus 77
bond 133, 166, 206
bonded to 128
bonding 133
bone 293
bone cell 58
bone layers 62
bone marrow 59, 160, 233, 239
bone matrix 62
bone structure 62
bone tissue 62, 160
boom-bust cycle 344
boost 279
booster 107
borage family 121
bostryx 114
botany 15
bottle bank 402
bottom-dwelling animal 376
botulinum toxin 321
boulder 383
bovine 241
bow and arrow 293
bowl 401
bowl shaped 292
Bowman's capsule 84

box elder 357
brachydactyly 197
bracket 36
brackish water 383
bract 105, 116, 118, 121
bract scale 100
bracteole 105
brain 68, 318, 326
brain skull 292
brainstem 69, 328
bran 117
branch 110
branched 315
brawn 314
Brazil nut 272
break down 171, 348
breakdown product 257
bream 383
breast 54
breast milk 241
breath cycle 82
breathing tube 375
breed 271
breeding 187, 282, 339
breeding bird 393
breeding site 393
brewer's yeast 257, 411
brightly-coloured 106
brightness value 324
bristle 185, 394
bristletail 359
brittle 93
broad 111
broad-leafed tree 48
broken down rocks 361
bromide 406
bronchioles 81
bronchitis 404
bronchus 54, 81
bronze 293
brood 338
brood care 222
brook 369
broom 368
brow ridge 292
brown bear 357
Brownian motion 174
bryophyta 94
bryophyte 48
bryozoan 413
BSE 89, 241
bubbler 381
bud 91, 101, 110
bud off 228

budding 411
buffer 362
buffer zone 400
buffered solution 140
bug 52
bugle 363
building block 128, 168
building block of proteins 167
building block principle 235
building density 385
building stage 368
bulb 110, 336, 356, 412
bulblet 412
bulbous corydalis 356
bullying 314
bumblebee 53
Bunsen burner 28
buoyancy 374, 376
buoyant density 177
burrow 333
bursa of Fabricius 233
burst 190, 240
burst through 108
bush-cricket 365
bushy gills 394
butanoate-producing bacterium 145
buttercup 363
buttercup family 118
butterfly 52, 106, 364
buttress 109
butyric acid 145, 167
buzz pollination 106
buzzard 51, 358
by eye 37
by magnifying glass 37
by microscopy 37
bycatch 395
C segment 236
C-horizon 361
C_0t-curve 245
C4 photosynthesis 152
cabbage family 120
cactus 49
caddisfly 52, 370
caesalpiniaceae 119
caesium 407
cage 299
calanoida 371
calcitonin gene 218
calcium carbonate crystals 325
calcium phosphate 261
callus 412
callus culture 271

425

calyptra 95
calyx 101, 124
cambium ring 99
camouflage 240, 282, 340
camouflaged 240
campodea 359
Canada goldenrod 367
Canadian pond weed 374
canal 219, 369
cancer 228, 270, 407
cancer cell 236
cancer therapy 229
cannibalism 343
canopy 356
cap 210, 213, 355, 419
capillary 54, 79, 233
capillary action 148
capillary force 361
capillary transfer 244
capillary wall 80
capital letter 180
capping 210
capping process 210
capsid 89, 240
capsule 95, 114, 204
capsule lid 95
captivity 313
carapace 394
carbohydrate 75, 117, 164, 170
carbohydrate-rich 121
carbon 349
carbon atom 167
carbon dioxide 350, 403
carbon dioxide acceptor 151
carbon dioxide transport 82
carbon monoxide 350, 403
carbon particle 229
carbon reduction 388
carbonate 350
carboniferous era 95
carbonyl compound 167
carbonyl group 167
carboxyl group 167
carboxylic acid 167
carcinogen 229, 261
carcinogen-mouse 275
carcinogenic 228
carcinoma 228
cardiac cycle 79
cardiac output 79
carline thistle 368
carnation family 121
carnivore 346
carnivorous 346

carnivorous plant 368
carotene 147
carotenoid 147, 163
carp 51, 274, 371
carpel 102, 120, 180, 194
carpel margin 102
carrier 196
carrier protein 175
carrying capacity 343, 344
cartilage cell 58
cartilage tissue 59, 160
caryopsis 114, 117
cascade 226, 383, 419
case 384
casein 257
Casparian strip 161
catabolism 125
catalase 129
catalyse 129, 406
catalyst 129
catalytic converter 404
cataract 383
Catastrophism 280
caterpillar 364
cathode 179
cation 179
catkin 105, 124
cattle 187, 241, 401
cave 294
cave painting 294
cavity 102, 222, 384
cDNA 253, 267
cDNA library 268
cease 242
caecum 77
celery family 119
cell 16, 158, 188, 207
cell culture 177
cell debris 177
cell differentiation region 415
cell division 91
cell division control gene 229
cell division region 415
cell elongation region 415
cellextension 315
cell marker 87
cell membrane 63, 162
cell organelle 287
cell plate 190
cell sap 163
cell sorter 177
cell surface molecule CD4 240
cell suspension 177
cell theory 159

cell tissue 412
cell type 58, 237
cell wall 161
cellobiose 170
cellular element 78
cellular respiration 141, 227
cellulose 152, 161, 170, 407
cement 76
centiMorgan 185
centipede 359
central axis 100
central nervous system 68, 326
centrifugation 176, 258
centrifugation tube 209
centrifuge 21, 28, 176, 190, 208, 259
centriole 164, 414
centromere 189
centromeric 190
centrosome 164
cereal 117, 187
cerebellum 69, 328
cerebral cortex 69, 327
cerebral hemisphere 69, 327
cerebrum 69, 292, 327
cervix 71, 74
CFCs 404
CFTR gene 198
chaetognath 370
chaffinch 358, 368
chain 66, 143, 323
chain termination method 248
chalaza 103, 417
chamber of the eye 66
chamomile 48
change the social position 314
channel for chloride ions 198
channel protein 175, 275
chanterelle 355
chaparral 353
character 179
characteristic 217, 410
characteristic feature 13
Chargaff's rule 206
charge 136, 179, 243
chart 41
chemical 63, 322, 386
chemical communication 303
chemical composition 170
chemical evolution 286
chemical mutagen 220
chemical scissors 261
chemical treatment 389
chemical-free 401

chemistry 15
chemosynthesis 153
chemosynthesiser 153
chemotaxis 91
chest 198
chi-square test 39
chiasma 185, 192
chiasmatic 185
chick 372
chiffchaff 368
childbirth 74
chimney 403
chimney sweeper 228
chin 292
chironimid 370
chironomid 191
chlamydomonas 92
chlorination 390
chlorine 405, 406
chlorophyll 147, 163
chloroplast 147, 163, 182
chlorotic 331
CHO cell 268
cholera 90
cholesterol 171
chopper 293
Chorea Huntington 197
chorionic gonadotropin 74
chorionic villus 415
chorionic villus sampling 201
chorismic acid 218
choroid 67
chromatid 189
chromatin 189, 207
chromatogram 23, 151
chromatography 23
chromoplast 163
chromosomal mutation 220
chromosomal walking 252
chromosome 182, 189, 287
chronic inflammatory
  rheumatism 239
chylomicron 77
chymotrypsin 129
cider 367
ciliary muscle 67
ciliate 112, 359, 370
cilium 81, 161
cinnabar 186
circle of cilia 375
circle of friends 313
circular DNA 259
circular 112
circular DNA 287

circular pattern 305
circulate 377
circulation 377
circulation system 284
circulatory system 54, 60
cis region 163
citric acid 142, 167
citric acid cycle 142
citrulline 218
city forest 354
Cl⁻ ions 317
claret 185
clarifier retention time 390
clarify 390
class 16
class switching 236
classical conditioning 300
classification 16
classify 12, 191
claw 290
clawed frog 222
clay 361
clay mineral 362
clay mud 380
clay soil 337
clay-humus complex 361
cleaning of tanks 395
cleavage 73, 141, 261, 415
cleavage furrow 189
cleavage type 223
cleave 205, 261, 415
cleave off 268
cleft jaw 201
cleft lip 201
cleft palate 201
cleistogamy 104
click beetle 365
climax community 381
climax succession 381
climbing root 109
climbing stem 110
clinging property 384
clinical trials 277
clinker 402
clitoris 54, 71
clone 87, 236, 252, 265, 411, 420
close up 100
closed system 350
closed vessel 255
clot 140
cloud cover 407
clover 48, 363
cloverleaf 214
club moss 95

club-shaped 94
cluster 100, 333
cnidarian 193, 370
CO_2 fixation 151
coagulate 257
coagulation 390
coal seam 95
coarse adjustment knob 25
coarse grain sediment 385
coastal waters 394
coat 182, 237
coated particle 261
coating 177
cobnut 122
coccyx 285
cochlea 65, 325
cochlear duct 66, 325
cock 309
cockroach 52
cocksfoot 363
cocoa 409
cod 395
code 249
coding 217
coding region 259
coding strand 210
codominant 199
codon 213
coelacanth 289
coenocarpium 115
coenzyme 130
coevolution 280
coexist 338
cofactor 130
cognition 325
cognitive ability 310
coil 207
coitus 72
colchicine 190
cold 61
coleoptile 117
coleorhiza 117
collect data 35
collecting duct 84
collection 64
collide 135
colon bacterium 260
colon cancer 229
colony 204, 266, 307, 340, 413
colony hybridisation 252
colony lift 252
colour change 266
colour triangle 324
colourless 237

colpidium 26
coltsfoot 48
comb 243, 305
combat 404
combustion 141, 349, 404
combustion of methane 156
commensal 340
commensalism 340
comment fighting 307
commercial 139
commercialisation 279
commitment step 138
common 237
common bedstraw 364
common bent 363
common eiders 393
common evening primrose 367
common hermit crab 394
common lizard 380
common moorhen 372
common noctule 358
common pigeon 367
common quaking grass 363
common redshank 394
communication 293
community 329
community ecology 329
compaction 385
companionship 313
compare 251
comparison 13
compartment 173
compatibility 238
compatible 242, 265
compensation depth 373
compensation level 373
compete 337
competition 254, 281, 337
competitive 254
competitive inhibition 138
competitive inhibitor 138
complement 247
complement system 86, 231
complementary 206, 213, 244, 265
complementation analysis 185
complete flower 101
complete medium 217
complex ring structure 147
complexity 127, 245
component 165, 329
composite flower 118
compost 401
compost heap 402

compound 166
compound eye 323
compound leaf 111
concentration gradient 174, 225, 317, 419
conception 73
concern 279
conciliation 314
conclude 18
conclusion 18
concur 419
concurrence 342
condensation 169
condense 169, 188, 192, 349
condensed 192
condition 19, 298
condom 74, 241
conduct 317
conductive tissue 94
conductor 196
cone 66, 98, 194, 323
confluence 382
confuse 13
congenital disease 196
congenital disorder 196
conifer 48, 98, 194
coniferous forest 354
coniine 321
conjugation 94, 183
connective tissue 61, 79, 102, 160, 198
connective tissue cell 58
conscience 200
consensus 253
consequence 201
conservation 396
conservative 209
conspecies 338
conspecific 310
constant 39, 344
constant pressure 126
constant region 235
constituent 14
constituent monosaccharides 151
constitutive 215
constrict 332
construct 266
consume 348
consume energy 125
consumer 346
contact allergy 237
contact behaviour 311
contaminant 256, 387

contaminate 256, 397
contamination 387, 397
continue 248
continuous conduction 319
continuous fermentation 256
continuous variation 196
contraception 74
contraceptive 408
contract 63, 66
contracted 63
contractile vacuole 335
contraction 81
contrast 324
control 271
controller 64, 323
convection 377
convenience packaging 402
converge 223
convergence 284, 342
convergent 284
conversion 124
convert 65, 124
convert into 23
cooling 332
cooling agent 388
copepod 371
copper 216
copulate 193
copulation 193, 308
copy 310
coral 407
coral fungus 355
coral reef 370
coral species 412
corda 223
core body temperature 332
cork 99
cork oak 123
corm 110
cormorant 51
corn 49
cornea 66, 238
corolla 101
coronary blood vessel 54
coronary vessel 140
corpus callosum 69, 327
corpus cavernosum 55
corpus luteum 71, 73
correlate 334, 385
correlation 39
cortical reaction 193
corydalis 49
corymb 114
cosmid 252

cotton ball 29
cotton boll worm 272
cotton bud 29
cotton wool 29
cotyledon 98, 117, 216
cough 198, 322
counterconditioning 301
countercurrent heat exchange system 333
countercurrent multiplier system 84
counting mechanism 227
couple 129
coupled 185
coupled reaction 129
course gradient 381
course of disease 240
courtship 331
courtship ritual 304
cover over 379
covering 97
coverslip 27
cow brain 89
cow parsley 363
cow pox 90
cowslip 363
CpG-island 198
crab spider 365
crack 212
cramp 238, 321
crane fly 365
cranesbill family 121
crash 344
crassulacean acid metabolism 153
crawling motion 311
crayfish 52
cream 257
create 125
creating traditions 310
Creationism 280
creek 381
creeping buttercup 412
creeping soft grass 363
crenate 112
crested dog's-tail 363
Creutzfeldt-Jakob disease 242
crevice 366, 384
cricket 52
criminology 249
Cro-Magnon 291
crocus 49
crop 187, 271, 272
crop wild relative 187

crops 401
cross 181, 187
cross pollenise 103
cross pollination 103
cross section 216
cross species 242
cross-linking 220
crossbreed 104, 181
crossing over 192
crossing scheme 181
crossing-over 185
crossover value 185
crowding 343
crown 76, 182
crown gall 271
crucible tongs 28
crustacean 17, 371
cryptic coloration 282
cryptogam 95
CsCl-gradient 209
cuckoo 50
cuckoo flower 363
'cuckoo spit' 365
cucumber 48
culm 116
cultigen 188
cultivate 187, 255, 267
cultural evolution 293
cultural landscape 366
culture 255, 310
culture medium 154, 209, 266, 350
culture supernatant 236
cumulative 387
cupula 325
cupule 122, 123
curb 404
curd 257
curiosity behaviour 311
curled 185
curled pond weed 374
curlew 394
current 316, 381
current-induced 383
current-resisting property 384
curtail 396
curve 41
cushion plant 335
cut 246, 262
cut down 362
cuticle 100, 159
cutting 412
cutting site 250
cyanobacteria 161

cycad 98
cycle 247
cycle of matter compounds 347
cyclic curve 344
cyclic electron flow 150
cyclic pattern 378
cyclops 371
cyclostomata 230
cylinder glass 28
cylindrical 99, 219
cyme 114
cyst 391
cystic fibrosis 198, 275
cytidine triphosphate 192
cytochrome 143
cytochrome C 285
cytogenetics 188
cytokine 234
cytokinesis 188, 193
cytology 15
cytometer 177
cytoplasm 59, 159, 162
cytoplasmic channel 183
cytoplasmic strand 94
cytopyge 161
cytosine 205
cytoskeleton 164
cytosol 141
cytostatic 229
cytostome 161
cytotoxic T cell 87, 233
D segment 236
dachshund 185
dahlia 412
dairy 187
dairy produce 401
daisy 48, 364
daisy family 118
dam 369, 385
dam up 385
damage limitation 396
damaging fight 307
dance language of honey bees 305
dandelion 48, 363
danger 397
daphnia 371
Darwinism 280
data 18, 38, 42
data point 39
daughter cell 189, 412
daughter tumour 228
day-neutral plant 332

day-night oxygen fluctuation 382
ddNTP 248
DDT 398
deacidification 153
deadnettle 49, 412
death 227
death sentence 228
debris 208
decant 21, 177
decay 107, 273, 349
decaying matter 95
decide 200
deciduous forest 353
deciduous plant 110
decision 200
decolourise 23
decompose 145
decomposer 346
decomposition 66, 323
decomposition reaction 406
decrease 318
decussate 112, 120
deduce 419
deep 382
deep frozen 208
deep sea 370
deep sea vent 156
deepening 382
defence 230
defence of a nest 308
defend 230
deficiency 408
deficiency mutant 217
defined 242
deforestation 349
degenerate 103, 104, 213, 227
degenerative stage 369
degradable 402
degradation 117, 219, 231, 386
degrade 215, 219, 228, 231, 267, 273, 348
degree of hardness 391
degree of relationship 245
dehiscence 102
dehiscent 102, 114
dehydrate 176
dehydration 258
delayed hypersensitivity reaction type 88
delayed type 238
deletion 220
delicate 397
demand 338

denaturate 250
denature 136, 179, 245, 263
denaturing 245, 250
dendrite 315
denitrification 154, 351
dense leaf litter 123
density 209, 376
density gradient 209
dental arcade 292
dental root 76
dental structure 76
dentine 76
denucleate oocyte 420
deoxygenation 386
deoxyribose 205
depend on 136
deplasmolysis 175
deplete 405
depletion 405
depolarisation 318
depolarisation phase 318
deposit 93, 225, 349
deprivation 296
depth 382
derivative 60
dermis 61
desalination 391
descend 375
descend from 279
describe 12, 296
description 296
desensitisation 88, 238, 301
desert 353
desertification 401
desmosome 59
destaining 216
destroy 125
destruent 346
desulphurisation 157
detach 214, 215
detachment 215
detailed bone structure 62
detect 67, 217, 250, 325, 418
detection 140, 178, 217, 269
detergent 139, 179
deteriorate 227
deterioration 227
determination 58, 160, 224, 417
determine 217, 222, 224, 417
detritivorous 346
detritus rain 373
deuterostome 416
devastate 398
develop 244

developed country 408
developing country 90, 274, 408
development 74, 221
development aid 409
development stage 338
developmental disturbance 418
developmental fate 416
developmental genetics 221
developmental regulation 419
developmental stage 191
deviation 39
devoid 377
dew 335
dextrorse twining 110
diabetes 276
diabetes mellitus 88, 196
diabetes mellitus type 1 239
diabetic 276
diagnose 254
diagnosis 139, 254, 269
diagnostic 254
diagnostic character 13
diagram 41
dialypetal 113
diaphragm 25, 54, 74, 81
diaphysis 62
diarrhoea 260
diastolic pressure 80
diatom 93
diatomaceous earth 93
diatomic molecular oxygen 406
dichasium 114
dichogamous 104
dichogamy 104
dichotomous key 370
dicotyledons 118
dictyosome 163
die 227, 379
diencephalon 69, 328
diet 75, 409
differ 339
difference in pH value 143
differentiate 190, 224, 233
differentiated cell 419
differentiation 58, 98, 160, 224
diffracted light 24
diffuse 225
diffuser 381
diffusion 174
digest 231, 414
digested sludge 389
digester 389
digester gas 389
digestion 53, 76, 231, 389

digestive gland 76
digestive juice 76, 129
digestive organ 76
digestive process 407
digestive system 60
digestive tract 76
digit 290
digitate 112
diglyceride 171
dike 393
dilate 332
dilation 238
dilute 20
dilution 386
dimorphic flower 104
dioecious 97, 124, 306
dioxin 403
dipeptide 168
diploid 91, 191, 192, 413
diplophase 194
dipole 166
dipper 372
direct light 24
direction 175
disability 197, 201
disabled 201
disaccharide 129, 170
disaccharide sucrose 151
disadvantage 340
disc floret 118
discriminate 237
discrimination 314
discussion 35
disease 343
disinfectant 409
disinfection 390
disintegrate 108, 189, 193
dislodge 106
disorder 127
disparity 408
dispersal 360
dispersed 209
display 314
disposable bottle 402
disposal 402
dispose 216
dispose of 261
disposition 278
disrupt 136, 183
disrupted 347
dissecting needle 27
dissecting pan 27
dissociate 133
dissociation curve 82

dissolve 20, 348
dissolved ions 317
dissolved organic matter 383
dissolved oxygen 386
distal tubule 84
distichous 112
distill 21
distillation 21, 391
distilled water 190
distinct 13
distinct optimum pH 137
distinctive 249
distinguish 102, 230, 237
distinguish between 13
distribute 105
distribution 45, 330
disulphide bond 235
disulphide bridge 268
diurnal 331
diurnal acid rhythm 153
dive 376
divergence 283
divergent 283
diversity of proteins 270
divide 193, 408
divide vegetatively 96
divided feathery leaf 337
divided leaf 111
division 90
DNA 165, 205, 207
DNA analysis 249
DNA chip 216, 254
DNA ligase 265
DNA melting 247
DNA microarray 254
DNA polymerase 208, 246, 248
DNA probe 263
DNA sequence 212
DNA synthesis 188
DNase 205
dNTP 246
dock 363
dog rose 366
domestic coal fire 404
domesticate 187
domestication 187, 282
domestication of animals 294
dominance 354
dominant 180, 196
domino effect 242
donor 183, 238, 259, 418
dormancy 359
dorsal 224
dorsal root 68, 326

dot matrix 254
double 135
double helix 206
double-s-shaped 291
double-stranded DNA 247
downy hair 333
dragon fly 370
dragonfly 51
drain away 348
drain pipe 402
drainage basin 378, 382
drawing 26
drawing paper 34
dredge 385
dredging 380
drift 384
drinking water 388
drinking water reservoir 385
drinking water treatment 389
drone 414
drooping 105
drooping raceme 124
drop off 227
droplet infection 90
dropper 28
Drosophila melanogaster 185
drought 407
drug 70, 274
drug addict 241
drug intolerance 238
drupe 114
dry forest 354
dry fruit 114
dry season 383
dry stone wall 366
Duchenne muscular dystrophy 198
duck 51
duck bird 372
duckweed 105, 374
duct 72
dump 402
dune 393
dunnock 368
duodenum 53, 77, 129
duplicate 188, 208
duplicating stamp 266
dye 29, 140, 243
dynein 164
dysentery 409
dysfunctional enzyme 277
eagle 51
ear 63, 322
ear bones 65

ear canal 65
ear muscles 285
eardrum 65
earlobe 197
early atmosphere 286
early detection 140
early maturity onset 345
earth slide 343
earthworm 52, 141
earthworm burrow 361
earwax 65
earwig 52, 359
ebony 185
echinoderm 413
echolocation 107
ecogeographic rule 334
ecological 329
ecological equivalence 342
ecological farming 401
ecological niche 281, 330
ecological optimum 339
ecological potential 345
ecologically beneficial 396
ecology 15, 329
ecosystem 329
ectoderm 223, 416
ectoparasite 341
eczema 237
edge of the woods 354
edible 123, 355
edit 210
education 408
eel 51, 371
effector 215, 266, 322
efferent arteriole 84
efficient 347
egg 221
egg type 223
egg white 222
eggshell 399
8-oxoguanine 220
80S ribosome 213
ejaculation 72
elder 356
electricfield 179, 248, 317
electric pulse 261
electrical field 243
electrical impulse 65, 315, 318
electrocardiogram 79
electrode 179, 316
electrodialysis 390
electrogenic pump 317
electromagnet 270
electromagnetic wave 146

electron 142, 149, 166
electron carrier 143
electron microscope 24, 176
electron transport chain 150
electronegative 144
electronegativity 166
electrophoresis 23, 129, 179, 243, 248
electroporation 261
electrostatic interaction 166
electrotonic conduction 319
elevate 254
elevational 354
elevator effect 313
eliminate 251
ELISA 87, 237
elliptic 112
elm 357
elodia canadensis 105
elongate 331
elongation 213
elymus 393
embed 176, 415
embedding 415
embody 311
embryo 74, 91, 117, 201
embryo sac cell 194
embryoblast 415
embryogenesis 225
embryonic cell 58
embryophyta 94
emergent plant 373
emigration 343
emission 403
emission filter 404
emit 351, 403
empirical 38
EMS 220
emulsify 20, 171
enable 205
enamel 76
encephalopathy 241
enclose 102
encode 65
ENCODE 270
end 262
end product 138
end product repression 215
endanger 397
endocrine gland 70
endocrine system 60
endocytosis 175, 287
endoderm 223, 416
endometrium 71, 73

endoparasite 341
endoplasmic reticulum 163, 213
endorphin 70
endoskeleton 223
endosperm 98, 117, 216
endospermous 108
endosymbiotic theory 287
endothelium 79
endothermic reaction 127
enemy 304
energetically wasteful 138
energy 286
energy balance 75, 410
energy barrier 132
Energy Conservation Act 410
energy consumption 175, 403, 410
energy content 75
energy conversion 125
energy currency 128
energy demand 410
energy efficiency 144
energy flow 347
energy independent 175
energy profile 131
energy source 151
energy yield 145
energy-coupling 129
energy-harvesting reaction 140
energy-investing reaction 140
enhance 231
enjoyment 306
enlarge 100, 414
enrich 377
enter 271
enthalpy 126, 132
entropy 127
ENU 220
envelope 240
environment 180, 395
environment compatible 396
environmental 180, 396
environmental stress 396
environmentalist 395
environmentally friendly 396
enzymatic defect 217
enzymatic hydrolysis 76
enzyme 129, 178
enzyme concentration 134
enzyme-linked 226, 237
enzyme-substrate complex 133
eon 287
eosin 29
epibiotic organism 379

epicotyl 108
epidemic 90, 409
epidermis 59, 61, 159
epididymis 72
epigenetics 199
epiglottis 77, 81
epilimnion 377
epiphysis 62, 69, 328
epithelial cell 58, 277
epithelial tissue 160
epithelium 81
epitope 87, 232
equation 145
equatorial 224
equatorial plate 189
equilibrium 127, 131, 317, 397
Erlenmeyer flask 28
erosion 95
error 64, 323
erythrocyte 78, 82
erythropoietin 78, 276
eosophagus 53
essential oils 117
establish sb's guilt 249
ester bond 171
estrogen 73
estuary 370
ethanal 144
ethanol 29, 167, 208
ethical values 200
ethidium bromide 220
ethnical group 203
ethogram 296
ethologist 295
ethology 15, 295
ethyl alcohol 144
etiolation 331
euglena 26
euhominid 291
eukaryote 159, 287
eukaryotic cell 58, 159, 287
Eurasian coot 372
European adder 358
European spindletree 356
European spoonbill 393
euryhaline 335
eurypotent 330
eurytherm 332
Eustachian tube 65
eutrophic 378
evaluate 23, 296
evaluation 296
evaporate 21, 332, 349
evaporation 348, 407

evapotranspiration 378
even out 344
evergreen 99
evidence 204, 342
evolution 15, 249, 280
evolutionary 280
evolutionary synthesis 280
evolve 153
ex-vivo gene transfer 277
examine 23
exceed 344
excess of substrate 135
exchange 192, 348, 377
exchange of information 293, 303
exchange pool 349
excise 264
excision repair 221
excitation 149
excitatory postsynaptic potential 320
excitatory synapses 321
excited state 149
excitement 306
exclude 251
excrete 175
excretion 54, 83, 175, 223, 335
excretory system 60
exendospermous 108
exhalation 81
exhaust 403
exhaust fumes 404
exine 97
existence 330
exocytosis 175
exon 210, 253
exoskeleton 223
exothermic reaction 127
expecting mother 200
expecting parents 200
experience 298
experiment 18, 19
experimenter 19
explain 12, 23
exploit 409
exploitation 279
exponential 247
expose 105, 178, 329
exposition 178
express 209
expression level 254
expression profile 216, 226
expression vector 267
extend 168, 247

extension 168, 247
external defence 86
external respiration 141
extinct 396
extinction 280, 299, 396, 399
extinction risk 399
extirpate 396
extracellular body fluid 68, 317, 326
extracellular digestion 76
extracellular matrix 173
extracellular recording 317
extracellular space 161
extrachromosomal 182
extract 139, 261
extract from 207
extranuclear 182
extraplasmic space 161
extrapolate 42
extratentacular budding 413
extremities 333
eye 63, 284, 322
eye muscle 67
eye spot 92
eyepiece 25
F-plasmid 183
facial bone 292
facilitated diffusion 175
facilities 296
FACS 178
factor 39, 329
factor VIII 197, 275
facultative 215
FAD 142
faeces 78, 155, 335, 351, 386
falcon 51
fallopian tube 54, 414
fallout 407
family 16, 313
family based genetic association study 204
family planning 408
family tree 196, 201
fan 332
farming 274
fascia 62
fast motion 227
fat 75, 152, 171
fat cell 333
fate 223
fatherhood 251
fatty acid 167, 171
fatty deposit 335
faulty 198

433

favourable 410
feasible 19
feather 289
feathers 182, 289
feathery 102
feathery stigma 117
feature 408
fecundity 343
feeble 397
feedback 215, 407
feedback inhibition 138
feeder river 378
feeding 308
feeding ground 393
feeding relationship 346
Fehling's solution 29
Fehling's test 29
female 183, 309
female cone 100
female organ 92
fen peat 380
fermentation 144, 255
fermentation process 407
fermenter 255, 276
fern 48, 95, 194, 356, 411
ferret 358
ferrissia wautieri 371
ferro-oxidizing bacteria 156
ferrous sulphide 352
fertilisation 193, 221, 413
fertilisation membrane 414
fertilise 193, 278
fertilised 414
fertiliser 386
fertility factor 183, 259
fertilizer 401
fetus 201, 416
fibre 99, 187
fibrilline 197
fibrin 78
fibrinogen 78
fibrous root 109
field bindweed 367
field maple 356
field research 296
field scabious 363
field work 30, 379
fieldfare 368
figure 37, 39
figwort family 121
filament 102
filamentous 94
filial generation 181
filial imprinting 301

filter 21, 83, 208
filter feeder 375
filtering facilities 403
filtrate 21
filtration 21, 83, 257
fin 290
final electron acceptor 144
final stage 240
finch 50
fine adjustment knob 25
fine grain sediment 385
fingerprinting 249
finings 257
fir 48, 362
fir forest 354
fir tree 99
fire 293
firefly 128
firm 273
firmness 273
1st 267
first aid kit 31
first division 414
first trimester 74
fish 17, 371
FISH 190
fish characteristic 290
fish elevator 385
fish pass 385
fish stock 395
fishing quota 395
fishlike 290
fission 411
fit 132
fitness 203, 281, 344
5' 210
5-bromouracil 220
fix 176, 190, 251
fixation 251
fixed 237
fixed action pattern 297, 309
fixed retreat 384
flagellum 92, 160, 162, 164
flanking sequence 268
flat 111, 292
flatten out 134
flatworm 413
flavour 256, 257
flavour molecule 152
Flavr Savr tomato 273
fleshy 115
fleshy fruit 114
flexible 198
flint 293

flip over 174
float 105
floatation 387
floating leaf 337, 374
floating material 388
floating solid 387
flocculation 387
flocculation basin 390
flock 307, 340, 387
flock of birds 376
flood 343, 383, 392, 407
flood protection 385
floral diagram 101
floral organ 101
floral whorl 101
flounder 383, 395
flow characteristic 379
flow rate 382
flower 101
flower cluster 105
flu 90
fluctuation 344
fluid 65
fluid mosaic model 174
fluorescence 149
fluorescence detector 248
fluorescence dye-linked
 nucleotide 248
fluorescence picture 37
fluorescent 217
fluorescent dye 151, 178, 237, 263
fluorescently labelled 254
fly 107
foam 405
focus 66
fodder 117
foerna 360
foetus 74
folding 136
foliage 362
follicle 71, 114
follicle cell 221
follicle-stimulating hormone 72, 328
follow 301
food additive 258
food call 304
food chain 347, 399
food composition 75
food cycle 93
food hopper 299
food industry 139
food plant 121, 364

food pyramid 75
food source 305
food web 347
food-related signal 304
foot bone 62
footnote 36
footprint 62
forage 117, 305
forager 305
foramen magnum 292
foreign DNA 261, 264
foreign gene 264
foreign invader 230
foreign protein 264
forensic scientist 249
foreskin 54
forest 353
forest area 354, 400
forest clearance 354
forest clearing 354
forest cultivation 354
forest damage 354
forest decline 354
forest floor 355, 360
forest floor organic layer 355
forest industry 354
forest management 400
forest reserve 400
forest soil 355
forest stand 354
forest use plan 354
form 14
formation 93, 283
formyl-methionine 213
forward 246
forward and reverse reaction 127
fossil fuel 403
fossil intermediary 289
fossil remains 98
founder 279
founder effect 203, 280
fovea 67, 323
fox 50, 358
fraction 178
fragile 397
fragile X syndrome 198
fragment 242, 248, 261
fragment length 250
fragmentation 91, 413
fragrance molecule 152
frame shift mutation 214, 220
free energy 126
free nitrogen of the air 152

free oxygen atom 406
free radical 406
free-floating plant zone 374
freeze tolerant 360
freeze-etching 176
freeze-fracturing 176
frequency 64
frequency code 320
fresh water 92, 369, 383
freshwater ecosystem 369
freshwater green alga 93
freshwater leech 371
freshwater shrimp 52
friction 126
frightening behaviour 314
frog 51, 316, 372
froghopper 365
frond 96, 356
front 292
front limbs 284
frost-tolerant 187
fructan 117
fructose 170
frugivorous 360
fruit 75
fruit fly 185, 222
fruit wall 117
frustration 314
fuel efficiency 404
fuel molecule 129
full length cDNA 267
full-grown 225
fume hood 28
function 14, 385
functional sequences 270
funeral rites 294
fungicide 398
fungus 17, 48, 230, 272, 411
funiculus 103
funnel 28
furnace 403
further afield 403
fuse 174, 231, 236, 412, 414
fusion 174
fusion protein 268
G-banding 190
G_0-Phase 188
G_1-Phase 188
G_2-Phase 188
gaggle of geese 301
gain access 209
galago 309
gall bladder 53, 76
gall former 360

gallant soldier 367
gametangium 193
gamete 91, 182, 413
gametophyte 92, 94, 96, 194
ganglion cell 323
gannet 51
gap gene 225
gap junction 59
garden phlox 122
garden spider 365
garlic mustard 367
gas exchange 80
gas outlet 256
gas supply 28
gas valve 28
gasometer 389
gastric juice 77
gastrula 222, 416
gastrulation 416
GC-rich region 245
gel 243, 250
gel electrophoresis 250, 263
gel pocket 179
gelatinous 67
gemmule 412
gene 179, 258, 280
gene activitiy 198
gene expression 209, 215
gene flow 203, 280
gene frequency 280
gene lethality 204
gene library 268
gene pharming 274, 278
gene pool 188, 203, 280
gene regulation 211, 215, 419
gene shuttle 264
gene therapy 277
gene transfer 258
gene vehicle 271
gene-environment interaction 196
gene-silencing 274
genealogy 285
genealogy database 279
generate 141, 246, 272
generation 281
generative cell 102, 107
generative nucleus 108
genesis 380
genetic 179, 204, 258, 280
genetic association 196, 203
genetic code 212
genetic counselling 200
genetic dialect 214

genetic distance 185
genetic diversity 401
genetic drift 203, 280
genetic egoism 308
genetic engineering 258
genetic fingerprint 249
genetic information 209
genetic map 185
genetic marker 269
genetic material 192
genetic programme 227
genetic tool 261
genetic variability 411
genetic variance 104
genetically 179
genetically modified 273
genetically modified organism 255
geneticist 258
genetics 15
genital 54
genome 258
genomic library 252
genomic mutation 221
genotype 180, 217
genotyping 254
gentian 368
genus 16
geosphere 347
germ 108
germ layer 223, 416
germ line 224
germinable 415
germinal disc 224
germinate 91, 108, 257
germination 91, 109, 359, 415
germline 192
germline gene therapy 278
germline mutation 229
gesture 304
giant chromosome 191
giant hogweed 400
giant mouse 274
gibberelin 216
Giemsa-staining 190
gill 335, 355
gill appendage 384
gill arch 284
gill pouch 284
gill slit 284
ginkgo 98, 289
girth 30
glacial 380
glacial acetic acid 190

glacial rubble 380
glacier 369, 380, 407
gland 65
glandular 103
glandular cell 58
glans 55
glans penis 72
glass rod 208
glass stirrer 208
glial cell 315
global warming 406
global warming potential 407
globalisation 90
globe shaped 102
globulin 117
glomerulus 84
glottis 81
glove 20
glow-worm 365
glucose 170
glue 28
glume 116
glutamic acid 276
gluteal muscle 292
glutenin 117
glyceraldehyde 3-phosphate 151
glycerine 167
glycerol 171
glycocalyx 173
glycogen 140, 171
glycolipid 199
glycolysis 141
glycolytic 141
glycoprotein 173, 197, 240, 241, 268
glycosylation 268
GMO 188
GNP 409
goggles 19
golden oriole 358
goldfish 51
golgi apparatus 163
golgi vesicle 163
gonad 193, 223
gonadotropin-releasing hormone 72
Gondwana 286
gonosomal 196
gonosome 196
goose 51
gorge 383
gorse 49
goshawk 358

gradient 259
graduated cylinder 28
graft 238, 412
graft onto 419
graft-versus-host disease 88
grafting 412
grain 49
grain size 361
gram-positive 162
graminaceae 152
gramme 42
granite 361
granulocyte 87, 233
granum 147
grape phylloxera 400
graph 41
graph paper 34, 41
grass 48
grass snake 51, 372
grasses 356
grasshopper 52, 365
grassland 353
gravel 382
gravity 65
grazing 369
grazing regime 364
great crested grebe 372
great reed warbler 372
great ringed plover 394
great wood rush 356
green alga Spirogyra 148
green fly 365
green gene technology 278
green petals 285
green-white mottled 182
greenhouse 405
grey crescent 224, 418
grey matter 68, 326
greylag 301
greyling 382
grille 402
grip 292
grist 257
gross primary production 347
ground beetle 365
ground breeder 360
ground state 149
ground water 348, 369, 387
groundsel 367
group member 306
grow 16, 344
growing season 334
growth 16, 271, 344
growth factor 228

growth hormone 274
growth medium 177
growth rate 343
growth stage 368
grub 359, 365
guanine 205
guanosine triphosphate 192
gulf stream 407
gum 76
gymnosperm 98, 194
habitable 396
habitat 295, 337
habitat map 399
habitat network 399
habitat system 399
haem 130
haemoglobin 78, 82
haemophile 276
haemophilia 197, 275, 276
hair 61
hair cell 66
hair follicle receptor 325
hair-covered plants 334
hairy 102
half 192, 216
half-breed 187
halibut 395
halobacteria 157
halophyte 337, 393
halophytic 337, 393
halve 192
hammer 65
hand bone 62
hand lens 27, 31
hang out 105
haplodiploid system 184
haploid 90, 191, 192, 413
haploid pollen grain 97
haplophase 194
haplorrhini 309
haplotype 199
hard glass capillary 316
hardiness 360
hardy 187
Hardy-Weinberg principle 203
hare 50, 357
harmful 398
harmless 204
harvest 187, 256
harvesting of energy 140
harvestman 52, 365
hatch 301, 339
HATCH-SLACK-cycle 153
haustorium 109

hawkbit 363
hawthorn 356
hay fever 87, 237
hay infusion 381
hazard 398
hazel 122, 356
hazelnut 356
head 53, 114, 414
headwaters 382
health hazard 386
Health Impact Assessment 90
health prevention 90
health risk 279
heart 54, 239
heart attack 140
heart disease 79
heart failure 228
heart rate 79
heart valve 54
heart-shaped 112, 121
heat 22, 61, 126
heat conduction 332
heat dissipation 333
heat of respiration 141
heat radiation 331
heat-inactivated 205
heat-inactivation 205
heat-stable 247
heated lid 246
heath 368
heath family 121
heather 49, 368, 380
heather shoot 369
heavy chain 235
heavy DNA 209
heavy metal 216
heavy metal ion 176
heavy metal sulphate 157
heavy metal sulphide 156
hedge 366
hedgehog 50, 358
helical 206
helicase 208
heliozoan 26
helmet-shaped 120
helper T cell 87, 233, 240
hemizygous 192
hemlock 321
hemoglobin 276
hemoglobin-rich tail end 376
hen harrier 394
hens and chicks plant 366
hep 115
hepatic portal vein 77

herb layer 356
herbal tea 121
herbicide 272, 398
herbivore 346
herbivorous 346
herd 307
hereditary 204, 269, 411
hereditary disease 196
hermaphrodite 97, 184
heron 372
hesperidium 115
heteroecious 342
heteroecism 342
heterogametic 184
heterogenesis 342
heterostyly 104
heterothermic 332
heterozygosity testing 269
heterozygous 180, 192
HFR strain 259
hibernate 333
hibernation 333
hibernator 333
hiding place 343
hierarchically classified 306
hierarchy 306
high energy rays 229
high forest 354
high point 42
high soil salinity 337
high-yielding 187
highest value 42
Hill reaction 150
hippocampus 69, 327
histamine 88, 238
histone 206, 287
HIV 89, 240
HIV-positive 89, 240
HLA system 88
hnRNA 209
hole-nesting bird 360
hollow 222, 373
hollow stem 116, 119
homeostasis 335
hominid 291
hominisation 291
hominoid 291
Homo erectus 291
Homo habilis 291
Homo sapiens 291
Homo sapiens sapiens 291
homoeobox 225, 419
homoeodomain 225
homoeostasis 70

homoeotic gene 225, 419
homogametic 184
homogenate 177, 207
homogeneity 270
homogeneous 177
homogenise 177, 207
homoiothermic 332
homoiotherms 332
homologous 190
homology 284
homology criterion 284
homozygous 180, 192
hooked 115
hoopoe 367
hop 257
horizontal 38
horizontal cell 323
horizontal movement 174
horizontally 66
hormonal 234
hormonal balance 343
hormone 69, 70, 216, 234, 295, 326
horn 182
hornbeam 122
hornet 52, 359
hornwort 105, 374
horsefly 52
horsetail 95, 356
horticulture 187
host 89, 342, 418
host cell 265
hot plate 28
hot spring 247
hot volcanic spring 156
house keeping gene 198
housefly 52
household 388
hover 106
hoverfly 282, 365
hox cluster 225
hox gene 225
huddle 333
HUGO 251
human 309
human cell 58
human chorionic gonadotropin hormone 415
human evolution 280
human genome project 251, 269
human leucocyte antigen 238
human oogenesis 73
human skeleton 61

humane husbandry 401
humic acid 380
humidity 349
hummingbird 107
humoral 235
hump backed 185
humus 337
humus tank 388
hunter-gatherer 293
hunting ground 307
husbandry 401
husk 122
hybrid 180, 181
hybridisation 217, 244
hybridisation probe 263
hybridise 244, 251, 254
hybridoma cell 236
hydra 375, 412
hydrangea 122
hydration 166
hydro-electric power station 388
hydrocarbon 350, 403
hydrocarbon tail 167
hydrogen 166
hydrogen ion 142, 150
hydrogen oxidizing bacteria 156
hydrogen peroxide 140, 391
hydrogen sulphide 155
hydrogen sulphide gas 352
hydrogen-oxygen reaction 144
hydrolyse 128
hydrolysis 128
hydronium ion 153
hydrophilic 169, 172
hydrophily 105
hydrophobic 169, 172
hydrophyte 374, 393
hydrophytic 336
hydrosphere 347
hydrostatic function 375
hydrostatic pressure 174
hydroxyl 406
hydroxyl group 167
hydroxyl radical 220
hydrozoan 193
hygiene 409
hygienic 409
hygrophyte 337, 356, 393
hymen 71
hymenoptera 184
hyperpolarisation 318, 321
hypertonic 174

hyphen 411
hyphydrus ovatus 370
hypocotyl 108
hypodermis 61
hypolimnion 377
hypophysis 69, 328
hypothalamus 69, 328
hypothesis 17, 34
hypotonic 174, 190
hyracotherium 286
ice cover 376
ichthyostega 290
identification 237, 249
identification marking 296
IgA 235
IgD 235
IgE 235
IgE class 87
IgG 235
IgG antibody 88
IgM 235, 239
illuminate 24
illuminating system 25
image 37
imagination 310
imbalance 347, 397
imitation 295, 302, 310
immediate type 237
imminent 397
immission 403
immit 403
immobilise 139
immobilisation 139
immortal 236
immortalise 236
immune and lymphatic system 60
immune response 233
immune suppression 88, 238
immune system 230
immunisation 86, 232
immunise 236
immuno-staining 226
immunoglobulin 234
immunological 229
immunological tolerance 88, 239
immunology 230
immunosuppressed 238
impact 397
impaired 276
impede 375
imperil 398
imperilled 398

impermeable 174, 193
implanted cannula 301
import 400
imposing behaviour 314
impregnated 93
imprint 301
imprinting 198, 295, 301
impulse 63
in equilibrium 256
in situ 178
in situ hybridisation 226
in vitro fertilisation 74
in-line 419
in-vivo gene transfer 277
inactivate 137
inactivated 215
incalculable 279
incinerating plant 402
income 408
incoming signal 315
incompatibility 239
incomplete flower 101
incomplete oxidation 145
inconspicuous 104
incorporate 183, 248, 255, 265, 348
increase 201, 215, 274, 318
increase exponentially 135
increasing 238
incross 181
incubate 22, 205
incubation period 86, 232
incubator 28, 177, 301
indehiscent 114
indehiscent fruit 122
indentation 111
indication rule 200
indicator 21, 29
indicator species 30
indigenous 339
indigenous species 400
individual 280
individual distance 313
individual fitness 308
indole 218
induce 215, 225, 271, 415, 418
induced fit 133
inducible promoter 259, 267
induction 215, 225, 418
indusium 96
industrial farming 401
industrial melanism 282
industrial plant 403
industrial waste water 386

ineffective 400
infant marriage 408
infant mortality 408
infect 260
infection 86, 232
infectious 241
infectious disease 85, 90
inferiority 314
infertile 401
infertility 343
infestation 341
infested 341
infiltrate 228
inflammation 86, 232
inflammatory rheumatism 88
inflorescence 113
inflow 378
influenza 341
influenza-like 341
influx 317
information flow 320
information transfer 303
infructescence 114
infusion of hay 26
ingest 231
ingestion 76
inhabitable 396
inhalation 81
inhale 277
inherit 269
inheritable 196
inheritance 183
inherited disease 275
inhibit 193, 205, 299
inhibition 137, 299
inhibitor 137
inhibitory postsynaptic potential 321
inhibitory synapses 321
initiate 131, 229
initiation 213
inject 226
injection 200
innate immunity 86
inner ear 64
innermost whorl 102
inoculate 86, 232, 409
inoculation 86, 232, 409
inorganic 129
inorganic sulphur 157
input 64, 256, 323
insect 17
insect-pollinated 106
insecticide 272, 398

insectivorous plant 368
insemination 193, 413
insensitive 260
inseparable 117
insert 264
insert preparation 252
insertion 220, 264
insertion point 113
insidious 398
insight learning 312
insoluble starch 151
instinct 295
instrumental conditioning 298
insulate 333
insulation 333, 404
insulin 276
insulin production 239
intact 277
integrase 240
integrate 183
integument 98
integumentary system 60
Intelligent Design 280
intense crying 311
intense sun 152
intensify 406
intensity of respiration 141
interact 138, 166
interaction 132, 338, 418
intercalary meristem 116
intercalating 220
intercellular 60
intercellular space 140
interconnect 348
interconversion 124
interconvert 124
intercross 181
interfere with 205
interference 226
intermediate 129, 180
intermediate compound 153
intermediate product 138
intermembrane space 147
internal defence system 230
internal respiration 141
internode 116
interphase 188
interpolate 42
interpret 18, 23, 297
interpretation 18, 23, 297
interrelation 338
interspecific 339
interspecific communication 303

439

interstitial fluid 80
intertidal ecosystem 370
interval 263
interval between 301
intestinal 239
intestine 53
intine 97
intra-tentacular budding 412
intracellular digestion 76
intrasexual competition 308
intraspecific 339
intraspecific communication 303
introduce 400
introduced species 400
introduction 34
intron 210, 264
invade 230
invader 230
invaginate 223
invasive species 400
inverse 273
inversely proportional 146
inversion 221, 404
invertebrate 17
investigate 34
investigation 34
invisible 24
involuntary reflex action 300
iodine-potassium solution 216
ion 165
ion concentration 317
ion exchange 390
ion pump 175
ion theory of excitation 318
ionisation 136
ionising 220
iris 67
iris family 115
iron 156, 293
iron salt 361
iron sulphide 157
irradiance 331
irradiate 407
irradiation 220
irregular flowers 118
irreversibility 418
irreversible 137, 418
irrigation 388
islet of Langerhans 239
isogamete 91
isogamy 413
isolate 203, 207, 246, 261
isolation 203, 246, 283

isolation experiment 418
isolecital 223
isotonic 174
isotope 150, 209
Italian ryegrass 363
ivy 49
J segment 236
jackdaw 50
jar 30
Java man 291
jaw 290, 292
jaw bone 76
jaw joint 284
jawed vertebrates 230
jelly coat 413
jellyfish 52, 193, 414
joint 53, 62, 198
joint cartilage 62
joint inflammation 239
jolt up 120
jotter 34
jumping gene 245
junction 60
juncture 111
juniper bush 368
juniper heathland 368, 399
juxtaglomerular apparatus 85
K^+ions 317
K-selected species 345
Kaposi's-sarcoma 240
karyogram 190
karyotype 190
KCl solution 317
keel petal 119
Kentish plover 394
keratinised 59, 160
keratinous 61
kernel 123
kestrel 367
keto-enol-tautomerism 220
ketone 167
key 133
key hole 133
key reaction 144
kidney 54, 84, 175, 238, 335
killed 204
kinetochore 189
knapweed 363
knee joint 322
knock in 226
knock out 226
knockout animal 275
knockout method 419
knowingly 400

knuckle-walking 292
Krebs cycle 142
krill 371
lab 19, 27
lab coat 20
lab equipment 27
lab procedure 19
lab report 34
label 26, 38, 244, 251
labia majora 71
labia minora 71
labiate family 120
labium 54
lable 231
laboratory 19
laboratory experiment 296
labour 74
labyrinth 325
lac^+-strain 260
lack 217
lacking 104
lactalbumine 275
lactate fermentation 144
lactation 74
lacteal 77
lactic acid 144, 257
lactose 170, 215, 260, 275
ladybird 359, 365
lag phase 344
lag time 231
lagoon 370
lake 369
lake basin 378
lake bottom 378
Lamarckism 280
lambda library 252
lambda phage 252
lance-shaped 112
land use 349
landing platform 107
landrace 188
lane 179
language 293
larch 48
large 292
large batch production 255
large intestine 77
large scale 255
large scale production 255
large skipper 364
larva 223, 370
larval form 414
larynx 53, 81
lateral erosion 382

lateral inhibition 324
lateral root 109
laterally inverted 38
latitude 334
Laurasia 286
lava filter 391
law of independent assortment 181
law of segregation 181
layer 355
layer of cells 59, 159
layer of fat 333
layer of tissue 101
leach 348
leaching 379
leaching of nutrients 386
lead 404
leading strand 264
leadwort family 122
leaf 110
leaf axil 411
leaf base 111
leaf blade 111, 368
leaf browser 360
leaf bud 411
leaf litter 360
leaf miner 360
leaf rosette 366
leaf shape 112
leaf sheath 116
leaflet 112
leafy canopy 382
leafy shoot 101
lean-burn engine 404
leap up 385
learn 310
learned attachment 301
learning 295, 298
learning by imitation 312
leatherjacket 365
leave 153
lecithine 171
left atrium 78
leg bone 62
legend 42
legume 114, 187, 364
legume family 119
leguminous plant 152
lemma 116
lemur 309
lens 25, 66
lens eye 285
lenticel 110
less supportive tissue 337

less vascular tissue 337
lesser calendine 411
lethal 186, 201, 398
lethal allele 204
lethal factor 186, 204
leucocyte 78, 233
leucoplast 163
level off 134
Leydig cell 72
lichen 17, 48, 203, 355
life 16
life cycle 72, 91
life expectancy 198, 227, 408
life sciences 15
life-threatening 237
lifespan 345
ligase 209
ligate 253, 265
light 61, 63, 105, 322
light chain 235
light compensation point 360
light dependence 331
light intensity 331
light meter 379
light quantum 324
light reaction 146
light receptor cell 66, 323
light saturation 360
light-dependent reaction 146
light-harvesting complex 148
light-independent reaction 146
lighting 404
lightness value 324
lightning 286, 296
lignin 161
lignonberry 355
ligule 116
lilac 49
lily family 115
lily-of-the-valley 356
limb 53
limbic system 68, 326
lime 357, 361
lime tree 121
limestone 350, 380
limit 228
limiting factor 330
limiting resource 338, 376
limnetic zone 385
limulus 289
line 41
line of descent 291
line of progression 284
line of regression 284

lineage 285
lineage tracing 226
linear 112, 217
link 171, 178, 214, 265
link to 266
linkage analysis 185
linkage disequilibrium 204
linkage group 185
linking reaction 167, 171
linoleic acid 171
linolenic acid 171
lipid 164, 171
lipid bilayer 317
lipid catabolism 219
lipid mebrane 173
lipofection 261
lipophilic 169, 172
lipophobic 169, 172
liposome 163, 173, 261, 277
liquid 376
lithosphere 286, 347
litmus 29
litmus paper 21
litter decomposing animal 360
litter layer 355
little bittern 372
live birth 201
liver 76, 239
liverwort 94
livestock 187, 274
living conditions 342, 410
living fossil 289
living space 407
living system 125
living thing 165
lizard 51, 366
loach 371
load 214, 397
loaded t-RNA 213
loading 378
loading solution 140
lobe 186
lobed 112
lobed margin 123
lobster 52
locate 178
lock 133, 385
lock-and-key model 133
lock-and-key principle 87, 234
loculus 103
locust 52
locust infestation 409
lodicule 117
Loligo 318

lomentum 114
long generation time 345
long horned beetle 365
long hydrocarbon "tail" 147
long term 279
long-day plant 331
long-lived 227, 345
long-term memory 312
long-toed water beetle 371
longevity 345
longitudinal 411
longitudinal section 216
longitudinal slit 102
loop 65, 209
loop of Henle 84
loose 105
loris 309
loss 128, 335, 419
lotic systems 381
Lottka-Voltera equations 345
Lottka-Voltera models 345
low point 42
low solubility 350
low-lying land 369
lower 131, 254
lower case letter 180
lower lip 120
lower reaches 382
lowest value 42
luciferase 128
luciferin 128
Lugol's solution 29
lugworm 394
luminescent 128
lung 54, 80
lung volume 81
lung-breathing snail 384
lutein 147
luteinising hormone 72
luxury item 314
lycopodium 356
Lyme disease 341
lymph 80, 233, 241
lymph node 80, 86
lymphatic organ 86
lymphatic system 80, 86, 233
lymphatic vessel 80
lymphocyte 87, 233, 236
lymphoid lineage 233
lymphoid progenitor 233
lymphoid tissue 87
lymphoma 240
lynx 49, 357
lyse 252

lysine 276
lysosome 163, 231
lysozyme 86
macromere 417
macromolecule 130, 171
macrophage 86, 87, 231, 234
macroscopic 24
macula 64
mad cow disease 241
magma 286
magnesium atom 147
magnetic lens 176
magnification 26
magnify 26
magnifying glass 27, 31
magnolia 102
magpie 50
maidenhair tree 357
main stem 110
maintain 410
maize 116, 152, 272
major histocompatibility
  complex 238
major leaf vein 116
major source 117
malaria 90, 398
malate 153
male 183, 308
male catkins 123
male cone 100
male organ 92
malignant 228
mallard 372
malleus 284
mallow 121
mallow family 121
malnutrition 75, 409
malt 257
malting 257
maltose 170
mammal 17, 222, 309
mammalian 222
mammary gland 54, 71, 275, 278
mane 182
mangrove 370
mangrove forest 354
manipulate 271
manipulation 271
mantis 52
manure 401
map 251, 418
map butterfly 365
maple 48, 357
maquis 353

marbled white butterfly 364
Marfan's syndrome 197
margin 112
marginal 119
marginal zone 415
marguerite 48
marine 395
marine ecosystem 370
marine life 395
marine organism 128
mark 219
marlin 395
marsh 373, 392
marsh beetle larva 371
marsupial 17
marten 50
Marvel of Peru 182
mash 257
mask 93
mass blossoming 395
mass production 276
mass reproduction 222, 395
mass screen 255
mass spectrometry 270
massive tree 95
mast cell 87, 234
matching degree 302
mate 128
materials 35
maternal 182, 198, 222
maternal effect 225
maternal gene 225
mathematical model 345
mating call 303
mating ritual 309
mating system 309
matrix 147, 179
matter 346
maturation 233, 273
mature 233
mature stage 369
maturity 273
maximum 42
maximum level of product 256
maximum rate 134
maximum value 135
mayfly 52, 370
meadow 48, 363
meadow ant 365
meadow brown butterfly 364
meadow fescue 363
meadow foxtail 363
meadow melick 363
meadow orchard 366

meadow saffron 49
mean 39
meander straightening 385
meandering 382
measles 409
measurable 22
measure 22, 35, 296
measurement 316
measurement error 22
measuring 296
mechanical cleaning device 390
mechanical small sewage treatment plant 389
median 39
mediate 238
medical research 139
medical science 275
medulla oblongata 69, 328
medusa 414
megagametophyte 103
megasporocyte 103
meiosis 181, 192, 413
meiotic 90
Meissner's corpuscle 325
melanin 277, 282
melt 245, 376
melting curve 245
melting point 245
melting temperature 247
meltwater 380, 383
membrane 120, 173, 287
membrane flow 174
membrane model 174
membrane potential 317
membrane protein 173, 317
membrane-bound 229
membranous 228
membranous cisterna 163
membranous disk 323
memory 312
memory cell 86, 232, 235
menace 398
menopause 73
menstrual cycle 72
menstruation 72
mental retardation 277
meridional 224
meristem 160
Merkel nerve ending 325
Merkel's disc 325
mesencephalon 69
mesoderm 223, 416
mesophyll 159
mesophyte 337

mesophytic 337
mesotrophic 378
metabolic 227, 332
metabolic compartment 287
metabolic intermediate 171, 218
metabolic marker 266
metabolic pathway 138, 218
metabolic rate 80
metabolic reaction 165
metabolism 16, 83, 124, 215
metabolite 215
metabolise 16, 124
metacentric 190
metal grid 176
metal response element 216
metal transcription factor 216
metalimnion 377
metallisation 176
metallise 176
metamorphosis 223, 417
metaphase 188
methane 156, 401, 407
methane-forming bacteria 156
methanol 190
method 35
methyl group 147
methyl orange 29
methylating 220
methylation 198
methylene blue solution 29
metronome 301
MHC-protein 238
micelle 173
Michaelis-Menten constant 134
microarray 216
microbial 155, 351
microbial ammonification 155, 351
microbial degradation 387
microbial mats 157
microfilament 164
microinjection 278
micromere 222, 417
microorganism 26, 85, 230, 255, 395
micropylar end 98
micropyle 98
microsatellite 250
microscope 24, 27
microscope slide 25, 27
microscope stage 25
microscopic 24
microscopy 24
microspore mother cell 97

microtitre plate 237
microtubule 164, 190
microvilli 77
midbrain 328
middle ear 64
middle piece 414
middle reaches 382
middle-term memory 312
migrate 179, 223, 243, 248
migration 203, 331, 343
migratory 331
migratory bird 393
migratory fish 385
mildew 411
mildew resistance 187
millet 116
milling 257
millipede 359
mimesis 282, 340
mimic 107, 340
mimicry 282, 304, 340
mimosaceae 119
mineral 75, 286
mineralisation 155, 346, 351
mineralise 346
minimal medium 217
minimal nutrient medium 258
minimum 42
minus gamete 91
mis-imprinting 301
miscarriage 200
miscarry 200
misdirect 228
mismatch 245
missing link 289
mite 359
mitochondrion 163, 287, 414
mitosis 188
mitotic 188
mitotic division 410
mix 205, 377
mixed beech forest 353
mixed cultivation 401
mixed deciduous forest 353
mixed oak forest 353
mobile phase 148
model 31, 302
model organism 222
modelling 31
modern reproductive technology 74
modification 280, 298, 299
modified 248
modified stem 110

443

modify 180, 248, 299
moisture-loving 337, 356
mold 411
mole 50
molecular cue 419
molecular formula 145, 165
molecular pharming 274
molecular weight standard 243
molecule 125
mollusc 371
monitor 254, 256
monitoring 269
monkey 291, 309
monocarpellary 113, 119
monoclonal antibody 87, 236
monocotyledonous 115
monocotyledons 115
monocultural farming 401
monoculture 354, 401
monocyte 87, 234
monoecious 97, 122, 123
monogamy 309
monoglyceride 171
monolayer 173, 177
monophyletic group 285
monosaccharide 129, 170
monosomy 191
monosynaptic 322
moor burning 369
moose 49
moraine 380
morel 356
morphogen 225
morphogen gene 419
morphogenesis 416
morphogenic 225
morpholino 226
mortality rate 343
mortar 27, 207
morula 222, 415
mosaic development 225
mosaic embryo 418
mosquito 52, 399
moss 94, 411
moss layer 355
moth 106
motivation 297
motor end plate 321
motor nerve 322
motor nerve cell 318
mottled 182
mould 217, 257
mouse 50, 222, 357
mouth 53, 76

mouth of a river 383
movable 209
move 16
movement 16
movement disorder 197
mRNA 209, 213, 253
mucilaginous secretion 100
mucosa 53
mucous 81
mucus 81, 198
mud bottom 383
mudworm 371
mulberry family 124
multicellular 94
multicellular organism 58, 160
multichannel learning 312
multifactorial inheritance 196
multiples of four 118
multiples of three 115
multiply 235
multipotent 224
multistep metabolic pathway 141
municipal wastewater 154, 351
murein 162
muscle 53, 198
muscle fibre 62
muscle spindle 319, 322
muscle tissue 59, 160
muscular system 60
mussel 52, 371
mutagen 219, 229
mutagenesis 219, 226, 269
mutagenic 229
mutagenic potential 220
mutate 219, 240
mutation 219, 280, 286
mutual dependency 345
mutual trust 311
muzzle 292
mycelium 361
mycoprotein 256
mycorrhiza 361
mycorrhiza fungus 99, 352
myelin 315
myelin sheath 197
myelinated axons 319
myelocyte 233
myeloid lineage 233
myeloid progenitor 233
myeloid stem cell 87
myeloma cell 236
myofibril 63
myogenic contraction 79

myoma 228
myosin 164, 321
myosin filament 63
myriapod 17
N fertilizer 272
Na^+ ions 317
NAD^+ nicotinamide adenine dinucleotide 142
$NADH^-$ electron donor 142
name 14
narrow 292
narrow tube 106
narrowed 180
nasal cavity 81
nasopharynx 76
native wood 362
natural catastrophe 343
natural family planning 74
natural monument 400
natural selection 203
natural source 351
nature conservancy 399
nature reserve 400
nautilus 289
Neanderthal 291
neck 76
neck muscles 292
neck-canal cell 92
necrosis 228
nectar 103
nectariferous gland 124
nectarivore 107
nectary 103
needle 100
negative feedback circuit 85
negative pressure breathing 81
negative reinforcement 299
nekton 374
nematode 222, 225, 359
Neolithic Revolution 294
neophyte 339
neozoen 339
nephron 84, 335
nerve 76, 315
nerve cell 58
nerve fibre 62, 64
nerve-muscle tissue 316
nervous system 60, 64, 315
nervous tissue 59
nesting behaviour 331
net 30, 384
net ecosystem productivity 347
net energy 142
net primary production 347

net-veined 118
nettle 49, 363
neural crest 416
neural groove 417
neural mechanism 295
neural plate 416
neural tube 416
Neuraspora 217
neuro-degenerative 198
neurobiology 315
neurocranium 292
neurodermatitis 237
neurogenic 79
neuromuscular junction 321
neuromuscular synapse 63
neuron 68, 295, 315, 326
neurosciences 15
neurotoxin 321
neurotransmitter 320
neurula 222
neurulation 416
neuston 374
neutral 21
neutral fat 171
neutral red 29
newborn 200
newly industrialised country 90
newt 51, 372
niche 338
nidifugous bird 301
night blindness 324
nightingale 50
nightshade 321
nine-plus-two pattern 164
nipple 54
Niskin bottle 379
nitrate ion 154, 350
nitric oxide 406
nitrification 154, 350, 388
nitrifiying bacteria 154, 350
nitrite ion 154, 350
nitrite-oxidizing bacteria 154, 350
nitrobacter 154, 350
nitrogen 83, 154, 350
nitrogen-poor 368
nitrogenous base 205
nitrogenous base adenine 128
nitrosomonas 154, 350
nitrous oxide 403
nocturnal 106, 333
node 116, 331
node of Ranvier 315, 319
nodulation 272

nodule 272, 364
nomad 293
non-allosteric enzyme 138
non-coding 217
non-coding strand 210
non-cyclic electron flow 150
non-native habitat 339
non-protein molecular partners of enzymes 130
non-self 230
non-verbal communication 304
nonessential 333
nonsense mutation 214, 220
NOR 191
noradrenalin 68, 327
Northern blot 244
northern lapwing 394
northern red oak 357
Northern Shoveler 372
nose 53, 63, 292, 322
nosepiece 25
nostril 81
notebook 34
notepad 34
notice 23
notochord 284, 416
noxious 398
NTP 191
nucellus 98
nuclear envelope 188
nuclear power plant 407
nuclear transplantation 419
nuclear waste 408
nucleic acid 165, 204
nucleoid 162
nucleolus 163
nucleoside 205
nucleosome 206
nucleotide 128, 205
nucleus 63, 163, 209, 315
null hypothesis 39
number of offspring 345
nurse cell 222
nut 114, 123
nuthatch 358
nutlet 121
nutrient 151, 222, 352
nutrient condition 274
nutrient cycle 347
nutrient leaching 362
nutrient risk analysis 273
nutrient source 103
nutrient-free soil 391
nutritional niche 375

nutritional value 106
nutritious 409
nutritive 222
nutritive fluid 107
nylon membrane 244, 251, 263
nymphs 365
oak 123, 357
oak forest 353
oar 375
oat 49
oats 116
obesity 278
objective 25
oblong 112
observable 127
observation 23, 226, 296
observe 23, 296
observer 296, 302
obstruction 215
occur 166, 197
ocean 350, 370
ocean dumping 395
odour 326, 390
oesophagus 77
oestrus 72
offspring 181, 281, 308, 410
oil 152, 171
oil platform 395
oil rig 395
oil separator 388
oil spill 394
Okazaki fragment 209
old growth forest 354
oleic acid 171
olfactory communication 303
olfactory sensory neuron 326
oligoprimer 267
oligonucleotide 246
oligopeptid 168
oligotrophic 378
omnipotent 224
omnivore 76, 346
omnivorous 346
oncogene 228, 261
one cotyledon 115
one furrow pollen 115
one-celled ovule 124
one-seeded 122, 123
ontogeny 74, 284, 415
oocyte 193, 221, 413
oogamy 413
oogenesis 221
oogonium 73
open chain form 170

open dish 107
open fermenter 256
open reading frame 214
operant conditioning 298
operant learning 312
operator 215
operon 215, 266
operon model 215
opportunistic 345
opposable thumb 293
opposite 112
opsin 324
optic 66
optic chiasma 66, 325
optic fibre 66
optic nerve 66, 323
optic vesicle 416
optical axis 67
optimise 342
optimum 42
optimum level 330
oral cavity 76
oral disc 412
oral groove 161
oral mucosa cell 58
orchid 49, 364
orchid family 115
order 14, 16, 127
ordinate 41
ore 156
ORF 253
organ 16, 60, 162
organ donation 88
organ of Corti 65, 325
organ structure 385
organ system 60
organelle 59, 159, 162
organic 129
organic detritus feeder 346
organic layer 360
organic nitrogen 155, 351
organiser 224, 418
organism 16, 162
organogenesis 74, 416
orgasm 72
origin 233, 259
origin of replication 208
ornamental tree 121
ornithine 218
ornithologist 399
oscillate 344
oscilloscope 316
osmoconformer 335
osmolarity 83

osmoregulation 83, 335
osmoregulator 335
osmosis 83, 174
osmotic equation 175
osmotic phase diagram 175
osteoblast 62
ostracod 371
otolith 325
outcome 35
outdoor cultivation 401
outer barrier 230
outer covering 335
outer ear 64
outfall 386
outflow 378
outlast 366
output 64, 256, 323
outsider 314
outweigh 330
oval window 65
ovarian cycle 73
ovary 54, 71, 102, 180, 193, 221
ovate 112
overall energy relief 131
overcome 230
overfishing 395
overgrazing 369
overhang 242, 262
overlap 148, 339
overlapping fragment 252
overload 348, 386
overpopulation 408
overshoot 318
overturn 377
overwintering plant 360
oviduct 71
oviparous 345, 413
ovoviparous 413
ovulation 71, 73
ovule 98
ovuliferous scale 99, 100
ovum 73, 91, 193, 221
ovum of newt 418
owl 51, 358
ox-eye daisy 363
oxaloacetate 142, 153
oxidation 141, 143
oxidise 348
oxidise ammonia 154
oxidising agent 143
oxygen atom 167
oxygen concentration 82
oxygen debt 144
oxygen deficiency 379

oxygen depletion 379
oxygen radical 227
oxygen supply 141
oxygen transport 82
oxygen-dependent bacterium 148
oxyhydrogen 144
oyster 52
oystercatcher 394
ozonation 391
ozone 391
ozone hole 405
ozone layer 405
ozone-oxygen cycle 405
P-site 213
p53 228
PAC 252
Pacinian corpuscle 325
pack 307
package 206
paddy field 401
pain 61
painted lady 365
pair 214
pairing 308
palaeontology 287
palatine 233
palatine tonsil 80
palea 116
palindromic 242, 262
palisade layer 159
palm 115
palmar grasp 311
palmitic acid 167, 171
pancreas 53, 70, 76, 129, 238
pandemic 90
Pangaea 286
panicle 114, 116
panmixia 203
pant 145, 332
panting 349
paper clip 29
paper towel 244
papilionaceae 119
papillae 326
parabiosis 340
parabolic 293
paraffine 176
parallel 116
parallel-veined blade 116
paralyse 375
paralysis 321
paramecium 26, 370
parameter 39

parasite 230, 341
parasitism 341
parasympathetic 68, 326
parathyroid 219
parched 409
parenchyma 60, 160
parenchyma cell 58
parent 411
parental care 345
parental generation 181
parents 181
parthenogenesis 221
parthenogenetic 345, 414
parthogenesis 414
partial pressure 82
partial-shade plant 359
partially broken-down rock 361
partially digested 252
participant 19
particle gun 261
partner choice 308
pass on 347
pass through 239
passive transport 175
paste 265
pasteurise 256
pastoral forest 354
pasture 367
pasture field 364
patent 275
patented 275
paternal 182, 198
paternity testing 269
pathogen 86, 230
pathogenic 230
pathway 70
patient sample 254
pattern 191, 251, 263
pattern formation 419
pattern of inheritance 196
PCR 23, 246
PCR-step 247
pea plants 152
peach 48
pear 48
Pearson's chi-square test 204
peat bog 95
peat moss 95
peat soil 368
pectin 93, 273
pectinase 273
pectoral girdle 61
pedicel 101, 114
pedigree 201

pedosphere 347
peduncle 113
peg root 109
pellet 177, 259
pelvic girdle 62, 285, 290
pelvis 292
pencil 34
pencil sharpener 34
penetrate 108, 234, 361, 373
penicillin 255, 341
penis 54, 72
pentose 205
pepo 115
peppered moth 203, 283
pepsin 77
pepsinogen 77
peptide 168
peptide bond 214
peptidoglycan 162
per capita 343
per cent 39
peraeopod 375
percentage 39
perception 67, 325
perch 371
perennial 99, 336, 364
perennial plant 115
perform 316
performance-enhancing drug 276
perianth 101
perigone 101
peril 397
period of frost 360
period of growth 359
period of quiescence 109
period rule 200
periodic cycle 344
periodicity 331
periosteum 62
peripatus 289
peripheral nervous system 68, 326
periphery 224
perish 227
peristalsis 76
peritubular capillary 84
periwinkle family 121
permanent mount 25
permanent tissue cell 190
permanently 392
permeability 233
permeable 174, 261
pernicious anaemia 239

peroxisome 152, 163
persistent calyx 119
persistent leaf base 96
perturbed 352
pest 272, 398
pesticide 344, 398
pestle 27, 207
petal 101, 105
petiole 111
petri dish 28, 177, 266
petrified fern forest 95
petroleum 93
petunia 182
pH 21
pH value 136
phage 162, 183, 260
phagocyte 86, 87, 231
phagocytosis 86, 175, 231
phanerogam 98
phantom midge 370
pharmaceutical 274
pharmaceutics 274
pharmacogenomics 278
pharyngeal arch 416
pharyngeal cleft 416
pharyngeal pouch 416
pharynx 77, 81
phase 188
pheasant 50
phenomenon 17, 66
phenotype 179, 217
phenylalanine 277
phenylketonuria 197, 277
pherograph 248
pheromone 107, 303
phloem 111
phlox family 122
phosphatase 265
phosphate 205, 352
phosphate group 265
phosphoenolpyruvate 153
phospholipid 171
phospholipid layer 287
phosphorous cycle 352
phosphorus source 361
phosphorylate 128
phosphorylation 128
photographic emulsion 178
photolysis 150
photomorphogenesis 331
photon 146
photoperiodism 331
photophosphorylation 150
photoreceptor cell 284

photorespiration 152
photorespire 153
photosynthesis 145, 350
photosynthetic 145
photosynthetic reaction centre 148
phylogenetic 233
phylogenetic tree 285
phylogeny 284
phylum 16
physical attack 314
physical mutagen 220
physics 15
physiological optimum 339
physiological saline 83
physiological salt solution 174
physiology 15
phyto-remediation 386
phytoplankton 92, 399
phytoplankton net 379
pig 50
pigeon 50, 358
pigment 147, 284
pigment layer 67
pigmented 224, 417
pike 51, 372
pilewort 49
pin curler 206
pin head 89, 240
pinch off 411, 413
pine 48
pineal body 70
pinhole eye 285
pinna 65
pinnate 112
pinocytosis 175
pioneer plant 95
pioneer species 381
pioneer stage 368
pioneer zone 392
pipeline 394
pipette 27
pipetteman 27
pistil 102, 180
pistillate 97, 122, 124
pit 161
pit eye 284
pitch 64
pitcher plant 368
placenta 74, 96, 103, 199, 201, 239, 416
placentation 103
plague 90
plankton 375

plant 17, 48
plant cell 158
plant indicator 387
plant juice sucker 346
plant tissue feeder 346
plantain 363
plantar aponeurosis 62
plasma 78, 197
plasma cell 87, 233
plasmid 162, 259, 265
plasmodesmata 161
plasmolysis 175
plastid 163, 182, 287
plastidial DNA 147
plastoglobule 147
plate 266
plate out 266
platelet 78
platypus 289
play behaviour 311
playfulness 306
pleiotrop 217
pleiotropy 217
pleuston 374
pliable 337, 373
plot 42, 345
plumule 98
pluripotent 224
plus gamete 91
pluteus 223
pneumonia 204, 240
pod 180
poikilosmotic 335
poikilotherm 332
point mutation 220
poison 398
poisonous 121, 355, 398
polar molecule 166
polar nucleus 103
pole 189
pollen 180
pollen lobe 102
pollen sac 97
pollen tube 107
pollen tube cell 100
pollenise 97
polleniser 97
pollinate 97, 180, 182
pollinated 97
pollination 97, 180
pollination by insects 106
pollinator 97, 360
pollutant 227, 387, 397
pollute 397

polluted 203, 397
polluting 397
pollution 203, 397
poly-A tail 210, 213
polyadenylation 210
polyandry 309
polychaeta 370
polycistronic 210
polycistronic messenger 215
polygalacturonase 273
polygenetic 196
polygenic 180, 217
polygenic inheritance 217
polygyny 309
polymer 390
polymerase chain reaction 23
polyp 193, 228
polypeptide 130, 168
polyploid 191
polypoloidisation 221
polypore 356
polysaccharide 170
polysynaptic 322
polytene chromosome 191
pome 114
pond 369
pond skater 371
pond snail 371
ponding 392
pons 69, 328
poor soil 368
poplar 48, 123
poppy family 121
population 203, 280, 329
population bottleneck 203, 280
population count 387
population density 343
population ecology 343
population growth 408
population size 343
pore 102, 179
positive charge 317
positive reinforcement 299
possible explanation 35
post-transcriptional gene silencing 211
poster 37
posterior 224
posterior horn 68, 326
posterior vena cava 79
postsynaptic 320
posttranslational modification 268
posture 304, 333

potable 389
potable water 389
potato 121, 412
potato family 121
potential 143
poultry 187
poverty 90, 408
power station 404
Prader-Willi syndrome 198
preadaptation 282
precipitate 208
precipitation 208, 349
precipitation agent dispensing installation 389
precise 19
precision grip 292
precursor 107, 218, 223, 274
predation 343
predator 128, 281, 304, 340
predatory 340
predatory fish 372
predetermine 225
predispose 278
predisposed 229
predisposition 229, 282
preen 333
preen gland 333
preen oil 333
prefer 301
preference 214
pregnancy 201
pregnancy test 415
prehominid 291
preimplantation genetic diagnosis 201
preliminary level 277
premature 219
premature birth 417
premature death 277
prenatal diagnosis 201
prenatal diagnostic 269
prepuce 72
prerequisite 203
present 234
preservation 396
pressure 61
pressure wave 66
presynaptic 320
presynaptic inhibition 322
prevent 199, 265, 396
preventative 396
prevention 396
prey 281, 304, 340
primary antibody 237

primary clarifier 388
primary coloniser 381
primary colour 324
primary endosperm 100
primary oocyte 73
primary root 109
primary sensory cell 319
primary spermatocyte 73
primary succession 381
primate 291, 309
primer 209, 246
primeval forest 362
primitive gut 222, 416
primrose family 122
principle of competition exclusion 338
principle of uniformity 181
printout 248
prion 89, 241
prior 239
prism 146
privet 49, 366
pro-choice 200
pro-life 201
pro-virus 240
probability 39, 203, 250
probe 27, 217, 244, 251
problem 17
proboscis 184
process 64, 210, 323, 409
producer 346
product 126, 132
product removal 256
progenitor 233
progesterone 73
progress curve 134
progress of reaction 134
progressive 198
progressively 136
prohibit 278
prokaryote 183, 287
prokaryotic cell 161, 287
prokaryotic promoter 267
proliferation 266, 410
proliferative phase 73
promoter 211, 215, 266
proof 204
prop root 109
propagate 267
propagation 410
property 128, 168, 279
prophase 188
propose 206
proprietary company 306

prospective 223
prospective fate 418
prospective potency 418
prostate 55
prostate gland 72
prosthetic group 130
protease 129, 205, 219, 240
proteasome 164, 219
protect 396
protection 241, 396
protection forest 354
protective 216
protective measure 399
protein 75, 130, 165, 199, 204
protein decomposition 155
protein-coding gene 250
protein-rich 117, 123, 364
proteinaceous infectious particle 241
proteinase resistant 242
proteome 270
proterandrous 104
proterandry 104
proterogynous 104
proterogyny 104
prothallium 194
prothallus 96
protist 160
proto-oncogene 228
protobiont 287
proton 142, 150
proton acceptor 136
proton concentration gradient 143
proton donor 136
proton gradient 150
proton motive force 144, 150
proton pump 144
protonema 94
protoplast 271
protostome 416
protozoa 85
protozoan 230, 390
protrude 94
protruding 242, 262
prove 204
provide with 266
proximal tubule 84
PrP 241
pseudanthium 114
pseudocarp 115
pseudoscorpion 359
psilophyte 95
psoralene 220

psychological 198
psychopharmaca 70
PTC taster 196
public transport 404
puff 191
puff up 191
puffball 355
puffin 51
pulmonary artery 78
pulmonary vein 78
pulp cavity 76
pulse 54, 79
punish 299
punishment 299
Punnet square 181
pupal enclosure 384
pupil 67
pupillary reflex 67
purification 268, 389
purify 139, 237, 263, 389
purine 206
purple moorgrass 380
purview 329
pus 86, 232
putrefaction 145
putrefying bacteria 145
pyloric sphincter 77
pyramid of net production 347
pyramid of numbers 347
pyrenoid 93
pyrimidine 206
pyruvate 141
quack grass 412
quadrate 31
quadruped 291
quadruple 135
qualitative 38
quality of life 396
quantifiable 23
quantitative 38
quantity 39, 41
quaternary structure 130
queen bee 305, 414
R cells 204
R-banding 190
r-selected species 345
rabbit 50
raceme 114
rachis 114, 124
racoon 357
radially symmetrical 118
radiation 126, 146, 229, 270, 406
radical 98
radioactive 178, 244, 251

radioactive nucleotide 248
radioactively marked 191
radioactivity 178, 286
radioisotope 150
radioisotope labelling experiments 151
radiolarian 26
radish 182
raditation 220
raft 174
rain forest 362
rainfall 352
rainwater 95
raised bog 380
ramshorn snail 371
random 252, 261
randomly 127
randomness 127
range of pH 137
range of temperature 332
rank before 306, 314
rank below 306, 314
rannoch-rush 380
rape 272
rapid 410
rapid sand filter 390
raspberry 48
rat 50
rat chow pellet 299
rate 39
rate of evolution 280, 286
rate of photosynthesis 334
rate of yield 279
ratio 207
ravage 398
raven 51
raw material 151
raw milk 257
raw water 390
ray 99
ray floret 118
razor 27
re-establish 226
re-orient 418
reach adulthood 301
react 16, 171
reactant 125, 132
reacting organ 322
reaction 16
reaction volume 246
reagent 29
reanneal 245
rear 187
rearrangement 235

reassociation kinetics 245
reassociation study 245
rebedding 382
receive 102
receiving water 389
receptacle 101
receptive field 324
receptor 322
receptor cell 64, 319
receptor mediated phagocytosis 231
receptor molecule 228, 231, 326
receptor potential 319
receptor protein 229
recessive 180, 196
recipient 183, 238, 259, 303
reciprocal altruism 308
recoginition 230
recognition sequence 261
recognize 219, 231, 234, 242
recombination 183, 192, 258, 280
recombination nodule 192
recombination reaction 406
recombine 192, 258
record 30, 35
recorder 248
recording electrode 319
recording site 318
recreational forest 354
rectum 78
recycle 402
recycling 402
red blood cell 78, 199, 239, 276
red bone marrow 62, 80
red cabbage 175
red deer 49, 357
red gene technology 278
red kite 358
Red List 399
red-backed shrike 367
red-green colour blindness 197
reddening 237
redox reaction 143
redtop 363
reduce 348
reduced root system 337
reducing agent 143, 149
reduction 143
reductional division 192
redundant 213
redwood 357
reed 373
reef-building 412

reference 36
reference person 311
reference value 64, 323
refine 409
reflect 148
reflected light 24
reflex 300, 322
reforestation 350, 362, 369
refractory period 318
refrigerant 404
refuse to do 299
regenerate 142, 271
regeneration 411
regular 118
regular flowers 118
regular sampling 256
regulate 417
regulation 417
regulative development 225
regulative embryo 418
regulator protein 228
regulatory gene 215, 419
regulatory protein 419
regulatory subunit 138
regulatory system 70
reincorporate 348
reindeer 49
reinforce positively 299
reintroduce 277
reject 102
rejection 238
related 342
relationship 309
relaxation 306
relaxed 63
release 238, 240
release energy 125
releaser 297
relief 254
religion 294
religious values 200
remove 265
renal artery 84
renal calyx 84
renal cortex 84
renal function 175
renal medulla 84
renal pelvis 84
renal vein 84
renaturalisation 386
renaturalise 386
renature 245
renaturing 245
renewable 403

renin-angiotensin-aldosterone system 85
rennet 257
repeat 214, 247
repetitive DNA 245
repetitive sequence 250
replacement 266
replenish 348, 377
replicate 188, 208, 260
replication 191, 208, 259, 264
replication complex 264
replication-enzyme complex 227
repolarisation 318
reporter gene 266
repress 215, 401
repressor 211, 215
reprocessing plant 408
reproduce 16
reproducible 19
reproduction 16, 281, 410
reproductive apparatus 101
reproductive behaviour 308
reproductive cell 58
reproductive cycle 331
reproductive organ 71
reproductive success 281
reproductive system 60
reproductive unit 411
reprogramming 265
reptile 17
reptile characteristic 290
require energy 124
research 35, 275
resemble 229
reserve 399
reservoir 349, 369, 385
residence 349
residence time 390
residual disinfectant 391
residual group 168
residual volume 82
residue 167
resin 99, 176
resistance 266, 272
resistance gene 259, 266
resistant 260
resolve 213
resorption 343
resource 106, 339, 396
respective 214
respiration 53, 141, 349
respiration by gills 417
respiratory disorder 403

respiratory pigment 82
respiratory substrate 80
respiratory surface 80
respiratory system 60
respond 216, 231, 418
response 63, 231
responsive 216
resting 317
resting potential 317
restoration 381
restore 396
restriction digestion 262
restriction endonuclease 250
restriction enzyme 242, 250, 261
restriction fragment 242, 250
restriction site 242, 262
result 18, 23, 35
resuspend 177
retain 136
retention period 407
reticulate 118
retina 66, 323
retinal 130, 324
retinoblastoma 229
retroviral insertion 245
retrovirus 89, 240
Rett syndrome 198
return activated sludge 388
returnable bottle 402
reuse 219
reverse 246
reverse osmosis 390
reverse reaction 131
reverse transcribe 267
reverse transcriptase 89, 240, 267
reverse transcriptase inhibitor 240
reverse transcription 89, 240, 267
reversible 19, 137
reversible reaction 131
Rh-negative 88
Rh-positive 88
RhD negative 199
RhD positive 199
rhesus factor 88
rhesus system 87, 199, 239
rheumatoid factor 88, 239
rhizobial bacterium 272
rhizoid 94
rhizomania 272
rhizome 96, 110, 336, 356
rhodopsin 66, 324

rhythm method 74
rib 290
rib cage 62, 81
ribbon-like 94
ribose 128, 170
ribosome 164, 213
ribosome attachment site 214
ribulose 1,5-bisphosphate 151
rice 49, 116
rickets 197
right and left hemisphere 69
right atrium 79
rind 257
ring clamp 28
ring form 170
ring of teeth 95
ring stand 28
Ringer's solution 29
riparian forest 353
riparian zone 385
ripen 273
ripening 257, 273
rising phase 318
risk 254, 398
risk analysis 229
risky 398
rival 314
river 369, 381
river basin 382
river bed 381
river bed composition 385
river bed structure 385
river depression 380
river limpet 384
riverine traffic 385
riverine vegetation 385
riverine zone 385
rivulet 381
RNA 89, 165, 209
RNA editing 219
RNA polymerase 209
RNAi 211, 226
roach 372
robin 50, 358
rock bottom 383
rock flour 380
rocky 378
rod 66, 323
rodent 342
roe deer 49, 357
rook 50
roosting site 393
root 76
root cap 415

root free soil core 355
root layer 355
root nodule 152
root stock 109
root system 109
root tissue 361
root tuber 412
root tubercle bacterium 152
rooted floating-leaved plant
   zone 374
rooting 361
rooting system 355
rootstock 412
rose 49
rose family 118
rosette plant 335
rosulate 113
rotifer 414
rotting mud 386
rough 204
roughage 75
roughness 382
round 180
round dance 305
round window 65
rove beetle 365
royal 197
rRNA 210
rubber 34
rubber band 29
rubber glove 31
rubbish 402
RuBisCo 151
rudd 371
rudiment 416
rudimentary 285
rudimentary cell 100
rudimentary metacarpals 285
rudimentary organ 285
rugged 99
rule 31
ruler 34
run-off rainwater 386
rung 206
runner 110, 412
runner bean 152
running water 388
runoff 349
rusella 355
rush 373
rye 49, 116
S cells 204
S-phase 188
S-shaped curve 344

saccharose 117, 170
safety cord 384
safety precautions 19
salamander 51
saline 21
salinity 21, 157, 337, 392, 393
saliva 53, 137
salivary amylase 77
salivary gland 53, 76, 191
salmon 51, 395
salmonidae 382
salt 165
salt bladder 393
salt exclusion 393
salt excretion 337, 393
salt gland 393
salt indifferent 393
salt marsh 370
salt solution 316
salt water 93, 383
saltatory conduction 319
samara 114
sample 25, 30, 35, 249
sample container 30
sample DNA 263
sample jar 379
sampling 30, 387
sand 361
sandhopper 52
sandy 378
sanitation 409
sap feeder 360
saprophyte 346
saprophytic 346
sarcoma 228
SARS 90
satellite DNA 245
saturated 20, 166, 391
saturation 376, 392
saturation point 20
saturation value 344
savanna 353
saxifrage family 122
scaffolding of fibrin 140
scale 94
scale leaf 99
scales 27
scalpel 27
scaly 99
scan 255
scanner 217, 254
scanning electron microscope
   176

scanning tunneling microscope 176
scar 110
scarcity 408
scattered 115
scavenge 231
scavenger 51, 346
scene of crime 249
scent 304
scented 106
schizocarp 114
school of fish 376, 395
scion 412
scissors 28
sclera 67
sclerophyllous vegetation 353
scrap iron 402
scrap yard 402
scrape 241
scrapie 241
screen 226, 269
screening 388, 390
scrotum 55, 72
scrubber 403
sculpin 371
sculpture 294
scutellum 117
scythe 367, 399
sea anemone 413
sea eagle 399
sea floor 370
sea lavender 122, 393
sea level 407
sea purslane 393
sea thrift 122, 393
sea urchin 52, 222
seagull 51
seal 100
seasonal 331
seasonal phase 376
seasonal pond 369
Secchi disc 379
second messenger molecules 324
second trimester 74
secondary antibody 237
secondary coelom 416
secondary growth 99, 118
secondary immune response 86
secondary oocyte 73
secondary spermatocyte 73
secrete 65, 91, 159, 235, 236, 271
secretion 84

secretory cell 58
section 25, 37
sedentary 294
sedentism 294
sedge 122, 152
sedge family 122
sediment 177, 208, 373
sediment of the lake 376
sedimentation 177, 386
sedimentation basin 390
seed 98, 216
seed capsule 119
seed dormancy 415
seed embryo 257
seed predator 360
seedling 194, 216, 356
seedpod 120
seep 378
seepage 378
segmentation gene 225, 419
select 187, 253, 342
selectable marker 266, 271
selected 342
selection 187, 281
selection medium 266
selection pressure 282, 309
selection-neutral 249
selective ion channel 317
selective pressure 342
selective reabsorption 84
self 230
self tolerance 239
self-assembly 417
self-awareness 310
self-compatible 104
self-digestion 257
self-fertile plant 104
self-incompatible 104
self-knowledge 310
self-organisation 417
self-purification 386
selfheal 363
Sellotape™ 29
semen 72, 241
semi-conservative 209
semi-parasite 364
semicircular canal 64
seminal vesicle 72
seminiferous tubule 72
semipermeable 174
semipermeable membrane 84
sender 303
sender recipient relationship 303

sense 63
sense codon 219
sense organ 312
sensitisation 87
sensitive 260, 397
sensitive phase 301
sensor 64, 323
sensor for rotation 325
sensory 297
sensory cell 318, 323
sensory nerve 322
sensory organ 63, 322
sensory receptor 61
sepal 101
separate 179, 205, 236, 243, 248, 412
separate sewage system 388
separation 243
separation step 192
sequence 169, 246
sequencing 246, 248, 251
sequencing by hybridisation 252
sequencing primer 248
sequencing reaction 248
sequoia 289
seral stage 381
serosa 417
serrated 112
sessile 111, 394
sessile polyp 414
set of data 38
set square 34
set up 19
settlement 294
settling sediment 388
70S ribosome 162, 213
sever 192
sewage 386
sewage plant 154, 351, 388
sewer 402
sex 183
sex characteristic 71
sex chromosome 183
sex determination 183
sex education 408
sex hormone 73
sex organ 223
sex pilus 259
sex-chromosome 190
sex-linked 185, 190
sexual conduct 295
sexual reproduction 90, 193, 221

sexual reproduction pattern 343
sexual selection 309
sexually mature 184
seymuria 289
shade leaf 359
shade plant 359
shadow box 296
shake 20
shallow 379
shallow water zone 383
shape 133, 179, 191
share 13
shaven 186
shear 253
sheath 111
shed 97
shed leaves 336
sheep grazing 399
shelf life 273
shell 93, 122
shellfish-eating bird species 394
shelter 367, 384
shikimic acid 218
shiver 333
shoal 307
shock 237
shoot 99, 109, 356
shoreline 373
shoreline erosion 379
shoreline forest 380
short tandem repeats 250
short-day plant 332
short-eared owl 394
short-lived species 345
short-term change 318
short-term memory 312
shot 296
shotgun library 253
shoulder girdle 290
shrimp 395
shrub 110
shrub layer 356
shuffle 193
shuttle vector 267
sibling 181
sickle cell anemia 203, 276
side chain 168
signal 303
signal molecule 152
significant 270
silage 364
silent mutation 220

silica 93
silicle 120
silicon 254
silicone oil 246
silicule 114
silique 114, 120
silkworm 124
silt 383
silt up 380
silting 380
silver bromide 178
silver grain 178
silver maple 357
similar sequence 419
simple leaf 111
simplification 344
simplify 344
sing in alternation 303
single copy DNA 245
single nucleotide polymorphism 250
single ovary 124
single-stranded DNA 247, 263
sinistrorse twining 110
sinoatrial node 79
sinuate 112
site 34
size 179, 191
skate 395
skeletal muscle 62
skeletal system 60
skeleton 53
sketch 26
skewed 44
skim off 388
skin 61, 63, 323
skin cancer 407
skin colour 196
Skinner box 296, 299
skull 61, 292
slash burning 362, 368
slaughter weight 274
slide 37, 208
slime layer 162
sloe 366
slope 44
slot 243
slow motion 45
slow motion picture 296
slowed growth 362
sludge 388
sludge bulking 389
sludge digestion 389
sludge disposal 389

sludge tank 389
sludge tower 389
sludge trap 388
slug 52, 359
slurry 380
small intestine 77, 129
small tortoiseshell 365
smog 404
smooth 112, 204
smooth meadow-grass 363
smooth muscle 79
smooth muscle cell 58
smooth surface 384
snail 52, 359
snail shell 65
snake 358
snap mechanism 120
snap shut 368
sneezing 237
snipe fly 370
snowdrop 49
snowflake 49
SNP 198, 220
soakaway 389
social 184
social benefits 408
social contact 313
social life 313
social position 306, 314
social relationship 306
social security 408
society 306
sodium channel 319
sodium hydroxide 250
sodium-potassium pump 175, 317
soft 273
soft brome 363
soft ground 337
soft palate 76
soft wired 217
soft wood 121
soft-spined husk 123
soil amendment 95
soil bacteria 271
soil density 361
soil erosion 401
soil exhaustion 401
soil fertility 401
soil sampler 31
soil sealing 385
soil texture 361
solar irradiation 331
solar radiation 152, 377

solar water disinfection 391
solid 222, 376
solitary flower 114
solubility 376
soluble 20
solute 20, 83
solution 20, 29
solve 177
solvent 20, 29, 148, 405
soma 224, 315, 321
somatic cell 277
somatic mutation 229
somatic recombination 87, 235
somitogenesis 416
somitomere 416
sonar 395
song thrush 368
soot 203, 229, 283
sorghum 152, 409
sorosis 115
sorus 96, 194
sound 64
sound waves 63, 322
source 349, 382
Southern blot 244, 251
Southern Blotting 263
soybean 273, 409
spadix 114
sparger 256
sparrow 50, 367
sparrow hawk 358
sparsely toothed 123
spatial 66, 168, 207, 323
spatial perception 67
spatial structure 242
spatially 339
spatula 27
spawning ground 393
special case 414
special waste 402
speciation 283
species 16, 283
species difference 271
species' range 339
species-specific 222
specific 178, 242
specific antibody 226
specific gravity 177
specificity 132
specimen 25
spectral range 324
spectrometrically 246
speed of rotation 21
Spemann's organiser 225

sperm 414
sperm cell 73, 92, 100
sperm head 193
sperm tail 193
spermatogenesis 73
spermatogonium 73
spermatozoa 193, 221
sphagnum 380
sphagnum moss 373, 392
sphincter 76
sphingolipid 172
sphingosine 172
spider 52
spike 114
spikelet 116
spin down 176
spinal cord 68, 322, 326
spinal ganglion 68, 326
spinal nerve 68, 326
spindle apparatus 189, 190
spindle fibre 190
spine 61, 68, 198, 291, 326, 366
spine / thorn 336
spinneret 384
spiny 112, 115
spiral 113
spirogyra 93
spleen 80, 233, 236
splice 210, 265
splice variants 254
splicing 210, 218, 265
splicing machinery 264
split off 101
spongiform 241
spongy mesophyll 160
spool 208
sporangium 96, 193
spore 92, 193, 411
sporophyll 96
sporophyte 91, 92, 193
spotted 182
spotted sedge 370, 384
spread 106
spring 369
spring flower 49
spring forest geophyte 49, 359
spring runoff 383
spring snowflake 356
spring water 387
spring-fed brook 383
springtail 359
spruce 48, 362
spruce moth 359
spruce swamp 392

spur 106
square stems 120
squash preparation 25
squirrel 50, 357
SRY gene 184
stable 132
stable habitat 410
stacking interaction 206
stage 188, 408
stagnant 383
stagnant water zone 383
stagnation 377
stain 26, 29, 190, 237, 243
stalk 94, 375
stalk cell 100
stalked 96
stamen 102, 120, 180, 194
staminate 97, 122
staminate flower 124
staminum 116
standard 119
standing water 388
stapes 284
staple diet 121
starch 129, 137, 140, 170, 216
starch grain 147
starch suspension 129
starchy nutritious tissue 117
starling 367
start methionine 213
starting material 138
state 215
state of aggregation 376
statement of interest 306
static state 127
stationary phase 148
statistical significance 204
statistics 39
stats 39
steady state 349
steam sterilised 255
steam turbine 402
stearic acid 171
steepness 381
stem 109, 153, 180
stem cell 58, 78, 224, 277
stem tendril 110
stem tuber 412
stem-clasping 116
stenohaline 335
stenopotent 330
stenotherm 332
step 311
steppe 353

sterical 206
sterile 22
sterile nutrient 256
sterilisation 22
sterilise 22
sternum 290
steroid 171
stick blender 207
stick insect 52, 414
sticky 102
sticky end 242
sticky hair 368
sticky tape 29
stigma 102, 180
stimulate 234
stimulating current 318
stimulation 318
stimulation electrode 319
stimulus 16, 63, 297, 300, 318, 322
stimulus-response theory 300
stinging nettle 364
stipule 111
stir 208
stirrer 256, 381
stirring rod 28
stirrup 65
stoat 358
stolon 117
stoma 336
stomach 53, 77
stomatum 100, 153
stomium 96
stone 293
stonecrop 366
stonefly 370
stonework 404
stonewort 374
stop codon 219
stop watch 28
stopper 28
storage 335
storage organ 151
store 335
store oil 93
stored 351
stork 50
stork's nest 362
storm sewage 388
stormwater 388
stowaway 400
straight ditch 385
strain 258
strand 206, 208, 245

strata 379
stratification 355
straw 29
strawberry 48, 412
stream 369, 381
stream narrowing 385
stream pool 383
strepsirrhini 309
streptomycin 266
stress 274
stress tolerance 279
string 206
stroke 140, 228
stroke volume 79
stroma 147
strong 292
strong company 306
structural formula 165
structural gene 215
structure 14, 169
study 34
stunted growth 334, 361, 362
style 102, 180
sub unit 162
subcloning 253
subcutis 61
subfamily 152
subject 19
sublingual immunotherapy 238
submerge 105
submerged 336, 374
submergent plant 374
submissive behaviour 314
subordinated 226
subsequent 191
substance 29, 165
substrate 132, 178, 263
substrate concentration 134
substrate-binding region 133
subtractive colour mixing 324
subunit 130
succession 67, 381
succession process 381
succulent 153, 336, 366
suck 311
sucking reflex 311
sucrose-rich 106
suction pump 81
Sudan 29
suffer 200, 254
suffocate 404
sugar 117
sugar beet 272
sugar cane 152

sugar phosphate ester 205
sugarcane 117
suitable 411
suitable condition 268
sulphate 156, 351
sulphate aerosol 352
sulphate-reducing bacteria 156
sulphide 155, 157
sulphide ore 156
sulphite 157
sulphur 155, 351
sulphur cycle 351
sulphur dioxide 352
sulphur removal 157
sulphur trioxide gas 157
sulphuric 157
sulphuric acid 157, 352
summarise 12, 23
summation 321
summer egg 414
summer polder 393
sun leaf 360
sundews 368
superficial fascia 61
superior 219
superior ovary 116
superiority 314
supernatant 21, 177, 208
supernatant fluid 259
supersaturated 20
supplement 259, 266
support 201
supporting structure 64
surface 132, 140, 173, 231
surface aerated basin 388
surface antigen 199
surface appendage 259
surface effluent 378
surface influents 378
surface marker 229
surface molecule 231, 237
surface of the earth 407
surface sealing 385
surface skin 375
surface water 387
surgery 201
surplus 228
surround 222
survival 408
survival strategy 329
survive 266, 408
suspect 249
suspended particle 373
suspended solid 390

suspension 20, 129
suspension culture 177
suspensory ligament 67
sustainability 396
sustainable 396
Swabian highlands 368
Swabian mountains 400
swallow 50
swallowing 76
swamp 373, 392
swamp thicket 373
swamp zone 373
swap 192
sweat 332
sweating 349
sweet cherry 356
sweet vernal-grass 363
swell 190, 216, 233
swift 50, 367
swine flu 90
switch off 215
swollen 87
swollen leaf stalk 336
swordfish 395
symbiont 287
symbiosis 99, 341
symmetrical 44, 121
sympathetic 68, 326
sympetalous 113
symport 175
symptom 240
synapse 315, 320
synaptic knob 315, 320
syncarpous 113
synecological 329
synecology 329
synergid cell 103
syngonium 115
synthesis 163
synthesise 163
synthesise adequately 276
synthesise artificially 276
synthetic gene 268
system of veins 111
systolic pressure 80
T cell 87
T cell receptor 234
T cell receptor 87
t-test 39
table 41
table apple 366
tadpole 227, 372, 417
tag 266, 268
taiga 353

tail 414
tail end 394
take up 175, 178, 183, 205
tamper-proof 249
tandem repeat 245
tannin content 123
tansy 367
tap root system 109, 119
tap-root 99
tape measure 31
tapeworm 342
taproot 336
Taq polymerase 246
tar 229
tarsier 309
taste 390
taste bud 326
Tay-Sachs disease 197
TDF 184
tectorial membrane 66
teeth fungus 356
telomere 190, 227
telomeric 190
telophase 188
temperature dependence 334
temperature dependent 184
temperature-depending 141
template 208, 247
temporal 207
temporarily 392
temporary 183
tending strategy 399
tendon 53, 62
tens of thousands 406
tension 314
tent 294
tentacle 375
term 14
terminal bud 96
terminal stigma 119
terminate 209, 211
termination 214
terminator 211, 215
tern 394
terrace 366
terrestrial ecosystem 353
territorial behaviour 313
territorial call 303
territory 281, 307
tertiary structure 132
test 22
test strip 140
test substance 29
test tube 28, 237, 246

testa 98
testicle 55, 193
testis 72
testosterone 73
tetrad 192
texture 256
thalamus 69, 328
thallus 91
the effect of sth 135
the effect on sth 135
the use 139
theory of evolution 280
therapeutic 277
therapeutic benefit 277
therapeutic option 89, 240
thermal cycling steps 247
thermal energy 126
thermal power station 388
thermal radiation 406
thermal stratification 377
thermocline 377
thermocycler 246
thermometer 28
thermophilic digestion 389
thermophilus aquaticus 247
thermoregulation 60, 61
thick cuticle 336
thin 111
thin-layer chromatography 147
thiosulphate 157
third trimester 74
30 nm chromatine fibre 207
thistle 363
thoracic cavity 81
thoracic duct 80, 87
thorax 53
thorn 110, 334
thread 384
thread cell 375
thread-like 208, 242
threat 398
threaten 398
three furrow pollen 118
3' 210
three-angled nut 123
3-carbon sugar phosphate 151
three-dimensional 38, 135, 168
three-lobed 120
three-point analysis 185
threshold effect 330
threshold voltage 318
throat 65
thrombus 78
throw-away 402

thumb 292
thylakoid 162
thylakoid membrane 147
thymine 206
thymine dimer 221
thymus 80, 86, 233
thyroid 239
thyrsus 114
Ti plasmid 271
tibia 62
tick 341, 359
tidal creek 392
tidal flats 352, 392
tidal volume 82
tight 66
tight junction 59
tiller 117
timber 362
time-lapse microscopy 226
time-lapse photography 45
time-lapse shot 296
timothy 363
tinsel syndrome 362
tip of shoot 94
tissue 16, 59, 159, 207
tissue transplantation 418
tissue-plasminogen-activator 275
tit 50, 358
toad 51, 358, 372
toe biter 371
tolerance 187, 329
tomato 48
tongue 63, 76, 196, 322
tongue roller 196
tool 30, 293
toothed 112
topsoil 361
torpor 333
torrent 383
torso 53
tortoise 51
total 39
total energy 126
totally submerged rooted plant 374
totipotency 410
totipotent 58, 160
town 294
toxic 197, 398
toxic load 386
toxic metabolite 197
toxicity 140, 277
toxin 137, 344

toxoplasmosis 240
trabecula 62
trace element 216
trace of blood 241
tracer method 151
trachea 76, 81
tracheid 96, 99
track down 269
trait 187, 196
transcriptional 192
trans region 163
transcribe 209
transcription 209, 270
transcription factor 211, 228, 419
transcriptional regulatory factor 419
transduce 64
transduction 64, 183, 323
transect 30
transfer 65, 97, 205, 244, 259, 263
transference 97
transform 258, 348
transformation 183, 205, 258, 266, 348
transfuse 238
transfusion 238
transgenic 255, 278
transition 220
transition country 408
transition zone 393
transitional fossil 289
transitional phase 105
translate 212
translation 212, 270
translocation 191, 221
transmembrane proteine 198
transmission 64, 241
transmission electron microscope 176
transmit 318, 341
transmitter 296
transmitting substance 320
transpiration 348
transpire 348
transplant rejection 88
transplantate 238
transplantation 238
transplantation antigen 238
transplantation experiment 224
transposable element 245
transversal section 216
transverse 411

transversion 220
trap 368
travel advice 90
trawl net 395
treat 238, 261
treatment 139, 238, 261
tree 110
tree layer 356
tree limit 354
tree of heaven 357
tree ring analysis 362
trial-and-error learning 298, 312
triatomic ozone molecule 406
tributary 382
tricarboxylic acid cycle 142
tricarpellary 113
trigger 63, 300, 322
triglyceride 171
trinucleotide expansion 198
triops 289
triple test 201
triplet 213
tripod 28
trisomy 191
^{3}H 191
tRNA 210, 214
trophic level 347
trophoblast 74, 415
tropical wood 362
trout 51, 274, 382
true grasses 115
trunk 356
trypsin 129
tryptophan 277
tryptophan synthesis 218
tubal ligation 74
tube 25, 94, 107
tube cell 102, 107
tube nucleus 107
tuber 110, 336, 356
tuberculosis 409
tuberous root 109
tubular calyx 120
tubular corolla 106
tubulin 190
tufted duck 372
tumour 228, 240, 261
tumour marker 140
tumour suppressor gene 228, 278
tumour-inducing 271
tuna 395
tundra 353
tungsten 261

turbid 373
turbidity 379, 383, 390
turbulence 382
turgid 174
turgor pressure 174
turn of energy policies 410
turning point 42
turnover number 135
turtle 51
tussock 364
tweezers 27, 31
twig 110
twilight 324
twining stem 110
twisted rope ladder 206
two dimensional
  electrophoresis 270
two-chamber 120
two-hit hypothesis 229
two-lobed style 124
two-valved capsule 124
2C 189
2n 189
tying experiment 224
tympanic canal 325
type of learner 312
typhoid 409
tyrosine 277
U- or J-shaped-burrow 394
U-shaped 293
ubiquitin 219
udder cell 420
ultra-thin section 176
ultra-violet nectar guide 106
ultramicrotome 176
ultrasound examination 201
umbel 114, 119
umbilical cord 201
unaffected 196
unborn 240
unbound probe 263
unbranched 94
uncertainty 306
under side 100
underground 351
underground storage stem 96
understand 310
undifferentiated cell 58, 415
undisturbed 224
undulated 112
unequal 417
unfavourable 410
unfold 219
unicellular organism 411

uniform 377
unintentional 279
unisexual 97, 99
unisexual catkins 123
unit 39, 41
universal 213
universal solvent 166
unknowingly 400
unpigmented 163
unprecedented 407
unpredictable 407
unprotected sex 241
unrelated 342
unsaturated fat 123
unstable 132
unstained 26
untranslated region 214
unusable energy 126
unwind 209
upper lip 120
upper reaches 382
upper surface 100
upright 291
uptake 175, 178, 183, 205
uracil 206, 210
urbanisation 408
urbanise 408
urbanophil 367
urbanophobic 367
urea 155, 351
ureter 54, 84
urethra 54, 72, 84
uric acid 155, 351
uridine 210
uridine triphosphate 192
urinary bladder 84
urine 335
use a microscope 24
uterus 54, 71, 201, 278
UTP 210
UV irradiation 221
UV radiation 286, 391
UV rays 229
UV spectrometer 246
V segment 235
V-shaped structure 166
vacant 213
vaccinate 86, 232
vaccination 86, 232, 409
vaccine 240, 341, 409
vacuole 92, 161, 163
vagina 54, 71
vaginal secretion 241
valve 78

van't Hoff equation n 334
van't Hoff's rule 135
variability 283
variable 41, 240, 344
variable region 235
variance 411
variant 254
variation 180
Varroa mite 400
vary 180
vas deferens 55, 72
vasa recta 84
vascular 95
vascular bundle 111, 115, 118
vascular cambium 412
vascular plant 98
vascular system 96
vasectomy 74
VDJ recombination 235
vector 264, 341, 399
vegetable 75
vegetal pole 223, 415
vegetation period 334
vegetative cell 102, 107
vegetative propagation 117
vegetative reproduction 411
vein 54, 78, 79, 96, 111
velocity 380
velvet stamp 266
venation 111
venous valve 54
venter 92
venter canal cell 100
ventral 224
ventral root 68, 326
ventricle 54, 78
ventricular systole 79
venule 79
Venus flytrap 368
Venus of Willendorf 294
vermiform appendix 80, 233
vermilion 186
vernalisation 415
vertebrate 17, 371
vertical 38
vertical movement 174
vesicle 162, 228, 231
vessel-less 99
vestibular apparatus 65
vestibule 71
vestigial 285
vetch 363
vibrate 106
vibration 106, 325

vicinity 403
vicious circle 397
vie 338
view 38
villus 77
vineyard 366
violet 49
viral envelope 89
viral particle 277
viral vector 277
virtual water 391
virulent 204
virus 162, 229, 230
viscosity 276
visible 24, 67, 188, 244
visible spectrum 146
visual acuity 67
visual attraction 308
visual communication 304
visual field 67, 323
vital capacity 82
vitality 330
vitamin 75
vitamin A rice 274
vitamin Biotin 258
vitelline layer 414
vitreous body 67
viviparous 345, 413
VJ recombination 235
vocal communication 303
vocal cord 53
vocal fold 81
volcanic eruption 351
volcano 286
voltage 316
voltage-gated channels 318
volunteer 19
volva 355
vorticella 26
vulture 51
vulva 54, 71
Wadden Sea 392, 400
wader species 394
wag 305
waggle dance 305
waggle pattern 305
wall contact behaviour 313
warm-blooded 332
warn 282
warning 282
warning colour 282
warning colouration 304
warning cry 303
wash 263

wash bottle 27
wash into 348
wash out 386
washing powder 208
washing-up liquid 208
wasp 53
waste heat 406
waste management 402
waste product 83, 142, 150
waste substance 256
waste water 386
watch glass 28
watch spring 96
water 29, 75
water balance 334
water bath 22, 28
water boatman 371
water clarity 378
water column 379
water conditioning 391
water consumption 391
water current 375
water discharge 386
water flea 51, 371
water fluoridation 391
water holding capacity 361
water income 378
water level 383
water logged 363
water milfoil 374
water molecule 165
water quality 389
water quality assessment 379
water reservoir 348
water shortage 336, 391
water smart weed 374
water storage 95
water strider 51
water surface tension 385
water tiger 371
water transparency 378
water-dependent 94
water-purifying plant 391
waterlogged 337
waterlogged soil 391
waterlouse 371
waterproofs 31
watershed 378, 382
wave 376
wavelength 64, 146, 246
waxy 159
waxy layer 336
weak 292
weasel 357, 366

weather 351
weathered stones 361
weathering 351
weed 401
weevil 272, 365
weir 390
wellington 31
Werner syndrome 227
Western blot 244
wetland 369, 391
wheat 49, 116
whelk 394
whey 257
white blood cell 78, 232
white film 381
white gene technology 278
white matter 68, 326
white swan 372
white water lily 374
whooping cough 409
whorl 99
whorled 113
wide 292, 382
width 382
wild boar 357
wild carrot 367
wild-type mice 274
wildcat 50, 357
wildlife activist 396
wildtype 182
willow 48, 123, 357
willow family 123
wilted 175
wind 208
wind dispersal 98
wind-borne 97
wind-dispersed 121
wind-pollinated 104
windfall 367
windpipe 54
wing 101, 185
wing petal 119
winged 115, 121
winter egg 414
winter fur 333
wire gauze 28
wireworm 359, 365
wishbone 289
wither 98
withstand 329
wobble hypothesis 214
wolf 49, 358
wolf spider 359
wood grouse 358

wood sorrel family 122
wood-boring insect 360
woodbine 356
woodlouse 52
woodpecker 50, 358
woodruff 122
woodrush beech forest 353
woody 99
woody debris 360, 392
woody plant 110
woody tissue 118
wordplay 274
work bench 19
worker 305, 414
working forest 354
World Health Organization 90
worm 230, 359
wort 257
wound 271
wrap 207
wren 358
wrinkled 180
write up 34

write-up 34
X-chromosome-linked 196
X-ray 206, 220, 226
X-ray film 151, 244, 251
X-ray photograph 37
X-ray resistant 242
X-rays 229
χ-square 204
xantophyll 147
xenopus 419
xerophyte 336, 366
xerophytic 100
XX-X0 system 184
xylem 111
xylem vessel 99
Y-shaped 235
YAC 252
yarrow 363
yeast 144, 257, 264
yeast cell 216, 255, 268
yellow bone marrow 62
yellow chamomile 367
yellow oatgrass 363

yellow spot 67
yellow-rattle 364
yew 48
yield 187
yield of product 256
yolk 222, 417
yolk sac 417
zebrafish 222
zero growth rate 344
zig-zag pattern 305
zipper 208
zoning 372
zoology 15, 295
zooplankton 370, 399
zooplankton net 379
zoospore 93
zygomorphic 118
zygomorphic flower 119
zygospore 93
zygote 91, 182, 193, 222, 413
zygotic gene 225

Deutsches Stichwortregister

A-Horizont 360
a-Satelliten-DNA 245
A-Stelle 213
Aal 51, 371
Aasfresser 51, 346
AB0-System 87, 199, 239
Abbau 219, 231
Abbau durch Mikroorganismen 387
Abbau von Kohlenstoffverbindungen zu Kohlenstoffdioxid 388
abbaubar 402
abbauen 215, 219, 228, 231, 267, 273, 348, 414
Abbauprodukt 257
Abbildung 37
Abbrechen 91, 183, 211, 413
Abbruch 214
abdecken 93
Abfall 402
Abfall fressend 346
abfallen 227
Abfallprodukt 83, 142, 150
Abfallstoff 256
abflachen 134
Abfluss 349, 378
Abflussrohr 402
Abgase 403
abgetötet 204
abhängig sein von 136
abholzen 362
abiotisch 329
abiotische Bestäubung 104
abiotischer Faktor 281
Abkömmling 60
Abkühlen 332
ablagern 403
Ablagerung 93, 373, 386
Ablaufwasser 386
Ablehnung 238
ablöschen 250
ablösen 214, 215, 412
Ablösung 215
abnehmen 318
abschnüren 228, 411
Abschnürung 413
abschöpfen 388
Absetz- oder Vorklärbecken 388
absinken 375
absondern 271
absorbieren 148, 246

Absorption 77, 231, 246
abspalten 268
abstammen von 279
Abstammung 285
Abstammungslinie 285
Abstand 263
Abszisse 41
Abtragung 386
Abtreibung 74
abtrennen 101
Abwärme 406
Abwasser 386
abwechseln mit 92
abwechselnd singen 303
abweichende Entwicklung 418
Abweichung 39, 191
abzentrifugieren 176
Abzug 28
Acetabularia 419
Acetyl 142
Acetylcholin 68, 320, 326
Achene 114
Achse 41
Achsel 99
8-Oxoguanin 220
80S Ribosom 213
Ackerbau 294
Ackerwinde 367
Ackerwitwenblume 363
Actin 164
adaptieren 215, 324
additive Farbmischung 324
Adenin 205
Adenosin-Triphosphat 192
Adenosintriphosphat 317
Ader 111
Aderhaut 67
Adersystem 111
Aderung 111
Adhäsionskultur 177
Adler 51
ADP – Adenosindiphosphat 128
Adrenalin 68, 327
Aerenchym 336, 373
aerob 141
aerobe Schlammbehandlung 389
aerober Abbauprozess 386
Affe 291, 309
afferente Arteriole 84
Affinitätschromatografie 268
After 53

Agar 258
Agar-Platte 266
Agglutination 88, 235
agglutinieren 235
Aggregatzustand 376
Aggressionsverhalten 314
Aggressivität 343
agouti 182
Agrobacterium tumefaciens 271
ähneln 229
ähnliche Reihenfolge 419
Ahorn 48, 357
Ährchen 116
Ähre 114
AIDS 89, 240, 409
Airlift Reaktor 256
Akklimatisierung 330
Akrosom 193, 414
Akrosomen-Reaktion 221
akrozentrisch 190
Aktin 321
Aktionspotential 318
Aktivator 211, 215
aktiver Transport 175
aktives Zentrum 132
aktivieren 234
aktiviert 215
Aktivierungsenergie 131
Aktivkohle 390
akustische Anlockung 308
akzessorisches Pigment 148
Albinismus 197
albino 182
Albumin 117
Aldehyd 167
Aldehydgruppe 147
Aldosteron 85
Aleuronschicht 117, 216
Alge 17, 92, 287, 374, 411
Algenblüte 395
Algenrasen 379
alkalische Lösung 250, 263
Alkaloid 121
Alkanol 167
Alkohol 29, 167
Allantois 417
alle Staubblätter zusammen 102
Allel 181, 277, 280
Allelfrequenz 203
Allen-Regel 334

462

Allergen 87, 237, 272
Allergie 87, 237, 272
allergisch 272
allergischer Schock 88
allergisches Asthma 237
Alles-oder-Nichts-Gesetz 318
allesfressend 346
Allesfresser 76, 346
allosterische Hemmung 138
allosterisches Enzym 138
allosterisches Zentrum 138
α-Amylose 170
als Abort abgehen 200
Alteisen 402
Alter 227
altern 227
alternativer Exongebrauch 218
alternatives Spleißen 236
Altglascontainer 402
Altmundtiere 416
Altruismus 308
altruistisches Verhalten 308
Alveole 54, 81
am Boden eines Sees lebende Tiere 376
Amakrinzelle 323
Amboss 65, 284
Ameise 52, 359
Amerikanische Roteiche 357
Ames-Test 220
Amin 167
Aminoacyl-tRNA-Synthetase 214
Aminogruppe 167
Aminosäure 168
Aminosäure-Kette 212
Aminosäure-Sequenz 212
Aminosäurebindungsstelle 214
Aminosäurestoffwechsel 197
Ammoniak 154, 350
Ammonifikation 155, 351
Ammonium 83
Ammonium oxidieren 154
Ammoniumion 154, 350
Ammoniumsalze 154, 350
Amnion 417
Amniozentese 201
Amöbe 26, 359
Ampfer 363
Amphibie 222, 290
Amphibium 17
amphipatisch 172
amphoter 169
Amplifikation 246

amplifizieren 246, 249
Amplitude 64
Amplituden-Code 320
Ampulle 65
Amsel 50, 358
Amylase 129, 257
an der Mikropyle 98
Anabolismus 124
anaerob 144
anaerobe Bedingungen 378
anaerobe Schlammbehandlung 389
anaerober Abbauprozess 386
Anaerobier 144
analog 284
analoge Struktur 342
Analogie 284, 342
Analyse 297
analysieren 12, 297
Analyst 297
Anaphase 188
anaphylaktisch 237
Anatomie 15, 53
anatomischer Bau 284
Anbau in Monokulturen 401
anbauen 187
ändern 136, 343
Androgen 73
Androhung 398
Andrözeum 102
Aneuploidie 191
anfällig 397
angeboren 269
angeborene Immunität 86
angeborene Krankheit 196
angeborene Störung 196
Angelman-Syndrom 198
angeschwollen 87
Angiosperme 194
Angiotensin II 85
Ängstlichkeit 306
anhalten 190
anhäufen 249, 317
Anhäufung 227
anheften 231, 234
animaler Pol 223, 415
Anion 179
Anisogamie 413
anisolecital 223
Anlage 416
Anlage des Stammes im Embryo 98
anlagern 214, 231, 247
Anlagerung 247, 386

anlegen 253
anlocken 101
Anlockung mittels Duftstoffen 308
Annäherung 345
annotieren 253
Annulus Zelle 95
Anode 179
Anopheles 399
Anordnung 14, 254
anorganisch 129
anorganische Schwefelverbindungen 157
anpassen 67
Anpassung 136, 281, 324, 329, 384
Anpassungsgrad 302
anregen 271
Anregung 149
Anregungszustand 149
anreichern 178, 344, 348, 377, 398
Anreicherung 178, 344, 348
Anreicherung eines schwer bis nicht abbaubaren Stoffes 398
ansammeln 148
Ansammlung 148
Ansatzpunkt 113, 318
Ansäuerung 153
Ansaugen von Luft 385
Anschluss 60
anschwellen 233
Anschwemmung 386
Ansicht 38
Ansicht mit Lupe 37
Ansicht unter dem Mikroskop 37
Anspruch 338
ansteckend 409
anstehendes Gestein 361
ansteigen 44
anteilige Monosaccharide 151
Antennapedia 225
Antenne 375
anterior 224
Antheridium 92
Antheridium Mutterzelle 100
Anthocyan 163
Anthranilsäure 218
Anthropologie 15
Anti-A 88
Anti-B 88
anti-D-Antikörper 200
anti-D-Prophylaxe 199

463

Anti-Matsch-Tomate 273
Antibabypille 74
Antibiotikum 260, 266
antidiuretisches Hormon 85
Antigen 86, 232, 234
Antigen-Antikörper-Reaktion 87
Antigen-präsentierendes Protein 238
Antigenrezeptor 234
Antikörper 86, 140, 176, 178, 231
Antikörper produzierend 235
Antikörperbildung 200
Antikörperklasse 235
Antikörperproduktion 234
Antikörpervielfalt 235
antiparallel 206
Antipod 103
Antiport 175
Antisense-Technik 211, 274
Antwort 231
antworten 216, 231
anwenden 12
Anwendung 139
anziehen 166
Aorta 54, 78
Apex 66
Apfel 48
Apikalmeristem 415
Apoenzym 130
Apolipoprotein B 219
Apoptose 227
Appendix 76
Aquakultur 395
aquatisches Ökosystem 369
äquatorial 224
Äquatorialplatte 189
Arbeit vor Ort 379
Arbeiterin 305, 414
Arbeitstisch 19
Archaea 156
Archäopteryx 289
Archebakterien 162
Archegonium 92
Arginin 277
Arginin-Synthese 218
Armknochen 62
Armleuchteralge 374
Armspanne 198
Armut 90, 408
Aroma 274
aromatisch 273
Art 16, 283
Artbildung 283

Arten, die verstädtern 367
Arten, die Verstädterung vermeiden 367
Artengrenze 271
Artenvielfalt 283, 396, 401
Arteria renalis 84
Arterie 54, 78, 79
Arteriole 79
Artgenosse 310, 338
artgerechte Tierhaltung 401
Artgrenzen überwinden 242
artspezifisch 222
Arzneimittelherstellung 274
Arzneimittelunverträglichkeit 238
Äsche 382
assimilieren 349
assoziatives Lernen 300
Ast 110
Asthma 403
asymmetrisch 44
asymptotisch 344
AT-reiche Region 245
Atavismus 285
atavistisch 285
Atemvolumen 82
Atemwurzel 141
ätherische Öle 117
Atmosphäre 347
atmosphärische Überwachung 405
atmosphärische Zusammensetzung 405
atmosphärisches Aerosol 405
atmosphärisches Ozon 405
atmosphärisches Wasser 349
Atmung 53, 141, 349
Atmung via Unterdruck 81
Atmungsintensität 141
Atmungspigment 82
Atmungssubstrat 80
Atmungssystem 60
Atmungswärme 141
Atmungszyklus 82
Atom 165
Atomkraftwerk 407
Atommüll 408
ATP – Adenosintriphosphat 128
ATP Synthase 150
ATP-abhänging 265
Atrioventrikularknoten 79
Auerhahn 358
aufbauschen 191
Aufbaustadium 368

aufeinander stoßen 135
Aufenthaltszeit 390
auffalten 219
auffüllen 348
aufgeblasener Blattstiel 336
aufgenommen werden 348
Aufhängepparat 67
Auflicht 24
auflösen 108, 189
Auflösung 343
Aufmerksamkeit auf sich ziehen 314
Aufnahme 37, 175, 178, 183, 205
aufnehmen 175, 178, 183, 205, 231, 304
aufplatzen 190
Aufplatzen des Staubbeutels 102
aufplatzend 102, 114
aufpropfen 419
aufrecht 291
Aufrechtgänger 291
Aufregung 306
aufreinigen 263
aufsaugen 231
Aufschaukelungskreis 344
Aufschmelzen der DNA 247
aufschreiben 34
aufspalten 171
Aufspaltung 73
aufspüren 269
aufstauen 385
Aufstrich 318
auftragen 42
Auftragstasche 179
Auftrennung 243
auftreten 166
Auftrieb 374, 376
auftriebgebende Funktion 375
aufwickeln 208
aufwinden 207
Aufwuchsorganismus 379
aufzeichnen 35
aufziehen 187
Aufzucht 339
Auge 63, 284, 322
Augenblase 416
Augenfleck 92
Augenkammer 66
Augenmuskel 67
Augentierchen 26
Ausatmung 81
Ausbaggern 380, 385
ausbeuten 409

Ausbeutung 279
ausbleichen 407
ausdehnen 168
Ausdehnung 168
ausdifferenzierte Zelle 419
Ausdruck 248
Ausfall 419
ausfällen 208
Ausfaulung 389
Ausflockung 387
ausführen 316
Ausgangsprodukt 138
Ausgangsstoff 125, 151
ausgeglichen 347
ausgestorben 396
ausgleichen 344
Ausläufer 110, 117, 412
auslaugen 348
Auslaugen des Bodens 401
auslösen 63, 131, 229, 322, 418
Auslöser 297, 300
ausplatieren 266
Auspuffgase 404
ausrotten 396
ausschalten 215
ausscheiden 91, 159, 175, 236
Ausscheidung 54, 223, 335
ausschlaggebend sein 330
ausschließen 251
ausschütten 97
Außenkiemen 394
Außenohr 64
Außenschicht 335
Außenseiter 314
Außenskelett 223
äußere Abwehr 86
äußere Atmung 141
äußere Barriere 230
äußere Hüllschicht 97
außerhalb des Zellkerns 182
aussetzen 105, 178, 329, 400
Aussterben 396, 399
Ausstoß 403
ausstoßen 351, 403
Austausch 266, 348, 377
austauscharme Wetterlage 404
austauschen 192, 348
Austauschwert 185
Auster 52
Austernfischer 394
Australopithecus afarensis 291
Auswahl 187
auswählen 187, 253
Auswanderung 343

Auswaschen der Nährsalze 362
auswerten 18, 23, 296
Auswertung 18, 296
Auswirkung 397
Auszeichnung 314
Autoantikörper 88, 239
Autoimmunerkrankung 88, 239
Autoimmungstörung 239
Autoimmunität 88
Autökologie 329
autökologisch 329
autonom 260
autonomes Nervensystem 68, 326
Autoradiografie 178, 192, 244, 248
Autosom 190, 196
autosomal 196
autotroph 93
Auwald 353
auxotroph 258
Axon 68, 315, 326
Axonmembran 317
Aye-Aye 309
Azidität 136
Azidothymin 89, 240
B-Horizont 361
B-Zelle 87, 233
BAC 252
Bach 369, 381
Bachflohkrebs 52
Bächlein 381
Bäckerhefe 411
Baculum 72
Bakterie 230, 359
bakterielle Proteinfragmente 234
bakterielle Verunreinigung 128
bakterielles Plasmid 267
Bakterienkolonie 259
Bakterienkultur 260
Bakterienrasen 157, 259
Bakterienstamm 204
Bakterienstämme mit Fertilitätsfaktor 259
Bakterienzellwand 162
Bakterium 17, 161, 234, 255, 287
Balance 397
Balgfrucht 114
Balken 69, 327
Ballaststoff 75
Balz 331
Balzritual 304
Banangewächse 115

bandartig 94
Bande 179, 191, 243, 251
Bandenmuster 264
Bandwurm 342
Bannwald 354
Bannwald im Sinne von Schonwald 400
Bär 49
Barbe 382
Bärlapp 95
Bärlappgewächs 356
Barriere 173
Barriere-Verhütungsmittel 74
Barsch 371
Bartholin-Drüse 71
Basalmembran 79
Basenanalogon 220, 240
Basenpaar 206, 243, 262
basierend auf 298
Basilarmembran 325
Basis 66
basisch 21
basisches Milieu 137
Basizität 136
Basstölpel 51
Batch-Kultur 255
Bau 14
Bauch 53
Bauchkanalzelle 100
Bauchspeicheldrüse 53, 70, 76, 129, 238
Baukastenprinzip 235
Baum 110
Baumgrenze 354
Baumringanalyse 362
Baumschicht 356
Baumwollkapselwurm 272
Baustein 128, 168
Baustein der Proteine 167
Baustoff 151
bearbeiten 64
Bebauungsdichte 385
Becherglas 28
Becken 292, 383
Beckengürtel 62, 285, 290
Bedenken 279
Bedingung 19
bedrohen 397, 398
Bedrohung 398
beenden 209
Beere 114
Beerenfrucht der Kürbisfamilie 115
Beerenfruchtverband 115

465

befähigen 205
Befall 341
befallen 341
befestigen 254
befestigt 237
befruchten 193, 278
befruchtet 414
Befruchtung 193, 221, 413
Befruchtungsmembran 414
begrenzen 396
begrenzender Faktor 330
Begriff 14
behalten 136
behandeln 238, 261
Behandlung 139, 238, 261
Behandlungsmöglichkeit 240
beheizter Deckel 246
behindert 201
Behinderung 197, 201, 215
bei niedrigerer Temperatur wieder aneinander lagern 245
Beifang 395
Beinknochen 62
bekämpfen 404
Bekundung von Interesse 306
beladene t-RNA 213
belasten 397
Belastung 378
Belebtschlammbecken 388
Belebungstank 388
Beleuchtung 25, 296, 404
Beleuchtungsstärke 331
beliebig 261
Belüfter 381
Belüftung 373, 381, 386
bemerken 23
benachbarte Antennenpigmente 148
benachbarte Zelle 418
benennen 14
Benzanthrazen 220
beobachtbar 127
beobachten 23, 254, 296
Beobachter 296, 302
Beobachtung 23, 226, 296
Bereich 329
Bereich mit geringer Strömung 383
Bergeidechse 380
Bergmann-Regel 334
Bernsteinschnecke 371
Besamung 413
Beschädigungskampf 307

Beschaffenheit 256
beschichten 237
beschichteter Partikel 261
Beschichtung 177, 237
beschleunigen 131
beschreiben 12, 296
Beschreibung 296
beschriften 26, 38
Beschriftung 26, 38
Beschwichtigung 314
Beseitigung 402
Besitz 279
Besorgnis 306
Bestandteil 14, 165, 329
bestäuben 97, 180, 182
Bestäuber 97, 360
bestäubt 97
Bestäubung 97, 180
Bestäubung durch Brummen 106
Bestäubung durch Fledermäuse 107
Bestäubung durch Insekten 106
Bestäubung durch Lebewesen 106
Bestäubung durch Vögel 107
Bestäubungstropfen 100
Bestehen 330
Bestimmungsschlüssel 370
bestrafen 299
Bestrafung 299
Bestrahlung 220, 229
Bestrahlungsstärke 331
Beta-Carotin 274
Beta-Galactosidase 268
beträchtlich 270
betroffen 196
Beute 281, 304, 340
Beuteltier 17
Bevölkerungswachstum 408
bevorstehend 397
bevorzugen 301
Bewässerung 388
bewegen 16
beweglich 198, 209
Bewegung 16
Bewegungsstörung 197
Beweidung 369
Beweidungsverlauf 364
Beweis 204
beweisen 204
bewohnbar 396
bewusst 400
bezahlbar 276

Bezugsperson 311
bezwingen 230
Biber 50, 399
biegsam 337, 373
Biene 53, 106
Bienenkönigin 305
Bienenstock 305
Bierhefe 411
Bierwürze 257
bilateral symmetrisch 120
Bildung 408
Bindegewebe 61, 79, 160, 198
Bindegewebezelle 58
binden 132, 133, 216
Bindung 133, 206, 301
Bindungsparter 219
Bindungszentrum 133
Binokular 24
Binse 373
Biochemie 15
Bioethik 15
Biogas 156
biogeochemischer Kreislauf 349
Bioindikator 387
Biologe 15
Biologie 15
biologisch 15
biologische Klärstufe 388
biologische Reinigung 390
biologischer Merkmale 342
biologischer Sauerstoffbedarf 379, 387
Biolumineszenz 128
Biom 353
Biomasse 145, 347
Biomembran 173
Biorhythmus 331
Biosensor 140
Biosphäre 347, 407
Biosphärenreservat 400
Biotechnologie 15, 255
biotisch 329
biotischer Faktor 281
Biotop 329
Biotopkarte 399
Biotoporrdnung 399
Biotopschutz 399
Biotopverbundnetz 399
Biotopverbundsystem 399
Biotopvernetzung 399
Biowissenschaften 15
Biozönose 329
bio~ 15

Bipedie 61
bipolare Nervenzelle 68, 326
bipolare Zelle 324
Birke 48, 203
Birkengewächse 122
Birkenspanner 203, 283
Birkenwald 353
Birne 48
Bitterstoff 152
Biuret-Test 29
Biuretreaktion 29
Blähschlammbildung 389
Bläschendrüse 72
Blasdüsenrohr 381
Blasenauge 285
Blasenkeim 417
Blässhuhn 372
Blastocoel 222
Blastocyste 74, 415
Blastom 228
Blastomere 222, 415
Blastopore 222
Blastula 222, 417
Blatt 110, 153
Blattachsel 411
Blattader 96
Blättchen 112
Blätter abwerfen 336
Blätterdach 382
Blätterpilz 355
Blattform 112
Blattfuß 375
Blattfußkrebs 371
Blattgrund 111
Blatthäutchen 116
Blatthöcker 96
Blattknospe 411
Blattkreis 101
Blattlaubfall 360
Blattlaus 365, 414
Blattminierer 360
Blattrosette 366
Blattscheide 111, 116
Blattscheide des Keimblattes 117
Blattspreite 111, 368
Blattstiel 111
Blattwerk 362
Blaualge 162, 359
Blei 404
Bleistift 34
Blende 25
Blinddarm 77
Blinder Fleck 67, 323

blinder Passagier 400
Blindschleiche 51
Blitz 286
Block 246
blockieren 215, 273
„Blot" 244
„blotten" 244
Blumenbinsen 380
Blut 54, 59, 160
Blut-Stammzelle 87
Blutaustausch 200, 239
Blutdruck 79, 238
Blüte 101
Blüten treiben 359
Blütenblatt 101, 105
Blütenboden 101
Blütendiagramm 101
Blütenhülle 101
Blütenorgan 101
Blütenpflanze 98
Blütenspindel 114, 124
Blütenstand 113
Blütenstängel 114
Blütenstiel 101, 113
Bluter 276
Bluterkrankheit 276
Blütezeit 359
Blutgefäß 54, 62, 67, 76, 79, 84, 332
Blutgerinnsel 78, 275
Blutgerinnung 78, 197
Blutgerinnungsfaktor 276
Blutgruppe 87, 199
Blutgruppe A/B/AB/0 239
Blutgruppensystem 199, 239
Blutkreislaufsystem 70
Blutplättchen 78
blutsaugendes Insekt 346
Blutspender 197
Blutspur 241
Bluttransfusion 88, 239
Blutzelle 58
Bockkäfer 365
Bodenbakterium 271
Bodenbeschaffenheit 361
Bodenbrüter 360
Bodendichte 361
Bodenerosion 401
Bodenfruchtbarkeit 401
Bodennutzung 349
Bodentier 376
Bohr-Effekt 82
Bolus 77
Borke 99

Borkenkäfer 358
Borreliose 341
Borste 185, 394
bösartig 228
Botanik 15
Botulinum-Toxin 321
Bovist 355
Bowmannsche Kapsel 84
Brachse 383
Brackwasser 383
Brandrodung 362, 368
Brauhefe 257
Braunbär 357
Braunelle 363
Braunwurzgewächse 121
breit 111, 292, 382
Breite 382
Breitengrad 334
Bremse 52
Brennnessel 49, 364
Brenztraubensäure 141
Brettwurzel 109
Bromatom 406
Brombeere 48
Bronchiolen 81
Bronchitis 404
Bronchus 54, 81
Bronze 293
Brown'sche Molekularbewegung 174
Bruchmoor 392
Bruchwald 373
Brücke 69, 328
Brückenmolekül 231
Brückentier 289
Brust 54
Brustbein 290
Brustdrüse 71
Brusthöhle 81
Brustkorb 53, 62, 81, 198
Brustlymphgang 80, 87
Brustwarze 54
Brut 338
Brutpflege 222, 345
Brutschrank 28, 301
Bruttoprimärproduktion 347
Bruttosozialeinkommen 409
Brutverhalten 331
Brutvogel 393
Brutzwiebel 412
Bryophyta 94
BSE 89, 241
Buche 48
Buchengewächse 123

Buchenmischwald 353
Buchfink 358, 368
buckelig 185
buhlen 338
Bunsenbrenner 28
Büroklammer 29
Bursa Fabricii 233
Bürzeldrüse 333
Bürzeldrüsenfett 333
Büschel 100
Büschelmücke 370
Buschwindröschen 49
Bussard 51, 358
Butterblume 363
Buttersäure 145, 167
Buttersäurebakterie 145
C- Horizont 361
C-Region 236
C_0-Kurve 245
Caesium 407
Calcitonin-Gen 218
Calcium-Phosphat 261
Cap 210, 213
„capping" 210
Carbonat 350
Carnivore 368
Carotin 147
Carotinoid 147, 163
Carrier-Protein 175
cDNA 253, 267
cDNA Bibliothek 268
Cellobiose 170
CentiMorgan 185
Centriol 414
Cerebellum 69, 328
CFTR-Gen 198
Chalaza 103
Chargaff-Regel 206
Chemie 15
Chemikalie 63, 322, 386
chemische Evolution 286
chemische Kommunikation 303
chemische Verfahren 3. Klärstufe 389
chemischer Aufbau 170
chemisches Mutagen 220
Chemosynthese 153
Chemosynthese betreibender Mikroorganismus 153
Chemotaxis 91
Chi-Quadrat-Test 39
Chiasma 185, 192
chiasmatisch 185
Chironomus 191

Chlamydomonas 92
Chlor 405
Chloratom 406
Chlorierung 390
Chlorophyll 147, 163
Chlorophyllmangel 331
Chloroplast 147, 163, 182
CHO-Zelle 268
Cholera 90
Cholesterol 171
Chorea Huntington 197
Choriongonadotropin 74
Chorionzotten 415
Chorionzottenbiopsie 201
Chorisminsäure 218
Chromatid 189
Chromatin 189, 207
Chromatografie 23
Chromatogramm 23, 151
Chromoplast 163
Chromosom 182, 189, 287
„Chromosomal-Walking" 252
Chromosomenmutation 220
chronischer entzündlicher Rheumatismus 239
Chylomikron 77
Chymotrypsin 129
Cilie 81
Cis-Seite 163
Citrullin 218
Cl^- Ionen 317
Cnidaria 193
CO_2 Akzeptor 151
CO_2-Fixierung 151
Cochlea 65, 325
codogener Strang 210
Codon 213
Coevolution 280
Colchizin 190
Coniin 321
Copepode 371
Corda 223
Corpus luteum 71, 73
Corti-Organ 65
cortisches Organ 325
Cosmid 252
CpG-Insel 198
Crassulaceen 153
Creutzfeldt-Jakob-Krankheit 242
Cromagnonmensch 291
Crustacee 17
CsCl-Gradient 209
Cupula 325

Cyanobakterien 161
Cyste 391
cystische Fibrose 198, 276
Cytidin-Triphosphat 192
Cytochrom 143
Cytochrom C 285
Cytogenetik 188
Cytokin 234
Cytokinese 188, 193
Cytologie 15
Cytometer 177
Cytoplasma 162
Cytoplasmabrücke 183
Cytosin 205
Cytoskelett 164
Cytosol 141
Cytostatikum 229
Cytotoxische T-Zelle 87
D-Region 236
Dach-Hauswurz 366
Dachs 50, 357
Dackel 185
Dahlie 412
Dämmerung 324
Dampfturbine 402
Danksagung 36
Darm 53
Darmbakterium 260
Darm~ 239
darstellen 345
Darwinismus 280
Daten 18, 38, 42
Daten sammeln 35
Datenbank der Genealogie 279
Datenpunkt 39
Datensatz 38
dauerfeucht 337
Dauergewebezelle 190
Dauerknospe 412
Dauerpräparat 25
Daumen 292
DDT 398
deaktiviert 215
Debris 208
Deckgläschen 27
Deckschuppe 100
Deckspelze 116
Deckungsgrad 354
definiert 242
degenerieren 227
degeneriert 213
Dehydration 258
Deich 393
dekantieren 21, 177

Deletion 220
Demutsverhalten 314
denaturieren 136, 179, 245, 250
Denaturierung 245, 250
Dendrit 315
Denitrifikation 154, 351
Dentin 76
Deplasmolyse 175
Depolarisation 318
Depolarisationsphase 318
deponieren 225
der Einfluss auf etw. 135
der Einfluss von etw. 135
Dermis 61
Desensibilisierung 88, 238, 301
Desinfektion 390
Desinfektionsmittel 390, 409
desintegrieren 193
Desmosom 59
Desoxyribose 205
Destillation 21, 391
destillieren 21
destilliertes Wasser 190
Destruent 346
detaillierte Knochenstruktur 62
Detektion 217
Detergenz 139, 179
Determination 58, 160, 417
determinieren 224, 417
Determinierung 224
Detritivor 346
Detritusregen 373
Dia 37
Diabetes 276
Diabetes mellitus 196
Diabetes mellitus Typ 1 239
Diabetiker 276
Diabetis mellitus 88
Diagnose 139, 269
Diagnostik 254
diagnostisch 254
diagnostizieren 254
Diagramm 41
Diaphragma 74
Diaphyse 62
diastolischer Druck 80
Dichasium 114
dichogam 104
Dichogamie 104
Dichte 177, 209, 376
Dichtegradient 209
dichter Laubabfall 123
Dickdarm 77
Dickdarmkrebs 229

dicke Kutikula 336
Dickenwachstum 99
dickes Filament 63
Didesoxynukleotid-Triphosphat 248
die Nutzung 139
die soziale Stellung wechseln 314
die Umwelt betreffend 396
Diencephalon 69, 328
differenzieren 190, 224, 233
Differenzierung 58, 98, 160, 224
Differenzierung des dorsalen Mesodermstreifens Somit 416
Differenzierungszone 415
diffundieren 225
Diffusion 174
Diglyderid 171
Dikotylen 118
Diktyosom 163
Dioxin 403
Dipeptid 168
Diplo-Haplo-Mechanismus 184
diploid 91, 191, 192, 413
Diplophase 194
Dipol 166
Disaccharid 129, 170
Disaccharid Saccharose 151
Discoblastula 224
Diskriminierung 314
Diskussion 35
Dissoziationskurve 82
distaler Tubulus 84
Distel 363
Distelfalter 365
Disulfidbrücke 235, 268
diurnaler Säurerhythmus 153
divergent 283
Divergenz 283
DNA 165, 205, 207
DNA Doppelstrang 247
DNA Einzelstrang 247
DNA Probe 263
DNA-Analyse 249
DNA-Chip 216, 254
DNA-Ligase 265
DNA-Polymerase 208, 246, 248
DNA-Ring 259
DNA-Sequenz 212
DNA-Synthese 188
DNase 205
dNTP 246
Dohle 50

Dolde 114, 119
Doldenrispe 114
Domestikation von Tieren 294
domestizieren 187
Domestizierung 187, 282
dominant 180, 196
Dominoeffekt 242
Donor 183, 259
Doppelfüßer 359
Doppelhelix 206
Doppelschicht 173
Doppelschwanz 359
doppelt S-förmig 291
Dorn 334, 336, 366
dornig gezähnt 112
dorsal 224
Dorsalwurzel 68, 326
Dorsch 395
Dotter 222, 417
Dottersack 417
Drahtnetz 28
Drahtwurm 359, 365
Drehgeschwindigkeit 21
Drehsinnesorgan 325
3' 210
3-lippig 120
3-Phosphoglycerat 151
dreiatomiges Ozonmolekül 406
dreidimensional 38, 135, 168
dreifruchtblättrig 113
Dreifurchenpollen 118
Dreifuß 28
dreikantige Nüsse 123
Dreipunktanalyse 185
30-nm-Chromatinfaser 207
dreizählig 115
Drogenabhängiger 241
Drohne 414
Drohverhalten 314
Drosophila melanogaster 185
Druck 61
Druckwelle 66
Drüse 65
Drüsenzelle 58
drüsig 103
Ductus 72
duftend 106
Duftstoff 152, 304
Düne 393
Dung 401
Düngemittel 386, 401
dünn 111
Dünndarm 77, 129
dünnes Filament 63

Dünnschichtchromatografie 147
Duplizier-Stempel 266
duplizieren 188, 208
durch Dampf sterilisiert 255
durch den Wind verbreitet 121
durch Wind übertragen 97
durchbrechen 108
durchdringen 373
Durchfallerkrankung 260
Durchflussmenge 382
durchgehender DNA-Strang 264
durchlässig 174, 261
Durchlässigkeit 233
Durchlaufgäranlage 256
Durchlicht 24
Durchlüftung 361
durchmischen 377
Durchschnitt 39
durchschnittlich 39
durchschnittliche Fragmentlänge 262
durchsickern 239
Durchtrennung der Samenleiter 74
Dürre 407
Dychennsche Muskeldystrophie 198
Dynein 164
Ebenholz 185
Echolot 395
Edelreiser 412
editieren 210
Edukt 132
Efeu 49
Effektor 215, 266, 322
efferente Arteriole 84
effizient 347
Ei 221
Eibe 48
Eiche 123, 357
Eichel 55, 72, 123, 357
Eichelhäher 358
Eichenmischwald 353
Eichenwald 353
Eichhörnchen 50, 357
Eidechse 51
Eiderente 393
Eier legend 345, 413
Eierstock 54, 71, 193, 221
eiförmig oval 112
Eigenschaft 41, 128, 168, 187, 410

Eigenschaft, die ein Verdriften verhindert 384
Eigenschaft, die hilft, der Wasserströmung Widerstand zu leisten 384
Eileiter 54, 71, 414
Eileiterabschnürung 74
ein Fruchtknoten 124
ein Keimblatt 115
Ein-Zellschicht 177
einander beeinflussen 166
Einatmung 81
einbauen 183, 248, 255, 348
einbetten 176
eindämmen 404
eindringen 108, 230, 234, 271, 361
Eindringling 230
eine Fehlgeburt haben 200
eine Traube bilden 333
einfach gekrümmt 291
einfaches Blatt 111
einfruchtblättrig 113, 119
einfügen 264
Einfuhr 400
Einfurchenpollen 115
Eingabe des Sollwerts 64, 323
eingeengt 180
eingepflanzte Kanüle 301
eingeschlechtlich 97, 99
eingeschlechtliche Kätzchen 123
eingeschleppte Art 400
Eingeweide 401
einhäusig 97, 122, 123
einheimisches Holz 362
Einheit 39, 41
einheitlich 377
einjährig 110, 336
einjährige Art 364
einjährige Pflanze 115
Einkeimblätterige 115
einkeimblättrig 115
Einkerbung 111
einklammern 36
Einkommen 408
Einleitung 34, 386
einnisten 415
Einnistung 415
einordnen 12
einpflanzen 265
einsamig 122, 123
einsamiges Nüsschen 118
Einschleusung 264

einschließen 102
einschwemmen 348
Einsiedlerkrebs 394
einstellen 242
Einstellung 324
Einstrom 317
Eintagsfliege 52, 370
eintreffendes Signal 315
Einwegflasche 402
Einzelblüte 114
Einzeller 160
einzellige Samenanlage 124
einzelliger Organismus 411
Einzelschicht 173
Einzelstrang DNA 263
Eirinde 414
Eischale 399
Eisdecke 376
Eisen 156, 293
Eisen-Salz 361
Eisenbakterien 156
Eisensulfat 352
Eisensulfid 157
Eisessig 190
eiszeitlich 380
Eiter 86, 232
Eityp 223
Eiweiß 75, 222, 417
eiweißreich 117, 123, 364
Eizelle 91, 193, 221, 413
Ejakulation 72
Ektoderm 223, 416
Ektoparasit 341
Ekzem 237
Elch 49
elektrischer Impuls 65, 315, 318
elektrischer Puls 261
elektrisches Feld 179, 243, 248, 317
Elektrode 179, 316
Elektrodialyse 390
elektrogene Pumpe 317
Elektrokardiogramm 79
Elektromagnet 270
elektromagnetische Welle 146
Elektron 142, 149, 166
elektronegativ 144
Elektronegativität 166
Elektronen liefernder Stoff 149
Elektronenmikroskop 24, 176
Elektronenträger 143
Elektronentransportkette 150
Elektrophorese 23, 129, 179, 243, 248

Elektroporation 261
elektrostatische Wechselwirkung 166
elektrotonische Leitung 319
eliminieren 251
ELISA 237
ELISA-Test 87
elliptisch 112
Elster 50
Eltern 181, 411
Elterngeneration 181
Embryo 74, 91, 201
Embryo-Zelle 58
Embryoblast 415
Embryogenese 225
Embryophyta 94
Embryosackzelle 194
Emissionsfilter 404
Empfänger 183, 238, 303
Empfängerzelle 265
Empfängnis 73
empfindlich 260, 397
empirisch 38
emulgieren 20, 171
ENCODE 270
Ende 262
Endknöpfchen 315, 320
Endknospe 96
Endocytose 175, 287
Endoderm 416
endokrine Drüse 70
endokrines System 60
Endometrium 73
Endoparasit 341
endoplasmatisches Retikulum 163, 213
Endorphin 70
Endosperm 98, 117, 216
Endosperm erhaltend 108
Endosperm verbrauchend 108
Endosymbiontenhypothese 287
Endothelium 79
endotherme Reaktion 127
Endprodukt 138
Endprodukthemmung 215
endständige Narbe 119
energetisch verschwenderisch 138
energetische Kopplung 129
energetischer Wirkungsgrad 144
Energie 286
Energie benötigen 124

Energie bindende Reaktion 140
Energie freisetzen 125
Energie freisetzende Reaktionen 140
Energie verbrauchen 125
Energie-Umwandlung 125
Energieausbeute 145
Energiebedarf 410
Energiebetrag 131
Energiebilanz 75, 410
Energiediagramm 131
Energieeinsparung 404
Energieeinsparungsgesetz 410
Energiefluss 347
Energiegehalt 75
Energiegewinnung 140
energiereiche Strahlung 229
Energieschwelle 132
Energieträger 151
energieunabhängig 175
Energieverbrauch 175, 403, 410
Energiewährung 128
Energiewende 410
enge Röhre 106
enger Zusammenhalt 306
Engerling 359, 365
Enspannung 306
Entbehrung 296
Entbindung 74
entdecken 250, 325
Entdeckung 140
Ente 51
Entengrütze 105, 374
Entenvogel 372
entfärben 23
Entfärbung 216
entfernen 265
Entfernen des Produkts 256
entgegengesetzt 273
Enthalpie 126, 132
entkernte Eizelle 420
Entnahme 256
Entoderm 223
Entropie 127
Entsalzung 391
Entsäuerung 153
entscheiden 200
Entscheidung 200
Entschwefelung 157
entsorgen 216
entspannt 63
entsprechen 132
entsprechend 214
Entstehung 93, 283

Entstehung der Körpergestalt 416
Entstehungsgeschichte 380
Entwaldung 349
entwässern 176
entwickeln 244
Entwicklung 74, 221
Entwicklungsgenetik 221
entwicklungsgeschichtlich 233
Entwicklungshilfe 409
Entwicklungsland 90, 274, 408
Entwicklungsstadium 191, 338
Entwicklungssteuerung 419
entwinden 209
entzündliches Rheuma 88
Entzündung 86, 232
entzündungshemmendes Mittel 341
Enzephalopathie 241
Enzian 368
Enzym 129, 178
Enzym-Substrat-Komplex 133
Enzym-verknüpft 226
Enzymaktivität 137
enzymatische Hydrolyse 76
Enzymdefekt 217
Enzymkonzentration 134
Eosin 29
Epidemie 90
Epidermis 59, 61, 159
Epigenetik 199
Epiglottis 77
Epikotyl 108
Epilimnion 377
Epiphyse 62, 69, 70, 328
Epithel 160
Epithelium 81
Epithelzelle 58, 277
Epitop 87, 232
Equilibrium 397
erben 269
Erbgang 196
Erbgut 192, 258
Erbinformation 209
Erbkoordination 297
Erbkrankheit 196, 275
Erb~ 204, 411
Erdbeere 48, 412
Erdbohrer 31
Erderwärmung 406
Erdhöhle 333
Erdkruste 286, 347
Erdoberfläche 407
Erdöl 93

Erdrutsch 343
Erdschnake 365
Erdversiegelung 385
Erfahrung 298
ergänzen 266
Ergänzung 259, 266
Ergebnis 18, 23, 35
erhalten 102, 410
Erhaltung 396
erhitzen 22
erhöhen 201, 215, 254
Erholungswald 354
erkennen 217, 219, 230, 231, 234, 242, 325, 418
Erkennungsmerkmal 13
Erkennungssequenz 261
erklären 12, 23
Erkrankung der Atemwege 403
Erle 48, 122
erleichterte Diffusion 175
Erleichterung 254
Erlenbruchwald 380
Erlenmeyerkolben 28
erlernen 310
erleuchten 24
ermangeln 217
Ermittlung der Zahl der Individuen einer Population 387
ernährend 222
Ernährung 75
Ernährungsbedingung 274
Ernährungsquelle 103
erneuerbar 403
Ernte 187
ernten 187, 256
Erosion 95
Erosion an den Uferböschungen 382
erregende Synapsen 321
erregendes postsynaptisches Potential 320
erreichen 131
erscheinen 217
Erscheinung 66, 217
Erschütterung 106
erschweren 375
erste Teilung 414
Erste-Hilfe-Tasche 31
erstes Drittel 74
ersticken 404
Erststrangsynthese 267
Ertrag 187
Ertragsrate 279
ertragsreich 187

erwachsen 225
Erwachsenenalter erreichen 301
Erweiterung 238
erworbene Krankheit 275
Erythropoietin 78, 276
Erythrocyte 78, 82
Erz 156
erzeugen 125
Erzlaugung 157
Esche 48
Eschenahorn 357
essbar 123, 355
Essigsäure 167
Esterbindung 171
Ethanal 144
Ethanol 29, 144, 167, 208
Ethidiumbromid 220
ethische Werte 200
ethnische Gruppe 203
Ethogramm 296
Ethyl-Methyl-Sulfonat 220
Etikett 231, 244
Etoilement 331
Eucyte 287
Euhominidae 291
Eukaryot 159, 287
eukaryotische Zelle 58, 159
Eule 51, 358
euryhalin 335
euryök 330
eurytherm 332
Eustachische Röhre 65
Euterzelle 420
eutroph 378
Evapotranspiration 378
Evertebrat 17
Evolution 15, 249, 280
Evolution des Menschen 280
evolutionär 280
Evolutionsrate 280, 286
Evolutionstheorie 280
Ex-vivo-Gentransfer 277
Exkretion 83, 175
Exkretionssystem 60
Exocytose 175
Exon 210, 253
exotherme Reaktion 127
Experiment 19
experimentieren 18
exponentiell 247
exponentiell erhöhen 135
Exposition 178
Expressionsprofil 216, 226

Expressionsvektor 267
exprimieren 209
Extinktion 280
extrachromosomal 182
extrahieren 139, 261
extrahieren aus 207
Extrakt 261
extraplasmatischer Raum 161
extrapolieren 42
extrazelluläre Ableitung 317
extrazelluläre Körperflüssigkeit 317
extrazelluläre Matrix 173
extrazelluläre Verdauung 76
extrazellulärer Raum 161
Extrazellulärflüssigkeit 68, 326
Exzisionsreparatur 221
F-Plasmid 183
Fabrik 403
fächeln 332
FACS 178
FAD Flavin-Adenin-Dinukleotid 142
Faden 384
fadenförmig 94
fädig 208, 242
fädig zerschlitztes Blatt 337
Fahne 119
Fahrstuhleffekt 313
Fäkalien 386
Faktor 39, 329
Faktor VIII 197, 275
fakultativ 215
Falke 51
Falle 350, 368
Fällmittelöseanlage 389
Fallobst 367
Fällung 208
fälschungssicher 249
Faltung 136
Familie 16, 313
Familie der Doldengewächse 119
Familie der Hahnenfußgewächse 118
Familie der Hülsenfrüchtler 119
Familie der Korbblütler 118
Familie der Kreuzblütler 120
Familie der Lippenblütler 120
Familie der Rosengewächse 118
Familie der Sauergräser 122
familienbasierte genetische Assoziationsstudie 204
Familienplanung 408

472

Familienstammbaum 201
Fangarm 375
Fangnetz 30
Fangquote 395
Farbdreieck 324
Färbemittel 26, 29
färben 26, 190, 237, 243
Färberhundskamille 367
farblos 237
Farbstoff 29, 140, 237, 243
Farbumschlag 266
Farn 48, 95, 194, 356, 411
Fasan 50
Faser 99, 187
Faserwurzel 109
Faszie 61, 62
Faulaffe 309
Faulbehälter 389
Faulgas 389
Fäulnis 107, 145
Fäulnis von Eiweißen 155
Fäulniserreger 145
Fäulnisprozess 386
Faulschlamm 386, 389
Faulturm 389
Faustkeil 293
FCKWs 404
Feder 289
federartiger Narbenast 117
federig 102
„feed-back"-Hemmung 138
fehlend 104
fehlerhaft 198
Fehlernährung 75
Fehlgeburt 200
Fehlingprobe 29
Fehlingsche Lösung 29
Fehlpaarung 245
Fehlprägung 301
fehlsteuern 228
Feind 304
feinkörniges Sediment 385
Feintrieb 25
Feldahorn 356
Feldforschung 30
Feldfrucht 187
Feldfrüchte 401
Fell 182
felsig 378
Felstrümmer 361
Fermenter 255, 276
Fernglas 31
Fertilitätsfaktor 183, 259
fest 66, 376

festes Handlungsmuster 309
festgeheftete Wohnröhre 384
festgewachsen 394
festhalten an 102
Festigkeit 273
festlegen 217, 222, 225
festsitzender Polyp 414
Fett 75, 152, 171
Fettabbau 219
Fettgewebe 61, 333
Fettleibigkeit 278
Fettsäure 167, 171
Fettschicht 333, 335
Fettzelle 333
Fetus 74
Feuchtbiotop 391
Feuchtgebiet 369
Feuchtigkeit 349
feuchtigkeitsliebend 337, 356
Feuchtnasenaffe 309
Feuer 293
Feuerstein 293
Fibrillin 197
Fibrin 78
Fibringerüst 140
Fibringen 78
Fichte 48, 362
Fichtenspanner 359
Filialgeneration 181
Filmaufnahme 296
Filter 208
Filteranlage 403
Filteranlagen 403
Filterung 390
Filtrat 21
Filtration 21, 83, 257
filtrieren 21, 83, 208
Filtrierer 375
Finger 290
Fink 50
Fisch 17, 371
fischähnlich 290
Fischaufzug 385
Fischbestand 395
Fischschwarm 376, 395
Fischtreppe 385
FISH 190
Fitness 203, 281
fixieren 176, 190, 251
Fixierung 139, 251, 263
flach 111, 292, 379
flacher Blütenboden 107
Flachwasserzone 383
flankierende Sequenz 268

Flaschenbauch 92
Flaschenhalseffekt 203, 280
Flaschenhalszelle 92
Flechte 17, 48, 203, 355
Fledermaus 50
fleischfressend 346
Fleischfresser 346
fleischig 115, 336, 366
Flieder 49
Fliege 107
Fließeigenschaft 379
Fließgewässer 381, 388
Fließgewässerraum 385
Flocke 387
Flockenblume 363
Flockungsbecken 390
Floß 174
Flosse 290
Flügel 101, 119, 185
Flügelfrucht 114
Flunder 383, 395
Fluoreszenz 149
Fluoreszenz-Detektor 248
fluoreszenz-markiert 254
Fluoreszenzaufnahme 37
Fluoreszenzfarbstoff 151, 237, 263
Fluoreszenzfarbstoff-gekoppeltes Nukleotid 248
fluoreszierend 217
fluoreszierender Farbstoff 178
Fluoridierung des Wassers 391
Fluss 369, 381
Flussbecken 382
Flussbegradigung 385
Flussbett 381
Flussbettstruktur 385
Flussbettzusammensetzung 385
flüssig 376
Flüssig-Mosaik-Modell 174
Flüssigkeit 65
Flüssigschlamm 380
Flusskrebs 52
Flussmützenschnecke 384
Flusssenke 380
Flussverkehr 385
fokussieren 66
Folge 201
folgen 301
folgend 191
Follikel 71
follikelstimulierendes Hormon 72, 328

Follikelzelle 221
Foramen magnum 292
Forelle 51, 274, 382
Forensiker 249
Form 14, 133, 179, 191, 257
Förna 355, 360
Forschung 35, 275
Forschungsstation 296
forstliche Bewirtschaftung 400
Forstschaden 354
Fortpflanzung 16, 281
Fortpflanzungsapparat 101
Fortpflanzungserfolg 281
Fortpflanzungsmuster 343
Fortpflanzungspotential 344
Fortpflanzungssystem 60
Fortpflanzungsverhalten 308
Fortpflanzungszelle 58, 411
Fortpflanzungszyklus 331
Fortsatz 375
fortschreitend 198
fortsetzen 248
fossiler Brennstoff 403
fossiles Überbleibsel 98
fotografische Emulsion 178
Fotomorphose 331
Fotophosphorylierung 150
Fotosynthese 145, 350
fotosynthetisch 145
Fötus 201, 416
Fovea 67, 323
Fragiles-X-Syndrom 198
Fragment 242, 248
fragmentieren 242
Fragmentlänge 250
Fraktion 178
frei 213
freie Energie 126
freie Wasserzone 385
freies Radikal 406
freies Sauerstoffatom 406
Freilandbeobachtung 296
Freilandhaltung 401
freilassen 238
freisetzen 106, 240
Freiwillige 19
Fremd-DNA 261, 264
fremdbestäuben 103
Fremdbestäubung 103
Fremdgen 264
Fremdprotein 264
Frequenz 64
Frequenzcode 320
Fressfeind 128, 281

Frettchen 358
Freude 306
Freundeskreis 313
Fristenlösung 200
Frosch 51, 316, 372
Frostperiode 360
Frostschutzmittel 360
frosttolerant 187, 360
Frucht 75
Fruchtbarkeit 343
Fruchtbecher 122, 123
Fruchtblatt 102, 120, 180, 194
Fruchtblätter nicht verwachsen 113
Fruchtblätter verwachsen 113
Fruchtblattrand 102
Früchte fressend 360
Fruchtfliege 185, 222
Fruchtknoten 102, 180
Fruchtschuppe 99, 100
Fruchtstand 114
Fruchtwand 117
Fruchtwasser 417
Frühblüher 49
frühe Geschlechtsreife 345
Früherkennung 140
Frühgeburt 417
Fruktan 117
Fruktose 170
Frust 314
Fuchs 50, 358
Fühler 64, 323
führen 317
5' 210
5-Bromuracil 220
fungieren 14
Funiculus 103
Funktion 14, 385
funktionale Sequenzen 270
für Protein codierendes Gen 250
„für-das-Leben" 201
„für-die-Wahl" 200
furchen 415
Furchung 415
Furchungstyp 223
Fusion 174
fusionieren 174, 231, 236
Fusionsprotein 268
Fußabdruck 62
Fußgewölbe 292
Fußknochen 62
Fußnote 36
Futterpflanze 121, 364

Futterquelle 305
Futterschale 299
Fütterung 308
G-Bänderung 190
G_0-Phase 188
G_1-Phase 188
G_2-Phase 188
Gabelbein 289
Galago 309
Gallbildner 360
Galle 77, 271
Gallenblase 53, 76
gallertartig 67
Gallerthülle 413
Gamet 182, 413
Gametangium 193
Gametophyt 92, 94, 96, 194
Ganglionzelle 323
Gans 51
Gänseblümchen 48, 364
Gänseschar 301
Garnele 395
Gartenbau 187
Gärung 144, 255
Gärungsprozess 407
Gasaustausch 80
Gasaustritt 256
Gashahn 28
Gasometer 389
Gastrula 222, 416
Gastrulation 416
Gaszufuhr 28
Gattung 16
Gaumen 233
Gaumenmandel 80
Gaumenspalte 201
GC-reiche Region 245
Gebärmutter 54, 201
Gebärmuttermund 71, 74
Gebärmutterschleimhaut 71
gebeugtes Licht 24
gebogener Griffel 119
gebuchtet 112
Geburtenrate 343, 408
Gedächtnis 312
Gedächtniszelle 86, 232, 235
geeignet 411
geeignete Bedingung 268
Gefahr 397
gefährden 398
gefährdet 398
Gefährdung 397, 398
Gefährdungsgrad 399
Gefälle des Flussverlaufs 381

Gefangenschaft 313
Gefäßpflanze 98
Gefäßsystem 60, 96
Gefäß~ 95
Gefieder 182, 289
gefiedert 112
gefingert 112
gefleckt 182
Geflügel 187
geflügelt 115, 121
Gefrierätzen 176
Gefrierbruch 176
Gegenkonditionierung 301
gegenseitige Abhängigkeit 345
Gegenspieler 63
gegenständig 112
Gegenstrom-Wärmeaustausch- 333
Gegenstromverstärker-System 84
Gehirn 68, 318, 326
Gehirn einer Kuh 89
Gehörkanal 65
Gehörknöchelchen 65, 284
Gehörnerv 65
Geier 51
Geißblatt 356
Geißel 92, 160, 162, 164
geistige Behinderung 277
gekerbt 112
gekoppelt 185
gekoppelte Reaktion 129
Gel 243, 250
gelappt 112
gelappter Rand 123
Gelbe Wiesenameise 365
gelber Punkt 67
gelbes Knochenmark 62
Gelbrandkäfer 371
Gelelektrophorese 250, 263
Gelenk 53, 62, 198
Gelenkentzündung 239
Gelenkknorpel 62
gelockt 185
gelöste Ionen 317
gelöste Substanz 20, 83
gelöster Sauerstoff 386
gelöstes organisches Material 383
gelöstes Teilchen 373
Gemeine Nachtkerze 367
Gemeiner Schotendorn 357
Gemeines Labkraut 364
Gemeines Ruchgras 363

gemeinsam 237
gemeinsam haben 13
Gemüse 75
Gen 179, 258, 280
Gen-Pharming 274, 278
Gen-Umwelt-Interaktion 196
Genaktivität 198
Genbibliothek 268
Gendrift 203, 280
Generation 281
Generationswechsel 91, 193, 342
generative Zelle 102, 107
generativer Nukleus 108
generieren 141, 272
Genetik 15
Genetiker 258
genetisch 179, 204, 258, 280
genetisch manipuliert 273
genetisch modifizierter Organismus 255
genetische Assoziation 196, 203
genetische Beratung 200
genetische Entfernung 185
genetische Karte 185
genetische Marker 269
genetische Scheren 261
genetische Vielfalt 104, 411
genetischer Code 212
genetischer Dialekt 214
genetischer Egoismus 308
genetischer Fingerabdruck 249
genetisches Programm 227
genetisches Werkzeug 261
Genexpression 209, 215, 254
Genfähre 264
Genfluss 203, 280
Genhäufigkeit 280
Geninaktivierung 274
Genom-Bibliothek 252
Genommutation 221
Genotyp 180, 217
Genotypisierung 254
Genpool 188, 203, 280
Genregulation 211, 215, 419
Gensonde 263
Gentaxi 271
Gentechnologie 258
Gentherapie 277
Gentransfer 258
Geodreieck 34
Geosphäre 347
gerader Graben 385
Gerät 30, 405

Geräusch 64
geringer 131
gerinnen 257
Gerinnsel 140
Geröll 383
Gerste 49, 116, 257
Geruch 390
Geruchsstoff 326
gesägt 112
Gesamtenergiemenge 126
Gesamtmenge der freigesetzten Energie 131
Gesamt~ 387
Gesäßmuskulatur 292
gesättigt 20, 166, 391
geschädigt 276
Geschiebe 383
Geschlecht 183
geschlechtliche Fortpflanzung 90, 193, 221
Geschlechtsbestimmung 183
Geschlechtschromosom 183, 190
geschlechtsgekoppelt 185, 190
Geschlechtshormon 73
Geschlechtsmerkmal 71
Geschlechtsorgan 54, 223
geschlechtsreif 184
geschlossen 114
geschlossener Behälter 255
geschlossenes System 350
Geschmack 257, 390
Geschmacksknospe 326
Geschmackspapillen 326
Geschmacksstoff 152, 256
Geschwindigkeit 380
Geschwindigkeit des Blutstroms 79
Geschwister 181
Geschwisterkreuzung 181
Gesellschaft 306
Gesichtsfeld 67, 323
Gesichtsschädel 292
gespeichert 351
gesprenkelt 182
Gesteinsmehl 380
Gesteinssplitter 361
gestielt 96
Gestik 304
gestört 347, 352
Gesundheitsgefährdung 386
Gesundheitsrisiko 279
Gesundheitsverträglichkeitsprüfung 90

Gesundheitsvorsorge 90
getarnt 240
geteiltes Blatt 111
Getreide 49, 117, 187
getrenntgeschlechtlich 306
Gewebe 16, 59, 159, 207
Gewebe mit luftgefülltem
  Hohlraum 141
Gewebe-Plasminogen-Aktivator
  275
Gewebefresser 346
Gewebeschicht 101
Gewebetransplantation 418
gewimpert 112
Gewissen 200
gezähnt 112
Gibberelin 216
Giemsa-Färbung 190
Gift 137, 344
giftig 121, 355, 398
Giftigkeit 277
Giftstoffbelastung 386
Ginkgo 98, 289, 357
Ginster 49, 368
Glas 30
Glaskörper 67
Glasrührer 208
Glasstab 28, 208
glatt 112, 204
glatte Muskelzelle 58
glatte Oberfläche 384
glatter Muskel 79
Glatthafer 363
Gleichgewicht 64, 127, 131, 317
Gleichgewichtsorgan 65
Gleichgewichtszustand 349
Gleichung 145
gleichwarm 332
Gleichwarme 332
Gletscher 369, 380, 407
Gliazelle 315
Gliederfüßer 17
Gliederhülsen 114
Gliederschote 114
Gliederung 355
Gliedmaßen 53, 333
Globalisierung 90
Globulin 117
Glockenblume 363
Glockenblumengewächse 120
glockenförmig 107
Glockentierchen 26, 375
Glomerulus 84
Glühwürmchen 128, 365

Glukose 170
Glutaminsäure 276
Gluten 117
Glycerin 167, 171
Glycokalyx 173
Glycoprotein 173, 241, 268
Glycosylierung 268
Glykogen 140, 171
Glykolipid 199
Glykolyse 141
glykolytisch 141
Glykoprotein 197, 240
GMO 188
Goldfisch 51
Goldraute 367
Golfstrom 407
Golgi-Apparat 163
Golgi-Vesikel 163
Gonade 193, 223
gonadotropin-freisetzendes
  Hormon 72
Gondwana 286
Gonosom 196
gonosomal 196
Götterbaum 357
Gottesanbeterin 52
Gradient 259
gram positiv 162
Gramm 42
Granit 361
Granne 117
Granulocyt 87, 233
Granum 147
Gras 48
Gräser 152, 356
Grashorst 364
Grashüpfer 52, 365
Graslandschaft 353
Grasnelke 122
Grasnelkengewächse 122
graue Substanz 68, 326
grauer Halbmond 224, 418
Graugans 301
Graureiher 372
greifen 292
Greifreflex 311
Grenze 228
Griffel 102, 180
Griffelbeine 285
Grille 52
Grippe 90, 341
grippeähnlich 341
grobkörniges Sediment 385
Grobtrieb 25

Groppe 371
groß 292
Großbuchstabe 180
Größe 39, 179, 191
große Schamlippen 71
Großer Abendsegler 358
Großer Brachvogel 394
Großes Ochsenauge 364
Großhirn 69, 292, 327
Großhirnhemisphäre 69, 327
Großhirnrinde 69, 327
Großserienfertigung 255
Grubenauge 284
grün-weiß panaschiert 182
Grünalge Spirogyra 148
Grund des Grases 364
Gründereffekt 203, 280
Gründer~ 279
Grundfarbe 324
Grundgestein 378
Grundmuster 416
Grundnahrung 121
Grundwasser 348, 369, 387
Grundzustand 149
grüne Blütenblätter 285
grüne Gentechnologie 278
Grünfutter 117
Gruppenmitglied 306
Guanin 205
Guanosin-Triphosphat 192
Gummiband 29
Gummihandschuh 31
Gummistiefel 31
günstig 410
gutartig 228
Gymnosperme 194
H+ 150
Haar 61
Haarfollikel-Rezeptor 325
haarig 102
Haarzelle 66
Habicht 358
Habitat 295
Hafer 49, 116
Haftwurzel 109
Hagebutte 115
Hagelschnur 417
Hainbuche 122
Hainsimsen-Buchenwald 353
Hakenkäferlarve 371
halbieren 192
Halbschattenpflanze 359
Halbschmarotzer 364
Hälfte 192, 216

Halligflieder 122
Halm 116
Halobakterien 157
Halophyt 393
halophytisch 337, 393
Hals 76
haltbar 273
Haltbarkeit 273
Häme 130
Hammer 65, 284
Hämoglobin 78, 82, 276
Hämophilie 197, 275
Hand-im-Handschuh-Prinzip 133
Handknochen 62
Handschuh 20
hängend 105
hängende Traube 124
haploid 90, 191, 192, 413
haploider Pollenkorn 97
Haplophase 194
Haplotyp 199
Hardy-Weinberg-Gesetz 203
Harnblase 54, 84
Harnleiter 54, 84
Harnröhre 54, 72, 84
Harnsäure 155, 351
Harnstoff 155, 351
Hartboden 383
Härtegrad 391
hartes Glaskapillar 316
Hartlaubzone 353
Harz 99
Hase 50, 357
Hasel 122, 356
Haselnuss 122, 356
Hatch-Slack-Zyklus 153
Haube 95
Haubentaucher 372
Häufigkeit 330
Haupt-Histokompatibilitäts-komplex 238
Hauptblattader 116
Hauptquelle 117
Hauptstamm 110
Hauptwurzel 109
Hausbrand 404
Haushalt 388
Haushaltsgen 198
Hausrotschwanz 367
Haut 61, 63, 323
Hautfarbe 196
Hautflügler 184
häutiger Bogengang 64

häutiger Schneckengang 66, 325
Hautkrebs 407
Hebel 299
Hebelmechanismus 120
hecheln 145, 332, 349
Hecht 51, 372
Hecke 366
Heckenbraunelle 368
Heckenrose 366
Hefe 144, 257, 264
Hefezelle 216, 255, 268
heftig schütteln 20
Heide 49, 368
Heidekraut 380
Heidekrautfamilie 121
Heidelbeere 48, 355
Heideschössling 369
Heilbutt 395
heimisch 339
heimische Art 400
heiße Quelle 247
heiße vulkanische Quelle 156
Heizplatte 28
helfen 93
Helfer 308
Helicase 208
helikal 206
Helligkeitswert 324
helmförmig 120
hemizygot 192
hemmen 299
hemmende Synapsen 321
Hemmstoff 137
Hemmung 137, 299
Henlesche Schleife 84
herabsetzen 131
heraufspringen 385
heraushängen 105
herauspülen 386
herausragen 94
herausschneiden 264
Herbstlöwenzahn 363
Herbstzeitlose 49
Herde 307
Hermaphrodit 184
Hermelin 358
herstellen 246
Herz 54, 239
herzförmig 112, 121
Herzinfarkt 140
Herzinsuffizienz 228
Herzkammer 54
Herzklappe 54

Herzkrankheit 79
Herzkranzgefäß 54, 140
Herzkreislaufsystem 284
Herzzeitvolumen 79
Herzzyklus 79
Hesperidium 115
heterogametisch 184
Heterostylie 104
heterozygot 180, 192
Heterozygotentest 269
Heterozygotenvorteil 203
Heuaufguss 26, 381
Heupferd 365
Heuschnupfen 87, 237
Heuschrecke 52
Heuschreckenbefall 409
Heutierchen 26
hierarchisch geordnet 306
Hill-Reaktion 150
Himbeere 48
hin- und herschwingen 376
Hin- und Rückreaktion 131
Hinterende 394
Hinterende mit hoher Hämo-globinkonzentration 376
Hinterhorn 68, 326
Hinterleib 375
Hinweis 204
Hippocampus 69, 327
Hirnanhangdrüse 69, 328
Hirnschädel 292
Hirnstamm 69, 328
Hirsch 49
Hirse 116, 152, 409
Histamin 88, 238
Histon 206, 287
Hitze 61
hitzeinaktiviert 205
Hitzeinaktivierung 205
hitzestabil 247
HIV 89, 240
HIV-positiv 89, 240
HLA-System 88
hnRNA 209
Hochblatt 121
Hochmoor 380
Hochmoorwald 354
Hochpunkt 42
hochschnellen 120
höchste Produktmenge 256
höchster Wert 42
Hochwald 354
Hochwasserschutz 385
Höckerschwan 372

477

Hoden 55, 72, 193
Hodenkanälchen 72
Hodensack 55, 72
höhenbedingt 354
höher im Rang sein 314
hoher Salzgehalt des Bodens 337
hohl 222, 373
Höhle 294
Höhlenbrüter 360
Höhlenmalerei 294
hohler Stängel 116, 119
Hohlraum 102, 222, 384
Holunder 356
Holz 362
Holzabfall 360, 392
Holzbohrer 360
Holzgewebe 118
holzig 99
Holzverarbeitungsindustrie 354
Homeostase 335
Homo erectus 291
Homo habilis 291
Homo sapiens 291
Homo sapiens sapiens 291
homogametisch 184
homogen 177
Homogenat 177, 207
homogenisieren 177, 207
Homogenität 270
homolog 190
Homologie 284
Homologiekriterium 284
Homöobox 225, 419
Homöodomäne 225
Homöostase 70
homöotisches Gen 225, 419
homozygot 180, 192
Hopfen 257
horizontal 38, 66
horizontale Bewegung 174
Horizontalzelle 323
Hormon 69, 70, 216, 234, 295, 326
hormonell 234
hormonelles Gleichgewicht 343
Horn 182
Hornblatt 105
Hornhaut 66, 238
hornig 61
Hornisse 52, 359
Hornkraut 374
Hortensie 122
Hox-Cluster 225

Hox-Gen 225
Huflattich 48
Hüllblatt 118
HUGO 251
Hülle 97, 122
Hüllschicht 98
Hüllspelze 116
Hülse 180
Hülsenfrucht 114, 187
Hülsenfrüchtler 152
Human choriongonadotropin 415
humanes Leukocyten-Antigen 238
Humangenomprojekt 251, 269
Hummel 53
Hummer 52
humoral 235
Humus 337, 355
Humussäure 380
Hundertfüßer 359
Hundsgiftgewächse 121
Hüpferling 371
Husten 198, 322
Hut 355
Hutewald 354
Hybride 180, 181
hybridisieren 244, 251, 254
Hybridisierung 217, 244
Hybridomazelle 236
Hybridsequenzierung 252
Hydration 166
Hydrolyse 128
hydrolysieren 128
hydrophil 169, 172
Hydrophilie 105
hydrophob 169, 172
Hydrophyt 374, 393
hydrophytisch 336
Hydrosphäre 347
hydrostatischer Druck 174
Hydroxyl 406
Hydroxyl-Radikal 220
Hydroxylgruppe 167
Hydrozoe 193
Hygiene 409
hygienisch 409
Hygrophyt 337, 356, 393
Hymen 71
Hyperpolarisation 318, 321
hyperton 174
Hyphen 411
Hypodermis 61
Hypokotyl 108

Hypolimnion 377
Hypothalamus 69, 328
Hypothese 17, 34
hypoton 174, 190
Ibisfliege 370
Ich-Bewusstsein 310
Ichthyostega 290
Identifizierung 237, 249
Identifizierung durch Fingerabdruck 249
IgA 235
IgD 235
IgE 235
IgE Klasse 87
Igel 50, 358
IgG 235
IgG-Antikörper 88
IgM 235, 239
im Gleichgewicht 256
im Rang höher sein 306
im Rang nachstehen 314
im Rang niedriger sein 306
immergrün 99
Immission 403
immortalisieren 236
Immun- und Lymphgefäßsystem 60
Immunantwort 233
Immunfärbung 226
immunisieren 236
Immunisierung 86, 232
Immunoglobulin 234
Immunologie 230
immunologisch 229
immunologische Toleranz 88, 239
Immunsuppression 88, 238
immunsupprimiert 238
Immunsystem 230
impfen 86, 232, 409
Impfstoff 240, 341, 409
Impfung 86, 232, 409
Imponierverhalten 314
imprägniert 93
Imprinting 198
Impuls 63
in ausreichenden Mengen synthetisieren 276
in großem Maßstab 255
in situ 178
In-situ-Hybridisierung 226
In-vivo-Gentransfer 277
inaktivieren 137
inäqual 417

Indikationslösung 200
Indikator 21, 29
Individualdistanz 313
individuelle Fitness 308
Individuum 280
Indiz 342
Indol 218
Induktion 215, 225, 418
Industrieabwasser 386
industrielle Landwirtschaft 401
Industriemelanismus 282
Industrieschornstein 403
Industriestaat 408
induzierbarer Promotor 259, 267
induzieren 215, 225, 415
Infektion 86, 232
Infektionskrankheit 85, 90
infektiös 241
infiltrieren 228
infizieren 260
Informationsaustausch 293, 303
Informationsfluss 320
Informationsübertragung 303
inhalieren 277
inhibitorisches postsynaptisches Potential 321
Initialstadium 368
Initiation 213
Injektion 200
injizieren 226
Inkubationszeit 86, 232
Inkubator 177
inkubieren 22, 205
Innenohr 64
innerartlich 339
innerartliche Kommunikation 303
innere Atmung 141
innere Hüllschicht 97
innere Uhr 331
innerer Antrieb 297
inneres Abwehrsystem 230
inneres Skelett 223
innergeschlechtliche Konkurrenz 308
innerster Kreis 102
Insekt 17
insektenbestäubt 106
Insektenvernichtungsmittel 272, 398
Insektivore 368
Insemination 193

Insert-Herstellung 252
Insertion 220
instabil 132
Instinktverhalten 295
instrumentelle Konditionierung 298
Insulin 276
Insulinproduktion 239
intakt 277
Integrase 240
integrieren 183
Integumentsystem 60
Intelligent Design 280
interagieren 138
Interferenz 226
interkalierend 220
intermediär 180
Internodie 116
Interphase 188
interpolieren 42
Interpretation 23, 297
interpretieren 23, 297
interstitielle Flüssigkeit 80
intrazelluläre Verdauung 76
Intron 210, 264
invaginieren 223
invasive Art 400
Inversion 221
Inzucht 181
Ion 165
Ionenaustausch 390
Ionenkonzentration 317
Ionenpumpe 175
Ionentheorie der Erregung 318
ionisierend 220
Iris 67
irreversibel 137
Isogameie 413
Isogamet 91
Isolation 203, 283, 333
Isolationsversuch 418
isolecital 223
isolieren 203, 207, 246, 261, 333
Isolierung 246, 404
isoton 174
Isotop 150, 209
Isotopen Markierungsversuche 151
Sollwert 64, 323
J-Region 236
Jagdrevier 307
Jäger und Sammler 293
jahreszeitlich bedingt 331

jahreszeitlich bedingte Phase 376
Javamensch 291
Joch 94
Jochkäferlarve 371
Jod-Kaliumiodid-Lösung 216
Johannisbrotgewächse 119
juxtamedullärer Apparat 85
K^+Ionen 317
K-Strategen 345
Käfer 53, 107
Käfig 299
Kahlfläche 354
Kahmhaut 381
Kakao 409
Kaktus 49
Kalk 361, 380
Kalkkristalle 325
Kalkstein 350
Kallus 412
Kalluskultur 271
Kälte 61
Kältestarre 333
Kambium der Leitbündel 412
Kambiumring 99
Kameradschaft 313
Kamille 48
Kamin 403
Kamm 182, 243
Kammersystole 79
Kammgras 363
Kampfverhalten 304
Kanadische Wasserpest 374
Kanal 219, 369
Kanal für Chlorid-Ionen 198
Kanalprotein 175, 275
Kaninchen 50
Kannenpflanze 368
Kannibalismus 343
Kapazitätsgrenze 344
Kapillare 79, 233
Kapillargefäß 54
Kapillarkraft 148, 361
Kapillartransfer 244
Kapillarwand 80
Kaposi-Sarkom 240
Kapsel 95, 114, 204
Kapseldeckel 95
Kapsid 89, 240
Karbonylgruppe 167
Karbonylverbindung 167
Karbonzeit 95
Karboxylgruppe 167
Karboxylsäure 167

479

Karpfen 51, 274, 371
Karte 251
kartieren 418
Kartoffel 121, 412
kartografieren 251
Karyogramm 190
Karyopse 114, 117
Karyotyp 190
karzinogen 228, 229, 261
Karzinom 228
Käsebruch 257
Kasein 257
Kaskade 226, 419
Kasparischer Streifen 161
Katabolismus 125
Katalase 129
Katalysator 129, 404
katalysieren 129, 406
Katastrophentheorie 280
Kathode 179
Kation 179
Kätzchen 105, 124
Kaulquappe 227, 372, 417
KCl-Lösung 317
Kehldeckel 81
Kehlkopf 53, 81
Keim 108
Keimbahn 192, 224
keimbahnbetreffende Gentherapie 278
Keimbahnmutation 229
Keimblatt 98, 117, 216, 223, 416
keimen 91, 108, 257
keimfähig 415
Keimhöhle 415
Keimling 194, 216, 257, 356
Keimruhe 109, 359, 415
Keimscheibe 224
Keimung 91, 109, 359, 415
Keimung nach einer Frostperiode 415
Keimzelle 91
Kelch 101, 124
Kelchblatt 101
Kellerassel 52
Kernäquivalent 162
Kernhülle 188
Kernkörperchen 163
Kernobst 114
Kerntransplantation 419
Keto-Enol-Tautomerie 220
Keton 167
Kette 66, 143, 323
Kettenabbruchmethode 248

Kettenform 170
Keuchhusten 409
keulenförmig 94
Kiebitz 394
Kiefer 48, 290, 292
Kiefergelenk 284
Kieferknochen 76
Kiefermäuler 230
Kieferspalte 201
Kieme 335
Kiemenanhang 384
Kiemenatmung 417
Kiemenbogen 284, 416
Kiemenspalt 416
Kiemenspalte 284
Kiementasche 284, 416
Kies 382
Kieselalge 93
Kieselgur 93
Kieselsäure 93
Kinderehe 408
Kindersterblichkeit 408
Kinetochor 189
Kinn 292
Kittel 20
Klappe 78
Kläranlage 154, 351, 388
Klärmittel 257
Klasse 16
Klassenwechsel 236
klassifizieren 191
klassische Konditionierung 300
Klausenfrucht 114
Klebeband 29
kleben 265
klebrig 102
klebrige Haare 368
klebriges Ende 242
Klebstoff 28
Klee 48, 363
Kleeblatt 214
Kleiber 358
Kleie 117
Kleinbuchstabe 180
kleine Schamlippen 71
Kleiner Fuchs 365
Kleiner Klappertopf 364
Kleistogamie 104
Kletterstamm 110
Kletterwurzel 109
Klimawirksamkeit eines Gases 407
Klimaxgesellschaft 381
Klimaxphase 369

Klimaxstadium 381
klinische Versuchsreihen 277
Klitoris 54, 71
Klon 87, 236, 252, 265, 411
klonieren 265, 420
Kluft 408
knacken 212
Knallgas 144
Knallgasbakterien 156
Knallgasreaktion 144
Knäulgrass 363
Knaus-Ogino-Methode 74
Kniegelenk 322
Knoblauchrauke 367
Knöchelgang 292
Knochen 293
Knochenbälkchen 62
Knochenbildungszelle 62
Knochengewebe 62, 160
Knochenhaut 62
Knochenmark 59, 160, 233, 239
Knochenmatrix 62
Knochenschichten 62
Knochenstruktur 62
Knochenzelle 58
Knock-in 226
Knock-out 226
Knock-out Verfahren 419
Knockout-Tier 275
Knöllchen 272, 364
Knöllchenbakterie 152
Knöllchenbildung 272
Knolle 110, 336, 355, 356
knopfförmig 102
Knopfkraut 367
Knorpelgewebe 59, 160
Knorpelzelle 58
Knospe 91, 101, 110
Knospung 413
Knospung im Fangarmbereich 412
Koagulation 390
Koboldmaki 309
kochen 22, 391
Köcher 384
Köcherfliege 52, 370
Kochsalzlösung 83
Köder 394
kodieren 249
kodierend 217
kodierender Bereich 259
kodominant 199
Koenzym 130
koexistieren 338

Kofaktor 130
kognitive Fähigkeit 310
Kohlenflöz 95
Kohlenhydrat 75, 117, 164, 170
kohlenhydrathaltig 121
Kohlenmonoxid 403
Kohlenstoff 349
Kohlenstoffatom 167
Kohlenstoffdioxid 350, 403
Kohlenstoffdioxid-Transport 82
Kohlenstoffmonoxid 350
Kohlenstoffpartikel 229
Kohlenwasserstoff 350, 403
Kohlenwasserstoff-Schwänzchen 167
Koitus 72
Kolben 114
Kolibiri 107
Kolonie 204, 266, 307, 340
Koloniehybridisierung 252
„Kolonielift" 252
Kommensalismus 340
Kommentkampf 307
Kommerzialisierung 279
kommunale Abwässer 154, 351
Kommunikation 293
Kommunikationskontakt 59
kompakt 222
Kompartiment 173
kompatibel 242, 265
Kompatibilität 238
Kompensationsebene 373
kompetitiv 254
kompetitive Hemmstoffe 138
kompetitive Hemmung 138
komplementär 206, 213, 244, 265
Komplementationsanalyse 185
Komplementsystem 86, 231
Komplexauge 323
komplexe Ringstruktur 147
Komplexität 127, 245
Kompost 401
Komposthaufen 402
Kondensation 169
kondensieren 169, 188, 192, 349
kondensiert 192
konditionieren 298
Kondom 74, 241
Konifere 194
Königin 414
königlich 197
Konjugation 94, 183
Konkurrenz 254, 337

Konkurrenzausschlussprinzip 338
konkurrieren 337
Konnektiv 102
Konsensus 253
konservativ 209
konstant 344
Konstante 39
konstante Region 235
konstanter Druck 126
konstitutiv 215
Konstrukt 266
Konsument 346
Kontaktallergie 237
Kontaktverhalten 311
kontinuierliche Leitung 319
kontinuierliche Variabilität 196
kontrahieren 63, 66
kontrahiert 63
Kontraktion 81
Kontrast 324
Kontrazeption 74
kontrollieren 256
Kontrollprotein 228
Konvektion 377
konvergent 284
Konvergenz 284, 342
konvergieren 223
Konzentrationsgradient 174, 225, 317, 419
Kopf 53, 114, 414
koppeln 129, 178, 266
Kopplungs-Ungleichgewicht 204
Kopplungsanalyse 185
Kopplungsgruppe 185
Kopulation 193
kopulieren 193
Koralle 407
Korallenart 412
Korallenpilz 355
Korallenriff 370
Kork 99
Korkeiche 123
Kormoran 51
Kormus 110
Korngröße 361
Kornweihe 394
Körperabwehrmechanismus 61
Körperachse 224, 419
Körperanhang 334
Körperfett 399
Körperflüssigkeit 241
Körperform 385

körperfremder Eindringling 230
Körpergröße 196
Körperhaltung 304, 333
Körperkerntemperatur 332
körperlicher Angriff 314
Körpermasse 196, 334
Körperproportion 334
Körperzelle 58
Korrelation 39
korrelieren 334, 385
Kost 409
Kot 78, 155, 335, 351
Krabbenspinne 365
Kraftwerk 404
Kralle 290
Krallenfrosch 222
Krampf 238, 321
Krankheit 343
Krankheitsverlauf 240
kratzen 241
Krauses Laichkraut 374
Kräutertee 121
Krautschicht 356
Kreationismus 280
Krebs 228, 270, 407
Krebsbehandlung 229
krebserregendes Gen 261
Krebsmaus 275
Krebstier 371
Krebszelle 236
Krebszyklus 142
kreisförmiges Muster 305
Kreislauf der Stoffe 347
Kreislaufsystem 54
kreuzen 104, 181, 187
kreuzgegenständig 112, 120
Kreuzkraut 367
Kreuzotter 358, 380
Kreuzspinne 365
Kreuzung 181
Kreuzungsschema 181
Kriebelmückenlarve 370
Kriechbewegung 311
Kriechender Günsel 363
Kriechender Hahnenfuß 412
Krill 371
Kriminalistik 249
Krokus 49
Krone 101, 356
Kröte 51, 358, 372
Krüppelwuchs 361, 362
Kryptogam 95
Küchenschabe 52
Kuckuck 50

Kuckucksspeichel 365
Kugelschwimmer 370
Kühlmittel 404
Kühlwasser 388
Kuhpocken 90
Küken 372
kultivieren 255, 267
Kultur 255, 310
kulturelle Evolution 293
Kulturlandschaft 366
Kulturmedium 177, 209, 266
Kulturüberstand 236
Kunst 294
Kunstharz 176
künstlich hergestellt 254
künstlich herstellen 276
künstliche Befruchtung 74
künstliche Interferenz 226
künstliche Mutation 269
künstliche Selektion 282
künstliches Gen 268
Kupfer 216
Kurve 41
Kurzfingringkeit 197
Kurzflügler 365
kurzfristige Veränderung 318
kurzlebige Art 345
Kurztagspflanze 332
Kurzzeitspeicher 312
Küstengewässer 394
Kutikula 100, 159
Lab 257
Labor 19, 27
Laborexperiment 296
Laborgeräte 27
Labyrinth 325
lac$^+$-Stamm 260
Lachs 51, 395
Lackmus 29
Lackmuspapier 21
laden 214, 243
Ladung 136, 143, 179, 243
Ladungsverhältnis 136
Lagerapfel 367
Lagerstätte 349
Lagphase 344
Lagune 370
lähmen 375
Laichplatz 393
Laktalbumin 275
Laktose 170, 215, 260, 275
Lamarckismus 280
Lambda-Bibliothek 252
Lambda-Phage 252

Lamelle 355
Lamettasyndrom 362
Landeplatz 107
Landkärtchen 365
Landrasse 188
Landschaftsschutzgebiet 400
Landwirtschaft 187, 271, 274, 349, 388
lange Generationszeit 345
lange Kohlenwasserstoffkette 147
Langerhans'sche Insel 239
langfristig 279
langlebig 227, 345
Langlebigkeit 345
länglich 112
länglicher Einriss 102
längs 411
Längsschnitt 216
Langtagspflanze 331
Langzeitgedächtnis 312
lanzettlich 112
Lappen 186
Lärche 48
Larve 223, 370
Larvenform 414
Last 397
laterale Inhibition 324
Laubbaum 48
Laubfresser 360
Laubmischwald 353
Laubmoos 94
Laubspross 101
Laubwald 353
Laufkäfer 365
Laufmittel 148
Laurasia 286
Lava-Filter 391
Leben 16
lebend gebärend 345, 413
„lebendes Fossil" 289
lebendes System 125
Lebendgeburt 201
Lebensbedingungen 342, 410
lebensbedrohlich 237
Lebensdauer 345
Lebenserwartung 198, 227, 408
Lebensgemeinschaft 329
lebensmittelchemische Risikountersuchung 273
Lebensmittelindustrie 139
Lebensmittelzusatzstoff 258
Lebensqualität 396
Lebensraum 337, 407

Lebenszyklus 72, 91
Leber 76, 239
Lebermoos 94
Leberpfortader 77
Lebewesen 165
Lecitin 171
Lederhaut 67
Legende 42
Leguminose 364
Lehmboden 337
leicht 105
leicht gesägt 123
leichte Kette 235
leiden 200, 254
Leistenpilz 355
leistungssteigernde Droge 276
Leitbündel 111, 115, 118
Leitersprosse 206
Leitgefäße 94
Lemur 309
Lentizelle 110
Lerchensporn 49, 356
Lernen 295, 298
Lernen am Erfolg 312
Lernen duch Einsicht 312
Lernen durch Nachahmung 312
Lernen durch Versuch und Irrtum 298, 312
lernfähig 86
Lerntyp 312
Leserastermutation 214, 220
letal 201
letales Allel 204
Letalfaktor 186, 204
Letalität aufgrund eines genetischen Defekts 204
letztes Drittel 74
letztes Stadium 240
leuchtend farbig 106
Leukoplast 163
Leukocyt 78, 233
Leydig-Zelle 72
Libelle 51, 370
Licht 61, 63, 322
lichtabhängige Reaktion 146
Lichtabhängigkeit 331
Lichtatmung 152
Lichtatmung betreiben 153
Lichtblatt 360
Lichtkompensationspunkt 360
Lichtquant 324
Lichtrezeptorzelle 66, 323
Lichtsammelkomplex 148
Lichtsättigung 360

Lichtsinneszelle 284
Lichtwert 324
Lidschlagreflex 322
Ligase 209
ligieren 253
Lignin 161
Liguster 49, 366
Liliengewächse 115
limbisches System 68, 326
Linde 48, 121, 357
Lineal 34
linealisch 112
linear 217
linkes Atrium 78
linksdrehend 110
Linolensäure 171
Linolsäure 171
Linse 25, 66
Linsenauge 285
Lipid 164, 171
Lipid-Doppelschicht 317
Lipidtröpfchen 147
Lipofektion 261
lipophil 169, 172
lipophob 169, 172
Liposom 163, 173, 261, 277
Lippenspalte 201
Literaturangabe 36
Lockenwickler 206
Lockstoff 304, 413
Loculus 103
Löffelente 372
Löffler 393
logistische Kurve 344
lokalisieren 178
Loligo 318
Löschpapier 244
Löschung 299
lose 105
lösen 20, 177, 213, 348
löslich 20
Löslichkeit 376
Lösung 20, 29
Lösungsmittel 20, 29, 405
Lottka-Voltera Modelle 345
Lottka-Voltera Regeln 345
Löwenzahn 48, 363
Luchs 49, 357
Luciferin 128
Lückengen 225
Luft 81
Luft-Wasser-Gemisch Rührer 381
Luftdruck 81

luftführendes Stängelteil 373
Luftgewebe 105
Luftkammer 417
Luftröhre 54
Luftsack 97
Luftstickstoff 152
Lufttaschen 375
Luftverschmutzung 386, 403
Luftwurzel 109
Lugolsche Lösung 29
lumineszent 128
Lunge 54, 80
Lungenarterie 78
lungenatmende Schnecken 384
Lungenentzündung 204, 240
Lungenvene 78
Lungenvolumen 81
Lupe 31
Lutein 147
luteinisierendes Hormon 72
Luxmeter 379
Luxusartikel 314
Luziferase 128
lymphatisches Organ 86
lymphatisches System 80, 86
Lymphe 80, 233, 241
Lymphgewebe 87
Lymphkapillare 80
Lymphkapillare des Dünndarms 77
Lymphknoten 80, 86
Lymphocyt 87, 233, 236
lymphoide Linie 233
lymphoide Vorläuferzelle 233
lymphoide Zelllinie 233
Lymphom 240
Lymphsystem 233
lysieren 252
Lysin 276
Lysosom 163, 231
Lysozym 86
M = „dritter Stoßpartner" 406
Macchie 353
machbar 19
Macula 64
Magen 53, 77
Magensaft 77
Magermotor 404
Magma 286
Magnesiumatom 147
magnetische Linse 176
Magnolie 102
mähen 399
Mahlen 257

Mahlgut 257
Mähne 182
Maiglöckchen 356
Mais 49, 116, 152, 272
Maische 257
Makromer 417
Makromolekül 130, 171
Makrophage 86, 87, 231, 234
makroskopisch 24
Malaria 90, 398
Malat 153
Maltose 170
Malve 121
Malvengewächse 121
Malz 257
Mälzen 257
Mammutbaum 289, 357
Mangel 408
Mangelernährung 409
Mangelmutante 217
Mangrove 370
Mangrovenwald 354
Manipulation 271
manipulieren 271
Männchen 308
männlich 183
männliche Kätzchen 123
männliches Geschlechtsorgan 92
Marder 50
Marfan-Syndrom 197
Margerite 48, 363
Marienkäfer 359, 365
marines Ökosystem 370
markieren 219, 231, 244, 251, 266
Markierung 268, 296
Markstrahl 99
Marlin 395
Marsch 392
Märzenbecher 49, 356
Masern 409
Maßband 31
Massenauftreten 395
Massenproduktion 255, 276
Massenreproduktion 222
Massenscreen 255
Massenspektrometer 270
Massenvermehrung 395
Mastdarm 78
Mastzelle 87, 234
Material 346
Materialien 35
maternal 198

maternaler Effekt 225
maternales Gen 225
maternell 182
mathematisches Modell 345
Matrix 147, 179
matschig 273
Mauerritze 366
Mauersegler 50
Mauerwerk 404
Maulbeerbaumgewächse 124
Maulbeerkeim 415
Maulwurf 50
Maus 50, 222, 357
Mäusestamm 274
Mauswiesel 366
maximal mögliche Rate 134
maximal möglicher Wert 135
Maximum 42
meandrierend 382
mechanische 1. Stufe einer Kläranlage 388
mechanische Kleinkläranlage 389
mechanische Säuberungseinrichtung 390
Median 39
Medikament 70, 274
mediterranes Biom 353
Medizin 275
medizinische Forschung 139
Meduse 414
Meer 370
Meeresboden 370
Meereslebewesen 128, 395
Meeresspiegel 407
Meeres~ 395
Megaprothallium 100
Megasporenmutterzelle 103
Mehltau-Resistenz 187
Mehltaupilz 411
mehrjährig 99, 336, 364
mehrjährige Pflanze 115
mehrkanaliges Lernen 312
mehrschrittiger Stoffwechselweg 141
Mehrwegflasche 402
Meiose 181, 192, 413
meiotisch 90
Meise 50, 358
Meissner-Körperchen 325
Melanin 277, 282
Membran 173, 287
Membranfluss 174
membrangebunden 229

Membranmodell 174
Membranpotential 317
Membranprotein 173, 317
Membranscheibchen 323
membranumschlossen 228
Membranzisterne 163
Menopause 73
Mensch 309
Menschenaffe 291, 309
Menschenartiger 291
Menschenskelett 61
menschlich bedingt 347
menschliche Oogenese 73
menschliche Zelle 58
Menschwerdung 291
Menstruation 72
Menstruationszyklus 72
meridional 224
Meristem 160
Merkel-Zelle 325
Merkmal 179, 196, 217, 408
Merkmal der Fische 290
Mesencephalon 69, 328
Mesoderm 223, 416
Mesophyll 159
Mesophyt 337
mesophytisch 337
mesotroph 378
messbar 22
Messelektrode 319
messen 22, 35, 296
Messfehler 22
Messstelle 318
Messung 316
Messzylinder 28
metabolischer Marker 266
Metabolismus 124
Metalimnion 377
Metall-Transkriptionsfaktor 216
Metallgewinnung durch Mikroben 157
metallisieren 176
Metallisierung 176
Metallnetz 176
metallresponsives Element 216
Metamorphose 223, 417
Metaphase 188
metazentrisch 190
Methan 401, 407
Methanbildner 156
Methangas 156
Methanol 190
Methode 35
Methylenblau 29

Methylgruppe 147
methylierend 220
Methylierung 198
Methylorange 29
MHC-Protein 238
Michaelis-Menten Konstante 134
Micropyle 98
Miesmuschel 52
Migration 203
migratorisch 331
Mikroarray 216
mikrobiell 155, 351
mikrobielle Ammonifikation 155, 351
Mikrofilament 164
Mikroinjektion 278
Mikromer 417
Mikromere 222
Mikroorganismen 395
Mikroorganismus 26, 85, 230, 255
Mikroprothallium Zelle 100
Mikrosatellit 250
Mikroskop 24, 27
Mikroskopie 24
mikroskopieren 24
mikroskopisch klein 24
Mikrosporenmutterzelle 97
Mikrotiterplatte 237
Mikrotubulus 164, 190
Mikrovilli 77
Milbe 359
Milchdrüse 54, 275, 278
Milchsäure 144, 257
Milchsäuregärung 144
Millimeterpapier 34, 41
Milz 80, 233, 236
Mimese 282, 340
Mimikry 282, 304, 340
Mimosengewächse 119
Mineral 75, 286
mineralisieren 346
Mineralisierung 155, 346, 351
mineralstoffarmer Boden 368
Minimalmedium 217
Minimalnährmedium 258
Minimum 42
Minus Gamet 91
mischen 193, 205
Mischkulturen 401
Mischling 187
Mischwasser 388
„Missing Link" 289

mit doppelter Blütenhülle 113
mit einem Enzym gekoppelt 237
mit Häkchen versehen 115
miteinander verwoben sein 348
Mitochondrium 163, 287, 414
Mitose 188
mitotisch 188
mitotische Teilung 410
mittelfristiger Gedächtnisspeicher 312
Mittellauf 382
Mittelohr 64
Mittelstück 414
Mizelle 173
Mobbing 314
mobile Phase 148
Modell 31
Modellbildung 31
modellieren 31
Modellorganismus 222
moderne Reproduktionstechnik 74
Modifikation 280
modifizieren 180, 248
modifiziert 248
modifizierter Stamm 110
mögliche Erklärung 35
Mohngewächse 121
Molch 51, 372
Molchei 418
Molekül 125
Molekül, das Energie liefert 129
Molekulargewichtsstandard 243
Molke 257
Molkerei 187
Molkereiprodukte 401
monoklonaler Antikörper 87
Monoclycerid 171
Monocyt 87, 234
Monogamie 309
monoklonaler Antikörper 236
Monokultur 354, 401
monophyletische Gruppe 285
Monosaccharid 170, 129
Monosomie 191
monosynaptisch 322
Moor 392
Moorbrand 369
Moos 48, 411
Moosschicht 355
Moostierchen 413
Moräne 380

Moränenschotter 380
Morchel 356
Morphogen 225, 419
Morphogenese 416
Morpholino 226
Mörser 27, 207
Morula 222
Mosaikentwicklung 225
Mosaiktyp 418
Most 367
Motoneuron 318
motorische Endplatte 321
motorischer Nerv 322
Motte 106
Möwe 51
mRNA 209, 213, 253
Mukoviszidose 275
Müllbeseitigung 402
Müllhalde 402
Müllverbrennungsanlage 402
multifaktorielle Vererbung 196
multipotent 224
Mund 53, 76
Mundfeld 161
Mundhöhle 76
Mundöffnung 412
Mundschleimhautzelle 58
Mündungsbereich 383
Mündungsgebiet 370
Murein 162
Muschel 52, 371
Muschelkrebs 371
Muskel 53, 198
Muskelfaser 62
Muskelgewebe 59, 160
Muskelkraft 314
Muskelspindel 319, 322
Muskelsystem 60
Muster 191, 251, 263
Musterbildung 419
Mutagen 219, 229
mutagenes Potential 220
Mutagenese 219, 226
Mutation 219, 280, 286
mutieren 219, 240
mütterlich 222
Muttermilch 241
Mützenschnecke 371
Mycoprotein 256
Myelin 315
myelinisierte Axone 319
Myelinscheide 197
Myelocyt 233
myeloide Vorläuferzelle 233

myeloide Zelllinie 233
Myelomazelle 236
Mykorrhiza 361
Mykorrhizapilz 99, 352
Myofibrille 63
Myom 228
Myosin 164, 321
N-Ethyl-N-nitrosoharnstoff 220
N-Formyl-Methionin 213
Na^+ Ionen 317
Nabelschnur 201
nach Futter suchen 305
nachahmen 107, 310, 340
Nachahmung 295, 302, 310
Nachbarschaft 403
Nachfolgeprägung 301
nachgeschaltet 419
nachhaltig 396
Nachhaltigkeit 396
Nachklärbecken 388
Nachkomme 181, 281, 308, 410
Nachkommenzahl 345
nachtaktiv 333
Nachtblindheit 324
Nachteil 340
Nachtigall 50
nächtlich 106
Nachtschattengewächs 321
Nachtschattengewächse 121
Nachweis 22, 178, 269
Nachweismittel 29
Nackenmuskulatur 292
Nacktsamer 98
Nacktschnecke 52, 359
NAD 142
Nadel 100
Nadelbaum 48, 98
Nadelkopf 89, 240
Nadelwald 354
NADH 142
Nagetier 342
Nährflüssigkeit 107
nahrhaft 409
Nährlösung 154, 350
Nährsalz 352
Nährsalzauswaschung 386
nährsalzfreie Erde 391
Nährstoff 222
Nährstoffkreislauf 347
Nahrungsaufnahme 76
Nahrungsbereich 393
Nahrungsbeziehung 346
nahrungsbezogenes Signal 304
Nahrungsgrundlage 411

485

Nahrungskette 347, 399
Nahrungskreislauf 93
Nahrungsnetz 347
Nahrungsnische 375
Nahrungspyramide 75, 347
Nahrungsruf 304
Nahrungszusammensetzung 75
Nährwert 106
Nährzelle 222
Name 14
Narbe 102, 110, 180
Narzissengewächse 115
Nase 53, 63, 292, 322
Nasenhöhle 81
Nasenloch 81
Nasenrachen 76
Nationalpark Bayerischer Wald 400
Natrium-Kalium-Pumpe 175, 317
Natriumhydroxid 250
Natriumkanal 319
Naturdenkmal 400
Naturkatastrophe 343
natürliche Familienplanung 74
natürliche Quelle 351
natürliche Selektion 203
Naturschutz 399
Naturschützer 396
Nautilus 289
Neandertaler 291
Nebenblatt 111
Nebenfluss 382
Nebenhoden 72
Nebenschilddrüse 219
Nebenwurzel 109
negative Rückkopplung 85
negative Verstärkung 299
Nekrose 228
Nektar 103
Nektarblatt 103
Nektardrüse 124
Nektarivor 107
Nekton 374
Nelkengewächse 121
Nematode 222, 225, 359
Neolithische Revolution 294
Neophyt 339
Neozoen 339
Nephron 335
Nerv 76, 315
Nerv-Muskel-Gewebe 316
Nervenfaser 62, 64
Nervengewebe 59
Nervensystem 60, 64, 315

Nervenzelle 58
Nessel 363
Nesseltier 370
Nesselzelle 375
Nestflüchter 301
Nestverteidigung 308
Netto-Ökosystem-Produktivität 347
Nettoprimärproduktion 347
Netz 384
netzartig 118
Netzhaut 66
Netzhautkrebs 229
netznervig 118
neu orientieren 418
Neugeborenes 200
Neugierverhalten 311
9+2-Muster 164
Neuntöter 367
Neuralplatte 416
Neuralrinne 417
Neuralrohr 416
Neuralwulst 416
Neuraspora 217
Neurobiologie 315
neurodegenerativ 198
Neurodermitis 237
neurogen 79
neuromuskuläre Endplatte 321
neuromuskuläre Synapse 63
Neuron 68, 295, 315, 326
neuronale Kontrolle 295
Neurotoxin 321
Neurotransmitter 320
Neurowissenschaften 15
Neurula 222
Neurulation 416
Neuston 374
neutral 21
Neutralfett 171
Neutralrot 29
nicht allosterisches Enzym 138
nicht betroffen 196
nicht codogener Strang 210
nicht heimischer Lebensraum 339
nicht kodierend 217
nicht verwandt 342
nicht voraussagbar 407
nicht zyklische Fotophosphorylierung 150
Nicht-selbst 230
Niederschlag 349
Niederschlagsgebiet 378, 382

niedriger Wuchs 334
niedrigster Wert 42
Niere 54, 84, 175, 238, 335
Nierenbecken 84
Nierenfunktion 175
Nierenkelch 84
Nierenmark 84
Nierenrinde 84
Niesen 237
Nische 338
Nistplatz 393
Nitratbakterien 154, 350
Nitrationen 154, 350
Nitrifikation 154, 350
nitrifizierende Bakterien 154, 350
Nitrifizierung 388
Nitritionen 154, 350
Nitrobakter 154, 350
Nitrosomonas 154, 350
Nitroxyl 406
noch nie da gewesen 407
Nomade 293
nonverbale Kommunikation 304
NOR 191
Noradrenalin 68, 327
„Northern-Blot" 244
Notizblock 34
Notizbuch 34
Notizheft 34
Notochord 284, 416
NPT 191
Nucellus 98
Nukleinsäure 165, 204
Nukleosid 205
Nukleosom 206
Nukleotid 128, 205
Nukleus 209
Nullhypothese 39
Nullwachstumsrate 344
Nuss 114
Nüsschen 121
Nussfrucht 123
Nussfruchtverband 115
Nutzen 298
Nutzen des Verhaltens 295
Nutzenergie 142
Nutznießer 340
Nutzpflanze 271, 272
Nutztiere 274
Nylonmembran 244, 251, 263
Nymphen 365
Oberboden 361

Oberfläche 132, 140, 173, 231
Oberflächenabfluss 378
Oberflächenantigen 199
Oberflächenhäutchen 375
Oberflächenmarker 229
Oberflächenmolekül 231, 237
Oberflächenversiegelung 385
Oberflächenwasser 387
Oberflächenzufluss 378
Oberlauf 382
Oberlippe 120
Oberseite 100
oberständiger Fruchtknoten 116
Objekt 25
Objektiv 25
Objekttisch 25
Objektträger 25, 27
offener Fermenter 256
offenes Leseraster 214, 253
öffentlicher Verkehr 404
ohne chemische Stoffe 401
ohne sein 377
ohne Tracheen 99
Ohr 63, 322
Ohrenschmalz 65
Ohrläppchen 197
Ohrmuschel 65
Ohrmuskeln 285
Ohrwurm 52, 359
Okazaki-Fragment 209
ökogeografische Regel 334
Ökologie 15, 329
ökologisch 329
ökologische Landwirtschaft 401
ökologische Nische 281, 330
ökologische Potenz 345
ökologisches Optimum 339
Ökosystem 329
Ökosystem der Binnengewässer 369
Ökosystem Wattenmeer 370
Okular 25
Öl 152, 171
Öl speichern 93
Ölabscheider 388
Ölbohrplattform 395
oligo-Primer 267
Oligonukleotid 246
Oligopeptid 168
oligotroph 378
Ölpest 394
Ölplattform 395
Ölsäure 171

omnipotent 224
Onkogen 228
Ontogenese 74, 284, 415
Oocyt I. Ordnung 73
Oocyt II. Ordnung 73
Oocyte 193, 221
Oogamie 413
Oogenese 221
Oogonium 73
operante Konditionierung 298
Operation 201
Operator 215
Operon 215, 266
Operon-Modell 215
opponierbarer Daumen 293
opportunistisch 345
Opsin 324
optimieren 342
Optimum 42, 330
Optimumskurve 42
optisch 66
optische Achse 67
optische Anlockung 308
optische Kommunikation 304
optisches Chiasma 325
Orchidee 49, 364
Orchideen 115
Ordinate 41
Ordnung 16, 127
Organ 16, 60, 162
Organell 159
Organelle 59, 162
Organisator 224, 418
organisch 129
organische Auflage 360
organischer Stickstoff 155, 351
Organismus 16, 162
Organogenese 74, 416
Organspende 88
Organstruktur 385
Organsystem 60
Orgasmus 72
Ornithin 218
Ort des Austauschs von Stoffen 349
Ortung durch Echolot 107
Osmokonformer 335
Osmolarität 83
Osmoregulation 83, 335
Osmoregulierer 335
Osmose 83, 174
osmotische Zustandsgleichung 175

osmotisches Zustandsdiagramm 175
Ösophagus 77
Osteocyt 58
Östrogen 73
Östrus 72
Oszilloskop 316
Otolith 325
ovales Fenster 65
Ovarialzyklus 73
ovovivipar 413
Ovulation 71, 73
Ovum 73
Oxalacetat 153
Oxalessigsäure 142
Oxidation 143
Oxidationsmittel 143
oxidieren 348
Oxonium-Ionen 153
Ozean 350
Ozon 391
Ozon-Sauerstoff Kreislauf 405
Ozonisierung 391
Ozonloch 405
Ozonschicht 405
P-Stelle 213
P53 228
paaren 214
Paarung 308
Paarungsakt 308
Paarungsritual 309
Paarungsruf 303
Paarungssystem 309
PAC 252
Pacini-Körperchen 325
Paläontologie 287
palindromisch 242, 262
Palisadenschicht 159
Palme 115
Palmfarn 98
Palmitinsäure 167, 171
Pandemie 90
Pangäa 286
Panmixie 203
Pantoffeltierchen 26, 370
Papageitaucher 51
Papierhandtuch 244
Pappel 48, 123
Parabiose 340
parabolisch 293
Paraffin 176
parallel 116
parallelnervige Blattspreite 116
Paralyse 321

Parameter 39
Paranuss 272
Parasit 230, 341
Parasitismus 341
parasympathisch 68, 326
Parenchym 60, 160
Parenchymzelle 58
Parkbaum 121
Parthenogenese 221, 414
parthenogenetisch 345, 414
Partialdruck 82
Particle-Gun 261
Partnerwahl 308
passiver Transport 175
pasteurisieren 256
patentieren 275
patentiert 275
paternal 198
paternell 182
Pathogen 86, 230
Patientenprobe 254
Paukentreppe 325
PCR 23, 246
PCR-Schritt 247
Pearsons χ 204
Pedosphäre 347
Pektin 93, 273
Pektinase 273
Peleusball 27
Pellet 177
pendeln 344
Penicillin 255, 341
Penis 54, 72
Pentose 205
Pepsin 77
Pepsinogen 77
Peptid 168
Peptidbindung 214
Peptidoglykan 162
Perigon 101
periodische Schwankungen 344
Periodizität 331
Peripatus 289
peripheres Nervensystem 68, 326
Peripherie 224
Peristaltik 76
peritubuläre Kapillaren 84
Perle 206
Perlgras 363
permanent 392
perniziöse Anämie 239
Peroxisom 152, 163

Pest 90
Pestizid 344
Petrischale 28, 177, 266
Petunie 182
Pfaffenhütchen 356
Pfahlwurzel 99, 336
Pfahlwurzelsystem 109, 119
Pfeifengras 380
Pfeil 347
Pfeil und Bogen 293
Pfeilschwanzkrebs 289
Pfeilwurm 370
Pfirsich 48
Pflanze 17, 48
Pflanzen mit Behaarung 334
pflanzenfressend 346
Pflanzenfresser 346
Pflanzensauger 346
Pflanzenspross 356
pflanzliche Zelle 158
pflanzlicher Leitorganismus 387
Pflegemaßnahme 399
pfropfen 412
Pfützenbildung 392
pH-Toleranz 137
pH-Wert 21, 136
Phage 162, 183, 260
Phagocyt 86, 87
Phagocyte 231
Phagocytose 86, 175
Phänomen 17
Phänotyp 179, 217
Pharmakogenomik 278
pharmazeutisch 274
Pharynx 77
Phase 188
Phenylalanin 277
Phenylketonurie 197, 277
pherografieren 248
Pheromon 107, 303
Phloem 111
Phlox 122
Phosphat 205, 352
Phosphat-Gruppe 265
Phosphatase 265
Phosphoenolpyruvat 153
Phospholipid 171
Phospholipidschicht 287
Phosphorquelle 361
phosphorylieren 128
Phosphorylierung 128
Photolyse 150
Photon 146

Photoperiodismus 331
Photosyntheseleistung 334
Phylogenese 284
Physik 15
physikalisches Mutagen 220
Physiologie 15
physiologische Kochsalzlösung 174
physiologisches Optimum 339
Phytoplankton 92, 399
Phytoplanktonnetz 379
Pigment 147
pigmentiert 224, 417
Pigmentschicht 67, 284
Pilz 17, 48, 230, 272, 411
Pilzgeflecht 361
Pilzvernichtungsmittel 398
Pinocytose 175
Pinzette 27, 31
Pionierart 381
Pionierorganismus 381
Pionierpflanze 95
Pionierzone 392
Pipeline 394
Pipette 27
Pirol 358
Pistill 27, 207
Plakat 37
Plankton 370, 375
Plantaraponeurose 62
Plasma 78, 197
Plasmafortsatz 259
Plasmazelle 87, 233
Plasmid 162, 259, 265
Plasmodesmata 161
Plasmolyse 175
Plastid 163, 182, 287
Plastiden DNA 147
Plastik 294
Platte 266
Plattwurm 413
platzen 240
Plazenta 74, 103, 199, 201, 239, 416
Plazentation 103
Pleuston 374
Ployandrie 309
pluripotent 224
Plus Gamet 91
Pluteus 223
Poaceen 115
poikilosmotisch 335
Pol 189
polares Molekül 166

Polkern 103
Pollen 180
Pollensack 97
Pollenschlauch 107
Pollenschlauchzelle 100
Polsterpflanze 335
poly-A-Schwanz 210, 213
Polyadenylierung 210
Polychaeta 370
polycistronisch 210
polycistronische mRNA 215
Polygalacturonase 273
polygen 180, 217
polygenetisch 196
Polygenie 217
Polygynie 309
Polymer 390
Polymerase-Kettenreaktion 23
Polyp 193, 228
Polypeptid 130, 168
Polyphänie 217
polyphänisch 217
polyploid 191
Polyploidisierung 221
Polysaccharide 170
polysynaptisch 322
Polytänchromosom 191
Population 203, 280, 329
Populationsdichte 343
Populationsgröße 343
Populationsökologie 329, 343
Pore 102, 179
Porling 356
Portulak-Salzmelde 393
positiv verstärken 299
positive Ladung 317
positive Verstärkung 299
post-transkriptionelles Gene Silencing 211
posterior 224
Posthornschnecke 371
postsynaptisch 320
posttranslationale Modifikation 268
Präadaptation 282
Prader-Willi-Syndrom 198
prädisponiert 229
Prädisposition 229, 282
prägen 301
Prägung 295, 301
Präimplantationsdiagnostik 201
Pränataldiagnostik 201
pränatale Diagnostik 269

Präpariernadel 27
präsentieren 234
präsynaptisch 320
präsynaptsiche Hemmung 322
Präzipitat 208
präzise 19
Präzisionsgriff 292
Preiselbeere 355
Priel 392
Primär-Antikörper 237
primäre Sinneszelle 319
primäre Sukzession 381
Primärprozess 146
Primat 291, 309
Primelgewächse 122
Primer 209, 246
Prion 89, 241
Prisma 146
Privatgesellschaft 306
Pro-Kopf 343
Proband 19
Probe 27, 30, 35, 217, 244, 249, 251
Proben entnehmen 30
Probenentnahme 30, 387
Probengefäß 30
Probenglas 379
Probequadrat 31
Problem 17
Procyte 287
Produkt 126, 132
Produktertrag 256
Produzent 346
Progesteron 73
Progressionsreihe 284
Prokaryot 183, 287
prokaryotische Zelle 161
prokaryotischer Promotor 267
Promotor 211, 215, 266
Propfung 412
Prophase 188
prospektiv 223
prospektive Bedeutung 418
prospektive Potenz 418
Prostata 55
Prostatadrüse 72
prostethische Gruppe 130
Protease 129, 205, 219, 240
Proteasom 164, 219
Protein 130, 165, 199, 204
proteinöser infektiöser Partikel 241
Proteom 270
Prothallium 194

Proto-Onkogen 228
Protobiont 287
Proton 142, 150
Protonema 94
Protonen bewegende Kraft 144, 150
Protonengradient 143, 150
Protonenpumpe 144
Protonenrezeptor 136
Protonenspender 136
Protoplast 271
Protostomier 416
Protozoa 85
Protozoon 230, 390
Provirus 240
proximaler Tubulus 84
Prozent 39
Prozentsatz 39
Prozess des „Cappings" 210
prozessieren 210
PrP 241
Pseudoskorpion 359
Psilophyt 95
Psoralen 220
psychologisch 198
Psychopharmaka 70
PTH-Schmecker 196
Puff 191
Puffer 362
Pufferlösung 140
puffern 362
Pufferzone 400
Pulpahöhle 76
Puls 54, 79
Pulsfrequenz 79
pulsierende Vakuole 335
Punktmutation 220
Punktraster 254
Punnet-Quadrat 181
Pupille 67
Pupillenreflex 67
Puppenhülle 384
Pürierstab 207
Purin 206
putzen 333
Pyrenoid 93
Pyrimidin 206
Pytalin 77
qualitativ 38
Qualle 52, 193, 414
quantifizierbar 23
quantitativ 38
Quartärstruktur 130
Quastenflosser 289

Quecke 393, 412
Quellbach 383
Quelle 349, 369, 382
Quellgebiet 382
Quellmoos 374
Quellwasser 387
quer 411
Querschnitt 216
quervernetzend 220
Quetschpräparat 25
R-Bänderung 190
r-Stratege 345
R-Zellen 204
Rabe 51
Rachen 65, 81
Rachitis 197
Rädertierchen 414
radiärsymmetrisch 118
Radiergummi 34
Radieschen 182
radioaktiv 178, 244, 251
radioaktiv markiert 191
radioaktiver Niederschlag 407
radioaktives Nukleotid 248
Radioaktivität 178, 286
Radioisotop 150
Rahm 257
Rainfarn 367
Rand 112
Randzone 415
Rangordnung 306
Ranvier-Schnürring 315, 319
Raps 272
Raseneisenerz 157
Rasierklinge 27
rasiert 186
Rasterelektronenmikroskop 176
Rastplatz 393
Rate 39
Ratte 50
Rattenfutter-Pellet 299
rau 204
Räuber 304, 340
Räuber-Beute-Beziehung 343
räuberisch 340
Raubfisch 372
Raublattgewächse 121
Raubvogel 51, 399
räumlich 66, 168, 207, 323, 339
räumliche Struktur 242
räumliche Wahrnehmung 67
Raupe 364
Reagens 29

Reagenzglas 28, 237, 246
reagieren 16, 171, 418
reagierend 216
reagierendes Organ 322
Reaktion 16
Reaktionskette 70
Reaktionsraum 287
Reaktionsverlauf 134
Reaktionsvolumen 246
Reaktionszentrum des Lichtsammelkomplexes 148
Reassoziationskinetik 245
Reassoziationsstudie 245
Reblaus 400
rechte und linke Hemisphäre 69
Rechtes Atrium 79
rechtsdrehend 110
Redoxreaktion 143
Reduktion 143
Reduktionsmittel 143
Reduktionsschritt 192
Reduktionsteilung 192
redundant 213
reduzieren 348
reflektieren 148
Reflex 300, 322
Refraktärzeit 318
Regelgröße 64, 323
regelmäßig 121
regelmäßige Probeentnahme 256
Regen 352
Regeneration 411
regenerieren 142, 271, 377
Regenkleidung 31
Regenwald 362
Regenwasser 95, 388
Regenwasser, das in Fluss gelangt 386
Regenwurm 52, 141
Regenwurmfraßgang 361
Regler 64, 323
Regressionsreihe 284
Regulation 417
Regulationsentwicklung 225
Regulationssystem 70, 264
Regulationstyp 418
Regulatorgen 215, 419
regulatorisches Protein 419
regulieren 417
Reh 49
Rehwild 357
Reibung 126

reich an Rohrzucker 106
reif 233
Reifegrad 273
reifen 233, 273
Reifung 233, 257, 273
Reihenfolge 169
Reiherente 372
reinigen 139, 231, 237, 263, 389, 390
Reinigung 268, 389
Reis 49, 116
Reisetipp 90
Reisfeld 401
Reißverschluss 208
Reiz 16, 63, 297, 300, 318, 322
Reiz-Reaktionstheorie 300
Reizbeantwortung 63
Reizelektrode 319
Rekombination 183, 192, 258, 280
Rekombinationsknoten 192
Rekombinationsreaktion 406
rekombinieren 192, 258
Rekorder 248
Religion 294
religiöse Werte 200
Renaturalisierung 386
renaturieren 245, 386
Renaturierung 245
Renin-Angiotensin-Aldosteron- 85
Rentier 49
repetitive DNA 245
repetitive DNA-Sequenz 250
Replikation 191, 208, 259, 264
Replikations-Enzym-Komplex 227
Replikationsursprung 208
replizieren 188, 208, 260
Repolarisation 318
Reportergene 266
Repressor 211, 215
reprimieren 215
Reproduktionsorgan 71
reproduzierbar 19
Reptil 17
Reptilienmerkmal 290
Reservoir 349
resistent gegenüber Proteinase 242
resistent gegenüber Röntgenstrahlen 242
Resistenz 266, 272
Resistenzgen 259, 266

respiratorische Oberfläche 80
Ressource 106, 339, 396
Rest 167
Restgruppe 168
restistent 260
Restluftmenge 82
Restriktionsendonuklease 250
Restriktionsenzym 242, 250, 261
Restriktionsfragment 242, 250
Restriktionsschnittstelle 242
Restriktionsverdau 262
resuspendieren 177
Retina 323
Retinal 130, 324
retrovirale Insertion 245
Retrovirus 89, 240
Rettsyndrom 198
Reuse 390
revers transkribieren 267
reverse Transkriptase 89, 240, 267
reverse Transkriptase-Inhibitor 240
reverse Transkription 89, 240, 267
reversibel 19, 137
Revier 281
Revierruf 303
Revolver 25
rezeptives Feld 324
Rezeptor 322
Rezeptormolekül 228, 231, 326
Rezeptorpotential 319
Rezeptorprotein 229
rezeptorvermittelte Phagocytose 231
Rezeptorzelle 64, 319
rezessiv 180, 196
Rezipient 259
reziproker Altruismus 308
RGT-Regel 135, 334
Rh-negativ 88
Rh-positiv 88
Rhesus-negativ 199
Rhesus-positiv 199
Rhesusfaktor 88
Rhesussystem 87, 199, 239
Rheumafaktor 88, 239
Rhizoid 94
Rhizom 96, 110, 356
Rhodopsin 66, 324
Ribose 128, 170
Ribosom 164, 213
Ribosomenbindungsstelle 214

Ribulose-(1,5)-bisphosphat 151
Richtung 175
Riechsinneszelle 326
Riedtorf 380
Riesenbärenklau 400
Riesenchromosom 191
Riesenmaus 274
riesiger Baum 95
Riff aufbauend 412
Rinde 123, 257
Rindenbohrer 360
Rindenreaktion 193
Rinder 187, 241, 401
Rinder-betreffend 241
Rinderwahnsinn 241
Ring 96
Ring kleiner Zähnchen 95
Ringelnatter 51, 372
Ringerlösung 29
Ringform 170
ringförmige DNA 287
ringförmige DNA-Struktur 162
Rippe 290
Risiko 254, 398
Risikoanalyse 229
riskant 398
Rispe 114, 116
Rivale 314
RNA 89, 165, 209
RNA-Editing 219
RNA-Polymerase 209
RNAi 211, 226
Rochen 395
Rodung 354
Roggen 49, 116
Rohmilch 257
Röhre 107
Röhrenblüte 118
röhrenblütige Korbblütler 118
röhrenförmige Blütenkrone 106
röhrenförmiger Blütenkelch 120
Röhrling 355
Rohrsänger 372
Rohwasser 390
Roller 196
Röntgenaufnahme 37
Röntgenfilm 151, 244, 251
Röntgenstrahl 206, 220
Röntgenstrahlen 226
Röntgenstrahlung 229
Rose 49
Rosette 335
rosettig 113

Rost 402
Rostfarbiger Dickkopffalter 364
Rot-Grün-Blindheit 197
Rotauge 372
rote Blutzelle 78
rote Gentechnologie 278
Rote Liste 399
Rötegewächse 122
rotes Blutkörperchen 199, 239, 276
rotes Knochenmark 62, 80
Rotes Straußgras 363
Rotfeder 371
Rotkehlchen 50, 358
Rotkohl 175
Rotmilan 358
Rotschenkel 394
Rötung 237
Rotwild 357
rRNA 210
RubisCo 151
Rückenmark 68, 322, 326
Rückenschwimmer 370, 371
Rückgrat 61, 68, 198, 223, 326
Rückhaltezeit 390
Rückkopplung 215, 407
Rücklaufschlamm 388
Rückmutation 220
Rückgrat 205
Rückreaktion 131
rückschließen 419
Rückstand 259
Rückstände des Desinfektionsmittels 391
rückwärts 246
Rudel 307
Ruder 375
Ruderfußkrebs 371
Rudiment 285, 416
rudimentär 285
ruhend 317
Ruhepotential 317
Ruhr 409
rühren 208
Rührer 256
Rumpf 53
rund 180
rundes Fenster 65
rundlich 112
Rundmäuler 230
Rundtanz 305
runzlig 180
Ruß 203, 229, 283
Rüssel 184

Rüsselkäfer 272, 365
S-Phase 188
S-Zellen 204
Saatkrähe 50
Saccharose 117, 170
Säftesauger 360
Saftfrucht 114
Salamander 51
Salatgurke 48
Salmoniden 382
saltatorische Erregungsleitung 319
Salz 165
Salz-indifferent 393
Salzausscheidung 337, 393
Salzausschluss 393
Salzblase 393
Salzdrüse 393
Salzgehalt 21, 157, 337, 392, 393
Salzlösung 21, 316
Salzmarsch 370
Salzpflanze 337
Salzwasser 93, 383
Samen 98, 117, 216
Samenanlage 98
Samenfresser 360
Samenhülse 120
Samenkapsel 119
Samenkern 123
Samenleiter 55
Samenschale 98
Samenzelle 73
Sammeln 64
Sammelrohr 84
Sammlung 27
Sand 361
sandig 378
Sandregenpfeifer 394
Sanierung 381
Sanierung durch Pflanzen 386
Sanitäreinrichtungen 409
Saprophyt 346
saprophytisch 346
Sarkom 228
SARS 90
Satelliten-DNA 245
Sättigung 376, 392
Sättigungskurve 134
Sättigungspunkt 20, 344
Säubern von Tanks 395
sauer 121
Sauerkleegewächse 122
Sauerstoffatom 167
Sauerstoffkonzentration 82

sauerstoffliebende Bakterie 148
Sauerstoffmangel 379
Sauerstoffradikal 227
„Sauerstoffschuld" 144
Sauerstofftransport 82
Sauerstoffversorgung 141
Sauerstoffzehrung 379, 386
saugen 311
Säugetier 17, 222, 309
Säugetier~ 222
Saugpumpe 81
Saugreflex 311
Saugwurzel 109
saure Bedingungen 77
Säuregehalt 21, 386
Säuremantel 86
saurer Regen 352, 354, 403
saurer Torf 392
saures Milieu 137
Säurestoffwechsel 153
Savanne 353
„scannen" 255
Scanner 254
Schachbrett 364
Schachtelhalm 95, 356
Schädel 61, 292
Schadensbegrenzung 396
schädlich 398
Schädling 272, 398
Schädlingsbekämpfungsmittel 398
Schadstoff 227, 387, 397
Schadstoffanreicherung 387
Schafbeweidung 399
Schafgarbe 363
Schale 93, 122, 494
schalentierfressende Vogelart 394
Schallwellen 63, 322
Schamlippe 54
Scharbockskraut 49, 411
Scharfer Mauerpfeffer 366
Schattenblatt 359
Schattenpflanze 359
Schaukasten 296
Schaumstoff 405
Schaumzikade 365
Scheide 54, 71
Scheidensekret 241
Scheidewand 120
Scheinblüte 114
Scheinfrucht 115
Schere 28

scheren 253
Schichten 379
Schicksal 223
Schieber 208
Schienbein 62
Schierling 321
Schiffchen 119
Schilddrüse 239
Schildkröte 51
Schilfrohr 373
Schilfrohrzone 373
Schimmelpilz 217, 411
Schirm 419
Schlachtgewicht 274
Schlacke 402
Schlaganfall 140, 228
Schlagvolumen 79
Schlamm 388
Schlammbecken 389
Schlammbeseitigung 389
Schlammfang 388
Schlammfaulung 389
Schlammfliege 370
Schlammröhrenwurm 371
Schlammschnecke 371
Schlange 358
Schlauchnukleus 107
Schlauchzelle 102, 107
Schlaufe 209
Schlehdorn 356
Schlehe 366
schleichend 398
Schleier 96
Schleife 65
Schleim 81, 198
Schleimhaut 53
schleimig 81
Schleimkapsel 162
Schleppnetz 395
Schleuse 385
Schlick 383
schließen 18, 100
Schließfrucht 120, 122
Schließmuskel 76
Schließmuskel des Magenpförtners 77
Schließöffnung 100
Schließzelle 336
Schloss 133
Schlucht 383
Schlucken 76
schlüpfen 301, 339
Schlüssel-Schloss-Modell 133

492

Schlüssel-Schloss-Prinzip 87, 234
Schlüsselblume 363
Schlüsselloch 133
Schlüsselreaktion 144
Schlussfolgerung 18
schmal 292
schmelzen 245, 376
Schmelzkurve 245
Schmelzpunkt 245
Schmelztemperatur 247
Schmelzwasser 380, 383
Schmerle 371
Schmerz 61
Schmetterling 52, 106, 364
Schmetterlingsblütler 119, 152
Schnabeltier 289
Schnakenlarve 365
Schnauze 292
Schnecke 52, 359
Schneckenhaus 65
Schneeglöckchen 49
Schneeschmelze 383
schneiden 246
schnell 410
Schnelldurchlauf 227
schneller Sandfilter 390
Schnellkäfer 365
Schnitt 25, 37, 261, 262
Schnittanfertigen 25
Schnittstelle 250, 262
Schnittstück 261
Schnorchel 375
Schnur 206
Schnürungsexperiment 224
Schock 237
Schöpfflasche 379
Schornsteinfeger 228
Schötchen 120
Schote 114, 120
Schraubel 114
Schraubenalge 93
schraubig 113
schreiten 311
Schreiweinen 311
Schritt für Schritt 136
Schrotschuss-Bibliothek 253
Schrottplatz 402
Schulter- und Beckengürtel 285
Schultergürtel 61, 290
Schuppe 94
Schuppe des Langtriebs 99
Schuppenblatt 105
schuppig 99

Schüssel 133
schüsselförmig 292
schütteln 20
Schutz 241, 384, 396
Schutzbrille 19
schützen 396
schützend 216
Schutzgebiet 399
Schutzmaßnahme 399
Schutzwald 354
Schwäbische Alb 368, 400
schwach 292, 397
Schwalbe 50, 367
schwammförmig 241
Schwammschicht 160
Schwangerschaft 201
Schwangerschaftsabbruch 200
Schwangerschaftstest 415
Schwankung 344
Schwänzelmuster 305
schwänzeln 305
Schwänzeltanz 305
Schwanzteil 414
Schwarm 307, 340
Schwärme bilden 376
Schwärmer 92
Schwarze Witwe 321
schwärzen 244, 251
schwarzer Raucher 286
Schwebedichte 177
schweben 106
Schwebfliege 282, 365
Schwebstoff 390
Schwebstoffe 388
Schwefel 155, 351
Schwefeldioxid 352
Schwefelkreislauf 351
Schwefelsäure 157, 352
Schwefelwasserstoff 155, 352
Schwefel~ 157
Schwein 50
Schweinegrippe 90
schwellen 190, 216
Schwellenspannung 318
Schwellenstaat 408
Schwellenwerteffekt 330
Schwellkörper 55, 117
Schwemmland 383
schwere DNA 209
schwere Kette 235
Schwerkraft 65
schwerlöslich 350
Schwermetall 216
Schwermetall-Ion 176

Schwermetallsulfid 156
Schwermetallsulfat 157
Schwertfisch 395
Schwertlilien 115
Schwimmaufbereitung 387
Schwimmblatt 337, 374
Schwimmblattpflanzenzone 374
Schwimmpflanzenzone 374
Schwimmstoff 387
Schwimmwanze 371
schwitzen 332, 349
Screen 226
Scutellum 117
Secchi-Scheibe 379
Sediment 177, 208
Sedimentation 177
Sedimentationsbecken 390
See 369
Seeadler 399
Seebecken 378
Seeboden 378
Seebodenschlamm 376
Seeigel 52, 222
Seepocke 52
Seeregenpfeifer 394
Seerose 374
Seeschildkröte 51
Seeschwalbe 394
Seestern 413
Segelklappe 79
Segge 122, 152
Segmentierungsgen 225, 419
Sehfaser 66
Sehgenauigkeit 67
Sehne 53, 62
Sehnerv 66, 323
Sehnervenkreuzung 66
Seidenraupe 124
Seitenkette 168
Seitentrieb 362
seitenverkehrt 38
Sekret 65
Sekretion 84
sekretorische Zelle 58
Sekundär-Antikörper 237
sekundäre Botenstoffe 324
sekundäre Immunantwort 86
sekundäre Leibeshöhle 416
sekundäres Dickenwachstum 118
Sekundärprozess 146
Selbst 230
selbstbefruchtende Pflanze 104

Selbstkenntnis 310
Selbstkonstruktion 417
Selbstorganisation 417
Selbstreinigung 386
Selbsttoleranz 239
Selbstverdauung 257
selektierbarer Marker 266
selektieren 342
selektiert 342
Selektion 281
selektionierbarer Marker 271
Selektionsbedingung 342
Selektionsdruck 282, 309
Selektionsnährboden 266
selektionsneutral 249
selektive Rückresorption 84
selektiver Ionenkanal 317
semikonservativ 209
semipermeabel 174
semipermeable Membran 84
Sender 296, 303
Sender-Empfänger-Beziehung 303
Senkwurzel 109
Sense 367
Sensibilisierung 87
sensible Phase 301
sensorischer Nerv 322
Sequenz 246
Sequenzbildung 251
sequenzieren 246
Sequenzierprimer 248
Sequenzierreaktion 248
Sequenzierung 246, 248
Serosa 417
sesshaft 294
Sesshaftigkeit 294
Seuche 409
Sexpilus 259
Sexualpartner 128
sexuelle Aufklärung 408
sexuelle Selektion 309
sexuelles Verhalten 295
Seymuria 289
sezernieren 235
Sezierwanne 27
Shikimisäure 218
Shuttle-Vektor 267
sich auf etw. auswirken 135
sich fortpflanzen 16
sich gegenseitig umwandeln 124
sich herausbilden 153
sich trennen 192

sich überschlagen 174
sich unterscheiden 339
sich verhalten 146
sich weigern etw. zu tun 299
sich weiten 332
sich wiederholende Abschnitte im Erbgut 250
sich zusammendrängen 333
sich zusammenziehen 332
Sichelzellanämie 203, 276
Sicherheitsleine 384
Sicherheitsvorkehrungen 19
sichtbar 24, 67, 188, 244
sichtbar werden 266
sichtbares Licht 146
Sichttiefe 378
Sickeranlage 389
70S Ribosom 162, 213
Siedepunkt 22
Siedlung 294
Signal 303
Signalstoff 152, 419
Silage 364
Silberahorn 357
Silberbromid 178
Silberdistel 368
Silberfisch 359
Silberkorn 178
Silikonöl 246
Silizium 254
Singdrossel 368
single-copy-DNA 245
Sinkstoff 388
Sinn 63
Sinncodon 219
Sinnesorgan 63, 312, 322
Sinnesrezeptor 61
Sinneszelle 318, 323
Sinnes~ 297
Sinusknoten 79
sitzend 111
Skalpell 27
Skanner 217
Skelett 53
Skelettmuskel 62
Skelettsystem 60
Skinner Box 296, 299
Skizze 26
skizzieren 26
Skrapie 241
„Slot" 243
Smog 404
SNP 198, 220, 250
Soforttyp 237

Sojabohne 273, 409
Sollbruchstelle des Rings 96
Soma 315, 321
somatische Mutation 229
somatische Rekombination 87, 235
somatische Zelle 277
Sommereier 414
sommergrüne Pflanze 110
Sommerpolder 393
Sonderfall 414
Sondermüll 402
Sonneneinstrahlung 152, 331, 377
Sonnentau 368
Sonnentierchen 26
Sorus 194
Southern Blotting 263
„Southern-Blot" 244, 251
sozial 184
soziale Beziehung 306
soziale Enge 343
soziale Stellung 306, 314
sozialer Kontakt 313
soziales Zusammenleben 313
Sozialleistungen 408
Sozialversicherungssystem 408
Spalte 384
spalten 205, 263
Spaltöffnung 153
Spaltung 141
Spaltungsregel 181
Spannung 314, 316
spannungsabhängige Kanäle 318
Spatel 27
Spättyp 88
Spatz 367
Spatz, Sperling 50
Specht 50, 358
Speichel 53, 137
Speicheldrüse 53, 76, 191
speichern 335
Speicherorgan 151
Speicherung 335
Speiseröhre 53
Spektralbereich 324
spektrometrisch 246
Spemannscher Organisator 225
Spender 238, 418
Sperber 358
Sperma 72, 241
Spermatocyt I. Ordnung 73
Spermatocyt II. Ordnung 73

Spermatogenese 73
Spermatogonium 73
Spermatoza 193, 221
Spermazelle 100
Spermienkopf 193
Spermienschwanz 193
Spermium 414
Sperrkrautgewächse 122
spezifisch 178, 242
spezifische Antikörper 226
spezifisches Immunsystem 231
spezifisches pH Optimum 137
Spezifität 132
Sphingolipide 172
Sphingosin 172
Spielverhalten 311
Spinalganglion 68, 326
Spinalnerv 68, 326
Spindelapparat 189, 190
Spindelfaser 190
Spinndrüsen 384
Spinne 52
Spinnentier 17, 341, 365
Spitzer 34
Spleißen 210, 218, 265
Spleißmechanismus 264
Spleißvarianten 254
spontane Muskelkontraktion 79
Spore 92, 193, 411
Sporenkapsel 96
Sporenkapselhäufchen 96
sporenkapseltragendes Blatt 96
Sporn 106
Sporophyt 91, 92, 193
Sprache 293
Spray 277
Spraydose 404
springendes Gen 245
Springschwanz 359
Spritzflasche 27
Sproangium 193
spröde 93
Spross 109
Sprossachse 153
sprossbürtige 96
sprossbürtige Stützwurzel 109
sprossbürtige Wurzel 115, 116
Sprossknolle 412
Sprossknoten 331
Sprossspitze 94
Sprossung 411
Sprungschicht 377

Spülmittel 208
Spur 179
Spurenelement 216
SRY-Gen 184
Stab 186
Stäbchen 66, 323
Stabheuschrecke 52, 414
stabil 132
stabiler Lebensraum 410
Stachelhäuter 413
stachelig 115
Stachelpilz 356
Stadium 188, 408
Stadt 294
Stadtwald 354
Stagnation 377
Stamm 16, 109, 258, 356
Stammbaum 196, 201, 285
Stammdornen 110
Stammlösung 140
Stammranke 110
Stammzelle 58, 78, 224, 277
Standort 34
Standzylinder 28
stängelumfassend 116
Stangenbohne 152
Stapel-Wechselwirkung 206
Star 367
stark 292
Stärke 129, 137, 140, 170, 216
starke Sonneneinstrahlung 152
starke Zunahme 266
Stärkeaufschwemmung 129
stärkehaltiges Nährgewebe 117
Stärkekorn 147
Startmethionin 213
stationäre Phase 148
Statistik 39
statistische Signifikanz 204
Stativ 28
Stativring 28
stattfinden 197
Staubbeutel 102
Staubblatt 102, 116, 120, 180, 194
Staubblüte 97, 122
Staubfaden 102
Staubkätzchen 124
Staudamm 369, 385
Stausee 369, 385
Stearinsäure 171
Stechmücke 52, 399
Steckling 412
stehendes Gewässer 388
Steigbügel 65, 284

steigend 238
steigern 279
Steigerung 274
Steigung 44
Steilheit 381
Stein 293
Steinbrechgewächse 122
Steinfliege 370
Steinfrucht 114
Steinfruchtverband 115
Steißbein 285
Stellenäquivalenz 342
Stempel 102, 180, 266
Stempelblüte 97, 122
Stempelkätzchen 124
Stengelknoten 116
stenohalin 335
stenök 330
stenotherm 332
Steppe 353
sterben 227
Sterberate 343
steril 22
steriler Nährstoff 256
Sterilisation 22
sterilisieren 368
sterisch 206
Sternchen 36
Steroid 171
steuern 271
Stickstoff 83, 154, 350
stickstoffarm 368
Stickstoffdünger 272
stickstoffhaltige Base 205
stickstoffhaltige Base Adenin 128
Stickstoffoxid 403
Stiel 94, 180, 375
Stiellupe 27, 31
Stielzelle 100
stille Mutation 220
Stillphase 74
„Stillstand" 127
stillstehend 383
Stillwasserzone 383
Stimmband 53
Stimmlippe 81
Stimmritze 81
Stimulation 318
stimulieren 234
stimulierende Strömung 318
Stirn 292
Stockente 372
Stockwerk 355

Stoff 29, 165
Stoffkreislauf des Phosphors 352
Stoffwechsel 16, 83, 215
Stoffwechsel haben 16, 124
stoffwechselgesteuert 332
Stoffwechselkette auslösende Reaktion 138
Stoffwechselprodukt 215
Stoffwechselprozess 138, 218
Stoffwechselrate 80
Stoffwechselreaktion 165
Stoffwechselzwischenprodukt 171, 218
Stoffwechsel~ 227
Stopcodon 219
Stopfen 28
Stoppuhr 28
Storch 50
Storchennest 362
Storchenschnabelgewächse 121
Störung der Entwicklung 418
strahlenblütige Korbblütler 118
Strahlentierchen 26
Strahlung 126, 146, 220, 270, 406
Strand-Grasnelke 393
Strandflieder 393
Strandfloh 52
Strang 206, 208, 245
Strang aus Zytoplasma 94
Straßentaube 367
Stratum basale 61
Strauch 110
Strauchschicht 356
Straußgras 363
Streptomycin 266
Stresstoleranz 279
Streuobstwiese 366
Streuzersetzer 360
Strom 316, 369, 381
Stroma 147
Stromschnelle 383
strömungsbedingt 383
Strömungsleitrohr 256
Struktur 169
Strukturformel 165
Strukturgen 215
Stubenfliege 52
Stufe der Sukzession 381
Sturzbach 383
„Subcloning" 253
sublinguale Immuntherapie 238

Substrat 132, 178
Substratkonzentration 134
subtraktive Farbmischung 324
Sudan 29
Sukkulente 153, 336, 366
Sukzession 67, 381
sukzessiver Prozess 381
Sulfat 156, 351
Sulfat Aerosol 352
sulfatreduzierende Bakterien 156
sulfidisch 155
sulfidische Erze 156
Sulfidschwefel 157
Sulfit 155, 157
Sulfitgas 157
Summation 321
Summe 39
Summenformel 145, 165
Summengleichung 141
Sumpf 373, 392
sumpfig 368
sumpfiges Dickicht 373
Sumpfland 369
Sumpfohreule 394
Sumpfpflanze 373
Suspension 20, 129
Suspensionskultur 177
Süßwasser 92, 369, 383
Süßwasser Grünalge 93
Süßwasseregel 371
Süßwasserpolyp 375, 412
süßwasser~ 92
Symbiont 287
Symbiose 99, 341
symmetrisch 44
sympathisch 68, 326
Symport 175
Symptom 240
Synapse 315, 320
Synergid 103
Synökologie 329
synökologisch 329
Synthese 163
synthetische Evolutionstheorie 280
synthetisieren 163
Systematik 16
systolischer Druck 80
T-Helfer-Zelle 233, 240
T-Helferzelle 87
T-Killerzelle 233
t-Test 39
T-Zelle 87

T-Zellrezeptor 87, 234
Tabelle 41
Tafelapfel 366
Tag-Nacht-Sauerstoffschwankungen 382
Tages~ 331
tagneutrale Pflanze 332
Taiga 353
Taktmesser 301
Tandem-Wiederholung 245
Tanne 48, 362
Tannenwald 354
Tanningehalt 123
Tanzsprache der Honigbienen 305
Taq-Polymerase 246
tarnen 340
Tarnfärbung 282
Tarnung 240, 282, 340
Tastscheibe 325
Tatort 249
Tau 335
Taube 50, 358
Täubling 355
Taubnessel 49, 412
Tauchgang 376
Tauchpflanze 374
tauschen 192
Tausendblatt 374
Tausendfüßer 17
Tay-Sachs-Syndrom 197
TDF 184
technische Hilfsmittel 296
Teer 229
Teich 369
Teichralle 372
teilen 193
Teilung 90, 411
Teilungsfurche 189
teilweise verdaut 252
Tektorialmembran 66
Telomer 190, 227
telomerisch 190
Telophase 188
temperaturabhängig 141, 184
Temperaturabhängigkeit 334
Temperaturschichtung 377
Temperaturschwankung 332
Template 208, 247
temporärer Teich 369
terminaler Elektronenakzeptor 144
Terminator 211, 215
Terrasse 366

terrestrisches Ökosystem 353
Territorialverhalten 313
Territorium 307
Tertiärstruktur 132
Tesafilm 29
Testosteron 73
Teststäbchen 140
Tetrade 192
Teufelskreis 397
Thalamus 69, 328
Thallus 91
Theka 102
therapeutisch 277
therapeutische Alternative 89
therapeutischer Nutzen 277
Thermocycler 246
Thermometer 28
thermophile Faulung 389
thermophiles Bakterium 247
Thermoregulation 60, 61
thermoregulatorische Verhaltensweise 333
Thiosulfat 157
Thylakoid 162
Thylakoid-Membran 147
Thylakoidmembran 147
Thymin 206
Thymin-Dimer 221
Thymus 80, 86, 233
Ti Plasmid 271
Tiefe der Kompensationsebene 373
tiefgefroren 208
Tiefpunkt 42
Tiefsee 370
Tiefseeschlote 156
Tiegelzange 28
Tier 17
Tierhaltung 187
tierische Emotionen 295
tierische Kommunikation 295
tierische Zelle 158
tierischer Leitorganismus 387
Tierstock 413
Tochtergeschwulst 228
Tochterindividuum 412
Tochterzelle 189
Tod 227
Todesurteil 228
tödlich 186, 398
Toleranz 187, 329
Tomate 48
Ton 361
Ton-Humus Komplex 361

Tonhöhe 64
Tonmineral 362
Tonmudde 380
Torfboden 368
Torfmoor 95
Torfmoos 95, 373, 380, 392
Totenkult 294
totipotent 58, 160
Totipotenz 410
toxisch 197
toxisches Stoffwechselprodukt 197
Toxizität 140
Toxoplasmose 240
Tracermethode 151
Trachea 76, 81
Tracheide 96, 99
Traditionsbildung 310
Tragblatt 116
tragen 94
Träger 196
Trägermaterial 263
Trans-Seite 163
Transduktion 64, 183, 323
transduzieren 64
Transekt 30
transferieren 244
Transformation 183, 205, 258, 266
transformieren 258
transfundieren 238
Transfusion 238
transgen 255, 278
Transition 220
Transkiption 209
transkribieren 209
Transkription 270
transkriptionell 192
Transkriptionsfaktor 211, 228, 419
Transkriptionsregulationsfaktor 419
translatieren 212
Translation 212, 270
Translokation 191, 221
Transmembranprotein 198
Transmissionselektronenmikroskop 176
Transpiration 348
transpirieren 348
Transplantat 238
Transplantat-gegen-Wirt-Reaktion 88
Transplantatablehnung 88

Transplantation 238
Transplantationsantigen 88, 238
Transplantationsexperiment 224
transplantieren 238
transponierbares Element 245
Transversion 220
Traube 114
traubenartige Blütenbüschel 105
treiben 105
Treibhaus 405
trennen 133, 179, 205, 236, 243, 248
Trennkanalisation 388
Tricarbonsäurezyklus 142
Trichter 28
Trieb 99, 117
Triglycerid 171
trinkbar 389
Trinkhalm 29
Trinkwasser 388, 389
Trinkwasseraufbereitung 389
Trinkwasserspeicher 385
Trinukleotid-Expansion 198
Triops 289
Triosephosphat 151
Tripeltest 201
Triplett 213
Trisomie 191
^{3}H 191
tRNA 210, 214
Trockenfrucht 114
Trockenfutter 117
Trockengebiete 336
Trockenmauer 366
Trockennasenaffe 309
trockentolerant 187
Trockenwald 354
Trockenzeit 383
Trommelfell 65
Tröpfcheninfektion 90
Tropfpipette 28
Trophieebene 347
Trophoblast 74, 415
tropisches Holz 362
trübe 373
Trübung 390
Trübungsgrad des Wassers 378
Trypsin 129
Tryptophan 277
Tryptophan-Synthese 218
Tuberkulose 409

Tubulin 190
Tubus 25
Tumor 228, 240, 261
Tumor-Unterdrücker-Gen 228, 278
tumorerregend 271
Tumormarker 140
Tundra 353
Tunfisch 395
Tunnelelektronenmikroskop 176
Tüpfel 161
turgeszent 174
Turgor 174
Turmfalke 367
Typhus 409
Tyrosin 277
U- oder J-förmige Röhre 394
U-förmig 293
Überaugenwulst 292
Überbevölkerung 408
überdauern 366
überdauernde Stielreste 96
überdauernder Kelch 119
übereinstimmen 419
Übereinstimmung 342
Überfischung 395
überflüssig 228
Überflutung 407
überfrachten 348
überführen 249
Übergangsform 289
Übergangsphase 105
Übergangszone 393
übergeordnet 219
Überhang 242, 262
überhängend 242, 262
Überkreuzung 185, 192
überlappen 148
überlappendes Fragment 252
Überlastung 274, 386
überleben 266, 408
Überlebensstrategie 329
Überlegenheit 314
übermitteln 318
übersättigt 20
überschneiden 339
überschreiten 344
Überschuss 318
Überschuss an Substraten 135
Überschwemmung 343, 383, 392
Überstand 21, 177, 208, 259
übertragen 65, 97, 205, 263, 341

Überträger 196, 341, 399
Überträgerstoff 320
Übertragung 64, 97, 259
Überwachung 269
Überweidung 369
überwinternde Pflanze 360
Ubiquitin 219
Uferbewaldung 380
Uferbewuchs 385
Ufererosion 379
Uferfiltration 390
Uferzone 373, 385
Uhrfeder 96
Uhrglas 28
Ulme 357
Ultradünnschnitt 176
Ultramikrotom 176
Ultraschalluntersuchung 201
ultraviolettes Blütenmal 106
unempfindlich 260
Umfang 30
umgeben 222
umgekehrt proportional 146
Umkehrosmose 390
Umkehrreaktion 127
umkippen 379
Umlagerung 235
Umprogrammierung 265
umsetzen in 23
umwälzen 377
Umwälzung 377
umwandeln 65, 124, 348
Umwandlung 124, 348
Umwelt 180, 395
umweltbedingt 180
Umweltbelastung 396
Umweltfaktor, der am weitesten vom Optimum entfernt ist 338, 376
umweltfreundlich 396
Umweltkapazität 343
umweltschädlich 397
umweltschonend 396
Umweltschützer 395
umweltverschmutzt 397
Umweltverschmutzung 203
umweltverträglich 396
unabänderlich 418
Unabänderlichkeit 418
Unabhängigkeitsregel 181
unauffällig 104
unbeabsichtigt 279
unbeweglich machen 139
unbewohnbar 396

unbewusst 400
undifferenzierte Zelle 58, 415
undurchlässig 174, 193
Unebenheit 382
unerwünscht 237
unfruchtbar 401
Unfruchtbarkeit 343
ungeboren 240
ungefärbt 26
ungesättigte Fettsäure 123
ungeschlechtliche Fortpflanzung 91, 193, 221
ungeschützter Geschlechtsverkehr 241
ungestört 224
Ungleichgewicht 347, 397
Ungleichheit 408
ungünstig 410
ungünstige Immunreaktion 87
Uniformitätsregel 181
universales Lösungsmittel 166
universell 213
unkalkulierbar 279
Unkraut 401
Unkrautvernichtungsmittel 272, 398
unlösliche Stärke 151
Unordnung 127
unpigmentiert 163
Unregelmäßigkeit 376
unschädlich 204
unschädlich machen 261
Unsicherheit 306
unsichtbar 24
Unsinnsmutation 214, 220
unsterblich 236
unter Wasser 336, 374
Unterboden 355
unterbrechen 136
unterdrücken 193, 205, 401
Untereinheit 162
Untereinheiten 130
Unterfamilie 152
untergeordnet 226
Unterhaut 61
unterirdisch 351
unterirdischer Speicherstamm 96
Unterlage 412
Unterlauf 382
Unterlegenheit 314
Unterlippe 120
unterscheiden 102, 230, 237
unterscheiden zwischen 13

Unterscheidungsmerkmal 13
Unterschied im pH-Wert 143
unterschiedlich 13
Unterschlupf 367
Unterseite 100
unterstützen 201
unterstützende Struktur 64
untersuchen 22, 23, 34, 35, 269
Untersuchung 34
Untersuchungsbericht 34
Untersuchungsobjekt 25
untertauchen 105
Unterwasserpflanze 374
untranslatierte Region 214
untrennbar 117
unvergrößert 37
unverträglich gegenüber dem eigenen Pollen 104
Unverträglichkeit 239
unverwechselbar 249
unverzweigt 94
unvollständige Blüte 101
unvollständige Veratmung 145
unwichtig 333
unwillkürliche Reflexhandlung 300
Unzulänglichkeit 408
unzureichendes Enzym 277
Uracil 206, 210
Uratmosphäre 286
Urdarm 222, 416
Urdarmhöhle 416
Uridin 210
Uridin-Triphosphat 192
Urin 335
Urmund 416, 419
Urpferdchen 286
Ursprung 233, 259
Urwald 354, 362
Uterus 71, 278
UTP 210
UV-Bestrahlung 221, 391
UV-Spektrometer 246
UV-Strahlung 229, 286
V-förmige Struktur 166
V-Region 235
Vakuole 92, 163
variabel 240
Variabilität 283
Variable 41, 344
variable Region 235
Variante 254
Variation 180
variieren 180

Varroa Milbe 400
Vas deferens 72
Vasa recta 84
Vaterschaft 251
Vaterschaftsgutachten 269
VDJ-Rekombination 235
Vegetationsperiode 334
vegetativ teilen 96
vegetative Fortpflanzung 411
vegetative Verbreitung 117
vegetative Zelle 102, 107
vegetativer Pol 223, 415
Veilchen 49
Vektor 264
Vena cava anterior 79
Vena cava posterior 79
Vena renalis 84
Vene 54, 78, 79
Venenklappe 54
ventral 224
Ventralwurzel 68, 326
Ventrikel 78
Venule 79
Venus von Willendorf 294
Venusfliegenfalle 368
verändern 131, 299
Veränderung 298, 299
Veränderung des Bachbetts 382
verankern 373, 384
Verankerung 337
Veranlagung 278
Veranlagung vorgeben 278
verarbeiten 323
verästelt 315
Veratmung 141
Verband 306
Verbesserung der Erde 95
verbieten 278
verbinden 166, 171, 265
Verbindung 166
Verbindungsreaktion 167, 171
Verbindungsstelle 111
verbrauchen 348
verbraucherfreundliche Verpackung 402
verbreiten 105, 106
Verbreitung 330, 360
Verbreitung der Art 339
Verbrennung 141, 349, 404
Verbrennung von Methan 156
verbunden mit 128
Verdächtiger 249
verdauen 231

Verdauung 53, 76, 231
Verdauungsdrüse 76
Verdauungsorgan 76
Verdauungsprozess 407
Verdauungssaft 76
Verdauungssäfte 129
Verdauungssystem 60
Verdauungstrakt 76
Verdichtung 385
verdoppeln 135
Verdopplungszyklus 247
verdörrt 409
Verdriftung 384
verdrillte Strickleiter 206
verdünnen 20
verdünnt 20
Verdünnung 386
verdunsten 21, 332, 349
Verdunstung 348, 407
veredeln 409
vereinfachen 344
Vereinfachung 344
vereinigen 414
Verengung des Strombetts 385
vererbbar 196
Vererbung 183
Verfall 227
verfallen 227
verfangen 100
Verfolgung einer Zelllinie 226
Verfügbarkeit 274
vergehen 227
vergiften 398
Vergleich 13
vergleichen 251
vergrößern 26, 100, 318, 414
Vergrößerung 26
Vergrößerungsglas 27
Verhalten 70, 295
Verhaltensbiologie 15
Verhaltensforscher 295
Verhaltensforschung 295
Verhaltensmuster 297
Verhaltenswissenschaften 15
Verhaltens~ 295
Verhältnis 207
verhindern 199, 265, 396
Verhinderung 396
verholzte Pflanze 110
verhornt 59, 160
Verhütungsmittel 408
Verklappung 395
verknüpfen 214, 265
verkümmern 103

verkümmert 285
Verkümmerung 117
verlanden 379, 380
Verlandung 380
verlängern 247, 331
verlängertes Mark 69, 328
Verlängerung 213, 247
verlangsamtes Wachstum 362
Verletzung 271
Verlust 128, 335
vermehren 267
Vermehrung 410
Vermehrungsphase 73
vermeiden 201, 238, 299
Vermeidung 299
vermindern 254
vermitteln 238
verpacken 206
verringern 405
Verringerung 405
verrotten 107
verrottendes Material 95
Verschiedenheit 411
verschlüsseln 65
Verschlusskontakt 59
verschmutzen 397
verschmutzt 203
Verschmutzung 397
verschoben 44
verseuchen 397
Verseuchung 397
versickern 348, 378
Versickerung 378, 379
versiegeln 100
versorgen mit 266
Verspieltheit 306
verstädtern 408
Verstädterung 408
Verständigung durch Gerüche 303
Verständigung durch Laute 303
verstärken 65, 231, 406
Verstärker 107
Versteck 343
verstehen 310
versteinerter Farnwald 95
Versteppung 401
verstrahlen 407
verstreut 115
Versuch 18
Versuchsanleitung 19
Versuchsaufbau 19
Versuchsbeschreibung 34
Versuchsleiter 19

Versuchsstadium 277
verteidigen 230
Verteidung 230
verteilt 209
Verteilung 45
Vertiefung 382
vertikal 38
vertikale Bewegung 174
verträglich gegenüber dem eigenen Pollen 104
Vertrauensverhältnis 311
verunreinigen 256
verunreinigende Substanz 256
Verunreinigung 387
vervielfachen 235
vervierfachen 135
vervollständigen 247
verwachsen 412
verwachsenkronblättrig 113
verwandt 342
verwandt sein 309
Verwandtschaft 309
Verwandtschaftsgrad 245
verwechseln 13
Verweildauer 349, 407
verwelken 98
verwerfen 102
verwesen 145
Verwesung 273
Verwirbelung 382
verwittern 351
verwittertes Gestein 361
Verwitterung 351
Verwurzelung 361
verwüsten 398
verzögerter Typ 238
Verzögerung 231
Vesikel 162, 228, 231
Vibration 325
vibrieren 106
Vieh 187
Viehhaltung 401
Vielfalt der Proteine 270
Vielzeller 58, 160
vielzellig 91
Vierbeiner 291
viereckiger Stamm 120
vierzählig 118
viraler Partikel 277
viraler Vektor 277
virtuelles Wasser 391
virulent 204
Virus 162, 229, 230
Virushülle 89, 240

Viscosität 276
Vitalität 330
Vitalkapazität 82
Vitamin 75
Vitamin A-Reis 274
Vitamin B7 258
VJ-Rekombination 235
Vogel 17
vogelähnlich 289
Vogelgrippe 90
Vogelkirsche 356
Vogelkundler 399
Vogellied 303
Vogelmännchen 309
Vogelmerkmal 289
Vogelschwarm 376
Volllängen-cDNA 267
Vollmedium 217
vollständige Blüte 101
von C4- Pflanzen betriebene Photosynthese 152
Voraussetzung 203
vorbeugend 396
Vorbild 302
Vorblatt 105
Vordergliedmaßen 284
Vorderhorn 68, 326
Vorfahr 181, 291
Vorfahrenreihe 291
Vorfluter 389
Vorfreude 306
Vorhaut 54, 72
vorherig 239
Vorhof 54, 71
Vorhof- und Kammerdiastole 79
Vorkeim 96
Vorläufer 223, 233
Vormännlichkeit 104
Vormensch 291
vorschlagen 206
Vorspelze 116
vorstäubend 104
Vorstellungsvermögen 310
Vorstufe 107, 218, 274
Vorteil 139, 340
vorübergehend 183
vorwärts 246
vorweiblich 104
Vorweiblichkeit 104
vorzeitig 219
vorzeitiges Ableben 277
Vorzug 214
Vulkan 286
Vulkanausbruch 351

Vulva 54, 71
Waage 27
Wabe 305
Wacholderbusch 368
Wacholderdrossel 368
Wacholderheide 368, 399
wachsartig 159
wachsen 16, 344
Wachsschicht 336
Wachstum 16, 271, 344
Wachstumsfaktor 228
Wachstumshormon 274
Wachstumsperiode 334, 359
Wachstumsphase 368
Wachstumszone 116
wahllos 127
wahrnehmen 67
Wahrnehmung 67, 325
Wahrscheinlichkeit 39, 203, 250
Wald 353
Wald-Hainsimse 356
Waldbestand 354
Waldbewirtschaftung 354
Waldboden 355, 360
Walderde 355
Waldfläche 354, 400
Waldfrühblüher 49, 359
Waldfunktionsplan 354
Waldkiefer 99
Waldmeister 122
Waldrand 354
Waldsterben 354
Wanderbewegung 331
Wanderfisch 385
wandern 179, 223, 243, 248
Wanderung 343
Wandkontaktverhalten 313
wandständige 119
Wanze 52
warmblütig 332
Wärme 126
Wärmeabstrahlung 333
Wärmeenergie 126
Wärmekraftwerk 388
Wärmeleitung 332
Wärmestrahlung 331, 406
warnen 282
Warnfärbung 282, 304, 340
Warnruf 304
Warnschrei 303
Warnung 282
Waschbär 357
Waschpulver 208
Wasser 29, 75

Wasser hinzufügen 171
wasserabhängig 94
Wasseramsel 372
wasserarm 152
Wasserassel 371
Wasseraufbereitung 391
Wasserbad 22, 28
Wasserdesinfektion durch Sonnenbestrahlung 391
Wassereinzugsgebiet 378, 382
Wasserfall 383
Wasserfloh 51, 371
wasserführende Schicht 369
wassergesättigt 363
wassergesättigter Boden 391
Wassergütebestimmung 379
Wasserhaushalt 334
wässerige Lösung 139
Wasserknöterich 374
Wasserkörper 379
Wasserkraftwerk 388
Wasserläufer 51, 371
Wassermangel 336, 391
Wassermolekül 165
Wasseroberflächenspannung 385
Wasserpest 105
Wasserpflanze 336, 374
Wasserqualität 389
wasserreinigende Pflanze 391
Wasserseelchen 370, 384
Wasserspeicher 348
Wasserspeicherfähigkeit 361
Wasserspeicherkapazität 361
Wasserspeicherung 95
Wasserstand 383
Wasserstoff 166
Wasserstoffion 142
Wasserstoffperoxid 140, 391
Wasserstrom 375
Wassertrübung 379, 383
Wasserverbrauch 391
Wasserzufluss 378
Watt 352
Watte 29
Wattenmeer 392, 400
Wattestäbchen 29
Wattfläche 392
Wattvogelart 394
Wattwurm 394
Weberknecht 52, 365
Wechselbeziehung 338
wechselseitige Umwandlung 124

wechselständig 112
wechselwarm 332
Wechselwarmer 332
wechselwirken mit 205
Wechselwirkung 132, 338, 418
Wechselzahl 135
Wedel 96, 356
Wegerich 363
Wegwerf- 402
wegwerfen 402
Wehe 74
Weibchen 309
weiblich 183
weibliche Zapfenblüte 100
"weiblicher" Gametophyt 103
weibliches Geschlechtsorgan 92
weich verdrahtet 217
Weichboden 383
Weiche Trespe 363
weicher Gaumen 76
weicher Untergrund 337
Weiches Honiggras 363
Weichholz 121
weichstachelige Hülle 123
Weichtier 371
Weide 48, 123, 357, 364, 367
Weidelgras 363
Weidengewächse 123
Weinberg 366
weinrot 185
Weißdorn 356
weiße Blutzelle 78
weiße Gentechnologie 278
weiße Substanz 68, 326
weißes Blutkörperchen 232
Weißkopf-Seeadler 399
weit 382
Weite 382
weiter weg 403
Weitergabe 241
weitergeben 347
weiterverarbeiten 409
Weizen 49, 116
welk 175
Wellenlänge 64, 146, 246
Wellhornschnecke 394
wellig 112
Weltgesundheitsorganisation 90
Wendepunkt 42
werdende Eltern 200
werdende Mutter 200
Werkzeug 293

Werner-Syndrom 227
wesentliches Glied 93
Wespe 53
„Western-Blot" 244
Wettbewerb 281
Wicke 363
Wickel 114
wickeln 207
widerstehen 329
Wiedehopf 367
wieder einschleusen 277
Wiederaufbereitungsanlage 408
Wiederaufforstung 350, 362, 369
wiederherstellen 226, 396
wiederholen 214, 247
wiederkehrendes Muster 378
wiederverwenden 219
wiederverwerten 402
Wiederverwertung 402
Wiese 48, 363
Wiesel 357
Wiesen-Lieschgras 363
Wiesenfuchsschwanz 363
Wiesenkerbel 363
Wiesenrispengras 363
Wiesenschaumkraut 363
Wiesenschnake 365
Wiesenschwingel 363
wild wachsende Verwandte 187
Wildbeuter 305
Wilde Möhre 367
Wildkatze 50, 357
Wildschwein 357
wildtyp 182
Wildtyp 182
willkürlich 343
Wimper 161
Wimpernkranz 375
Wimpertierchen 359, 370
windbestäubt 104
Windbestäubung 97
winden 208
windender Spross 110
Windverbreitung 98
Wintereier 414
Winterfell 333
winterhart 187
Winterhärte 360
Winterschlaf 333
Winterschlaf halten 333
Winterschläfer 333
Wirbelsäule 291

Wirbeltier 17, 371
Wirkgruppen 130
Wirkstoff 255
wirkungslos 400
Wirkungsspektrum 148
Wirt 89, 342, 418
Wirtel 99
wirtelständig 113
wirtschaftlich 139
Wirtschaftswald 354
Wirtswechsel 342
Wirtswechsel betreibend 342
Wobbelhypothese 214
Wolf 49, 358
Wolfram 261
Wolfsspinne 359
Wolkendecke 407
Wollhaar 333
Wortspiel 274
Wunderblume 182
Wurm 230, 359
Wurmfortsatz 80, 233
Wurzel 76, 98
Wurzelbakterie 272
Wurzelbärtigkeit 272
Wurzelgewebe 361
Wurzelhaube 415
Wurzelknöllchen 152
Wurzelknöllchen durch Knöllchenbakterien 119
Wurzelknolle 109, 336, 412
Wurzelscheide 117
Wurzelschicht 355
Wurzelstock 109, 336
Wurzelsystem 109
Wurzelwerk 355
Wüste 353
X-chromosomal 196
χ-Quadrat 204
Xantophyll 147
Xenopus 419
Xerophyt 336, 366
xerophytisch 100
XX-X0-System 184
Xylem 111
Xylem Gefäß 99
Y-förmig 235
YAC 252
Zahl 39
Zahlenpyramide 347
Zählwerk 227
Zahnbogen 292
Zahnfleisch 76
Zahnkrone 76

Zahnschmelz 76
Zahnstruktur 76
Zahnwurzel 76
Zahnzement 76
Zapfen 66, 98, 194, 323
Zapfenblüte 100
Zauneidechse 366
Zaunkönig 358
Zebrafisch 222
Zecke 341, 359
zehntausende 406
Zeichenpapier 34
Zeichnung 26
Zeigerart 30
Zeitabstand zwischen 301
Zeitalter 287
zeitlich 207
Zeitlupe 45
Zeitlupenaufnahme 296
Zeitraffer-Mikroskopie 226
Zeitrafferaufnahme 45, 296
zeitweilig 392
Trümmer 177
Zellafter 161
Zellatmung 141, 227
Zelle 16, 158, 188, 207
Zellfortsatz 315
Zellfressen 231
Zellgewebe 412
Zellkern 63, 163, 315
Zellkörper 224
Zellkultur 177
Zellmarker 87
Zellmembran 63, 162
Zellmund 161
Zelloberflächenmolekül CD4 240
Zellorganelle 287
Zellplasma 59, 159
Zellplatte 190
Zellsaft 163
Zellsaftraum 161
Zellschicht 59, 159
Zellsortierer 177
Zellstreckungszone 415
Zellsuspension 177
Zellteilung 91
Zellteilungskontrollgen 229
Zellteilungszone 415
Zelltheorie 159
Zelltyp 58, 237
zelluläres Element 78
Zellulose 152, 161, 170, 407
Zellwand 161

Zellzwischenraum 140
Zelt 294
zentrale Blütenachse 100
zentrales Nervensystem 68, 326
Zentrifugation 176, 258
Zentrifugationsröhrchen 209
Zentrifuge 21, 28, 208, 259
zentrifugieren 21, 176, 190, 208
Zentriole 164
Zentromer 189
zentromerisch 190
Zentrosom 164
Zerfall 323
Zerfallsereignis 406
Zerfallsphase 369
Zerfallsprozesse 349
zerfurcht 99
zerschneiden 261
Zersetzer 346
Zersetzung 66
zerstören 125, 398
Zick-Zack-Muster 305
Ziel 34
Ziliarmuskel 67
Zilpzalp 368
Zinnober 186
zinnoberrot 186
Zirkulation 377
Zitronensäure 142, 167
Zitronensäurezyklus 142
Zittergras 363
zittern 333
Zollstock 31
Zonierung 372
Zoologie 15, 295
Zooplankton 399
Zooplanktonnetz 379
Zoospore 93
Zotte 77
Zucht 187, 282

züchten 271
Züchtung 188
Zucker 117
Zucker-Phosphat-Ester 205
Zuckerrohr 117, 152
Zuckerrübe 272
Zuckmücke 370
zufällig 252, 261
Zufälligkeit 127
Zufluss 378
Zugabe 256
Zugang bekommen 209
Zugvogel 393
zum Ausdruck bringen 311
Zunge 63, 76, 196, 322
Zungenblüte 118
zuordenbar 274
zuordnen 249
zur Schau stellen 314
zur selben Art gehörend 310
zurückeinbauen 348
zurückgebildet 104
zurückgebildetes Leitbündelgewebe 337
zurückgebildetes Stützgewebe 337
zurückgebildetes Wurzelwerk 337
zusammenbrechen 344
Zusammenbruch 344
zusammenfassen 12, 23
Zusammenfluss 382
zusammengesetzte Blüte 118
zusammengesetztes Blatt 111
zusammenkleben 210
zuschnappen 368
Zustand 215
Zuwachsrate 343
zwei Blütenformen an einer Pflanze 104

Zwei-Treffer-Theorie 229
zweiatmiges molekulares Sauerstoffmolekül 406
2C 189
2D-Gelelektrophorese 270
zweifruchtblättrig 113
zweigeißelig 94
zweigeschlechtlich 97
zweihäusig 97, 124
zweijährige Pflanze 115
zweikammerig 120
zweilappige Narbe 124
2n 189
zweischalige Kapsel 124
zweiseitig symmetrisch Blüte 119
Zweiteilung 411
zweites Drittel 74
zweizeilig 112
Zwerchfell 54, 81
Zwergdommel 372
Zwiebel 110, 356, 412
zwischenartlich 339
zwischenartliche Kommunikation 303
Zwischenmembranraum 147
Zwischenprodukt 129, 138, 153
zwischenzellulär 60
Zwitter 97
zwittrig 97, 106
Zwölffingerdarm 53, 77, 129
zygomorph 118
Zygospore 93
Zygote 91, 182, 193, 222, 413
zygotisches Gen 225
zyklische Fotophosphorylierung 150
zyklische Schwankungen 344
Zyklus 247
zylindrisch 99, 219

503

Übersicht über die Infoboxen

Classification – the wolf	16
Passive voice	37
Participle constructions	37
Quantities and their units	40
Prefixes and their abbreviations	40
The human ear: functional areas	66
Methods in brain research:	69
Food pyramid	75
Stages of food processing	77
Water balance	83
From blood filtrate to urine	85
Anthers	113
Ovaries and flowers	113
Forms of energy	125
Examples of prosthetic groups and coenzymes	130
Types of enzymes	134
Oxidative decarboxylation reaction	142
Light	146
Four classes of biomolecules in living organisms	165
Chemical elements of biomolecules	166
Classification of amino acids	169
Lipids	172
Fatty acids	172
Sex determination	184
Commonly used mutations in Drosophila Genetics	186
Cell cycle	189
Meiosis I	194
Meiosis II	195
Subdivision of prophase I	195
Examples of different patterns of inheritance in humans	199
Examples of different mutations affecting humans	202
RNA polymerase	210
Differences between DNA and RNA	211
Differences between procaryotic and eucaryotic mRNAs	212
Definitions: Gene, genotype, genome and others	218
Prospective fate of the germ layers	223
The innate and the aquired immune system	232
White blood cells	234
Terminology: Genetic fingerpriting	249
Amino acids	259
Genetic tests	270
Early atmosphere	286
Eon	288
Neurobiology: practicals	316
Parasympathetic nervous system	327
Sympathetic nervous system	328
Law of tolerance	330
Parabiosis – commensialism	340
Alliance	341
Symbiotic relationship	342
Water quality testing	387
Virtual water content and water footprint	391
Indigenous Wadden Sea species	394
Climate	405
Agenda 21	410

Abb. 1 Hypotheses and experiments S. 17

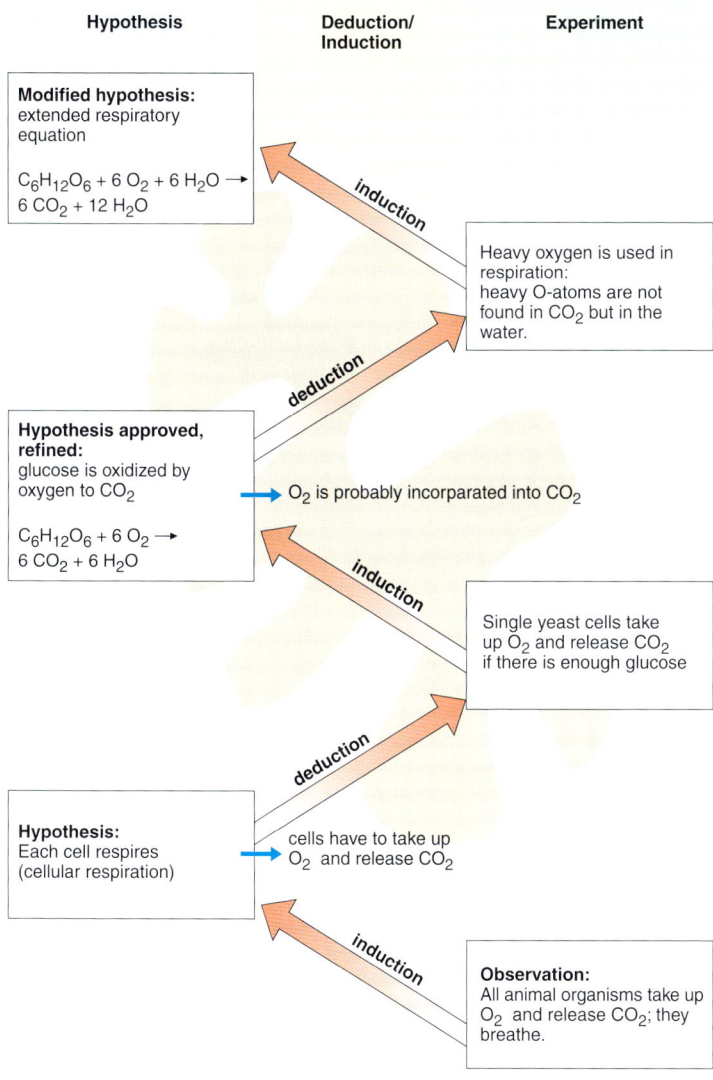

Abbildungen

Abb. 2 In the lab   S. 27

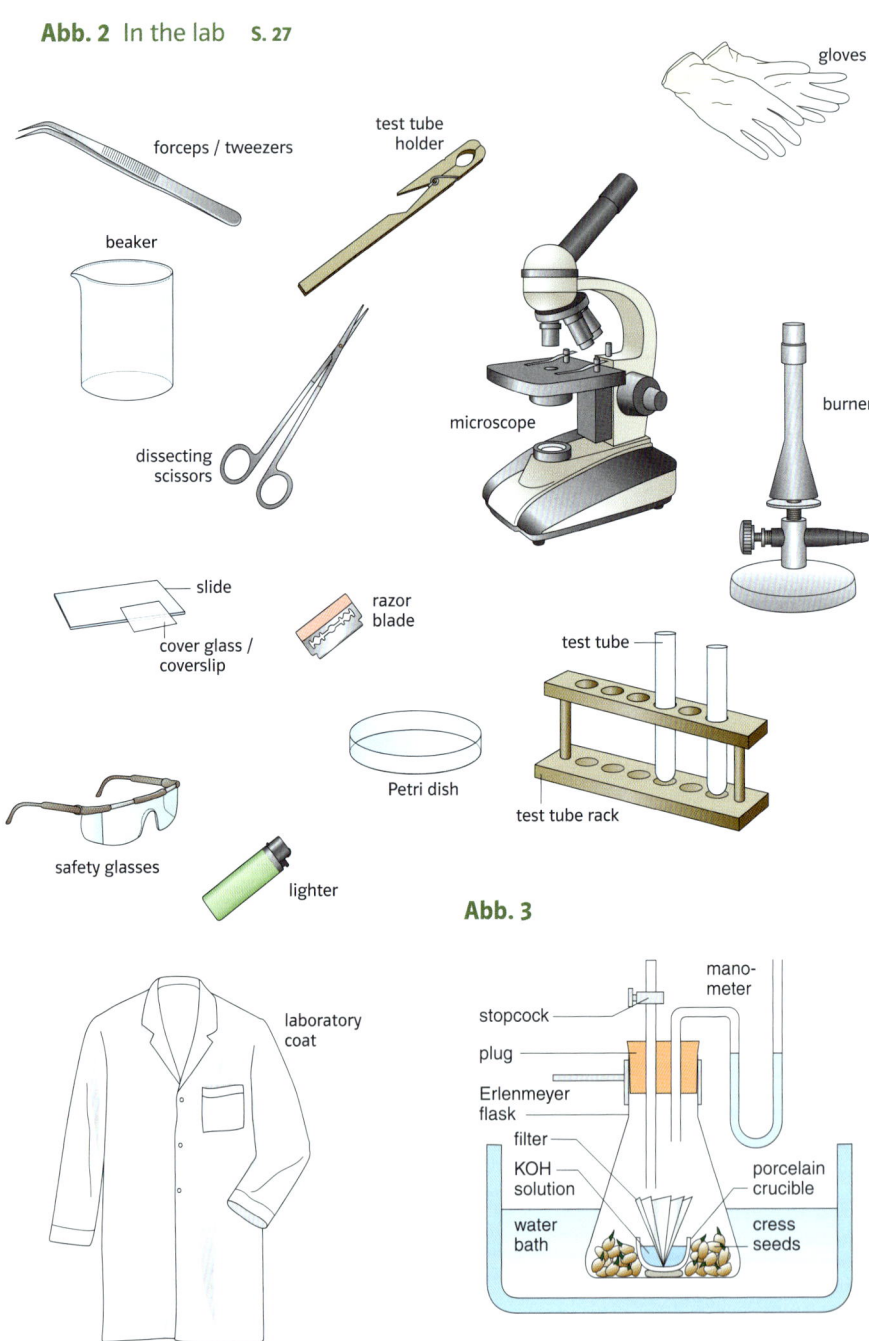

Abb. 4 The microscope S. 24, 27

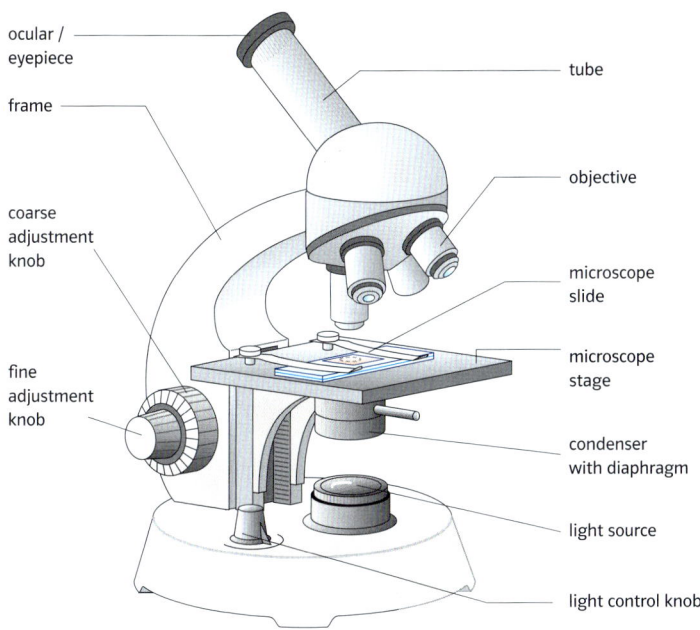

Abb. 5

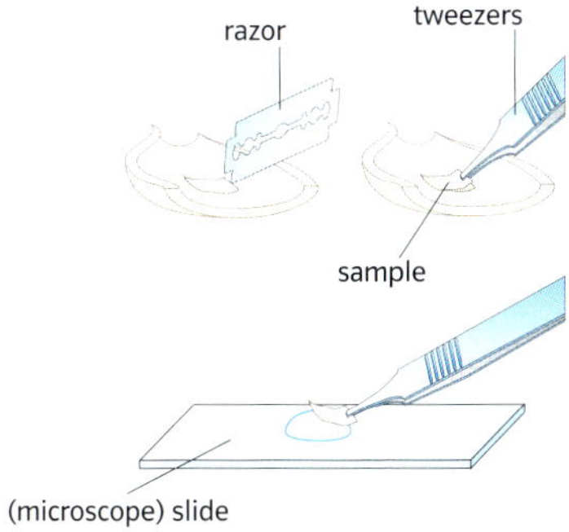

Abb. 6

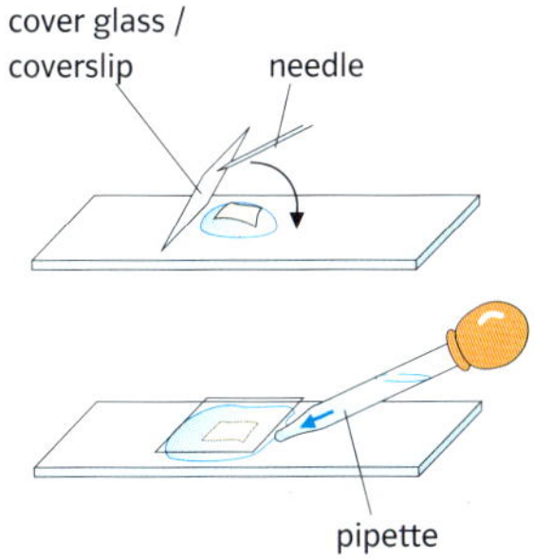

Abbildungen

Abb. 7 Light microscopy

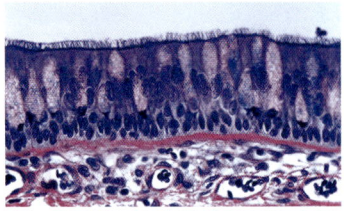

Abb. 8 Electron microscopy

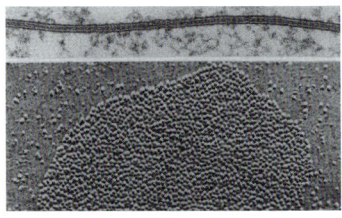

Abb. 9 Dark-field microscopy

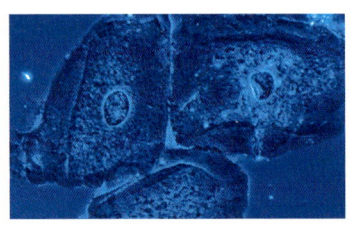

Abb. 10 Bright-field microscopy

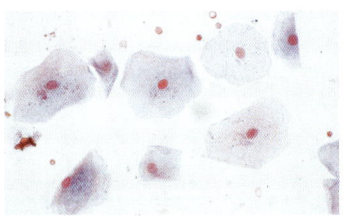

Abb. 11 Polarised-light microscopy

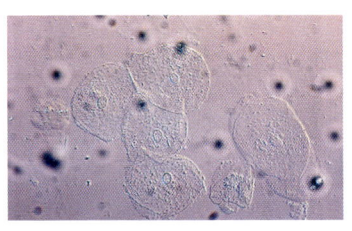

Abb. 12 Phase-contrast microscopy

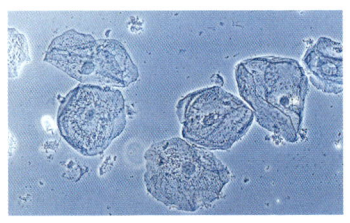

Abb. 13 Fluorescence microscopy

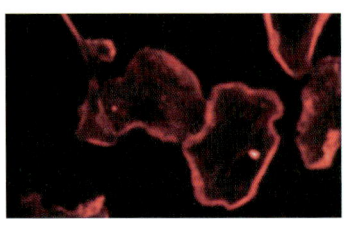

Abb. 14 Cross section

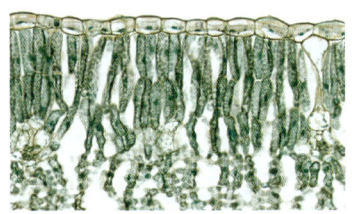

S. 24, 37, 176

Abbildungen

Abb. 15 Bar chart   S. 41

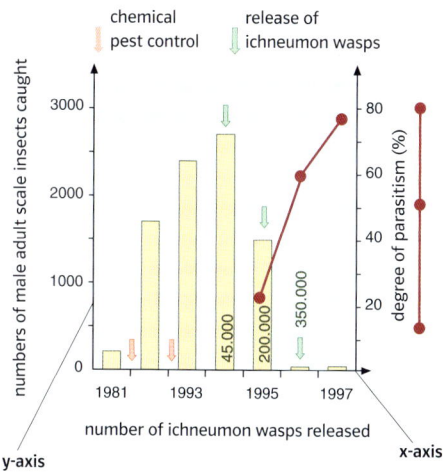

bar chart/vertical bar chart

Abb. 16 Pie chart

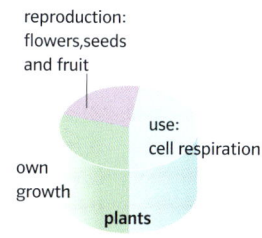

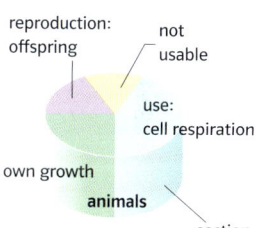

Abb. 17 Line graph

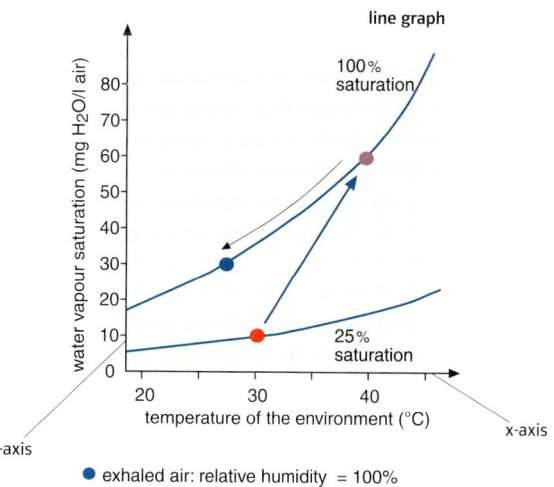

- exhaled air: relative humidity = 100%
- air saturated with water vapour in the lungs = 38%
- inhaled air: relative humidity = 25%

509

Abb. 18 Describing a scene or a picture **S. 37**

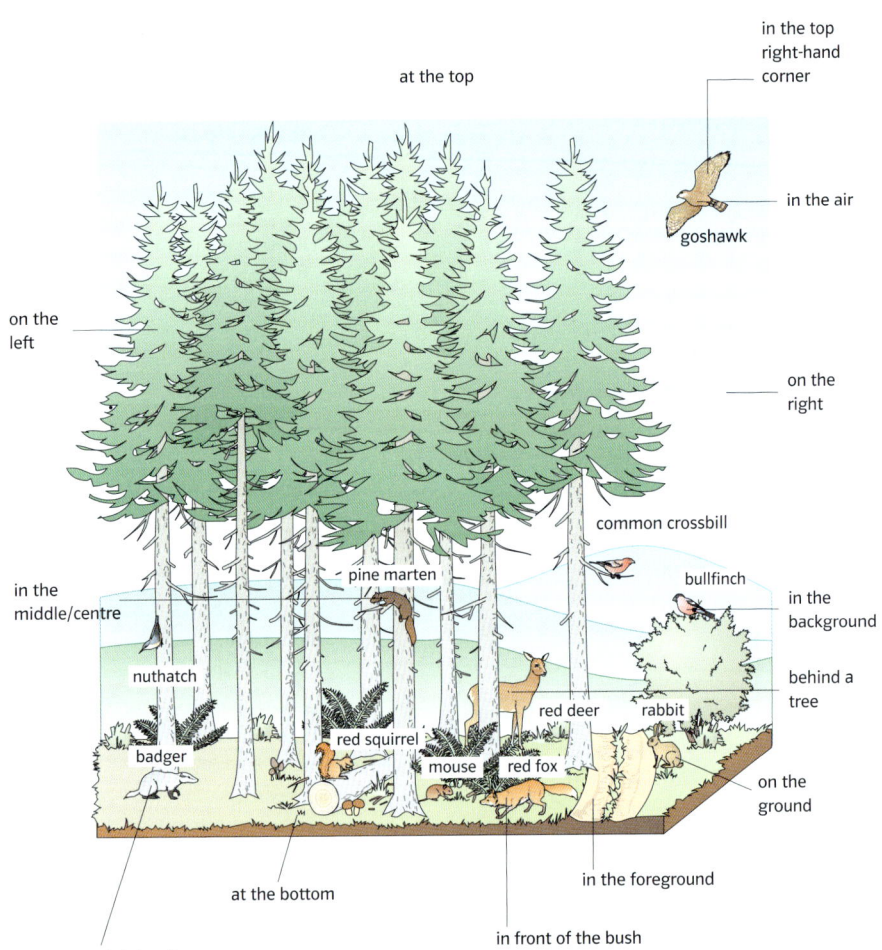

Abb. 19 The human body S. 53, 61

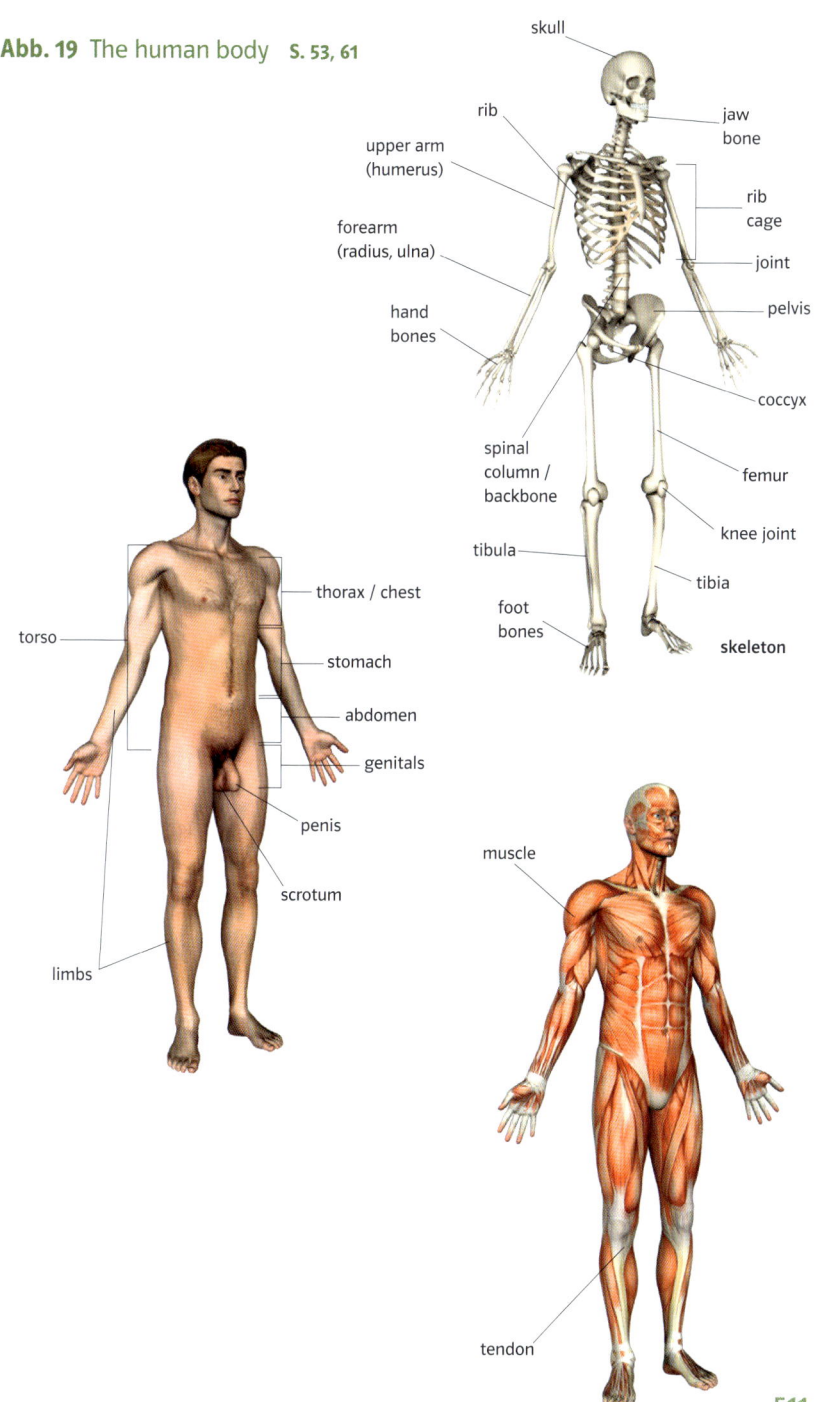

Abbildungen

Abb. 20 Intestines S. 53

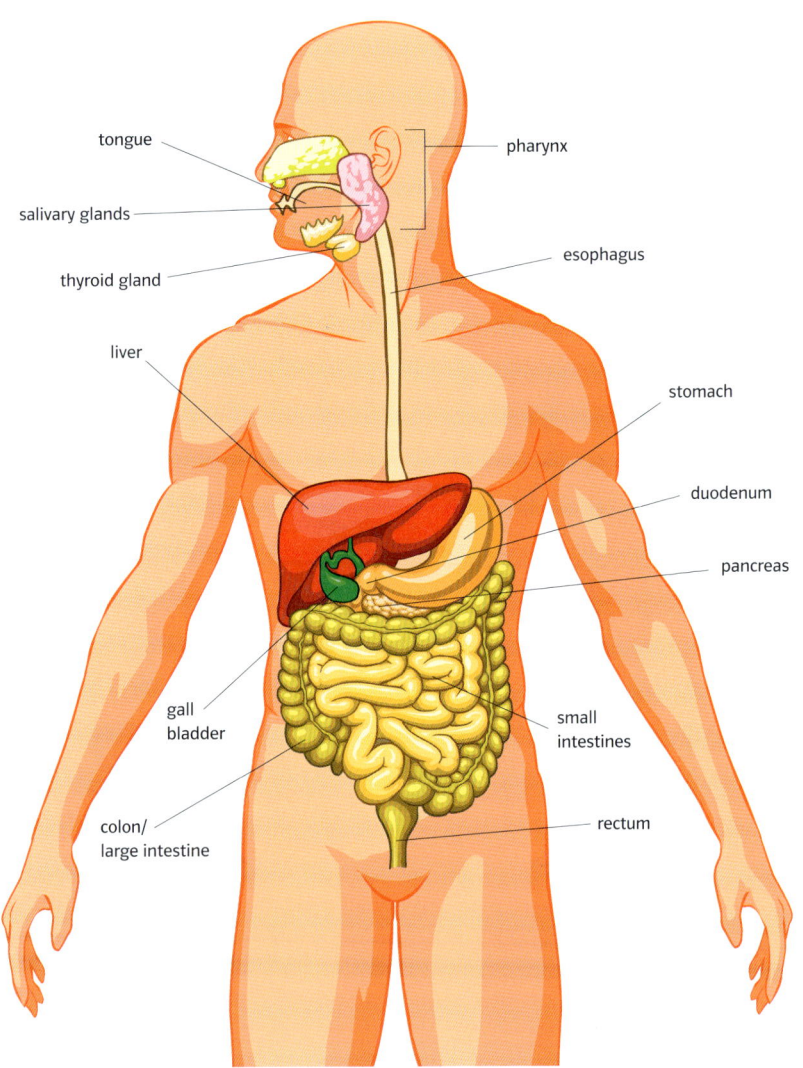

Abb. 21 Lymphatic system S. 80

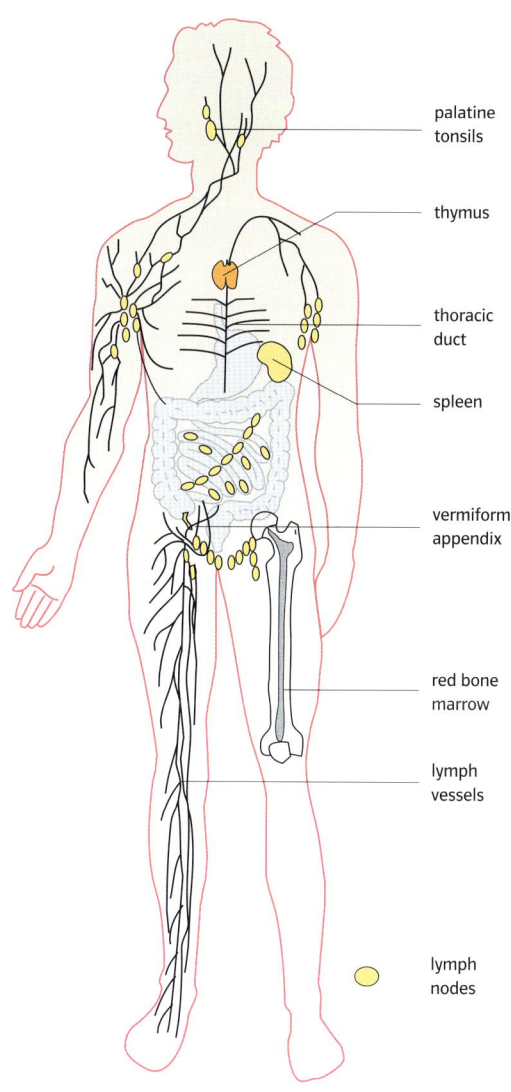

Abbildungen

Abb. 22 The brain S. 68

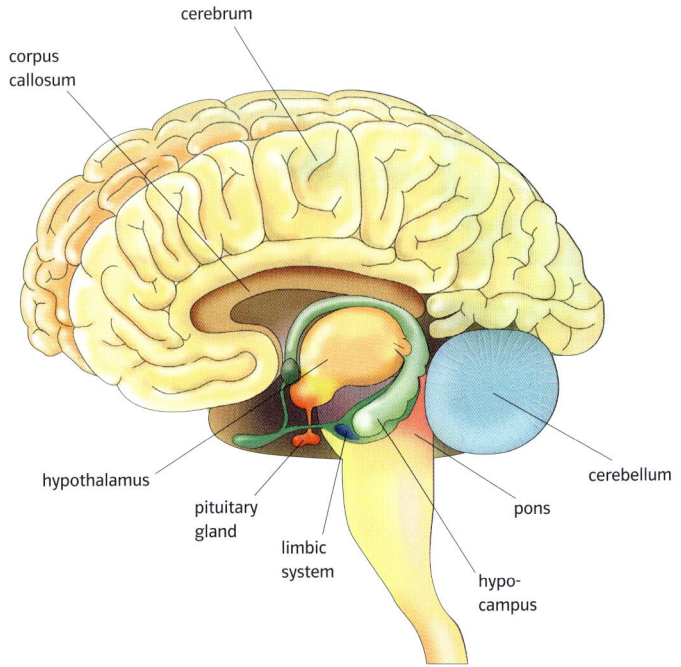

Abb. 23 Skin S. 61, 63

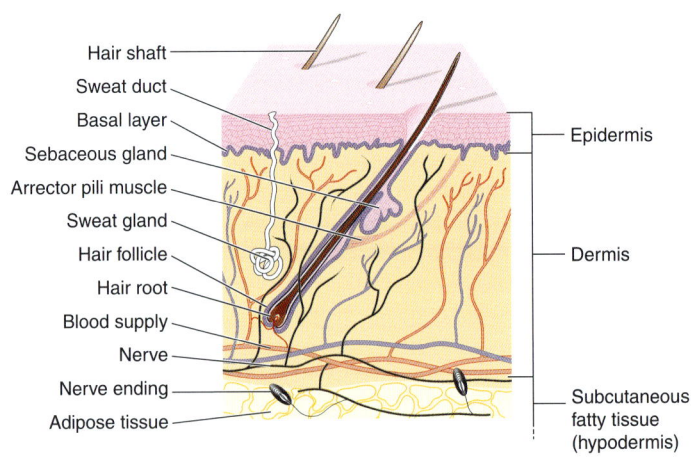

Abbildungen

Abb. 24 The ear S. 64

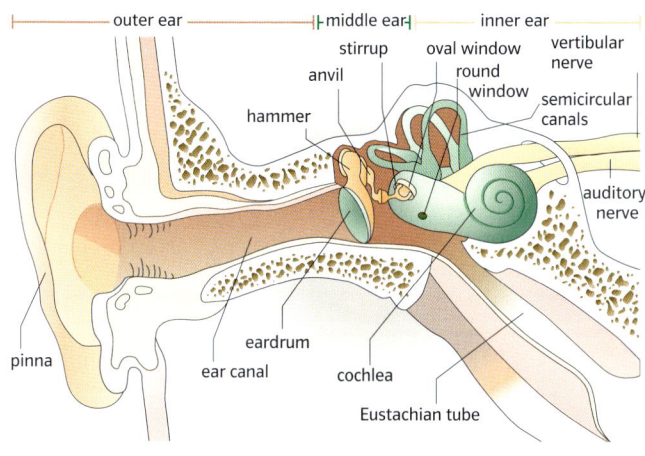

Abb. 25 Detail

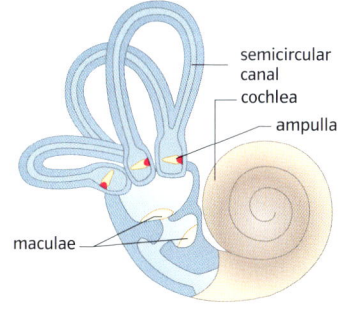

Abb. 26 Producing sound

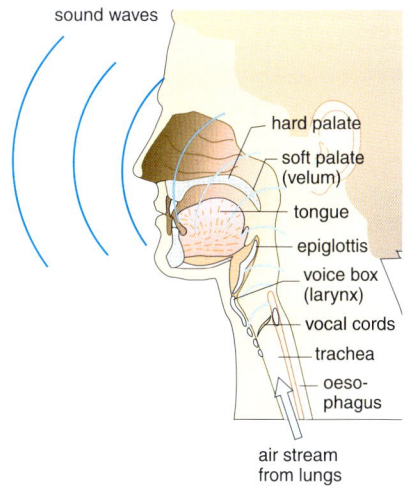

Abbildungen

Abb. 27 The eye S. 66, 323

Abb. 29 Compound eye S. 323

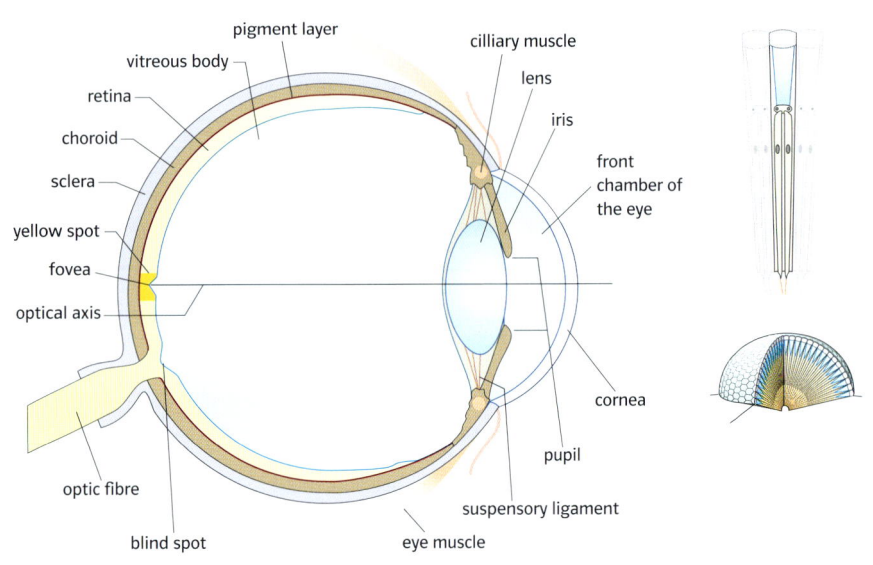

Abb. 28 Eye muscles

Abb. 30 The colour triangle S. 324

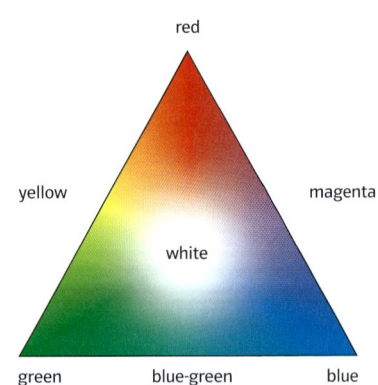

Abb. 31 Reflex arc of the knee jerk (patellar) reflex S. 68, 320, 322

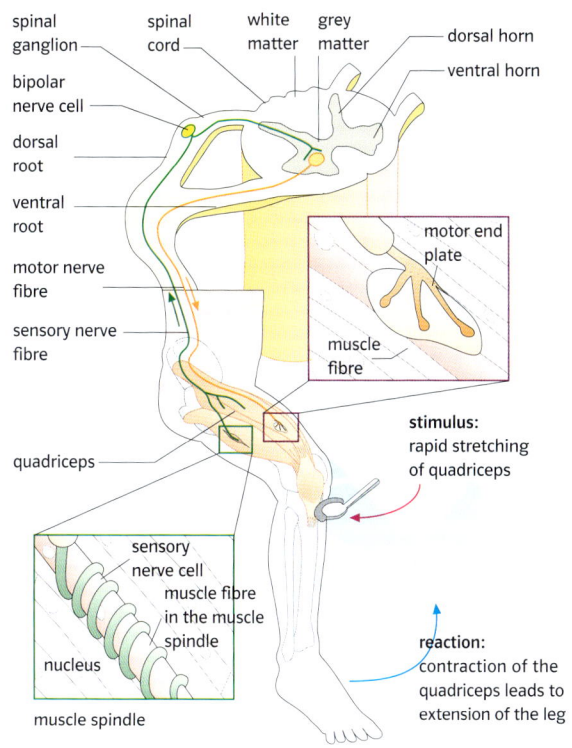

Abb. 32 Spinal cord

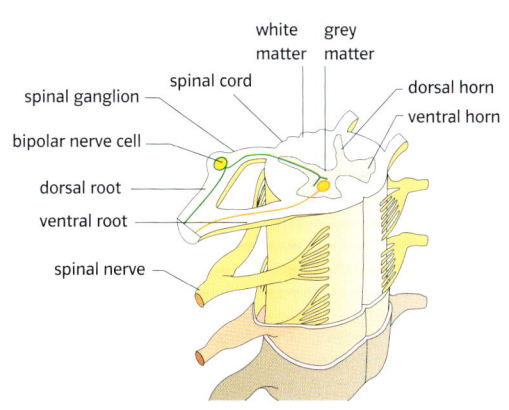

Abbildungen

Abb. 33 Neuron S. 315

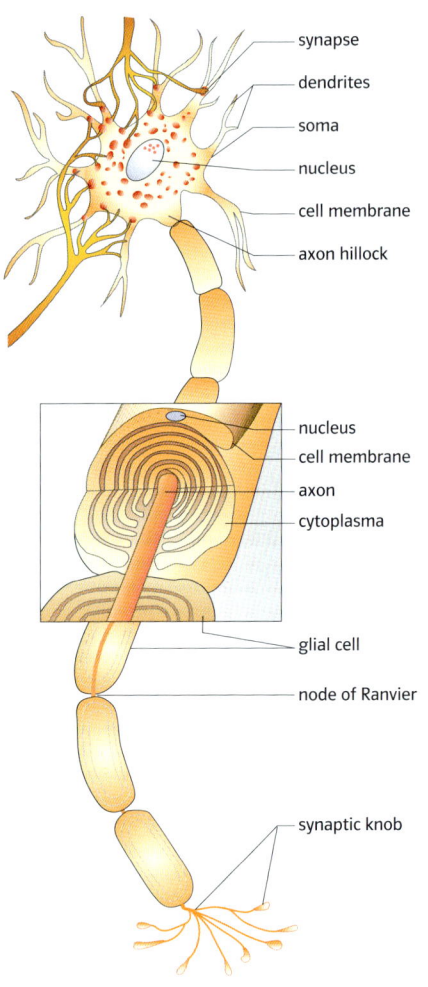

Abb. 34 Saltatory conduction S. 319

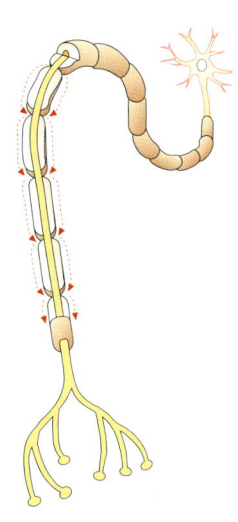

Abb. 35 Ion pump S. 316

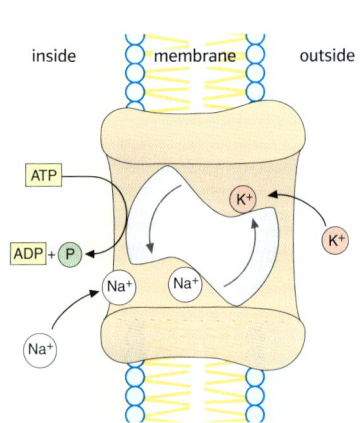

Abb. 36 Food and diet S. 75

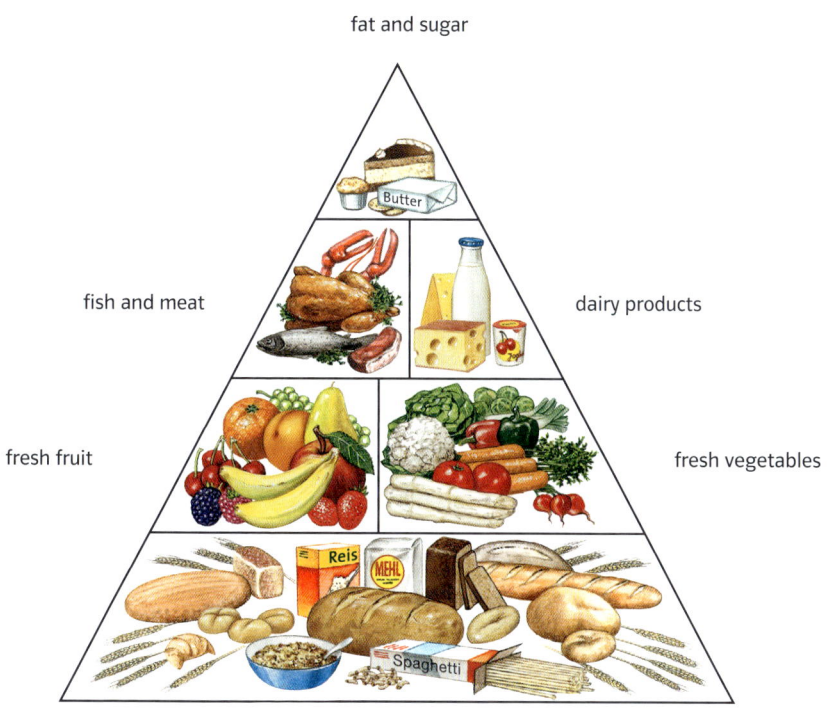

Abbildungen

Abb. 37 Prokaryotic cell S. 161

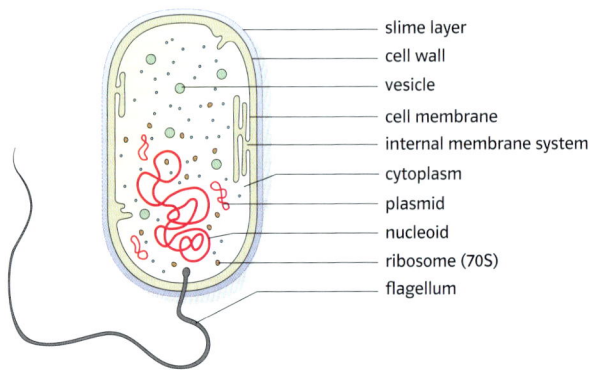

Abb. 38 Plant cell S. 158

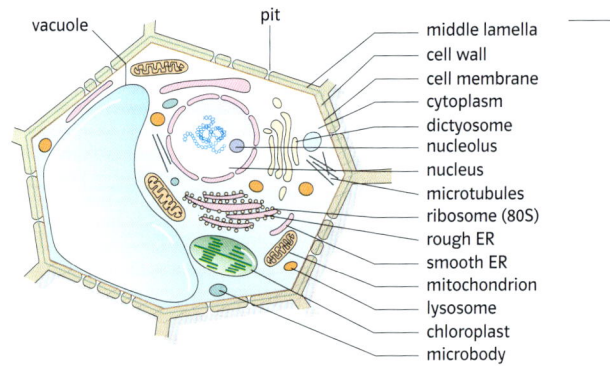

Abb. 39 Animal cell S. 158

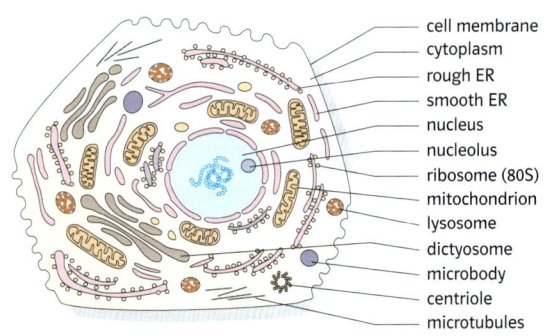

Eukaryotic cells

Abbildungen

Abb. 40 Tissue S. 58, 159

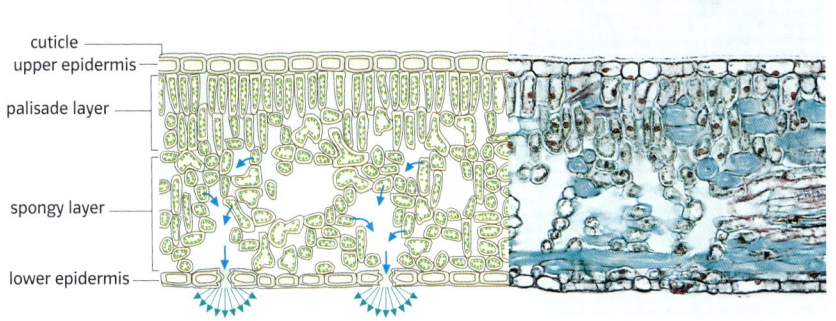

Abb. 41 Lock-and-key model S. 133

Abb. 42 Lock-and-key model

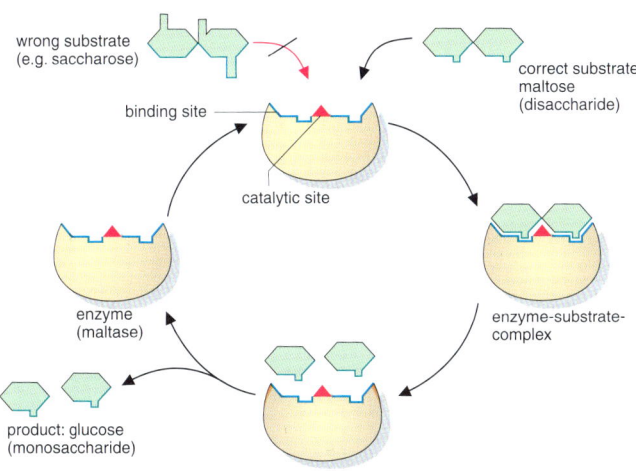

Abbildungen

Abb. 43 The structure of an amino acid S. 168

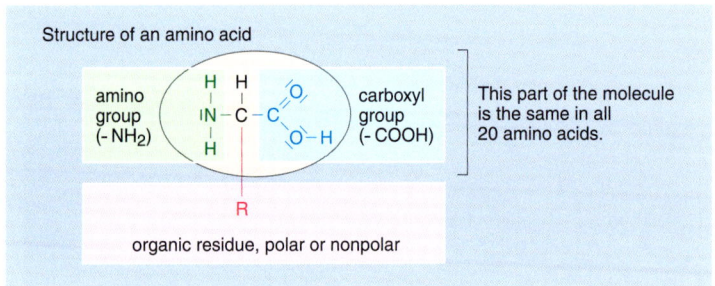

Abb. 44 Biomembrane S. 173

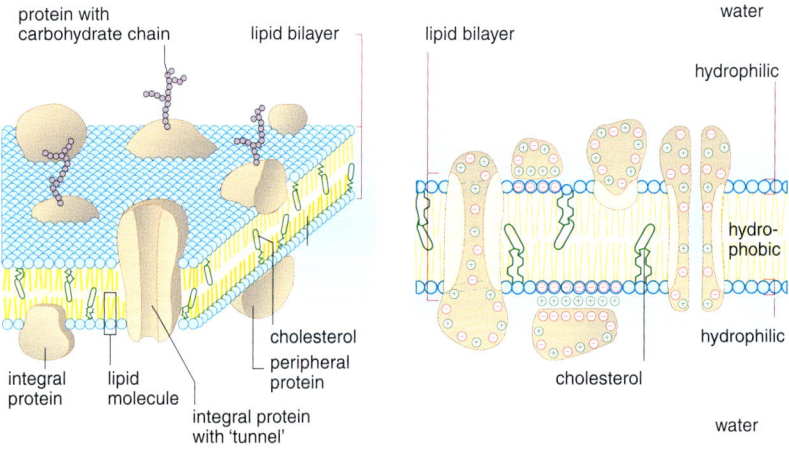

522

Abb. 45 Cell cycle S. 188

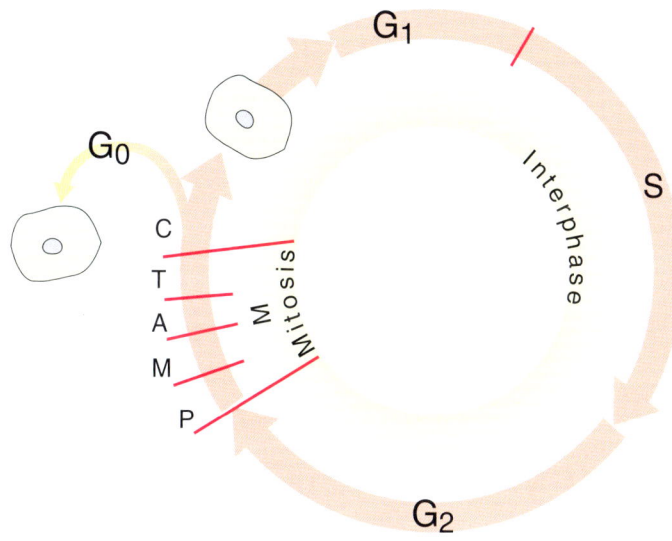

G_1 – cell growth with intensive metabolism and multiplication of cell organelles

G_2 – further growth and preparation for mitosis

M – mitosis with its parts Pro- (P), Meta- (M), Ana- (A), Telophase (T)

C – cytokinesis

S – synthesis of new DNA (replication)

G_0 – differentiation to a permanent cell

Abb. 46 Meiosis S. 192

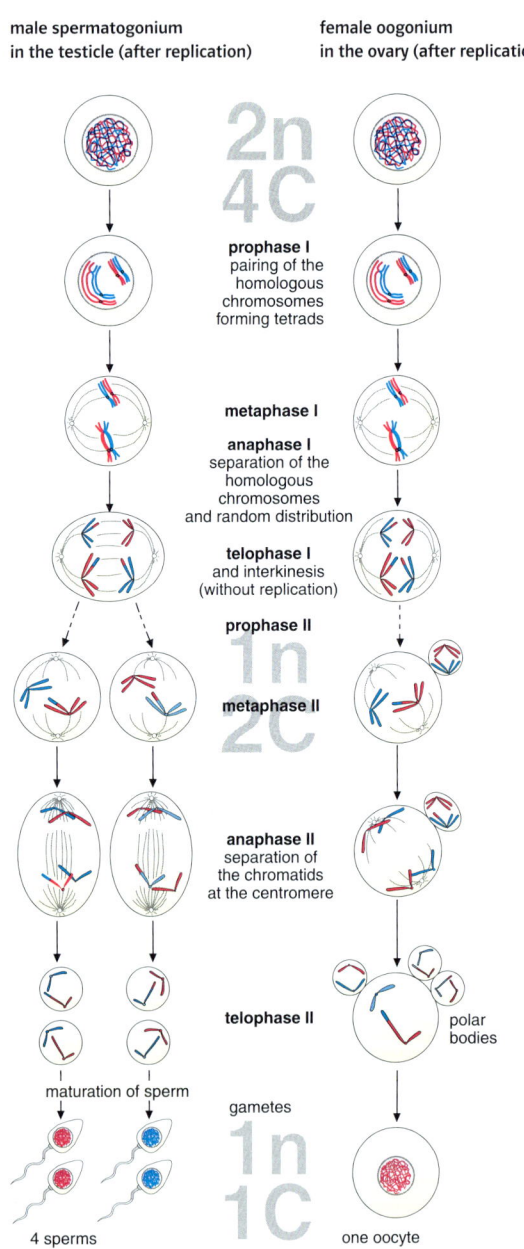

Abbildungen

Abb. 47 Double helix S. 205

Abb. 48 Codon codes S. 213

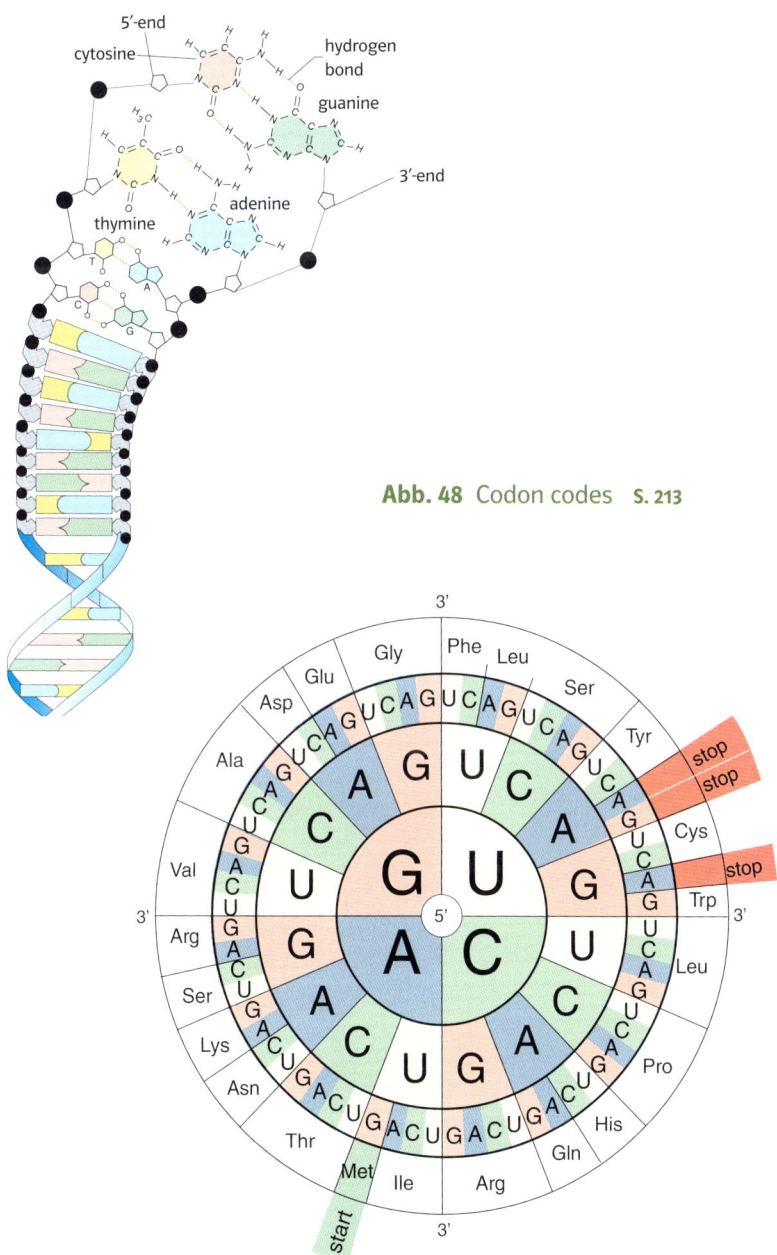

Abbildungen

Abb. 49 Polymerase chain reaction S. 246

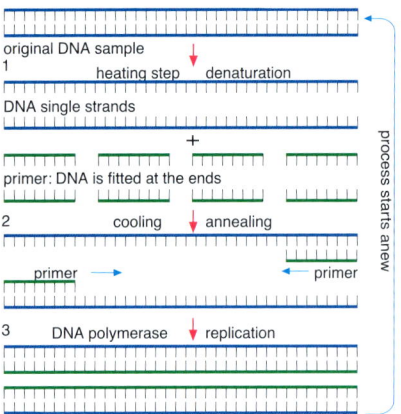

Abb. 50 Insulin production: classic and gene engineering method S. 239, 276

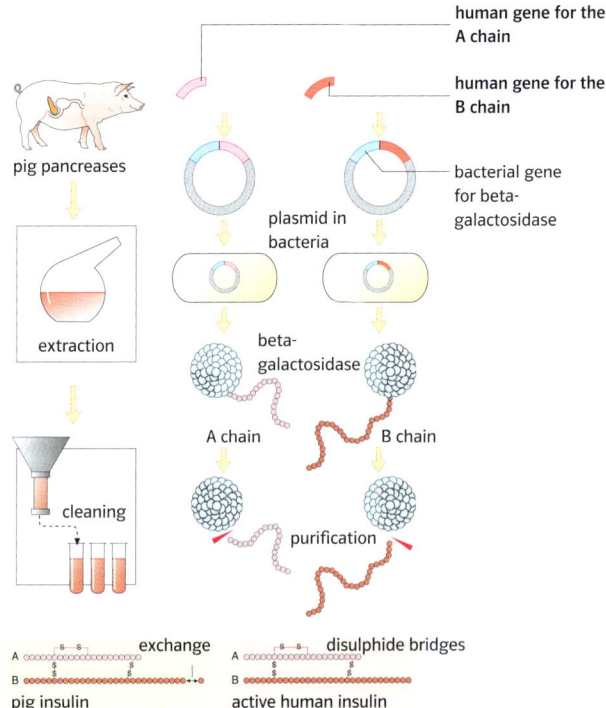

Abb. 51 HI virus: replicate cycle   S. 240

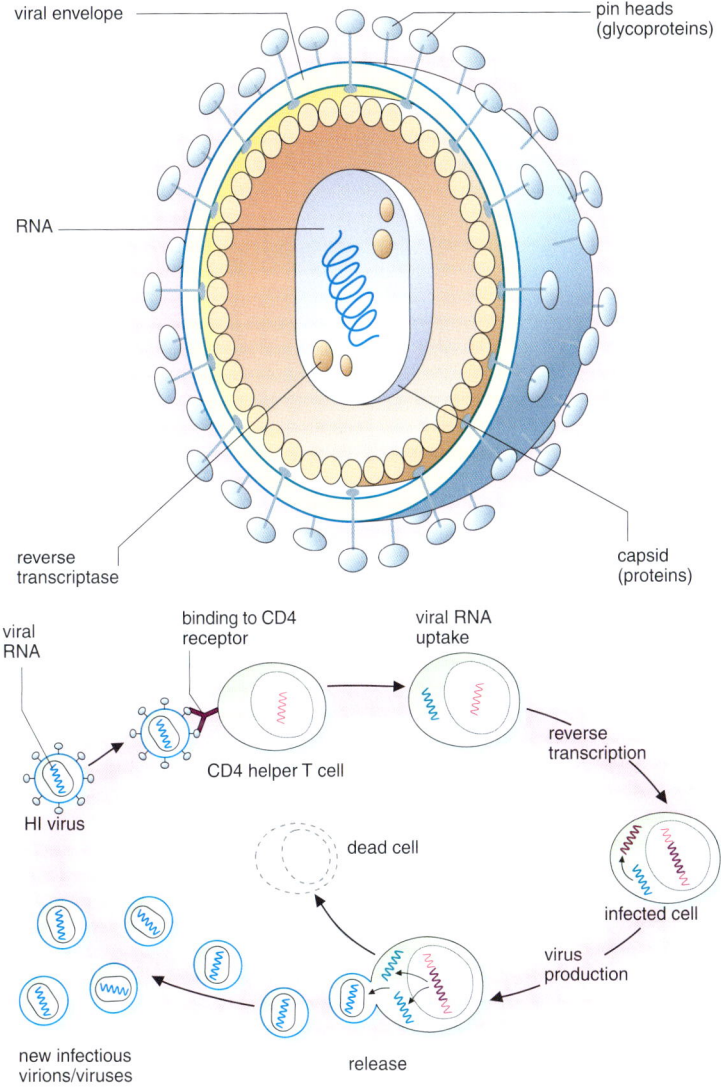

Abbildungen

Abb. 52 Tolerance and preference – an example S. 329

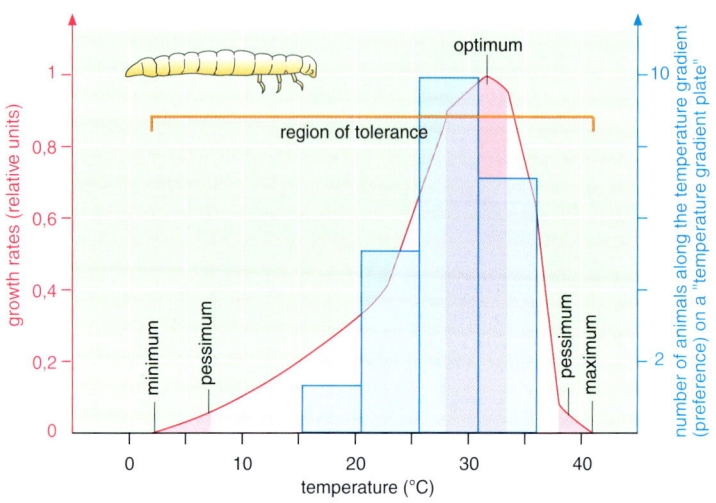

Abb. 53 Osmoregulation – example saltwater and freshwater fish S. 335

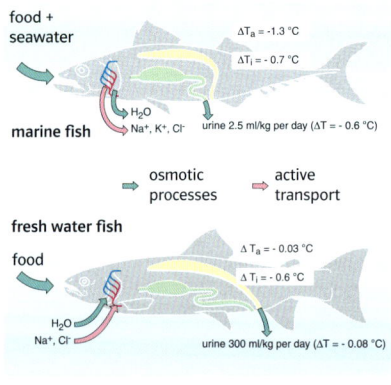

Abb. 54 Homoiosmotic and poikiosmotic S. 335

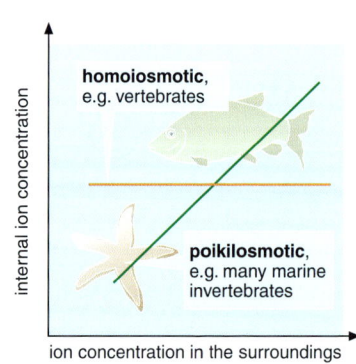

Abbildungen

Abb. 55 Competition - ecological factors and resources (example common buzzard)   S. 337

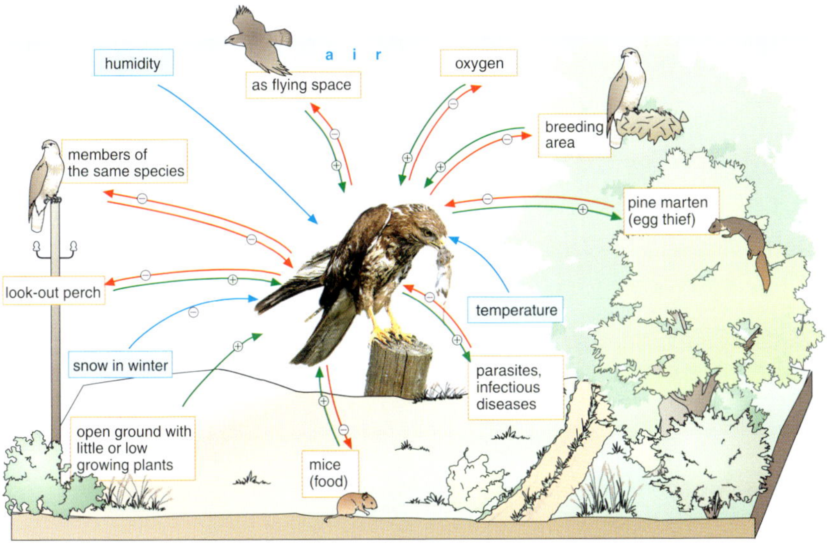

humidity

air as flying space

oxygen

breeding area

members of the same species

pine marten (egg thief)

look-out perch

temperature

snow in winter

parasites, infectious diseases

open ground with little or low growing plants

mice (food)

arrows   proportional effect: A ⊕→ B   inverse effect: A ⊖→ B

the more A, the more B   the more A, the less B

the less A, the less B   the less A, the more B

Abb. 56 Ecological pyramid (example terrestrial ecosystems)   S. 347

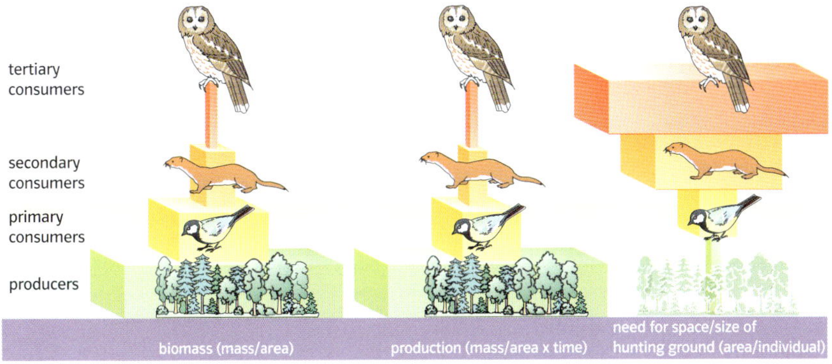

tertiary consumers

secondary consumers

primary consumers

producers

biomass (mass/area)   production (mass/area × time)   need for space/size of hunting ground (area/individual)

Abb. 57 Carbon cycle   S. 349

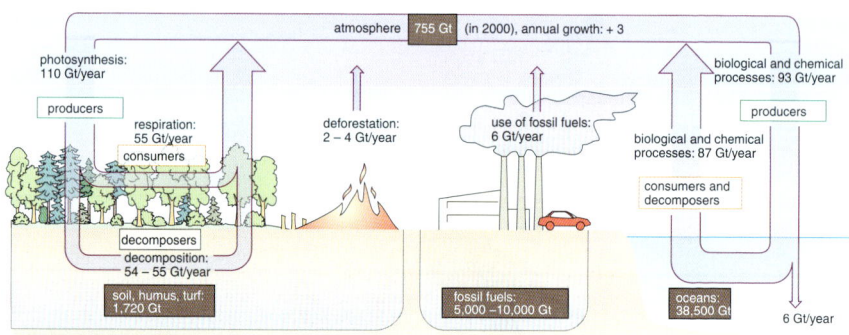

Gt = gigaton (here: gigatons/year)

Abb. 58 Nitrogen cycle   S. 350

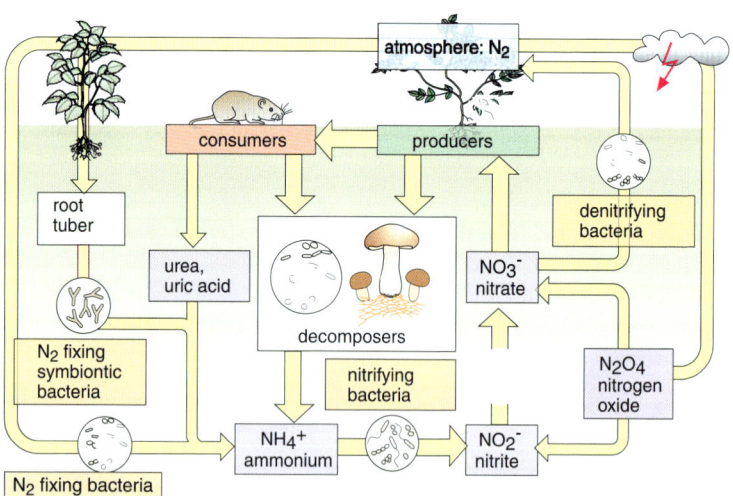

Abb. 59 Endangered forest S. 362

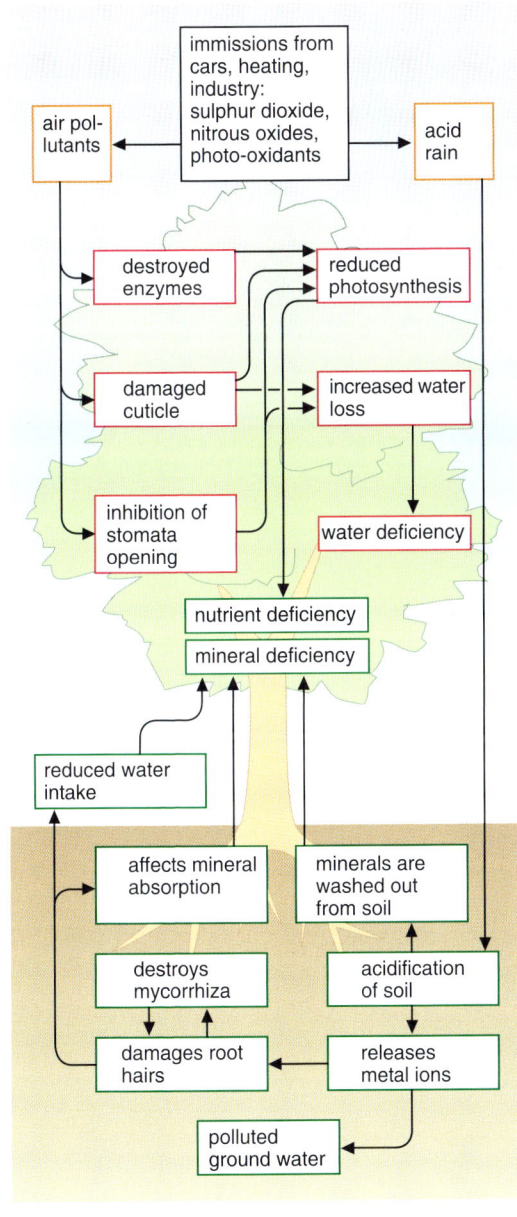

Abb. 60 Layers of the lake S. 372

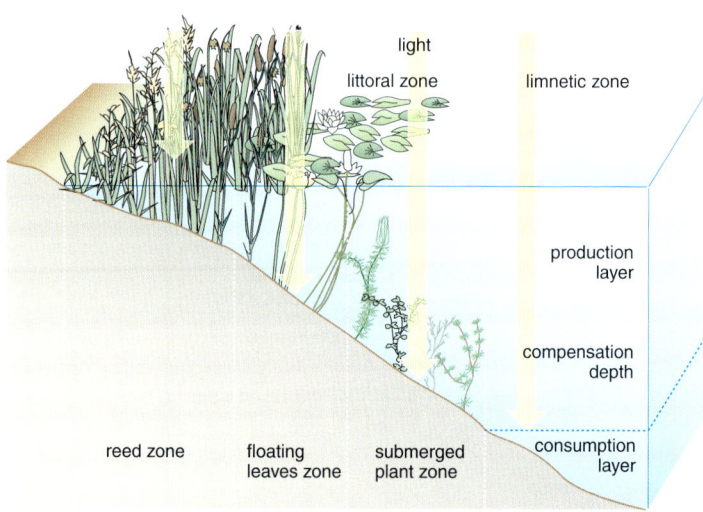